# ESPRIT Basic Research Series

Edited in cooperation with
the European Commission, DG III

Editors: P. Aigrain  F. Aldana  H. G. Danielmeyer
O. Faugeras  H. Gallaire  R. A. Kowalski  J. M. Lehn
G. Levi  G. Metakides  B. Oakley  J. Rasmussen  J. Tribolet
D. Tsichritzis  R. Van Overstraeten  G. Wrixon

Springer
*Berlin*
*Heidelberg*
*New York*
*Barcelona*
*Budapest*
*Hong Kong*
*London*
*Milan*
*Paris*
*Tokyo*

B. Randell   J.-C. Laprie   H. Kopetz
B. Littlewood  (Eds.)

# Predictably Dependable Computing Systems

With 159 Figures and 33 Tables

 Springer

Editors

Brian Randell
University of Newcastle upon Tyne
Department of Computing Science
Claremont Tower, Claremont Road
Newcastle upon Tyne NE1 7RU, UK

Jean-Claude Laprie
LAAS-CNRS
7 Avenue du Colonel Roche
F-31077 Toulouse, France

Hermann Kopetz
Technische Universität Wien
Institut für Technische Informatik
Treitlstraße 3/182
A-1040 Wien, Austria

Bev Littlewood
The City University
Centre for Software Reliability
Northampton Square
London EC1V 0HB, UK

CR Subject Classification (1991): C.4, D.2.4-5, D.4.5, D.4.7

ISBN 3-540-59334-9 Springer-Verlag Berlin Heidelberg New York

CIP data applied for

Publication No. EUR 16256 EN of the European Commission, Dissemination of Scientific
and Technical Knowledge Unit, Directorate-General Information Technologies and
Industries, and Telecommunications, Luxembourg. Neither the European Commission
nor any person acting on behalf of the Commission is responsible for the use which might
be made of the following information.

Typesetting: Camera-ready by authors/editors
SPIN 10502070      45/3142 - 5 4 3 2 1 0 - Printed on acid-free paper

# Preface

The first ESPRIT Basic Research Project on Predictably Dependable Computing Systems (No. 3092, PDCS) commenced in May 1989, and ran until March 1992. The institutions and principal investigators that were involved in PDCS were: City University, London, UK (Bev Littlewood), IEI del CNR, Pisa, Italy (Lorenzo Strigini), Universität Karlsruhe, Germany (Tom Beth), LAAS-CNRS, Toulouse, France (Jean-Claude Laprie), University of Newcastle upon Tyne, UK (Brian Randell), LRI-CNRS/Université Paris-Sud, France (Marie-Claude Gaudel), Technische Universität Wien, Austria (Hermann Kopetz), and University of York, UK (John McDermid).

The work continued after March 1992, and a three-year successor project (No. 6362, PDCS2) officially started in August 1992, with a slightly changed membership: Chalmers University of Technology, Göteborg, Sweden (Erland Jonsson), City University, London, UK (Bev Littlewood), CNR, Pisa, Italy (Lorenzo Strigini), LAAS-CNRS, Toulouse, France (Jean-Claude Laprie), Université Catholique de Louvain, Belgium (Pierre-Jacques Courtois), University of Newcastle upon Tyne, UK (Brian Randell), LRI-CNRS/Université Paris-Sud, France (Marie-Claude Gaudel), Technische Universität Wien, Austria (Hermann Kopetz), and University of York, UK (John McDermid).

The summary objective of both projects has been "to contribute to making the process of designing and constructing dependable computing systems much more predictable and cost-effective". In the case of PDCS2, the concentration has been on the problems of producing dependable distributed real-time systems and especially those where the dependability requirements centre on issues of safety and/or security.

As the original PDCS Proposal remarked, the great problem about dependability is that it is a systems issue, since virtually all aspects of a computing system, and of the means by which it was specified, designed and constructed, can affect the system's overall dependability. Users gain little satisfaction from being assured that particular system components are functioning faultlessly or that particular parts of the design process have been carried out absolutely correctly if the overall system does not provide a level of dependability commensurate with the level of dependence that they have to place on it.

A major characteristic of the projects has therefore been their concentration on exploring links, and gaps, between topics that are often investigated separately, but whose interactions could be of considerable relevance to issues of overall system dependability. The second major characteristic has been the stress we have put on the use of quantitative assessments of system dependability. Clearly there will be limits to the extent that many process and product characteristics can be meaningfully and accurately quantified. Nevertheless, we feel that our concentration on techniques which could help to lay the foundations of increased use of quantitative methods has been fully justified by the results we have achieved.

There have been approximately 40 staff involved at any one time in the two projects. Over two hundred resulting papers have been published in journals and technical conferences. This book is made up of a carefully-chosen selection of these papers. Our aim in making the selection has been to provide a good general overview of the work of the two projects, as well as coverage of most of the major research achievements.

At the time when what became the ESPRIT Basic Research Programme was being planned, the hope was that it would provide the means whereby hitherto independent, and relatively small, research groups in various member states could form themselves into strong broad-based European research teams, capable of tackling much more ambitious research projects than had previously been commonly possible. This certainly was the thinking that led to the formation of PDCS — we are happy to leave readers to judge how successfully these hopes have been fulfilled in this case. However, from our vantage point, we can confirm that the whole experience has been very stimulating intellectually, as well as very pleasant. We are thus most grateful to the ESPRIT Research Programme for the support that made this work possible.

Brian Randell<br>
Jean-Claude Laprie<br>
Hermann Kopetz<br>
Bev Littlewood

# Contributors to this Volume

TOM ANDERSON, University of Newcastle upon Tyne, Department of Computing Science, Claremont Tower, Claremont Road, Newcastle Upon Tyne, NE1 7RU, UK

JEAN ARLAT, LAAS-CNRS, 7 avenue du Colonel Roche, 31077 Toulouse, France

NEIL AUDSLEY, University of York, Department of Computer Science, Heslington, York, Y01 5DD, UK

CHRISTIAN BÉOUNES,[†] LAAS-CNRS, 7 avenue du Colonel Roche, 31077 Toulouse, France

ANDREA BONDAVALLI, CNUCE-CNR, Via Santa Maria 36, I-56126 Pisa, Italy

SARAH BROCKLEHURST, The City University, Centre for Software Reliability, Northampton Square, London, EC1V 0HB, UK

ALAN BURNS, University of York, Department of Computer Science, Heslington, York, Y01 5DD, UK

RAM CHAKKA, University of Newcastle upon Tyne, Department of Computing Science, Claremont Tower, Claremont Road, Newcastle Upon Tyne, NE1 7RU, UK

SILVANO CHIARADONNA, CNUCE-CNR, Via Santa Maria 36, I-56126 Pisa, Italy

PIERRE-JACQUES COURTOIS, Université Catholique de Louvain, Unité d'Informatique, Place Sainte-Barbe, 2, 1348 Louvain-la-Neuve, Belgium

YVES CROUZET, LAAS-CNRS, 7 avenue du Colonel Roche, 31077 Toulouse, France

ROB DAVIS, University of York, Department of Computer Science, Heslington, York, Y01 5DD, UK

ROGÉRIO DE LEMOS, University of Newcastle upon Tyne, Department of Computing Science, Claremont Tower, Claremont Road, Newcastle Upon Tyne, NE1 7RU, UK

YVES DESWARTE, LAAS-CNRS, 7 avenue du Colonel Roche, 31077 Toulouse, France

FELICITA DI GIANDOMENICO, IEI del CNR, Via Santa Maria 46, I-56126 Pisa, Italy

---

[†] Christian Béounes passed away on 23 April 1993.

JOHN DOBSON, University of Newcastle upon Tyne, Department of Computing Science, Claremont Tower, Claremont Road, Newcastle Upon Tyne, NE1 7RU, UK

JEAN-CHARLES FABRE, LAAS-CNRS, 7 avenue du Colonel Roche, 31077 Toulouse, France

NORMAN ELLIOTT FENTON, The City University, Centre for Software Reliability, Northampton Square, London, EC1V 0HB, UK

PETER FOLKESSON, Chalmers University of Technology, Department of Computer Engineering, S-41296 Göteborg, Sweden

MARIE-CLAUDE GAUDEL, LRI, Bâtiment 490, Université de Paris-Sud, 91405 Orsay, France

DIETER GOLLMANN, Universität Karlsruhe, Department of Computer Science, Zirkel 2, 76128 Karlsruhe, Germany

ERIC JENN, LAAS-CNRS, 7 avenue du Colonel Roche, 31077 Toulouse, France

ERLAND JONSSON, Chalmers University of Technology, Department of Computer Engineering, S-41296 Göteborg, Sweden

KARAMA KANOUN, LAAS-CNRS, 7 avenue du Colonel Roche, 31077 Toulouse, France

MOHAMED KAÂNICHE, LAAS-CNRS, 7 avenue du Colonel Roche, 31077 Toulouse, France

JOHAN KARLSSON, Chalmers University of Technology, Department of Computer Engineering, S-41296 Göteborg, Sweden

HERMANN KOPETZ, Technische Universität Wien, Institut für Technische Informatik, Treitlstrasse 3, A-1040 Vienna, Austria

JEAN-CLAUDE LAPRIE, LAAS-CNRS, 7 avenue du Colonel Roche, 31077 Toulouse, France

PASCALE LE GALL, LRI, Bâtiment 490, Université de Paris-Sud, 91405 Orsay, France

GÜNTHER LEBER, Technische Universität Wien, Institut für Technische Informatik, Treitlstrasse 3, A-1040 Vienna, Austria

BEV LITTLEWOOD, The City University, Centre for Software Reliability, Northampton Square, London, EC1V 0HB, UK

MINYAN LU, The City University, Centre for Software Reliability, Northampton Square, London, EC1V 0HB, UK

BRUNO MARRE, LRI, Bâtiment 490, Université de Paris-Sud, 91405 Orsay, France

ELIANE MARTINS, LAAS-CNRS, 7 avenue du Colonel Roche, 31077 Toulouse, France

JOHN MCDERMID, University of York, Department of Computer Science, Heslington, York, Y01 5DD, UK

PETER MELLOR, The City University, Centre for Software Reliability, Northampton Square, London, EC1V 0HB, UK

ISI MITRANI, University of Newcastle upon Tyne, Department of Computing Science, Claremont Tower, Claremont Road, Newcastle Upon Tyne, NE1 7RU, UK

VINCENT NICOMETTE, LAAS-CNRS, 7 avenue du Colonel Roche, 31077 Toulouse, France

JOAKIM OHLSSON, Chalmers University of Technology, Department of Computer Engineering, S-41296 Göteborg, Sweden

TOMAS OLOVSSON, Chalmers University of Technology, Department of Computer Engineering, S-41296 Göteborg, Sweden

STELLA PAGE, The City University, Centre for Software Reliability, Northampton Square, London, EC1V 0HB, UK

TANGUY PÉRENNOU, LAAS-CNRS, 7 avenue du Colonel Roche, 31077 Toulouse, France

DAVID POWELL, LAAS-CNRS, 7 avenue du Colonel Roche, 31077 Toulouse, France

BRIAN RANDELL, University of Newcastle upon Tyne, Department of Computing Science, Claremont Tower, Claremont Road, Newcastle Upon Tyne, NE1 7RU, UK

JOHANNES REISINGER, Technische Universität Wien, Institut für Technische Informatik, Treitlstrasse 3, A-1040 Vienna, Austria

MARCUS RIMÉN, Chalmers University of Technology, Department of Computer Engineering, S-41296 Göteborg, Sweden

ALEXANDER ROMANOVSKY, University of Newcastle upon Tyne, Department of Computing Science, Claremont Tower, Claremont Road, Newcastle Upon Tyne, NE1 7RU, UK

CECILIA M.F. RUBIRA, University of Newcastle upon Tyne, Department of Computing Science, Claremont Tower, Claremont Road, Newcastle Upon Tyne, NE1 7RU, UK

AMER SAEED, University of Newcastle upon Tyne, Department of Computing Science, Claremont Tower, Claremont Road, Newcastle Upon Tyne, NE1 7RU, UK

WERNER SCHÜTZ,[1] Technische Universität Wien, Institut für Technische Informatik, Treitlstrasse 3, A-1040 Vienna, Austria

PIERRE SEMAL, Université Catholique de Louvain, Unité d'Informatique, Place Sainte-Barbe, 2, 1348 Louvain-la-Neuve, Belgium

ANDREAS STEININGER, Technische Universität Wien, Institut für Technische Informatik, Treitlstrasse 3, A-1040 Vienna, Austria

LORENZO STRIGINI,[2] IEI del CNR, Via Santa Maria 46, I-56126 Pisa, Italy

ROBERT J. STROUD, University of Newcastle upon Tyne, Department of Computing Science, Claremont Tower, Claremont Road, Newcastle Upon Tyne, NE1 7RU, UK

PASCALE THÉVENOD-FOSSE, LAAS-CNRS, 7 avenue du Colonel Roche, 31077 Toulouse, France

KEN TINDELL, University of York, Department of Computer Science, Heslington, York, Y01 5DD, UK

HÉLÈNE WAESELYNCK, LAAS-CNRS, 7 avenue du Colonel Roche, 31077 Toulouse, France

ANDY WELLINGS, University of York, Department of Computer Science, Heslington, York, Y01 5DD, UK

DAVID WRIGHT, The City University, Centre for Software Reliability, Northampton Square, London, EC1V 0HB, UK

ZHIXUE WU, University of Newcastle upon Tyne, Department of Computing Science, Claremont Tower, Claremont Road, Newcastle Upon Tyne, NE1 7RU, UK

JIE XU, University of Newcastle upon Tyne, Department of Computing Science, Claremont Tower, Claremont Road, Newcastle Upon Tyne, NE1 7RU, UK

---

[1] Now with Alcatel Austria, Wien

[2] Now with The City University, Centre for Software Reliability, Northampton Square, London EC1V 0HB, UK

# Table of Contents

# Chapter I

# Basic Concepts

The paper contained in this chapter gives precise definitions of dependability, its attributes (reliability, availability, safety, confidentiality, integrity, maintainability), its impairments (faults, errors, failures), and its means (fault prevention, fault tolerance, fault removal, fault forecasting).

The features of the PDCS and PDCS2 projects which have been pointed out in the preface to this book, i.e. concern for system aspects and the exploration of links between topics often investigated separately, have been a strong incentive to the work on the formulation of the basic concepts of dependability. The fault-error-failure model is central to understanding and mastering the various impairments which may affect a system, and enables a unified presentation of these impairments, though preserving their specificities via the various fault classes that are defined. The model provided for the means for dependability has proved to be extremely useful in classifying the projects' activities, as these means are much more orthogonal to each other than is the case with the usual classification according to the attributes of dependability, with respect to which the design of any real system has to perform trade-offs, due to the fact that these attributes tend to be in conflict with each other.

# Dependability – Its Attributes, Impairments and Means*

Jean-Claude Laprie

LAAS-CNRS

**Abstract.** This paper gives the main definitions relating to dependability, a generic concept including as special cases such atributes as reliability, availability, safety, security, maintainability. The various impairments to dependability (faults, errors, failures) and means for dependability (especially fault tolerance, fault removal, fault forecasting) are emphasized.

## 1    Introduction

This paper is aimed at giving precise definitions characterizing the various attributes of computing systems dependability. Dependability is first introduced as a global concept which subsumes the usual attributes of reliability, availability, safety, security, maintainability. The basic definitions given in the first section are then commented on, and supplemented by additional definitions, in the subsequent sections. Boldface characters are used when a term is defined, italic characters being an invitation to focus the reader's attention. The guidelines which have governed this presentation can be summed up as follows: (i) search for a reduced number of concepts enabling the dependability attributes to be expressed, and (ii) emphasis on integration (as opposed to specialization).

This paper can be seen as a minimum consensus within the community in order to facilitate fruitful interactions. In this view, the associated terminology effort is not an end in itself: words are only of interest in so far as they unequivocally label concepts, and enable ideas and viewpoints to be shared. The paper is devoid of any pretension of being a state-of-the-art or "Tablets of Stone"; the concepts that are presented have to evolve with technology, and with our progress in understanding and mastering the specification, design and assessment of dependable computer systems.

## 2    Basic Definitions

**Dependability** is that property of a computer system such that reliance can justifiably be placed on the service it delivers. The **service** delivered by a system is its behaviour *as it is perceived* by its user(s); a **user** is another system (physical, human) which *interacts* with the former.

Depending on the application(s) intended for the system, different emphasis may be put on different facets of dependability, i.e. dependability may be viewed according to different, but complementary, *properties,* which enable the *attributes* of dependability to be defined:

- the property *readiness for usage* leads to **availability**;
- the property *continuity of service delivery* leads to **reliability**;

---

* This paper is based largely on material in [48, 49].

- the property *non-occurrence of catastrophic consequences on the environment* leads to **safety**;
- the property *non-occurrence of unauthorized disclosure of information* leads to **confidentiality**;
- the property *non-occurrence of improper alterations of information* leads to **integrity**;
- the property *aptitude to undergo repairs and evolution* leads to **maintainability**.

Associating integrity and availability with respect to authorized actions, together with confidentiality, leads to **security**.

A system **failure** occurs when the delivered service deviates from fulfilling the system **function**, the latter being what the system *is intended for*. An **error** is that part of the system state which is *liable to lead to subsequent failure*: an error affecting the service is an indication that a failure occurs or has occurred. The *adjudged or hypothesized cause* of an error is a **fault**.

The development of a dependable computing system calls for the *combined* utilization of a set of methods that can be classed into:

- **fault prevention**: how to prevent fault occurrence or introduction;
- **fault tolerance**: how to provide a service capable of fulfilling the system function in spite of faults;
- **fault removal**: how to reduce the presence (number, seriousness) of faults;
- **fault forecasting**: how to estimate the present number, the future incidence, and the consequences of faults.

The notions introduced up to now can be grouped into three classes (Fig. 1):

- the **impairments** to dependability: faults, errors, failures; they are undesired — but not in principle unexpected — circumstances causing or resulting from un-dependability (whose definition is very simply derived from the definition of dependability: reliance cannot, or will not any longer, be placed on the service);
- the **means** for dependability: fault prevention, fault tolerance, fault removal, fault forecasting; these are the methods and techniques enabling one (i) to provide the ability to deliver a service on which reliance can be placed, and (ii) to reach confidence in this ability.
- the **attributes** of dependability: availability, reliability, safety, confidentiality, integrity, maintainability; these (i) enable the properties which are expected from the system to be expressed, and (ii) allow the system quality resulting from the impairments and the means opposing to them to be assessed.

# 3   On System Function, Behaviour, and Structure

Up to now, a **system** has been — implicitly — considered as a whole, emphasizing its externally perceived behaviour. A definition complying with this "black box" view is: an entity having interacted or interfered, interacting or interfering, or likely to interact or interfere with other entities, i.e., with other systems. These other systems have been, are, or will constitute the **environment** of the considered system. A system **user** is that part of the environment which *interacts* with the considered system: the user provides inputs to and/or receives outputs from the system, its distinguishing feature being to *use the service* delivered by the system.

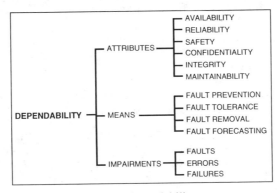

**Fig. 1.** The dependability tree

As already indicated in section 2, the function of a system is what the system is intended for [43]. The **behaviour** of a system is what the system *does*. What *makes it do what it does* is the **structure** of the system [82]. Adopting the spirit of [3], a system, from a structural ("white box" or "glassbox") viewpoint, is a set of components bound together in order to interact; a **component** is another system, etc. The recursion stops when a system is considered as being **atomic**: any further internal structure cannot be discerned, or is not of interest and can be ignored. The term "component" has to be understood in a broad sense: layers of a system as well as intralayer components; in addition, a component being itself a system, it embodies the interrelation(s) of the components of which it is composed. A more classical definition of system structure is what a system *is*. Such a definition fits in perfectly when representing a system without accounting explicitly for any impairments to dependability, and thus in the case where the structure is considered as *fixed*. However, we do not want to restrict ourselves to systems whose structure is fixed. In particular, we need to allow for structural changes caused by, or resulting from, dependability impairments.

From its very definition (the user-perceived behaviour), the service delivered by a system is clearly an *abstraction* of the system's behaviour. It is noteworthy that this abstraction is highly dependent on the application that the computer system supports. An example of this dependence is the important role played in this abstraction by time: the time granularities of the system and of its user(s) are generally different, and the difference varies from one application to another. In addition, the service is of course not restricted to the outputs only, but encompasses all interactions which are of interest to the user; for instance, scanning sensors clearly is part of the service expected from a monitoring system.

Of special interest with respect to dependability are timeliness properties. A **real-time function or service** is a function or service that is required to be fulfilled or delivered within finite time intervals *dictated by the environment*, and a **real-time system** is a system which fulfils at least one real-time function or delivers at least one real-time service [64].

Of central role in dependability is the system **specification**, i.e. an *agreed* description of the system function or service. The system function or service is usually specified first in terms of what *should* be fulfilled or delivered regarding the system's primary aim(s) (e.g. performing transactions, controlling or monitoring an industrial process, piloting a plane or a rocket, etc.). When considering safety- or security-related systems, this specification is generally augmented by an indication of what *should not* happen (e.g. the hazardous states from which a catastrophe may ensue, or the disclosure of sensitive information). Such a specification may in turn lead to specifying (additional) functions or services that the system *should* fulfill or deliver in order to reduce the likelihood of what should not happen (e.g. authenticating a user and checking his or her authorization rights).

Expressing the functions of a system is an activity which naturally starts during the very first steps of a system development. It is however not generally limited to this phase of a system's life; experience shows that specifying a system's functions is pursued during all the system's life, due to the difficulty in identifying what is expected from a system.

## 4    The Attributes of Dependability

The attributes of dependability have been defined in section 2 according to different properties, which may be more or less emphasized depending on the application intended for the computer system under consideration: (i) availability is always required, although to a varying degree depending on the application; (ii) reliability, safety, confidentiality may or may not be required according to the application.

Integrity is a pre-requisite for availability, reliability and safety, but may not be so for confidentiality (for instance when considering attacks via covert channels or passive listening). The definition given for integrity — absence of improper alterations of information — generalizes the usual definitions, which relate to the notion of authorized actions only (e.g. prevention of the unauthorized amendment or deletion of information [16], assurance of approved data alterations [40]; naturally, when a system implements an authorization policy, "improper" encompasses "unauthorized".

The definition given for maintainability goes deliberately beyond **corrective maintenance**, aimed at preserving or improving the system's ability to deliver a service fulfilling its function (relating to reparability only), and encompasses via evolvability the other forms of maintenance: **adaptive maintenance**, which adjusts the system to environmental changes (e.g. change of operating systems or system data-bases), and **perfective maintenance**, which improves the system's function by responding to customer — and designer — defined changes, which may involve removal of specification faults [68]. Actually, maintainability conditions a system's dependability all along its life-cycle, due to the unavoidable evolutions during its operational life.

Security has not been introduced as a single attribute of dependability, in agreement with the usual definitions of security, which view it as a *composite* notion, namely «the combination of confidentiality, the prevention of the unauthorized disclosure of information, integrity, the prevention of the unauthorized amendment or deletion of information, and availability, the prevention of the unauthorized withholding of information [16].

# 5    The Impairments to Dependability

Failure occurrence has been defined in section 2 with respect to the function of a system, not with respect to its specification. Indeed, if an unacceptable behaviour is generally identified as a failure due to a deviation from the compliance with the specification, it might happen that such behaviour complies with the specification, and be however unacceptable for the system user(s), thus uncovering a specification fault. In such situations, recognizing that the event is undesired (and is in fact a failure) can only be performed after its occurrence, for instance via its consequences[1].

A system may not, and generally does not, always fail in the same way. The ways a system can fail are its *failure modes*, which may be characterized according to three viewpoints as indicated in Fig. 2: domain, perception by the system users, and consequences on the environment.

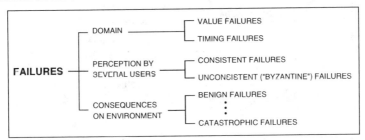

**Fig. 2.** The failure classes

A class of failures relating to both value and timing are the **halting failures**: system activity, if any, is no longer perceptible to the users. According to how the system interacts with its user(s), such an absence of activity may take the form of (i) frozen outputs (a constant value service is delivered; the constant value delivered may vary according to the application, e.g. last correct value, some predetermined value, etc.), or of (ii) a silence (no message sent in a distributed system). A system whose failures can be — or more generally are to an acceptable extent — only halting failures, is a **fail-halt system**; the situations of frozen outputs and of silence lead respectively to **fail-passive systems** and to **fail-silent systems** [66]. A system whose failures can only be — or more generally are to an acceptable extent — benign failures is a **fail-safe system**.

Faults and their sources are extremely diverse. They can be classified according to five main viewpoints which are their phenomenological cause, their nature, their phase of creation or of occurrence, their situation with respect to the system boundaries, and their persistence. The resulting fault classes, which can be termed as elementary fault classes, are given in Fig. 3.

If all the combinations of fault classes according to the five viewpoints of Fig. 3 were possible, there would be 48 different fault classes. In fact, the number of likely

---

1   In fact, what has to be recognized is that, although it is generally desirable that specifications can be stated at the beginning of, or during, the system development, there are some specifications which can only be derived from the observation of the system in its context and environment.

combinations is more restricted: 15 combinations are indicated in Fig. 4, which also
gives the usual labelling of these combined classes of faults. These labels are
commonly used in order to point in a condensed manner at one or several combined
fault classes.

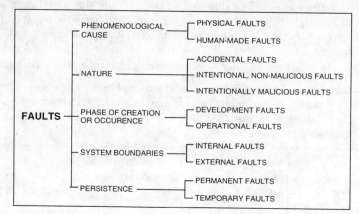

**Fig. 3.** Elementary fault classes

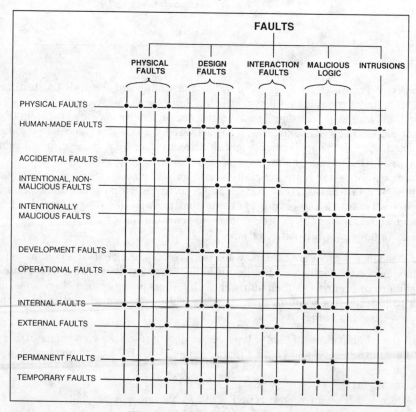

**Fig. 4.** Combined fault classes

The label *physical faults* relates to the various combinations which precisely share physical faults as elementary faults. A few comments regarding the human-made fault classes:

1) Intentional, non-malicious, design faults result generally from tradeoffs, either (i) aimed at preserving acceptable performances, at facilitating the system utilization, or (ii) induced by economic considerations; such faults can be sources of security breaches, under the form of *covert channels*. Intentional, non-malicious interaction faults may result from the action of an operator either aimed at overcoming an unforeseen situation, or deliberately violating an operating procedure without having developed the consciousness of the possibly damaging consequences of his or her action. These classes of intentional non-malicious faults share the property that, often, it is realized they were faults only *after* an unacceptable system behaviour, thus a failure, has ensued.

2) Malicious logics encompass development faults such as *Trojan horses*, logic or timing *bombs*, *trapdoors*, as well as operational faults (for the considered system) such as *viruses* or *worms* [47].

3) Intrusions, in order to be successful, necessitate the existence of design faults; there are interesting and obvious similarities between an intrusion and an accidental external fault "exploiting" a lack of shielding. It is in addition noteworthy that the external character of intrusions does not exclude that they be attempted by system operators or administrators which exceed their rights.

It is noteworthy that the very notion of fault is *arbitrary,* and is in fact a facility provided for stopping the recursion induced by the causal relationship between faults, errors and failures. Hence the definition given: *adjudged or hypothesized* cause of an error. This cause may vary depending upon the chosen viewpoint: fault tolerance mechanisms, maintenance engineers, repair shop, developer, semiconductor physicist, etc. In fact, *a fault is nothing else than the consequence of a failure of some other system* (including the developer) *that has delivered or is now delivering a service to the given system.* A computing system is a human artifact and as such any fault in it or affecting it is ultimately human-made since it represents human inability to master all the phenomena which govern the behaviour of a system. Going further, *any fault can be viewed as a permanent design fault.* This is indeed true in an absolute sense, but is not very helpful for the developers and assessors of a system, hence the usefulness of the various fault classes when considering (current) methods and techniques for procuring and validating dependability.

The creation and manifestation mechanisms of faults, errors, and failures may be summarized as follows:

1) A fault is **active** when it produces an error. An active fault is either (i) an internal fault which was previously **dormant** and which has been activated by the computation process, or (ii) an external fault. Most internal faults cycle between their dormant and active states. Physical faults can directly affect the hardware components only, whereas human-made faults may affect any component.

2) An error may be latent or detected. An error is **latent** when it has not been recognized as such; an error is **detected** by a detection algorithm or mechanism. An error may disappear before being detected. An error may, and in general does, propagate; by propagating, an error creates other — new — error(s). During

operation, the presence of active faults is determined only by the detection of errors.

3)  A failure occurs when an error "passes through" the system-user interface and affects the service delivered by the system. A component failure results in a fault (i) for the system which contains the component, and (ii) as viewed by the other component(s) with which it interacts; the failure modes of the failed component then become fault types for the components interacting with it.

These mechanisms enable the "fundamental chain" to be completed:

$$\cdots \rightarrow \text{ failure } \rightarrow \text{ fault } \rightarrow \text{ error } \rightarrow \text{ failure } \rightarrow \text{ fault } \rightarrow \cdots$$

The arrows in this chain express a causality relationship between faults, errors and failures. They should not be interpreted in a restrictive manner: by propagation, several errors can be generated before a failure occurs; an error can lead to a fault without a failure being observed, if the observation is not performed, as a failure is an event occurring at the interface between two components.

Two final comments, relative to the words, or *labels*, "fault", "error", and "failure":

1)  their exclusive use in this paper does not preclude the use in special situations of words which designate, succinctly and unambiguously, a specific class of impairment; this is especially applicable to faults (e.g. bug, defect, deficiency) and to failures (e.g. breakdown, malfunction, denial-of-service);

2)  the assignment made of the particular terms fault, error, failure simply takes into account current usage: i) fault prevention, tolerance, and diagnosis, ii) error detection and correction, iii) failure rate.

# 6   The Means for Dependability

In this section, we examine in turns fault tolerance, fault removal and fault forecasting; fault prevention is not dealt with as it clearly relates to "general" system engineering. The section ends with a discussion on the relationship between the several means for dependability.

## 6.1  Fault tolerance

Fault tolerance [7] is carried out by error processing and by fault treatment [3]. **Error processing** is aimed at removing errors from the computational state, if possible before failure occurrence; **fault treatment** is aimed at preventing faults from being activated — again.

*Error processing* can be carried out via three primitives:

•  **error detection**, which enables an erroneous state to be identified as such;

•  **error diagnosis**, which enables assessment of the damages caused by the detected error, or by errors propagated before detection;

•  **error recovery**, where an error-free state is substituted for the erroneous state; this substitution may take on three forms.

   -  **backward recovery**, where the erroneous state transformation consists of bringing the system back to a state already occupied prior to error occurrence; this involves the establishment of **recovery points**, which are points in time during the execution of a process for which the then current state may subsequently need to be restored;

- **forward recovery**, where the erroneous state transformation consists of finding a new state, from which the system can operate (frequently in a degraded mode);
- **compensation**, where the erroneous state contains enough redundancy to enable its transformation into an error-free state.

When backward or forward recovery are utilized, it is necessary that error detection precedes error recovery. Backward and forward recovery are not exclusive: backward recovery may be attempted first; if the error persists, forward recovery may then be attempted. In forward recovery, it is necessary to perform error diagnosis, something which can — in principle — be ignored in the case of backward recovery, provided that the mechanisms enabling the transformation of the erroneous state into an error-free state have not been affected [3].

The association into a component of its functional processing capability together with error detection mechanisms leads to the notion of a **self-checking component**, either in hardware [14, 62, 77] or in software [50, 81]; one of the important benefits of the self-checking component approach is the ability to give a clear definition of *error confinement areas* [72]. When error compensation is performed in a system made up of self-checking components partitioned into classes executing the same tasks, then state transformation simply consists of switching within a class from a failed component to a non-failed one. On the other hand, compensation may be applied systematically, even in the absence of errors, so providing **fault masking** (e.g. in majority vote). However, this can at the same time correspond to a redundancy decrease whose extent is not known. So, practical implementations of masking generally involve error detection, which may then be performed *after* the state transformation. As opposed to fault-masking, implementing error processing via error recovery *after* error detection has taken place, is generally referred to as **error detection and recovery**.

The first step in *fault treatment* is **fault diagnosis**, which consists of determining the cause(s) of error(s), in terms of both location and nature. Then come the actions aimed at fulfilling the main purpose of fault treatment: preventing the fault(s) from being activated again, thus aimed at making it(them) passive, i.e. **fault passivation**. This is carried out by preventing the component(s) identified as being faulty from being invoked in further executions. If the system is no longer capable of delivering the same service as before, then a **reconfiguration** may take place, which consists of modifying the system structure in order that the non-failed components enable the delivery of an acceptable service, although degraded; a reconfiguration may involve some tasks to be given up, or re-assigning tasks among non-failed components.

If it is estimated that error processing could directly remove the fault, or if its likelihood of recurring is low enough, then fault passivation need not be undertaken. As long as fault passivation is not undertaken, the fault is regarded as a **soft fault**; undertaking it implies that the fault is considered as **hard**, or **solid**. At first sight, the notions of soft and hard faults may seem to be respectively synonymous to the previously introduced notions of temporary and permanent faults. Indeed, tolerance of temporary faults does not necessitate fault treatment, since error recovery should in this case directly remove the effects of the fault, which has itself vanished, provided that a permanent fault has not been created in the propagation process. In fact, the notions of soft and hard faults are useful due to the following reasons:

- distinguishing a permanent fault from a temporary fault is a difficult and complex task, since (i) a temporary fault vanishes after a certain amount of time, usually before fault diagnosis is undertaken, and (ii) faults from different classes may lead to very similar errors; so, the notion of soft or hard fault in fact incorporates the subjectivity associated with these difficulties, including the fact that a fault may be declared as a soft fault when fault diagnosis is unsuccessful;

- the ability of those notions to incorporate subtleties of the modes of action of some transient faults; for instance, can it be said that the dormant internal fault resulting from the action of alpha particles (due to the residual ionization of circuit packages), or of heavy ions in space, on memory elements (in the broad sense of the term, including flip-flops) is a *temporary* fault? Such a dormant fault is however a *soft* fault.

The preceding definitions apply to physical faults as well as to design faults: the class(es) of faults that can actually be tolerated depend(s) on the fault hypothesis that is being considered in the design process, and thus relies on the *independence* of redundancies with respect to the process of fault creation and activation. An example is provided by considering tolerance of physical faults and tolerance of design faults. A (widely-used) method of achieving fault tolerance is to perform multiple computations through multiple channels. When tolerance of physical faults is foreseen, the channels may be identical, based on the assumption that hardware components fail independently; such an approach is not suitable for providing tolerance to design faults where the channels have to provide *identical services* through *separate designs and implementations* [8, 29, 69], i.e. through **design diversity** [9].

An important aspect of the coordination of the activity of multiple components is that of preventing error propagation from affecting the operation of non-failed components. This aspect becomes particularly important when a given component needs to communicate some information to other components that is private to that component. Typical examples of such *single-source information* are local sensor data, the value of a local clock, the local view of the status of other components, etc. The consequence of this need to communicate single-source information from one component to other components is that non-failed components must reach an *agreement* as to how the information they obtain should be employed in a mutually consistent way. Specific attention has been devoted to this problem in the field of distributed systems (see e.g. atomic broadcast [20], clock synchronization [42, 45] or membership protocols [19]). It is important to realize, however, that the inevitable presence of structural redundancy in any fault-tolerant system implies distribution at one level or another, and that the agreement problem therefore remains in existence. Geographically localized fault-tolerant systems may employ solutions to the agreement problem that would be deemed too costly in a "classical" distributed system of components communicating by messages (e.g. inter-stages [44], multiple stages for interactive consistency [31]).

Fault tolerance is (also) a recursive concept: it is essential that the mechanisms aimed at implementing fault tolerance be protected against the faults which can affect them.

Examples are voter replication, self-checking checkers [14], "stable" memory for recovery programs and data [46].

Fault tolerance is not restricted to accidental faults. Protection against intrusions traditionally involves cryptography [24]. Some mechanisms of error detection are directed towards both intentional and accidental faults (e.g. memory access protection techniques) and schemes have been proposed for the tolerance to both intrusions and physical faults [30, 67], as well as for tolerance to malicious logic [41].

## 6.2 Fault removal

Fault removal is composed of three steps: verification, diagnosis, correction. **Verification** is the process of checking whether the system adheres to properties, termed the *verification conditions* [17]; if it does not, the other two steps have to be undertaken: diagnosing the fault(s) which prevented the verification conditions from being fulfilled, and then performing the necessary corrections. After correction, the process has to be resumed in order to check that fault removal had no undesired consequences; the verification performed at this stage is usually termed (non-)**regression verification**. Verification conditions can take two forms:

- general conditions, which apply to a given class of systems, and are therefore — relatively — independent of the specification, e.g. absence of deadlock, conformance to design and realization rules;
- conditions specific to the considered system, directly deduced from its specification.

Verification techniques can be classed according to whether or not they involve exercising the system. Verifying a system without actual execution is **static verification**. Such verification can be conducted:

- on the system itself, in the form of (i) *static analysis* (e.g. inspections or walk-through [61], data flow analysis [63], complexity analysis [56], compiler checks, etc.) or (ii) *proof-of-correctness* (inductive assertions [18, 36]);
- on a model of the system behaviour (e.g. Petri nets, finite state automata), leading to *behaviour analysis* [25].

Verifying a system through exercising it constitutes **dynamic verification**; the inputs supplied to the system can be either symbolic in the case of **symbolic execution**, or valued in the case of verification testing, usually simply termed **testing**.

Testing a system exhaustively with respect to all its possible inputs is generally impractical. Methods for the determination of the test patterns can be classed according to two viewpoints: criteria for selecting the test inputs, and generation of the test inputs.

Techniques for selecting the test inputs may in turn be classed according to three viewpoints:

- the purpose of the testing: checking whether the system satisfies its specification is **conformance testing**, whereas testing aimed at revealing faults is **fault-finding testing**;

- the system model: depending on whether the system model relates to the function or the structure of the system, leads respectively to **functional testing** and **structural testing**;

- fault model: the existence of a fault model leads to **fault-based testing** [60], aimed at revealing specific classes of faults (e.g. stuck-at-faults in hardware production [71], physical faults affecting the instruction set of a microprocessor [74], design faults in software [23, 33, 38]); if there is no fault model, one is then led to **criteria-based testing**, where the criteria may relate, for software, to path sensitization [37], to utilization of the program variables [70], to input boundary values [61], etc.

Combining the various viewpoints leads to various testing approaches, where the distinction between hardware and software is important since hardware testing is mainly aimed at removing production faults, whereas software testing is concerned only with design faults:

- structural testing when applied to hardware generally means fault-finding, fault-based testing, whereas it generally means fault-finding, non-fault-based testing when applied to software;

- functional testing when applied to hardware generally means fault-finding, fault-based testing, whereas it generally means either conformance or fault-finding, criteria-based testing when applied to software;

- *mutation testing* of software [23] is fault-finding, structural, fault-based, testing.

The *generation* of the test inputs may be deterministic or probabilistic:

- in **deterministic testing**, test patterns are predetermined by a selective choice according to the adopted criteria,

- in **random**, or **statistical**, **testing**, test patterns are selected according to a defined probability distribution on the input domain; the distribution and the number of input data are determined according to the adopted criteria [22, 28, 75].

Observing the test outputs and deciding whether they satisfy or not the verification conditions is known as the *oracle* problem [2]. The verification conditions may apply to the whole set of outputs or to a compact function of the latter (e.g. a system signature when testing for physical faults in hardware [21], or a "partial oracle" when testing for design faults of software [78]). When testing for physical faults, the results — compact or not — anticipated from the system under test for a given input sequence are determined by simulation [53] or from a reference system ("golden unit"). For design faults, the reference is generally the specification; it may also be a prototype, or another implementation of the same specification in the case of design diversity ("back-to-back testing", see e.g. [10]).

Some verification methods may be used in conjunction, e.g. symbolic execution may be used (i) for facilitating the determination of the testing patterns [2], or (ii) as a proof-of-correctness method [13].

As verification has to be performed throughout a system's development, the above techniques apply naturally to the various forms taken by a system during its development: prototype, component, etc.

Verifying that the system *cannot do more* than what is specified is especially important with respect to what the system should not do, thus with respect to safety and security [32].

Designing a system in order to facilitate its verification is termed **design for verifiability**. This is well developed for hardware with respect to physical faults, where the corresponding techniques are then termed *design for testability* [57, 79].

Fault removal during the operational phase of a system's life is **corrective maintenance**, which can take two forms:

• **curative maintenance**, aimed at removing faults which have produced one or more errors and have been reported;

• **preventive maintenance**, aimed at removing faults before they produce errors; these faults can be physical faults that have appeared since the last preventive maintenance actions, or design faults having led to errors in other similar systems [1].

These definitions apply to non-fault-tolerant systems as well as to fault-tolerant systems, which can be maintainable on-line (without interrupting service delivery) or off-line. It is finally noteworthy that the frontier between corrective maintenance and fault treatment is relatively arbitrary; in particular, curative maintenance may be considered as an — ultimate — means of achieving fault tolerance.

## 6.3  Fault forecasting

Fault forecasting is conducted by performing an *evaluation* of the system behaviour with respect to fault occurrence or activation. Evaluation has two aspects:

• *qualitative*, aimed at (i) identifying, classifying and ordering the failure modes, or at (ii) identifying the events combinations (component failures or environmental conditions) leading to undesired events;

• *quantitative*, aimed at evaluating in terms of probabilities some of the attributes of dependability, which may then be viewed as *measures* of dependability.

Methods and tools enabling qualitative and quantitative evaluations are either specific (e.g. failure mode and effect analysis for qualitative evaluation, or Markov chains for quantitative evaluation), or can be used for performing both forms of evaluation (e.g. reliability block diagrams, fault-trees).

The definition of the measures of dependability necessitates first defining the notions of correct and incorrect service:

• **correct service**, where the delivered service fulfills the system function;

• **incorrect service**, where the delivered service does not fulfill the system function.

A failure is thus a transition from correct to incorrect service, and the transition from incorrect to correct service is a **restoration**. Quantifying the alternation of correct-incorrect service delivery then enables reliability and availability to be defined as measures of dependability:

• **reliability**: a measure of the *continuous* delivery of correct service — or, equivalently, of the *time to* failure;

• **availability**: a measure of the delivery of correct service *with respect to the alternation* of correct and incorrect service.

A third measure, **maintainability**, is usually considered, which may be defined as a measure of the time to restoration from the last experienced failure, or equivalently, of the continuous delivery of incorrect service.

As a measure, safety can be seen as an extension of reliability. Let us group the state of correct service together with the state of incorrect service subsequent to benign failures into a safe state (in the sense of being free from catastrophic damage, not from danger); **safety** is then a measure of continuous safeness, or equivalently, of the time to catastrophic failure. Safety can thus be considered as reliability with respect to catastrophic failures.

In the case of multi-performing systems, several services can be distinguished, as well as several modes of service delivery, ranging from full capacity to complete disruption, which can be seen as distinguishing less and less correct service deliveries. Performance-related measures of dependability for such systems are usually grouped under the notion of **performability** [58, 73].

When performing an evaluation through *modelling*, the approaches differ significantly according to whether the system is considered as being in a period of stable reliability or in one of reliability growth, which may be defined as follows [51]:

- **stable reliability**: the system's ability to deliver correct service is *preserved* (stochastic identity of the successive times to failure);
- **reliability growth**: the system's ability to deliver correct service is *improved* (stochastic increase of the successive times to failure).

Evaluation of the dependability of systems in stable reliability is usually composed of two main phases:

- *construction* of the model of the system from the elementary stochastic processes which model the behaviour of the components of the system and their interactions;
- *processing* the model in order to obtain the expressions and the values of the dependability measures of the system.

Evaluation can be conducted with respect to (i) physical faults [76], (ii) design faults [5, 54], or (iii) a combination of both [52, 65]. The dependability of a system is highly dependent on its environment, either in the broad sense of the term [35], or more specifically its load [15, 39].

Reliability growth models, be they for hardware [26], for software [55, 59, 80], or for both [51], are aimed at performing reliability predictions from data relative to past system failures.

When evaluating fault tolerant systems, the coverage of error processing and fault treatment mechanisms has a very significant influence [6, 12]; its evaluation can be performed either through modelling [27] or through testing, then called *fault-injection* [4, 34].

## 6.4  Dependencies between the means for dependability

All the "how to's" which appear in the basic definitions given in section 2 are in fact goals which cannot be fully reached, as all the corresponding activities are human activities, and thus imperfect. These imperfections bring in *dependencies* which explain why it is only the *combined* utilization of the above methods — preferably at each step of the design and implementation process — which can best lead to a dependable computing system. These dependencies can be sketched as follows: in spite of fault prevention by means of design methodologies and construction rules (imperfect in order to be workable), faults are created. Hence the need for fault removal. Fault removal is itself imperfect, as are the off-the-shelf components — hardware or software — of the system, hence the importance of fault forecasting. Our increasing dependence on computing systems brings in the requirement for fault tolerance, which is in turn based on construction rules; hence fault removal, fault forecasting, etc. It must be noted that the process is even more recursive than it appears from the above: current computer systems are so complex that their design and implementation need computerized tools in order to be cost-effective (in a broad sense, including the capability of succeeding within an acceptable time scale). These tools themselves have to be dependable, and so on.

The preceding reasoning illustrates the close interactions between fault removal and fault forecasting, and motivates their gathering into the single term **validation**. This is despite the fact that validation is often limited to fault removal, and associated with one of the main activities involved in fault removal, verification: e.g. in "V and V" [11]; in such a case the distinction is related to the difference between "building the system right" (related to verification) and "building the right system" (related to validation). What is proposed here is simply an extension of this concept: the answer to the question "am I building the right system?" (fault removal) being complemented by "for how long will it be right?" (fault forecasting). In addition, fault removal is usually closely associated with fault prevention, forming together **fault avoidance**, i.e. how to *aim at* a fault-free system. Besides highlighting the need for validating the procedures and mechanisms of fault tolerance, considering fault removal and fault forecasting as two constituents of the same activity — validation — is of great interest in that it enables a better understanding of the notion of coverage, and thus of an important problem introduced by the above recursion: *the validation of the validation,* or how to reach confidence in the methods and tools used in building confidence in the system. **Coverage** refers here to a measure of the representativity of the situations to which the system is submitted during its validation compared to the actual situations it will be confronted with during its operational life[2]. Imperfect coverage strengthens the relation between fault removal and fault forecasting, as it can be considered that the need for fault forecasting stems from imperfect coverage of fault removal.

The *assessment* of whether a system is truly dependable — justified reliance on the delivered service — or not thus goes beyond the validation techniques as they have been addressed in the previous sections for, at least, the three following reasons and limitations:
• checking with certainty the coverage of the design or validation assumptions with respect to reality (e.g. relevance to actual faults of the criteria used for determining test inputs, fault hypotheses in the design of fault tolerance

---

[2] The notion of coverage as defined here is very general; it may be made more precise by indicating its field of application, e.g.: (i) coverage of a software test wrt its text, control graph, etc., (ii) coverage of an integrated circuit test wrt a fault model, (iii) coverage of fault tolerance wrt a class of faults, (iv) coverage of a design assumption wrt to reality.

mechanisms) would imply a knowledge and a mastering of the technology used, of the intended utilization of the system, etc., which exceeds by far what is generally achievable;

- performing a probabilistic evaluation of a system according to some attributes of dependability with respect to some classes of faults is currently considered as infeasible or yielding non-significant results: probability-theoretic bases do not exist or are not — yet — widely accepted; examples are safety with respect to accidental design faults, security with respect to intentionally malicious faults;
- the specifications "against" which validation is performed are not generally fault free — as any system.

## 7    Summary and Conclusions

This paper has introduced the main concepts which are useful for the specification, design, realization and operation of dependable computing systems. The attributes of dependability and the means aimed at making a system dependable have been defined independently of specific classes of impairments. The fault-error-failure model is central to the understanding and mastering of the various impairments which may affect a system, and it enables a unified presentation of these impairments, though preserving their specificities via the various fault classes which have been defined.

## Acknowledgements

What has been presented in this paper has benefited from many discussions held with many colleagues, from LAAS, from the other PDCS and PDCS2 partners, and from IFIP WG 10.4 on *Dependable Computing and Fault Tolerance*. Special thanks go to Tom Anderson, Al Avizienis, Alain Costes, Yves Deswarte, David Powell, Brian Randell, and Pascale Thévenod.

# References for Chapter 1

[1]     E. Adams, "Optimizing Preventive Service of Software Products", *IBM Journal of Research and Development*, 28 (1), pp.2-14, 1984.

[2]     W. R. Adrion, M. A. Branstad and J. C. Cherniavsky, "Validation, Verification and Testing of Computer Software", *Computing Surveys*, 14 (2), pp.159-92, 1982.

[3]     T. Anderson and P. A. Lee, *Fault Tolerance — Principles and Practice,* Prentice Hall, 1981.

[4]     J. Arlat, Y. Crouzet and J.-C. Laprie, "Fault Injection for Dependability Validation of Fault-Tolerant Computing Systems", in *Proc. 19th Int. Symp. on Fault Tolerant Computing (FTCS-19),* (Chicago, IL, USA), pp.348-55, IEEE Computer Society Press, 1989.

[5]     J. Arlat, K. Kanoun and J.-C. Laprie, "Dependability Evaluation of Software Fault Tolerance", in *Proc. 18th Int. Symp. on Fault-Tolerant Computing (FTCS-18),* (Tokyo, Japan), pp.142-7, IEEE Computer Society Press, 1988.

[6]     T. F. Arnold, "The Concept of Coverage and its Effect on the Reliability Model of Repairable Systems", *IEEE Transactions on Computers*, C-22 (3), pp.251-4, 1973.

[7]     A. Avizienis, "Design of Fault-Tolerant Computers", in *Proc. Fall Joint Computer Conf.,* pp.733-43, 1967.

[8]     A. Avizienis, "Fault Tolerance, the Survival Attribute of Digital Systems", *Proceedings of the IEEE*, 66 (10), pp.1109-25, 1978.

[9]     A. Avizienis and J. P. J. Kelly, "Fault Tolerance by Design Diversity: Concepts and Experiments", *IEEE Computer Magazine*, 17 (8), pp.67-80, 1984.

[10]    P. G. Bishop, "The PODS Diversity Experiment", in *Software Diversity in Computerized Control Systems (Proc. IFIP Working Conf. "Design Diversity in Action", Baden, Austria, June, 1986)* (U. Voges, H. Kopetz and J.-C. Laprie, Eds.), Dependable Computing and Fault-Tolerant Systems, 2, (A. Avizienis, Ed.), pp.51-84, Springer-Verlag, Vienna, Austria, 1988.

[11]    B. W. Boehm, "Guidelines for Verifying and Validating Software Requirements and Design Specifications", in *Proc. EURO IFIP'79,* (London, UK), pp.711-9, 1979.

[12]    W. G. Bouricius, W. C. Carter and P. R. Schneider, "Reliability Modelling Techniques for Self-Repairing Computer Systems", in *Proc. 24th. National Conference,* pp.295-309, ACM Press, 1969.

[13]    W. C. Carter, W. H. Joyner, D. Brand, H. A. Ellozy and J. L. Wolf, "An Improved System to Verify Assembled Programs", in *Proc. 8th Int. Symp. Fault-Tolerant Computing (FTCS-8),* (Toulouse, France), pp.165-70, IEEE Computer Society Press, 1978.

[14]  W. C. Carter and P. R. Schneider, "Design of Dynamically Checked Computers", in *Proc. IFIP'68 World Computer Congress,* (Amsterdam, The Netherlands), pp.878-83, 1968.

[15]  X. Castillo and D. P. Siewiorek, "Workload, Performance and Reliability of Digital Computing Systems", in *Proc. 11th Int. Symp. on Fault Tolerant Computing (FTCS-11),* (Portland, ME, USA), pp.84-9, IEEE Computer Society Press, 1981.

[16]  *Information Technology Security Evaluation Criteria*, Provisional Harmonised Criteria, Version 1.2, Office for Official Publications of the European Communities, 1991.

[17]  M. H. Cheheyl, M. Gasser, G. A. Huff and J. K. Miller, "Verifying Security", *Computing Surveys*, 13 (3), pp.279-339, 1981.

[18]  D. Craigen, "Strengths and Weaknesses of Program Verification Systems", in *Proc. 1st European Software Engineering Conf.,* (Strasbourg, France), pp.421-9, 1987.

[19]  F. Cristian, "Agreeing on Who is Present and Who is Absent in a Synchronous Distributed System", in *Proc. 18th Int. Symp. on Fault-Tolerant Computing (FTCS-18),* (Tokyo, Japan), pp.206-11, IEEE Computer Society Press, 1988.

[20]  F. Cristian, H. Aghali, R. Strong and D. Dolev, "Atomic Broadcast: From Simple Message Diffusion to Byzantine Agreement", in *Proc. 15th Int. Symp. on Fault-Tolerant Computing (FTCS-15),* (Ann Arbor, MI, USA), pp.200-6, IEEE Computer Society Press, 1985.

[21]  R. David, "Signature Analysis of Multiple Output Circuits", *IEEE Transactions on Computers*, C-35 (9), pp.830-7, 1986.

[22]  R. David and P. Thévenod-Fosse, "Random Testing of Integrated Circuits", *IEEE Transactions on Instrumentation and Measurement*, IM-30 (1), pp.20-5, 1981.

[23]  R. A. DeMillo, R. J. Lipton and F. G. Sayward, "Hints on Test Data Selection: Help for the Practicing Programmer", *IEEE Computer*, pp.34-41, 1978.

[24]  D. E. Denning, *Cryptography and Data Security,* Addison-Wesley, 1982.

[25]  M. Diaz, "Modelling and Analysis of Communication and Cooperation Protocols Using Petri Net Based Models", *Computer Networks*, 6 (6), pp.419-41, 1982.

[26]  J. T. Duane, "Learning Curve Approach to Reliability Monitoring", *IEEE Transactions on Aerospace*, 2, pp.563-6, 1964.

[27]  J. B. Dugan and K. S. Trivedi, "Coverage Modelling for Dependability Analysis of Fault-Tolerant Systems", *IEEE Transactions on Computers*, 38 (6), pp.775-87, 1989.

[28]  J. W. Duran and S. C. Ntafos, "An Evaluation of Random Testing", *IEEE Transactions on Software Engineering*, SE-10 (4), pp.438-44, 1984.

[29]  W. R. Elmendorf, "Fault-Tolerant Programming", in *Proc. 2nd Int. Symp. on Fault-Tolerant Computing (FTCS-2)*, (Newton, MA, USA), pp.79-83, IEEE Computer Society Press, 1972.

[30]  J.-M. Fray, Y. Deswarte and D. Powell, "Intrusion-Tolerance using Fine-Grain Fragmentation-Scattering", in *Proc. 1986 Symp. on Security and Privacy*, (Oakland, CA, USA), pp.194-201, IEEE Computer Society Press, 1986.

[31]  S. G. Frison and J. H. Wensley, "Interactive Consistency and its Impact on the Design of TMR Systems", in *Proc. 12th IEEE Int. Symp. on Fault Tolerant Computing (FTCS-12)*, (Santa Monica, CA, USA), pp.228-33, IEEE Computer Society Press, 1982.

[32]  M. Gasser, *Building a Secure Computer System*, Van Nostrand Reinhold, 1988.

[33]  J. B. Goodenough and S. L. Gerhart, "Toward a Theory of Test Data Selection", *IEEE Transactions on Software Engineering*, SE-1 (2), pp.156-73, 1975.

[34]  U. Gunneflo, J. Karlsson and J. Torin, "Evaluation of Error Detection Schemes Using Fault Injection by Heavy-ion Radiation", in *Proc. 19th Int. Symp. Fault-Tolerant Computing (FTCS-19)*, (Chicago, IL, USA), pp.340-7, IEEE Computer Society Press, 1989.

[35]  H. Hecht and E. Fiorentino, "Reliability Assessment of Spacecraft Electronics", in *Proc. 1987 Annual Reliability and Maintainability Symp.*, IEEE Computer Society Press, 1987.

[36]  C. A. R. Hoare, "An Axiomatic Basis for Computer Programming", *Communications of the ACM*, 12 (10), pp.576-83, 1969.

[37]  W. E. Howden, "Reliability of the Path Analysis Testing Strategy", *IEEE Transactions on Software Engineering*, SE-2, pp.208-14, 1976.

[38]  W. E. Howden, *Functional Program Testing and Analysis*, McGraw-Hill, 1987.

[39]  R. K. Iyer, S. E. Butner and E. J. McCluskey, "A Statistical Failure/Load Relationship: Results of a MultiComputer Study", *IEEE Transactions on Computers*, C-31 (7), pp.697-706, 1982.

[40]  J. Jacob, "The Basic Integrity Theorem", in *Proc. 1991 Int. Symp. on Security and Privacy*, (Oakland, CA, USA), pp.89-97, IEEE Computer Society Press, 1991.

[41]  M. K. Joseph and A. Avizienis, "A Fault Tolerance Approach to Computer Viruses", in *Proc. 1988 Symp. on Security and Privacy*, (Oakland, CA, USA), pp.52-8, IEEE Computer Society Press, 1988.

[42]  H. Kopetz and W. Ochsenreiter, "Clock Synchronization in Distributed Real-Time Systems", *IEEE Transactions on Computers*, C-36 (8), pp.933-40, 1987.

[43]    B. Kuipers, "Commonsense Reasoning about Causality: Deriving Behaviour from Structure", in *Qualitative Reasoning about Physical Systems* (D. G. Bobrow, Ed.), pp.169-203, MIT Press, 1985.

[44]    J. H. Lala, "A Byzantine Resilient Fault Tolerant Computer for Nuclear Power Plant Applications", in *Proc. 16th Int. Symp. on Fault Tolerant Computing (FTCS-16)*, (Vienna, Austria), pp.338-43, IEEE Computer Society Press, 1986.

[45]    L. Lamport and P. M. Melliar-Smith, "Synchronizing Clocks in the Presence of Faults", *Journal of the ACM*, 32 (1), pp.52-78, 1985.

[46]    B. W. Lampson, "Atomic Transactions", in *Distributed Systems — Architecture and Implementation* Lecture Notes in Computer Science 105, Chap. 1, Springer-Verlag, Berlin, Germany, 1981.

[47]    C. E. Landwher, A. R. Bull, J. P. McDermott and W. S. Choi, *A Taxonomy of Computer Program Security Flaws, with Examples*, Naval Research Laboratory , Washington, DC, USA, Report, N°NRL/FR/5542—93-9591, November 1993.

[48]    J.-C. Laprie (Ed.), *Dependability: Basic Concepts and Terminology in English, French, German, Italian and Japanese*, Dependable Computing and Fault Tolerance, 5, 265p., Springer-Verlag, Vienna, Austria, 1992.

[49]    J.-C. Laprie, "Dependability: From Concepts to Limits", in *Proc. SAFECOMP'93*, (Poznan, Poland), pp.157-68, Springer-Verlag, 1993.

[50]    J.-C. Laprie, J. Arlat, C. Béounes and K. Kanoun, "Definition and Analysis of Hardware-and-Software Fault-Tolerant Architectures", *IEEE Computer*, 23 (7), pp.39-51, 1990.

[51]    J.-C. Laprie, C. Béounes, M. Kaâniche and K. Kanoun, "The Transformation Approach to the Modelling and Evaluation of the Reliability and Availability Growth of Systems in Operation", in *Proc. 20th Int. Symp. on Fault-Tolerant Computing (FTCS-20)*, (Newcastle-upon-Tyne, UK), pp.364-71, IEEE Computer Society Press, 1990.

[52]    J.-C. Laprie and K. Kanoun, "X-ware Reliability and Availability Modelling", *IEEE Transactions on Software Engineering*, 18 (2), pp.130-47, 1992.

[53]    Y. Levendel, "Fault Simulation", in *Fault-Tolerant Computing, Theory and Techniques* (D. K. Pradhan, Ed.), pp.184-264, Prentice-Hall, Englewood Cliffs, 1986.

[54]    B. Littlewood, "A Software Reliability Model for Modular Program Structure", *IEEE Transactions on Reliability*, R-28 (3), pp.241-6, 1979.

[55]    B. Littlewood, "Forecasting Software Reliability", in *Software Modelling and Identification* (S. Bittani, Ed.), pp.140-209, Springer-Verlag, 1988.

[56]    T. J. McCabe, "A Complexity Measure", *IEEE Transactions on Software Engineering*, SE-2 (4), pp.308-20, 1976.

[57]   E. J. McCluskey, "Design for Testability", in *Fault-Tolerant Computing, Theory and Techniques* (D. K. Pradhan, Ed.), pp.95-183, Prentice Hall, Englewood Cliffs, NJ, USA, 1986.

[58]   J. F. Meyer, "On Evaluating the Performability of Degradable Computing Systems", in *Proc. 8th Int. Symp. on Fault-Tolerant Computing (FTCS-8)*, (Toulouse, France), pp.44-9, IEEE Computer Society Press, 1978.

[59]   D. R. Miller, "Exponential Order Statistic Models of Software Reliability Growth", *IEEE Transactions on Software Engineering*, SE-12 (1) 1986.

[60]   L. J. Morell, "A Theory of Fault-Based Testing", *IEEE Transactions on Software Engineering*, 16 (8), pp.844-57, 1990.

[61]   G. J. Myers, *The Art of Software Testing*, John Wiley & Sons, New York, 1979.

[62]   M. Nicolaïdis, S. Noraz and B. Courtois, "A Generalized Theory of Fail-Safe Systems", in *Proc. 19th Int. Symp. on Fault Tolerant Computing (FTCS-19)*, (Chicago, IL, USA), pp.398-406, IEEE Computer Society Press, 1989.

[63]   L. J. Osterweil and L. D. Fodsick, "DAVE — A Validation Error Detection and Documentation System for FORTRAN Programs", *Software Practice and Experience*, pp.473-86, 1976.

[64]   *Real-Time Systems*, Specific Closed Workshop, PDCS - ESPRIT Basic Research Action no. 1092, Workshop Report N°W6, 1990.

[65]   P. I. Pignal, "An Analysis of Hardware and Software Availability Exemplified on the IBM 3725 Communication Controller", *IBM Journal of Research and Development*, 32 (2), pp.268-78, 1988.

[66]   D. Powell, G. Bonn, D. Seaton, P. Veríssimo and F. Waeselynck, "The Delta-4 Approach to Dependability in Open Distributed Computing Systems", in *Proc. 18th Int. Symp. on Fault-Tolerant Computing Systems (FTCS-18)*, (Tokyo, Japan), pp.246-51, IEEE Computer Society Press, 1988.

[67]   M. O. Rabin, "Efficient Dispersal of Information for Security, Load Balancing and Fault Tolerance", *Journal of the ACM*, 36 (2), pp.335-48, 1989.

[68]   C. V. Ramamoorthy, A. Prakash, W.-T. Tsai and Y. Usuda, "Software Engineering: Problems and Perspectives", *IEEE Computer*, 17 (10), pp.191-209, 1984.

[69]   B. Randell, "System Structure for Software Fault Tolerance", *IEEE Transactions on Software Engineering*, SE-1 (2), pp.220-32, 1975.

[70]   S. Rapps and E. J. Weyuker, "Selecting Software Test Data Using Data Flow Information", *IEEE Transactions on Software Engineering*, SE-11 (4), pp.367-75, 1985.

[71]   J. P. Roth, W. G. Bouricius and P. R. Schneider, "Programmed Algorithms to Compute Tests to Detect and Distinguish Between Failures in Logic Circuits", *IEEE Transactions on Electronic Computers*, EC-16, pp.567-79, 1967.

[72]  D. P. Siewiorek and R. S. Swarz, *The Theory and Practice of Reliable System Design,* Digital Press, 1982.

[73]  R. M. Smith, K. S. Trivedi and A. V. Ramesh, "Performability Analysis: Measures, An Algorithm and a Case Study", *IEEE Transactions on Computers,* 37 (4), pp.406-17, 1988.

[74]  S. M. Thatte and J. A. Abraham, "A Methodology for Functional Level Testing of Microprocessors", in *Proc. 8th Int. Symp. on Fault-Tolerant Computing (FTCS-8),* (Toulouse, France), pp.90-5, IEEE Computer Society Press, 1978.

[75]  P. Thévenod-Fosse, "Software Validation by Means of Statistical Testing: Retrospect and Future Direction", in *Proc. 1st IFIP Int. Working Conf. on Dependable Computing for Critical Applications (DCCA-1),* (A. Avizienis, J.-C. Laprie, H. Kopetz and J.-C. Laprie, Eds.), (Santa Barbara, CA, USA), Dependable Computing and Fault-Tolerant Systems, 4, (A. Avizienis, Ed.), pp.23-50, 1989.

[76]  K. S. Trivedi, "Reliability Evaluation for Fault-Tolerant Systems", in *Mathematical Computer Performance and Reliability* (G. Iazeolla, P. J. Courtois and A. Hordijk, Eds.), pp.403-14, North-Holland, Amsterdam, The Netherlands, 1984.

[77]  J. Wakerly, *Error Detecting Codes, Self-Checking Circuits and Applications,* Elsevier North-Holland, New York, 1978.

[78]  E. J. Weyuker, "On Testing Non-Testable Programs", *The Computer Journal,* 25 (4), pp.465-70, 1982.

[79]  T. W. Williams, "Design for Testability — A Survey", *Proceedings of the IEEE,* 71 (1), pp.98-112, 1983.

[80]  S. Yamada and S. Osaki, "Software Reliability Growth Modelling: Models and Applications", *IEEE Transactions on Software Engineering,* SE-11 (12), pp.1431-7, 1985.

[81]  S. S. Yau and R. C. Cheung, "Design of Self-Checking Software", in *Proc. Int. Conf. on Reliable Software,* (Los Angeles, CA, USA), pp.450-7, IEEE Computer Society Press, 1975.

[82]  B. P. Zeigler, *Theory of Modelling and Simulation,* John Wiley & Sons, New York, 1976.

# Chapter II

# Fault Prevention

Fault prevention and fault tolerance are the two complementary techniques to achieve the stated goal of highly dependable systems. This chapter highlights the most significant results that have been achieved in the PDCS project in the area of fault prevention. In this area the focus of the PDCS work was on safety-critical distributed real-time systems.

The first paper in this chapter, "Analysis of Safety Requirements for Process Control Systems" presents a systematic method for the development of high-quality requirements specification that put special emphasis on the safety relevant behavior. For this purpose a new approach is introduced that is based on three related aspects: modeling, analysis, and documentation. To be able to analyze the interactions between a computing system and its environment, proper models of the computing system and its environment must be constructed. To obtain a hierarchical model, successive structural decompositions and behavioral refinements are performed on the system and its components. The models are then used to perform a safety analysis. The results and interrelationships of the requirements analysis and safety analysis are documented in a structured form in a safety specification graph, a piece of evidence that assists in the certification of safety critical systems.

The second paper, "Real-Time Scheduling", reports about the significant contributions to the field of scheduling that have been produced by the Real-Time Systems Research group at the University of York. The scheduling theories for fixed priority preemptive scheduling have been advanced to the point that a genuine engineering approach to the construction of real-time systems is possible. Whereas in many of today's system the "tuning" of the system's parameters to meet the deadline is achieved by trial and error, the advances in the field of schedulability analysis make it possible to carry out off-line schedulability test that ascertain that under the stated conditions all tasks will meet their deadlines all the time. This work on schedulability is based on the assumption that the real-time operating system exhibit a predictable behavior with efficient context switching and an ample range of priorities.

The third paper, "The Time-Triggered Approach to Real-Time System Design", examines the basic assumption that govern the design of time-triggered distributed real-time systems. In a time-triggered(TT) architecture all system activities are initiated by the progression of time. There is only one interrupt in the system, the periodic clock interrupt, which partitions the continuum of time into a sequence of equidistant granules. TT architectures delegate a high degree of autonomy to their subsystems. The strict data sharing interfaces between the subsystems of a TT architecture help to isolate the subsystems from each other and eliminate the possibility of control error propagation from one subsystem to another subsystem. Since a properly designed TT application is replica determinate, it is relatively easy to introduce active redundancy to tolerate transient and permanent faults.

The fourth paper, "Software Measurement: A Necessary Scientific Basis" argues that software measurement, like measurement in any other discipline, must adhere to the science of measurement if this is to gain widespread acceptance and validity. It is shown that the search for general-purpose, real-valued software 'complexity' measures is doomed to failure. The most promising approach is to identify specific attributes of complexity and to measure these separately. Finally, a framework is introduced which enables us to view apparently diverse software measurements activities in a unified way.

# Analysis of Safety Requirements for Process Control Systems[*]

Tom Anderson   Rogério de Lemos   Amer Saeed

University of Newcastle upon Tyne

**Abstract.** An essential basis for the development of software for safety-critical systems is to establish high-quality requirements specifications. This paper describes an approach to the incremental and iterative analysis of requirements for safety-critical systems. Safety specifications are developed to ensure that hazard states are avoided and the system's integrity is maintained even in the presence of failures in system components.

## 1   Introduction

The use of software in safety-critical systems has increased to such an extent that now failures in software can directly lead to accidents. These are systems for which, the development and certification of software is essential for their deployment. A major problem that developers of safety-critical software must confront is that safety-related concerns are often addressed too late in the software lifecycle, with the consequence that major re-work of designs and implementations is necessary when conceptual problems are identified in the later phases of software development.

The aim of the work presented in this paper is to move many of the concerns that can arise during the later phases of software development within the scope of the phase of requirements analysis, thereby reducing significantly the number of iterations through the phases of development and the amount of re-work involved in each iteration. The specific safety concerns that we will address, during the requirements phase, are as follows:

- *System context.* Software safety can only be examined in the context of the system into which it will be embedded. Furthermore, a precise understanding of the relationship between the system and its environment must be established to determine if the risk associated with the system, and thereby its software, is acceptable.
- *Failure behaviours.* Safety-critical systems must strive to maintain safe behaviour, even in the presence of failures of system components and when the behaviour of the environment deviates from that which was expected.

The extent to which effort typically employed in the later phases of software development can be beneficially transferred to the requirements phase depends upon having the ability to develop requirements specifications (and their respective support models) that facilitate an earlier and more effective examination of safety concerns. The basic aspects of the proposed approach are as follows:

- *Modelling.* Modelling the system (and its environment) into which the software will be embedded is perceived to be an integral part of requirements analysis, because such models provide the context in which requirements are expressed

---

[*] This paper is based on [22, 19, 23].

and examined. The activity of modelling is concerned with the description of system structure and behaviour.

- *Analysis*. Both requirements analysis and safety analysis must be undertaken. Requirements analysis is the process of eliciting and modelling the service to be provided by a system and the constraints imposed on that system, which leads to the production of the requirements specification. Safety analysis is the process of determining whether the risk associated with a requirements specification is acceptable.

- *Documentation*. Linkages between the outputs obtained from the different phases of analysis are documented in a format which provides support for subsequent analysis, and for system certification.

In our approach, the activities of modelling and analysis are closely interrelated. Modelling provides the context in which the analysis is to be conducted, and from the process of analysis we obtain the information which enables the development of more detailed models of a system. To delineate a part of the system for modelling and analysis activities, suppressing irrelevant detail about the overall system, we adopt the following abstractions:

- *Levels of analysis*. A level of analysis slices the model of the system into layers, providing vertical abstraction.

- *Domains of analysis*. A domain of analysis delineates a particular scope of analysis, providing partial knowledge of a level of analysis (horizontal abstraction).

- *Perspectives of analysis*. A perspective of analysis is a set of facts observed and modelled according to a particular modelling aspect and viewpoint [46], providing partial knowledge of a domain of analysis (viewpoint abstraction).

The rest of this paper will consider the basic aspects of the approach in more detail. In section 2, we discuss the role of modelling in requirements analysis. In section 3, we describe how the domains of analysis are established, and outline the analysis activities to be conducted within a domain. Section 4 presents a structure for recording the results of the analysis. Sections 5 and 6 describe in more detail the activities to be conducted during requirements analysis and safety analysis. Finally, section 7 presents some concluding remarks.

## 2    Modelling

The activity of modelling is concerned with the description of a structure and a behaviour of the system and its environment.

### 2.1    System Model

The aim of a system model is to describe a structure and behaviour of the system, thereby providing a context for the expression and examination of requirements.

A system will be modelled in terms of its components, each representing a coherent part of the system with an associated behaviour. Alternatively, the behaviour of the system is the composition of the behaviour of its components and their interactions. A detailed description of the interaction between components consists of the definition of the interface between the components (static part) and the behaviour observed at that interface (dynamic part) by each component.

The behaviour of a system is captured in terms of a model of the system's input and output variables. This model (known as the input-output model or the black-box model), depending on the analysis to be conducted, may not be adequate for expressing all of the relevant behaviour of a system. A more comprehensive approach enriches this model by taking into account the state variables of the system. In this model, known as the state space model, the future behaviour of the system can be determined from its state (captured by the state variables) and the sequence of inputs.

A system model is composed from models of its components, which, in turn, considered as system models (recursively, a component can be considered to be another system) are comprised of models of *their* components. Thus to obtain a hierarchical model of a system, successive structural decompositions and behavioural refinements are performed on the system and its components. Each layer of the hierarchical model corresponds to a step in the decomposition/refinement process (level of analysis). This process ceases when a component is considered to be atomic.

Once a system model has been constructed for a particular system within an application domain, it is possible to abstract a generic model that establishes key levels of analysis within which common structure and behaviours for the systems in the application domain can be obtained. Such a generic model can then be used as a basis for conducting the requirements analysis of other systems within the same application domain. The generic model can be specialized for a particular system by enriching it with additional structural and behavioural requirements that are specific to the system under consideration.

## 2.2    Environment Model

The aim of the environment model is to assist the development of a system by describing and analysing aspects of the environment into which the system is to be embedded. The environment of a system is considered to be all the other systems with which it interacts. The environment model for a system characterizes the constraints imposed on the structure and behaviour of the system, thereby enabling the requirements crucial to the integration of the system into its environment to be identified.

## 2.3    Modelling Concepts

The principal modelling abstraction used in the proposed approach is based on the *interactor* [26], an object-based concept. The variant of interactors that we employ provides a means for specifying collections of objects that model features of the system under development or its environment [19]. An interactor corresponds to a class in object-based terms and is described by a template with the following fields: a *name*, a collection of *components*, declarations of *constants* and *variables*, and a *behaviour specification*. In order to specify the behavioural composition between a group of instances of interactors we employ a mechanism similar to a *contract* [35]; this is also specified by means of templates.

In order to describe the behaviour of systems for the different abstractions, we adopt an event/action model (E/A model) as a common foundation for models of system behaviour [24]. System behaviour is modelled in terms of system predicates, i.e. formulae over relational operators parametrized, in particular, by system variables. The E/A model is based on the following primitive concepts. A *state* of a system is the information that, together with the system input, determines the future behaviour of the system. A *transition* represents a transformation of the system state. The system state is modified by the occurrence of events and the execution of actions. An *event* is a temporal marker of no duration which causes or marks a transition. An *action* is the basic unit of activity, which implies duration. The motivation for selecting these primitive concepts is twofold: they have been used as primitives in several real-time specification languages, and they have meaningful interpretations for the different abstractions. These concepts provide flexibility, enabling descriptions to be given of system behaviour ranging from the activities of the physical entities of the plant to the temporal ordering of the computational tasks of the controlling system. The main features of the E/A model are: the primitive concepts can be expressed in different classes of formalisms, both discrete and dense time structures are supported, and timing constraints can be depicted graphically.

## 3    Analysis

In the previous section, the concern was to describe modelling aspects that are relevant for the process of requirements analysis. In this section, we describe how the analysis is conducted in terms of domains of analysis, how these are established from the structure of the system, and their role in the analysis of safety requirements.

### 3.1 System Structure

Process control systems can be grouped into application domains, such as chemical, aerospace, nuclear and transport, and for each application domain we can identify systems possessing similar structures.

A hierarchical system structure is obtained by establishing levels of analysis. The following levels of analysis are often used for the class of process control systems. At the highest level of analysis – the *environment level* – the scope of the system is defined within its environment. At the next level of analysis – the *system level* – the basic components of the system and their interactions are identified. For process control systems, three basic components are defined: the physical process or plant, the controller, and the operator. By associating domains of analysis with each of these components, other components are identified and successively decomposed. For example, at the controller level, apart from the *control system* which can be a computer based system, we identify those components of the controller that interface to the plant and the operator. These are, respectively, the *plant interface* (sensors and actuators) and the *operator interface*. Fig. 1 illustrates this generic structure for the class of process control systems. Boxes represent components and arrows represent the main interactions between them, that is, their inputs and outputs. Alternatively, the structure of the system could be represented as a hierarchy in which each layer would correspond to a level of analysis; each box at a level would represent a domain of analysis.

### 3.2    Establishing Domains of Analysis

For each level of analysis of a system, the approach involves identifying essential domains of analysis. These domains provide partial knowledge of the level of analysis, and are established by the entities and their interactions, identified for that level. Once a domain is established, analysis is conducted by applying the process to be presented in section 3.3. Depending upon the particular domain under analysis, appropriate techniques and notations have to be employed to emphasize pertinent characteristics of the domain. Domains of analysis are associated with system components, and dependencies between the domains are derived from the interactions between the components.

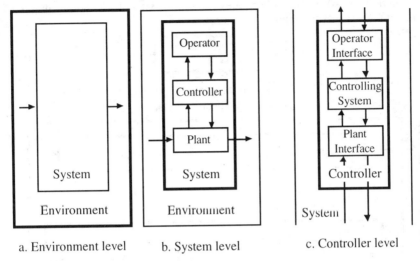

a. Environment level          b. System level          c. Controller level

**Fig.1.** Levels of analysis for process control systems

The approach for conducting the analysis is characterized as a framework that partitions the analysis of requirements into smaller domains and provides directives for conducting the analysis. This framework is defined in terms of a set of phases (corresponding to the domains), and an ordering relationship between phases (corresponding to dependencies between domains). Since the concern of this paper is the analysis of safety requirements, and safety is essentially a property of the system, the requirements analysis is most effectively conducted in a hierarchical manner, starting from the system concept. The aim is to identify levels of analysis that contain those system components which are relevant for the software being developed, thereby constructing an environment model for the software.

From the generic structure proposed above, we define the framework for requirements analysis which is illustrated in fig. 2. The boxes depict the phases of the framework, and the arrows represent the information flow between the phases. The aim of the framework is to obtain the safety requirements specification of the controlling system (a component of the controller), hence the need to perform the controller analysis from the perspective of the plant and operator.

### 3.3   Analysing a Domain

Our approach to systematising the analysis of safety requirements is based upon two interrelated activities: requirements analysis, which produces safety specifications, and safety analysis, which assesses whether or not the risk associated with a safety specification is acceptable. The aim is to conduct in tandem, within each phase of analysis, the requirements and safety analyses. The safety specifications obtained from the requirements analysis of the domain will feed into the safety analysis, and any identified defects will be used to guide the modification of the safety specifications before proceeding to the next phase. The main benefits of conducting the safety analysis at each phase (rather than at the last phase of analysis) are that this minimizes the effects of faults propagating through the sequence of safety specifications, considers respecification as early as possible (the preferred method for the reduction of risk [53], and reduces the complexity of the safety analysis by scoping it into smaller domains.

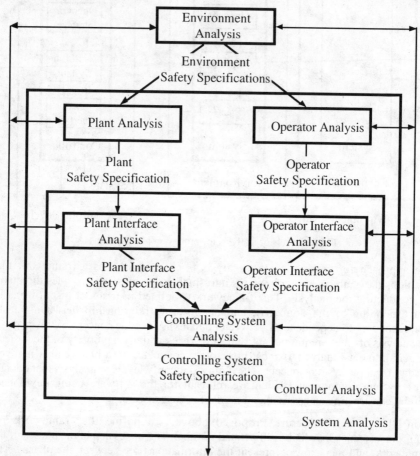

**Fig.2.** A framework for requirements analysis

The relationships between requirements analysis and safety analysis within a phase of analysis are shown in the SADT diagram [59] in fig. 3. If the result of the safety analysis of a safety specification is that the risk associated with the specification is acceptable, then *evidence* that can be used in a safety case must be produced. On the other hand, if the safety analysis concludes that the risk is unacceptable then the result of the analysis is to identify the *defects* in the safety specification. Because of the iterative nature of the requirements and safety analyses, the overall process should be thought of as cyclic rather than sequential.

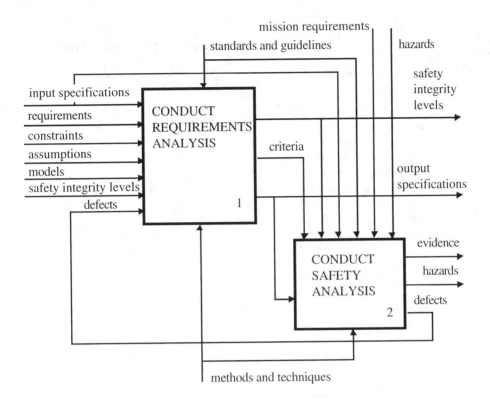

**Fig.3.** Relationships between requirements analysis and safety analysis

Within each phase, the requirements analysis consists of the following notions:

- *Input specifications* are the safety specifications produced from the previous phase of the framework; they will be refined to produce the *output specifications*. The latter characterize safe behaviour over the entities of the domain.

- *Requirements*, which are imposed on the entities of the domain, can either be functional or non-functional.

- *Constraints* are non-negotiable requirements.

- *Assumptions* are hypotheses over the behaviour of the entities of the domain.

- *Models* of the domain support the analysis by identifying the entities of the domain, capturing their behaviour and describing their interactions; the models input to the requirements analysis will be refined and become part of the *output specifications*.

- *Safety integrity level* indicates the likelihood of a safety specification achieving its required safety features under all stated conditions within a stated measure of use [53]. New safety integrity levels are associated with the output specifications.

- *Defects* can refer either to output specifications that do not comply with input specifications or to output specifications that do not attain the established safety integrity levels.

- *Standards and guidelines* impose constraints on the safety specifications, and may prescribe *methods and techniques* to be employed during requirements analysis.

- For each output specification, specific *criteria* are defined to provide the basis for checking whether or not the safety integrity levels are attained. Essentially, these criteria relate to the functionality of the safety specifications.

Within each phase, the safety analysis consists of the following notions:

- The *output specifications* are verified against the *input specifications* and validated against the *mission requirements*.

- Verification and validation of the output specifications are performed in order to confirm that the respective *safety integrity levels* have been attained, following general *criteria* established by the *standards and guidelines*, and specific *criteria* associated with a particular safety specification defined during requirements analysis. Either the risk associated with an output specification is acceptable and *evidence* has to be produced to support this, or *defects* are identified.

- The *methods and techniques* employed in the verification and validation of the output specifications should yield part of the evidence that the specifications are able to attain their associated safety integrity levels. Formal techniques can be employed, together with formal proofs, for the verification, and animation techniques can be employed for validation. Depending on the safety integrity levels, the standards and guidelines impose, or suggest, the methods and techniques to be used for the safety analysis, and the evidence that has to be produced.

# 4    Safety Specification Graph

A crucial concern in the development of safety-critical systems is to provide quality documentation that records the results of the analysis in a well structured format. Poor, or incomplete, documentation is often a major obstacle to the certification of a system. For the proposed approach we provide the notion of a *Safety Specification Graph* (SSG) as a means for recording the results of the requirements and safety analyses, and their interrelationships [22]. The structure provided by the SSG supports the selection of information to be recorded, and records the selected information in a format that facilitates further analysis.

An SSG is represented as a linear graph, in which a *node* denotes a safety specification and an *edge* denotes a relationship between a pair of safety specifications. For those systems whose behaviour is described through modes of operation, a separate SSG is constructed for each mode. For a mode of operation with $p$ identified accidents, the SSG consists of $p$ component graphs. A component graph organizes the safety specifications into layers, thereby providing a hierarchical structure.

## 4.1    SSG Structure

**Safety Specifications.** The nodes of an SSG record the information associated with individual safety specifications, and the relationship between safety specifications of the same layer. For each node, this involves recording the following notions:

- The safety specification represented by a node, comprising some of the following three elements:

- *Safety strategy*: a scheme for maintaining safe behaviour, defined as a set of conditions imposed on controllable factors;
- *Assumptions*: hypotheses about the behaviour of the system at the level of analysis being considered;
- *System states*: states of the system considered unsafe for the level of analysis being considered.
- The safety integrity level associated with the safety specification.

Relative weights can be associated with the safety specifications of the same layer in order to provide a notion of relative risk for alternative safety specifications. However, the relative weights do not give the necessary assurance that a particular safety specification, or set of safety specifications, is able to meet the required safety integrity level.

**Relationships between Safety Specifications.** The edges of an SSG encode the relationships between safety specifications at consecutive layers of component graphs. Each edge records the relationship between two safety specifications, the specification defined at the originating node (the input specification) and the specification defined at the terminating node (the output specification). For each edge, this involves recording the following notions:

- The *evidence* produced by the safety analysis to confirm that the output specification has attained the required safety integrity level and complies with the input specification.
- The *criteria* used to judge that the output specification complies with the input specification and related standards.

When more than one specification is related to a specification in a previous layer, then two interpretations are possible; either the specifications are exclusive alternatives and a choice will have to be made in later phases of analysis to select and refine a single safety specification, or the safety specifications complement each other and all are needed to attain sufficient confidence that the safety integrity levels can be achieved.

### 4.2   SSG Role

The structured record of the safety specifications and their relationships, embodied in an SSG, will provide assistance for subsequent certification and maintenance activities. An SSG establishes a bridge between the safety analysis of the system and that of the software. This enables the risk associated with the software to be assessed in the system context. An SSG can also support a number of specific tasks during the requirements and safety analyses.

- A key concern when safety specifications are refined or modified is *traceability*, that is the ability to trace back from a specification to its origins and to trace forwards to the specifications which are derived from it.
- Internal consistency of the safety specifications of an SSG is verified by conducting horizontal and vertical checks. The *horizontal checks* establish that at each layer of an SSG the safety specifications are not in conflict with each other. The *vertical checks* are applied between different layers of an SSG, and confirm that safety is maintained down an SSG; the relationships that must be established follow from the edges of an SSG.

- An SSG supports the construction and organisation of a *safety case*. The basic safety arguments which constitute the safety case follow from the evidence recorded at the edges, and the structure of an SSG provides a regime in which to organize the safety arguments into a coherent safety case.

# 5    Requirements Analysis

## 5.1    The Method

The process of conducting requirements analysis within a domain consists of identifying relevant entities, specifying their behaviour and interactions with other entities, and confirming that the composition of the behaviour of the entities complies with the behaviour of the domain. The entities obtained from the decomposition of the domain are analysed at lower levels of analysis.

The behaviour of an entity is specified in terms of its *standard, failure* and *exceptional* behaviours. The motivation for adopting such a partition is to attempt to characterize the complete behavioural space of an entity. By specifying the failure behaviour of the entities we are also able to establish how the behaviour of the domain can be made more robust in the presence of failures of its entities. The specification of the exceptional behaviour of an entity takes into account those situations when it becomes impossible for the entity to deliver the specified standard behaviour.

## 5.2    Techniques

The utilisation of formal techniques in the different phases of software development has been advocated as a means of improving confidence in the dependability of the final product [61]. During the phase of requirements analysis there is a demand for utilising techniques whose features and expressive power match the characteristics of the activities. Formal techniques have been classified in a number of different ways; in the context of our approach we identify the following two classes [20]:

- *Property-oriented formalisms* describe a system in terms of the properties that are exhibited by the system. A property-oriented specification should only state the necessary constraints on system behaviour to minimize the restrictions imposed on possible implementations. Temporal Logic and Timed History Logic are examples of property-oriented formalisms.
- *Operational formalisms* describe a system in terms of a model that simulates its behaviour. Two relevant characteristics that operational formalisms should possess are the ability to explicitly specify non-determinism and concurrency. Petri nets and Statecharts are examples of operational formalisms.

# 6    Safety Analysis

The purpose of the safety analysis of the safety specifications is to increase assurance that the contribution of a specification to the overall system risk is acceptable. The results of a safety analysis are used during the requirements phase for *risk reduction* and subsequently for *certification* of the system. For risk reduction, safety analysis must identify the defects in the safety specifications that make the greatest contribution to the risk, providing guidance for the inclusion of additional safety precautions. For certification, safety analysis must provide evidence that can be used in the preparation of a safety case.

A method for the safety analysis of safety specifications, from qualitative and quantitative perspectives, was presented in earlier work [62]. In the rest of this paper, we will be focusing on the qualitative analysis, since:

- Most current standards subject software to safety targets that are expressed in qualitative terms [11].

- A detailed quantitative analysis should not be conducted too early, particularly when there is limited confidence in the data on which the analysis will be based – as is the case during the requirements phase.

## 6.1   The Method

For safety specifications, qualitative safety analysis must confirm that, under normal circumstances, the safety specifications will prevent the system from entering a hazard state, and should also identify possible defects in the safety specifications and investigate their impact on safety. Consequently the qualitative analysis is partitioned into two activities, *preliminary analysis* and *vulnerability analysis*. The relationships between these two activities are shown in the SADT diagram in fig. 4.

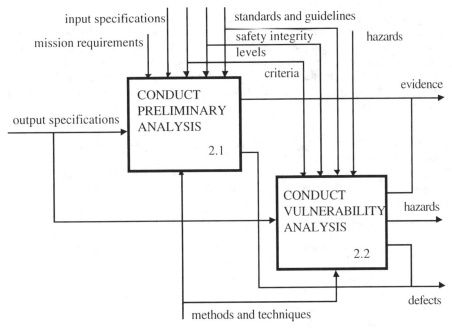

**Fig.4.** Relationships between preliminary and vulnerability analyses

**Preliminary Analysis.** The preliminary analysis activity must ensure, under clearly defined circumstances, that the safety specifications are adequate for maintaining the absence of hazards. Preliminary analysis aims to increase the assurance in the safety specifications by *verification* and *validation*. Verification is the process of checking that the safety specifications are internally consistent (i.e. the requirements captured by the specifications are not contradictory), and that they conform to the specifications stipulated at the previous layer. Validation is the process of checking that a safety specification accurately reflects the requirements and constraints imposed on the system by the user, or some other authority, and does not conflict unduly with the mission requirements.

Verification should not be used as the only source of evidence that an output specification is able to attain the required safety integrity levels. It must also be shown that an output specification does not affect the safe behaviour of the system, for example, by influencing hazards from which it is not derived.

**Vulnerability Analysis.** The vulnerability analysis is similar in intent to that for a traditional safety analysis. Vulnerability analysis probes the safety specifications to find defects which can affect the safe behaviour of the system; once such defects are identified the safety specifications can be modified to reduce their contribution to the system risk.

The notions associated with the vulnerability analysis are similar to those defined in section 3.3. However, the method and techniques utilized are different, because different evidence is sought for a different category of defect (namely, safety specifications that are based on unsound assumptions).

The method proposed for vulnerability analysis closely follows the principles that underpin the Hazards and Operability Studies (HAZOPS) method. Consequently, the analysis is partitioned into the following activities: identification of the failure modes of the safety specification; determining causes of the failure modes; and determining the consequences of the identified failure modes on the safe behaviour of the system. The relationships between the vulnerability analysis activities are shown in the SADT diagram in fig. 5.

After completing the vulnerability analysis, defective safety specifications might be identified, and new hazards might be identified whose causes are the safety specifications that have altered the original design of the system. If at this stage of the safety analysis, a safety specification is considered neither to be defective, nor to introduce new hazard states, then this constitutes evidence in support of a claim that the criteria demanded have been fulfilled.

## 6.2    Methods and Techniques

Typically, qualitative safety analysis is conducted by examining the causal relations between events and states in sequences connecting failures of components to hazard states of the system. There are two basic styles for analysing causal relations: *inductive analysis* and *deductive analysis* [36].

- *Inductive analysis.* Inductive analysis starts from a particular set of facts and reasons (forwards) to more general facts. When employed for safety analysis, inductive analysis starts with a set of failure events and seeks to discover any dangerous consequences (i.e. hazards) which could result from those events. The inductive analysis approach is typified by Failure Modes and Effects Analysis (FMEA) and Event Tree Analysis (ETA).
- *Deductive analysis.* Deductive analysis starts with a general fact and reasons (backwards) towards the more particular. When employed for safety analysis, deductive analysis starts with a hazard and seeks to uncover possible failures that could lead to the hazard. The deductive analysis approach is typified by Fault Tree Analysis (FTA).

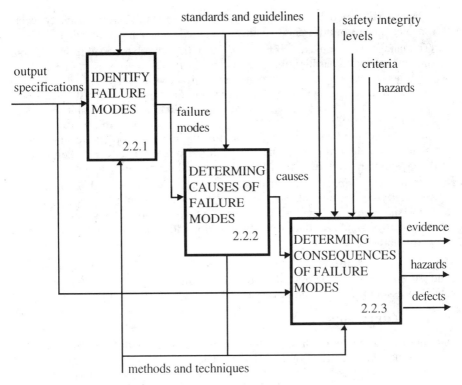

**Fig.5.** Relationships between the activities of the vulnerability analysis

Some methods and techniques employ both inductive and deductive analysis; examples include HAZOPS and cause-consequence analysis [54].

Both analytical styles can be employed during vulnerability analysis in order to analyse defects of the safety specifications. The role of deductive analysis is to determine the causes of failure behaviour, and the role of inductive analysis is to determine the consequences of failure behaviour. The degree of application of one style of analysis versus the other varies according to the level of analysis being considered and the technique employed for representing the safety specification. At higher levels of analysis there is a natural tendency to use deductive analysis, since the description of the safety specifications is more general. Inductive analysis is more appropriate at lower levels of analysis, since then information about the elements of a safety specification and their inter-relationships will be more particular.

## 7    Conclusions

This paper has presented a systematic approach to the development of high-quality requirements specifications. The approach is based upon three related aspects: *modelling*, *analysis* and structured *documentation*.

- *Modelling* is employed as the means for explicitly providing a context for the analysis. Two types of model have been presented: environment model and system model. To describe the behaviour of entities a set of primitive modelling concepts (E/A model) were suggested. The flexibility of these primitive concepts enables models of different domains to be based on a common foundation.

- To manage the complexity of the *analysis*, a framework (derived from a system model) is used to partition the overall analysis into smaller phases. The analysis within a phase consists of two interrelated activities: *requirements analysis* which produces the requirements specifications; and *safety analysis* which has to assess whether the risk associated with a specification is acceptable. For both activities, partitioning the analysis into phases makes the analysis more manageable and facilitates employment of the most appropriate techniques; in addition conducting safety analysis within a phase reduces the likelihood of defects in specifications propagating through to later phases.

- For *documentation* a graphical structure, the SSG, was presented as a means for explicitly recording linkages between the elements of the products of the analysis. These linkages can be exploited to support change control, and verification and validation activities; in addition the SSG can support certification.

The feasibility of different aspects of the approach have been demonstrated by conducting a number of case studies, based on: railway systems [20, 63], chemical batch processing [21], and avionics systems [24].

## Acknowledgements

Our approach to modelling has benefited from interaction with M. D. Harrison and his colleagues, in particular Bob Fields, at the University of York. The authors would like to acknowledge the financial support of British Aerospace (Dependable Computing Systems Centre), and the EPSRC (UK) SCHEMA project, as well as PDCS.

# Real-Time System Scheduling

Neil Audsley   Alan Burns   Rob Davis   Ken Tindell   Andy Wellings

Real-Time Systems Research Group, Department of Computer Science,
University of York

**Abstract.** Scheduling theories for fixed priority pre-emptive scheduling are now sufficiently mature that a genuine engineering approach to the construction of hard real-time systems is possible. In this paper we review recent advances. A flexible computational model is adopted that can accommodate periodic and sporadic activities, different levels of criticality, task interaction and blocking, co-operative scheduling (deferred pre-emption), release jitter, precedence constrained processes, arbitrary deadlines, deadlines associated with specific events (rather than the end of a task's execution) and offsets. Scheduling tests for these different application characteristics are described. The paper also considers the issues involved in producing safe and predictable kernels to support this computational model.

## 1  Introduction

Recent developments [5] in the analysis of fixed priority pre-emptive scheduling have made significant enhancements to the model introduced by Lui and Layland in their seminal 1973 paper [49]. These developments, taken together, now represent a body of analysis that forms the basis for an engineering approach to the design, verification and implementation of hard real-time systems. In this paper we review much of this analysis in order to support the thesis that safety critical real-time systems can, and should, be built using these techniques.

Pre-emptive priority based scheduling prescribes a run-time environment in which tasks, with a priority attribute, are dispatched in priority order. Priorities are, essentially, static. Tasks are either runnable, in which case they are held on a notional (priority ordered) run queue; delayed, in which case they are held on a notional (time-ordered) delay queue; or suspended, in which case they are awaiting an event which may be triggered externally (via an interrupt) or internally (from some other task).

Most existing hard real-time systems are implemented using a static table-driven schedule (often called a cyclic executive). Priority based scheduling has many advantages over this static approach (see Locke [50] for a detailed discussion of this issue). In essence these advantages all relate to one theme: increased flexibility. However, in order to challenge the role of static scheduling as the premier implementation model, priority based scheduling must:
- provide the same level of predictability (in terms of temporal behaviour);
- allow a wide range of application characteristics to be accommodated;
- enable dependable (safe) implementations to be supported.

All of these issues are addressed in this review. The remainder of this introduction outlines a simple model of task attributes and shows how worst case response times can be calculated. Section 2 considers the necessary run-time kernel and shows how its temporal characteristics can be accommodated and how its implementation can be made safe. Section 3 extends the simple model to include a number of important application characteristics. Section 4 presents our conclusions.

## 1.1    Calculating Response Times

We restrict our considerations to single processor systems. The techniques are, however, applicable in a distributed environment with a static allocation of tasks to processors [70]. The processor must support a bounded, fixed, number of tasks, $N$. The general approach is to assign (optimally) a unique priority ($P_i$) to each task, $\tau_i$ and then to calculate the task's worst case response time, $R_i$. This value can then be compared, trivially, with the task's deadline, $D_i$. This approach is illustrated with the derivation of appropriate analysis for a simple computational model.

Each of the $N$ tasks is assumed to consist of an infinite number of invocation requests, each separated by a minimum time $T_i$. For periodic tasks this value defines its period, for sporadic tasks $T_i$ is the minimum inter-arrival time for the event that releases the task. Each invocation of task $\tau_i$ requires $C_i$ computation time (worst case). During this time the task does not suspend itself. Tasks are independent of each other apart from their use of shared protected data. To bound priority inversion, a ceiling priority protocol is assumed (for access to the protected data) [64, 8]. This gives rise to a maximum blocking time of $B_i$, i.e. the maximum time task $\tau_i$ can be blocked waiting for a lower priority task to complete its use of protected data. Our simple model has the restriction that each task's deadline must be less than, or equal to, its inter-arrival time (i.e. $D_i \le T_i$). We also assume that context switches, etc., take no time (this optimistic assumption is removed in Section 2).

For this simple model, optimal priority assignment is easily obtained. Leung and Whitehead [48] showed that deadline monotonic assignment is optimal, i.e. the shorter a task's deadline the higher its priority.

The worst case response time for the highest priority task (assuming task $\tau_1$ has the highest priority) is given by:

$$R_i = B_i + C_i$$

For the other tasks, it is necessary to calculate the worst case interference suffered by the task. Interference results from higher priority tasks executing while the task of interest is pre-empted. It can be shown, for this simple computational model, that maximum interference occurs when all higher priority tasks are released at the same time (known as the critical instant) as the task under consideration. This leads to the following relation:

$$R_i = B_i + C_i \sum_{j \in hp(i)} \left\lceil \frac{R_i}{T_j} \right\rceil C_j$$

where $hp(i)$ is the set of tasks of higher priority than task $\tau_i$.

As $R_i$ appears on both sides of this equation, a simple solution is not possible [38]. Rather a recurrence relation is derived. Let $w$ be a window (time interval) into which we attempt to insert the computation time of the task. We expand $w$ until all of $C_i$ can be accommodated:

$$w_i^{n+1} = B_i + C_i + \sum_{j \in hp(i)} \left\lceil \frac{w_i^n}{T_j} \right\rceil C_j \tag{1}$$

Iteration starts with $w_i^0 = C_i$ (although more optimal start values can be found). It is trivial to show that $w_i^{n+1} \geq w_i^n$. If $w_i^n > D_i$ then task $\tau_i$ cannot be guaranteed to meet its deadline. However if $w_i^{n+1} = w_i^n$ then iteration terminates and $R_i = w_i^n$.

The derivation of this result together with examples of its use can be found in [38, 3, 6]. Note that $w_i$ is referred to as the priority $i$ busy period since the priority of the executing tasks does not fall below priority $i$ during this period.

In section 3 we show how this simple model can be extended. But first we must consider the implementation of pre-emptive priority based scheduling.

## 2 Safe and Predictable Kernels

It is undoubtedly true that the support needed to implement pre-emptive priority based dispatching is more complicated than static scheduling — although the difference is not as large as it would first appear. It should be noted that a full operating system is not required, only a micro-kernel with efficient context switching and an ample range of priorities.

The production of a correct kernel necessitates the development of a formal specification of the interface to the kernel and its behaviour following calls to that interface. Formal notations such as Z have been used to give precise definitions to such kernels [66, 13].

The notion of a safety kernel was introduced by Rushby [60] to imply a kernel that was not only built correctly but had a positive role in ensuring that various negative behaviours (of the application) were inhibited. A prototype run-time support system for a restricted subset of Ada 95 has been built along these lines [17]. It monitors all application tasks to make sure that they do not use more resources (in particular CPU processing time) than was assigned to them during the scheduling analysis of the application. If a task attempts to run over its budget, it has an exception raised to enable it to recover (the exception handler also has a budget defined).

In addition to engineering the kernel to an appropriate level of reliability, it is also critically important for the timing characteristics of the kernel to be obtainable. This is true both in terms of models of behaviour and actual cost (i.e. how long does each kernel routine take to execute). The following sections address these issues.

### 2.1 Predicting Overheads

Simple scheduling models ignore kernel behaviour. Context switch times and queue manipulations are, however, significant and cannot usually be assumed to take negligible time unless a purpose built processor is used. For example, the FASTCHART [67] processor can genuinely claim to have zero overheads.

Even if a scheduling co-processor is used to perform context switches (in parallel with the application/host processor) there will be some context switch overhead. When a software kernel is used, models of actual behaviour are needed. Without these models excessively pessimistic overheads must be assumed. The interrupt handler for the clock will usually also manipulate the delay queue. For example, in one implementation [17], when there are no tasks on the delay queue then a cost of 16s is experienced. If an application has 20 periodic tasks that all share a critical instant then the cost of moving all 20 tasks from the delay queue to the run queue is 590s: i.e. 38 times more.

Context switch times can be accounted for by adding their cost to the task that causes the context switch. For a periodic task, the cost of placing itself on the delay queue (and switching back to the lower priority task it pre-empted) is, however, not necessarily a constant. It depends on the size of the delay queue (i.e. on the number of periodic tasks in the application).

To model the delay queue manipulations that occur, in the clock interrupt handler, adequately (i.e. at one of the top priority levels), it is necessary to address the overheads caused by each periodic task directly. It is possible to model the clock interrupt handler using two parameters: $C_{CLK}$ (the overheads occurring on each interrupt assuming tasks are on the delay queue but none are removed), and $C_{PER}$ (the cost of moving one task from the delay queue to the run-queue). Each periodic task now has a fictitious task with the same period $T$ but with computation time $C_{PER}$. Equation (1) thus becomes :

$$w_i^{n+1} = B_i + C_i + \sum_{j \in hp(i)} \left\lceil \frac{w_i^n}{T_j} \right\rceil C_j + \left\lceil \frac{w_i^n}{T_{CLK}} \right\rceil C_{CLK} + \sum_{f \in fpt} \left\lceil \frac{w_i^n}{T_f} \right\rceil C_{PER} \qquad (2)$$

where $fpt$ is the set of fictitious periodic tasks.

Our analysis of kernels indicates that this model is itself over simplistic and hence too pessimistic. There is usually a cost saving when two or more tasks are transferred between the queues together. In this case, a three parameter model is more appropriate, see Burns, Wellings and Hutcheon [17] for a derivation of this model.

In addition to supporting periodic behaviour, the kernel will also have to accommodate interrupt handling and the release of sporadic tasks following an interrupt. This again gives rise to parameters that must be established before full scheduling analysis can be undertaken [15].

## 2.2    Tick Driven Scheduling

In all the above analysis, periodic tasks are assumed to have periods which are exact multiples of the clock period. They can thus be *released* (i.e. put on the run queue) as soon as they arrive. If the release time is not equal to the arrival time then the task is said to suffer from release jitter. Although it would usually be a poor engineering decision to have release *jitter*, there are situations where it might be inevitable.

Sporadic tasks are also assumed to be released as soon as the event on which they are waiting has occurred. A tick driven scheduler will, however, poll for these events as part of the clock interrupt handling routine. This has the advantage of clearly defining the times at which new tasks can become runnable. It also allows safety checks to be implemented that can ensure that sporadic tasks are not released too often. With this implementation scheme, sporadic tasks are bound to suffer release jitter.

Let $J_i$ represent the worst case release jitter suffered by task $\tau_i$ (i.e. the maximum time between arrival and release). Two modification to equation (1) are now required. First, the response time calculated according to equation (1) is from release, not arrival. The true (desired) maximum response time is measured from arrival:

$$R_i^{TRUE} = R_i + J_i$$

Second, the interference that this task has on lower priority tasks is increased. This is because two releases of the task can be closer together than the minimum inter-arrival $T_j$. If one arrival suffers maximum release jitter, but the next does not, then the two releases have a time gap of only $T_j - T_j$. The interference factor in equation (1) must be modified as follows [3]:

$$w_i^{n+1} = B_i + C_i + \sum_{j \in hp(i)} \left\lceil \frac{w_i^n + J_j}{T_j} \right\rceil C_j \qquad (3)$$

## 2.3   Co-operative Scheduling

The kernels described above all implement true pre-emptive dispatching. In this section an alternative scheme is outlined: the use of deferred pre-emption. This has a number of advantages but can still be analysed by the scheduling technique embodied in equation (1). In equation (1), there is a blocking term $B_i$ that accounts for the time a lower priority task may be executing while a higher priority task is runnable. In the application domain this may be caused by the existence of data that is shared (under mutual exclusion) by tasks of different priority. Blocking can, however, also be caused by the kernel. Many systems will have the non-pre-emptable context-switch as the longest blocking time (e.g. the release of a higher priority task being delayed by the time it takes to context switch to a lower priority task — even though an immediate context switch to the higher priority task will then ensue).

One of the advantages of using the immediate ceiling priority protocol [8] (to calculate and bound $B$) is that blocking is not cumulative. A task cannot be blocked both by an application task and a kernel routine — only one could actually be happening when the higher priority task is released.

Co-operative scheduling exploits this non-cumulative property by increasing the situation in which blocking can occur. Let $B^{MAX}$ be the maximum blocking time in the system (using a conventional approach). The application code is then split into non-pre-emptive blocks, the execution times of which are bounded by $B^{MAX}$. At the end of each of these blocks the application code offers a "de-scheduling" request to the kernel. If a high priority task is now runnable then the kernel will instigate a context switch; if not, the currently running task will continue into the next non-pre-emptive block.

Although this method requires the careful placement of de-scheduling calls, these could be automatically inserted by the worst case execution time analyser which is itself undertaking a control flow analysis of the code.

The normal execution of the application code is thus totally co-operative. A task will continue to execute until it offers to de-schedule. To give some level of protection over corrupted (or incorrect) software, a safe kernel could use an interrupt mechanism to abort the application task if any non-pre-emptive block lasts longer than $B^{MAX}$. The use of co-operative scheduling is illustrated by the DIA architecture [65]. Here, a kernel support chip deals with all interrupts and manages the run queue. The de-scheduling call is a single instruction and has negligible cost if no context switch is due.

The use of deferred pre-emption has two important advantages. It increases the schedulability of the system, and it can lead to lower values of $C$. In equation (1) as the value of $w$ is being extended, new releases of higher priority tasks are possible that will further increase the value of $w$. With deferred pre-emption, no interference can occur during the last block of execution. Let $F_i$ be the execution time of the final block, such that when the task has consumed $C_i - F_i$ the last block has (just) started. Equation (1) is now solved for $C_i - F_i$ rather than $C_i$:

$$w_i^{n+1} = B_i + C_i - F_i + \sum_{j \in hp(i)} \left\lceil \frac{w_i^n}{T_j} \right\rceil C_j \tag{4}$$

When this converges (i.e. $w_i^{n+1} = w_i^n$) the response time is given by:

$$R_i = w_i^n + F_i$$

In effect the last block of the task has executed with a higher priority (the highest) than the rest of the task.

The other advantage of deferred pre-emption comes from predicting more accurately the execution times of a task's non-preemptable basic blocks. Modern processors have caches, prefetch queues and pipelines that all significantly reduce the execution times of straight-line code. Typically estimations of worst case execution time are forced to ignore these advantages and obtain very pessimistic results because pre-emption will invalidate caches and pipelines. Knowledge of non-pre-emption can, however, be used to predict the speed up that will occur in practice. Zhang et al have shown how a 20% reduction in worst case execution time ($C$) can be obtained by modelling the prefetch queue directly [75]; Harmon et al have shown how the pipeline on a 68020 can be analysed at the micro-code level [34]; and cache advantages can also be predicted. If modern processors are to be used in real-time systems then this type of analysis is necessary.

## 3    An Extendible Model

Application requirements rarely (if ever) fit the simple model described in the introduction. An appropriate scheduling theory is one that can be extended to meet the particular needs of application requirements. In this section we consider a number of extensions to the basic model:

(1) Variations in $C$ and $T$

(2) Precedence Relations and Multi-Deadline Tasks

(3) Arbitrary Deadlines (i.e. $D > T$)

(4) Internal Deadlines (i.e. not all $C$ has to be completed by $D$)

(5) Offsets and Phased Executions

We then consider how priorities can be assigned optimally when the simple rate monotonic or deadline monotonic policies are not optimal.

## 3.1 Variation in Computation Time and Period

Where it can be shown that a task will not execute for its maximum time on each release, it is pessimistic to assume that it does. For example, a periodic task may do a small amount of data collection in each period but every, say, 10 periods analyses this data using a much more expensive algorithm. This behaviour can simply be modelled, in equation (1), as two tasks, one running every period (with a small computation time) and the other running every *10T* (with a larger computation time).

Variations in period are also possible. Bursts of activity involving a number of short periods are following by inactivity. Sporadic tasks released by interrupts can behave in this manner. For example, a sporadic task could have a worst case (minimum) arrival interval of 1ms but have the restriction that no more than 5 releases can occur within a 100ms interval. If the worst case arrival interval is very small then it is acceptable to collapse the 5 releases into a single task (with a period of 100ms). However, a more accurate prediction of the interference this task will impose on lower priority tasks, in the window $w$, can be derived [3]. Let $T_j$ be the outer period (e.g. 100ms in the above example) and $t_j$ be the inner period (e.g. 1ms). Also let $n_j$ be the number of releases in the outer period (e.g. 5). Task $\tau_j$ will have an interference ($I_i^j$) on each lower priority task $\tau_i$ as follows:

$$I_i^j = \left\lfloor \frac{w_i''}{T_j} \right\rfloor n_j C_j + \min\left[ \left\lceil \frac{w_i'' - \left\lfloor \frac{w_i''}{T_j} \right\rfloor T_j}{t_j} \right\rceil , n_j C_j \right] \tag{5}$$

This can then be incorporated into equation (1). The first term in equation (5) gives the cost of complete cycles (outer period) contained within $w_i''$. The second term gives the additional cost of minor cycles, this is upper bounded by cost of a complete burst, $n_j C_j$.

## 3.2 Precedence Relationships and Multi-Deadline Tasks

A common paradigm for structuring real-time software is as a set of tasks linked via precedence relations (i.e. task B cannot start until task A has completed). Data is often passed along these precedence links, but as the tasks involved never execute together, mutual exclusion over this data need not be enforced.

For illustration consider a simple straight line "transaction" involving three tasks : *L*, which must run before *Q*, which runs before *S*. Table 1 contains the given timing attributes for these tasks. Note that the periods of the three tasks are identical and that the overall deadline is 16.

**Table 1:** An Example Task Set

|   | C | D | T | P |
|---|---|---|---|---|
| L | 2 | 5 | 20 | 2 |
| Q | 2 | 4 | 20 | 1 |
| S | 4 | 7 | 20 | 3 |

A naive application of, say, deadline monotonic analysis will assign priorities (P) as given in Table 1. The schedulability test will then assume that all tasks are released at the same time and deem the task set to be unschedulable.

The critical instant assumption (i.e. all task released simultaneously) is clearly too pessimistic for precedence constrained tasks. We know that they never wish to execute together. Both $Q$ and $S$ require an offset. That is, they cannot execute at the start of the period.

**Table 2:** Transformed Task Set

|         | C | D  | T  | P |
|---------|---|----|----|---|
| $L$     | 2 | 5  | 20 | 1 |
| $Q^T$   | 2 | 9  | 20 | 2 |
| $S^T$   | 4 | 16 | 20 | 3 |

A simple transformation can be applied to tasks with offsets that share the same period. We relate the deadlines of all tasks not to their start times but to the start time of the transaction. This will not effect $L$ but it will mean that $Q$ and $S$ have their deadlines stretched (we refer to the new tasks as $Q^T$ and $S^T$). Table 2 now has the new deadlines and priorities for the task set.

The priority model will now ensure that $L$ executed first then $Q^T$ and then $S^T$. Moreover, the new task set is schedulable and would actually allow other tasks to be given priorities interleaved with this transaction. Note that tasks $L$ and $Q^T$ must not undertake any external blocking as this would free the processor to execute $Q^T$ or $S^T$ early. This formulation results in tasks having lower priorities for later positions down the precedence relationship (i.e. $S$ lower than $L$). Lehoczky *et al* have shown that by increasing the priority (and imposing some mechanism to stop the later tasks starting too early) can result in greater schedulability [33].

Finally it should be noted that precedence relations can be implemented with real offsets (i.e. $Q$ not being released until time 5). (See section 3.5.)

The above approach for dealing with precedence constrained tasks has a further property that enables multi-deadline tasks to be accommodated. Processes can exist that have more than one deadline: they are required to complete part of their computations by one time and the remainder by a later time. This can occur when a task must read an input value very early in its period and must produce some output signal at a later time.

To implement multi-deadline tasks it is necessary for the run-time system interface to facilitate dynamic priority changes. The task is modelled as a precedence related transaction. Each part of the transaction is thus assigned a priority (as described above). The task actually executes in a number of distinct phases, each with its own priority; for example a high priority to start with until its first deadline is met, then a lower priority for its next deadline.

## 3.3    Arbitrary Deadlines

To cater for situations where $D_i$ (and hence potentially $R_i$) can be greater than $T_i$ we must adapt the analysis. The following outlines the approach of Tindell [71]. When deadline is less than (or equal) to period, it is only necessary to consider a single release of each task. The critical instant, when all higher priority tasks are released at the same time, represents the maximum interference and hence the response time following a release at the critical instant must be the worst case. However, when deadline is greater than period, a number of releases must be considered. We assume that the release of a task will be delayed until any previous releases of the same task have completed. For each potentially overlapping release we define a separate window $w(q)$, where $q$ is just an integer identifying a particular window and invocation of $\tau_i$ (i.e. $q = 0, 1, 2, ...$). Equation (1) can be extended to have the following form:

$$w_i^{n+1}(q) = B_i + (q+1)C_i + \sum_{j \in hp(i)} \left\lceil \frac{w_i^n(q)}{T_j} \right\rceil C_j \qquad (6)$$

For example with $q$ equal to two, three releases of task $\tau_i$ will occur in the window. For each value of $q$, a stable value of $w(q)$ can be found by iteration — as in equation (1). The response time is then given as

$$R_i(q) = w_i^n(q) - qT_i \qquad (7)$$

e.g. with $q=2$ the task started $2T_i$ into the window and hence the response time is the size of the window minus $2T_i$.

The number of releases that need to be considered is bounded by the lowest value of $q$ for which the following relation is true:

$$R_i(q) \le (q+1)T_i \qquad (8)$$

At this point the task completes before the next release and hence subsequent windows do not overlap. The worst case response time is then the maximum value found for each $q$:

$$R_i(q) = \max_{q = 0,1,2...} R_i(q) \qquad (9)$$

Note that for $D \le T$ relation (8) is true for $q=0$ (if the task can be guaranteed), in which case equations (6) and (7) simplify back to the original equation.

## 3.4    Internal Deadlines

In a recent report [32], Gerber argues that it is only meaningful to attach a deadline to the last observable event of a task. Moreover this last observable event may not be at the end of the task's execution, i.e. there may be a number of internal actions after the last output event.

When the model for analysis is enhanced to include kernel overheads (as described in section 2), it is necessary to "charge" to each task the cost of the context switch that allows it to pre-empt a lower priority task plus the cost of the context switch back to a lower priority task once the higher priority task has completed. For realistic context switch times (i.e. not zero) it is meaningless to attach the "deadline" to the end of the context switch.

In the following we denote by $C^D$ the computation time required by the real internal deadline and by $C^T$ the total computation time of the task in each period. Note there is no requirement to complete $C^T$ by $T$ as long as $C^D$ is completed by $D$. Hence an adaptation of the arbitrary deadline model (see previous section) is required.

If we include the two phases of computation into equation (6) we get:

$$w_i^{n+1}(q) = B_i + q\,C_i^T + C_i^D + \sum_{j \in hp(i)} \left\lceil \frac{w_i^n(q)}{T_j} \right\rceil C_j^T \qquad (10)$$

This when combined with (7), (8) and (9) allows the worst case response time for $C_i^D$ to be calculated (assuming maximum $C_i^T$ interference from earlier releases of the same task). Equation (6) could be used directly to calculate the response time for $C_i^T$ but this value is not directly relevant to this formulation. It can be shown, trivially, that for utilisation less than 100% there exists bounded response times for all tasks. What is important is that $R_i^D$ is less than $D_i$.

The above analysis can be applied to the simple task set introduced and discussed by Gerber [32]. Table 3 shows the characterisation of three tasks, note that $D = T$ for all entries, and that no task experiences blocking. With rate monotonic analysis task 3 cannot be guaranteed. However, Gerber shows that by transforming this task, of the 653 units of computation only 493 are required to be completed by the deadline. He then shows how an implementation scheme can be used to guarantee task 3. However, the above analysis furnishes a value for $R_3^D$ of 2493, which is just before the deadline (and period). Hence standard pre-emptive priority based dispatching will satisfy the timing requirements of this task set. No transformation is needed. Note, for completeness, that the worst case response time of $R_3^T$ is 2653.

**Table 3**: Gerber's Task Set

| Task   | $T$  | $C^D$ | $C^T$ | $D$  | $R^D$ | $R^T$ |
|--------|------|-------|-------|------|-------|-------|
| task 1 | 1000 | 400   | 400   | 1000 | 400   | 400   |
| task 2 | 1600 | 400   | 400   | 1600 | 800   | 800   |
| task 3 | 2500 | 493   | 653   | 2500 | 2493  | 2653  |

### 3.5    Offsets and Phased Executions

Perhaps the most extreme restriction of the basic model is that it assumes that all tasks could be released at the same time (the critical instant). This assumption simplifies the analysis but it is not applicable on many occasions. Cyclic executives (static scheduling), for example, explicitly use offsets to order executions and obtain feasible schedules. Without offsets, priority based systems are often too pessimistic; with offsets, equivalent behaviour to cyclic executives can be obtained [7]. (Consider a set of periodic tasks with 100% utilisation, all of which have deadlines equal to the LCM of the task set; clearly within the LCM no idle tick is present and no task executes for more than its computation time and hence all deadlines must be met.) For example, a recent case study [16] of the Olympus satellite AOCS (Attitude and Orbital Control System), containing some 30 tasks, was deemed unschedulable by the standard deadline monotonic test (i.e. equation (1) modified to include kernel overheads). On inspection it contained three tasks of identical period that could not all be scheduled. Table 4 gives the details of these tasks.

**Table 4:** Three Offset Tasks

| Task Name | Period | Comp. Time | Offset | Deadline |
|-----------|--------|-----------|--------|----------|
| Command Actuators | 200 | 2.13 | 50 | 14 |
| Request DSS Data | 200 | 1.43 | 150 | 17 |
| Request Wheel Speeds | 200 | 1.43 | 0 | 22 |

The only requirement on these tasks were their periods (and deadlines), they did not have to be released together. By giving "Command Actuators" an offset of 50ms and "Request DSS Data" an offset of 150ms, their execution was spread out. From an analysis point of view it was possible to replace these three tasks by just one (see Table 7). This task has a computation time requirement equal to the greatest of the original three, and a deadline which is the shortest. The task set (including this new one but not the originals) now passed the schedulability test.

**Table 5:** Combined Task

| Task Name | Period | Comp. Time | Offset | Deadline |
|-----------|--------|-----------|--------|----------|
| Combined Task | 50 | 2.13 | 0 | 14 |

Hence a simple transformation, that actually increases the load on the system (as it notionally executes every 50ms), can increase schedulability by incorporating offsets.

In the more general case of arbitrary offset relationships, it would be desirable to have an exact feasibility test. One way of testing feasibility is just to simulate the behaviour of the system. Leung shows that the length of interval that should be examined is twice the LCM of the task set plus the largest offset (assuming tasks have been normalized to have offsets less than period) [47]. For task sets with periods that are relative primes this implies a computationally infeasible test.

Recently Tindell [69, 7] has developed a feasible, but inexact (sufficient but not necessary) test, using the window approach outlined earlier for arbitrary deadlines. The derivation of this result is, however, beyond the scope of this review.

### 3.6 Priority Assignment

The formulations given in the last three sections (i.e. arbitrary deadlines, internal deadlines and offsets) have the common property that no simple algorithms (such as rate or deadline monotonic) gives the optimal priority ordering. In Fig. 1 we reproduce Audsley's algorithm [4] (in Ada) for assigning priorities in these situations.

Variable 'set' is an array of tasks that is ordered by priority, 'set(1)' being the highest priority, 'set($N$)' the lowest. The procedure 'task_test' tests to see whether task $K$ is feasible at that place in the array. The double loop works by first swapping tasks into the lowest position until a feasible result is found, this task is then fixed at that position. The next priority position is then considered. If at any time the inner loop fails to find a feasible task the whole procedure is abandoned. Note that a concise algorithm is possible if an extra swap is undertaken.

```
procedure assign_pri(set : in out process_set; N : natural;
                     OK : in out boolean) is
    begin
    for K in reverse 1..N loop
      for next in reverse 1..K loop
        swap(set,K,next);
        task_test(set,K,OK);
        set(K).P := K;
        exit when OK;
      end loop;
      exit when not OK;
    end loop;
end;
```

**Fig. 1.** Audsley's Priority Assignment Algorithm

If the feasibility test is exact (necessary and sufficient) then the priority ordering is optimal. Thus for arbitrary deadlines and internal deadlines (without blocking), an optimal ordering is found. Where a non-exact test is used (for example with the offset test) the priority ordering reflects the quality of the test.

## 4    Conclusions

In this paper simple scheduling models have been extended to account for realistic kernel behaviour and necessary application requirements. The result is a flexible computational model supported by a rich set of analysis techniques.

The overheads due to implementing fixed priority scheduling do reduce processor utilisation but the use of internal deadlines and offsets can move utilisation close to 100%. A final technique is worth noting for some tasks sets that still cannot be scheduled by the fixed priority approach. Even when 100% utilisation is needed it is not necessary to move to a fully earliest deadline approach. It has been shown that a dual priority scheme is adequate [14]. Here some low priority tasks are given an intermediate deadline at which their priority is raised (if they still have work to do).

We can conclude that fixed priority scheduling now represents an appropriate (and arguably, a mature) engineering approach. Although the many equations and relationships must be embedded in trusted tools, this is no different from many other engineering disciplines. The real-time systems designer now has the techniques available to engineer systems rather than just build them and then see if they meet their timing requirements during extensive (and expensive) testing.

## Acknowledgements

The research reported on here has been sponsored, in part, by the Engineering and Physical Science Research Council of Great Britain GR/H39611, as well as PDCS.

# The Time-Triggered Approach to Real-Time System Design

Hermann Kopetz

Technical University of Vienna

**Abstract**: In this paper the basic assumptions that govern the design of time-triggered(TT) real-time systems are examined and the characteristic properties of these architectures are analyzed. The paper introduces a real-time system model and discusses the important concept of temporal accuracy of real-time data. The fundamental paradigm behind the time-triggered design approach is explained in detail. The services and the basic design principles of the time-triggered communication protocol TTP are presented. Finally, the services of a TT architecture are assessed from the points of view of predictability, testability, resource utilization, and assumption coverage.

## 1    Introduction

A real-time computer system has to meet the deadlines dictated by its environment, otherwise it has failed. In this paper we focus on applications, where such a failure can have catastrophic consequences, e.g. a flight control system, a drive by wire system, or a nuclear power control system. In these applications a high level of assurance concerning the proper operation of the computer system — both in the domain of values and in the domain of time — is demanded. We call these type of real-time systems *hard real-time systems*. Designing hard real-time systems is challenging: the functional specifications must be met within the specified deadlines. The strict observance of these deadlines complicates the solutions of many problems that are well understood if no time constraints have to be considered.

From a user's point of view it makes little difference whether a specified service is provided by a fault-tolerant distributed system or by a highly reliable central system. While the timeliness requirement is a service attribute at the user/system interface, distribution and fault-tolerance are implementation characteristics. They are, however, the most promising implementation technologies for the design of cost effective dependable real-time systems.

For our purpose it is useful to classify a system architecture as either even-triggered (ET) or time-triggered (TT). In an ET architecture a system activity is initiated as an immediate consequence of the occurrence of a significant event in the environment or the computer system. A TT architecture observes the state of the environment periodically and initiates system activities at recurring predetermined points of the globally synchronized time. While TT-designs are prevailing in safety critical real-time applications, the ET-designs are common in non-safety critical real-time applications.

In this paper the basic assumptions that govern the design of time-triggered real-time systems are examined and the characteristic properties of these architectures are analyzed. We start by presenting a real-time system model and introduce the important concept of temporal accuracy of real-time data. In the next section the time-triggered design approach is explained in some detail. The services and the basic design principles of the time-triggered communication protocol TTP are presented in section four. In the final section we assess the services of a TT architecture from the point of view of predictability, testability, resource utilization, and assumption coverage.

## 2    A Real-Time System Model

A real-time application can be decomposed into a set of subsystems, called *clusters*, e.g. a controlled object (i.e. the machine that is to be controlled), the controlling computer system, and the operator. The controlling computer system has to react to stimuli from the controlled object within an interval of real-time that is dictated by the dynamics of the controlled object.

We make the following assumptions:

(1)  The distributed computer system (Fig. 1) consists of a set of self-contained computers, the nodes, which communicate via a Local Area Network by the exchange of messages only.

(2)  All clocks in the nodes are synchronized such that an approximate global time base of sufficiently small granularity is available to all clients in the different nodes of the distributed computer system [45].

(3)  The nodes are fail-silent and messages which are mutilated by the communication system can be detected and discarded.

(4)  Some nodes, the interface nodes, support a connection to the intelligent instrumentation, i.e. the sensors and actuators, which are at the interface to the controlled object.

We call a *physical sensor* with an associated microcontroller an *intelligent sensor*. It is the purpose of an intelligent sensor to encapsulate and hide the detailed technical interface of the physical sensor from the client computer and to provide a preprocessed abstract high level sensor reading to the client computer.

### 2.1    RT Entities and Observations

From the point of view of the control system designer, the behaviour of a real-time application can be modeled by a set of computational processes operating on representations of *real-time (RT) entities*. A RT-entity [44] is a state variable of interest for the given purpose, either in the controlled object (an external RT-entity) or in the computer system (an internal RT-entity). A RT-entity has a time-dependent internal state. Examples of RT-entities are the temperature of a particular vessel (external RT-entity), the speed of a vehicle (external RT entity), or the intended position of a specific control valve (internal RT-entity).

Every RT-entity is in the *sphere of control* of a subsystem (e.g. in the controlled object or in a particular node of a distributed computer system) that establishes the value of this RT-entity at any point in real-time. From outside its sphere of control, the state of an RT-entity can only be observed, but not modified. We call the atomic tuple

$$O = <\text{entity name,value,point of observation}>$$

an *observation* O(e,v,t) of an RT-entity e with value v at time t. The value v of an observation represents an estimation of the state of the RT-entity at time t.

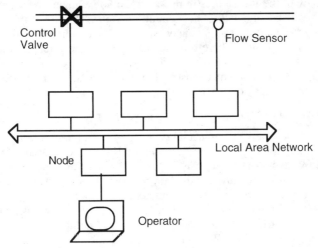

**Fig. 1.** A Real-Time Application

In typical real-time applications, the computer system has to perform a multitude of different functions concurrently, e.g. the display of observations to the operator, the monitoring of observations (both their value and rate of change) to detect alarm conditions, the processing of observations by process models in order to find new setpoints, etc.. In distributed computer systems, these different functions are normally allocated to different nodes. To guarantee a consistent behaviour of the distributed computer system as a whole, it must be assured that all nodes operate on the same versions of the observations at about the same time.

## 2.2    Downcalls and Upcalls

We distinguish between two different types of observations, *downcalls* and *upcalls*. The first is normally related to the notion of sampling, the second to the notions of interrupt in ET systems and polling in TT systems.

In the downcall mode (sampling) the intelligent sensor delivers the most recent observation about the state of the RT-entity either as a consequence of receiving a request (a downcall) from its client or at predetermined points in time (the sampling points). We call the data that is related to a downcall *sampled data* or s-data. The periodic observation of a RT-entity, e.g. a temperature, is a typical example of the generation of s-data. s-data is always "fresh" since it has been collected immediately before its delivery.

In the upcall mode the intelligent sensor reports to the client about a significant state change that has occurred in the RT entity in recent history. We call the data that is related to an upcall *occurrence data* or o-data. Whereas in an ET system o-data is reported immediately by the interrupt mechanism, the o-data is stored in a memory element at the control-object/system interface in a TT system and the delivery of the o-data can be delayed by up to one observation granule, the polling period of the TT system.

Consider the case of a pipe rupture in a reactor. Such a rare, but nevertheless very important, event will result in correlated important changes of state (i.e. significant events) in many of the RT-entities in the controlled object, causing many coincident o-data elements to be signaled to the computer system. It is impossible to service all these coincident events instantaneously, since every computer system has only a finite processing capacity. Therefore mechanisms for the intermediate storage of these *"event showers"* and for the restriction of the flow of information from the controlled object to the computer must be put into place at the interface between the computer system and the control object.

## 2.3   Temporal Accuracy

Observations of the controlled object taken at a particular point in time form the basis of computer internal *RT-images* of the observed RT-entities that are transmitted to, manipulated by, and stored within *RT-objects* [44] in the nodes of the computer system. This transportation and manipulation of the observations take a certain span of real-time, determined by the delay characteristics of the communication protocols and the processing speed within the nodes. Thus an RT-image that is available to the client of a RT-object in a remote node at a particular point in time t-use is already aged by this span of real-time. We call the length of this time-span, i.e. the difference between the point of use of an RT-image and the point in time that the RT-entity has possessed this value (normally the point of observation), the *temporal accuracy* of the RT-image. An observation that is inaccurate, either in the domain of value or in the domain of time, can cause a failure in the service of the real-time computer system.

The patterns of change of a RT-entity, i.e. the dynamics of the RT-entity, determine the response time requirements on the computer system. If the response time of the computer system is much longer than the time between significant changes in the state of the RT-entity, then it is difficult to perform any real-time control of the controlled object. Real-time control is only feasible if the speed of the computer system matches the dynamics of the controlled object.

## 3   The Time-Triggered Design Approach

In a time-triggered architecture all system activities are initiated by the progression of time. There is only one interrupt in the system, the periodic clock interrupt, which partitions the continuum of time into a sequence of equidistant granules. It is assumed that all clocks are synchronized and every observation of the control object is timestamped with this synchronized time. The granularity of the global time must be chosen such that the temporal order of any two observations taken anywhere in a distributed TT system can be reestablished from their time-stamps [44].

### 3.1   The TT-View of the World

The time-triggered paradigm of a real-time system rests on a distinctive view of the world: the observer (the computer system) is not driven by the events that happen in its environment, but decides autonomously when to look at the world. It is therefore impossible to overload a time-triggered observer!

A TT system takes a snapshot of the world, *an observation,* at recurring predetermined points in time determined by the current value of its synchronized local clock. This snapshot is disseminated within the computer system by a synchronized time-triggered protocol to update the RT-images in the remote RT-objects with minimal delay. As soon as the time difference between *now* and the point in time that is associated with the current value of the RT image (normally the time of observation of the RT entity) has grown beyond an application-specific limit, the RT image loses its temporal accuracy. It is possible to improve the accuracy of real-time images by *state estimation*. Based on knowledge about the laws of change of a RT entity, a procedure within the RT-object in the computer system can periodically modify the corresponding RT image to bring it into better agreement with the current state of the external RT entity and to even stretch out the validity of a RT-image to some point of use in the future. Good temporal accuracy of RT-images can therefore be realized either by frequent observations of the controlled object or by a good state estimation model. Within limits it is possible to replace observation and communication actions by computational actions and vice versa.

The semantics of the periodic messages transported in a TT system is a *state-message semantics,* i.e. a new version of a message overwrites the previous version and a message is not consumed on reading. This semantics is well suited to handle the transport of the RT images of the state variables used in control applications. The state message semantics provides a predefined constant load on the communication system and eliminates the delicate problem of dynamic buffer management.

### 3.2   Autonomy

TT architectures delegate a high degree of autonomy to their subsystems. TT systems are not pushed by the events that happen in the environment and which are outside the *sphere of control* of the computer system. In a TT system temporal control always remains inside the controlling subsystem.

Flow control in a TT system is *implicit*. During system design appropriate observation, message, and task activation rates are determined for the different state variables based on their given dynamics. It has to be assured during the design that all receiver processes can handle these rates. If the state variables change faster than specified then some short-lived intermediate states will not be reflected in the observations. Yet, even in a peak load situation, the number of messages per unit time, i.e. the message rate, remains constant.

This implicit flow control will only function properly if the instrumentation of the TT system supports the previously discussed *state view*. If a significant *event*, i.e. o-data, (or a short-lived state that can be smaller than a polling cycle) has to be observed, local logic in the interface has to recognize this event (or state) and must transform it into a state representation with a state duration of more than one polling cycle.

Consider the example of a push button, which is a typical *event sensor*. The local logic in this sensor must assure that the state "push button pressed" is true for an interval that is longer than the polling cycle. If the push button is pressed a number of times within a single polling cycle, then the system will only observe the first button push and will neglect all others. The behaviour that is outside the specification, i.e. the state changes that happen faster than specified, are suppressed at the computer-system/environment interface. Even in this overload situation a TT system will observe all state changes that are within the specification without any additional delay. This example shows how a TT system protects itself from overload caused by an unspecified behaviour of a malign environment.

## 3.3   Temporal Firewalls

The strict data sharing interfaces between the subsystems of a TT architecture help to isolate the subsystems from each other and eliminate the possibility of control error propagation from one subsystem to another subsystem. Since the subsystems derive their control signals autonomously from the progression of time, the interfaces can be designed as data-sharing interfaces without any control signals passing the interface. We call such an interface that blocks any control error propagation a *temporal firewall*. Three of these temporal firewalls within a distributed time-triggered architecture deserve special mention:

(1) the interface between the control object and the computer system

(2) the interface between the application software within a node and the communication system, the message-base interface (MBI), and

(3) the gateway interface between clusters.

In a TT architecture the interface between the control object and the computer system is a data sharing interface free of any control signals. A TT architecture does not have to make any assumptions about the proper generation of control signals (interrupt signals) by an external subsystem that is outside its sphere of control. There is no possibility for a malicious external device to upset the computer by generating unspecified sporadic interrupts.

The message base interface (MBI) separates the communication within a cluster from the processing within a node. It is a data sharing interface that hides the communication system from the application software within the client node behind a memory abstraction. This abstraction is implemented in a dual-ported random access memory (DPRAM) that is accessible by both, the communication controller and the client CPU that executes the application tasks. The communication controller autonomously updates the images of the state variables of the MBI. Whenever an TT application task needs a timely image, it just reads the specified DPRAM area (potential access conflicts are not possible in the preplanned schedules).

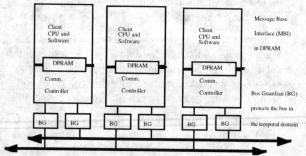

**Fig. 2.** Structure of a Fault-Tolerant Unit (FTU) consisting of three nodes

If the temporal accuracy of the real-time data is longer than the longest time interval between the point of observation and the point of use of this data element, then the application process at the receiver end can always assume that the real-time data in the MBI is temporally valid. If the data is phase sensitive, i.e. the above cited condition is not satisfied, then the receiving task must be synchronized with the sending task on the basis of the a priori known receive time of the data, and/or a state estimation task must be executed at the receiving end to improve the temporal accuracy of the real-time image. Since there is no control signal crossing the MBI other than the synchronized ticks of the clock, the control of any one of the subsystems (communication controller, host CPU) cannot be interrupted by a failure in the control of any of the other subsystems.

The gateway interface between clusters implements the relative views of interacting clusters. It is an application specific data-sharing interface. The gateway interface software collects the information in the sending cluster that is relevant for the receiver and transforms it to a representation that conforms to the information representation expected by the receiving cluster. There are no control signals passing through a gateway component, i.e. a gateway does not reduce the autonomy of control of the interconnected clusters.

## 3.4    Static Temporal Control Structures

In a TT system the temporal control structure of the tasks is data independent and static. By taking the maximum execution time of a task as the basis for the generation of the static schedules, data dependence of the temporal control structure is eliminated in a TT system. It is thus possible to separate the design and validation of the temporal control structure of a system from the design and validation of the sequential data transformation functions. The price paid for this reduction in complexity is reduced flexibility and an increase in resource requirements.

The analysis of field data about the failure patterns of complex real-time software leads to the conclusion that the complexity in the dynamic data-dependent task coordination and synchronization is the cause for many software failures. This failure cause is eliminated in TT architectures.

**Maximum Execution Time of Programs.** The application tasks in a TT system have a linear structure, starting with the reading of the input data and the previous internal task state, calculating the specified data transformation, and terminating with the output of the results and the new internal state. There is no need for any explicit synchronization points within a TT task (e.g. a *wait* statement) since all potential access conflicts are avoided by the implicit synchronization designed into the static schedule. It is thus possible to determine the maximum execution time of a TT task off-line in isolation from all other tasks, provided the programmer has observed a set of programming rules that lead to terminating tasks [73]. It is a challenge to find tight bounds on the maximum execution time of real-time programs. Recently a number of researchers have focussed on the solution of this problem, e.g. [57].

**Scheduling**. TT operating systems are based on a set of static predetermined schedules, one for each operational mode of the system. These schedules guarantee the deadlines of all time-critical tasks, observe all necessary task dependencies (precedence, mutual exclusion) and provide implicit synchronization of the tasks at run time. At run time a simple table lookup is performed by the dispatcher of the operating system to determine which task has to be executed at the next point in real time, the grid points of the *action grid*. The difference between two adjacent grid points of the action grid determines the *basic cycle time* of the real-time executive. The basic cycle time is a lower bound for the responsiveness of a TT system. In TT systems all input/output activities are preplanned and realized by sampling the appropriate sensors and actuators at the specified times. Access to the common communication channel is also predetermined, e.g. by a synchronous time division multiple access protocol (TDMA). The calculation and test of the static schedules is performed off line for each operating mode of a TT system [31]. The mode changes can be initiated dynamically at run time. The mode changes are thus the only means of bringing data dependency into the temporal control structure of a TT system.

**Testing for Timeliness.** The temporal encapsulation of the tasks and the nodes, achieved by the TT task schedules and the TT communication protocol, and the replica determinism (discussed below) support constructive testing for timeliness: The temporal control structure is data independent and can be tested in isolation from the data transformations. In a TT system, the results of the performance test of every system task can be compared with the a priori established maximum execution time. The proper operation of the TT communication system can be tested without consideration of the application software, since there is no control transfer across the MBI. Since the time-base is discrete and determined by the precision of the global clock synchronization [41], every input case can be reproduced precisely in the domains of time and value.

## 3.5    Fault Tolerance

In a properly designed TT architecture tolerance of hardware faults can be realized by the provision of active redundancy [42]. Redundancy management is performed by the communication system at the cluster level and does not affect the MBI, the interface between the communication system and host computer executing the application software. Fault tolerance is thus transparent to the application software.

In a TT-system we distinguish between the mechanisms for the detection of timing errors and the mechanisms for the detection of value errors.

**Error Detection in the Temporal Domain.** The a priori global knowledge about the expected temporal behaviour of all nodes forms the basis for the prompt detection of timing errors. If a message has not arrived by the specified time at the receiver, the receiver immediately knows that either the message has been lost or the sending node has failed. The regular transmission of periodic message rounds that are observed by all receivers makes it possible to implement efficient membership protocols in TT architectures [43]. Such a membership protocol that consistently informs all nodes about any node failure within a short latency is the basis for an atomic multicast service that can be provided by the TT communication system. The most critical timing failure in any bus system is the *babbling idiot* failure, in which a faulty node forwards messages to the common channel at arbitrary points in time and thereby obstructs communication between any of the other nodes. In a TT architecture babbling idiot failures can by avoided by the implementation of an intelligent bus guardian that denies access to the channel outside the a priori known TDMA timeslot (see Fig. 2 ). In a safety-critical environment the intelligent bus guardian (BG) is an independent autonomous hardware unit with its own clock and its own power supply that will only allow the node to access the common resource bus during the a priori specified time-slot.

**Error Detection in the Value Domain.** Mechanisms for the detection of value failures can be provided at two levels. At the communication level the inclusion of a CRC field in every message allows detection with high probability of message mutilation during transport. At the application level end-to-end error detection mechanisms that cover the complete trajectory between the sending task and the receiving task can be implemented to increase error detection coverage. Transient data errors can be detected by time-redundant execution of the application tasks or by the implementation of triple modular redundancy (TMR) with voting.

**Active Redundancy.** Active redundancy is implemented in a TT architecture by replicating the nodes and grouping them into Fault-Tolerant Units (FTUs — see Fig. 2). As long as any one of the fail-silent nodes of an FTU provides its service, the FTU is operational. Alternatively it is possible to mask errors by triplicating non fail-silent nodes and by majority voting (TMR) on the results of each triple. The error detection mechanism in the temporal domain assures that even a maliciously faulty node cannot interfere with the time slots of the other nodes of the triple. The loss of n physical messages can be tolerated in the communication system by masking, if every logical message is sent n+1 times. Necessary prerequisites for the proper operation of such a replication scheme are the maintenance of *replica determinism* among the fail-silent units of an FTU and the *idempotency of messages*.

Replica determinism means that replicated nodes visit the same states at about the same points in time. It requires that all decisions within the architecture and the application software are deterministic. The preplanned time-triggered temporal control structure eliminates the need for random conflict resolution mechanisms at the architectural level. If the application software avoids nondeterministic constructs, e.g. such as a *wait* statement for explicit synchronization, then deterministic behaviour of the total node can be guaranteed. Detailed discussion about all implications that follow from the replica determinism requirement is beyond the scope of this paper. The reader is referred to [55] for a thorough analysis of this subject.

State messages are idempotent by definition. Since state messages are not queued and a new version of a state message replaces the present version, no special mechanisms have to be introduced to eliminate replicated physical messages.

# 4    The Time-Triggered Communication Protocol

In a time-triggered architecture, the occurrence of all significant events (sampling the environment, scheduling the tasks, etc.) is known *a priori* at design time. It is possible to use this a priori information to design a responsive and efficient time-triggered communication protocol. In this section we present an overview of the time-triggered protocol TTP. The interested reader is referred to [43] to find a comprehensive description of the protocol.

## 4.1    Principle of Operation

TTP is an integrated time-triggered protocol that provides the following services without the strict separation of concerns proposed in the layered OSI model
- prompt transmission of messages
- responsive membership service
- fault-tolerant clock synchronization service
- mode change service
- error detection with short latency

- redundancy management
- high data efficiency

We consider the OSI model an excellent *conceptual* model for reasoning about the different design issues. We do not feel that the OSI model is a good *implementation* model for the development of time-critical protocols, since timeliness was not a goal in the development of the OSI model.

In a time-triggered architecture much information about the behaviour of the system, e.g. which node has to send what type of message at a particular point in time of a sparse time base, is known a priori — at design time — to all nodes of the ensemble. TTP tries to make best use of this a priori information to reduce the number and size of messages, to increase the error detection coverage, and to reduce the error detection latency.

In a time-triggered architecture, a receiver can only interpret the frame sent by a sender if sender and receiver agree about the controller state at the time of sending and receiving. In TTP this controller state (the C-state) consists of three fields: the mode, the time and the membership. The mode field contains the identification of the current operational mode of the system. The time field contains the global internal time. The membership field reveals which FTUs have been active and which FTUs have been inactive at their last membership point. To enforce C-state agreement between a sender and a receiver, in TTP the CRC of a normal message is calculated over the message contents concatenated with the local C-state (Fig 3). The C-state itself is not transmitted in the message.

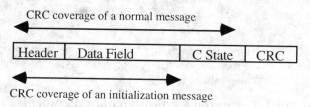

**Fig. 3.** CRC Calculation in TTP

In case the C-state of the sender is different from the C-state of the receiver, any message sent by the sender will be discarded by the receiver on the basis of an invalid CRC check.

TTP is based on the assumption that the communication channels have only omission failures and the nodes support the fail-silent abstraction in the temporal domain, i.e. a node either delivers a message at the correct point in time or does not deliver a message. This property, which will be discussed at length in the rest of this paper, helps to enforce error confinement at the system level and simplifies the implementation of fault tolerance.

TTP is based on a sparse time base, i.e. all actions in the sphere of control of the distributed computer system will occur at the lattice points of a predefined space-time lattice. This property helps to simplify the solution of the agreement problems in fault-tolerant distributed systems.

## 4.2 Data Formats

Fig.4 presents the format of a TTP frame on the network. Since sender and receiver know a priori when a particular message will be sent, it is not necessary to carry the message identifier in the TTP frame. This helps to reduce the length of messages.

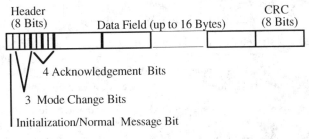

**Fig. 4.** Format of a TTP Frame

Since TTP messages are *state* messages, i.e. a new version of a message overwrites the previous version and a message is not consumed by reading it, the TTP network can be hidden behind the memory abstraction. The MBI interface to the application software is formed by the TTP message base, i.e. a section of memory that contains the set of TTP input and output messages (Fig.5). The attributes of these messages are described in a Message Descriptor List (MEDL).

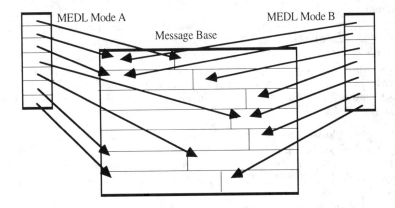

**Fig. 5.** Message Base Interface (MBI)

The TTP controller periodically and autonomously reads the messages from and writes the messages to the message base interface.

## 4.3 Fault Handling Strategy

At the system level TTP assumes that all nodes exhibit a fail-silent behaviour in the temporal domain, i.e. a node either sends

- a correct message (correct operation) at the specified point in time or
- no message (crash failure or omission failure) or
- a detectable incorrect message at the correct point in time.

A detectable incorrect message, e.g. a message with a CRC field such that the corruption of the message can be detected by recalculating the CRC polynomial, must be discarded by the receiver. At a higher level of abstraction we can therefore assume that a message is either correct or no message has arrived. We call any failure of the above indicated type a "clean node failure". Note that a difference in the C-state of the sender from that of the receiver will also result in a "missing message" because of the CRC calculation technique explained above.

The fault handling strategy of TTP is based on a two level approach: At the system level the protocol must detect and manage clean node failures promptly. At the component level it must be ensured that all internal failure modes of a node are mapped into a clean node failure at the node/network service interface of the node.

To tolerate the loss of messages, every FTU can send multiple copies of the same logical message on the physical network. If an FTU consists of two actively redundant nodes and every node is connected to two redundant communication channels, then four physical copies of every message, — one on each channel from each node of the FTU — can be transmitted. Up to three of these four messages can be corrupted without any effect on the application. In any case, there will be only a single correct message presented to the application software at the TTP/application software interface, the MBI interface (Fig. 2), i.e. the redundancy is hidden from the application.

To tolerate the failure of a node, a Fault-Tolerant Unit (FTU) can be configured to consist of two replicated nodes operating in active redundancy. In this configuration the system level fault model requires that node failures are "clean failures", i.e. every message accepted by the receiver is a correct and timely message. As long as any one of the two active replicas is sending messages, the FTU service is provided. If clean node failures in the value domain cannot be assumed, it is possible to configure an FTU as a Triple-Modular Redundant (TMR) unit that will detect and mask a wrong message by majority voting. Note that fail-silence in the time domain is enforced by the Bus Guardians (see Fig. 2) that block incorrectly timed messages based on the *a priori* known send time.

TTP provides a global time base by executing the distributed FTA (Fault-Tolerant-Average) clock synchronization algorithm in each node. In a time-triggered architecture, such as TTP, the intended send times and receive times of all messages are known a priori to all nodes. The difference between the actual receive time and the expected receive time of a message is thus a measure of the difference between the state of the sender clock and the state of the receiver clock. Using this knowledge, the distributed FTA algorithm periodically calculates a correction factor for the local clock in each node by sorting the clock differences according to size, eliminating the k-largest positive and negative values, and taking the average of the remaining N-2k clock difference terms. This clock correction factor is used to align the rate of the local clock (by hardware means in the TTP controller) such that the local time will stay within a predefined interval — the precision of the clock synchronization — of the global notion of time. This algorithm is capable of handling up to k arbitrary (Byzantine) clock failures, provided N, the number of nodes in the ensemble, is larger than 3*k [45].

# 5    Conclusions

TT systems require careful planning during the design phase. First it is necessary to establish the observation lattice for the RT-entities and then the maximum execution time of time-critical tasks must be determined. After the allocation of the tasks to the nodes and the allocation of the communication slots on the LAN, appropriate execution schedules have to be constructed off line. Because of this accurate planning effort, detailed plans for the temporal behaviour of each task are available and the behaviour of the system in the domain of time can be predicted precisely. In a TT system all schedules are fixed and planned for the peak load demand in the specified operating mode. The time slot assigned to a specific task must be at least as long as the maximum execution time of this task. If the difference between the average and the maximum execution time of a task is large, then only a fraction of the allocated time slot will be needed by this task. From a temporal point of view, every task of a TT system is encapsulated. There are no control signals crossing the interface between two TT subsystems. Every subsystem exercises autonomous control derived from the progression of the synchronized time that is available locally.

In an ET system it is not necessary to develop such a set of detailed plans during the design phase, since the data dependent execution schedules are created dynamically as a consequence of the actual demand. Depending on the sequence and timing of the events that are presented to the system in a specific application scenario, different schedules unfold dynamically. Confidence in the timeliness of an ET system can only be established by off-line schedulability tests or by extensive system tests. In a system where all scheduling decisions concerning the task execution and the access to the communication system are dynamic, no *temporal encapsulation* exists, i.e. a variation in the timing of any task can have consequences on the timing of many other tasks in different nodes.

In an ET-system only those tasks that have been activated under the actual circumstances have to be scheduled. Since the scheduling decisions are made dynamically, the CPU will be available again after the actual (and not the maximum) task execution time. On the other hand, run-time resources are required for the execution of the dynamic scheduling algorithm and for synchronization and buffer management. If load conditions are low or average, then the resource utilization of an ET system will be much better than that of a comparable TT system. In peak load scenarios the situation can reverse, since the time available for the execution of the application tasks is reduced by the increasing processing time required for executing the scheduling algorithms, buffer management, and explicit synchronization of the tasks.

Every control system is built on a set of assumptions concerning the behaviour of the controlled object and of the computer. The probability that these assumptions are violated limits the dependability of the whole application [56]. We denote those assumptions that refer to the behaviour of the controlled object the *external assumptions* and those that refer to the behaviour of the computer system the *internal assumptions*. In a TT system the critical external assumptions refer to the rate of change of the values of the RT-entities. The dynamics of a RT-entity determines the granularity of the observation lattice and thus the required minimum duration of states that can be guaranteed to be observed. If these assumptions are violated, short lived states may evade the observation. The dominant internal assumption in a TT-system refers to the maximum execution time of tasks, which must be evaluated during the design. In an ET-system, the critical external assumption is the conjectured distribution of the event occurrences, both in normal and peak load situations. This distribution forms the basis for the system test and predictions about the ability of the system to meet the specified deadlines. If this assumed distribution is not representative of the distributions that evolve in the real world, then the basis for predicting the timeliness of the system is compromised. The critical internal assumption in ET system concerns the services of the dynamic scheduler. Will the scheduler find a feasible solution for the evolving task scenario within the given time constraints?

As a consequence of the detailed planning phase required for the implementation of a TT application, the temporal behaviour of a TT design is predictable. If an ET design is chosen, this detailed planning phase is not necessary. On the other hand, the verification of an ET design demands much more extensive system tests than the verification of a TT design. Since an ET design does not support any temporal encapsulation, it does not scale as well as a TT design. From the point of view of resource utilization an ET-design will, in many cases, be superior to that of an TT design. The investigation of whether the advantageous properties of these two contrary architectures can be combined into a single coherent architecture is an interesting research issue. One possible solution is the application of an ET-design within a node, but a TT design for the communication between the nodes of a distributed system. Such an architecture would support temporal encapsulation between the nodes and thus provide excellent testability at the architectural level, while increasing flexibility of scheduling and resource utilization within the nodes.

# Software Measurement:
# A Necessary Scientific Basis*

Norman Elliott Fenton

CSR, City University, London EC1V 0HB

**Abstract.** Software measurement, like measurement in any other discipline, must adhere to the science of measurement if it is to gain widespread acceptance and validity. The observation of some very simple, but fundamental, principles of measurement can have an extremely beneficial effect on the subject. Measurement theory is used to highlight both weaknesses and strengths of software metrics work, including work on metrics validation. We identify a problem with the well known Weyuker properties, but also show that a criticism of these properties by Cherniavsky and Smith is invalid. We show that the search for general software complexity measures is doomed to failure. However, the theory does help us to define and validate measures of specific complexity attributes. Above all, we are able to view software measurement in a very wide perspective, rationalising and relating its many diverse activities.

## 1    Introduction

It is over eleven years since DeMillo and Lipton [25] outlined the relevance of measurement theory to software metrics. More recent work such as [52, 76, 27] has taken the measurement theory basis for software metrics considerably further. However, despite the important message in this work, and related material, it has been largely ignored by both practitioners and researchers. The result is that much published work in software metrics is theoretically flawed. This paper therefore provides a timely summary and enhancement of measurement theory approaches, which enables us to expose problems in software metrics work and show how they can be avoided.

In Sect.2 we provide a concise summary of measurement theory. In Sect.3 we use the theory to show that the search for general-purpose, real-valued software 'complexity' measures is doomed to failure. The assumption that fundamentally different views of complexity can be characterized by a single number is counter to the fundamental concepts of measurement theory. This leads us to re-examine critically the much cited Weyuker properties [74]. We explain how the most promising approach is to identify specific attributes of complexity and measure these separately. In Sect.4 we use basic notions of measurement to describe a framework which enables us to view apparently diverse software measurement activities in a unified way. We look at some well-known approaches to software measurement within this framework, exposing both the good points and bad points.

---

* This paper is based on [29]

# 2     Measurement Fundamentals

## 2.1    What is measurement?

*Measurement* is defined as the process by which numbers or symbols are assigned to attributes of entities in the real world in such a way as to describe them according to clearly defined rules [58]. An *entity* may be an object, such as a person or a software specification, or an event, such as a journey or the testing phase of a software project. An *attribute* is a feature or property of the entity, such as the height or blood pressure (of a person), the length or functionality (of a specification), the cost (of a journey), or the duration (of the testing phase).

Just what is meant by the numerical assignment 'describing' the attribute is made precise within the representational theory of measurement presented below. Informally, the assignment of numbers or symbols must preserve any intuitive and empirical observations about the attributes and entities. Thus, for example, when measuring the height of humans bigger numbers must be assigned to the taller humans, although the numbers themselves will differ according to whether we use metres, inches, or feet. In most situations an attribute, even one as well understood as height of humans, may have a different intuitive meaning to different people. The normal way to get round this problem is to define a *model* for the entities being measured. The model reflects a specific viewpoint. Thus, for example, our model of a human might specify a particular type of posture and whether or not to include hair height or allow shoes to be worn. Once the model is fixed there is a reasonable consensus about relations which hold for humans with respect to height (these are the empirical relations). The need for good models is particularly relevant in software engineering measurement. For example, even as simple a measure of length of programs as lines of code (LOC) requires a well defined model of programs which enables us to identify unique lines unambiguously. Similarly, to measure the effort spent on, say, the unit testing process we would need an agreed `model' of the process which at least makes clear when the process begins and ends.

There are two broad types of measurement: direct and indirect. *Direct measurement* of an attribute is measurement which does not depend on the measurement of any other attribute. *Indirect measurement* of an attribute is measurement which involves the measurement of one or more other attributes. It turns out that while some attributes can be measured directly, we normally get more sophisticated measurement (meaning a more sophisticated scale, see below) if we measure indirectly.

**Uses of measurement: assessment and prediction.** There are two broad uses of measurement: for *assessment* and for *prediction*. Predictive measurement of an attribute $A$ will generally depend on a mathematical model relating $A$ to some existing measures of attributes $A_1,...,A_n$. Accurate predictive measurement is inevitably dependent on careful (assessment type) measurement of the attributes $A_1,...,A_n$. For example, accurate estimates of project resources are *not* obtained by simply 'applying' a cost estimation model with fixed parameters. However, careful measurement of key attributes of completed projects can lead to accurate resource predictions for future projects. Similarly, it is possible to get accurate predictions of the reliability of software in operation, but these are dependent on careful data collection relating to failure times during alpha-testing [12].

For predictive measurement the model alone is not sufficient. Additionally, we need to define the procedures for a) determining model parameters and b) interpreting the results. For example, in the case of software reliability prediction we might use Maximum Likelihood Estimation for a) and Bayesian statistics for b). The model, together with procedures a) and b), is called a *prediction system*. Using the same model will generally yield different results if we use different prediction procedures.

It must be stressed that, for all but the most trivial attributes, proposed predictive measures in software engineering are invariably stochastic rather than deterministic. The same is true of proposed indirect measures.

**Measurement activities must have clear objectives.** The basic definitions of measurement suggest that any measurement activity must proceed with very clear objectives or goals. First you need to know whether you want to measure for assessment or for prediction. Next, you need to know exactly which entities are the subject of interest. Then you need to decide which attributes of the chosen entities are the significant ones. The definition of measurement makes clear the need to specify both an entity and an attribute before any measurement can be undertaken (a simple fact which has been ignored in much software metrics activity). Clearly, there are no definitive measures which can be prescribed for every objective in any application area. Yet for many years software practitioners expected precisely that: 'what software metric should we be using?' was, and still is, a commonly asked question. It says something about the previous ignorance of scientific measurement in software engineering that the Goal/Question/Metric paradigm [9] has been hailed as a revolutionary step forward. GQM spells out the above necessary obligations for setting objectives before embarking on any software measurement activity.

## 2.2 Representational theory of measurement

**The issues addressed**. Although there is no *universally* agreed theory of measurement, most approaches are devoted to resolving the following issues: what is and what is not measurement; which types of attributes can and cannot be measured and on what kind of scales; how do we know if we have really measured an attribute; how to define measurement scales; when is an error margin acceptable or not; which statements about measurement are meaningful. Here we present a brief overview of the *representational* theory of measurement [58].

**Empirical relation systems**. Direct measurement of a particular attribute possessed by a set of entities must be preceded by intuitive understanding of that attribute. This intuitive understanding leads to the identification of empirical relations between entities. The set of entities $C$, together with the set of empirical relations $R$, is called an *empirical relation system (C,R)* for the attribute in question. Thus the attribute of 'height' of people gives rise to empirical relations like 'is tall', 'taller than', and 'much taller than'.

**Representation condition.** To measure the attribute that is characterized by an empirical relation system *(C,R)* requires a mapping $M$ into a *numerical relation system (N,P)*. Specifically, $M$ maps entities in $C$ to numbers (or symbols) in $N$, and empirical relations in $R$ are mapped to numerical relations in $P$, in such a way that all empirical relations are preserved. This is the so-called *representation condition*, and the mapping $M$ is called a *representation*. The representation condition asserts that the correspondence between empirical and numerical relations is two way. Suppose, for example, that the binary relation $\angle$ *is* mapped by $M$ to the numerical relation $<$. Then, formally, we have the following instance:

Representation Condition: $x \angle y \Leftrightarrow M(x) < M(y)$

Thus, suppose, $C$ is the set of all people and $R$ contains the relation 'taller than'. A measure $M$ of height would map $C$ into the set of real numbers $\Re$ and 'taller than' to the relation $>$. The representation condition asserts that person A is taller than person B if and only if $M(A) > M(B)$.

By having to identify empirical relations for an attribute in advance, the representational approach to measurement avoids the temptation to *define* a poorly understood, but intuitively recognisable, attribute in terms of some numerical assignment. This is one of the most common failings in software metrics work. Classic examples are where attributes such as 'complexity' or 'quality' are equated with proposed numbers; for example, complexity with a 'measure' like McCabe's cyclomatic number [51], and 'quality' with Kafura and Henry's fan-in/fan-out equation [39].

**Scale types and meaningfulness.** Suppose that an attribute of some set of entities has been characterized by an empirical relation system $(C,R)$. There may in general be many ways of assigning numbers which satisfy the representation condition. For example, if person A is taller than person B, then $M(A) > M(B)$ irrespective of whether the measure $M$ is in inches, feet, centimetres metres etc. Thus there are many different measurement representations for the normal empirical relation system for the attribute of height of people. However, any two representations $M$ and $M'$ are related in a very specific way: there is always some constant $c > 0$ such that $M = cM'$ (so where $M$ is the representation of height in inches and $M'$ in centimetres, $c = 2.54$). This transformation from one valid representation into another is called an *admissible transformation*.

It is the class of admissible transformations which determines the *scale type* for an attribute (with respect to some fixed empirical relation system). For example, where every admissible transformation is a scalar multiplication (as for height) the scale type is called *ratio*. The ratio scale is a sophisticated scale of measurement which reflects a very rich empirical relation system. An attribute is never of ratio type *a priori*; we normally start with a crude understanding of an attribute and a means of measuring it. Accumulating data and analysing the results leads to the clarification and re-evaluation of the attribute. This in turn leads to refined and new empirical relations and improvements in the accuracy of the measurement; specifically this is an improved scale.

For many software attributes we are still at the stage of having very crude empirical relation systems. In the case of an attribute like 'criticality' of software failures an empirical relation system would at best only identify different classes of failures and a binary relation 'is more critical than'. In this case, any two representations are related by a monotonically increasing transformation. With this class of admissible transformations, we have an *ordinal* scale type. In increasing order of sophistication, the best known scale types are: *nominal, ordinal, interval, ratio*, and *absolute*. For full details about the defining classes of admissible transformations, see .[58]

This formal definition of scale type based on admissible transformations enables us to determine rigorously what kind of statements about measurement are meaningful. Formally, a statement involving measurement is *meaningful* if its truth or falsity remains unchanged under any admissible transformation of the measures involved. Thus, for example, it is meaningful to say that 'Hermann is twice as tall as Peter'; if the statement is true (false) when we measure height in inches, it will remain true (false) when we measure height in any constant multiple of inches. On the other hand the statement 'Failure $x$ is twice as critical as failure $y$' is not meaningful if we only have an ordinal scale empirical relation system for failure criticality. This is because a valid ordinal scale measure $M$ could define $M(x)=6$, $M(y)=3$, while another valid ordinal scale measure $M'$ could define $M'(x)=10$, $M'(y) = 9$. In this case the statement is true under $M$ but false under $M'$.

The notion of meaningfulness also enables us to determine what kind of operations we can perform on different measures. For example, it is meaningful to use *means* for computing the average of a set of data measured on a ratio scale but not on an ordinal scale. *Medians* are meaningful for an ordinal scale but not for a nominal scale. Again, these basic observations have been ignored in many software measurement studies, where a common mistake is to use the mean (rather than median) as measure of average for data which is only ordinal.

**Representation theories.** The serious mathematical aspects of measurement theory are largely concerned with theorems which assert conditions under which certain scales of direct measurement are possible for certain relation systems. A typical example of such a theorem, due to Cantor, gives conditions for real-valued ordinal-scale measurement when we have a countable set of entities $C$ and a binary relation $b$ on $C$:

*Cantor's Theorem*: The empirical relation system $(C,b)$ has a representation in $(\Re, <)$ if and only if $b$ is a strict weak order. The scale type is ordinal when such a representation exists.

The relation $b$ being a 'strict weak order' means that it is:

(i) *asymmetric* ($xRy$ implies that it is not the case $yRx$), and
(ii) *negatively transitive* ($xRy$ implies that for every $z \in C$, either $xRz$ or $zRy$).

# 3    Measuring software 'complexity'

### 3.1    General complexity measures: the impossible holy grail

For many years researchers have sought to characterize general notions of 'complexity' by a single real number. To simplify matters, we first restrict our attention to those measures which attempt only to characterize control-flow complexity. If we can show that it is impossible to define a general measure of control-flow complexity, then the impossibility of even more general complexity measures is certain.

Zuse cites dozens of proposed control-flow complexity measures in [76]. There seems to be a minimum assumption that the empirical relation system for complexity of programs leads to (at least) an ordinal scale. This is because of the following hypotheses which are implicit in much of the work:

*Hypothesis 1*: Let $C$ be the class of programs. Then the attribute control-flow 'complexity' is characterized by an empirical relation system which includes a binary relation $b$ 'less complex than'; specifically $(x,y) \in b$ if there is a consensus that $x$ is less complex than $y$.

*Hypothesis 2*: The proposed measure $M: C \to \Re$ is a representation of complexity in which the relation $b$ is mapped to $<$.

Hypothesis 1 seems plausible. It does not state that $C$ is totally ordered with respect to $b$; only that there is some *general* view of complexity for which there would be a reasonable consensus that certain pairs of programs are in $b$. For example, in Fig.1, it seems plausible that $(x,y) \in b$ (from the measurement theory viewpoint it would be good enough if most programmers agreed this).

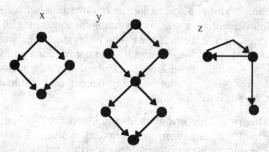

**Fig. 1**: Complexity relation not negatively transitive?

Some pairs appear to be incomparable, such as $x$ and $z$ or $y$ and $z$; if people were asked to 'rank' these for complexity they would inevitably end up asking questions like 'what is meant by complexity' before attempting to answer. Since $b$ is supposed to capture a general view of complexity this would be enough to deduce that $(x,z) \notin b$ and $(z,x) \notin b$ and also that $(z,y) \notin b$ and $(y,z) \notin b$. The idea of the inevitable incomparability of some programs, even for some specific views of complexity, has also been noted in [68].

Unfortunately, while Hypothesis 1 is plausible, Hypothesis 2 can be dismissed because of the Representation Condition. The problem is the 'incomparable' programs. While $b$ is not a total order in $C$, the relation $<$ *is* a total order in $\Re$. The measurement mapping $M$ might force an order which has to be reflected back in $C$. Thus, if for example $M(z) < M(y)$ (as in the case of McCabe's cyclomatic complexity measure in Fig.1 where $M(z)=2$ and $M(y)=3$) then, if $M$ is really a measure of complexity, the Representation Condition asserts that we must also have $z < y$ for which there is no consensus. Formally we can prove:

*Theorem 1*: Assuming Hypothesis 1, there is no general notion of control-flow complexity of programs which can be measured on an ordinal scale in $(\Re, <)$.

To prove this, the previous argument is made formal by appealing to Cantor's Theorem. It is enough to show that the relation $b$ is not a strict weak order. This follows since (according to our definition of $b$) it is reasonable to deduce that $(x,y) \in b$ but $(x,z) \notin b$ and $(z,y) \notin b$ (since it is not clear that any consensus exists about the relative complexities of $x$ and $z$ and $y$ and $z$).

The theorem should put an end to the search for the holy grail of a general complexity measure. However, it does not rule out the search for measures that characterize specific views of complexity (which is the true measurement theory approach). For example, a specific program complexity attribute is 'the number of independent paths'. McCabe's cyclomatic complexity is an absolute scale measure of this attribute. It might even be a ratio scale measure of the attribute of 'testability' with respect to independent path testing. Other specific attributes of complexity, such as the maximum depth of nesting, distribution of primes in the decomposition tree, and the number of paths of various types, can all be measured rigorously and automatically [27].

This idea of looking at measures with respect to particular viewpoints of complexity is taken much further by Zuse [76]. Zuse uses measurement theory to analyse the many complexity measures in the literature; he shows which viewpoint and assumptions are necessary to use the measures on different scales. The beauty and relevance of measurement theory is such that it clearly underlies some of the most promising work in software measurement even where the authors have not made the explicit link. Notable in this respect are the innovative approaches of Melton et al. [52] and Tian and Zelkowitz [68]. In both of these works the authors seek to characterize specific views of complexity. In [68] the authors do this by proposing a number of axioms reflecting viewpoints of complexity; in the context of measurement theory, the axioms correspond to particular empirical relations. This means that the representation condition can be used to determine the acceptability of potential measures.

Melton et al. [52] characterize a specific view of program complexity by specifying precisely an order relation $\leq$ on program flowgraphs; in other words they *define* the binary relation $b$ (of Hypothesis 1) as $\leq$. The benefit of this approach is that the view of complexity is explicit and the search for representations (i.e. measures of this view of complexity) becomes purely analytical. The only weakness in [52] is the assertion that a measure $M$ is 'any real-valued mapping for which $M(x) \leq M(y)$ whenever $x \leq y$'. This ignores the sufficiency condition of the Representation Condition. Thus, while McCabe's cyclomatic complexity [51] satisfies necessity, (and is therefore a 'measure' according to Melton et al), it is not a measure in the representational sense (since in Fig.1 $M(z) < M(y)$ but it is not the case that $z \leq y$). Interestingly, Tian and Zelkowitz also use the same weakened form of representation, but acknowledge that they 'would like the relationship' to be necessary and sufficient.

It follows from Cantor's theorem that there is no representation of Melton's $(F, <)$ in $(\Re, <)$. However, it is still possible to get ordinal measurement in a number system which is not $(\Re, <)$ (and hence for which it is not required that $<$ is a strict weak order), although the resulting measure is of purely theoretical interest. It is shown in [30] that there is a representation in $(Nat, | )$ where $Nat$ is the set of natural numbers and $|$ is the divides relation. The construction of the measurement mapping $M$ is based on ensuring incomparable flowgraphs are mapped to mutually prime numbers. For the flowgraphs of Fig1, $M(z) = 2$, $M(x)$ is a fairly large multiple of 3, and $M(y)$ is a very large multiple of 3.

## 3.2   The Weyuker properties

Despite the above evidence, researchers have continued to search for single real-valued complexity measures which are expected to have the magical properties of being key indicators of such diverse attributes as comprehensibility, correctness, maintainability, reliability, testability, and ease of implementation. A high value for a 'complexity' measure is supposed to be indicative of low comprehensibility, low reliability etc. Sometimes these measures are also called 'quality' measures [39]. In this case high values of the measure actually indicate low values of the quality attributes.

The danger of attempting to find measures which characterize so many different attributes is that inevitably the measures have to satisfy conflicting aims. This is counter to the representational theory of measurement. Nobody would expect a single number $M$ to characterize every notion of 'quality' of people, which might include the very different notions of a) physical strength, and b) intelligence. If such a measure $M$ existed it would have to satisfy a) $M(A)>M(B)$ whenever A is stronger than B and b) $M(A)>M(B)$ whenever A is more intelligent than B. The fact that some highly intelligent people are very weak physically ensures that no $M$ can satisfy both these properties. Nevertheless, Weyuker's list of properties [74] seems to suggest the need for analogous software 'complexity' measures. For example, two of the properties that Weyuker proposes any complexity measure $M$ should satisfy are:

*Property A*: For any program bodies $P,Q$; $M(P)\leq M(P;Q)$ and $M(Q) \leq M(P;Q)$.

*Property B*: There exist program bodies $P,Q$, and $R$ such that: $M(P)=M(Q)$ and $M(P;R)\neq M(Q;R)$.

Property A asserts that adding code to a program cannot decrease its complexity. This reflects the view that program *size* is a key factor in its complexity. We can also conclude from Property A that low comprehensibility is *not* a key factor in complexity. This is because it is widely believed that in certain cases we can understand a program *more* easily as we see more of it [68]. Thus, while a 'size' type complexity measure $M$ should satisfy property A, a 'comprehensability' type complexity measure $M$ cannot satisfy property A.

Property B asserts that we can find two program bodies of equal complexity which when separately concatenated to a same third program yield programs of different complexity. Clearly this property has much to do with comprehensibility and little to do with size.

Thus, properties A and B are relevant for very different, and incompatible, views of complexity. They cannot both be satisfied by a single measure which captures notions of size *and* low comprehensibility. Although the above argument is not formal, Zuse has recently proved [77] that, within the representational theory of measurement, Weyuker's axioms are contradictory. Formally, he shows that while Property A explicitly requires the ratio scale for $M$, Property B explicitly excludes the ratio scale.

The general misunderstanding of scientific measurement in software engineering is illustrated further in a recent paper [18] which was itself a critique of the Weyuker's axiom. Cherniavsky and Smith define a code based 'metric' which satisfies all of Weyuker's axioms but, which they rightly claim, is not a sensible measure of complexity. They conclude that axiomatic approaches may not work. There is no justification for their conclusion. On the one hand, as they readily accept, there was no suggestion that Weyuker's axioms were complete. More importantly, what they fail to observe, is that Weyuker did not propose that the axioms were *sufficient*; she only proposed that they were necessary. Since the Cherniavsky/Smith 'metric' is clearly not a measure (in our sense) of any specific attribute, then showing that it satisfies any set of necessary axioms for any measure is of no interest at all.

These problems would have been avoided by a simple lesson from measurement theory: the definition of a numerical mapping does not in itself constitute measurement. It is popular in software engineering to use the word 'metric' for any number extracted from a software entity. Thus while every measure is a 'metric', the converse is certainly not true. The confusion in [18], and also in [74], arises from wrongly equating these two concepts, and ignoring the theory of measurement completely.

# 4  Unifying framework for software measurement

## 4.1  A classification of software measures

In software measurement activity there are three classes of entities of interest [27]:

*Processes* which are any software related activities which take place over time.
*Products* which are any artefacts, deliverables or documents which arise out of the processes.
*Resources* which are the items which are inputs to processes.

We make a distinction between attributes of these which are *internal* and *external*:

*Internal attributes* of a product, process, or resource are those which can be measured purely in terms of the product, process, or resource itself. For example, length is an internal attribute of any software document, while elapsed time is an internal attribute of any software process.

*External attributes* of a product, process, or resource are those which can only be measured with respect to how the product, process, or resource relates to other entities in its environment. For example, *reliability* of a program (a product attribute) is dependent not just on the program itself, but on the compiler, machine, and user. *Productivity* is an external attribute of a resource, namely people (either as individuals or groups); it is clearly dependent on many aspects of the process and the quality of products delivered.

Software managers and software users would most like to measure and predict external attributes. Unfortunately, they are necessarily only measurable indirectly. For example, productivity of personnel is most commonly measured as a ratio of: size of code delivered (an internal product attribute); and effort (an internal process attribute). The problems with this oversimplistic measure of productivity have been well documented. Similarly, 'quality' of a software system (a very high level external product attribute) is often defined as the ratio of: faults discovered during formal testing (an internal process attribute); and size (measured by KLOC). While reasonable for developers, this measure of quality cannot be said to be a valid measure from the viewpoint of the user. Empirical studies have suggested there may be little real correlation between faults and actual failures of the software in operation [1].

## 4.2    Software metrics activities within the framework

The many, apparently diverse, topics within 'software metrics' all fit easily into the conceptual framework described above [27]. Here we pick out just two examples:

**Cost modelling** is generally concerned with *predicting* the attributes of *effort* or *time* required for the *process* of development (normally from detailed specification through to implementation). Most approaches involve a prediction system in which the underlying model has the form $E=f(S)$ where $E$ is effort in person months and $S$ is a measure of system size. The function f may involve other product attributes (such as complexity or required reliability), as well as process and resource attributes (such as programmer experience). In the case of Boehm's COCOMO [10], size is defined as the number of delivered source statements, which is an attribute of the final implemented system. Since the prediction system is used at the specification phase, we have to *predict* the product attribute size in order to plug it into the model. This means that we are replacing one difficult prediction problem (effort prediction) with another prediction problem which may be no easier (size prediction). This is avoided in Albrecht's approach [2], where system 'size' is measured by the number of function points (FP's). This is computed directly from the specification.

**Software quality models and reliability models** The popular quality models break down quality into 'factors', 'criteria', and 'metrics' and propose relationships between them. Quality factors generally correspond to *external* product attributes. The criteria generally correspond to *internal* product or process attributes. The metrics generally correspond to proposed measures of the internal attributes. In most cases the proposed relationships are based on purely subjective opinions. Reliability is one of the high-level, external product attributes which appears in all quality models. The only type of products for which this attribute is relevant is executable software. Reliability modelling is concerned with *predicting* reliability of software on the basis of observing times between failures during operation or testing. Thus internal attributes of processes are used to predict an external product attribute. The prediction systems used in reliability modelling typically consist of a probability distribution model together with a statistical inference procedure (such as maximum likelihood estimation) for determining the model parameters, and a prediction procedure for combining the model and the parameter estimates to make statements about future reliability.

## 4.3    The importance of internal attributes

The discussion in Sect.4.2 confirms that invariably we need to measure internal attributes to support the measurement of external attributes. This point has also been noted in [68]. Even the best understood external product attribute, *reliability* requires inter-failure time data to be collected during testing or operation. In many situations, we may need to make a prediction about an external product attribute before the product even exists. For example, given the detailed designs of a set of untested software modules, which ones, when implemented, are likely to be the most difficult to test or maintain? This is a major motivation for studying measures of internal attributes of products, and was the driving force behind much work on complexity measures.

Consider, for example, the product attribute modularity. Many modern software engineering methods and techniques are based on the premise that a modular structure for software is a 'good thing'. What this assumption means formally is that modularity, an internal software product attribute, has a significant impact on external software product attributes such as maintainability and reliability. Although a number of studies have investigated this relationship there is no strong evidence to support the widely held beliefs about the benefits of modularity. While the study in [72] sought evidence that modularity was related to maintainability, it presumed a linear relationship, whereas others believe that neither excessively high nor excessively low modularity are acceptable. However, the main problem with all the studies is the lack of a previously validated measure of modularity.

Using the representational approach, we need to identify the intuitive notions which lead to a consensus view of modularity before we can measure it. For example, it is widely believed that the average module size alone does not determine a system's modularity. It is affected by the whole structure of the module calling hierarchy. Thus the number of levels and the distribution of modules at each level have to be considered; module calling structures with widely varying widths are not considered to be very modular because of ideas of chunking from cognitive psychology.

### 4.4 Validating software measures

Validating a software measure in the assessment sense is equivalent to demonstrating empirically that the representation condition is satisfied for the attribute being measured. For a measure in the predictive sense, all the components of the prediction system must be clearly specified and a proper hypothesis proposed, before experimental design for validation can begin.

Despite these simple obligations for measurement validation, the software engineering literature abounds with so-called validation studies which have ignored them totally. This phenomenon has been examined thoroughly in [28].Typically a measure (in the assessment sense) is proposed. For example, this might be a measure of an internal structural attribute of source code. The measure is 'validated' by showing that it correlates with some other existing measure. What this really means is that the proposed measure is the main independent variable in a prediction system. Unfortunately, these studies commonly fail to specify the required prediction system and experimental hypothesis. Worse still, they do not specify, in advance, what is the dependent variable being predicted. The result is often an attempt to find fortuitous correlations with any data which happens to be available.

The search for rigorous software measures has not been helped by a commonly held viewpoint that no measure is 'valid' unless it is a good predictor of effort. An analogy would be to reject the usefulness of measuring a person's height on the grounds that it tells us nothing about that person's intelligence. The result is that potentially valid measures of important internal attributes become distorted. Consider, for example, Albrecht's function points [2]. In this approach the *unadjusted function count* UFC seems to be a reasonable measure of the important attribute of *functionality* in specification documents. However, the intention was to define a single size measure as the main independent variable in prediction systems for effort. Because of this, a *technical complexity factor* (TCF), is applied to UFC to arrive at the number of function points FP which is the model in the prediction system for effort. The TCF takes account of 14 product and process attributes in Albrecht's approach. This kind of adjustment (to a measure of system functionality) is analogous to redefining measures of height of people in such a way that the measures correlate more closely with intelligence. Interestingly, the studies [37] and [40] have shown that there was no significant differences between UFC and FP as effort predictors.

## 5    Summary

Contrary to popular opinion, software measurement, like measurement in any other discipline, must adhere to the science of measurement if it is to gain widespread acceptance and validity. The representational theory of measurement asserts that measurement is the process of assigning numbers or symbols to attributes of entities in such a way that all empirical relations are preserved. The entities of interest in software can be classified as processes, products, or resources. Anything we may wish to measure or predict is an identifiable attribute of these. Attributes are either internal or external. Although external attributes like reliability of products, stability of processes, or productivity of resources tend to be the ones we are most interested in measuring, we cannot do so directly. We are generally forced to measure indirectly in terms of internal attributes. Predictive measurement requires a prediction system. This means not just a model but also a set of prediction procedures for determining the model parameters and applying the results. These in turn are dependent on accurate measurements in the assessment sense.

We have used measurement theory to highlight both weaknesses and strengths of software metrics work, including work on metrics validation. Invariably, it seems that the most promising theoretical work has been using the key components of measurement theory. We showed that the search for general software complexity measures is doomed to failure. However, the theory does help us to define and validate measures of specific complexity attributes.

## Acknowledgements

This work was supported in part under EPSCR/IED project SMARTIE and ESPRIT project PDCS2. I would like to thank Bev Littlewood and Martin Neil for providing comments on an earlier draft of this paper, and Peter Mellor, Stella Page and Robin Whitty for sharing views and information which have influenced its contents. Finally I would like to thank four anonymous referees who made suggestions which clearly improved the paper.

# References for Chapter II

[1]   E. Adams, "Optimizing preventive service of software products", *IBM Research Journal*, 28 ( 1), pp.2-14, 1984.

[2]   A. J. Albrecht, "Measuring application development productivity", in *IBM Applic. Dev. Joint SHARE/GUIDE Symposium,* (Monterey, Cal.), pp.83-92, 1979.

[3]   N. Audsley, A. Burns, M. Richardson, K. Tindell and A. Wellings, "Applying New Scheduling Theory to Static Priority Pre-emptive Scheduling", *Software Engineering Journal*, 8 (5), pp.284-92, September 1993.

[4]   N. C. Audsley, *Optimal Priority Assignment and Feasibility of Static Priority Tasks With Arbitrary Start Times*, Dept. Computer Science, University of York, N°YCS 164, December 1991 1991.

[5]   N. C. Audsley, A. Burns, R. Davis, K. Tindell and A. J. Wellings, "Fixed Priority Pre-emptive Scheduling: An Historical Perspective", *Real-Time Systems*, 8 (2/3), pp.173-98, 1995.

[6]   N. C. Audsley, A. Burns and A. J. Wellings, "Deadline Monotonic Scheduling Theory and Application", *Control Engineering Practice*, 1 (1), pp.71-8, 1993.

[7]   N. C. Audsley, K. Tindell and A. Burns, "The End of the Line for Static Cyclic Scheduling", in *Proceedings of 5th Euromicro Workshop on Real-Time Systems, Oulu* pp.36-41, IEEE Computer Soc. Press, 1993.

[8]   T. P. Baker, "Stack-Based Scheduling of Realtime Processes", *Real-Time Systems*, 3 (1) 1991.

[9]   V. Basili and D. Rombach, "The TAME project: Towards improvement-orientated software environments", *IEEE Trans Software Eng.*, 14 (6), pp.758-73, 1988.

[10]  B. Boehm, *Software Engineering Economics,* Prentice Hall, 1981.

[11]  J. Brazendale and R. Bell, "Safety-Related Control and Protection Systems: Standards Update", *Computing and Control Engineering*, 5 (1), pp.6-12, February 1994.

[12]  S. Brocklehurst, P. Y. Chan, B. Littlewood and J. Snell, "Recalibrating Software Reliability Models", *IEEE Trans. Software Engineering*, 16 (4), pp.458-70, 1990.

[13]  A. Burns and A. J. Wellings, "Specifying an Ada Tasking Run-time Support System", *Ada User*, 12 (4), pp.160-86, 1991.

[14]  A. Burns and A. J. Wellings, "Dual Priority Assignment: A Practical Method for Increasing Processor Utilization", in *Proceedings of 5th Euromicro Workshop on Real-Time Systems, Oulu* pp.48-55, IEEE Computer Soc. Press, 1993.

[15]   A. Burns and A. J. Wellings, *"Implementing Analysable Hard Real-time Sporadic Tasks in Ada 9X"*, Ada Letters, 14 (1), 1994.

[16]   A. Burns, A. J. Wellings, C. M. Bailey and E. Fyfe, "The Olympus Attitude and Orbital Control System: A Case Study in Hard Real-time System Design and Implementation", in *Ada sans frontières: Proc. 12th Ada-Europe Conf., Lecture Notes in Computer Science* Springer-Verlag, 1993.

[17]   A. Burns, A. J. Wellings and A. D. Hutcheon, "The Impact of an Ada Run-time System's Performance Characteristics on Scheduling Models", in *Ada sans frontières: Proc. 12th Ada-Europe Conf., Lecture Notes in Computer Science 688* pp.240-8, Springer-Verlag, 1993.

[18]   J. C. Cherniavsky and C. H. Smith, "On Weyuker's axioms for software complexity measures", *IEEE Trans Software Eng.*, 17 (6), pp.636-8, 1991.

[19]   R. de Lemos, B. Fields and A. Saeed, "Analysis of Safety Requirements in the Context of System Faults and Human Errors", in *Proc. Int. Symp. on Systems Engineering of Computer Based Systems,* (Tucson, AZ), pp.375-81, IEEE Press, 1995.

[20]   R. de Lemos, A. Saeed and T. Anderson, "A Train Set as a Case Study for the Requirements Analysis of Safety-Critical Systems", *The Computer Journal (Special Issue on Security and Safety)*, 34 (2), pp.30-40, February 1992.

[21]   R. de Lemos, A. Saeed and T. Anderson, *Requirements Analysis for Safety-Critical Systems: A Chemical Batch Processing Example*, Department of Computing Science, University of Newcastle upon Tyne, Newcastle upon Tyne, UK, N°469, December 1993.

[22]   R. de Lemos, A. Saeed and T. Anderson, "On the Safety Analysis of Requirements Specifications", in *Proc. of the 13th Int. Conf. on Computer Safety, Reliability and Security (SAFECOMP'94),* (V. Maggioli, Ed.), (Anaheim, CA), pp.217-27, 1994.

[23]   R. de Lemos, A. Saeed and T. Anderson, "Analysing Safety Requirements for Process-Control Systems", *IEEE Software*, May 1995.

[24]   R. de Lemos, A. Saeed and T. Anderson, "Formal Techniques for Requirements Analysis for Safety-Critical Systems", in *Mathematics for Dependable Systems* (C. Mitchell and V. Stavridou, Eds.), pp.63-95, Oxford University Press, Oxford, UK, 1995.

[25]   R. A. DeMillo and R. J. Lipton, "Software project forecasting", in *Software Metrics* (Perlis, Ed.), pp.77-89, MIT Press, 1981.

[26]   D. Duke and M. D. Harrison, "Abstract Interaction Objects", *Computer Graphics Forum*, 12 (3), pp.25-36, 1993.

[27]   N. E. Fenton, *Software Metrics: A rigorous approach,* Chapman and Hall, London, 1991.

[28]   N. E. Fenton, "When a software measure is not a measure", *Software Eng J.*, 7 (5), pp.357-62, 1992.

[29] N. E. Fenton, "Software measurement: a necessary scientific basis", *IEEE Trans Software Eng*, 20 (3), pp.199-206, 1994.

[30] N. E. Fenton and B. A. Kitchenham, "Validating software measures", *J. Software Testing Verification and Reliability*, 1 (2), pp.27-42, 1991.

[31] G. Fohler, *Flexibility in Statically Scheduled Hard Real-Time Systems*, PhD Thesis, Technical University of Vienna, 1994.

[32] R. Gerber and S. Hong, *Semantic-Based Compiler Transformations for Enhanced Schedulability*, Department of Computer Science, University of Maryland, N°CS-TR-3071, 1993.

[33] M. G. Harbour, M. H. Klein and J. P. Lehoczky, "Fixed Priority Scheduling of Periodic Tasks with Varying Execution Priority", in *Proceedings 12th IEEE Real-Time Systems Symposium*, (San Antonio, TX, USA), 1991.

[34] M. G. Harmon, T. P. Baker and D. B. Whalley, "A Retargetable Technique for Predicting Execution Time", in *Proceedings of the 1992 IEEE Real-Time Systems Symposium* (L. Sha, Ed.), pp.68-77, IEEE Press, 1992.

[35] A. R. Helm, I. M. Holland and D. Gangopadhyay, "Contracts: Specifying Behavioural Compositions in Object-Oriented Systems", in *Proc. Conf. on Object-Oriented Programming Systems, Languages and Applications*, (Ottowa, Canada), SIGPLAN Notes, pp.169-80, ACM Press, 1990.

[36] E. J. Henley and H. Kumamoto, *Probabilistic Risk Assessment: Reliability Engineering, Design, and Analysis*, IEEE Press, New York, NY, 1992.

[37] D. R. Jeffery, G. C. Low and M. Barnes, "A comparison of function point counting techniques ", *IEEE Trans Software Eng.*, 19 (5), pp.529-32, 1993.

[38] M. Joseph and P. Pandya, "Finding Response Times in a Real-Time System", in *BCS Computer Journal*, pp.390-5, 1986.

[39] D. Kafura and S. Henry, "Software quality metrics based on interconnectivity ", *Journal of Systems & Software*, 2, pp.121-31 , 1981.

[40] B. A. Kitchenham and K. Kansala, "Inter-item correlations among function points ", in *IEEE Software Metrics Symposium*, (Baltimore), pp.11-5, 1993.

[41] H. Kopetz, "Sparse Time versus Dense Time in Distributed Real-Time Systems", in *Proc. 14th Int. Conf. on Distributed Computing Systems*, (Yokohama, Japan), pp.460-7, IEEE Press, 1992.

[42] H. Kopetz, A. Damm, C. Koza, M. Mulazzani, W. Schwabl, C. Senft and R. Zainlinger, "Distributed Fault-Tolerant Real-Time Systems: The MARS approach", *IEEE Micro*, 9 (1), pp.25-40, February 1989.

[43] H. Kopetz and G. Gruensteidl, "TTP — A Time-Triggered Protocol for Fault-Tolerant Real-Time Systems", in *Proc. 23rd IEEE International Symposium on Fault-Tolerant Computing (FTCS-23)*, (Toulouse, France), pp.524-32, IEEE Press, 1993.

[44]   H. Kopetz and K. Kim, "Temporal Uncertainties in Interactions among Real-Time Objects", in *Proc. 9th Symp. on Reliable Distributed Systems,* (Huntsville, AL, USA), pp.165-74, IEEE Computer Society Press, 1990.

[45]   H. Kopetz and W. Ochsenreiter, "Clock Synchronisation in Distributed Real-Time Systems", *IEEE Trans. Computers*, 36 (8), pp.933-40, August 1987.

[46]   J. C. S. P. Leite and P. A. Freeman, "Requirements Validation through Viewpoint Resolution", *IEEE Trans. on Software Engineering*, 17 (2), pp.1253-69, December 1991.

[47]   J. Y. T. Leung and M. L. Merrill, "A Note on Preemptive Scheduling of Periodic Real-Time Tasks", *Information Processing Letters*, 11 (3), pp.115-8, 1980.

[48]   J. Y. T. Leung and J. Whitehead, "On the Complexity of Fixed-Priority Scheduling of Periodic, Real-Time Tasks", *Performance Evaluation (Netherlands)*, 2 (4), pp.237-50, 1982.

[49]   C. L. Liu and J. W. Layland, "Scheduling Algorithms for Multiprogramming in a Hard-Real-Time Environment", *J. of the ACM*, 20 (1), pp.46-61, 1973.

[50]   C. D. Locke, "Software architecture for hard real-time applications: cyclic executives vs. fixed priority executives", *Real-Time Systems*, 4 (1), pp.37-53, 1992.

[51]   T. J. McCabe, "A complexity measure", *IEEE Trans Software Eng.*, 2 (4), pp.308-20, 1976.

[52]   A. C. Melton, D. A. Gustafson, J. M. Bieman and A. A. Baker, "Mathematical perspective of software measures research ", *IEE Software Engineering J.*, 5 (5), pp.246-54, 1990.

[53]   MoD, *Draft Interim Defence Standard 00-56: Hazards Analysis and Safety Classification of the Computer and Programmable Electronic System Elements of Defence Equipment*, UK Ministry of Defence, Glasgow, UK, April 1991.

[54]   D. G. Nielsen, *Use of Cause-Consequence Charts in Pratical System Analysis*, Atomic Energy Commission Research Establishment, Riso, Denmark, N°Riso-M 1743, 1974.

[55]   S. Poledna, *Replica Determinism in Fault-Tolerant Real-Time Systems,* PhD, Technical University of Vienna, 1994.

[56]   D. Powell, "Failure Mode Assumptions and Assumption Coverage", in *Proc. 22nd Int. Symp. on Fault-Tolerant Computing (FTCS-22),* (Boston, MA, USA), pp.386-95, IEEE Computer Society Press, 1992.

[57]   P. Puschner, *Zeitanalyse von Echtzeitprogrammen,* PhD, Technical University of Vienna, 1993.

[58]   F. S. Roberts, *Measurement Theory with applications to decision making, utility, and the social sciences*, Addison Wesley, 1979.

[59]   D. Ross, "Structured Analysis (SA): A Language for Communicating Ideas", in *Tutorial on Design Techniques* (P. Freeman and A. M. Wasserman, Eds.), pp.107-25, IEEE Computer Society Press, 1980.

[60]   J. Rushby, "Kernels for Safety?", in *Safe and Secure Computing Systems* (T. Anderson, Ed.), pp.310-20, Blackwell Scientific, 1987.

[61]   J. M. Rushby, *Formal Methods and Certification of Critical Systems*, SRI International, Menlo Park, CA, N°CSL-93-7, December 1993.

[62]   A. Saeed, R. de Lemos and T. Anderson, "Robust Requirements Specifications for Safety-Critical Systems", in *Proc. 12th Int. Conf. on Computer Safety, Reliability and Security (SAFECOMP'93)*, (J. Górski, Ed.), (Poznan-Kiekrz, Poland), pp.219-29, Springer-Verlag, 1993.

[63]   A. Saeed, R. de Lemos and T. Anderson, "An Approach for the Risk Analysis of Safety Specifications", in *Proc. 9th Annual Conf. on Computer Assurance (COMPASS'94)*, (Gaithersburg, MD), pp.209-21, 1994.

[64]   L. Sha, R. Rajkumar and J. P. Lehoczky, "Priority Inheritance Protocols: An Approach to Real-Time Synchronisation", *IEEE Transactions on Computers*, 39 (9), pp.1175-85, 1990.

[65]   H. R. Simpson, "A Data Interactive Architecture (DIA) for Real-time Embedded Multi-Processor Systems", in *RAe Conference, Computing Techniques in Guided Flight,* 1990.

[66]   J. M. Spivey, "Specifying a Real-time Kernel", *IEEE Software*, 7 (5), pp.21-8, 1990.

[67]   F. Stanischewski, "FASTCHART — Performance, Benefits and Disadvantages of the Architecture", in *Proceedings of 5th Euromicro Workshop on Real-Time Systems, Oulu* pp.246-50, IEEE Computer Soc. Press, 1993.

[68]   J. Tian and M. V. Zelkowitz, "A formal program complexity model and its applications", *Journal of Systems & Software*, 17, pp.253-66, 1992.

[69]   K. Tindell, *Using Offset Information to Analyse Static Pre-emptive Scheduled Task Sets*, Department of Computer Science, University of York, N°YCS 182, 1992.

[70]   K. Tindell, A. Burns and A. J. Wellings, "Allocating Real-Time Tasks (An NP-Hard Problem made Easy)", *Real Time Systems*, 4 (2), pp.145-65, 1992.

[71]   K. Tindell, A. Burns and A. J. Wellings, "An Extendible Approach for Analysing Fixed Priority Hard Real-Time Tasks", *Real-Time Systems*, 6 (2), pp.133-51, 1994.

[72]   D. A. Troy and S. H. Zweben, "Measuring the quality of structured design ", *Journal of Systems & Software*, 2, pp.113-20, 1981.

[73]   A. Vrchoticky, *The Basis for Static Execution Time Prediction,* PhD, Technical University of Vienna, 1994.

[74]   E. J. Weyuker, "Evaluating software complexity measures", *IEEE Trans Software Eng.*, 14 (9), pp.1357-65, 1988.

[75]   N. Zhang, A. Burns and M. Nicholson, "Pipelined Processors and Worst Case Execution Time", *Real-Time Systems*, 5 (4), pp.319-43, 1993.

[76]   H. Zuse, *Software complexity: measures and method,* de Gruyter, 1990.

[77]   H. Zuse, "Support of experimentation by measurement theory", in *Experimental Software Engineering Issues* (V. R. Basili and R. W. Selby, Eds.), 706, pp.137-40, Lecture Notes in Computer Science, Springer-Verlag, 1993.

# Chapter III

# Fault Tolerance

The issue of how best to achieve adequate dependability from systems, despite the likelihood of their suffering faults, has been a major topic of concern throughout the PDCS and PDCS2 Projects. The types of faults that have been considered range from design faults arising from unmastered complexity, typically in system and application software, through hardware faults, e.g. from component ageing, to faults due to actions in the system environment by users and operators, whether accidental or deliberate. These various types of fault can of course manifest themselves in the value domain and/or the time domain.

The first paper, "From Recovery Blocks to Concurrent Atomic Actions" surveys the development of error recovery structures, from the first schemes developed for purposes of tolerating design faults in sequential programs, through to our latest work on techniques for error recovery from software, hardware or environmental faults in concurrent systems. The unifying theme underlying this discussion is the use of new object-oriented structuring concepts. The second paper, "Definition and Analysis of Hardware-and-Software Fault-Tolerant Architectures", also stresses the issue of unification, in this case particularly of hardware and software fault tolerance as a whole, and of the importance that evaluation can play in guiding the design of well-engineered fault-tolerant systems. Such evaluation of course has to be based on assumptions about what sorts of failures, and hence faults, may or may not occur. The third paper, "Failure Mode Assumptions and Assumption Coverage", formalizes such assumptions as assertions on the types of errors that a component may induce in its enclosing system, and introduces the concept of assumption coverage to relate the notion of partially-ordered assumption assertions to the quantification of system dependability. Assumption coverage is shown to be extremely important in systems requiring very high dependability.

The next two papers concern techniques for improving the efficiency, from both the dependability and the performance viewpoints, of fault tolerance mechanisms. In the paper, "Rational Design of Multiple-Redundant Systems: Adjudication and Fault Treatment", two design problems in modular redundancy are studied. One is that of optimizing the derivation of a single correct result from the multiple results produced by the replicas in a redundant component. The other is how the decision can be made to remove a replica of a component, having classed it as permanently failed, on the basis of its history of agreement/disagreement with other replicas. The paper. "Dynamic Adjustment of Dependability and Efficiency in Fault-Tolerant Software" discusses the problem of attaining a dynamic compromise between using redundancy to improve software dependability and limiting the amount of redundancy so as to avoid unnecessary inefficiencies, and introduces a scheme called self-configuring optimal programming.

There follow two papers that rely heavily on the use of object-oriented programming ideas. The first, "Designing Secure and Reliable Applications using Fragmentation-Redundancy-Scattering", makes use of a technique called Fragmentation-Redundancy-

Scattering to provide reliable processing of confidential information, despite accidental, e.g. hardware component faults, and intentional faults (security intrusions) by system users and operators. This is followed by a paper, "Implementing Fault-Tolerant Applications using Reflective Object-Oriented Programming", which explores how the use of reflection can improve the transparency of fault tolerance mechanisms to the programmer. The paper does this by describing a number of reflection-based re-implementations of various classical replication schemes.

The final paper, "The PDCS Implementation of MARS Hardware and Software", provides a description of the most ambitious system experiment carried out within the PDCS Projects, namely the MARS fault-tolerant real-time distributed system. This system is notable for the success with which it demonstrated the merits, for critical hard real-time systems, of a periodic time-triggered (as opposed to event-triggered) structure, and the use of fail-silent processing nodes.

These papers, between them, though they do not by any means cover all the work undertaken on fault tolerance in PDCS and PDCS2, do provide a good indication of the breadth of this work, and of the progress that has been made in developing sophisticated yet effective means of tolerating the various kinds of fault that occur in practical computing systems.

# From Recovery Blocks to Concurrent Atomic Actions*

Brian Randell   Alexander Romanovsky   Cecilia M F Rubira
Robert J Stroud   Zhixue Wu   Jie Xu

University of Newcastle upon Tyne

**Abstract.** This paper reviews the development of error recovery structures that support general fault tolerance, and describes a new object-oriented scheme for error recovery in concurrent systems that generalizes existing schemes based on either conversations or transactions. This new scheme, which is based on what we term a Coordinated Atomic Action, is intended to facilitate the provision of means of tolerating hardware and software faults, and faults that have affected the environment of the computer system — and to do so for programs that involve cooperating concurrent processes, *and* the use of shared resources.

## 1    Introduction

A research project to investigate system reliability was initiated by the first author at the University of Newcastle upon Tyne in 1971. This was at a time when the problems of software reliability had come to the fore, for example through the discussions at the 1968 and 1969 NATO Software Engineering Conferences, concerning what at the time was termed the "software crisis". Such discussions were one of the spurs to research efforts, in a number of places, aimed at finding means of producing error-free programs. However, at Newcastle the opposite (or more accurately the complementary) problem, namely that of what to do in situations where the possibility of residual design faults could not be denied, was taken as an interesting and worthwhile goal. We thus started work on the subject of design fault tolerance.

We were well aware that if we were to develop techniques aimed explicitly at tolerating software faults we would have to allow for the fact that the principal cause of residual software faults is complexity. Therefore the use of appropriate structuring techniques would be crucial — otherwise the additional software that would be needed might well increase the system's complexity to the point of being counter-productive. Aided by what we had found in an examination of contemporary checkpoint and restart facilities, we came to realize that even though a variety of quite disparate error detection mechanisms could usefully be employed together in a system, it was critical to have a simple, coherent and general strategy for error recovery. Moreover it was evident that such a strategy ought to be capable of treating multiple errors, including errors that were detected during the recovery process itself.

The first structuring technique that we developed was in fact the basic *recovery block* scheme. This scheme was soon extended to concurrent processes, via the introduction of the concept of a *conversation* as a means of error recovery in concurrent systems. In what follows we use the object-oriented structuring concepts that have been

---

* This paper is based largely on material in [129, 176].

developed during the work of PDCS and PDCS2 projects to describe this basic
scheme, and of some of the ensuing research on recovery blocks carried out at
Newcastle and elsewhere, before discussing some of the latest ideas that we have
been investigating on error recovery in concurrent processes.

## 2    System Structuring

Our interest in the problems of structuring systems so as to control their complexity,
and in particular that of their fault tolerance provisions, led us early on to a style of
system design that is based on what we term *idealized fault-tolerant components* [8,
126]. Such components provide a means of system structuring that makes it easy to
identify *which* parts of a system have *what* responsibilities for trying to cope with
*which* sorts of fault.

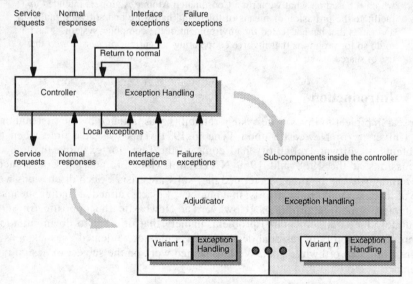

**Fig. 1.** Idealized component with diverse design.

We view a system as a set of components interacting under the control of a design
(which is itself a component of the system) [93]. Clearly, the system model is
recursive in that each component can itself be considered as a system in its own right
and thus may have an internal design that can identify further sub-components.
Components receive requests for service and produce responses. When a component
cannot satisfy a request for service, it will return an exception. An idealized fault-
tolerant component should in general provide both normal and abnormal (i.e.
exceptional) responses in the interface between interacting components, in a
framework that minimizes the impact of these provisions on system complexity.

Three classes of exceptional situation are identified. Interface exceptions are
signalled when interface checks find that an invalid service request has been made to
a component. These exceptions must be treated by the part of the system that made
the invalid request. Local exceptions are raised when a component detects an error
that its own fault tolerance capabilities could or should deal with. This is in the hope
that the component would return to normal operations after exception handling.
Lastly, a failure exception is signalled to notify the component which made the

service request that, despite the use of its own fault tolerance capabilities, it has been unable to provide the service requested of it (see the upper part of Fig. 1).

The notion of an idealized component is mainly concerned with interactions of a component with its environment. The structuring of exception handling is based on minimal assumptions about possible faults, and about the fault masking and the fault tolerance scheme adopted. Exception handling is often considered as being a limited form of software fault tolerance. However, such software cannot be regarded as truly fault-tolerant since some perceived departures from specification are likely to occur, although the exception handling approach can result in software that is robust in the sense that catastrophic failure can often be avoided.

However, to achieve effective design fault tolerance, capable of completely masking the effects of many residual software errors, it is necessary to incorporate deliberate redundancy, i.e. to make use of design diversity, in such systems. The structuring scheme described in [128] for describing and comparing the various existing software fault tolerance schemes, and for guiding their actual implementation, is illustrated in the lower part of Fig. 1.

This shows an idealized component which consists of several sub-components, namely an adjudicator and a set of software variants (modules of differing design aimed at a common specification). The design of the component, i.e. the algorithm that is responsible for defining the interactions between the sub-components, and establishing connections between the component and the system environment, is embodied in the controller. This invokes one or more of the variants, waits as necessary for such variants to complete their execution and invokes the adjudicator to check on the results produced by the variants. As illustrated in Fig. 1, each of these sub-components (even the adjudicator), as well as the component (controller) itself, can in principle contain its own provisions for exception handling, and indeed for full software fault tolerance, so the structuring scheme is fully recursive.

## 3    Basic Recovery Blocks

The basic recovery block is aimed at providing fault-tolerant functional components that may be nested within a sequential program [60, 125]. The usual syntax is as follows:

```
ensure      acceptance test
by          primary alternate
else by     alternate 2
                .
                .
else by     alternate n
else error
```

Here the alternates correspond to the variants of Fig. 1, and the acceptance test to the adjudicator, while the structure and semantics of the recovery block statement correspond to a description of the controller algorithm. On entry to a recovery block the state of the system must be saved by some underlying mechanism (which we termed a recovery cache) in order to provide backward error recovery. The primary alternate is executed and then the acceptance test is evaluated to provide an adjudication on the outcome of this primary alternate. If the acceptance test is passed then the outcome is regarded as successful and an exit is made from the recovery block, discarding the information on the state of the system taken on entry (i.e. checkpoint). However, if the test fails or if any errors are detected by other means during the execution of the alternate, then an exception is raised and backward error recovery is invoked. This restores the state of the system to what it was on entry. After such recovery, the next alternate is executed and then the acceptance test is applied again. This sequence continues until either an acceptance test is passed or all alternates have failed the acceptance test. If all the alternates either fail the test or result in an exception (due to an internal error being detected), a failure exception will be signalled to the environment of the recovery block. Since recovery blocks can be nested, then the raising of such an exception from an inner recovery block will invoke recovery in the enclosing block.

The overall success of the recovery block (RB) scheme rests to a great extent on the effectiveness of the error detection mechanisms used — especially (but not solely) the acceptance test. The acceptance test must be simple otherwise there will be a significant chance that it will itself contain design faults, and so fail to detect some errors, and/or falsely identify some conditions as being erroneous. Moreover, the test will introduce a run-time overhead which could be unacceptable if the test is very complex. The development of simple, effective acceptance tests can thus be a difficult task, depending on the actual specification of the component.

In fact, the acceptance test in a recovery block should be regarded as a last line of detecting errors, rather than the sole means of error detection. The expectation is that it will be buttressed by executable assertion statements within the alternates and by run-time checks supported by the hardware. Generally, any such exception raised during the execution of an alternate will lead to the same recovery action as for acceptance test failure. Should the final alternate fail, for example by not passing the acceptance test, this will constitute a failure of the entire module containing the recovery block, and will invoke recovery at the level of the surrounding recovery block, should there be one.

In other words, each alternate should itself be an idealized fault-tolerant component. An exception raised by run-time assertion statements within the alternate or by hardware error-detection mechanisms may be treated by the alternate's own fault tolerance capabilities. A failure exception is raised to notify the system (i.e. the control component in our model) that, despite the use of its own fault tolerance capabilities, the alternate has been unable to provide the service requested of it. The control component may then invoke another alternate.

In general, as described in [104], forward error recovery can be further incorporated in recovery blocks to complement the underlying backward error recovery. (In fact, a forward error recovery mechanism can support the implementation of backward error recovery by transforming unexpected errors into default error conditions [36].) If, for example, a real-time program communicated with its (unrecoverable) environment from within a recovery block then, if recovery were invoked, the environment would not be able to recover along with the program and the system would be left in an inconsistent state. In this case, forward recovery would help return the system and its environment to a mutually consistent state by sending the environment a pre-defined compensatory message.

Although each of the alternates within a recovery block endeavours to satisfy the same acceptance test, there is no requirement that they must all produce the same results [92]. The only constraint is that the results must be acceptable — as determined by the test. Thus, while the primary alternate should attempt to produce the desired outcome, the further alternate(s) may only attempt to provide a degraded service. This is particularly useful in real-time systems, since there may be insufficient time available for fully-functional alternates to be executed when a fault is encountered. An extreme case corresponds to a recovery block that contains a primary module and a null alternate [7, 6]. Under these conditions, the role of the recovery block is simply to detect and recover from errors by ignoring the operation where the fault manifested itself.

Most of the time, only the primary alternate of the recovery block is executed. (This keeps the run-time overhead of the recovery block to a minimum and makes good use of the system and hardware resources.) However, this could cause a problem: the alternates must not retain data locally between calls, otherwise these modules could become inconsistent with each other since not all of them are executed each time that the recovery block is invoked. Distributed (parallel) execution of recovery blocks [72] could solve this problem. An alternative solution is to design the alternate modules as memoryless functional components rather than as objects.

Unlike tolerance to hardware malfunctions, software fault tolerance cannot be made totally transparent to the application programmer although some operations related to its provision, such as saving and restoring the state of the system, can be made automatic and transparent. A programmer who wishes to use software fault tolerance schemes must provide software variants and adjudicators. Therefore, a set of special linguistic features or conventions is necessary for incorporating software redundancy in programs. The key point here is to attempt to keep the syntactic extensions natural and minimal.

Current work at Newcastle on such linguistic issues has been greatly influenced by the now very fashionable topic of object-oriented programming. It has been found convenient to try to exploit various characteristics of C++ [159], a language that has been used extensively at Newcastle in connection with work on distributed systems [149]. In particular, the recent extension of C++ to include generic classes and functions (*templates*), and exception handling (*catch* and *throw*) makes it possible to implement both forward and backward error recovery in C++ in the form of reusable components that separate the functionality of the application from its fault tolerance mechanisms [136]. This separation makes it feasible to design general reusable software components implementing various fault tolerance strategies (including generalizations and combinations of recovery blocks, and N-version programs [13], and encompassing the use of parallelism), and aids the re-use of application-specific software components [128]. For example, a set of pre-defined C++ classes can be organized to support a general linguistic framework based on the abstract model represented by Fig. 1, and described in Section 2 [136].

## 4    Extensions and Applications of Basic Recovery Blocks

Many applications and varieties of recovery blocks have been explored and developed by various researchers. Some typical experiments and extensions are considered below.

## 4.1    Distributed Execution of Recovery Blocks

H. Hecht was the first to propose the application of recovery blocks to flight control systems [57]. His work included an implementation of a watchdog timer that monitors the availability of output within a specified time interval and his model also incorporates a rudimentary system to be used when all alternates of the recovery block scheme are exhausted. M. Hecht *et al.* [58] reported some subsequent research and experiments.

K. H. Kim and his colleagues in the DREAM Laboratory have extensively explored the concept of distributed execution of recovery blocks, a combination of both distributed processing and recovery blocks, as an approach to the uniform treatment of hardware and software faults [72, 74, 73]. A useful feature of their approach is the relatively low run-time overhead it requires, making it suitable for incorporation into real-time systems. The basic structure of the distributed recovery block is straightforward: the entire recovery block, two alternates with an acceptance test, is fully replicated on the primary and backup hardware nodes. However, the roles of the two alternate modules are not the same in the two nodes. The primary node uses the first alternate as the primary initially, whereas the backup node uses the second alternate as the initial primary. Outside the distributed recovery block, forward recovery can be achieved; but the node affected by a fault must invoke backward recovery by executing an alternate for data consistency with the other nodes.

## 4.2    Consensus Recovery Blocks

The consensus recovery block (CRB) [144] is an attempt to combine the techniques used in the recovery block and N-version programming (NVP). It is claimed that the CRB technique reduces the importance of the acceptance test used in the recovery block and is able to handle cases where NVP would not be appropriate because there are multiple correct outputs. The CRB requires the design and implementation of $N$ variants of the algorithm which are ranked (as in the recovery block) in the order of service and reliance. On invocation, all variants are executed and their results submitted to an adjudicator, i.e. a voter (as used in N-version programming). The CRB compares pairs of results for compatibility. If two results are the same then the result is used as the output. If no pair can be found, then the results of the variant with the highest ranking are submitted to an acceptance test. If this fails then the next variant is selected. This continues until all variants are exhausted or one passes the acceptance test. However, the CRB is largely based on the assumption that there are no common faults between the variants. (This of course is often not the case, as was shown by such experiments as [77].) In particular, if a matching pair is found, there is no indication that the result is submitted to the acceptance test, so a correlated failure in two variants could result in an erroneous output and cause a catastrophic failure.

## 4.3    Retry Blocks with Data Diversity

The retry block developed by Ammann and Knight [3] is a modification of the recovery block scheme that uses data diversity instead of design diversity. Data diversity is a strategy that does not change the algorithm of the system, but does change the data that the algorithm processes. It is assumed that there are certain data values which will cause the algorithm to fail, and that if the data were re-expressed in a different, equivalent (or near equivalent) form the algorithm would function correctly. A retry block executes the single algorithm normally and evaluates the acceptance test. If the test passes, the retry block is complete. If the test fails, the algorithm executes again after the data has been re-expressed. The system repeats this process until it violates a deadline or produces a satisfactory output. The crucial elements in the retry scheme are the acceptance test and the data re-expression routine.

## 4.4   Other Applications

Self-configuring optimal programming (SCOP) [27, 175], developed within PDCS, is another attempt to combine some techniques used in RB and NVP in order to enhance efficiency of software fault tolerance and to eliminate some inflexibilities and rigidities. The gain of efficiency would be limited if the supporting system was intended for a specific application — the hardware resources saved by the SCOP scheme would then be merely left idle. It is perhaps more appropriate if the application environment is complex and highly variable, e.g. a large distributed computing system that supports multiple competing applications.

Sullivan and Masson developed an algorithm-oriented scheme, based on the use of what they term Certification Trails [160]. The central idea of their method is to execute an algorithm so that it leaves behind a trail of data (certification trail) and, by using this data, to execute another algorithm for solving the same problem more quickly. The outputs of the two executions are compared and considered correct only if they agree. An issue with the data trail is that the first algorithm may propagate an error to the second algorithm, and this could result in an erroneous output. Nevertheless, the scheme is an interesting alternative to the recovery block scheme, despite being perhaps of somewhat limited applicability.

## 5   Concurrent Programs

Work at Newcastle on this topic dates from 1975, when we began to consider the problems of providing structuring for error recovery among sets of cooperating processes. (Some research was also done on error recovery in the particular case of so-called competing processes, i.e. where the processes communicate only for resource sharing [148].) Having identified the dangers of what we came to term the *domino effect*, we came up with the notion of a *conversation* [125] — something that we later realized was a special case of a nested atomic action.

The activity of a group of components constitutes an atomic action if no information flows between that group and the rest of the system for the duration of the activity [96, 22, 93]. Atomic actions may be planned when the system is designed, or (less commonly) may be dynamically identified by exploratory techniques after the detection of an error [172]. Planned atomic actions must be maintained by imposing constraints on communication within the system.

When a system of cooperating processes employs recovery blocks, each process will be continually establishing and discarding checkpoints, and may also on occasion need to recover to a previously established checkpoint. However, if recovery and communication operations are not performed in a coordinated fashion, then the rollback of a process can result in a cascade of rollbacks that could push all the processes back to their starting points — the domino effect. This causes the loss of the entire computation performed prior to the detection of the error.

The conversation scheme provides a means of coordinating the recovery blocks of interacting processes so as to avoid the domino effect. A conversation, which generally involves two or more processes, constitutes a two-dimensional enclosure of recoverable activities of multiple interacting processes and creates a "time-space boundary" that process interactions may not cross. The boundary of a conversation consists of a recovery line, a test line, and two side firewalls. A recovery line is a coordinated set of recovery points for interacting processes that are relying on backward error recovery. Such a recovery line is established on entry to the conversation before any process interaction occurs. A test line is a correlated set of acceptance tests for the interacting processes. The two side firewalls define exclusive membership; that is, a process inside a conversation cannot interact with a process that is not in the conversation. Fig. 2 shows an example where three processes communicate within a conversation and the processes P1 and P2 communicate within a nested conversation. It is worth particular notice that there may in practice be some means, such as shared resources, by which information will break through the side firewalls and thus defeat the effect of error recovery — this problem is known as "information smuggling".

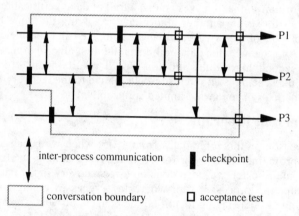

inter-process communication        ▮ checkpoint

conversation boundary              ☐ acceptance test

**Fig. 2.** Nested conversations.

Considerable research has been undertaken into the subject of concurrent error recovery, including improvements on the conversation and different implementations of it. There are at least two classes of approaches to preventing the domino effect: the coordination-by-programmer approach and the coordination-by-machine approach. With the first approach, the application programmer is fully responsible for designing processes so that they establish checkpoints in a well-coordinated manner [125, 137, 71]. Many authors have added language constructs to facilitate the definition of restorable actions based on this approach [138, 7, 55, 64]. In contrast, the coordination-by-machine approach relies on an "intelligent" underlying processor system that automatically establishes appropriate checkpoints of the interacting processes [70, 19, 79, 75]. If restorable actions are unplanned, so that the recovery mechanism must search for a consistent set of checkpoints, such actions would be expensive and difficult to implement. However, exploratory techniques have the advantage that no restrictions are placed on inter-process communication and that a general mechanism could be applied to many different systems [105, 172]. To reduce synchronization delays introduced by controlled recovery, some researchers have focused on improvements in performance, such as the lookahead scheme and the pseudo-recovery block [138, 147, 74, 124].

# 6     Error Recovery in Concurrent Object-Oriented Systems

Recently there has been work in PDCS2 on a framework for fault tolerance in concurrent object-oriented programs that integrates conversations, transactions and exception handling, thus supporting the use of both forward and backward error recovery techniques to tolerate hardware and software design faults, and also environmental faults (i.e. faults that exist in or have affected the environment of the computing system).

## 6.1     Exception Handling, Conversations and Transactions

If an exception is raised by one or several processes within a conversation, then an appropriate error recovery mechanism must be invoked. A coordinated error recovery strategy between *all* the processes in the conversation is required [31]. It is important that all the participating processes have corresponding exception handlers for a given exception (though the use of a default exception handler provided by the underlying system is permitted). These handlers may either invoke appropriate recovery measures, or signal a further exception. (A resolution scheme is used to combine multiple exceptions into a single exception if they are raised at the same time — the multiple exceptions are resolved into the exception that is the root of the smallest subtree containing all the raised exceptions.)

In the event of error recovery, the error handlers can use a mixture of forward and backward recovery techniques. For example, the state of a process may be rolled back to the recovery line or compensating actions may be performed to correct the erroneous state. Note that the incorporation of forward error recovery techniques into the conversation framework provides a basis for coordinating the recovery measures taken by the system and its environment (which is typically incapable of simple backward recovery).

A conversation is successful only if all of the interacting processes pass their acceptance tests (and a global test if required) at the test line. If one or more of the interacting processes fails an acceptance test, then an exception is raised and all of the processes within the conversation must attempt to recover. If backward error recovery is used, the original state of each process is restored before allowing participating processes to retry, perhaps using an alternate. (Where the aim is merely to tolerate operational, e.g. hardware, faults such alternates might simply perform a "retry" rather than be of deliberately diverse design.) In principle, if only forward error recovery is used, then there is no need to establish a recovery line on entry to the conversation. However such a recovery line will certainly be needed if there is a requirement to guarantee that a failure of the fault tolerance mechanisms within the conversation leaves the original state of the system unchanged.

The well-established transaction concept is a logical user action that performs a sequence of basic operations on shared data or objects. In general, such shared objects are designed and exist independently of the user processes. A transaction protects shared objects by providing the well known ACID properties — atomicity, consistency, isolation and durability — for all the operations carried out within the transaction [54]. Nested transactions [109] extend the transaction paradigm by providing the independent failure property for sub-transactions. Therefore, concurrency, i.e. concurrent sub-transactions, may be supported within a transaction. However, unlike a conversation in which multiple processes may enter the conversation asynchronously, concurrency between processes is hidden inside a transaction; that is, just one process can enter the transaction and exit later.

Transactions are usually intended to tolerate hardware-related failures such as node crashes and communication failures, and most transaction mechanisms do not deal with the possibility of software design faults within a transaction that could also be a cause of data inconsistency. Moreover, since transactions hide the effects of concurrency by guaranteeing serialisability, it is not possible for concurrent entities (i.e. interacting processes) to synchronize their activities according to the ordering of their transactions and this could be an additional source of faults.

Conversations provide a framework for programming explicit cooperative concurrency amongst a set of processes or objects that have been designed to interact with each other. In contrast, transactions are used to deal with concurrency implicitly by serialising accesses to objects that are shared by independently designed actions, i.e. objects that have simply been designed to be interacted with (typically termed *shared objects*). Since both kinds of interactions are important, we argue that fault-tolerant concurrent software should combine the mechanisms of conversations and transactions in order to resolve the problems caused by hardware and software faults in the presence of both shared objects and concurrent entities.

Because shared objects have been designed and implemented separately from the applications (i.e. objects) that make use of them, they thus have to be responsible for ensuring their own integrity in the face of concurrent updates and possible failures. However objects that have been designed to interact with each other are collectively responsible for their own integrity. For such objects it may well be possible to use forward error recovery since the designer will know what progress each of the set of objects is intended to make. Backward error recovery can be designed without the need of such knowledge and so is the typical form of recovery used for objects that are individually responsible for their own integrity.

Shared objects that are under the control of a transaction system will guarantee the ACID properties if all the operations on them are performed from within an atomic activity. We will describe these transactional objects as being *atomic* because they provide guarantees of atomicity for objects that interact with them. Interactions via shared objects that are not atomic should occur within the context of a conversation and will require explicit mechanisms for concurrency control and error recovery.

## 6.2    Object-Oriented Concurrency

Computations are carried out in concurrent systems by the cooperation of several separate (or asynchronous) execution threads. Features for supporting concurrency in an object-oriented (OO) programming language may be added as an extra layer on top of the OO features, or may be fully integrated with the language. We concentrate on the latter because such solutions encompass the concepts of object and process into a single abstraction.

In our proposed framework for coordinated error recovery we view a concurrent OO system as a collection of interacting objects. Concurrent execution threads correspond to executions of operations on a group of objects. What we are actually concerned with is concurrent executions of operation bodies and coordinated error recovery between a set of such executions. Consequently, there is no need to distinguish between active and passive objects at this level of abstraction. Since a general error recovery mechanism should make no assumptions about the synchronization mechanism that is being used, our model will not specify this mechanism. To avoid extra complexities, we assume in the model that an object must execute just one of its operations at a time. It is therefore conceptually correct by this model to consider objects, rather than individual operations, as participants of a coordinated activity.

## 6.3   Coordinated Atomic Actions

We use the term *coordinated atomic action* (or CA action) to characterize an activity between a group of interacting objects that combines properties of conversations and transactions and integrates exception handling. Objects that are involved in a CA action and not shared with other actions are called *participating* objects; objects that are shared with more than one CA action are called *external* objects and must be atomic.

A CA action has the following basic properties:

- A CA action that relies on backward error recovery must provide a recovery line in which the recovery points of the objects participating in the action are properly coordinated so as to avoid the domino effect.

- CA actions must provide a test line consisting of a set of acceptance tests, one for each participating object, and a global test for the whole.

- All the objects accessed by a CA action must invoke appropriate forward and/or backward recovery measures cooperatively once an error is detected inside the action, in order to reach some mutually consistent conclusion.

- Error recovery for participating objects in a CA action requires the use of explicit error coordination mechanisms within the CA action; objects that are external to the CA action and can be shared with other actions must be atomic and provide their own error coordination mechanisms (in order to prevent information smuggling).

- Nesting of CA actions is permitted.

On entry to a CA action, a participating object establishes a recovery point if backward error recovery is required and, thereafter, may only communicate with other objects participating in the action and with external objects that are atomic. Note that the participating objects in a particular CA action may enter the action asynchronously. Accessing an external atomic object from within a CA action in effect involves starting some kind of transaction. If all the current participants complete and pass their acceptance tests, then any recovery points taken on entry are discarded, transactions involving external atomic objects are committed and the CA action is exited. If, for any reason, some participating object fails to complete or to satisfy its acceptance test, appropriate recovery measures must be invoked. For this purpose, a CA action is organized as several *CA action attempts*. The first attempt is the normal activity that results from executions of the primary alternates of cooperative participating objects. Subsequent attempts either consist of the activity of the set of exception handlers, or of the activity of doing backward recovery followed by the next set of alternates. Transactions involving external atomic objects must be aborted during backward error recovery. New transactions started by subsequent attempts may involve different sets of external objects by reason of diverse design. The concept of a CA action thus suggests a quite general solution where both forward and backward recovery techniques can be used in a complementary or combined manner.

Through the use of appropriate protocols it is possible to have a CA action whose participating objects are held in various of the different computers forming a distributed computing system. Indeed users in the environment of a computing system can also be viewed as objects participating in a CA action if they adhere to appropriate protocols — the practicality of this possibility is greatly enhanced by the fact that a CA action can provide a structure and strategy for forward error recovery. For example, the system could send compensatory messages to users in order to correct earlier messages that were later discovered to have been erroneous. In this way, a CA action can effectively deal with cooperative activities between application programs and environments that cannot be rolled back, using forward error recovery.

Fig. 3 shows an example that combines different forms of error recovery into a single CA action in which object 1 uses the exception handler H to do forward recovery while object 2 is rolled back and then tries its second attempt. The effects of operations on external atomic objects are undone completely when the first attempt of the CA action fails.

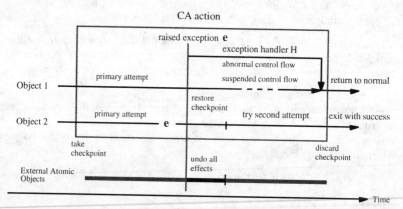

**Fig. 3.** Combined forms of coordinated error recovery.

The transaction mechanism that supports atomic objects is independent of the mechanism used to implement CA actions, and atomic objects can be being used by different CA actions concurrently. Atomic objects generally contain no design redundancy, but may have their own mechanisms for concurrent access control. Each execution of a CA action behaves like a transaction with respect to the external atomic objects it accesses, and each CA action attempt during execution may be thought of as a nested transaction. Since any effect that a CA action has on external atomic objects shared with other CA actions only becomes visible if the CA action terminates successfully, unexpected information smuggling between CA actions via external shared objects can effectively be avoided.

CA actions can be nested. A nested CA action is still atomic during its execution (even with respect to its parent and sibling actions). When it completes successfully, its results can only be revealed within its parent action. All the effects of the nested CA action can thus be undone by its parent if the need arises and appropriate recovery points have been taken. Concurrent nested CA actions behave like nested transactions with respect to external atomic objects involved in transactions with their parent action. Thus, although they may be allowed to use the external atomic objects held by their parent action, they must compete for them in a strictly controlled manner. Nested CA actions may also acquire some external atomic objects that are not held by the parent action. However, these external atomic objects cannot be simply released — they should be passed onto the parent action so as to enable possible error recovery. Within a CA action, new objects may be created and then destroyed. If it is necessary to keep the newly created objects after the completion of the creating CA action, the availability of the newly created objects will be strictly limited to the parent action.

## 6.4    Exception Handling in CA Actions

In object-oriented systems it is appropriate for exceptions to be represented by instances of classes and therefore have a type [37, 78]. This makes it possible to use the type hierarchy to group exceptions together and to define a single handler to cope with a group of related exceptions.

It should be noticed that different participating objects in a CA action may raise different exceptions concurrently. The exception tree proposed by Campbell and Randell [31] is an appropriate mechanism for combining these multiple exceptions into a single exception. For a given exception, the corresponding exception handlers may either invoke appropriate recovery measures, or signal a further exception. Similarly, transactions involving external atomic objects must be either aborted, or else, if practically possible, forward error recovery mechanisms must be used to compensate for any erroneous updates they have made to external atomic objects.

To ensure the proper combination of forward and backward recovery, the CA action structure will guarantee that an exception is raised if the acceptance test fails or a run-time error is detected before the acceptance test is reached. CA actions must be coordinated so as to either produce a result agreeable to all the participating objects or (if at all possible) to restore all the objects changed by the CA action to their prior states. Thus, the default exception handler will typically simply use backward error recovery to terminate the current CA action attempt.

## 6.5    Linguistic and Implementation Issues

In general, support for CA actions can be provided by either embedding the support into a new language or by extending an existing language. The former approach can offer powerful linguistic constructs and provide a fine degree of control because of its tight integration with the underlying language. An example is the Argus language which provides language constructs for the creation of top-level and nested transactions [94]. But a new language may have difficulty in finding practical acceptance. Providing a set of library objects to support CA actions is the simplest approach to implementation — for example, the Arjuna system [149] uses this approach to provide a transaction-based toolkit for writing reliable distributed programs in C++. However, the disadvantage of an approach based on the use of library classes is that it does not offer a good degree of control for coordinated actions because there is no linguistic link between the start and end of an action.

Linguistically, a CA action is like a multi-threaded procedure call and has some similarities to the proposal for a *multi-function* made in [17]. The programming language Arche [63] has a construct that supports N-version programming which is a simplified form of a multi-function called a multi-operation. However, a multi-operation call is a mechanism by which a single object can invoke the same operation on a set of objects that implement it in differing ways. In contrast, a CA action allows several different objects to cooperate in performing a task by coming together. Each participating object plays a different role in the CA action, in other words, each object executes a different operation. These roles should be declared as part of the specification of the CA action since the complete set of participating objects in a CA action must be known at run-time, so as to be able to ensure a synchronized exit from the action. Since a CA action is a mechanism by which a group of otherwise unrelated threads can rendezvous, the syntax and semantics for specifying a call to a CA action must make it possible to identify a particular instance of such an action because, unlike a conventional procedure call, a single invocation of a CA action is made up of several different calls. CA actions should be parameterized allowing them to be bound to different objects on each invocation. A further complication is the way in which variants of the different operations within the CA action should be specified. These language design considerations are the subject of on-going research — they are therefore not discussed further in this paper.

The most important implementation issue is the mechanism for coordinating the activity within a CA action. One approach would be to introduce a *CA action manager* object whose basic functions would be: (1) to register asynchronous entries of the participating objects; (2) to manage the transactions used to access external atomic objects; (3) to synchronize the exit of all participants; and (4) to enforce the correct nesting of CA actions.

On invocation of a CA action, i.e. when one or more objects begin to participate in the action, a globally unique identifier for the action must be generated. As each participating object enters the CA action, its identifier is passed onto the manager and recorded in the *Current-Participant-List* of the CA action. Whenever a CA action accesses an external atomic object (that hence is potentially visible to other CA actions executing concurrently), the manager must ensure that this access is recoverable, for example, the CA action must in effect start a transaction in order to access any atomic objects. If backward error recovery is being used, the manager is also responsible for establishing a recovery point for each participating object as the object enters the CA action. If the action completes successfully, any such recovery points are discarded; otherwise the previous states of the participating objects are restored and some recovery measures are invoked. The CA action may terminate with a failure exception despite the use of its own fault tolerance capabilities. Since CA actions can be nested, a failure exception of a sub-CA action will simply cause termination of the current attempt of the enclosing CA action. The outer CA action will then invoke appropriate recovery.

External atomic objects may be accessed concurrently by different CA actions and must have the semantics of atomic data types [169]. Either optimistic or pessimistic concurrency control policies can be used to implement atomic data types [169, 59]. The simplest approach is to lock all atomic objects exclusively for use only within a single CA action. This can be relaxed somewhat by allowing concurrent access to external atomic objects from several CA actions provided that none of them tries to modify such objects. Allowing concurrent updates to external atomic objects requires type-specific knowledge about the semantics of the atomic data type to prevent conflicts. However, note that concurrency control and error recovery for external atomic objects are the responsibility of those objects and not the CA actions that access them concurrently.

If exception handling is used to implement forward error recovery, a participating object may raise an exception during the execution of an operation within the CA action or if it fails its acceptance test at the end of the CA action. If an exception is raised, all the participating objects in the CA action should stop their normal computation and the process of exception resolution must be started. Any such exception must be first caught by the manager object which will then inform other participating objects that an exception has occurred so as to stop other normal computations. If several exceptions are raised concurrently, a resolution function is used to decide which single exception covers the entire set. Appropriate steps are then taken to handle that exception.

Finally, participating objects in a nested CA action may access external atomic objects that are already held by their parent CA action, but this must be done in a strictly controlled way in order to prevent information smuggling. A set of rules must be designed carefully, enforced and checked by the action manager. For example, once external atomic objects have been passed onto a nested CA action by the parent CA action, the parent action should not be allowed to access the external atomic objects until the nested action terminates.

## 7    Concluding Remarks

Although we believe that OO concepts provide a valuable perspective on the design of error recovery structures that support the provision of design fault tolerance in sophisticated programs, we have made only rather limited use of these ideas in this paper. Space constraints have precluded a more detailed discussion of the advantages that are provided by various object-oriented linguistic constructs (see however [125, 128, 136, 177], and also Paper III.G in this volume).

## Acknowledgements

Our research at Newcastle was originally sponsored by the UK Science and Engineering Research Council and by the Ministry of Defence, but in recent years it has been supported mainly by two successive ESPRIT Basic Research projects on Predictably Dependable Computing Systems (PDCS and PDCS2). Needless to say, as will be obvious from the references we have given, the work we have attempted to summarize here has been contributed to by a large number of colleagues. It would be invidious to name just some of them, but we are very pleased to acknowledge our indebtedness to all of them.

# Definition and Analysis of Hardware-and-Software Fault-Tolerant Architectures*

Jean-Claude Laprie   Jean Arlat   Christian Béounes[†]   Karama Kanoun

LAAS-CNRS

**Abstract.** This paper is devoted to the definition and the analysis of architectures aimed at tolerating hardware faults and software faults. The paper is composed of fourth sections. The second section is devoted to a unified presentation of the methods for software-fault tolerance; in addition to recovery blocks and N-version programming, a third type of method is identified from the careful examination of current, real-life systems: N self-checking programming. The third section presents a set of hardware-and-software fault-tolerant architectures. In the fourth section, an analysis and an evaluation of three of the defined architectures is performed.

## 1    Introduction

Tolerance of software faults by design diversity has become a reality in both experiments and real-life systems [166]. The currently privileged domain where design diversity is applied is that of safety-related systems. In such systems, extreme attention is paid to *design faults,* where the term "design" is considered in a broad sense, from the system requirements to realization, during initial system production as well as in possible future modifications. Design faults are a source of *common-mode* failures, which defeat fault tolerance strategies based on strict replication (thus intended to cope with physical faults), and have generally catastrophic consequences.

Pre-computer realizations of safety-related systems classically called for diversified designs, i.e. the production of two or more variants of a system or equipment intended to fulfill the same function through implementations based on different technologies. The aim of diversified designs is to minimize, as much as possible, the likelihood of occurrence of common-mode failures; a typical example is an hardwired electronic channel backed by an electro-mechanic or electro-pneumatic channel. In addition, the systems architecture was based on the *federation* of equipments each implementing one or several subfunctions of the system; one of the criteria for partitioning the system global function into subfunctions was that a failure of any equipment should be confined, and should not prevent the global function of the system to be performed, possibly in a degraded mode. When the transition was made to computer technology, the safety-related systems generally retained the federation approach. Each subfunction was then implemented by a "complete" computer: hardware, executive and application software. Examples of this approach may be found in airplane flight control systems (e.g. the Boeing 757/767) or nuclear plant monitoring (e.g. the SPIN system of Merlin Gerin). A prerequisite for confining computer failures is the auto-detection of the error(s) having led to failure. The auto-detection of errors due to design faults can be achieved through two main approaches:

---

*   This paper is a condensed version of [88]
†   Christian Béounes passed away on 23 April 1993.

- acceptance tests of the results by means of executable assertions which constitute a generalization and a formalization of the likelihood checks which are classical in process control;
- diversified design leading to two software variants whose results are compared; real-life examples are: (i) the Airbus A-300 and A-310, and (ii) the Swedish railways' interlocking system.

The federation approach generally leads to a very large number of processing elements, larger than what would be necessary in terms of the computing power required; for instance, the Boeing 757/767 flight management control system is composed of 80 distinct functional microprocessors (300 when redundancy is accounted for).

An additional step towards a better use of computers consists in having several subfunctions implemented by software, supported by the same hardware equipment. Such an approach, which can be termed as *integration,* comes up against software failures, which are due to design faults only; adopting the integration approach thus necessitates software-fault tolerance. Moreover, an evolution of some safety-related systems (e.g. the flight control systems) is towards limited, if any, back-up possibilities, either manual or by non-computer technologies. This is of course an additional incentive to software fault tolerance, since safe behavior of the system is then entirely dependent on reliable behavior of the software. Real-life examples are the NASA's space shuttle and the Airbus A-320.

This paper presents a structured definition of hardware-*and*-software fault-tolerant architectures. The paper results from an elaboration on a previously reported work [89]. A constant underlying guide-line in the production of this paper has been to adopt as much as possible a global view, specialization to specific classes of faults or technique being conducted only when necessary. More specific attempts to the definition of hardware-and-software fault-tolerant architectures have already appeared in the literature which concerns extensions of the recovery block approach [72] or which are based on N-version programming [84].

The paper is composed of four sections. The second section is devoted to a unified presentation of the methods for software-fault tolerance; in addition to the recovery blocks and N-version programming methods, a third type of method is identified from the careful examination of current, real-life systems: N self-checking programming. The third section presents a set of hardware-and-software fault-tolerant architectures. In the fourth section, an analysis and an evaluation of three of the defined architectures is performed.

## 2    Methods for Software-Fault Tolerance

### 2.1   The Methods and their Characteristics

*Design diversity* may be defined as the *production of two or more systems aimed at delivering the same service through separate designs and realizations.* The systems produced through the design diversity approach from a common service specification are termed *variants*. In addition to the existence of at least two variants of a system, tolerance of design faults necessitates a *decider*, aimed at providing an — assumed as being — error-free result from the variant execution; the variant execution has to be performed from consistent initial conditions and inputs. The common specification has to address explicitly the *decision points,* i.e. (i) when decisions have to be performed, and (ii) the data upon which  decisions have to be performed, thus the data processed by the decider.

The two most well documented techniques for tolerating software design faults are the *recovery blocks* [127] (see also paper III.A) and the *N-version programming* [12]. In the recovery block (RB) approach, the variants are termed alternates and the decider is an acceptance test, which is applied sequentially to the results provided by the alternates: if the results provided by the primary alternate do not satisfy the acceptance test, the secondary alternate is executed, and so on. In the N-version programming (NVP) approach, the variants are termed versions, and the decider performs a vote on all versions results.

The term *variant* is preferred in this paper as a unifying term to the terms *alternate* or *version* because (i) the term "alternate" reflects sequential execution, which is a feature specific to the recovery block approach, and (ii) the term "version" has a widely accepted different meaning: successive versions of a system resulting from fault removal and/or functionality evolution; during the life of a diversely designed system, several versions of the variants are expected to be generated.

The hardware-fault tolerant architectures equivalent to RB and to NVP are stand-by sparing and N-modular redundancy, respectively. The equivalent of a third approach to hardware-fault tolerance, active dynamic redundancy (very popular especially when based on self-checking components, as in the ATT ESSs, Stratus systems, etc.), does not appear to have been described in the published literature as a generic technique for software-fault tolerance. However, self-checking programming has long been introduced [178] a self-checking program results from the addition of redundancy into a program in order to check its own dynamic behavior during execution. A self-checking software component is considered as resulting either from the association of an acceptance test to a variant, or from the association of two variants with a comparison algorithm. Fault tolerance is provided by the parallel execution of N≥2 self-checking components. At each execution of the system so constituted, a self-checking component is considered as being acting (in the sense of the delivered service, and thus of the effective delivery of the results to the controlled or monitored application); the other self-checking components are considered as — "hot" — spares. Upon failure of the acting component, service delivery is switched to a self-checking component previously considered as a spare; upon failure of a spare component, service keeps being delivered by the acting component. Error processing is thus performed through error detection and — possible — switching of the results. In what follows, we shall term such a software fault tolerance approach *N self-checking programming* (NSCP).

Our aim is not so much "introducing" a "new" software fault tolerance approach as providing a clear classification of the various approaches which may be considered. In fact, most of the real-life systems mentioned in the introduction do not actually implement either RB or NVP, but are based on self-checking software. For instance, the computer-controlled part of the flight control systems of the Airbus A-300 and A-310 and the Swedish railways' interlocking system are based on the parallel execution of two variants whose results are compared, and they stop operation upon error detection. The flight control system of the Airbus A-320 is based on two self-checking components, each of them being in turn based on the parallel execution of two variants whose results are compared: tolerance to a single fault needs four variants; it is worth mentioning that the two self-checking components (each with two variants) do not exactly deliver the same service: when switching from the initially acting component to the other one, the critical functions are preserved whereas the non-critical functions are performed in a degraded mode.

Five additional comments can be made on NSCP:

*   when a self-checking software component is based on the assiociation of two variants, one of the variants only may be written for the purpose of fulfilling the functions expected from the component, the other variant being an extended acceptance test (e.g. different accuracy, inverse function when possible);

*   as in N-version programming, the fact that the components are being executed in parallel necessitates an input consistency mechanism;

*   the acceptance tests associated with each variant or the comparison algorithms associated to a pair of variants can be the same, or specifically derived for each of them — from a common specification;

*   it could be argued that NSCP is "parallel recovery block", however, in our opinion, the RB concept cannot be reduced to the association of alternates together with an acceptance test: the *backward* recovery strategy is an integral part of it;

*   the delivery or not of an acceptable result is the *responsibility* of each self-checking component in NSCP, whereas the judgement on result acceptability is *cooperative* in NVP.

| Method | Error Processing Technique | | Judgement on Result Acceptability | Variant Execution Scheme | Consistency of Input Data | Suspension of Service Delivery during Error Processing | Number of Variants for Tolerance of f Sequential Faults |
|---|---|---|---|---|---|---|---|
| Recovery Blocks (RB) | Error Detection by Acceptance Test and Backward Recovery | | Absolute, with respect to Specification | Sequential | Implicit, from Backward Recovery Principle | Yes, Duration Necessary for Executing One or More Variants | f+1 |
| N Self-Checking Programming (NSCP) | Error Detection and Result Switching | Detection by Acceptance Test(s) | | Parallel | Explicit, by Dedicated Mechanisms | Yes, Duration Necessary for Result Switching | |
| | | Detection by Comparison | Relative, on Variants Results | | | | 2(f+1) |
| N-Version Programming (NVP) | Vote | | | | | No | f+2 |

**Fig. 1** .   Main Characteristics of the Software-Fault Tolerance Strategies

The table of Fig. 1 summarizes the main characteristics of the three strategies considered. Of particular interest, with respect to the selection of a strategy for a given application, are the judgement on result acceptability and the suspension of service delivery on error occurrence. The table of Fig. 2 summarizes the main sources of overhead, from both structural and operational time viewpoints, involved in software fault tolerance. In this table, the overheads brought about by tests local to each variant such as input range checking, grossly wrong results, etc. are not mentioned: they are common to all approaches (in addition, they are — or should be — present in non fault-tolerant software systems as well).

| Method Name | Structural Overhead | | Operational Time Overhead | | |
|---|---|---|---|---|---|
| | Diversified Software Layer | Mechanisms (Layers Supporting the Diversified Software Layer) | Systematic | | On Error Occurrence |
| | | | Decider | Variants Execution | |
| Recovery Blocks (RB) | One variant and One Acceptance Test | Recovery Cache | Acceptance Test Execution | Accesses to Recovery Cache | One Variant and Acceptance Test Execution |
| N Self-Checking Programming (NSCP) — Error Detection by Acceptance Tests | One variant and Two Acceptance Tests | Result Switching | Acceptance Test Execution | Input Data Consistency and Variants Execution | Possible Result Switching |
| N Self-Checking Programming (NSCP) — Error Detection by Comparison | Three Variants | Comparators and Result Switching | Comparison Execution | | |
| N-Version Programming (NVP) | Two Variants | Voters | Vote Execution | Execution Synchronisation | Usually neglectable |

**Fig. 2**. Overheads Involved in Software-Fault Tolerance for Tolerance of One Fault (with respect to Non Fault-Tolerant Software)

## 2.2    Classes of Faults to be Considered

**Independence with respect to the Redundancy Scheme.** We consider *independent faults* and *related faults* [12]. Related faults result either from a specification fault — common to all the variants — or from dependencies in the separate designs and implementations. Related faults manifest under the form of *similar errors*, whereas independent faults usually cause *distinct errors*, although it may happen that independent faults lead to similar errors. Similar errors lead to *common-mode failures*, and distinct errors usually cause *separate failures*. These definitions are illustrated by Fig. 3.

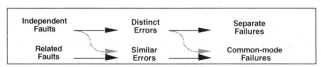

**Fig. 3.** Classes of Faults, Errors and Failures

**Persistence with respect to the Computation Process and Recoverability.** Faults are classified as *solid* or *soft* faults based on their persistence. Such a distinction is usual in hardware, where the solidity or softness character of a fault plays an important role in fault tolerance: a component affected by a solid fault has to be made passive after fault manifestation, whereas a component affected by a soft fault can be utilized in subsequent executions after error recovery has taken place. Stated in equivalent terms, a solid fault necessitates error processing *and* fault treatment, whereas error processing is sufficient for dealing with a soft fault. Typical examples are (i) permanent faults for solid faults, (ii) temporary faults (either transient or intermittent) for soft faults.

Let us now consider software faults of operational programs, i.e. programs which have been thoroughly debugged. The remaining sources of problems are more likely to be arising from subtle fault conditions than from easily identifiable faults: limit conditions, race conditions, or strange underlying hardware conditions. As a consequence of a slight change in the execution context, the corresponding fault conditions may not be gathered, and the software will not fail again. The notion of soft fault may thus be extended to software [53] in the sense that the likelihood of manifestation recurrence upon re-execution is low enough so as to be neglected.

Another important consideration is the notion of local and global variables for the components, in relation to error recovery actions. Let us call a *diversity unit* the program between two decision points. As a general rule, it can be said that recovery necessitates that the diversity units have to be procedures (in the sense that their activation and behavior do not depend on any internal remanant data). Stated in other terms, all the data necessary for the processing tasks of a diversity unit have to be global data. The globality of the data for a diversity unit may:

- originate directly from the nature of the application; an example is provided by the monitoring of a physical process (e.g. nuclear reactor protection) where tasks are initialized by acquisition of sensor data, and do not utilize data produced in previous processing steps;
- result from system partitioning, either naturally, or from the transformation of local data into global data, at the expense in the latter case of an overhead and of a possible decrease in diversity (the specification of the decision points has to be made more precise); a — deliberately over-simplified — example is provided by a filtering function which would constitute a diversity unit: the past samples should be made part of the global data.

The preceding discussion applies to all of the software fault tolerance methods. It is however noteworthy that some arrangements can be made to this general rule in some specific, application-dependent, cases. For example, if the above-mentioned overhead cannot be afforded, or if it is estimated that transforming local data into global data may lead to a too severe decrease in diversity, an alternative solution exists for NSCP and NVP: eliminate a failed variant from further processing, i.e. undertake fault treatment.

As a summary, we shall adopt the following definitions for soft and solid faults:

- a *soft* software fault is a fault whose likelihood of recurrence can be neglected *and* is recoverable,
- a *solid* software fault is a fault which is recurrent under normal operation *or* which cannot be recovered.

## 3      Definition of Hardware-and-Software Architectures

This section presents examples of architectures providing tolerance to both hardware and software faults. Emphasis will be put on: (i) the dependencies among the software and hardware fault tolerance and (ii) the impact of the solid and soft character of the software faults in the definition of the architectures.

Two levels of fault tolerance requirements are investigated: (i) architectures tolerating a single fault, and (ii) architectures tolerating two consecutive faults (These requirements can be related respectively, to the classical Fail Op/Fail Safe and Fail Op/Fail Op/Fail Safe requirements used in the aerospace community for hardware fault tolerance). The architectures will be identified by means of a condensed expression of the form: X/i/j/..., where label X stands for the acronym of the software fault tolerance method, X ∈ { RB, NSCP, NVP }, i is the number of hardware faults tolerated and j is the number of software faults tolerated. Further labels will be added to this expression when necessary.

Due to the scope of the paper, the architectures are described from a deliberately highly abstracted view. As a consequence, distinguishing features, such as (i) the overhead involved by intercomponent communication for synchronization, decision-making, data consistency, etc., and (ii) the differences in memory space necessary for each architecture, are not addressed.

## 3.1    Design Decisions when Implementing Design Diversity

Among the many issues which have to be dealt with design diversity [12], two of them are especially important — and correlated — *with respect to architectural considerations*: (i) the number of variants, and (ii) the level of fault tolerance application.

Independently from any economic consideration, the *number of variants* to be produced for a given software fault tolerance method is directly related to the number of faults to be tolerated (see Fig. 2). It will be seen in this section that the soft or solid character of the software faults has a significant impact on the architecture only when dealing with the tolerance of more than one fault. It has also to be remembered that an architecture tolerating a solid fault is also able to tolerate a (theoretically) infinite sequence of soft faults — provided there is no fault coincidence phenomenon. It is noteworthy that the relation between the likelihood of such faults and the number of variants is not simple: whether increasing the number of variants will increase or decrease the number of related faults depends on several factors, some of which are antagonistic [12]. However, in NVP, a reason to increase the number of variants is the fact that two similar errors can outvote a good result in a three-version scheme, whereas they would be detected in a four-version scheme, thus providing an increase in safety (situations contrary to safety being defined as corresponding to an undetected error).

The level of application of fault tolerance encompasses two aspects: (i) at what level of detail should one perform the decomposition of the system into components which will be diversified?, and (ii) which layers (application software, executive, hardware) have to be diversified? The answer to the first question should at first sight result from a trade-off between two opposite considerations: on the one hand, small size components enable a better mastering of the decision algorithms; on the other hand, large size components favor diversity. In addition, the decision points are "non diversity" points (and synchronisation points for NSCP and NVP); as such, they have to be limited: decision points are a priori necessary only for the interactions with environment (sensor data acquisition, delivery of orders to actuators, interactions with operators, etc.). However, additional compromises may result from performance considerations. Concerning the second question, the methods mentioned can be applied to any of the software layers, either of application software, or of the executive software. They can also be applied to the hardware layer(s) [166]. The states — with respect to the computation process — of distinct variants are different. A consequence is that when the variants are executed in parallel (NSCP and NVP), thus on distinct (redundant) hardware, diversity of a given layer leads to states of the underlying layers which are different, even if they are not diversified — except of course at the decision points. A decision concerning whether or not layers underlying the application software have to be diversified should include additional considerations, such as determining the influence of the portions of executive software and of hardware which are specifically designed for the particular application, and what confidence to place on experience validation for those parts which are off-the-shelf.

## 3.2 Structuring Principles for the Definition of Architectures

Structuring is a prerequisite to the mastering of complexity. This is especially true when dealing with fault tolerance [127]. A usual, and useful, principle when dealing with hardware fault tolerance is that the fault tolerance mechanisms should go along, and respect the structuring of a system into layers [151]. Especially, it is desirable that each layer be provided with fault tolerance mechanisms aimed at processing the errors produced in the particular layer, with respect (i) to performance considerations in terms of time to recover from an error and (ii) to the damage created by error propagation. Implementation of this principle at the hardware layer when dealing with software fault tolerance necessitates that the redundant hardware components are in the same state with respect to the computation process in the absence of error. Such a condition can obviously be satisfied only if the variants are executed sequentially, i.e. in the RB approach. However, the diagnosis of hardware faults may be made possible by taking advantage of the syndromes provided by the decider(s) of the particular software fault tolerance method considered.

Another useful structuring mechanism is the notion of **error confinement area** [151]. This notion cannot be separated from the architectural elements considered. In relation to the scope of this paper, the architectural elements considered will be:

- the elements providing the services necessary for an application software to be executed, i.e. hardware and the associated executive software; such elements will be termed — abusively, for sake of conciseness — as **hardware components**;
- the variants of the **application software**.

Consideration of both hardware and software faults leads to distinguishing hardware error confinement areas (HECAs) and software error confinement areas (SECAs). In our case, a HECA will cover at least one hardware component and a SECA will cover at least one software variant. It is noteworthy that, due to our definition of hardware component, a HECA corresponds to the part of the architecture that is made passive after occurrence of a solid hardware fault, and can thus be interpreted as a Line Replaceable Unit (LRU).

## 3.3 Architectures Tolerating a Single Fault

Three architectures are considered that correspond to the implementation of the three software fault-tolerance methods of section 2. Fig. 4 illustrates the configurations of the SECAs and HECAs for each case. The intersections between the SECAs and the HECAs characterize the software and hardware fault tolerance dependencies of the architectures.

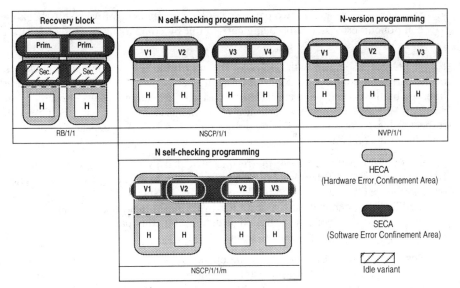

**Fig. 4.** Architectures Tolerating a Single Fault

**The RB/1/1 Architecture.** This architecture is obtained by the duplication on two hardware components of the RB composed of two variants. Two variants and their associated instances of the acceptance test constitute two distinct SECAs and intersect each HECA. Accordingly, each HECA is software-fault tolerant due to the RB method: the independent faults in a variant are tolerated, while the related faults between the variants are detected; however related faults between each variant and the acceptance test cannot be tolerated or detected.

The hardware components operate in hot standby redundancy and always execute the same variant. This allows the design of a high coverage concurrent comparison between the results of the acceptance tests and the results provided by the hardware components, in order to handle specifically the hardware faults. It is noteworthy that when a discrepancy between the results of the hardware components is detected during the execution of the primary alternate or of the acceptance test, it might be interesting to call for the execution of the secondary in order to tolerate the fault (should the fault be a soft fault). If the discrepancy persists (which would be the case upon manifestation of a solid fault), the failed HECA could be identified by running diagnosis programs on each HECA; thus, the failed HECA would be made passive and the continuity of service would be ensured .

It is worth noting that after this hardware degradation, (i) the architecture is still software fault-tolerant, and (ii) subsequent hardware faults can be detected either by means of the acceptance test or by periodic execution of the diagnosis.

**Examples of NSCP/1/1 Architectures.** The basic architecture (NSCP/1/1 in Fig. 4) is made up of:
- four hardware components grouped in two pairs in hot standby redundancy, each pair of hardware components forming a HECA;

- four variants grouped in two pairs; each pair constitutes a software self-checking component, error detection being carried out by comparison; each pair forms a SECA.

Each SECA is associated with a HECA. The comparison of the computational states of the hardware components cannot be directly performed due to the diversification imposed by the variants; however, the comparison between the results of each pair of variants also covers the two hardware components composing each HECA with respect to hardware faults (including design faults); a HECA is thus also a hardware self-checking component.

In case of discrepancy between the results provided by the paired variants in one HECA, irrespective of the type of fault, the associated HECA is possibly switched out and the results are delivered by the other HECA. Should the discrepancy occur repeatedly, thus characterizing a solid hardware fault, then the designated HECA would be made passive. The degraded structure after this passivation still enables both software and hardware faults to be detected.

Besides the nominal tolerance of an independent software fault, the architecture ensures supplementary tolerance and detection features: (i) tolerance of two simultaneous independent faults in a SECA, (ii) detection of a related fault among two variants (each pertaining to one of the two disjoint SECAs) and (iii) detection of three or four simultaneous independent software faults.

The NSCP/1/1 architecture corresponds to the principle of the architecture implemented in the Airbus A-320 [163] However, in some applications, the requirement of four variants would be prohibitive; it is worth noting that a modified architecture (NSCP/1/1/m) can be obtained, based on just three variants (Fig. 4).

The major significant difference in error processing between the NCSP/1/1 and NCSP/1/1/m architectures can be identified when considering the activation of a software fault in V2. It is important to note that this would result in a discrepancy in both self-checking component, thus implying an associated SECA covering all the four software components and preventing any software fault tolerance. As this is the only event that can lead to such a syndrome (under the hypothesis of single independent fault), the "correct" result is immediately available as the one provided by V1 or V3, hence, the SECA associated with V2 shown on Fig. 4. However, as a consequence, all the fault tolerance and detection capabilities of the NSCP/1/1 architecture termed above "supplementary" are lost.

**The NVP/1/1 Architecture.** The NVP/1/1 architecture is a direct implementation of the NVP method. It is made up of three hardware components, each running a distinct variant. The handling of hardware faults (including design faults) and of software faults is common and performed at the software layer by the decider of the NVP method. Besides tolerance to an independent fault in a single variant, the architecture allows detection of independent faults in two or three variants.

The problem of discrimination between hardware and software faults, in order that passivation of a hardware component occurs only upon occurrence of a solid fault, gives an example of the dependency between software and hardware fault tolerance. Due to the soft character considered for the software faults, a diagnosis of (solid) hardware fault could be easily implemented as the monitoring of a repeatedly disagreeing hardware component. After passivation of the failed hardware component, the decider has to be reconfigured as a comparator, which thus ensures a fail safe characteristic to the architecture in case of a subsequent activation of a hardware or a software fault.

### 3.4    Architectures Tolerating Two Consecutive Faults

When dealing with the tolerance of two faults, the distinction between soft and solid software faults comes immediately into play:

- if the software faults can be considered as soft faults, then the number of variants is unchanged with respect to the architectures aimed at tolerating one fault; so these architectures will be of the type X/2/1, $X \in \{$ RB, NSCP, NVP $\}$,
- if the software faults are to be considered as solid faults, then the number of variants must be increased in order to cope with the discarding of a failed variant from further execution; so the corresponding architectures will be of the type X/2/2.

The particular architectures for the tolerance of two faults are displayed on Fig. 5. According to the above discussion, the first three architectures (RB/2/1, NSCP/2/1 and NVP/2/1) are characterized by tolerance of two hardware faults and of a single software fault. The impact of the solid character of the software faults is illustrated in the case of an architecture using the NVP method; this structure (NVP/2/2) is designed to tolerate two consecutive (solid) faults in hardware or software.

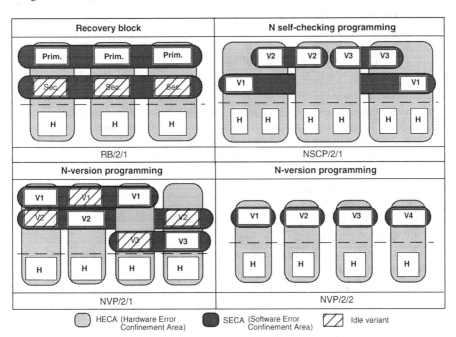

**Fig. 5.**  Architectures Tolerating Two Consecutive Faults

**The RB/2/1 Architecture.** This architecture is made up of three hardware components arranged in triple modular redundancy (TMR). Software fault tolerance capability is unchanged with respect to RB/1/1 architecture. Upon solid hardware fault manifestation, the architecture is degraded through the passivation of the corresponding hardware component, thus resulting in an architecture analogous to the RB/1/1 architecture.Accordingly, even if they are basically useless in handling the first hardware fault, local diagnosis must be incorporated in each hardware component.

**The NSCP/2/1 Architecture.** This architecture is a direct extension of the NSCP/1/1/m architecture. A supplementary duplex HECA is added that supports a software self-checking component made up of two variants. A symmetric distribution of the three SECAs among the three HECAs is thus obtained. It is noteworthy that the fact that all the variants are duplicated allows instantaneous diagnosis of the hardware faults from the syndrome obtained by comparing the results delivered by all the hardware components. The architecture allows also detection of simultaneous independent faults in two or three variants.

**The NVP/2/1 Architecture.** The NVP/2/1 architecture is derived from the NVP/1/1 architecture by addition of a hardware component without introducing another variant. In order to maintain the software fault tolerance capability after passivation of one hardware component, it is necessary that at least two instances of each variant pertain to two distinct HECAs. Thus six variant instances have to be distributed among the four HECAs. A possible configuration is the one shown in Fig. 5 (An enumeration of all the possible combinations reveals 18 solutions).

Among the two distinct variants associated with each HECA, one is active and the other is idle. At a given step, three hardware components execute three distinct variants and the fourth hardware component executes a replica of one of the variants (V1 in this configuration). Besides tolerance to an independent software fault, the architecture allows detection of two or three simultaneous independent faults.

The tolerance of an independent fault can be obtained by a decision based on a vote in which the knowledge that two variants are identical is incorporated. The unbalanced numbers of executions of the variants can be used to improve diagnosability with respect to hardware faults by the use of a double vote decision (each vote includes the results of the non-duplicated variants and only one of the results of the duplicated variant); this is illustrated by considering the following cases:

- activation of a hardware fault in one of the hardware components executing the duplicated variant (V1),
- activation of a software fault in the duplicated variant ,
- activation of a hardware fault in one of the hardware components executing the non duplicated variants (V2, V3) or of a software fault in one of these variants.

In the first case, the fault is of course easily tolerated and diagnosed as the obtained syndrome consists of (i) an agreement among the three results in one vote and (i) a discrepancy among the results of the second vote, hence, designating as false the result of the duplicated variant.

In the second case, the decider will identify a non-unanimity in both votes designating as false the results supplied by the duplicated variant; such a syndrome enables the duplicated variant to be diagnosed as failed and thus the "correct" result is immediately available as the one provided by the non duplicated ones.

In the last case, tolerance is immediate, but the votes do not enable the fault to be diagnosed. Based on the assumption of the non-recurrent nature of the software faults, diagnosis of a hardware fault can result from repeated failure of a hardware component. However, it is worth noting that another form of diagnosis is possible here that would allow one to relax this assumption: upon occurrence of a localized fault (i.e. imputable to either one SECA or one HECA) the next execution step is performed after a reconfiguration of the active variants that matches the duplicated variant with the identified HECA; the decider will then have to solve one of the two cases identified above. A systematic rotation of the duplicated variants would also contribute to such a diagnosis.

After passivation of a failed hardware component, the active variants are reconfigured so that the SECAs be distributed among the remaining HECAs in order to form disjoint areas. Fig. 6 shows the distribution of active and idle variants among the three remaining HECAs after passivation of any of the HECAs of the NVP/2/1 architecture. It is noteworthy that, in each case, the reconfiguration affects only a single HECA. The decision has to be modified to a vote among the remaining variants and thus the degraded architecture is the same as the NVP/1/1 architecture.

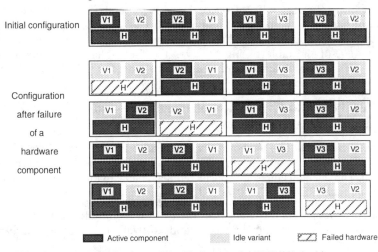

**Fig. 6.** Various Activations of the Variants in the NVP/2/1 Architecture

**The NVP/2/2 Architecture: An Example of Architecture Tolerating Two Solid Software Faults.** In order to illustrate the impact of the solid character of the software faults, on the design of architectures tolerating two faults, we consider the case of the NVP method. The definition of such an architecture requires the provision of four disjoint HECAs and SECAs, hence the NVP/2/2 architecture.

Although, this architecture appears as a direct extension of the NVP/1/1 architecture by addition of one HECA and one associated SECA, major differences exist in the processing of errors. The fault tolerance decision is now based on the identification, among the results provided by the four variants, of a single set of agreeing results made up of two or more results. Furthermore, after the first discrepancy among the results, the hardware component (and its associated variant) designated as failed is made passive without any attempt to diagnose the fault as a hardware or software fault. The decision is then modified as a vote among the remaining versions and the degraded architecture obtained is close to the NVP/1/1 architecture. However, the same discarding action as the one described above would be carried out upon manifestation of a subsequent fault.

Besides tolerance to two consecutive independent software faults, this architecture allows the system (i) to tolerate two simultaneous independent faults, (ii) to detect related faults among two variants and (iii) to detect simultaneous faults in three or four variants. The Fault-Tolerant Processor-Attached Processor (FTP-AP) architecture [84] may be seen as an implementation of this hardware-and-software fault-tolerant architecture: a quad configuration of the core FTP architecture is used as a support for the management of the execution of four diversified applications software that are run on four distinct application processors.

### 3.5   Summary

The table of Fig. 7 summarizes the main fault tolerance properties of the architectures introduced in the preceding paragraphs. Besides the generic notation identifying the software fault tolerance method, and the number of hardware faults and (independent) software faults tolerated, the table presents for each architecture, the number of hardware components and the number of variants required. Also, when applicable, some properties in addition to nominal fault tolerance are listed. Finally, the last field of the table of Fig. 7 gives the fault tolerance properties of the architecture that are obtained after tolerance of a hardware fault, that is, when a HECA has been made passive.

## 4   Analysis and Evaluation of Hardware-and-Software Fault-Tolerant Architectures

The aim of this section is to show how a dependability analysis of hardware-and-software fault-tolerant architectures can be conducted when adopting a Markov approach. Three architectures are considered that enable to tolerate a single hardware or software fault: RB/1/1, NSCP/1/1 and NVP/1/1 (see section 3.3).

Emphasis is first put on the analysis of the software fault tolerance features. Then, models accounting for both hardware and software behavior are derived and evaluated.

### 4.1   Analysis of Software Fault-Tolerant Architectures

Emphasis is put on the distinction between the different sources of failures: independent and related faults in variants and decider. In the analysis, it is assumed that only one type of fault(s), either independent or related, can be activated at each execution and produce error(s). In addition, the underlying fault tolerance mechanisms, i.e. (i) recovery point establishment and restoration for the RB, and (ii) synchronization of the versions, cross check-points establishment and the decision mechanisms for NSCP and NVP, are not accounted for. The failures will be classified according to two different viewpoints:

| Architecture | Hardware Comp. | Variants | Properties in Addition to Nominal Fault Tolerance | | Fault Tolerance Properties After an HECA has been Made Passive | |
|---|---|---|---|---|---|---|
| | | | Hardware Faults | Software Faults | Hardware | Software |
| RB/1/1 | 2 | 2 | Low error latency | – | Detection provided by local diagnosis | Tolerance of one independent fault |
| NSCP/1/1 | 4 | 4 | • Tolerance of 2 faults in hardware components of the same SECA<br>• Detection of 3 or 4 faults in hardware components | • Tolerance of 2 independent faults in the same SECA<br>• Detection of 2 related faults in disjoint SECA's<br>• Detection of 2, 3 or 4 independent faults | Detection | Detection of independent faults |
| NSCP/1/1/m | 4 | 3 | Tolerance of 2 faults in hardware components of the same SECA | – | Detection | Detection of independent faults |
| NVP/1/1 | 3 | 3 | Detection of 2 or 3 faults | Detection of 2 or 3 independent faults | Detection | Detection of independent faults |
| RB/2/1 | 3 | 2 | Low error latency | – | Identical to RB/1/1 | |
| NSCP/2/1 | 6 | 3 | Detection of 3 to 6 faults in hardware components | Detection of 2 or 3 independent faults | Identical to NSCP/1/1/m | |
| NVP/2/1 | 4 | 3 | Detection of 3 to 4 faults in hardware components<br>Tolerance of combinations of single fault in hardware component and independent software fault in non duplicated variant | Detection of 2 or 3 independent faults | Identical to NVP/1/1 | |
| NVP/2/2 | 4 | 4 | Detection of 3 or 4 faults in hardware components | • Detection of 2 related faults<br>• Tolerance of 2 independent faults<br>• Detection of 3 or 4 independent faults | Identical to NVP/1/1 | |

**Fig. 7.** Synthesis of the Properties of the Architectures

1) with respect to the type of faults whose activation has led to failure:

- *separate failures*, which result from the activation of independent faults in the variants,
- *common-mode failures*, which may result from the activation either of related faults or from independent faults in the decider; we shall distinguish among two types of related faults: (i) related faults among the variants, and (ii) related faults between the variants and the decider.

2) with respect to the detection of inability to deliver acceptable results:

- *detected failures*, when no acceptable result is identified by the decider and no output result is delivered,
- *undetected failures*, when erroneous results are delivered.

It is assumed in the sequel that the probability of fault activation is identical for all the variants of a given architecture. This assumption is performed in order to simplify the notation and does not alter the significance of the results obtained (the generalization to the case where the characteristics of the variants are distinguished can be easily deduced).

In order to characterize the probabilities of failure of the software fault-tolerant architectures considered, we introduce the following notation for the considered X/1/1 architectures with $X \in \{ RB, NSCP, NVP \}$:

- $q_{I,X}$ = P {activation of an independent fault in one variant of X | execution},
- $q_{ID,X}$ = P {activation of an independent fault in the decider of X | execution},
- $q_{nV,X}$ = P {activation of a related fault between n variants of X | execution},

- $q_{RVD,X} = P$ {activation of a related fault between the variants and the decider of $X$ | execution},
- $q_{S,D,X} = P$ {detected failure of $X$ | execution},
- $q_{S,U,X} = P$ {undetected failure of $X$ | execution},
- $q_{S,X} = q_{S,D,X} + q_{S,U,X} = P$ {failure of $X$ | execution}.

The table of Fig. 8 summarizes the obtained probabilities of failure and discriminates them with respect to both separate/common-mode and detected/undetected viewpoints.

| Architecture X/1/1 | Probability of Failure: $q_{S,X} = q_{S,D,X} + q_{S,U,X}$ | |
| --- | --- | --- |
| | Prob. of Detected Failure: $q_{S,D,X}$ | Prob. of Undet. Failure: $q_{S,U,X}$ |
| RB/1/1 | Separate: $(q_{I,RB})^2$ + <br> Common-mode: $q_{ID,RB} + q_{2V,RB}$ | Common-mode: $q_{RVD,RB}$ |
| NSCP/1/1 | Separate: $4 (q_{I,NSCP})^2 [1 - q_{I,NSCP} + \frac{(q_{I,NSCP})^2}{4}]$ <br> Common-mode: $q_{ID,NSCP} + 4 q_{2V,NSCP}$ | Common-mode: $q_{2V,NSCP} + 4 q_{3V,NSCP}$ <br> $+ q_{4V,NSCP} + q_{RVD,NSCP}$ |
| NVP/1/1 | Separate: $3 (q_{I,NVP})^2 [1 - \frac{2}{3} q_{I,NVP}] +$ <br> Common-mode: $q_{ID,NVP}$ | Common-mode: $3 q_{2V,NVP} + q_{3V,NVP}$ <br> $+ q_{RVD,NVP}$ |

**Fig. 8.** Probabilities of Failures

As could be expected, the table shows that, although the detected failures may correspond to either separate failures or common mode failures, the undetected failures correspond only to common mode failures.

The comparison of the various failure probabilities is difficult due to the difference in the values of the parameters characterizing each architecture. However, it is possible to make some interesting general remarks.

Although a large number of experiments have been carried out to analyze NVP, no *quantitative* study has been reported on the reliability associated to the decider. However, it has to be noted that the probabilities associated with the deciders can be significantly different. Due to the generic character and the simplicity of the functions performed by the deciders of the NSCP (comparison) and NVP (voting) architectures, it is likely that these probabilities are ranked as follows:

$$q_{ID,NSCP} \le q_{ID,NVP} \ll q_{ID,RB} \text{ and } q_{RVD,NSCP} \le q_{RVD,NVP} \ll q_{RVD,RB}$$

In the case of separate failures, the influence of the activation of independent faults differs significantly: for RB, the probability of separate failure is equal to the square of the probability of activation of independent faults, whereas it is almost triple for NVP and quadruple for NSCP. This difference results from the number of variants and the type of decision used. However, it does not mean that RB and NSCP are the only architectures that enable some related-fault combinations between the variants to be detected. All related faults in NVP result in undetected failures (it is worth noting that such a singularity is due to the limitation to the analysis of software redundancy for tolerating one fault; increasing the number of versions would also enable some related faults to be detected as pointed out in section 2).

Related faults between the variants have no impact on the probability of undetected failure of the RB architecture, whereas it is the major contribution for NSCP and

NVP. However, the comparison of the respective probabilities of undetected failures is not an easy task.

## 4.2    Evaluation of Hardware and Software Architectures

**Modeling Assumptions.** In order to model the behavior of the architectures the following is assumed:

- only one type of fault(s) can be activated at each execution and produce error(s), either hardware or software,
- after detection and recovery of an error, the variant is not discarded and at the next step it is supplied with the new input data, i.e. software faults are considered to be soft faults,
- constant failure rates are considered for the hardware components and the software-fault tolerant architectures.

**Models.** The hardware and software behavior for the RB/1/1, NSCP/1/1 and the NVP/1/1 architectures can be described as indicated by the generic model shown on Fig. 9-a. The table of Fig. 9-b gives the specific definitions for states $S_j$ and transitions $T_{jk}$ of the model; the expressions of the rates associated to the transitions of the model are based on the following notation:

- c is the hardware coverage factor of the RB/1/1 architecture, $\bar{c} = 1 - c$,
- $\lambda_{H,X}$ denotes the failure rate for a hardware component of the architecture X/1/1, $X \in \{RB, NSCP, NVP\}$,
- $\lambda_{S,D,X}$ and $\lambda_{S,U,X}$ denote respectively the detected and undetected failure rates for the fault-tolerant software X, $X \in \{RB, NSCP, NVP\}$; if $\gamma$ denotes the application software activation rate, then these failure rates can be expressed as functions of the failure probabilities given in Fig. 8 as:

$$\lambda_{S,D,X} = [ q_{S,D,X} ] \gamma \text{ and } \lambda_{S,U,X} = [ q_{S,U,X} ] \gamma$$

- $\lambda_{S,D,2V}$ and $\lambda_{S,U,2V}$ denotes respectively the application software detected and undetected failure rates of the NSCP/1/1 and NVP/1/1 architectures, after an HECA has been made passive; these rates are defined as:

$$\lambda_{S,D,2V} = [ q_{S,D,2V} ] \gamma \text{ and } \lambda_{S,U,2V} = [ q_{S,U,2V} ] \gamma$$

where the detected and undetected failure probabilities of the degraded 2V configuration are defined by:

$$q_{S,D,2V} = 2 q_{I,2V} (1 - \frac{q_I}{2V,2}) + q_{ID,2V} \text{ and } q_{S,U,2V} = q_{RVD,2V}$$

For the RB/1/1 architecture, it should be noted that a hardware failure does not alter the software fault tolerance capabilities and vice versa. It is assumed that a near-perfect detection coverage can be achieved for hardware faults since both HECAs run the same variant simultaneously. Thus, the coverage considered here for the hardware-fault tolerance mechanisms corresponds to a localization coverage due to (i) the diagnosis program and (ii) the capacity of the acceptance test to identify hardware failures.

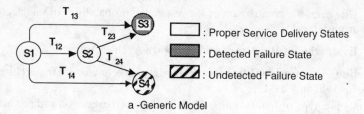

a -Generic Model

| States and Transitions | RB/1/1 | NSCP/1/1 | NVP/1/1 |
|---|---|---|---|
| $S_1$ | 2 (RB + Hardware Component) Operational | 2 (2 (Variant + Hardware Component)) Operational | 3 (Variant + Hardware Component)) Operational |
| $S_2$ | (RB + Hardware Component) Operational | 2 (Variant + Hardware Component) Operational | 2 (Variant + Hardware Component) Operational |
| $S_3$ and $S_4$ | Detected and Undetected Failures | | |
| $T_{12}$ | Covered Hardware Component Failure: $2c\ \lambda_{H,RB}$ | Hardware Component Failure: $4\ \lambda_{H,NSCP}$ | Hardware Component Failure: $3\ \lambda_{H,NVP}$ |
| $T_{13}$ | Non-Covered Hardware Component Failure or Detected RB Failure: $2\ \bar{c}\ \lambda_{H,RB}\ +\ \lambda_{S,D,RB}$ | Detected NSCP Failure: $\lambda_{S,D,NSCP}$ | Detected NVP Failure: $\lambda_{S,D,NVP}$ |
| $T_{14}$ | Undetected RB Failure: $\lambda_{S,U,RB}$ | Undetected NSCP Failure: $\lambda_{S,U,NSCP}$ | Undetected NVP Failure: $\lambda_{S,U,NVP}$ |
| $T_{23}$ | Covered Hardware Component Failure or Detected RB Failure: $c\ \lambda_{H,RB}\ +\ \lambda_{S,D,RB}$ | Hardware Component Failure or Detected 2Variant Failure: $2\ \lambda_{H,NSCP}\ +\ \lambda_{S,D,2V}$ | Hardware Component Failure or Detected 2Variant Failure: $2\ \lambda_{H,NVP}\ +\ \lambda_{S,D,2V}$ |
| $T_{24}$ | Non-Covered Hardware Component Failure or Undetected RB Failure: $\bar{c}\ \lambda_{H,RB}\ +\ \lambda_{S,U,RB}$ | Undetected 2 Variant Failure: $\lambda_{S,U,2V}$ | Undetected 2 Variant Failure: $\lambda_{S,U,2V}$ |

b - Specific State and Transition Definitions

Fig. 9.  Architecture Behavior

In the case of the NSCP/1/1 architecture, hardware and software fault tolerance techniques are not independent since the HECAs and the SECAs match. After the failure of a hardware component, the corresponding HECA (and hence, SECA) is discarded; the remaining architecture is composed of a pair of hardware components and a two-version software architecture that form a hardware- and software-fault self-checking architecture.

In the case of the NVP/1/1 architecture, again, hardware and software fault tolerance techniques are not independent: after a hardware unit has been made passive, the remaining architecture is analogous to the degraded architecture of the NSCP/1/1 architecture.

For both NSCP/1/1 and NVP/1/1 architectures, hardware faults are tolerated at the software layer through the decision algorithm (comparison or vote); accordingly, the associated coverage will be accounted for at the software level only and thus incorporated in the probability of activation of a fault in the decider.

In the degraded architectures obtained from NSCP/1/1 and NVP/1/1 after failure of a hardware component, the software is no longer fault-tolerant and thus the failure rates of the variants are of significant importance in the failure rate of the degraded configuration of the application software.

**Model Processing.** Processing models of Fig. 9-a, when accounting for the different transition rates of Fig. 9-b, enables one to derive the expressions for the time-dependent probabilities of detected failure and undetected failure of the considered hardware-and-software fault-tolerant architectures: $Q_{D,X}(t)$ and $Q_{U,X}(t)$, respectively, $X \in \{$ RB, NSCP, NVP $\}$. In practice, two types of probabilities are of interest:

- the reliability, $R_X(t) = Q_{D,X}(t) + Q_{U,X}(t)$,
- the probability of undetected failure, $Q_{U,X}(t)$.

For missions of short duration with respect to the mean times to failure, these expressions can be simplified to the following approximate expressions:

$$R_{RB}(t) \approx 1 - (2 \; \overline{c;} \; \lambda_{H,RB} + \lambda_{S,RB}) t \qquad Q_{U,RB}(t) \approx \lambda_{S,U,RB} \, t$$

$$R_{NSCP}(t) \approx 1 - \lambda_{S,NSCP} \, t \qquad Q_{U,NSCP}(t) \approx \lambda_{S,U,NSCP} \, t$$

$$R_{NVP}(t) \approx 1 - \lambda_{S,NVP} \, t \qquad Q_{U,NVP}(t) \approx \lambda_{S,U,NVP} \, t$$

These expressions show that – as could be expected – the reliability of the RB/1/1 architecture is strongly dependent on the coverage of the fault diagnosis in the hardware components. Furthermore, it is likely that the hardware component failure rate will be greater for the RB/1/1 architecture than for the other ones, due to the extra memory needed to store the second variant; also further hardware and/or software resources would be needed to perform the comparison among the results provided by each hardware processor so as to ensure a near-perfect detection coverage and storage would be needed for the acceptance test and the diagnosis program.

The expressions also reveal an identical influence of the failure rate of the application software for the three architectures. However, this has to be tempered by the differences between the associated probabilities identified in section 4.1.

## 5    Conclusions

What has been presented in this paper contributes to the field of fault tolerance in at least the following aspects:

1) The identification of N self-checking programming as a significant fault tolerance scheme with some important and interesting differences, compared to recovery blocks and N-version programming.

2) The integration of the topics of hardware and software fault tolerance, and the detailed analysis of the effectiveness of various architectures involving the above three fault tolerance schemes.

3) The modelling and evaluation of the dependability.

From a wider perspective, the emergence of hardware-fault tolerant commercial systems will increase the influence of design faults on the service delivered by computing systems to their users. As a foreseeable consequence, software fault tolerance aimed at providing service continuity to each system user, so calling for design diversity (as opposed to the software fault tolerance currently implemented in such systems, aimed at preserving the system core integrity through the abortion of erroneous tasks [53], is likely to spread out from its currently typical domain, i.e. safety-related systems. Accordingly the approaches and results presented in this paper are thus likely to be of a wider field of application.

## Acknowledgements

The authors want to acknowledge the highly useful comments received from the referees, the contribution by Tom Anderson (University of Newcastle upon Tyne) when discussing the recoverability issues, and the contribution of Catherine Hourtolle (now with CNES, the French Organization for Space) to the previous version of this paper.

# Failure Mode Assumptions and Assumption Coverage*

David Powell

LAAS-CNRS

**Abstract.** A method is proposed for the formal analysis of failure mode assumptions and for the evaluation of the dependability of systems whose design correctness is conditioned on the validity of such assumptions. Formal definitions are given for the types of errors that can affect items of service delivered by a system or component. Failure mode assumptions are then formalized as assertions on the types of errors that a component may induce in its enclosing system. The concept of assumption coverage is introduced to relate the notion of partially-ordered assumption assertions to the quantification of system dependability. Assumption coverage is shown to be extremely important in systems requiring very high dependability. It is also shown that the need to increase system redundancy to accommodate more severe modes of component failure can sometimes result in a decrease in dependability.

## 1    Introduction and Overview

The definition of assumptions about the types of faults, the rate at which components fail and how they may fail is an essential step in the design of a fault-tolerant system. The assumed *type* or nature of faults (see chapter I) dictates the type of redundancy that must be implemented within the system (e.g., space or time, replication or diversification,...). Similarly, the assumed *rates* of component failure influence the amount of redundancy needed to attain a given dependability objective. This paper is concerned with assumptions about *how* components fail — i.e., the components' failure modes — *independently of the actual cause or rate of failure*. Assumptions about component failure modes influence both the design and the degree of redundancy of a system's fault-tolerance mechanisms. For example, it is well-known that the tolerance of $k$ faults leading to stopping or "crash" failures [38] requires a redundancy of $k+1$ whereas the tolerance of $k$ faults leading to so-called "Byzantine" failures requires a redundancy of $3k+1$ [85].

A supposedly fault-tolerant system may fail if any of the assumptions on which its design is based should prove to be false. Indeed, when evaluating the lower bound of the dependability achieved by the system, it must be assumed that the system *will* fail if any assumption made during the system design is violated during system operation. At first sight, this observation favors a design approach based on "worst-case" assumptions since such assumptions are less likely to be violated in the real system. However, as illustrated by the example of "crash" versus "Byzantine" failures given above, when component failure modes become increasingly "arbitrary", the degree of redundancy required to ensure correct error processing must often be increased. Increasing the degree of redundancy not only raises the cost of the system, it also leads to an increase in the possible sources of failure — giving rise to a potential *de-*

---

\*   This is a revised version of [117].

*crease* in dependability. The designer of a fault-tolerant system is thus faced with the dilemma that although conservative failure mode assumptions are more likely to be true during system operation, the resulting increase in minimum redundancy necessary to enable a proof of correctness of the fault-tolerance mechanisms can lead to an overall decrease in system dependability.

The aim of this paper is to investigate this paradox by establishing a method for formally analyzing the failure mode assumptions on which the designs of fault-tolerant systems are based and for the evaluation of the dependability of systems whose design correctness is conditioned on the validity of such assumptions. The paper is organized as follows.

Section 2 introduces first a model of the service delivered by a system (or a component[1]) to a single user. This model specifies the service as the sequence of value-time tuples of service items that would be perceived by an *omniscient observer* of that service. Formal definitions are then given of various ways in which *individual* service items can be erroneous in the value and time domains. The service model is then augmented to embrace the case of a (single) service delivered to multiple users. Section 3 builds on the definitions of section 2 in order to give formal definitions of the *failure modes* of a system. A failure mode is defined in terms of an assertion on the *sequence* of value-time tuples that a failed or failing system is assumed to deliver. The definitions given in sections 2 and 3 are an extension, and an attempted unification, of concepts set forth by other authors, in particular, those presented in [38, 48, 49, 28, 86]

The formalism used for the failure mode assertions of section 3 allows them to be partially ordered by means of an "implication graph". Each path through this graph represents an ordered set of increasingly weaker assertions on system behavior or, equivalently, increasingly severe modes of failure. In terms of fault-tolerant system design, the existence of such orders on the failure modes that can be assumed for the system's components is of very practical significance. First, it enables the design of *families* of fault-tolerance algorithms that can accommodate failure modes of increasing severity. Second, it provides a framework for the analysis of the effect of failure mode assumptions on system dependability. The likelihood of a particular failure mode assertion being true in the real system can be formalized by the *assumption coverage* concept presented in section 4. The coverage of a failure mode assumption is defined as the probability that the assertion that formalizes the assumption is true, conditioned on the fact that the component has failed. In terms of the failure mode implication graph, if assertion $X$ implies assertion $Y$, then — *for a given component* — the coverage of the failure mode assumption embodied by assertion $Y$ must be greater than that embodied by $X$ since $Y$ is a weaker assertion than $X$. The directed edges of the implication graph therefore portray increasing assumption coverage.

Section 5 illustrates the effect of failure mode assumptions on system dependability by means of a case study. It is shown that, depending on the coverage of the failure mode assumptions, weaker assertions on component failure modes do not necessarily

---

[1]  Using the recursive definition of chapter I, a *system* is a set of interacting components and a *component* may be considered as another system. The *service* delivered by a system is its behavior as perceived by the system user - the *user* of a system can be viewed as another system (human or physical) interacting with the former.

lead to higher system dependability; in particular, it shows that the weakest design assumption of all — that of arbitrary failures — is not always the best decision for the design of predictably dependable systems.

## 2    Types of Errors

This section first introduces a model of system service delivered to a *single* user in terms of the sequence of service items that would be perceived by an *omniscient observer* of that service. Formal definitions are then given of various ways in which a *specified* service item can be incorrect in the value and time domains. The set of definitions is then extended to include the case of unspecified or *impromptu* service items that are spontaneously generated by a failed system. An extension of the service model for the case of a service delivered to *multiple* users is then considered.

### 2.1    Single-user Service

**Service Model.** The service delivered by a system with a single user can be defined in terms of a sequence of service items, $s_i$, $i = 1, 2, \ldots$ each characterized by a tuple $\langle vs_i, ts_i \rangle$ where $vs_i$ is the value or content of service item $s_i$ and $ts_i$ is the time[2] or instant of observation of service item $s_i$.

To define what is a *correct* service item (and from there, what are the different possible sorts of *incorrect* service items), an *omniscient observer* is considered that has complete knowledge of the specified sequence of service items that the system should deliver. For each observed service item, the omniscient observer can decide (i) whether the observed service item was indeed specified and (ii) whether its value and time are correct. The omniscient observer can base both decisions (i) and (ii) on a value-time domain specification for each service item $s_i$:

**Def. 1.** Service item $s_i$ is *correct* iff: $(vs_i \in SV_i) \wedge (ts_i \in ST_i)$ where $SV_i$ and $ST_i$ are respectively the specified sets of values and times for service item $s_i$.    ❑

Generally, $SV_i$ and $ST_i$ will be *functions* of the (history of) inputs to the system. However, the definitions given here do not need to refer to the system's inputs.

For many systems, the specified value and time sets are reduced to the special cases $SV_i = \{sv_i\}$ (a single value) and $ST_i = [st_{\min}(i), st_{\max}(i)]$ (a single time interval). Examples of systems where the general case must be considered are: for multiple value sets, one variant of a set of diverse-design software systems and, for multiple time period sets, a system accessing a shared channel by some time-slot mechanism.

A *real* (non-omniscient) observer may not (and usually, does not) have *a priori* knowledge of the specified value-time sets for each service item. Thus, in order for a real observer to detect whether a particular service item is correct in value and time, it must derive the *expected* value-time domains from some other information in its possession. For instance, the "correct" value domain $SV_i$ for a particular service item $s_i$

---

2    "Time" may be measured in seconds, clock ticks, instruction cycles,...; for simplicity, time may be interpreted here as meaning absolute time, although it could equally well be measured with respect to some reference instant.

could be obtained as a function (e.g., a majority vote) of the values of reference service items delivered by a set of similar (redundant) systems. Similarly, the "correct" time domain for a particular service item could be obtained from knowledge of the admissible delay between some reference event and the instant of delivery of the given service item; the reference event could be the delivery of an input to the system, the delivery of a previous service item from the same system or the delivery of one or more service items from other redundant systems. Such practicalities are not of interest when defining — in an absolute manner — what is and what isn't a correct service item. However, they *are* of interest in a practical system when reasoning about the way by which incorrect service items will be perceived (if at all).

**Errors in a Single-user Service.** A system fails whenever any service item is *incorrect*. In the overall service (the *sequence* of service items) delivered by a system, the relationship between various incorrect and correct items of delivered service is captured by the system's *failure mode*. Before defining more formally (in section 3) what is meant by such failure mode assumptions, we shall first consider how *individual* service items can be incorrect. We consider the viewpoint of an enclosing system wherein incorrect service items from a failed component will be perceived as *errors*. According to the definition of a correct service item (cf. definition 1), a distinction can be made between *value errors* and *timing errors*.

*Value errors.* The definition of a value error is immediately deduced as the corollary of definition 1. The adjective "arbitrary" underlines the fact that the general definition places absolutely no restriction on the erroneous value:

**Def. 2.** *Arbitrary value error:* $s_i$ : $vs_i \notin SV_i$                                    ❏

(The above definition reads: "given service item $s_i$, the value of $s_i$ (noted $vs_i$) does not fall within the set of values specified for $s_i$ (noted $SV_i$)".)

The values of individual service items are often restricted to a sub-set of the universe of values either by some specified syntax for values (e.g., a dictionary of valid symbols) or a range of "reasonable" values. The classic notions of the *theory of error-detecting codes* can thus be taken in a broad sense whereby the set of values that obey a given syntax, or which pass an "acceptance" test, define by extension a set of code values $CV$, $(CV \supseteq SV_i)$. Whenever such a "code" exists, it is therefore possible to define a sub-set of value errors called *noncode* value errors:

**Def. 3.** *Noncode value error:*  $s_i$ : $vs_i \notin CV$ where $CV$ defines a code.          ❏

Other authors (e.g., [49]) define the notion of a "null-value" error that is similar in spirit to the above definition of a noncode value error. Whenever the value of a service item is detectably incorrect by simple inspection (i.e., when it does not respect the "code"), an observer can choose to ignore the value or treat it *as if* it was "null". However, in pursuit of precision, the term "noncode value error" is preferred here since there may be several such noncode values and not just one single "null" value.

In [28] a distinction is made between the set of "legal outputs" (legal values) over *all* possible service items delivered by a system and the set of "coarse incorrect outputs" ("unreasonable" values) for a *particular* service item. The latter notion effectively defines a code that is specific to the particular service item based on the knowledge, for example, of previous service items or previous inputs to the system. This distinction is not made here — the important concept behind the notion of noncode values is that they are *detectable* as errors by simple inspection of the value of the service item — irrespectively of how the actual "code" is established.

*Timing errors.* A timing error is also defined from the corollary of definition 1. An (arbitrary) timing error occurs whenever a service item is delivered outside its specified set of times (this includes the case in which a service item is not delivered at all):

**Def. 4.** *Arbitrary timing error:*  $s_i$ : $ts_i \notin ST_i$                                    ❏

Since occurrences in the time domain can, by definition, be ordered, it is possible to distinguish the following classic sub-types for timing errors (e.g., [38]):

**Def. 5.** *Early timing error:* $s_i$ : $ts_i < \min(ST_i)$                              ❏

**Def. 6.** *Late timing error (or performance error):* $s_i$ : $ts_i > \max(ST_i)$        ❏

**Def. 7.** *Infinitely late timing error* or *omission error:* $s_i$ : $ts_i = \infty$         ❏

An omission error is defined here as a service item that is never delivered, i.e., from the omniscient observer's viewpoint, a service item that is "observed" at time infinity. In [48], an omission is defined as being *either* infinitely late timing *or* a "null-value" (i.e., a noncode value that is "ignored"). This viewpoint is valid when the "path" over which service items are delivered to the user is a dedicated one. However, if this path is shared with other systems and users, the unification of infinitely late timing and ignored noncode values as an "omission" is no longer appropriate. For instance, if the service items under consideration are messages over a bus, there is a fundamental difference between no message being sent and a noncode message being sent. In the former case, the bus remains "free" for another transmission whereas in the second case, the bus is "occupied" (albeit by an incomprehensible and therefore useless message) and is therefore not available for use by other systems.

*Impromptu errors.* Value errors and timing errors were defined above in terms of deviations of the values and times of a *specified* service item. Failure also occurs when a system spontaneously delivers a service item that was *not* specified — such unspecified service items can be termed *impromptu* errors. Since the correct value and time domains of any service item $s_i$ are given by the set tuple $\langle SV_i, ST_i \rangle$ then an *unspecified* service item $s_i$ is one for which $SV_i$ and $ST_i$ are undefined (noted " $\perp$ "):

**Def. 8.** *Impromptu error:* $s_i$ : $(vs_i = \perp) \wedge (ts_i = \perp)$                      ❏

If the actual value and time of an impromptu service item are considered, then, since the admissible value and time sets are undefined, then *a fortiori*:

$$s_i : (vs_i \notin SV_i) \wedge (ts_i \notin ST_i)$$

i.e., an impromptu service item is arbitrarily erroneous in both value and time.

From a practical viewpoint, a *real* observer could detect an impromptu error as *either* a value error *or* a timing error, depending on the particular error detection scheme that is used. A real observer (error detection mechanism) would declare an impromptu error to be a value error if it had deduced a value domain $SV_j$ and a time domain $ST_j$ for an expected service item $s_j$ and the impromptu service item $s_i$ falls within $ST_j$ but with $vs_i \notin SV_j$. Similarly, an impromptu error would be declared as a timing error if the impromptu service item $s_i$ was delivered outside any time window in which a service item was expected.

## 2.2 Multiple-user Service

The service model is now extended to the case of a (single) service delivered to multiple users. In this case, the service is defined as a set of sequences of *replicated* service items. This extension allows the formal definition of the uniformity — or *consistency* — of value-time tuples across the replicated service items.

**Service Model.** The service delivered by a system to $n$ users is a sequence of $n$ "replicated" service items, $s_i = \{s_i(1), \ldots, s_i(n)\}$, $i = 1, 2, \ldots$ Each service item "replica" is characterized by a tuple $\langle vs_i(u), ts_i(u) \rangle$, where $vs_i(u)$ is the *value* of replica $s_i(u)$, and $ts_i(u)$ is the time or instant of observation of replica $s_i(u)$. A processor with a private unidirectional multidrop bus is a typical example of such a multiple-user system in which the "users" are the receiving entities on each drop.

In the case of a non-failed system, each user should perceive consistent sequences of replicated service items. In the value domain, this is captured by the constraint: $\forall u \in [1,n]$, $vs_i(u) = vs_i$, i.e., all perceived values are equal to some value $vs_i$. Furthermore, if the set of replicated service item values is to be correct then this value must be within the specified set of values for service item $s_i$, i.e., $vs_i \in SV_i$.

Since the different users of a multiple-user service are not generally co-located, the instants of delivery of the service items cannot be exactly the same; some other definition of consistency is necessary for the time domain. A definition of consistent instants of occurrence that would appear to be meaningful is that the difference between occurrences should be bounded (on a pair-by-pair basis), i.e., $\forall u, v \in [1,n]$, $|ts_i(u) - ts_i(v)| \leq \theta_{uv}$. Furthermore, if the set of service item times is to be correct, then each observed occurrence must lie within a set of times for service item $s_i$ specified for that user, i.e., $\forall u \in [1,n]$, $ts_i(u) \in ST_i(u)$.

The considerations discussed above lead to the following definition of correctness for a service item delivered to multiple users:

**Def. 9.** A replicated service item $s_i = \{s_i(1), \ldots, s_i(n)\}$ is defined to be *correct* iff:

$$\forall u, v \in [1,n], \left( \left( vs_i(u) = vs_i \right) \wedge \left( vs_i \in SV_i \right) \right) \wedge$$
$$\left( \left( |ts_i(u) - ts_i(v)| \leq \theta_{uv} \right) \wedge \left( ts_i(u) \in ST_i(u) \right) \right) \qquad \square$$

**Errors in a Multiple-user Service.** An error occurs in a multiple-user service whenever the assertion in definition 9 is negated. All the definitions of the previous section can be extended to the multiple-user situation by considering errors in individual replicas of a given service item.

However, it is the notion of *consistency* that introduces a new and important dimension to the definition of error types since it allows assertions regarding the *uniformity* of value-time tuples across replicated service items — independently of whether or not the values and times are correct. It is the presence or absence of this uniformity that determines whether or not fault-free multiple users of the service can themselves continue to provide consistent service.

A consistent error occurs in the *value domain* when the value of a replica of a service item is incorrect yet the value consistency condition is respected. If this should occur, then all the replicas of a given service item are identically incorrect:

**Def. 10.** *Consistent value error:*

$$s_i = \{s_i(1),\ldots,s_i(n)\} \; : \; \forall u \in [1,n], \; \left(vs_i(u) = vs_i\right) \wedge \left(vs_i \notin SV_i\right) \qquad \square$$

Similarly, a consistent error in the *time domain* occurs when a replica of a given service item is delivered outside its specified set of times yet the overall time consistency condition is respected:

**Def. 11.** *Consistent timing error:*

$$s_i = \{s_i(1),\ldots,s_i(n)\} \; : \; \left(\exists u \in [1,n], \; ts_i(u) \notin ST_i(u)\right) \wedge$$
$$\left(\forall u,v \in [1,n], \; |ts_i(u) - ts_i(v)| \leq \theta_{uv}\right) \qquad \square$$

In the value domain, the notion of coded values allows the definition an interesting "semi-consistent" error scenario in which the values of *some* replicas of a service item are identically incorrect while the other replicas all have *noncode* values:

**Def. 12.** *Semi-consistent value error:*

$$s_i = \{s_i(1),\ldots,s_i(n)\} \; : \; \forall u \in [1,n], \; \left(\left(vs_i(u) = vs_i\right) \wedge \left(vs_i \notin SV_i\right)\right) \vee \left(vs_i \notin CV\right) \quad \square$$

Semi-consistent value errors can be observed in the practical case of a processor sending coded messages (e.g., with a CRC) over a multidrop bus. The receivers (the users of the service) may receive either incode *or* noncode messages; however, those receivers that receive *incode* messages, receive *identical* value messages. This is a lesser assumption than the atomicity implied by *consistent* value errors.

## 3    Failure Mode Assumptions

The previous section gave definitions of the ways by which *individual* service items can be correct or incorrect. In this section, we attempt to formalize the concept of an assumed *failure mode* by assertions on the (possibly infinite) sequence of service items delivered by a component. For simplicity, we restrict ourselves to the case of a single-user service and define first assertions that apply independently to the value and time domains. It should be noted, however, that the proposed set of assertions is given as an example; *many* meaningful sets of assertions could be defined.

### 3.1  Value Error Assertions

Assertions concerning the value of service items are noted $\mathcal{V}_X$ where $X$ denotes a particular assertion. Consider the following set of assertions regarding possible value errors produced by a component:

$\mathcal{V}_{none} := \forall i, \; vs_i \in SV_i \Rrightarrow$ *No value errors occur (every service item is of correct value).*

$\mathcal{V}_N := \forall i, \; \left(vs_i \in SV_i\right) \vee \left(vs_i \notin CV\right) \Rrightarrow$ *The only value errors that occur are noncode value errors (every service item value is either correct or noncode).*

$\mathcal{V}_{arb} := \forall i, \; \left(vs_i \in SV_i\right) \vee \left(vs_i \notin SV_i\right) \equiv true \Rrightarrow$ *Arbitrary value errors can occur.*

By inspection of the formal assertions, it can easily be seen that they may be represented as nodes of a simple oriented graph (fig. 1) in which an edge directed from node $X$ to node $Y$ means: assertion $X \Rightarrow Y$.

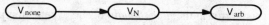

**Fig. 1.** Value error implication graph

## 3.2 Timing Error Assertions

Assertions concerning the timing of service items are noted $\mathcal{T}_X$ where $X$ denotes a particular assertion. Consider the following set of assertions regarding possible timing errors produced by a component:

$\mathcal{T}_{none} := \forall i, \; ts_i \in ST_i \Rrightarrow$ *No timing errors occur (every service item is delivered on time).*

$\mathcal{T}_O := \forall i, \; \left(ts_i \in ST_i\right) \vee \left(ts_i = \infty\right) \Rrightarrow$ *The only timing errors that occur are omission errors (every service item is delivered on time or not at all).*

$\mathcal{T}_L := \forall i, \; \left(ts_i \in ST_i\right) \vee \left(ts_i > \max\left(ST_i\right)\right) \Rrightarrow$ *The only timing errors that occur are late timing errors (every service item is delivered on time or too late)*

$\mathcal{T}_E := \forall i, \; \left(ts_i \in ST_i\right) \vee \left(ts_i < \min\left(ST_i\right)\right) \Rrightarrow$ *The only timing errors that occur are early timing errors (every service item is delivered on time or too early)*

$\mathcal{T}_{arb} := \forall i, \; \left(ts_i \in ST_i\right) \vee \left(ts_i \notin ST_i\right) \equiv true \Rrightarrow$ *Arbitrary timing errors can occur.*

All the assertions defined above effectively define component failure modes that, at the system level, denote *temporary* faults (either intermittent or transient faults). A further assertion of practical interest describes the situation in which a component delivers correctly timed service items up to a particular item and then ceases (omits) to deliver service items. This represents a failure mode that can be viewed at the system level as a *permanent* fault. We shall denote this as *permanent omission* or *crash* and the corresponding formalized assertion is:

$$\mathcal{T}_P := \forall i, \; \left(ts_i \in ST_i\right) \vee \left(\forall j \geq i, ts_j = \infty\right)$$

A weaker assertion of practical significance corresponds to the situation in which a component may omit to deliver some service items but, if more than $k$ contiguous items are omitted then all further items are omitted. In [165], the term *"bounded omission degree"* is used to characterize such an assumed behavior for a transmission channel. This assumption is formalized by the assertion:

$$\mathcal{T}_{B_k} := \forall i, \left(ts_i \in ST_i\right) \vee \left(\forall j \ge i, ts_j = \infty\right) \vee \left((ts_i = \infty) \wedge (\exists j \in [i+1, i+k]), \ ts_j \in ST_j\right)$$

The implication relationships between the various time domain error assertions defined above are represented by the graph of fig. 2.

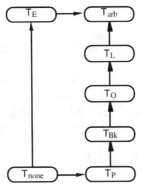

**Fig. 2.** Timing error implication graph

## 3.3 Failure Mode Assertions

The complete definition of a component failure mode entails an assertion on errors occurring in both the value and time domains. By taking the Cartesian product of the various definitions given in the two previous sections, 21 conjunctive assertions may be defined; the resulting implication graph is shown in Fig. 3.

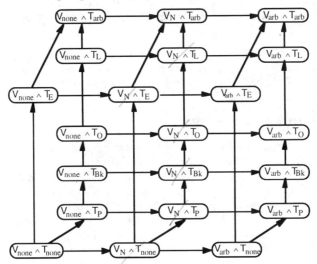

**Fig. 3.** Failure mode implication graph

The implication graph defines a partially-ordered set of assertions regarding the behavior of a component (the implications can be deduced from the formal definitions). The existence of such a partial order means that, if a system's fault-tolerance mechanisms will correctly process errors according to assertion $Y$, the same mechanisms will be able to process errors according to assertion $X$ if $X$ precedes $Y$ in the partial order. It is thus feasible to design *families* of fault-tolerance algorithms that can process errors of increasing severity [38, 48].

The source node of the implication graph $\mathcal{V}_{none} \wedge \mathcal{T}_{none}$ designates the strongest assumption that can be made about the behavior of a component, i.e., that the component never induces any errors in the enclosing system, neither in the value domain nor in the time domain.

At the opposite extreme, the sink node of the implication graph $\mathcal{V}_{arb} \wedge \mathcal{T}_{arb}$ defines the weakest "assumption" that can be made regarding component behavior, i.e., no assumption at all (the assertion $\mathcal{V}_{arb} \wedge \mathcal{T}_{arb}$ is always true). This means that the component may produce arbitrary errors in both the time and value domains (note that this also includes impromptu errors, cf. §2.1) — such a component may therefore be called a fail-uncontrolled component. It may even be imagined that the behavior of a fail-uncontrolled component is "malicious" in that the timing and the values of service items are malevolently calculated to cause havoc in the system; this viewpoint lies behind the original definition of "Byzantine behavior" [85].

Several other nodes in the implication graph are of very real practical significance. The assertion $\mathcal{V}_{none} \wedge \mathcal{T}_P$ defines the behavior of a fail-silent component [119], i.e., a perfectly self-checking component that, as soon as any fault within the component is activated, the component inhibits all outputs and ceases to provide service items (e.g., messages). From the viewpoint of the other components in the system, a fail-silent component either behaves correctly or remains permanently silent. Such a behavior is sometimes called "crash failure semantics" [38]and represents a sub-set of the properties of the various definitions of "fail-stop processors" [140, 142]. A weaker assertion (called weak fail-silence in [115] is represented by $\mathcal{V}_{none} \wedge \mathcal{T}_{B_k}$ in which a component may omit to deliver some service items but, if more than $k$ items are omitted, the component will remain forever silent. In both cases, the $\mathcal{V}_{none}$ part of the assertion implies that any service items that are delivered are service items with correct content. This has very important implications in the simplification of the design of a system's fault-tolerance mechanisms.

## 4    Assumption Coverage

The previous section established a set of failure mode assumptions that is partially-ordered due to the implications between the corresponding assertions — leading to failure modes producing errors of increasing "severity". This section introduces a new concept, called *assumption coverage* [114] that enables another interpretation of such partially-ordered assumptions. It establishes a link between an assumed component failure mode and the dependability of a fault-tolerant system whose design relies on that assumption. The importance of the concept is then illustrated in the next section by a case study.

If the fault-tolerance mechanisms of a system are designed with the assumption that any components that fail will do so according to a given failure mode assertion, then, if any component should fail in such a way that the assertion is violated, the system can fail. In fact, when assessing the dependability of the system, it is preferable to take the pessimistic view that the system *will* fail if a behavior assertion assumed during the system design is violated. In terms of quantitative assessment of dependability, the degree to which a component failure mode assumption proves to be true in the real system can be represented by the notion of the *coverage* of the assumption.

**Def. 13.** The failure mode *assumption coverage* $(p_X)$ is defined as the probability that the assertion $X$ defining the assumed behavior of a component proves to be true in practice conditioned on the fact that the component has failed:

$$p_X = \Pr\{X = true \,|\, \text{component failed}\} \qquad \Box$$

The partially-ordered set of assertions defined by an implication graph such as that on fig. 3 defines a set of possible modes of component failure that are of increasing severity. In terms of assumption coverage, the directed edges on the graph can be interpreted as indicating an increase in assumption coverage. Since the assumption of arbitrary timing/value errors $(\mathcal{V}_{arb} \wedge \mathcal{T}_{arb})$ is — by definition — true, its coverage is equal to 1. Any assumption of a more well-behaved failure mode can only have a coverage less than 1. The strongest assumption of all, that of a *failed* component causing no errors at all $(\mathcal{V}_{none} \wedge \mathcal{T}_{none})$, cannot possibly be true; its coverage is therefore 0. All intermediate assumptions thus have a coverage $p \in ]0,1[$ .

Note that the coverage of a given failure mode assumption is different from the coverage of the mechanisms of a fault-tolerant system designed to process errors that occur according to that assumption. The *overall coverage* of a given component failure is given by the product of the coverage of the error-processing mechanisms when errors occur according to a given component failure mode assumption and the coverage of that failure mode assumption, i.e.:

$$\Pr\{\text{correct error processing} \,|\, X = true\} \times \Pr\{X = true \,|\, \text{component failed}\}$$

In particular, although the coverage of an assumption of *arbitrary* timing/value errors is equal to 1, this does not mean that the coverage of the *mechanisms* of a fault-tolerant system designed to process such arbitrary errors is necessarily 1. However, it is presumed in the remainder of this paper that the mechanisms of a fault-tolerant system designed to process errors according to a particular failure mode assumption have been "proven" correct, such that the overall coverage is equal to the coverage of the corresponding assumption.

## 5    Influence of Assumption Coverage on System Dependability: a Case Study

The designer of a fault-tolerant system is faced with the dilemma that although conservative failure mode assumptions (i.e., more severe faulty behavior) will have a higher coverage, there is often an attendant increase in the redundancy that is necessary in order to enable a formal proof of correctness of the system's fault-tolerance mechanisms. This increase in redundancy can lead to an overall decrease in system dependability. This section is devoted to a simple case study that demonstrates that the designer's failure mode assumptions should be no weaker than those justifiable by the way that the components are implemented. If this is not the case, the dependability of the system may be less than what might have been achieved with stronger assumptions of less severe faulty component behavior.

## 5.1 System Definition

Consider a fault-tolerant architecture consisting of $n$ processors each connected to all other processors by a unidirectional multidrop message-passing bus. Each processor carries out the same computation steps and communicates the results of each processing step to all other processors. Each processor applies a decision function to the replicated results received from the other processors to mask errors and triggers other processing steps using the result of the decision function. Each processor must also communicate private information (e.g., local clock values, local sensor information, diagnosis views, etc.) to the other processors; the classical interactive consistency constraints must therefore be respected to ensure that non-faulty processors use such single-source information in a consistent way [85].

Each processor and its associated bus can be viewed as a single component or "fault containment domain" (for the purposes of this case study, we do not consider architectures with multiple types of fault containment domains, e.g., the "inter-stage" technique for interactive consistency [153]. Three possible failure mode assumptions for this composite "processor-bus" component are considered, each leading to a different assumption coverage and requiring a different degree of redundancy to ensure correct error processing in the presence of a given number of faulty components.

**Fail-silent Processor-bus.** If each message multicast over a processor's bus is accompanied by an error detection checksum then it is possible to assume that every processor that receives a message with a correct checksum receives the same message, i.e., transmission errors can only lead to semi-consistent value errors (cf. definition 12). If we further assume that any message sent by a processor is a correct message (an important property of the fail-silent processor assumption), then the corresponding assertion on the values of messages delivered by the composite processor-bus component is:

$$\mathcal{V}_{FS} = \forall i, \ \left( \forall u \in [1,n], \ \left( vs_i \in SV_i \right) \wedge \left( \left( vs_i(u) = vs_i \right) \vee \left( vs_i(u) \notin CV \right) \right) \right) \tag{1}$$

A fail-silent processor always produces messages on time or ceases to produce messages (forever). Furthermore we assume that, as long as the multidrop bus is intact, it delivers messages to all processors with consistent fixed propagation delays and, if the bus fails, then messages are not delivered to any processor. The corresponding assertion on the timing of messages delivered by the composite processor-bus component is thus that of consistent, permanent omission:

$$\mathcal{T}_{FS} = \forall i, \ \left( \left( \forall j \geq i, \ \forall u \in [1,n], \ ts_j(u) = \infty \right) \vee \right.$$
$$\left. \left( \forall u,v \in [1,n], \ \left( ts_i(u) \in ST_i(u) \right) \wedge \left( |ts_i(u) - ts_i(v)| \leq \theta_{uv} \right) \right) \right) \tag{2}$$

Since any messages delivered with correct checksums are identical, and since any message sent by a fail-silent processor is a correct message, the decision function (in the presence of at most $k$ faults) consists of selecting any message sent from a group of $k+1$ actively replicated processing steps. Furthermore, with semi-consistent value errors, the necessary condition for interactive consistency with $k$ faulty components is $n \geq k+1$ [108]. We postulate that the (strong) assertion $\mathcal{T}_{FS}$ allows synchronization of replica execution with $n \geq k+1$ With this pair of value-time failure mode assertions, the system can be configured to be $k$-fault-tolerant by letting $n = k+1$. Such a $k$-fault-tolerant configuration will be noted $FS(k)$.

**Fail-consistent Processor-bus.** The failure mode assertions are now relaxed to allow faulty processors to send erroneous values. However, all messages transmitted are error-checked so that it is still possible to assert that only semi-consistent value errors may occur:

$$\mathcal{V}_{FC} = \forall i, \; \left( \forall u \in [1,n], \; \left( vs_i(u) = vs_i \right) \vee \left( vs_i(u) \notin CV \right) \right) \qquad (3)$$

Similarly, the time-domain error assertion is weakened to allow consistent timing errors other than consistent omission:

$$\mathcal{T}_{FC} = \forall i, \; \left( \forall u, v \in [1,n], \; \left( \left| ts_i(u) - ts_i(v) \right| \le \theta_{uv} \right) \right) \qquad (4)$$

Since any messages delivered with correct checksums are identical, then the necessary condition for interactive consistency with $k$ faulty components is again $n \ge k+1$. However, it is no longer possible to assume that messages with correct checksums are indeed correctly-valued messages (a faulty processor can send an incorrect value but with a correct checksum). The decision function in this case must therefore rely on some sort of majority vote function requiring $n \ge 2k+1$ to be able to mask $k$ faulty values. We postulate that the assertion $\mathcal{T}_{FC}$ allows synchronization of replica execution with $n \ge 2k+1$ With this pair of value-time failure mode assertions, the system can be configured to be $k$-fault-tolerant by letting $n = 2k+1$. Such a $k$-fault-tolerant configuration will be noted $FC(k)$.

**Fail-uncontrolled Processor-bus.** The value and time-domain assertions are now relaxed to include both arbitrary value errors and arbitrary timing errors, i.e.

$$\mathcal{V}_{FU} = \forall i, \; \left( \forall u \in [1,n], \; \left( vs_i(u) \in SV_i \right) \vee \left( vs_i(u) \notin SV_i \right) \right) \qquad (5)$$

$$\mathcal{T}_{FU} = \forall i, \; \left( \forall u \in [1,n], \; \left( ts_i(u) \in ST_i \right) \vee \left( ts_i(u) \notin ST_i \right) \right) \qquad (6)$$

which are both — by essence — identically true.

Since arbitrary value and timing errors can now occur, the interactive consistency constraint is now $n \ge 3k+1$ [85]. The condition for being able to vote on replicated computation ($n = 2k+1$) is therefore also fulfilled. With this pair of value-time failure mode assertions, the system can be configured to be $k$-fault-tolerant by letting $n = 3k+1$. Such a $k$-fault-tolerant configuration will be noted $FU(k)$.

**Implication Graph and Assumption Coverages.** By inspection of the expressions 1 through 6, the implications between the combined value/time assertions are:

$$\mathcal{V}_{FS} \wedge \mathcal{T}_{FS} \Rightarrow \mathcal{V}_{FC} \wedge \mathcal{T}_{FC} \Rightarrow \mathcal{V}_{FU} \wedge \mathcal{T}_{FU}$$

The coverages $p_{fs}, \; p_{fc}, p_{fu}$ of the corresponding assumptions are thus related by:

$$0 \le p_{fs} \le p_{fc} \le p_{fu} = 1$$

In practice, the coverage of a *system-level* assumption about a component's mode of failure can be determined from knowledge about the way by which the *component* has been implemented. For example, if only hardware faults are considered, the claim embodied in assumption $\mathcal{V}_{FS}$ can be supported by the use of self-checking hardware and the coverage of assumption $\mathcal{V}_{FS}$ can be taken to be bounded by the error-detection coverage that is achievable by such techniques. We will assume that our knowledge about the processor's self-checking mechanisms allows us to place an upper bound on assumption coverage $p_{fs}$ of say 0.99 or 0.999. Assumption $\mathcal{V}_{FC}$, however, is based on the use of message checksums (to ensure that value errors are semi-consistent) and such an error-detection technique is amenable to mathematical demonstration of quite high coverage levels (depending on the ratio of the number of bits in the checksum to the maximum number of bits per message). It would therefore seem reasonable to expect an assumption coverage $p_{fc}$ greater than about 0.9999.

## 5.2 Dependability Expressions

Markov models of the three architectures $FS(k)$, $FC(k)$ and $FU(k)$ have been established for $k=1$ and $k=2$ [116]. Due to space limitations, only the results obtained from the models are given here. The same failure rate $\lambda$ is used in all three architectures since identical processors are considered — the *only differences* among the architectures result from the different assumptions that are made as to *how* failures manifest themselves.

For the case of systems without maintenance, table 1 gives the expressions for the system reliability $R$ in function of the unit reliability $r = e^{-\lambda t}$.

**Table 1.** Reliability expressions (without maintenance)

| | |
|---|---|
| $FS(1)$ | $r^2 + 2r\, p_{fs}(1-r)$ |
| $FS(2)$ | $r^3 + 3r^2 p_{fs}(1-r) + 3r\, p_{fs}^2(1-r)^2$ |
| $FC(1)$ | $r^3 + 3r^2 p_{fc}(1-r)$ |
| $FC(2)$ | $r^5 + 5r^4 p_{fc}(1-r) + 10r^3 p_{fc}^2(1-r)^2$ |
| $FU(1)$ | $r^4 + 4r^3(1-r)$ |
| $FU(2)$ | $r^7 + 7r^6(1-r) + 21r^5(1-r)^2$ |

When systems with maintenance are considered, it is assumed that the repair time is exponentially distributed with rate $\mu$. Table 2 gives the expressions of the "equivalent failure rate" $\lambda_{eq}$ [113] for the single repairman case when $\lambda/\mu \ll 1$ (i.e., the mean time to repair is much smaller than the mean time to failure). The equivalent failure rate can be used to express the system reliability (with maintenance), $R' - e^{-\lambda_{eq}t}$ and the asymptotic system availability, $A = 1 - \lambda_{eq}/\mu$.

We shall now consider the various architectures in two different applications: (i) a life-critical application without maintenance, and (ii) a money-critical application with maintenance.

**Table 2.** Equivalent failure rate expressions (with maintenance such that $\lambda/\mu \ll 1$)

| | |
|---|---|
| **FS(1)** | $2\lambda\left[\left(1-p_{fs}\right)+p_{fs}\lambda/\mu\right]$ |
| **FS(2)** | $3\lambda\left[\left(1-p_{fs}\right)\left\{1+2\left(p_{fs}\lambda/\mu\right)\right\}+2\left(p_{fs}\lambda/\mu\right)^{2}\right]$ |
| **FC(1)** | $3\lambda\left[\left(1-p_{fc}\right)+2\left(p_{fc}\lambda/\mu\right)\right]$ |
| **FC(2)** | $5\lambda\left[\left(1-p_{fc}\right)\left\{1+4\left(p_{fc}\lambda/\mu\right)\right\}+12\left(p_{fc}\lambda/\mu\right)^{2}\right]$ |
| **FU(1)** | $12\lambda\left(\lambda/\mu\right)$ |
| **FU(2)** | $210\lambda\left(\lambda/\mu\right)^{2}$ |

## 5.3  A Life-critical Application

Consider a system reliability objective of $R \geq 1-10^{-9}$ over 10 hours (corresponding to a typical civil aviation requirement for a fly-by-wire flight control system) and consider that the reliability of a single processor is given by $r = e^{-\lambda t}$ with $1/\lambda = 5$ years. Fig. 4 gives the unreliability $UR = 1-R$ at 10 hours plotted as a function of assumption coverage $p$ for a non-redundant system (noted $NR$) and the 1- and 2-fault-tolerant configurations.

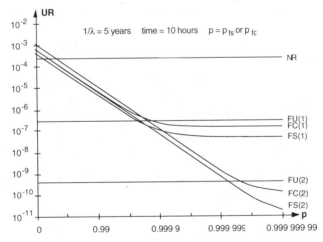

**Fig. 4.** Unreliability versus coverage (without maintenance)

It can be seen that configuration $FU(2)$ allows the $10^{-9}$ objective to be attained. However, configurations $FC(2)$ and $FS(2)$ also allow the objective to be attained *if* the coverage of the assumptions on which they are based is greater than 0.999999. Now, although this is not a reasonable value for $p_{fs}$, it does seem possible for $p_{fc}$ (cf. §5.1). In this case, the $FC(2)$ configuration with 5 processors can be considered a viable alternative to the $FU(2)$ configuration with 7 processors. If the coverage

$p_{fc}$ could be verified to be even higher, then fig. 4 shows that $FC(2)$ is better than $FU(2)$ even though worst-case (Byzantine) failures were not assumed in its design.

Careful inspection of fig. 4 also reveals that, for assumption coverages less than about 0.9995, configuration $FS(2)$ is less reliable than configuration $FS(1)$ although it is capable of tolerating two simultaneous faults instead of just one. The same is true for configuration $FC(2)$ with respect to $FC(1)$. This is an illustration of the well-known "point of diminishing returns" [157] that occurs with less-than-unity coverage — a degree of redundancy exists beyond which any further increase is detrimental to dependability.

Fig. 4 illustrates that, depending on the assumption coverage, the reliability achieved by solutions with restrictive failure mode assumptions can be higher than that in which less restrictive assumptions are made — including the 100% coverage case of assuming worst-case failure modes. Like the "diminishing returns" phenomenon mentioned above, this is due to the higher redundancy needed to process more complicated errors (leading to an increase in the possible sources of system failure).

## 5.4 A Money-critical Application

Consider now an application in which maintenance can be carried out and for which the dependability criterion is availability rather than reliability (for example, an electronic switching system). Fig. 5 gives the unavailability $UA = 1 - A$ plotted as a function of assumption coverage $p$ for the non-redundant system $NR$ and the 1- and 2-fault-tolerant configurations with $1/\lambda = 5$ years and $1/\mu = 1$ day.

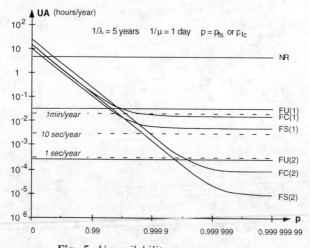

**Fig. 5.** Unavailability versus coverage

The curves on fig. 5 show that unavailability can be less than 6 minutes per year with the dual-redundant configuration $FS(1)$ (the cheapest fault-tolerant configuration) with an assumption coverage $p_{fs}$ of only 99% — which seems reasonable (cf. §5.1).

The QMR configuration $FU(1)$, tolerating the worst-case failure mode, achieves an unavailability of about 1 minute per year whereas the TMR configuration $FC(1)$, with an assumption coverage $p_{fc}$ of 0.9999, allows the yearly unavailability to be decreased to less than about 45 seconds per year. If even lower unavailability is required then a configuration tolerating two faults must be used. Note, however, that configuration $FC(2)$ enables a lower unavailability (less than 1/3 second per year) than configuration $FU(2)$ if the assumption coverage $p_{fc}$ is greater than about 0.99999 (such high figures may not be reasonable however for $p_{fs}$, cf. §5.1, so the theoretical best, $FS(2)$, may not a practical option).

Fig. 6 gives the unavailability of the various configurations as a function of mean repair time ($1/\mu$) when a particular set of (reasonable) values for $p_{fs}$ and $p_{fc}$ are taken, viz. $p_{fs} = 0.99$ and $p_{fc} = 0.9999$. The mean time between processor failures ($1/\lambda$) is again taken as equal to 5 years.

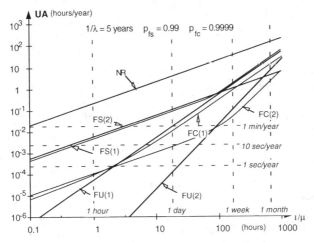

**Fig. 6.** Yearly unavailability versus repair time

Let us suppose now that the objective is to obtain an unavailability of less than 1 minute per year and consider three repair scenarios:

1) repair can be carried out, on average, within the *hour* (e.g., by personnel located on site); the most cost-effective configuration would be the dual-redundant configuration $FS(1)$ tolerating a single fault conditioned on it leading to a "silencing" failure mode (note again, that due to the diminishing returns phenomenon, the addition of an extra active spare, $FS(2)$, is in fact detrimental to availability),

2) repair can be carried out, on average, within a *day* (e.g., by personnel urgently dispatched to the site); the most cost effective solution would be a TMR system $FC(1)$ tolerating a single fault conditioned on it leading to a consistent failure mode,

3) repair can only be carried out, on average, within a *week*; there is no 1- or 2-fault-tolerant solution — however, the best possible solution (leading to an unavailability of about 3 minutes per year) would be the $FC(2)$ configuration (a 5

processor system tolerating 2 faults conditioned on them leading to a consistent failure mode); note that, even though configuration $FU(2)$ can tolerate two faults that lead to arbitrary failures, the long repair time considered here means that it is no longer the optimum solution.

# 6    Conclusions and Future Directions

This paper has attempted to provide a formalism for describing component failure modes in terms of the sequences and multiplicity of value and timing errors that a failed component may introduce into a system. The link between partially-ordered failure mode assertions and system dependability has been clarified by the notion of "assumption coverage". The importance of the latter has been underlined by means of a simple case study.

As stated in section 3, there are numerous possibilities for defining partially-ordered sets of value/timing error assertions and thus much scope remains for extension. In particular, the multiple-user error types defined in section §2.2, which include the important notion of consistency, introduce a new dimension to the definition of partially-ordered sets of failure modes that has not yet been fully explored.

A further extension of practical interest would be to include the concept of "fairness" that is necessary to prove the termination of protocols employing time-redundancy for ensuring delivery of messages over transmission channels that "lose" messages [122]. The assertion $V_{none} \wedge T_O$ (the "omission failure" semantics of [38]) does not portray a "fair" channel since it states that any *or all* service items may be omitted. On the contrary, a fair channel guarantees (with probability 1) that at least one item of an infinite sequence will be delivered.

Another area where further research would be useful is in the definition of necessary timing error assumptions in the design of fault-tolerant protocols. In section §5.1, we postulated that the timing assertions given in expressions (2) and (4) were sufficient to allow fault-tolerant synchronization with $k+1$ and $2k+1$ processors. Proof of these postulates (or similar) would be of interest.

Finally, it should be noted that the assumption coverage notion can be extended to any sort of assumption made during a system design (i.e., not just assumptions about component failure modes). For example, it could also be used to embrace assumptions about the peak-load submitted to a real-time system or about the independence of faults in redundant units.

# Acknowledgments

My particular thanks go to Jean-Claude Laprie with whom I have had many fruitful discussions that have helped no end in the clarification of the concepts set forth in this paper. I would also like to acknowledge the useful comments and ideas from discussion with or private communication from Tom Anderson, Jean Arlat, Paul Ezhilchelvan, Jack Goldberg, Brian Randell, Santosh Shrivastava, Luca Simoncini and Paulo Veríssimo.

# Rational Design of Multiple-Redundant Systems: Adjudication and Fault Treatment[*]

Andrea Bondavalli[1]  Silvano Chiaradonna[1]
Felicita Di Giandomenico[2]  Lorenzo Strigini[2]

[1] CNUCE-CNR  [2] IEI-CNR

**Abstract** - The design of fault-tolerant systems should ideally be based on rigorous predictions of the effects of design decisions on the achieved dependability. However, the complexity of the task is such that these decisions are typically based on ingrained, time-proven practice, without the benefit of thorough mathematical analysis. We analyse two specific problems in fault-tolerant design based on modular replication (with or without design diversity). First, we consider *adjudication*, i.e., the derivation of a single correct result from the multiple results produced by the replicas in a redundant component. Many designs have been proposed in the literature, supposed to improve upon simple majority voting, but without a unified, rigorous analysis to assist design choices. We describe such a general method for evaluating and comparing adjudicators, in probabilistic terms, and specify an *optimal adjudicator*, which yields the highest possible reliability for a redundant component, given the (probabilistic) failure characteristics of its subcomponents. Our analysis applies to components with and without a fail-safe mode. Second, we consider fault treatment: how the decision can be made to remove a replica of a component, considering it permanently failed, on the basis of its history of agreement/disagreement with other replicas. The problem is compounded by transient faults, which make it undesirable to disconnect a component at the first signs of errors, and by the use of dynamic error processing, in which the number of replicas executed depends on whether disagreements are observed. For this problem, we choose a scheme integrating dynamic error processing with diagnosis and disconnection of components that may be permanently failed, and show how its behaviour can be compared with alternative designs via simulation.

## 1    Introduction

One technique for making a system capable of tolerating faults is to build it with replicated hardware and/or software components. A *modular-redundant component* (MRC) is substituted instead of an ordinary component, and consists of a set of subcomponents (that we call *replicas*), each one implementing the same function as the whole component, plus some mechanism that, from the set of results produced by the replicas (*replica outputs*), obtains a single result (*adjudged output*) to be used as the output of the replicated component. It is convenient to depict this mechanism as an additional component called an *adjudicator* [5]. Adjudicators are usually based on a combination of majority voting (in one of the many forms possible) and self-checking by the replicas (*acceptance tests*). We consider a software-implemented MRC, where the replicas are software components (typically running on separate

---

[*] This paper is a compendium of [44] and [26].

processors). The replicas may be run in parallel, to minimise response time. As an alternative (*dynamic* error processing), one may run only enough replicas to detect possible errors (one replica, if it has sufficient self-checking capabilities), and additional replicas only if errors make it necessary.

In either case, the problem arises of *fault treatment*: if a replica becomes permanently faulty, keeping it in the redundant component increases the probability of having a majority of erroneous results at some future execution. It is desirable to be able to recognise and disconnect failed components; otherwise, a modular-redundant component may become, in the long run, less reliable than a non-redundant one based on one of its replicas. Fault treatment consists of disconnecting the failed (hardware or software) component, and either inserting a new component in its place, or carrying on the computation with decreased redundancy. *Diagnosis* is thus necessary. Luckily, the adjudication function provides useful diagnostic information, because it compares the results of the different replicas. However, this diagnosis is imperfect: first, faulty components do not necessarily produce erroneous results all the time. Second, many faults are *transient*: although they cause a replica to produce an erroneous result, and corrupt its internal state, the replica may recover a correct internal state and go back to behaving correctly. This behaviour appears in both hardware faults (e.g., caused by electromagnetic interference or *alpha* particles, which do not permanently damage the hardware affected) and software faults.

In short, although the concept of modular redundancy is straightforward, the design of modular-redundant components has many degrees of freedom, requiring many design decisions. Ideally, these decisions should be guided by a rigorous analysis of their expected consequences, so that the designer can then optimise the behaviour of the system for its specific requirements. This analysis is often difficult, and designers tend to adopt designs which have proven satisfactory in the past, or that appear to have some desirable characteristic, without full analysis. This is quite normal in engineering practice, as perfect prediction is impossible and detailed analyses may not be cost-effective. Nonetheless, it is often useful to analyse the design problem at least to fully understand the variables and trade-offs involved, and the analysis may then be applied to improving, if not optimising, the design. In this paper, we select two of the problems of designing modular-redundant components: adjudication and diagnosis (based on adjudication results, in the presence of transient faults), and perform an analysis susceptible of producing indications for design decisions.

In Section 2, we introduce the problem of designing adjudicators. In Section 3, we provide a systematic, probabilistic method for evaluating adjudicator designs, and show how an *optimal* adjudicator can be designed[1], which sets an upper bound on the reliability obtainable from an MRC, given the information input to the adjudicator; most of our results apply equally to hardware and to software redundancy. In Section 4, we extend these results to maximising utility functions different from reliability, and in particular to safety, and discuss practical application problems. In Section 5, we introduce a system with dynamic error treatment, and address the problem of diagnosis in the presence of transient faults. In Section 6, we describe a diagnostic algorithm and the trade-offs involved in tuning it to be more or less "pessimistic" in its diagnoses. Section 7 presents an instance of a hypothetical system and a

---

[1] This optimality result was originally presented independently in [44]and [25].

simulation comparing different combinations of error-processing and fault treatment strategies. Section 8 contains our conclusions.

## 2    The Adjudication Problem

A *modular-redundant component* (MRC) contains several *replicas* and an adjudication function, or adjudicator, implemented as one or more subcomponents. At each execution of the MRC, the adjudicator receives the outputs of the replicas and produces an output for the whole component. Outputs can be *normal outputs*, or *error signals*, indicating the detection of an internal error. The replicas are built to the same specification as the whole MRC, with the possible exception that the MRC may produce different error signals than the replicas (to signal different types of internal errors). Those replicas that are identical copies of a same component are said to belong to the same *variant*. In non-diverse redundancy, all replicas belong to the same variant.

The simplest adjudication function is *m-out-of-n majority voting*: if a certain result value is produced by at least m replicas out of the n constituting the MRC (usually n=2m-1, m=2,3,..), it is taken as the correct result. Sufficient conditions for this adjudicator to produce a correct output are: i) that no more than (n-m) replica outputs are erroneous; and ii) that all correct results are identical. Other adjudication functions have been used: e. g., selecting the *median* of the (numerical) replica outputs takes into account the possibility that replica outputs, for a given input, may be different and yet correct if contained within a specified interval [171, 97]. Different, correct results from different replicas may be due for instance to design diversity among the replicas, introduced to tolerate design faults [14, 167]; or to differences between the readings of replicated sensors, due to measurement error or non-simultaneous sampling.

A limitation with such simple adjudication functions is that they do not use all the information available about the trustworthiness of individual replica outputs: results of error detection mechanisms in the hardware, acceptance tests on results in the software, bounds (known to the designer) on the acceptable difference between correct results, etc. Using such additional information, an adjudicator could ideally obtain correct results under less restrictive fault hypotheses. For instance, replica outputs that are judged to be erroneous can be "filtered" out before the adjudged output is obtained from the remaining ones [5]. Examples of such two-step adjudication functions are found in [101, 145, 46, 97] and [100]. Other uses of additional information are shown in [46], where scores are assigned to each replica output; [66], where diagnostic information is used; and [84], where "ties" in a majority voter are resolved using a record of previous coincident failures for each pair of replicas. These refined designs attempt to correct perceived drawbacks of previous designs. Unfortunately, they are difficult to evaluate. The simpler schemes have at least the advantage that sufficient conditions (on the error situation) for the production of a correct adjudged result are easy to derive and use.

To clarify the issue of evaluating adjudicators, we may consider that an MRC is required to be more reliable than any of the replicas comprising it. It must produce correct results on a larger set of possible situations (including faults), where we will interpret "larger" as meaning "with a greater probability mass".

We ignore the details of how the system ensures that all the replicas receive consistent inputs, and that the adjudicator receives all the replica outputs. We assume that reliable watchdog timers detect replicas that are late, and feed the adjudicator error signals in place of their results. We thus isolate the problem of specifying the (combinatorial) adjudication function. We call *syndrome* the input to the adjudication function, consisting at least of the replica outputs, or some reduced set of information extracted from them. We shall consider as an example the (common) case in which the syndrome consists of the set of the n results of acceptance tests performed by the replicas on their own results (or other forms of self-checks by the replicas) and the set of the results of pairwise comparisons among the output values of all the replicas. We assume that the results of two replicas belonging to the same software variant, if correct, are identical (*deterministic* replicas), or, more generally, consistent according to a consistency relationship for which the transitive property holds. Each replica in the MRC performs an acceptance test on its own results, and signals any detected error to the adjudicator. As a further constraint, the adjudicator must choose as a result one of the replica outputs, or an error signal when it cannot extract an adjudged output with reasonable confidence.

To study the adjudication function for this example, let us consider Table 1, referring to an MRC with three replicas. Each row is a possible state of the MRC. The syndrome is what the adjudicator sees, and the "error state" is what the adjudicator must guess, i.e., which replicas are correct and which are erroneous. The output of the i-th replica is called $r_i$ and the result of the acceptance test on its result is called $T_i$ (i=1,2,3). $T_i=1$ means "accepted result". $r_{i,j}$ is the result of comparing the replica outputs $r_i$ and $r_j$, and $r_{i,j}=1$ means "$r_i$ and $r_j$ are in agreement". In the error state, $E_i=1$ means "$r_i$ is correct". The part of the table to the right of the double vertical line is the specification of the adjudicator: a table reporting, for each syndrome, the adjudged result. Different specifications have different values in the "adjudged result" column. Here, we have filled in some values on which presumably all designs would agree, and questions on more dubious cases. As the adjudicator only sees the syndrome, all the rows with the same syndrome must have identical values for the adjudged result. There are eight rows for each value of the syndrome, as each of the three replicas could be correct or erroneous (in Table 1, all the rows with the same syndrome are enclosed between thick horizontal lines). However, some of the rows describe impossible states and can be ignored in the specification. For instance, the first row marked "impossible" in Table 1 would have two correct replicas producing disagreeing results, which contradicts the assumed known behaviour of our replicas. Notwithstanding this simplification, the problem remains that a designer must specify only one adjudged result for each syndrome, while different error states are possible, though some of them may be improbable[2].

---

[2] Which error states are compatible with a syndrome is determined by the axioms of equality and by our assumption that correct results are consistent.

**Table 1.** The adjudication table (sorted by the values of the syndrome)

| Error state | | | Syndrome | | | | | | adjudged | |
|---|---|---|---|---|---|---|---|---|---|---|
| $E_1$ | $E_2$ | $E_3$ | $r_{1,2}$ | $r_{2,3}$ | $r_{3,1}$ | $T_1$ | $T_2$ | $T_3$ | result | *Notes* |
| 0 | 0 | 0 | 0 | 0 | 0 | 0 | 0 | 0 | error | |
| 0 | 0 | 1 | 0 | 0 | 0 | 0 | 0 | 0 | error | |
| .. | .. | .. | 0 | 0 | 0 | 0 | 0 | 0 | error | |
| 0 | 1 | 1 | 0 | 0 | 0 | 0 | 0 | 0 | impossible | |
| .. | .. | .. | 0 | 0 | 0 | 0 | 0 | 0 | error | |
| 0 | 0 | 0 | 0 | 0 | 0 | 0 | 0 | 1 | $r_3$ or error? | |
| .. | .. | .. | 0 | 0 | 0 | 0 | 0 | 1 | $r_3$ or error? | |
| .. | .. | .. | .. | .. | .. | .. | .. | .. | ....... | |
| .. | .. | .. | 1 | 0 | 0 | 1 | 0 | 1 | $r_1,r_2$,error? | |
| 0 | 0 | 0 | 1 | 0 | 0 | 1 | 0 | 1 | $r_1,r_2$,error? | *All wrong* |
| 0 | 0 | 1 | 1 | 0 | 0 | 1 | 0 | 1 | $r_1,r_2$,error? | $r_3$ *is correct* |
| 1 | 1 | 0 | 1 | 0 | 0 | 1 | 0 | 1 | $r_1,r_2$,error? | $r_1,r_2$ *are correct* |
| .. | .. | .. | 1 | 0 | 0 | 1 | 0 | 1 | $r_1,r_2$,error? | |
| .. | .. | .. | .. | .. | .. | .. | .. | .. | ....... | |
| .. | .. | .. | 1 | 0 | 0 | 1 | 1 | 0 | $r_1$ or $r_2$ | |
| .. | .. | .. | 1 | 0 | 0 | 1 | 1 | 0 | $r_1$ or $r_2$ | |
| .. | .. | .. | .. | .. | .. | .. | .. | .. | ....... | |
| .. | .. | .. | .. | .. | .. | .. | .. | .. | ....... | |
| | | | 1 | 1 | 1 | 1 | 1 | 1 | $r_1$, $r_2$ or $r_3$ | |

For some rows, the choice of an adjudged result is obvious, on the basis of natural probabilistic assumptions. For instance, we have marked some rows with the adjudged result "$r_1$ or $r_2$", because $r_1$ and $r_2$ form a majority, *and* their results pass their acceptance tests: they seem the least likely of the three results to be erroneous (they might be, though, maybe with low probability). But more ambiguous syndromes may occur, for instance in the rows marked "$r_1,r_2$,error?". Here, $r_1$ and $r_2$ form a majority (a hint that they are correct), but $r_2$ does not pass the acceptance test. Perhaps the acceptance test $T_2$ is erroneous and $r_1$ and $r_2$ are correct; if the acceptance test $T_2$ is correct, then $r_2$ (and $r_1$ as well) is erroneous, and the correct result, if any, is $r_3$; last, all three replica outputs could be erroneous: the adjudged output should be an error signal. To choose among these interpretations, that imply different adjudged outputs, we could use such considerations as:

- acceptance tests are often more trustworthy when judging a result erroneous than when passing it as correct (they check for necessary conditions for correctness). If this applies for this MRC, $T_2$ is stronger evidence than $T_1$ or $T_3$;

- if replicas 1 and 2 run on separate hardware modules and belong to diverse software variants, and many different output values are possible, the probability of their failing in identical ways is lower than it would be otherwise;
- if we have previous evidence of malfunctioning from replica 3, then we should not accept $r_3$ lightly;
- if the cost of producing an error signal as the adjudged output is low, maybe this is the best solution.

All rows with the same syndrome must have the same adjudged result, while the correct results may be different, depending on the values of the error state: so, *there is no adjudication function that can mask all conceivable error combinations*. Which result is correct for a given observed syndrome cannot be known *a priori*. However, probabilistic information is usually available. We shall show that this information can be used both for *evaluating* any given adjudication function and for building an *optimal adjudication function*.

## 3    Evaluation and Optimisation of Adjudication Functions

To choose between two candidate adjudication functions for a system, $A_i$ and $A_j$, some authors [46, 97] simply consider all the combinations of error states and syndromes and find the subsets, $C_i$ and $C_j$, in which the two adjudicators yield a correct result. If $C_i \subset C_j$, then $A_j$ is better than $A_i$. Unfortunately, given any adjudication function $A_i$, one can always build an $A_j$ such that none of the three conditions $C_i \subset C_j$, $C_j \subset C_i$, $C_i = C_j$ holds. A better criterion is based on the probabilities that the different adjudication functions produce a correct adjudged output (notice that we are still assuming perfectly reliable adjudicators; erroneous outputs from the MRC are only due to the fact that the adjudicator *cannot* always be right). This allows not only choices among alternative designs, but also absolute reliability assessment for the system employing the adjudicator. Let us define the *system state* as the set of variables (the syndrome plus the error state) that determine whether an adjudged output is correct. Let STATES be the set of all possible values for the system state, and STATES* $\subseteq$ STATES be the set of those states for which an adjudication function $A_k$ produces a correct output. Then, the probability that $A_k$ produces a correct adjudged output is:

$$P(A_k \text{ is correct}) = \sum_{x \in \text{STATES*}} P(x)$$

where $P(x)$ is the probability of occurrence of the system state x.

To use this equation, we could attach a probability to each row in Table 1. The total probability that an adjudication function produces a correct result, with the given system configuration and assigned probabilities, is found by selecting all the rows were the adjudged result is correct (that is, where, if the adjudged result is $r_i$, then $E_i=1$), and adding their probabilities.

We can use this evaluation criterion to define an *optimal adjudication function*. Stated informally, the best that can be done is to choose as the adjudged output a replica output which has the highest probability of being correct, given the observed syndrome. Referring to the example used in the previous section, for each given syndrome, one has to add the probabilities of all the rows with $E_1=1$, then of all those where $E_2=1$, and of all those where $E_3=1$, and set the adjudged result to be $r_1$, $r_2$, or $r_3$ depending on which sum is largest. We will consider later the possibility of generating an error signal instead of a normal output.

*An adjudication function that for any syndrome chooses that result which has the highest probability of being correct, conditional on the occurrence of that syndrome, is an optimal adjudication function,* i.e., it has the highest possible probability of producing a correct result for any input to a particular MRC. More precisely, if the adjudication function is to be a deterministic function of the syndrome only, then, once the information to be used as the syndrome has been chosen, our optimal adjudication function maximises the probability of a correct adjudged result on any individual invocation (from the distribution of invocations, i.e., of input values and error states, from which the probabilities of the system states - the rows of the adjudication table - are derived). This is a general result: it does not depend on which information constitutes the syndrome.

## 4   Extensions and Discussion

Our approach can be generalised if we consider that, for a given error state, different adjudged outputs yield different values of *utility* (or cost). The goal is still to optimise (the expected value of) this utility. The discussion this far can be seen as a special case in which correct adjudged results have utility 1, and erroneous ones have utility 0. An interesting special case is obtained considering an MRC which can choose to output, instead of one of the outputs of the replicas, a *fail-safe* error signal. Producing this signal causes a loss (e.g., non-optimal control), different from that caused by producing a normal, erroneous output (*unsafe* error). An adjudicator for this case can be specified starting from the adjudication table created above, and transforming it as follows. Let the three cost levels be: 0 for correct result, $C_s$ for fail-safe output, $C_f$ for unsafe error. For each syndrome, the following decision criterion applies. If $P_r$ is the probability that the adjudged result previously chosen for the syndrome is correct (conditional to the occurrence of that syndrome), this specified adjudged result must be changed to the fail-safe error signal if

$$1-P_r > C_s \, / \, C_f$$

> When the cost of the fail-safe output is equal to that of the unsafe error, the change is never worthwhile; when the cost of the unsafe error is so high that the condition is satisfied for all syndromes, the MRC is useless.

The main problem in applying these methods is of course estimating the probabilities of all the system states (under the usage conditions intended for the MRC). None of these probabilities can be known with certainty, which makes a certain degree of error unavoidable. This is *not* a limitation of our method: we have simply made explicit the probabilistic assumptions that are normally implicit in proposals of adjudication schemes. In practice, while the probabilities of the different states are difficult to predict (in particular in the design stage), failure statistics may be known, e.g., for the processors which execute the replicas. One can then try and derive the probabilities of error states, taking into account that an error by a replica may be caused by a hardware fault in its host and/or by a software fault in its variant, and using additional estimates of the probability of error conditional on these faults, on the joint probabilities of multiple faults and errors, and so on. Considering these additional details, of course, adds to the complexity of designing or evaluating an adjudicator (though not to the complexity of its operation). A software tool can be used to assist the procedure, in particular for sensitivity analysis.

An optimal adjudication function could have practical drawbacks (e.g., excessive computation time). However, it is still useful as a limiting case. The probability that an optimal adjudicator produces a correct result is an upper bound on the reliability of any MRC built with the given replicas and with a given choice of syndrome infomation. If it is insufficient, then a designer knows in advance that the MRC must be redesigned, e. g., using more reliable replicas, or providing additional relevant information to the adjudicator. In practice, the first assignments of probabilities may be rather tentative. However, our optimal adjudicator is specified as a look-up table (unlike most previously proposed adjudication algorithms), so that it can be recalibrated with information collected during the lifetime of the system. For instance, during a mission, the probabilities associated to different events can be reassigned based on observed symptoms. This is a formalised version of the "confidence voter" described in [84], or an extension of "self-purging redundancy" [98]: instead of disconnecting faulty components, one reduces the trust in components suspected of being faulty. In the longer term, the estimated reliability of a replica can be increased as it is observed to perform without failure, and decreased after catastrophic failures or new releases [90]. In particular, the adjudicator can be configured for arbitrarily asymmetric systems.

## 5    Diagnosis with Dynamic Error Processing: System Description and Fault Assumptions

We now move on to consider MRCs with dynamic error processing. Our MRCs are replicated application tasks in a multiprocessor system. An execution of an MRC now consists of running a minimum number of replicas, and then running more if these do not produce a result that appears trustworthy. For error-free executions, dynamic error processing saves resources and synchronisation overhead (improving both throughput and average response time) with respect to unconditionally executing all replicas. A simple dynamic design is a "2+1" scheme: two replicas are run at first, and if they disagree a third one is run, seeking a 2-out-of-3 majority. This can be seen as a special case of the SCOP scheme (see paper III.E in this volume). For simplicity's sake, we consider only hardware faults, and assume that the three replicas belong to the same variant and run on separate hardware units or lanes, "processors" for brevity. Each processor may suffer transient failures, which cause a replica to produce an erroneous result once, and permanent failures, after which every execution of a replica on that processor produces an error. As before, reliable watchdog timers detect timing failures and convert them into error signals to the adjudicator.

The diagnosis problem consists in deciding whether a processor, which produced results considered erroneous (minority results), is permanently failed, in which case it should be removed from the system. Replica errors due to transient faults, if detected, are always recovered completely, and we neglect the cost of this recovery action. There is a pool of enough processors for continuing the computation after the removal of one or more of them, and the removed processors are not replaced nor repaired. We are thus considering systems that are not maintained for the duration of a mission (avionics, remotely operated sites) or ever at all (space probes, satellites).

# 6    The Complete Fault Tolerance Strategy

## 6.1   Fault Treatment

Many different diagnosis strategies have been developed, appropriate for different application requirements and fault hypotheses. [120] presented the basic framework for system-level fault diagnosis (PMC model). In this model, processors in the system are able to test other processors by sending stimuli and analysing the responses. All this information (*syndrome*) is then collected by a reliable decision element that is able to decode it to obtain a diagnosis. This model was the starting point for much further research on system-level diagnosis [35, 102, 40, 130, 39, 173, 18]. A useful approach for systems with modular redundancy is to use, as a form of reciprocal testing between processors, the results of comparisons between application programs replicated on both processors [35]. [102] proposed to partition the system into subsystems to reduce the overhead due to diagnosis, at the price of reduced precision.

We do not consider the problem of distributed decoding of the syndrome (if two processors disagree, each one naturally "thinks" that the other one is faulty), but assume a reliable decision element which observes the results of adjudication and diagnoses which processors are permanently faulty. Our diagnosis model is inexpensive since it uses the work done by the error processing mechanism.

In our system, at each application task execution the error processing mechanism must select a result adjudged as the correct one. If this proves to be impossible, then the whole system fails. On this basis, we build the diagnostic mechanism as follows. For each not-yet-removed processor $u_i$, we keep memory of the history of (apparent) errors in a variable $\alpha_i$. $\alpha_i$ is initially set to 0. At each application task execution in which $u_i$ takes part, $\alpha_i$ is increased by a constant $H \geq 0$ if the result produced by $u_i$ disagrees with the adjudged result, and multiply it by another constant, $K$, $0 \leq K \leq 1$, if it agrees. When the value of $\alpha_i$ exceeds a pre-set threshold $\alpha'$, processor i is diagnosed as permanently faulty and is removed. The accuracy of the diagnosis depends on the parameters H, K and $\alpha'$. When H = 1, $\alpha'$ denotes the minimum number of consecutive failures after which a processor is diagnosed to be permanently faulty. Fig. 1 shows a possible history of the values of one of the $\alpha_i$ variables.

Clearly, a diagnostic strategy that reacts promptly to observed errors by removing the errant processor (i.e., a strategy with a small $\alpha'$) reduces the risk of keeping failed processors in the system. However, it increases the risk of removing non-faulty processors as a reaction to transient faults, and thus of the system failing from exhaustion of the available processors. The optimal combination of values for the parameters depends on the expected ratio between permanent and transient faults (and, of course, on the utility function that one chooses to optimise). If only permanent faults are expected, $\alpha'$ should be set to 1. If both permanent and transient faults are expected, the same processor is used many times and its failures must be detected and masked until it is diagnosed as being affected by a permanent fault. This approach to fault diagnosis avoids removing processors affected by transient faults, but introduces a delay in removing processors affected by permanent faults. This delay impacts the error processing mechanism and contributes to decrease the overall reliability of the system.

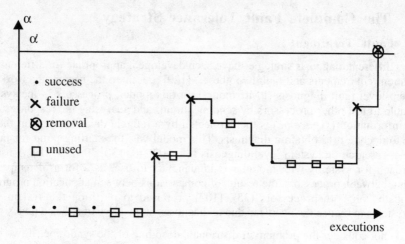

**Fig. 1.** A possible history of the values of one of the variable $\alpha_i$

## 6.2  Improving the Error Processing Mechanism

Continuing to use a failed processor increases the probability of having two failures while executing the same (redundant) task. This is the problem of so-called "latent faults" [132]: two faults occurring at different times in two distinct processors have the same effect as though they happened in the same time frame (during the execution of the same task), and may create a majority of erroneous results or a no-majority situation, decreasing the reliability of our "2+1" strategy. To address this problem, i.e. time intervals in which the system is using processors affected by permanent faults not yet diagnosed and removed, we consider a "2+2" error-processing strategy, in which two replicas are executed first, and in case of disagreement two more are executed in parallel (on two other processors). A result value is considered correct if agreed on by at least two processors. Therefore "2+2" can tolerate not just 1 processor error, as "2+1", but also two processor errors, if the two erroneous results are different. In terms of throughput, a "2+2" solution would not differ significantly from a "2+1" solution, as most executions are limited to the first phase, executing two replicas which produce consistent results.

The probability that two processor faults produce coincident errors may vary between systems. Two interesting cases (in a sense, the two extreme cases) are: 1) all failed processors produce the same erroneous result (for a given application task) and 2) a failed processor selects at random one of the possible erroneous values with a uniform probability distribution. In this latter case, the probability of a coincident error depends on how many values the type of the result has. To evaluate the effect on reliability of substituting "2+2" instead of "2+1", one would need to model the probabilities of having a faulty processor at the beginning of a redundant execution, as well as the probabilities of coincident errors.

## 7    Evaluation

In this section, we evaluate different combinations of the error processing and fault treatment strategies discussed so far. This is a preliminary evaluation carried out by simulation which, while not complete or extremely detailed, is useful to compare the different strategies considered. The simulation runs have been performed for only one, plausible setting of the parameter values.

Reliability and performability analyses (via analytic solutions of models) of the main error-processing schemes we have discussed in this paper are available in the literature (see [27, 162] and Paper III.B in this volume). We still consider useful to approach the evaluation by simulation since it allows us to investigate the different combinations of techniques and parameters with more freedom than is possible analytically. Analytical models tend to become extremely complex if one wishes to include many parameters, and the modelling approximations introduced to allow analytical solution of the models are often such that the resulting solutions loose precision and usefulness.

The behaviours of the error-processing and of the fault treatment strategies have complex relationships which vary with the values of their respective parameters. It becomes interesting to analyse different combinations of these techniques and parameters in order to determine, if possible, suitable settings. In our simulation we measured three quantities: 1) the average number of application tasks (MRC executions) the system correctly executes before its eventual failure, 2) the average number of processors that have been removed by the time the system fails, and 3) the average discrepancy between how many processors the fault treatment strategy removed and how many were actually faulty. The first measure gives a rough measure of combined dependability, performance and costs in systems without repair or replacement of faulty processors. The second is useful for checking the balance between the error-processing and fault treatment strategies, suggesting possible modifications to either strategy for better tuning. The third measure concerns only the fault treatment strategy and is useful to assess the quality of the diagnosis: large discrepancies indicate the need for further refinements to the adopted strategy.

The simulated system consists of 16 processors, without any time overhead for synchronisation or scheduling, to reach the highest parallelism permitted by the employed error-processing strategy, assuming an "infinite" load. Faults and errors in the different processors have been assumed to be statistically independent events, a simplifying assumption often made when considering only hardware faults. The system is assumed able to perform computations successfully so long as at least 9 processors are working. Under our hypotheses, the system can fail due to the exhaustion of available processors or to the production of an incorrect result. The system runs a mix of application tasks, each with constant execution time, and the execution times of the tasks are uniformly distributed in the interval 6-12 time units. When a processor fails, the task that it is executing produces an erroneous result selected at random (uniformly) among the possible values for the type of the result. Three types of results are assumed: Boolean, Char (256 different values) and Integer ($2^{32}$ different values) with probability 0.01, 0.09 and 0.9 respectively. Each processor has the same probability of experiencing a fault, which is divided into probabilities of permanent and transient fault. The complete set of parameter values is reported in Table 2.

**Table 2.** Parameters and values used in the simulation

| Parameters | Value |
|---|---|
| Number of processors in the system | 16 |
| Probability of permanent fault per execution | .0005 |
| Probability of transient fault per execution | .0045 |
| Probability of success per execution | .995 |
| Minimum number of processors for the system to be operational | 9 |
| Probability that the result of a service is Boolean | .01 |
| Probability that the result of a service is a character | .09 |
| Probability that the result of a service is an integer | .9 |
| Thresholds for considering a processor permanently faulty $(\alpha')$ | 2 |
| Increment in $\alpha_i$ in case of failure of processor i  (H) | 1 |
| Decremental factor of $\alpha_i$ in case of success of processor i  (K) | .9 |

We compare "2+1" and "2+2" with N-modular redundancy (NMR, i.e., with unconditional execution of all replicas) in combination with three fault treatment strategies:
1) a processor which fails is always immediately removed (optimal if only permanent
faults are possible); 2) processors are never removed (optimal if only transient faults
are possible); 3) the "$\alpha$ strategy" described in Section 6 is used with the threshold $\alpha'$
set to 2, H to 1, and K to 0.9. Fault treatment strategies 1) and 2) are the two ends of
the spectrum of possible strategies, and have been used to get an idea of the behaviour
of the system, although they are not appropriate if both transient and permanent
faults are possible (in our simulation, 90% of faults are transient). They have been
combined only with "2+1" and 3MR.

The results from 250 independent simulation runs [170] of a queuing model via the
Research Queueing Package (RESQ) Version 2, tool [139] are collected in the
following two tables. Table 3 shows two-sided confidence bounds for the expected
number of tasks correctly executed by the time of system failure.

**Table 3.** Successful task executions before system failure (confidence intervals with 95%
confidence level)

|  | NMR | | "2+1" or "2+2" | |
|---|---|---|---|---|
| 4 replicas, fault treatment strategy $\alpha$ | 3628 | 3969 | 7343 | 8043 |
| 3 replicas, fault treatment strategy $\alpha$ | 3766 | 4300 | 4674 | 5441 |
| 3 replicas, failed processors are always removed | 495 | 544 | 755 | 834 |
| 3 replicas, failed processors are never removed | 881 | 1060 | 1214 | 1494 |

It can be observed that the best results are obtained combining "2+2" error processing
with the $\alpha$ fault treatment strategy. "2+2" shows significant improvements over
"2+1" and much better results than NMR· the number of tasks executed by "2+2" is
about twice that executed by 4MR. "2+1" is better than 3MR by about 30-50%. The
number of tasks executed by 4MR is lower than that of tasks executed by 3MR:
executing an additional replica for each task is a very high price in our context of
infinite load (but it could be reasonable in other contexts). As expected, the two
extreme fault treatment strategies are inferior to the strategy $\alpha$, yielding a low number

of tasks. These results, although quite raw, confirm our conjecture: error-processing schemes which use more or less redundancy depending on the number of observed faults allow a more effective and efficient usage of the resources in a system.

**Table 4.** Number of removed and permanently faulty processors at system failure (confidence intervals with 95% confidence level)

| | Removed Processors | | Permanently Faulty Processors Removed | | Permanently Faulty Processors | |
|---|---|---|---|---|---|---|
| "2+2" | 7.79 | 7.99 | 7.57 | 7.79 | 7.58 | 7.80 |
| 4MR | 7.83 | 7.99 | 7.45 | 7.66 | 7.45 | 7.66 |
| "2+1" | 4.67 | 5.37 | 4.45 | 5.12 | 4.62 | 5.28 |
| 3MR | 5.97 | 6.60 | 5.66 | 6.28 | 5.78 | 6.37 |

Table 4 shows confidence bounds for the expected number of processors removed by the strategy $\alpha$, and the discrepancy between the removed processors and those which were really permanently faulty. It shows that the fault treatment strategy $\alpha$ is satisfactory, as it removes from the system almost all the permanently failed processors, and almost no processor that is not faulty, both in the case of "2+2"/"2+1" and NMR.

From Table 4 it can also be observed that combining the strategy $\alpha$ with "2+1" and 3MR leads the system to fail with a number of removed processors significantly smaller than the maximum allowed; the problem of latent faults causes the system to fail after only a few processors have been removed. On the contrary, using "2+2" and 4MR improves the utilisation of the available processors, as the system only fails when the number of operational processors is very close to the minimum allowed.

# 8    Conclusions

We have studied two design problems in modular redundancy, looking for ways to optimise an aspect of a fault-tolerant design on the basis of a clear model of the effects of the decisions.

First, we have considered the problem of specifying adjudicators for modular-redundant components, extending the specification of a voter so that it can use all the available evidence regarding the trustworthiness of the redundant results available. We have stated the problem of *evaluating* adjudication functions in general terms, showing what information is needed for comparing the worth of alternative designs in any specific environment. We have then derived the specification of an *optimal* adjudicator, with a precise definition of the kind of optimality achieved. Specifying the adjudication function as a table, rather than an algorithm, has allowed us to consider adapting it to systems for which the usual simplifying assumptions (like symmetry) do not hold, and recalibrating it on the basis of the observed behaviour of the components. These are very general results, in that they do not depend on which specific information is used as input to the adjudicator, and they are applicable both when the outputs are judged only in terms of their correctness and when a generic utility function is used.

An interesting speculative development of this work concerns the choice of utility functions for evaluating systems. Our choice, consistent with most other authors, has been to maximise the probability of producing a correct result on any individual invocation of a modular-redundant component, considered as isolated from all previous invocations, but others, taking into account utilities of sequences of executions, could conceivably be used.

Turning to the more complex problem of integrating fault treatment with error processing, we have assumed dynamic error processing, where normally only two replicas need to be executed, which offers the same reliability as triple-modular redundancy with better performance. We have described a simple diagnosis algorithm which uses the observed history of disagreements between the outputs of replicated tasks to discriminate between transient and permanent faults, and remove permanently faulty processors. We have shown the interplay of the parameters of this diagnostic algorithm in the necessary trade-off between the risk of discarding well-functioning processors and the risk of keeping permanently faulty processors connected. We have shown how the effects of the latter risk may be alleviated by executing two additional replicas at the second round instead of one. Via simulation, we have compared the effects of the different combinations of error processing and diagnosis strategies, and shown which combinations produces the best results, for a certain setting of the parameters of the model. Possible developments of this work include trying to define an optimal strategy in analytical terms, and considering a more detailed model of the system, including for instance faults that do not immediately cause failures, and probabilistic dependence between faults and errors of different replicas.

In conclusion, we have shown ways to apply mathematical prediction techniques to drive design decisions that are often taken on less rigorous grounds, due to the perceived complexity of their effects. It may be noticed that in both problems we have assumed that decisions are taken in a reliable centralised component, and neglected issues such as communication errors. Although this is an unrealistic simplification, virtual, reliable centralised decision elements can be built by replication, and the limits imposed by problems of distributed consensus with unreliable communication are well understood.

In the case of adjudicators, we have been able to obtain quite general results from very simple analytical considerations. This does not imply any simplification of the task of optimisation, as this depends on the knowledge of probabilistic characteristics of the components that are quite difficult to estimate. However, it allows one to specify clearly the design goals to be achieved. For the problem of diagnosis, we were able to identify the essential design trade-offs, and then simulation allowed us to study the behaviour of one particular design avoiding the difficulties of solving complex models. We are now seeking a useful optimality result for this problem as well.

# Dynamic Adjustment of Dependability and Efficiency in Fault-Tolerant Software[*]

Jie Xu[1]   Andrea Bondavalli[2]   Felicita Di Giandomenico[3]

[1]University of Newcastle upon Tyne   [2]CNUCE-CNR   [3]IEI-CNR

**Abstract.** In this paper we discuss the problem of attaining a dynamic compromise between using redundancy to improve software dependability and limiting the amount of redundancy so as to avoid unnecessary inefficiencies. A scheme, called *self-configuring optimal programming* (SCOP), is developed. SCOP attempts to reduce the resource cost of fault-tolerant software, both in space and time, by providing designers with a flexible redundancy architecture in which dependability and efficiency can be adjusted dynamically at run time. A design methodology is proposed to introduce support techniques for such dynamic adjustment. Our scheme also suggests a general control framework into which design diversity, data diversity and multiple copies can be incorporated selectively. A detailed dependability and efficiency evaluation shows that SCOP can achieve the same dependability level as those of other existing schemes, while making more efficient use of available resources.

## 1   Introduction

*Dependability* of a computing system refers to the quality of the service delivered by the system such that reliance can be justifiably placed on this service, and serves as a generic concept encompassing notions of reliability, availability, safety, security, performance, etc. (see Paper I.A in this volume, and [4]). A dependable system is capable of providing dependable service to its users over a wide range of potentially adverse circumstances. The development of dependable computing systems consists in the combined utilization of a large number of techniques, including *fault tolerance* techniques intended to cope with the effects of *faults* and avert the occurrence of *failures* or at least to warn a user that *errors* have been introduced into the state of the system. The provision of tolerance to anticipated hardware faults has been a common practice for many years, whereas a relatively new development is the techniques for tolerating unanticipated faults such as design (typically software) faults. (To avoid confusion in terminology, we will use in the following the term "fault-tolerant software" to characterize the software system that primarily treats software faults but may mask some hardware-related faults at the software level.)

Because software faults are permanent in nature, software fault tolerance in principle requires redundancy of design and/or data [3] although some software faults may be masked just by retry and message reordering [61]. Design redundancy, or design diversity, is the approach in which the production of two or more components of a system is aimed at delivering the same service through independent designs [15]. The components, produced through the design diversity approach from a common service specification, are called variants. Tolerance to design faults necessitates an adjudicator

---

[*] This paper is a revised version of [27]

[4] or a decision algorithm that provides an (assumed to be) error-free result from the execution of variants. The major advantage of design diversity is that dependable computing does not require the complete absence of design faults, but only that they should not produce similar errors in variants. Classical techniques for tolerating software faults are mostly based on some form of design diversity, including recovery blocks [125], N-version programming [13], N self-checking programming [89], $t/(n-1)$-variant programming [174], and some intermediate or combined techniques [72, 145].

There are two fundamental problems that need attacking. First, traditional approaches to software fault tolerance can be very costly. The cost of developing the variants and adjudicator may be many times more than that of programming a single version [87]. Despite of high cost, design diversity still has some difficulties in ensuring a routine-based improvement in software dependability. The interested reader is referred to [47] for details of such discussion. Experience has shown that some techniques such as rollback-and-retry may mask a range of software faults that produce transient effects [47]. The object-oriented programming paradigm has also shown much promise in reducing the development cost of fault-tolerant software through inheritance and polymorphism mechanisms [177].

Secondly, most of the methods for software fault tolerance are not particularly efficient, as will be discussed in Section 2, though *efficiency* remains an important aspect of software quality. Possible resolutions of the efficiency problem are the subject of this paper. Efficiency is defined in this paper as the good use of system and hardware resources, such as processors, internal and external memories, and communication devices [106]. Since the kind of applications which require software fault tolerance are often also likely to have stringent efficiency requirements, a good use of the available resources, both in space (hardware) and time (repetition), is highly desirable. In fact, the pursuit of increased efficiency in military computer-based systems, particularly in the economic and timely use of resources, is more apparent today than at any time in the past [107].

## 2    Tradeoff between Software Dependability and Efficiency

Recovery blocks (RB) are the first scheme designed to provide software fault tolerance. In this approach, variants are named alternates and the main part of the adjudicator is an acceptance test that is applied sequentially to the results produced by variants. The variants are organized in RB in a manner similar to the standby sparing techniques (dynamic redundancy) used in hardware, and may be executed serially on a single processor. The execution time of a recovery block is normally that of the first variant, acceptance test, and the operations required to establish and discard a checkpoint. This will not impose a high run-time overhead unless an error is detected and backward recovery required. In this regard, RB is highly efficient. Limitations of the RB method are mainly related to its acceptance test. This test is usually derived from the semantics of a given application, and close dependency between the test and variants may impact dependability of the whole system. Such a test will also introduce a run-time overhead which could be unacceptable if the test is complex. However, the development of simple, effective acceptance tests is a difficult task.

The next three approaches avoid use of an acceptance test by taking advantage of parallel execution of multiple variants and result's comparison (although sequential execution is conceptually possible just as parallel execution of RB alternates is possible). $N$-version programming (NVP) is a direct application of the hardware $N$-modular redundancy approach (NMR) to software. A voting mechanism determines a single adjudication result from a set or a subset of all the results of variants. $N$-self-checking programming (NSCP) provides fault tolerance through parallel execution of $N$ self-checking components. Each self-checking component is constructed from a pair of variants plus a result comparator (or from a variant associated with an acceptance test). One of them is regarded as the active component, and the others as "hot" standby spares. Upon failure of the active component, service delivery is switched to a "hot" spare. The $t/(n-1)$-variant programming scheme $(t/(n-1)$-VP) is based on the system diagnosis technique developed for hardware. This approach uses a particular diagnosability measure, $t/(n-1)$-diagnosability, and it can isolate the faulty variants within a set of at most $(n-1)$ variants. By applying a diagnosis algorithm to results produced by variants, a result is selected (the one that, among those produced, has the highest probability of being correct) as the system output.

The adjudication mechanisms used in these three schemes are usually based on result comparison and independent of semantics of the applications, thus the probability of common mode failure between the adjudicator and the variants is relatively low in these schemes. When variants are executed in parallel, NVP, NSCP and $t/(n-1)$-VP may have a fixed response time (without repetition), thereby guaranteeing timely responses in the presence of faults. However, these architectures utilize redundancy in a static manner and always execute all of their variants regardless of the normal or abnormal state of the system. They are intended to tolerate the maximum number of faults that may be present in the system; but, since such a "worst case" rarely happens, the amount of resources consumed is often higher than necessary. In this sense, they are not efficient.

All the fault tolerance approaches require some extra space or extra time, or both. Fig. 1 summarises space-time overheads in software fault tolerance schemes. The space is defined as the amount of hardware (e.g. the number of processors) needed to support parallel execution of multiple variants. The time is viewed here as the physical time needed to execute one or more variants sequentially. Note that efficient use of the available resources generally requires dynamic management and conditional execution of the software variants. This should come with a dynamic tradeoff between full parallel execution and totally sequential execution of the variants, as shown in the diagram. However, the majority of software fault tolerance schemes do not attempt to provide such a dynamic space-time tradeoff though it can in fact be achieved and so we would argue it should be provided. As a possible solution, we propose in the next section a new scheme, called Self-Configuring Optimal Programming (SCOP), which improves the efficiency of fault-tolerant software by diminishing the waste of resources without compromising software dependability.

Although the techniques discussed above generally require the use of diverse designs, multi-variant programming cannot always guarantee a signficant dependability improvement in a cost effective manner [47]. The work on using simple retry of programs to mask the effects of the faults that cause transient errors [54] seems to fit practical experience, but it is less complete and its effectiveness may be a matter of luck. Using data diversity to tolerate design faults in software systems [3] might provide a more cost effective alternative though such a technique is not generally applicable either. Given the existing problems in the area of software fault tolerance, SCOP is to be a general and conceptual scheme for coping with both dependability and efficiency. In order to tolerate software faults (and some hardware-related faults), an instance of our scheme may employ an application-specific strategy for masking the effect of faults, such as multiple versions of software, diversity in data space, or simple retry of programs, much depending upon special application requirements and considerations of cost effectiveness. Its mechanisms for combining dependability with efficiency rely on highly dynamic control and adaptive redundancy management, but basically independent of ways of redundancy for masking software faults.

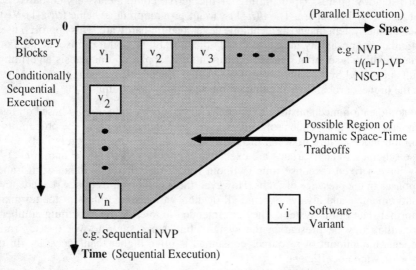

**Fig. 1.** Space and time redundancy in software fault tolerance.

In order to use redundancy in a dynamic or conditional manner, a scheme has to decide, at appropriate intermediate points of its execution, which of the following three execution states has been reached: (i) *End-state E* — a result exists that meets the stated *delivery condition* and can thus be delivered; (ii) *Non end-state N* — there is no result that meets the condition, but it is still possible to obtain such a result if further redundancy is employed; or (iii) *Failure state F* — there is no further possibility of producing a result that meets the condition. In reality, conditions for delivering a result are usually embedded in the adjudicator explicitly or implicitly. Note that different conditions in principle have different fault coverages though some conditions seem to be very similar. This influences both dependability and resource consumption. In further consideration of efficient use of the available resources, our proposed scheme is devised to admit different delivery conditions, thus becoming parametric to the level of fault tolerance.

Dynamic redundancy for the purpose of space-time tradeoff is a classical idea, e.g. Duplicated Configuration with a Spare and NMR with Spares used in hardware [65] Similar schemes have been applied to redundancy management in multiprocessors [95] or in distributed computing [16]. However, the existing proposals take only hardware faults into account, such as processor and communication faults. Our major concern in this paper is software faults and fault tolerance at software levels. We focus our attention on both dependability and efficiency, searching for a systematic way of using the minimum amount of hardware and time resources to attain the *required* software dependability. It is particularly emphasized here that a quality fault-tolerant software should be obligated to behave as precisely required (e.g. by different delivery conditions), but it should not be liable for anything outside of the specified requirement.

For non-real-time services whose specifications exclude any rigorous requirement on time, schemes based on dynamic redundancy would be the best technical and economical choice. However, in a real-time environment the uncontrolled application of time redundancy can lead to a delay in the production of output information and will result in such information being classed as invalid if deadlines are missed. The maximum possible delay in our approach must be determined carefully according to the response time required. Related work exists in the literature on the applicability of the schemes associated with time redundancy to real-time systems [57, 30, 73]. Integration of fault tolerance and real-time issues is addressed thoroughly in [29].

# 3  Self-Configuring Optimal Programming

## 3.1  Basic Architecture

The SCOP scheme consists of a set of software variants, $V=\{v_1, v_2, ..., v_n\}$, designed according to the principle of design diversity, an adjudication mechanism, and a controller that coordinates dynamic actions of the architecture. The main characteristics of SCOP include:

i)  *Dynamic Use of Redundancy*: SCOP always tries to execute the least number of variants strictly necessary for providing a result that meets the stated delivery conditions. To do this it organizes the execution of variants in phases, dynamically configuring a currently active set (CAS) $V_i$, a subset of $V$, at the beginning of the $i$th phase. An adjudication is made after the execution of $V_i$ in order to check if conditions for the release of a result are satisfied. The result will be output immediately and any further phases and actions will be ended once these conditions are met.

ii) *Growing Syndrome Space*: A syndrome is defined here as a set of information used by an adjudicator to perform its judgement as to the correctness of a result, in general involving those results produced by variants. The syndrome information in SCOP is accumulated with the increase of phases. All the results produced and the additional information collected so far are employed to support the selection of a correct result. This benefits dependability.

iii) *Flexibility and Efficiency*: SCOP can be designed to obey different delivery conditions. Since the different conditions will usually have different fault coverages, SCOP is therefore able to provide different levels of dependability. The different conditions may be dynamically chosen by different applications, according to their degrees of criticality, or by the same application at different times, according to the degradation of the system. The initial CAS $V_1$ in phase one can be determined and flexibly changed with respect to different delivery conditions. Furthermore, the set $V_i$ in the $i$th phase ($i>1$) can be constructed at run time based on information about the state of the system, so making efficient utilization of the available resources.

iv) *Generality*: Software variants used by SCOP can be simple copies of a program without using design diversity to cope with faults that lead to transient errors. These copies may be further associated with data diversity to mask the effects of another class of software faults.

```
begin
  i:= 0;                                  {index of the current phase, set to 0}
  State_mark := N;                        {set current state as non end-state}
  S_i = {};                               {set syndrome as empty}
  C := one of { delivery conditions };    {set required delivery condition}
  decide(max_phase);                      {based on time constraints}
  while State_mark = N and                {while current state is non end-state and
    i < max_phase do                      current phase < maximum allowed}
    begin
      i := i+1;                           {start new phase}
      configure(C, S_{i-1}, i, V_i);      {set new Currently Active Set}
      execute(V_i, S_i);                  {execute and obtain new syndrome}
      adjudicate(C, S_i, State_mark, res);{set new state mark and select result}
    end;
  if State = E                            {current state is end-state or failure state?}
    then deliver(res)
    else signal(failure);
end
```

The behaviour of SCOP can be described by the above control algorithm with comments on the right side. The `decide` procedure determines the maximum number `max_phase` of possible phases to be permitted by the specified timing constraints. Procedure `configure` constructs the CAS set $V_1$ in phase one according to the selected delivery condition and the given application environment, and establishes the CAS set $V_i$ ($i>1$) based on the syndrome $S_{i-1}$ collected in the ($i-1$)th phase and the information on phases. The execution of a CAS may lead to a successful state E. Note that variants in $V_i$ are selected from the variants that have not been used in any of the previous phases, i.e. $V_i$ is a subset of $V - (V_1 \cup V_2 \cup ... \cup V_{i-1})$. If the $i$th phase is the last, $V_i$ would contain all the remaining spare variants. The `execute` procedure manages the execution of the variants in CAS and generates the syndrome $S_i$, where $S_0$ is an empty set and $S_{i-1}$ is a subset of $S_i$. Procedure `adjudicate` implements the adjudication function using the selected condition $C$. It receives the syndrome $S_i$, sets the new `State_mark` and selects the result `res`, if one exists. The `deliver` procedure delivers the selected result and the `signal` produces a failure notification.

**Example:** Suppose that (i) three processors are available for execution of up to three software variants; (ii) seven software variants are provided; (iii) the maximum time delay permitted is three phases, and (iv) a result selected from at least three agreeing versions is considered as deliverable. An example of possible executions is illustrated in Table 1, where italics are used to indicate the correct results, bold characters to represent the incorrect, disagreeing results, and $V=\{v_1, v_2, v_3, v_4, v_5, v_6, v_7\}$.

**Table 1.** Execution example of SCOP.

| Phase | $V_i$ | Spares | Syndrome | Judgement & result |
|-------|-------|--------|----------|--------------------|
| 1 | $\{v_1,v_2,v_3\}$ | $\{v_4,v_5,v_6,v_7\}$ | $r_1, r_2, r_3$ | N |
| 2 | $\{v_4,v_5\}$ | $\{v_6,v_7\}$ | $r_1, r_2, r_3, r_4, r_5$ | $\Rightarrow$ E, $r_2$ |

This example shows how SCOP reaches the required dependability in a dynamic manner when the availability of hardware resources is fixed. The amount of available resources and real-time constraints may vary in practice. Particularly, in computing systems that function for a long period of time, the user may impose new requirements or modify the original requirements for timeliness, dependability etc. Also the user may program more variants when the need arises. These uncertain factors require more complicated and more dynamic control and management. SCOP is further intended to handle this.

## 3.2 Dynamic Behaviour in a Multiprocessor Environment

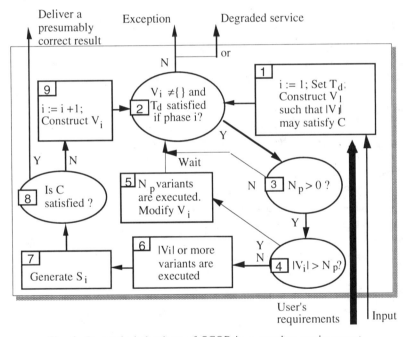

**Fig. 2.** Dynamic behaviour of SCOP in a varying environment.

In a large multiprocessor system, hardware resources can often be utilized by several competing concurrent applications. Furthermore, complex schemes for software fault tolerance may be necessary only for some critical part of the application that demands extra resources from the system. Dynamic management can make the allocation of resources more efficient. Let $N_p$ be the maximum number of software variants which can be executed in parallel on hardware resources currently allocated to the given application, and $T_d$ the time deadline that indicates the maximum response delay permitted for an application. Fig. 2 illustrates a possible organization for SCOP and its dynamic behaviour in such a varying environment.

Each step in the diagram is explained as follows.

1) For a given application, SCOP first establishes the delivery condition $C$ (or several delivery conditions that permit different levels of dependability), according to the user's requirements, and then configures the CAS set, $V_1$, from $V$, that includes the minimum number of variants needed to be executed to generate a result satisfying the condition $C$ in the absence of faults. The timing constraint, $T_d$, is also determined based on the response requirement.

2) Check whether the time deadline $T_d$ will be missed when the $i$th phase is initiated for the execution of $V_i$ ($i = 1, 2, 3, ...$) and whether $V_i$ is an empty set. If $T_d$ allows for no new phase or $V_i = \{ \}$, an exception will be raised to signal to the user that a timely result satisfying the required condition $C$ cannot be provided. In this case, a degraded service may be considered.

3) Check whether $N_p > 0$. $N_p = 0$ means that no variant can be executed at this moment due to the limitation of available resources in the system. Wait and go back to Step 2 to check $T_d$.

4) Check whether $|V_i| > N_p$. If $|V_i| > N_p$, only some of the variants in $V_i$ can be carried out within the current phase and thus additional time is needed for the execution of $V_i$.

5) $N_p$ software variants in $V_i$ are executed and $V_i$ is modified so that $V_i$ excludes the variants that have been executed. Back to Step 2.

6) Since $|V_i| \le N_p$, $|V_i|$ variants are executed and completed within the current phase. If the scheduler used by the supporting system allocates $N_p > |V_i|$ processors to SCOP during the $i$th phase, it is possible to consider the execution of $N_p$ variants (more than $|V_i|$). This avoids wasting the resources that would be left idle otherwise, and requires the ability to select the additional variants among those not yet used.

7) Syndrome $S_i$ is generated based on all the information collected up to this point.

8) Check whether a result exists that satisfies the delivery condition $C$. If so, deliver the result to the user; otherwise Step 9.

9) Set $i = i + 1$ and construct a new CAS set, $V_i$, from the spare variants according to the information about the syndrome, the deadline and the resources available; if no sufficient spare variants are available, set $V_i$ empty.

It is worth mentioning that the major purpose of this illustration is to outline the dynamic behaviour of SCOP. Practical applications will require deliberate designs. What we need is a design methodology for supporting this kind of dynamic management and control. However, in many existing methodologies for programming dependable applications, the dependability aspects of an application are fixed statically [1]. This is unsatisfactory for reasons of efficiency, flexibility and extendibility. We will propose in the next section a new methodology and show how (simple or complex) instances of SCOP could be derived automatically.

## 4    Design Methodology for SCOP

### 4.1  Description of a Design Methodology

In order to be able to adjust dependability and efficiency dynamically, the task of the control algorithm and of the adjudicator of SCOP may be very complex. This complexity could itself be a source of errors and thus defeat the proposed scheme. The development of a methodology for designing SCOP components is mainly meant to avoid such phenomena. Given the requirements to be fulfilled and proper information on the variants, an off-line activity is conducted for analyzing and collecting all the information regarding the possible (normal or abnormal) state of the software variants and the adjudicator. The correctness of the derived information can then be verified. Such off-line analysis and computation afford the major part of complexity of control and management, and could be made automatic by the construction and use of an appropriate tool. In this way, complexity of on-line control is greatly reduced. The adjudication mechanism and control algorithm of SCOP, which may be reusable for all SCOP instances, can take run-time actions by just identifying the states reached so far and by reading the associated information, without performing complex computation at each activation. This obviously improves dependability since the information collected in the off-line activity is made read-only and can be recorded on stable storage if necessary. The details of both off-line and on-line activities are illustrated in Fig. 3.

*Design Parameters*: The design parameters of a SCOP component should include:

i)   the number $N$ of available variants, an estimate of reliability of each variant and an estimate of the execution time of each variant; (Estimates of the probability of common-mode failures among the variants are also desirable, but they are very rarely available in practice.)

ii)  a timing constraint that the SCOP instance may be given for producing timely results; and

iii) the delivery condition(s) and the degree of flexibility in delivering results.

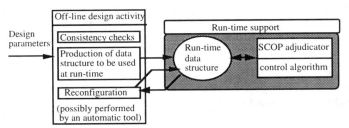

**Fig. 3.** Design and run-time organization of SCOP components.

In principle, a specific application has the freedom of establishing the delivery condition, whatever may satisfy the given dependability requirements. The degree of flexibility may range from only one fixed condition, which the SCOP component will try to verify for all the services, to many different conditions, one of which will be selected at run time by SCOP users through a run-time service parameter. Of course, permitting multiple delivery conditions will increase the amount of the off-line work necessary to provide the run-time information. Different delivery conditions may have respective fault coverages which may be difficult to compare. However, it is particularly useful to establish different delivery conditions whose coverages are totally ordered. A convincing example is the design of degradable systems: the same application may accept degraded services in the occurrence of faults. More generally, a given application may request different services under different conditions of the system state and its environment.

**Off-line Design.** The initial activity is, once the design parameters have been provided, to confirm their consistency: the parameters must admit solutions. For example if the response time required is shorter than the execution time of the variants, no timely services can be provided. It must also be verified that the design intended will be able to meet the delivery condition(s), probably using all the available redundancy when the need arises. Should the parameters prove to cause any inconsistency, they must be changed and the whole process started anew.

Next, a data structure, such as a directed graph or a table, is built. Each node or entry of the chosen structure will represent a possible state of execution of the scheme. It will contain, for each delivery condition, the corresponding state mark $E$ (end-states), $N$ (non end-states) or $F$ (failure states). In case of the state $N$ it will contain also the information on the necessary amount of redundancy to be further used. Each execution state corresponds to a set of syndromes that may lead to the same decisions under a given delivery condition. We will show later how such a graph may be actually built and discuss some minor differences when considering a table.

A further action is to define the initial state and to construct, for each delivery condition, the set of variants to start with, i.e. those to be executed in the first phase.

**Run-Time Support.** The run-time data structure is associated with the adjudicator and the control algorithm to support the SCOP run-time actions. Both the adjudicator and the control algorithm are independent of the data provided by the off-line design. At the end of each phase, the adjudication mechanism needs just to identify the syndrome collected (or the execution state) and then read from the data structure its classification ($N$, $E$ or $F$) with respect to the required delivery condition for that service. If the state is $N$, the control may dynamically configure a set of the variants for the next phase by looking up the information in the corresponding field of the data structure. The work at run-time is thus limited to following the information in the data structure, i.e. just moving from one element to another according to the observed syndrome.

**Reconfiguration.** The SCOP component will be operational waiting for service requests until affected by hard (permanent) faults. Although software components are usually modelled as being affected only by transient faults, the occurrence of hard faults should not be neglected. When hard faults need to be treated, a reconfiguration must be performed. The component will transit from an operational state to a reconfiguration state. For each variant that could be affected by a hard fault, the following off-line steps are performed to modify the data structure:

1)   all the states representing execution of all variants (syndromes of $N$ results) are erased from the data structure;
2)   the faulty variant is extracted from the set of available ones; and
3)   for each delivery condition, all the elements with the non end-states must be checked. If the reduced number of available variants no longer allows any end-state to be reached from a non end-state, then the state must be classified as a failure state.

This methodology consists essentially in providing the information off-line. Obviously algorithms for providing it may differ widely depending on the design parameters given. They could be made automatic and be grouped into a tool that helps use them appropriately. This automatic tool could then be used for designing SCOP instances and would be integrated into a programming environment for software development. Software designers could then use it to automatically derive instances of SCOP. They would just set the desired parameters without having to perform the analysis for any instance of SCOP they may want to design.

## 4.2 The Design of a SCOP Instance

We now describe, in order to show how the methodology can be applied, the off-line design process related to the following design parameters:

i)   five software variants are available, their maximum execution time and figures of reliability are given, and all variants have the same reliability figures;

ii)  there are no constraints on the response time for any service requests; and

iii) two different delivery conditions are defined: (1) $C_1$ — deliver a result if it is provably correct provided that no more than two variants produce incorrect results; and (2) $C_2$ — deliver a result if it is provably correct provided that no more than one variant produces incorrect results.

To check the consistency, we simply have to show that the condition $C_1$ can be met since $C_1$ has higher fault coverage than $C_2$ and no timing constraints are given. Note that some of the states reached by executing all the five variants can be marked as end-states, e.g. those representing at least three agreeing results. The requirement could also be met executing just three variants if all give agreeing results.

The second step consists in enumerating all the possible syndromes for each possible number $M$ ($1 \leq M \leq 5$) of variants needed to be executed. Here, the frequency of a result in a syndrome is defined as the times that the result appears in the syndrome. These syndromes are then partitioned into different classes, each of which is represented by an ordered string of numbers ($z_1, z_2, z_3, ...$) with $z_1 \geq z_2 \geq z_3 ...$, where $z_i$ is the frequency of the $i$th most frequent result in the syndrome. For example, when $M = 3$, the syndromes containing just two equal results belong to the class denoted as (2,1). Each class constitutes an execution state of the SCOP component we are designing, and is represented by a node in a directed graph.

In order to build such a directed graph we first define a relation among classes. The class $S_i{}^M$ ($i$th class while executing $M$ variants) is said to be related to the class $S_j{}^{M+1}$ ($j$th class while executing $M+1$ variants) if it is possible to obtain from any syndrome in $S_i{}^M$, when a further variant is executed, a syndrome belonging to $S_j{}^{M+1}$. For example, from any syndromes belonging to the class (2,1), the execution of a fourth variant may lead to a syndrome that belongs to (3,1), and the class (2,1) is thus related to the class (3,1). A directed graph can be thus created — nodes represent the states (or the syndrome classes) and directed arcs represent the defined relation among classes. In Fig. 4 the resulting graph is depicted. This directed graph structure has a nice property that one node is linked only to the states which may be reached by continuing execution; so any execution of the scheme can be monitored by following a path in the graph. A table structure where the strict linkage among reachable states is not directly represented would require a larger run-time effort for seeking the current state.

Next we will show how to derive the information to be associated with each node in the graph. For each node $S$ corresponding to the execution of $M$ variants (labelled with an ordered string of $j$ numbers $(z_1, z_2, ..., z_j)$ that indicates the result frequency), let $F_i(S) = M - z_i$ for $i = 1, 2, ..., j$, and $F_{j+1}(S) = M$. Note that $F_1(S)$ is the minimum number of variants that have failed and $F_{j+1}(S)$ represents the failure of all the $M$ variants. More generally, $F_i(S)$ is equivalent to the number of the variants that have failed when the $i$th result is correct. It follows that $F_1(S) \leq F_2(S) \leq ... \leq F_j(S) < F_{j+1}(S)$. Let $f_i$ be the maximum number of faulty variants admitted by the delivery condition $C_i$. We can label the nodes with respective states now.

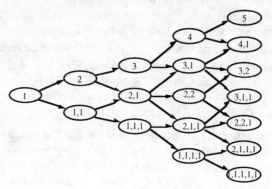

**Fig. 4.** Syndromes graph for $N = 5$.

For a given node, if $f_i < F_1(S)$, more than $f_i$ failures must have occurred. The node should be associated with the failure state. If $F_1(S) < F_2(S)$ and $f_i < F_2(S)$, then a most frequent result exists and the result can be unambiguously identified as correct. Otherwise, $F_1(S) = F_2(S)$ or $f_i \geq F_2(S)$ implies the result that appears $z_2$ times might be correct, whereas the result that appears $z_1$ times might be incorrect. Thus, the node should be labelled the non end-state. For example, the node (3) in Fig. 4 represents three agreeing results out of the execution of three variants. For the node, $F_1(\text{node } 3) = 0$ and $F_2(\text{node } 3) = 3$. The result can be unambiguously identified as correct if it is assumed that at most two variants can have failed (i.e. $f_i = 2$ and $F_1(\text{node } 3) < f_i < F_2(\text{node } 3)$). The node (3) can be therefore associated with the end-state. Formally, for a given value $f_i$ (induced from the condition $C_i$), a node $S$ is labelled: (i) end-state $E$ if $F_1(S) \leq f_i < F_2(S)$; (ii) non end-state $N$ if $F_2(S) \leq f_i$; or (iii) failure state $F$ if $F_1(S) > f_i$.

Unlike the nodes with the state $E$ or $F$, a node with the state $N$ should contain extra information on the minimum number $x$ of the variants to be further executed in the next phase so as to possibly reach an end-state. Now let $S = (z_1, z_2, ..., z_j)$ be a non end-state, where $F_2(S) \leq f_i$. Consider the best case in which the execution of the $x$ variants produces the results that agree with the most frequent result in the state $S$. A new state $S^* = (z_1+x, z_2,..., z_j)$ will be reached. Note that $F_1(S^*) = M + x - (z_1 + x) = M - z_1 = F_1(S) \leq f_i$, and $F_2(S^*) = M + x - (z_2) = F_2(S) + x$. By the rule of labelling, the state $S^*$ is an end-state if $f_i < F_2(S^*)$. Since $f_i < F_2(S^*)$ means $f_i < F_2(S) + x$, we have that $x > f_i - F_2(S)$, or $x = f_i + 1 - F_2(S)$.

The last step we have to take is to define the initial state and to set the number of variants to be executed in the first phase for the delivery conditions $\{C_i\}$. The initial state is defined as a null state with $F_1(0) = F_2(0) = 0$. Since it is a non-end state, the rule just described above can be applied and the initial number of variants to be executed is: $x = f_i + 1 - F_2(0) = f_i + 1$.

Table 2 summarizes all the data obtained at the end of the off-line activity. There are nineteen syndrome classes in this instance. Each class is associated with a state mark under the specific delivery condition. If the state mark is $N$, the corresponding $x$ shows the minimum number of variants needed to be executed in the next phase. (•• is used for cells with no information.) Note that the off-line activity also helps identify different delivery conditions. For example, consider a condition, $C^*$, that a result is deliverable if it is selected from three or more agreeing results. This condition seems to be the same as the condition $C_1$ used in the previous SCOP instance. However, they are actually different. The state (2, 1, 1) in Table 2 is an end-state under the condition $C_1$, but a non end-state according to the condition $C^*$.

**Table 2.** Off-line information obtained for the instance of SCOP with five variants.

| | $C_1 : [0, 2]$ | | $C_2 : [0, 1]$ | | | $C_1 : [0, 2]$ | | $C_2 : [0, 1]$ | |
|---|---|---|---|---|---|---|---|---|---|
| Class | Mark | $x$ | Mark | $x$ | Class | Mark | $x$ | Mark | $x$ |
| 5 | E | •• | E | •• | 2,1,1 | E | •• | F | •• |
| 4,1 | E | •• | E | •• | 1,1,1,1 | F | •• | F | •• |
| 3,2 | E | •• | F | •• | 3 | E | •• | E | •• |
| 3,1,1 | E | •• | F | •• | 2,1 | N | 1 | E | •• |
| 2,2,1 | F | •• | F | •• | 1,1,1 | N | 1 | F | •• |
| 2,1,1,1 | F | •• | F | •• | 2 | N | 1 | E | •• |
| 1,1,1,1,1 | F | •• | F | •• | 1,1 | N | 2 | N | 1 |
| 4 | E | •• | E | •• | 1 | N | 2 | N | 1 |
| 3,1 | E | •• | E | •• | 0 | N | 3 | N | 2 |
| 2,2 | N | 1 | F | •• | | | | | |

# 5 Evaluation

## 5.1 Dependability Aspects

We first analyse the SCOP scheme based on a configuration that makes it comparable with the other major schemes. Arlat *et al.* [Paper VI.E in this volume] developed complete fault classifications and constructed fault-manifestation models for RB, NVP and NSCP. We shall exploit their framework for modelling, with some slight adjustments, and use some of their results for the purpose of our comparison. Four schemes are considered: (i) the SCOP architecture involves three variants, the delivery condition associated with it requires that at least two variants produce the same results, and it thus executes just two variants in the first phase; (ii) the NVP architecture uses three variants based on the usual majority adjudication; (iii) the RB architecture consists of a primary block and an alternate block; and (iv) NSCP contains four variants organized as two self-checking components.

In our fault-manifestation model, two or more design faults among different components (e.g. variants and the adjudicator) are considered as "related" if they cause similar or identical errors; and they are regarded as "independent" if the errors they cause are distinct. In accordance with the consideration of general applicability, probabilities of independent and related faults are allowed here to be significantly high, with the upper bound up to one. The following analysis only concerns value correctness and does not deal with timing constraints. We focus here on reliability and safety as two attributes of dependability, but further extension could be made including other measures such as availability and performability [161].

**Basic Assumptions and Notation.** Let $X$ indicate one of the four schemes to be considered: SCOP, NVP, RB, NSCP. The analysis will be made using the following assumptions.

i)   Fault types and notation for probabilities of fault manifestation:

a)   independent fault(s) in the adjudicator or in the variant(s), given no a manifestation of related faults — the fault in the adjudicator manifests with probability $q_{A,X}$ while the fault in a variant with probability $q_{IX}$;

b)   a related fault between the variants and the adjudicator that manifests with probability $q_{VA,X}$;

c)   a related fault among $S$ variants that manifests with probability $q_{SV,X}$.

We condition the probability $q_{A,X}$ on a conservative base, namely, the fault will always cause the adjudicator to reject a result (or a majority) given the result (or the majority) is correct, or the adjudicator to output a result given the result is incorrect and no majority exists. Note that a comparison-based adjudicator is normally application-independent. We will not consider the fault type "b)" in the models for SCOP, NVP and NSCP, but in the model for RB.

ii)  The probability of a manifestation of an independent fault is the same for all variants.

iii) During the execution of Scheme $X$, only a single fault type may appear and no compensation may occur between errors of the variants and of the adjudicator.

iv)  For the reason of simplicity, it is assumed that an independent fault in the adjudicator will only manifest itself at the end of the final adjudication.

We can now compute the probability of software failure based on a discrete-time, finite-state Markov process. Due to the limitation of space, we have to omit all details of our dependability models. The interested reader is referred to [45]. For the $X$ approach, let $Q_{R,X}$ be the probability of software failure and $Q_{S,X}$ be the probability of undetected failure, we obtain that

$$Q_{R,SCOP} = (q_2 - 2q_Aq_2 + q_1q_1 - 2q_Aq_1q_1 + q_A)(1 - q_3 - q_4) + Q_{S,SCOP}$$
$$Q_{S,SCOP} = q_A(q_1q_1 + q_2)(1 - q_3 - q_4) + q_3 + q_4$$

where $q_1 = 2q_I(1-q_I)$, $q_2 = q_I^2$, $q_3 = 2q_{2V}$, and $q_4 = q_{2V} + q_{3V}$.
For the purpose of comparison with the NVP architecture, let $q_i = 3q_I^2(1-q_I) + q_I^3$ and $q_r = 3q_{2V} + q_{3V}$. It follows that

$$Q_{R,SCOP} = q_A(1-q_i)(1-q_r) + (1-q_A)q_i(1-q_r) + Q_{S,SCOP}$$
$$Q_{S,SCOP} = q_Aq_i(1-q_r) + q_r$$

Following a similar approach to dependability modelling, we conclude that

$$Q_{R,NVP} = q_A(1-q_i)(1-q_r) + (1-q_A)q_i(1-q_r) + Q_{S,NVP}$$

$$Q_{S,NVP} = q_A q_i (1-q_r)+q_r$$

$$Q_{R,RB} = q_A(1-q_I-q_{2V}-q_{VA})+q_A q_I(1-q_I)+(1-q_A)q_I^2+q_{2V}+Q_{S,RB}$$

$$Q_{S,RB} = q_A q_I^2+q_{VA}$$

$$Q_{R,NSCP} = q_A(1-q_{iv})(1-q_{rv})+(1-q_A)q_{iv}^2(1-q_{rv})+4q_{2V}+Q_{S,NSCP}$$

$$Q_{S,NSCP} = q_A q_{iv}^2(1-q_r)+q_{rv}-5q_{2V}$$

where $q_{iv} = 2q_I(1-q_I)+q_I^2$ and $q_{rv} = 6q_{2V}+4q_{3V}+q_{4V}$.

From these specific expressions for benign and catastrophic failures, we could claim that SCOP has the same level of dependability as NVP. However, the adjudicator in the SCOP architecture under consideration will be utilized twice if some faults are detected in the first phase. It is therefore possible that SCOP delivers an incorrect result in the early phase or rejects a correct majority, starting a new phase, because of a manifestation of a fault in the adjudicator. When such fault situations are taken into account, the dependability of SCOP would be slightly lower than that of NVP with a simple majority voter. In fact, probabilities associated with the adjudicator of NVP may also vary significantly since various complicated adjudicators may be employed [44].

RB seems to be the best, but an AT is usually application-dependent. The degree of design diversity between an AT and the variants could be different with respect to different applications so that $q_{VA,RB}$ (i.e. the probability of a related fault between an AT and the variants) may vary dramatically. Besides, the fault coverage of an AT is an indicator of its complexity, where an increase in fault coverage generally requires a more complicated implementation. NSCP could suffer from related faults among variants in spite of its low $q_{A,NSCP}$ (simple adjudication based on result comparison and switch).

## 5.2  Consumption of Resources

Let $T_X$ be the time necessary for the execution of a complete phase in the $X$ scheme, where $T_X$ consists of the execution time of the variants and the time for adjudication and control, and $f$ be the maximum number of variant failures to be tolerated by the scheme. We now conduct an analysis of resource consumption, referring to more general architectures (than those used in the dependability analysis): (i) the SCOP architecture involves $2f+1$ variants, with the delivery condition that requires at least $f+1$ identical results, executing $f+1$ variants in the first phase; (ii) the NVP architecture uses $2f+1$ variants based on the usual majority adjudication; (iii) the RB architecture consists of a primary block and $f$ alternate blocks; and (iv) NSCP contains $2(f+1)$ variants organized as $(f+1)$ self-checking components. (For NSCP, it must be further assumed that all the variant failures are independent.)

In the interest of concentrating on efficiency, we assume no timing constraints for the service and perfect adjudicators (and controllers). Table 3 reports some results about resource consumption, in which each cell of the NoVariant column indicates the total number of variants needed to be executed while a scheme attempts to complete its service, in direct proportion to the amount of hardware resources. Both the worst and the average case are shown. In the worst case, SCOP requires the amount of hardware resources that supports the execution of $(2f+1)$ variants, but on an average it needs the hardware support just for the execution of the $(f+1)$ variants. It would be therefore reasonable to rank SCOP as being more efficient than NVP and NSCP. RB would seem to be better again, relying to some extent on the use of acceptance tests.

SCOP will terminate any further execution if $(f+1)$ agreeing results are obtained in the first phase, i.e. the condition for delivering a result is satisfied. This scenario happens when (i) a related fault manifests itself and affects all the $(f+1)$ variants; or (ii) all the variants produce the same correct result. Events like the failure or success of individual variants are usually not independent but positively correlated under the condition that all the variants are executed together on the same input [76]. This factor determines that the probability of observing the event "ii)" would be higher than what might be expected assuming independence. Let $p_V$ be the probability that a single variant gives a correct result. The probability that SCOP would then stop at the end of the first phase > the probability that the $f+1$ variants would produce correct results > $p_V^{f+1}$. Experimental values of $p_V$ [76] are sufficiently high so that we would claim SCOP almost always gives the same fast response as NVP or even faster, as discussed later. Note that the worst case in which SCOP operates with the longest execution time $T_{SCOP}+fT_{SCOP}$ has in fact a very rare probability of occurrence. It occurs only when the first phase ends with $f$ agreeing results and every remaining variant, assigned to run in one of phases Two to $(f+1)$, produces a different result.

**Table 3.** Comparison of resource consumption.

| Scheme | NoVariant worst | NoVariant average | TIME worst | TIME average |
|--------|-----------------|-------------------|------------|--------------|
| SCOP | $(f+1)+f$ | $\cong(f+1)$ | $T_{SCOP}+fT_{SCOP}$ | $\cong T_{SCOP}$ |
| NVP | $2f+1$ | $2f+1$ | $T_{NVP}$ | $T_{NVP}$ |
| RB | $1+f$ | $\cong 1$ | $T_{RB}+fT_{RB}$ | $\cong T_{RB}$ |
| NSCP | $2(f+1)$ | $2(f+1)$ | $T_N+ft_{switch}$[†] | $\cong T_N$ |

[†] $t_{switch}$ is the time for switching the self-checking components

If timing constraints for delivering the result are considered, for example given that the maximum number of allowable phases is $p$ where $p \leq f+1$, the SCOP's worst case of execution time will become $pT_{SCOP}$. Note, however, that this limitation on the number of phases heavily impacts the average usage of variants only if $p = 1$ (in this case the execution of all the variants is required). Otherwise the first phase, very likely the only one, always involves just $(f+1)$ variants. The basic RB scheme will not be applicable directly to the case that $p < f+1$, as RB needs $f+1$ phases to deal with successive manifestations of $f$ faults. Parallel implementations of RB may be suitable, but they operate at the cost of more variants executed within a phase.

More precisely, the execution times of various adjudication functions (and control algorithms) can be significantly different with respect to specific fault coverages and algorithm complexity. Furthermore, the execution times of variants in a scheme can differ because of the requirements for design diversity and equivalent variant functionality. Since in SCOP the subsequent phases will be utilized much less than the first phase, the faster variants (those that correspond to more effective implementations and whose execution times are shorter) may be chosen in the first phase. The penalty caused by variant synchronization (that requires the system to wait for the slowest variant) can be thus reduced, as compared with NVP.

**Example: (Comparison of SCOP and NVP).** Table 4 gives the related figures of resource consumption in SCOP and NVP where $T_{SCOP} \leq T_{NVP}$ (i.e. $T_{SCOP1}$ $\leq T_{3VP}$, $T_{SCOP2} \leq T_{5VP}$, and $T_{SCOP3} \leq T_{7VP}$) and $p_V = (1 - 10^{-4})$ (the average reliability of the variants derived from the experiment in [76]. Data for SCOP have been obtained based on the assumption that just two phases are allowed. The table shows that SCOP consumes almost the same amount of time as NVP to provide services, but it requires just the amount of hardware resources that supports $(f+1)$VP (which only resists at most $f/2$ variant failures), rather than $(2f+1)$VP.

Table 4. Resource consumption of SCOP and NVP.

| | Scheme | No. of variants executed (Average) | Time consumption (Average) |
|---|---|---|---|
| Average Cost for General Case | SCOP | $(f+1)+(1-p_V^{f+1})f$ | $[1+(1-p_V^{f+1})]T_{SCOP}$ |
| | NVP | $2f + 1$ | $T_{NVP}$ |
| N = 3 f = 1 | SCOP | 2.0002 | $1.0002T_{SCOP1}$ |
| | NVP | 3 | $T_{3VP}$ |
| N = 5 f = 2 | SCOP | 3.0006 | $1.0003T_{SCOP2}$ |
| | NVP | 5 | $T_{5VP}$ |
| N = 7 f = 3 | SCOP | 4.0012 | $1.0004T_{SCOP3}$ |
| | NVP | 7 | $T_{7VP}$ |

## 6    Conclusions

In this paper we have discussed in detail the problem of attaining a flexible compromise between using redundancy to improve dependability and limiting the amount of redundancy for the purpose of efficiency. The SCOP approach has been developed with the aim of dynamically adjusting different characteristics that matter in fault-tolerant software. The results drawn from the evaluation of dependability show that SCOP could have the same level of dependability as other existing schemes. To attack the problem of complexity caused by highly dynamic behaviour, we have developed a methodology for devising various instances of SCOP, simplifying the on-line process at the price of the complex (but systematic and thorough) off-line design.

SCOP gives designers a general control framework into which multiple version software, diversity in data space, or simple copies of a program can be incorporated selectively, depending upon considerations of cost effectiveness and specific application requirements. The SCOP concept also admits different delivery conditions for the results produced. Since the different conditions may have different coverages SCOP could become parametric to dependability. This represents a significant novelty in software fault tolerance. SCOP makes it possible to impose additional dependability requirements for a system (or a server) or to provide gracefully degraded services flexibly as faults occur. What is to be sacrificed can be dynamically decided at run time with respect to the resources that are currently available.

In principle, SCOP provides the same basis as NVP and RB for achieving software fault tolerance and has no major implementation difficulties in any environments where NVP or RB has found considerable applications. A few existing applications have provided us with additional confidence for adopting SCOP in practical systems.

For example, four-version software and two-variant hardware are combined in a *dynamically reconfigurable* architecture to support the pitch control of the *fly-by-wire* A320 aircraft [163], which could be regarded as a limited or simplified form of the SCOP technique.

# Designing Secure and Reliable Applications using Fragmentation-Redundancy-Scattering: an Object-Oriented Approach*

Jean-Charles Fabre[1]   Yves Deswarte[1]   Brian Randell[2]

[1]LAAS-CNRS   [2]University of Newcastle upon Tyne

**Abstract.** Security and reliability issues in distributed systems have been investigated for several years at LAAS using a technique called Fragmentation-Redundancy-Scattering (FRS). The aim of FRS is to tolerate both accidental and intentional faults: the core idea consists in fragmenting confidential information in order to produce insignificant fragments and then in scattering the fragments so obtained in a redundant fashion across a distributed system, such as a large network of workstations and servers. Of these workstations, in principle just the user's own workstation needs to be regarded as trusted, whereas from this user's viewpoint the other workstations and servers, which in all probability are under someone else's control, can be untrusted devices.

This paper describes an object-oriented approach to the use of FRS, now under development at LAAS and Newcastle. This approach greatly eases the task of application programmers who seek to ensure reliable secure processing, as well as storage, of confidential information. The approach involves fragmenting a confidential object using its composition structure, i.e., in terms of a hierarchy of sub-objects (the *"is-part-of"* relation of the object model), each of course with its own subsidiary operations or "methods". The fragmentation process continues until the resulting sub-objects are as far as possible such as to be individually non-confidential. Replicas of non-confidential objects are then scattered among untrusted stations. By such means much of the processing of object methods, as well as the storing of much object state information, can be carried out safely on untrusted equipment.

## 1   Introduction

Mechanisms for fault tolerance in distributed systems are typically designed to cope with just a limited class of faults: usually just accidental, physical faults which occur during system operation (some designs take into account only an even more restricted subclass, such as crash failures). However, other classes of faults may also impede correct operation of distributed systems; nowadays a numerous such class is certainly that of intentional human interaction faults, i.e., intrusions. These are deliberate attempts at transgressing the security policy assigned to the system. They can originate from external intruders, registered users trying to exceed their privileges, or privileged users, such as administrators, operators, security officers, etc., who abuse their privileges to perform malicious actions.

Intrusions and accidental faults may have the same effects: that is the improper modification or destruction of sensitive information and the disclosure of confidential

---

* This paper is a revised version of [50].

information. The user will perceive these effects as a system failure: the service delivered by the system to the user no longer complies with the system specifications[1] [86]. In distributed systems composed of users' individual workstations and shared servers, users can generally trust their own workstation providing that they control it completely, while an individual user usually distrusts the servers and the other workstations because he/she cannot know directly if these servers and workstations are failing or have been penetrated by an intruder. On the other hand, server administrators and users distrust other workstations, for the same reasons. However the trustworthiness of the distributed system can be improved if it is fault-tolerant, i.e., if the failure of a server or of a workstation is not perceived at the other workstations, irrespective of the cause of the failure, be it an accidental physical fault or an intrusion.

Because they do not take intrusions into account classical fault tolerance techniques, such as data and processing replication, although they can help to tolerate accidental faults, do not provide means of preserving confidentiality. Indeed, if intrusions are to be taken into account and if confidentiality of sensitive information has to be maintained, simple replication will decrease system trustworthiness, since several copies of confidential information can be targets for an intrusion. This was the motivation for a technique which has been developed at LAAS for tolerating faults while preserving confidentiality, namely the fragmentation-redundancy-scattering (FRS) technique [42]. Fragmentation consists of breaking down all sensitive information into fragments, so that any isolated fragment contains no significant information. Fragments are then scattered among different untrusted sites of the distributed system, so that any intrusion into part of the distributed system only gives access to unrelated fragments. Redundancy is added to the fragments (by replication or the use of an error correcting code) in order to tolerate accidental or deliberate destruction or alteration of fragments. A complete information item can only be reassembled on trusted sites of the distributed system. The FRS technique has already been applied both to the storage of persistent files and to security management; this work has been described in several earlier papers, in particular in [42].

The aim of the present paper is to show how FRS, and in particular object-oriented FRS, can be used in the design and in the implementation of any application or system service so as to achieve not just reliable and secure storage but also secure processing of confidential information (e.g. protection from eavesdropping or interference). Secure processing of confidential information has been investigated elsewhere using more conventional ciphering approaches, i.e. the scheme of processing ciphered data described in [2]. Such approaches need specific ciphers ("Privacy Homomorphisms" [133], and are rather limited and relatively inefficient; simple attacks can manage to get clear information. The approach which is advocated in this paper is quite different since it relies on the fact that confidential information can very often be decomposed into a collection of non confidential items on which processing can be done in clear text. The original attempt to extend FRS to cover information processing [164] required significant manual redesign of the application

---

[1]  System specifications describe what the system should do, according to performance and reliability requirements, as well as what it should not, according to safety or security requirements (e.g. the hazardous states from which a catastrophe may ensue, or the sensitive information that must not be disclosed to or modified by unauthorized users).

programs whose execution was to be protected. In this paper we discuss how such requirements for application program redesign can be avoided by allying the FRS technique to an object-oriented approach to system design. In addition, we develop in this paper a scheme of "confidentiality constraints" expressed in terms of first-order logic formulae for defining the confidentiality requirements imposed on a given application, and provide a brief description of the first experiment on the use of FRS for information processing.

## 2 Distributed system architecture and assumptions

The distributed system architecture (cf. Fig. 1.) which we consider in this paper is composed of a set of trusted workstations (more exactly user workstations which are trusted by their respective users), and a set of untrusted machines which are the basis for providing a set of fault-tolerant secure servers. A user of a trusted workstation is responsible for the security of his/her workstation and also for taking all necessary physical security precautions for ensuring that such sensitive actions as logging in, and any required authentication are not being observed. During a session of usage of such a trusted workstation, that workstation resources are not sharable (e.g., remote access by others to the workstation is disallowed). Confidential information will be stored on such a workstation during a usage session. However, unless subsequent security precautions concerning access to that workstation are deemed adequate, such information will not be left on a workstation after completion of the session. (We do not consider network-related security and reliability issues in this paper, but would merely remark that analogous techniques to FRS, involving spread spectrum communications, already exist, as well of course as numerous conventional ones.)

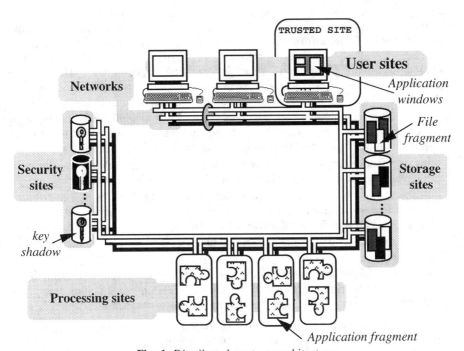

**Fig. 1.** Distributed system architecture

In this paper we assume the provision of two types of services already implemented using untrusted sites, namely the provision of storage and authentication/authorization. The use of conventional FRS for such provisions has been successfully demonstrated - see [42]. The authentication and authorization are realized by a security server implemented as a set of security sites, administrated by different operators. As long as a majority of security sites is free of faults and intrusions (including intrusions by the security administrators), user authentication and access control are reliably achieved and no sensitive information is disclosed. This security server can implement various security policies, including multi-level security (MLS) policies.

With regard to these services, our fault assumptions encompass accidental faults, physical faults that would affect untrusted sites, but also any type of intrusion that would affect the untrusted sites or the networks.

Although we admit the possibility of intrusions of untrusted sites, we nevertheless assume that such intrusions are not particularly easy to carry out, and that the effort an intruder will have to provide to intrude separately several sites is proportional to the number of sites involved. (Clearly, the mechanisms described in this paper are intended to ensure that successful intrusions at one or a small number of untrusted sites does not provide means of accessing or modifying data or processing activities that are the responsibility of any other untrusted site.)

## 3    FRS data processing

### 3.1  Principles

The aim of the original FRS technique was to provide a general framework for the reliable processing of confidential information, assuming that what matters is the confidentiality of the information being processed (the data) rather than the confidentiality of the operations performed on it (the program). This was later extended to provide confidentiality of information processing [164]. For any application program or system service, such use of FRS results in the transformation of the software into a fragmented form according to several basic rules:

1. the application including code and data is divided into application fragments in such a way that the cooperation of the application fragments satisfies the specifications of the initial (complete) application;

2. any application fragment shall not provide any confidential information to a potential intruder on the site where the application fragment is located;

3. all the application fragments shall be scattered among the sites of a distributed architecture (separation) in such a way that groups of fragments stored at a given site provide no significant information to an intruder;

4. appropriate redundancy must be introduced either during fragmentation or scattering;

5. as far as possible, an intruder shall not be able to identify fragments belonging to the same application process or to the same object, since application fragments shall be identified from the user site by enciphered references.

A major problem with the use of this original FRS technique was that of how to deal with fragment code, and in particular how to deal with global variables, a problem whose solution frequently involved partial redesign of the application programs involved. This problem provides much of the first motivation for the use of object-oriented techniques described in this paper.

## 3.2  Object view of FRS

The object model used here is not specific to any particular object-oriented programming language: we simply assume that *objects* are derived from *classes* and encapsulate data structures that can be manipulated only by a set of functions (*methods*); *objects* can be decomposed into *sub-objects* that can be identified by *references*. The use of *inheritance* is not discussed very much in this paper. Nevertheless, inheritance can be used for programming FRS applications in conjunction with other properties of object-oriented programming languages, such as *reflection* (see Section 5.4).

The main interest of the object model in connection with FRS is that the fragmentation, being in terms of objects, naturally encompasses program code as well as data. It can normally be applied to an existing application program without requiring the designer to reprogram the application - all that has to be done is to identify which object classes are to be used as the basis on which data and code is to be fragmented. Such identification involves deciding at what level of the object structuring it will be the case that the individual objects, when examined in isolation, do not contain confidential information. Thus the programmer simply has to provide what are in effect some additional declarations, rather than invent new fragmented algorithms (which is what the original method of extending FRS to information processing required).

The design approach which is proposed in this paper thus relies on the fact that the fragmentation of the application can be based, at design time, on the semantics of the information being processed. The designer of the application has therefore to find an appropriate design structuring to obtain non-confidential objects and thus to define application fragments. The object model offers a convenient design framework for several reasons: the object notion encapsulates information, objects can be decomposed into more elementary objects, and any object can readily be mapped onto an autonomous runtime unit on an appropriate fault-tolerant distributed system.

This approach can be used in different ways and for various applications. For example, in transaction-processing applications, large amounts of confidential information can be held in persistent objects but, in this case, the amount of processing may be relatively limited. The information and the operations performed can be organised (structured) in such a way that individual actions of a transaction are remotely executed by non-confidential objects. In other applications, such as numerical computations, processing is very intensive but objects are mainly temporary because there is little persistent state and thus all input parameters can be given for each activation. (In each case, the links i.e., the references, between objects belonging to the same application are kept secured at the trusted user workstation, where the application is started.)

The object-oriented approach to the use of FRS is thus attractive for implementing various types of applications that hold and process confidential information. A particular characteristic of the approach is that it provides application designers with a single unified design scheme for making their applications tolerant to both accidental *and* intentional faults.

# 4    Notion of confidential information

## 4.1  Principles

The notion of confidential information relates to the interpretation an intruder can have about its semantics in a given operational context. Information semantics may be confidential depending on its value: for instance, a string of characters might be sufficiently meaningful in isolation to be easily interpreted as a confidential information independently of any usage in a program. But this is not always the case; a numerical value is most unlikely to be interpreted as a confidential information without any knowledge of its internal representation or of its usage in a given application context. For example, the bit string corresponding to a salary variable that holds the value 20000 in the data segment of a program must be mapped to a real representation in the machine before it could be interpreted as a real value. However this is not sufficient, as a confidential information item is in fact a combination of sets of items that bring together information to a potential intruder. Such an intruder can get meaningful salary information if and only if he is able to associate together several information items such as: person name, salary amount, salary period and currency. This simple example shows that very often, thanks to its structure, a confidential information item is in fact a set of non-confidential data items.

This notion of confidential information defined as a set of public items may not be appropriate in some applications or for the management of unstructured objects (strings, keys, files, etc.) where the semantics is unknown. For instance, in the file storage system described in [42], FRS was applied to unstructured files (Unix files) and was based on the use of ciphering techniques and a scheme of regular fragmentation to produce fragments. Other techniques, such as threshold schemes[2], can also be used to deal with non-structured objects: a number of items higher than the threshold must be gathered to reconstruct the secret [146]. This technique has mainly been used for small information items such as cryptographic keys. A similar approach was also used at a coarse granularity in [123]. In the last two cases, fragmentation provides both redundancy and ciphering of the data.

The coexistence of both classes of fragmentation techniques can be illustrated by another example (in fact one which is used in our current major experiment): suppose a meeting of a group of people is a confidential information item. The information about the meeting is composed of a list of participants, a given topic, a venue and time/date items. A participant is defined by his/her personal identity which may be considered as public information; the same assumption can be made for other items such as the venue. However, the information about a meeting might be confidential because of the topic discussed and also because of the identities of the participants attending. Keeping the meeting information secret may involve ciphering the topic (given the lack of structural semantics of a character string) and scattering the list of participants ; only appropriate references to participants need then to be kept in the meeting object. An operation on the participant list itself is performed within the

---

[2]  Threshold schemes consist in generating, from a secret information, several shadows so that a given number T of shadows (T being the threshold) is necessary to reconstruct the secret information, whereas T-1 shadows does not reveal any confidential information. The number of shadows is greather than, or equal to T in order to tolerate faults and intrusions.

meeting object at a given site, while operations on the participant information are performed at other sites in the network where those participant objects are located.

## 4.2 Confidentiality constraints

The fragmentation principle relies on the notion of confidentiality constraints that define the confidential information used in the application. These confidentiality constraints are first expressed informally as part of the non-functional specifications of the application. These non-functional specifications are interpreted by the application designer so as to define an appropriate structuring so that each confidential information item is broken down into non-confidential items. In each object in the design, the information is structured in terms of a collection of sub-objects representing information items.

The interpretation of informal confidentiality constraints can be more formally described in terms of first order logic formulae. For instance, going back to the simple example given in Section 4, the confidential *meeting* information can be structured into more elementary objects such as *topic, time/date, venue, person_list* . The formula *{meeting == topic ∧ time/date ∧ venue ∧ person_list}* indicates first that meeting is decomposed into the aforementioned items and, second, that the conjunction of these items reveals sensitive information. Another example would be the following: *{meeting == (topic ∨ time/date ∨ venue) ∧ person_list}*; any combination of *person_list* and the topic discussed, or the location, or the date of the meeting is confidential. If the specifications indicate that the list of attendees is also a confidential information item for any meeting, then *{person_list == person [∧ person]\*}* indicates that any group of persons in the *person_list* is confidential information.

Such clauses specify in fact that the left hand side corresponding object is confidential because the right hand side logical formula composed of sub-objects may reveal confidential information to an intruder. Any sub-object in one formula may also be confidential and then be defined by another clause. Finally, a special clause is needed to specify the set of unstructured objects that are also confidential:

Unstructured confidential objects == *{<object> [ , <object>] \*}*

It is important to mention here that such a formal definition of confidentiality constraints by means of a set of clauses leads one to identify objects (in italic) used in further steps of the design process.

## 5    Object-oriented FRS

Based on the object model described in Section 3.2, the fragmentation design process operates on a strong structuring of the information in terms of a hierarchy (composition) of objects. In any object, confidential private information can be structured as a set of more elementary objects. The fragmentation is thus based on an appropriate structuring, as originally defined by the designer. The FRS design approach involves two main tasks:

i)    definition of basic objects (classes) that do not contain confidential information or whose confidential information is ciphered, based on the object composition hierarchy (fragmentation);

ii)   creation of autonomous instances of these basic objects in a large set of untrusted
      sites of a distributed computing system (scattering).

The main idea of the object oriented FRS is that it is a recursive design process that
operates on the hierarchical representation of the application and yields application
fragments; the recursion ends as soon as, on every branch of the design tree, an object
that does not process any confidential information is encountered, or, no further
decomposition exists already or can be applied (in which case the data in the object
must be enciphered if its confidentiality is to be protected). The corresponding runtime
fragments are then scattered among the distributed architecture and communicate via
messages. If fragmentation by itself does not introduce adequate redundancy, then
fragments are replicated before being scattered.

## 5.1  Fragmentation

The fragmentation design process can involve several design iterations, starting from a
first version of the design of the application, i.e., a first object composition tree. At
each iteration, the designer performs an analysis of the list of confidentiality
constraints of the application in order to identify the objects containing confidential
information. Then a new design step can be started if some confidential object can be
decomposed into, or is already defined in terms of, more elementary objects. This new
design step produces a refined version of the object composition tree. Then the
designer goes back to a new analysis of the confidentiality constraints that have not
been solved by the previous design  (see Fig. 2).

```
for any <object > in current design tree
do
        if object is confidential then
                decompose object further (fragmentation)
        or      apply ciphering technique
        or      leave it to a trusted site allocation
        end_if
end_for
```

**Fig. 2.** Fragmentation  principle

 This iterative design process with its analysis of the confidentiality constraints,
continues until non-confidential objects are obtained or a confidential leaf is reached,
and terminates when there are no more confidentiality constraints to solve in the list.
Finally, should there remain any confidential objects that cannot be structured into
more elementary objects, which might either be due to their granularity or their
functionality, ciphering techniques are used.

## 5.2  Redundancy

Several approaches can be used for adding redundancy to fragments. Various error
processing techniques may be used either when the runtime units corresponding to
design objects are created or at a early stage during the design of the application in
term of objects.

The underlying runtime system may offer a set of transparent error processing protocols that can be selected at configuration time to install runtime units in a redundant fashion, as in Delta-4 [115]. The latter relies on detection mechanisms and voting protocols implemented by the underlying multicast communication system. Several checkpointing strategies between passive replicas and synchronisation strategies between active replicas are available.

Another approach consists in defining the error processing technique at an early stage in the design using pre-defined system classes that are responsible for the implementation of a given solution. The idea is to use the notion of inheritance of the object model to derive a fault-tolerant implementation of any object. This solution consists in fact in making inheritable non functional characteristics, using appropriate system classes and programming conventions. This type of solution has been used in particular in the Arjuna project [149] where for example any object can be declared as recoverable.

This declaration means that any object from this class will be created in a redundant fashion, provided that some declarations are given by the object designer (virtual function definition, function overloading). System classes must provide by inheritance a large number of error processing protocols; the development of system classes can take advantage of basic system services such as error detection and recovery, atomic broadcast, various voting protocols, stable memory management. The first work on the use of object-orientation in connection with FRS assumed that conventional object-oriented inheritance would similarly be used to declare *secured* objects [52]. However, there are significant problems with such an approach, and we now think that the use of reflection is more promising approach (see Section 5.4).

## 5.3 Scattering

The scattering phase consists then in allocating object-fragments replicas to the computing sites; any object instance must be created as an autonomous computing unit, i.e., mapped onto a basic runtime unit of the underlying operating system. This aspect is discussed in Section 6.1.

```
for any <fragment> in current fragment set
do
            if object-fragment is still confidential then
                            allocate to a trusted site
      else
                    until a valid untrusted site is allocated
                            allocate to an untrusted site
                            if not creation of a confidential group of objects
                            then     this site is a valid site
                    end_until
            end_if
      end_for
```

Fig. 3. Scattering principle

The scattering phase is summarised in Fig. 3. The main problem in the scattering phase is to avoid creating sets of objects on the same site that correspond to a confidential information item. Confidentiality constraints between fragments must then be taken into account to identify such groups of fragments. The first simple rule is that object-fragments having the same parent object-fragment must be located on different sites. But this rule is not sufficient; scattering may group fragments which are not strictly brothers in the hierarchical design but that may reveal confidential information. A careful analysis of fragment groups must be done, especially if there are relatively few sites available to receive scattered fragments.

## 5.4  Use of inheritance and reflection

From an object-oriented programming language viewpoint, FRS leads to the scattering of sub-objects of a given object. This means that when the object is created, some or all of its sub-objects may need to be created remotely. Subsequently, the conventional scheme for invoking the methods of such remote sub-objects must be replaced by a scheme of remote method invocation.

The provision of means for so redefining what are normally basic internal operations (object creation and method invocation) of the language runtime system is not common. However some object-oriented languages do have the property that they provide access to such operations and the ability to modify them in the language itself: this property is known as *reflection*.

Clearly, even if it were possible, it would be undesirable for the application programmer to have to program such a redefinition scheme explicitly in the definitions of each class of objects whose confidentiality is to be protected. What is needed is a means of indicating, for any given class, that such a scheme is to be used. In other words, if one considers that a class is itself an object belonging to some meta-class, the requirement is to have some means of providing in the definition of the meta-class, the methods of object creation and method invocation that are to be used by any of its class objects. Such a *reflective* facility in fact would seem to be of great promise for not just for object-oriented FRS, but also for implementing various non functional characteristics using object-oriented languages .[158]

This type of facility was first provided in Common LISP, but has been recently implemented in a variant of C++ called OpenC++ [34], in which both method invocation and also access to local variables can be captured and re-defined at the meta-level. In OpenC++ the application programmer can readily redefine access behaviour at the meta-level. Inheritance of pre-defined meta-classes allows the definition of new meta-classes for any object class in the application. This scheme is now being investigated as a means of providing FRS facilities; the objective is to define meta-classes for every confidential class in the application, thus hiding object creation problems (including replication and scattering of sub-objects), but also remote access problems (including reference computation and access control mechanisms) from the application programmer.

## 5.5  Summary

The complete design process can be summarised in the several tasks that are represented in Fig. 4. This figure shows the major steps of the design and implementation of an FRS application. Several iterations on the design of the application taking into account confidentiality constraints on the information being manipulated, lead to the definition of non-confidential objects. These non-confidential objects are the application fragments. According to the runtime abstractions provided by the runtime system, application fragments are mapped onto autonomous runtime units. Adequate error processing protocols are then selected on an object-by-object basis leading to a set of autonomous runtime object replicas. This selection takes into account the functionality of the object and also the accidental fault assumptions that can be made regarding the available sites on the distributed configuration. The last phase of the design process consists in scattering these replicas. The scattering phase must take care to avoid gathering together groups of objects that can be perceived by an intruder as constituting a confidential information item. Confidentiality constraints between object replicas must thus be taken into account for the allocation of sites to runtime units. The set of replicas is in fact divided into two subsets: (i) object replicas that do not contain confidential information and that can be executed on untrusted stations, but also (ii) the set of some still confidential objects that must be executed on trusted sites of the distributed system.

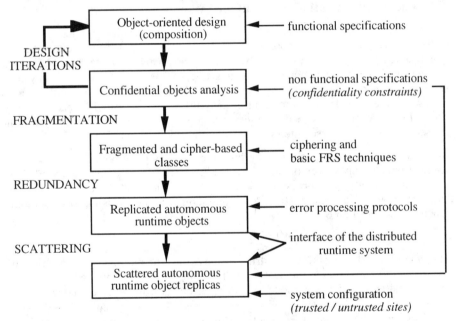

**Fig. 4.** FRS Application Design steps

# 6    Implementation issues

## 6.1  Distributed runtime environment

The degree of difficulty involved in implementing an object-based application largely depends on the abstractions provided by the distributed runtime system. Object fragments have to be mapped onto autonomous runtime units. The system we have used for our current major experiment, the Delta-4 system, does not provide the notion of object; instead it provides the notion of a server, though this is not far from the object notion as previously defined. It corresponds to a private address space and a set of operations with well-defined interfaces. Object mapping can be done in various ways: (i) any object instance corresponds at runtime to a server, or (ii) a server is responsible for any instance creation for a given class. The second of these approaches is the one we have used. The Delta-4 distributed runtime layer, namely Deltase[3], provides server mapping on top of Unix (the local executive) and a transparent multiple remote procedure call mechanism used for remote method invocation between object manager replicas. The set of servers provides an object management layer on top of the distributed runtime layer.

In the implementation of FRS, the object runtime layer may involve several instance managers (Deltase servers) per class. At one extreme, any site on the network may provide an instance manager for any class in the application. The scattering algorithm may then allocate any object instance on any site. Objects can be created dynamically by invoking the appropriate create operation of the corresponding instance manager. The Delta-4 distributed runtime system layer includes a set of error processing protocols used to install replicated servers.

## 6.2 User authentication and authorization

As indicated in Section 2, user authentication and authorization are achieved by a distributed security server composed of several security sites. A user is authenticated when at least a majority of security sites agree to authenticate him [42]. One authenticated, the user can request access to services. This request is evaluated by each security site according to user privileges, service access control list and security policy. All the sites decisions to grant or deny the access are voted on each security site and if a majority is reached to grant the access, an access key is transmitted from the security sites to the user site by means of a threshold scheme [146].

The access control approach, briefly presented in this paragraph, is used for any application, system server or simply any object (files) implemented by FRS on untrusted computing resources. The key which is gathered at the user site, will be used latter on by the application for referencing fragments using cryptographic functions (see Section 6.3.).

## 6.3 Reference management

The scattering of objects in a distributed environment requires an identification mechanism to allow remote invocation. In fact, most of the security of FRS relies on the fact that an intruder is not able to gather fragments from outside the trusted user site or to invoke objects (fragments) directly. The reference[4] management system must first ensure that related fragments (belonging to the same application) cannot be identified just by looking at object references. References can then be dynamically computed at the trusted site using the secret key, provided for this application and for this user by the authorization protocol.

Looking more carefully at a fragmented application (cf. Fig. 5), one can see that the application is in most cases implemented finally as a "star structure" whose centre is located at the trusted user site. The centre of the star is at least the root of the object composition tree.

---

[3]  DELTASE : DELTA-4 Application Support Environment.
[4]  A reference is viewed here as a generalisation of the notion of pointer in a distributed environment.

An ideal reference system must ensure: (i) unique identification of the remote object-fragment, (ii) authentication of the invoking application, and (iii) verification of permissions on the invoked object:

$$\text{reference} = E_k \text{ (object\_name, application\_name, object\_permissions)}.$$

A very simple way of using references can just be to consider them as capabilities: as soon as they are provided to an object manager (i.e., when the reference is known) then the corresponding object is activated. In this case, the ciphering algorithm $E$ is a one-way function and $k$ is the application secret key.

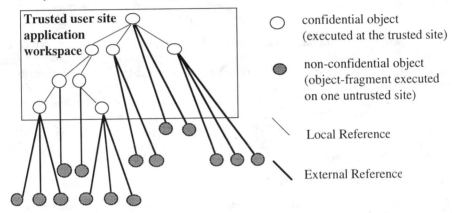

**Fig. 5.** Structure of a fragmented application - Local and External references

A more sophisticated solution would be to decipher the reference at the object manager site to check authenticity and permissions. In that case a shared secret key must be used to implement this solution; the key must then be kept securely in any station in a local trusted sub-system (local TCB [111]). In this case, the ciphering algorithm $E$ is based on a secret key cryptosystem and $k$ is a secret key shared by the user application at the user site and one of the untrusted sites (where one copy of the invoked object is located).

Finally, shared objects between two or more different applications will have different references, thus preventing search by induction on shared objects.

## 7    Experimentation

We have investigated the above FRS design approach on a detailed example, a distributed Electronic Diary, which has been implemented on the Delta-4 system. A more detailed description can found in [52]. We describe here this application using a small series of classes, so leading to a hierarchical design of the E-Diary. In this simple example, a number of confidentiality constraints on the processed information have been defined and taken into account. The processing facilities provided (i.e. the operations that can be performed on defined objects) are in fact very limited in the current version of the E-Diary application and the defined objects are persistent. Another possible type of application would be to have no persistence and heavy computation such as in numerical computations on sensitive information (e.g. missile trajectory computation). However, the E-Diary example provides a convenient means of illustrating the object-oriented FRS design steps described in Section 5.

## 7.1 Functional specifications

The functional specifications only address the definition of management operations on meetings day-by-day; the information related to a meeting is composed of a given topic, a group of people attending, a venue and time/date information. Any person attending is defined by several identification items. The information used for the management of meetings is stored in each of a set of *meeting* descriptors and can be summarised as follows:

- *topic:*            topic to be discussed during the meeting;
- *venue/time/date:*      place where the meeting is held and time/date information;
- *dynamic person list:*    list of persons attending the meeting.

These descriptors are the main leaves of a tree (a sub-tree) of the E-Diary which is considered as being an object which is private to a given user (the E-Diary is not shared by multiple users). Each *person* in the list is defined by several information items such as *name/firstname*, full *address*, and *phone_number*. Some periods like *days*, *weeks* or *months* may be locked for a given *reason* (travel abroad or any personal reason for instance). The E-Diary also includes a *note-pad* where *messages* may be stored on a day-by-day basis. The E-Diary provides functions to insert, list or remove any of the above defined objects. The italic words indicate most of the objects used in the design of E-Diary application.

## 7.2 Confidentiality constraints

The description of the example given in Section 7.1. can be augmented with an informal description of confidentiality constraints. These were chosen to be the following:

1.  Any two or more of items in a given *meeting* such as *topic, time/date, venue, person_list* considered as constituting confidential information.

2.  Personal identification items such as *name, address* and *phone number* can be individually considered as being public information; but any pair of such information items including person *name* is confidential.

3.  The group of *persons* attending the same *meeting* is considered as constituting a confidential information item.

4.  Any unstructured information items such as *topic* of a meeting, *message* in the note pad, and *locking reason* for a *day*, *week* or *month* is confidential.

The interpretation we have made of this informal description of the confidentiality constraints leads to the following formal description:

| Confidentiality clauses | Unstructured confidential objects |
|---|---|
| person == {name ∧ (address / phone number)} | {topic, message, locking_reasons} |
| meeting == {venue ∧ topic ∧ time/date ∧ [person]*, venue ∧ time/date ∧ [person]*, time/date ∧ [person]*, person ∧ [person]*} | |

These constraints have to be taken into account in order to refine the first design and to identify fragments. They are also used for scattering.

## 7.3  Final object-oriented design

Several design steps were performed to obtain the final design of the *E-Diary* objects and to identify fragments in the design. In the first design the *meeting* object was not decomposed into sub-objects as candidate fragments. The list of *persons* attending a *meeting* also did not appear . Since *meetings* and *persons* are confidential objects (see clauses 1 and 2) some decomposition into more elementary objects was performed such as represented in Fig. 6. Some of the object classes (and their component objects) forming the E-Diary application object are shown, where an asterisk indicates the possibility of there being several components of a given object class.

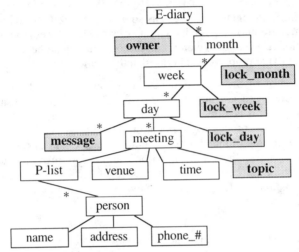

**Fig. 6.** The E-Diary object composition hierarchy (final version)

The object hierarchies presented in Fig. 6 illustrate the various components in the design of the E-Diary object down to elementary objects, the latter being a combination of elementary objects such as integers, booleans, strings, etc. Some of the elementary objects represented by grey boxes are confidential leaves of the tree that according to our assumptions cannot be usefully decomposed into smaller objects; for instance owner, messages, locking reason and meeting topic are strings that are assumed to be ciphered to ensure confidentiality as soon as they are entered by the user in the system.

Pre-defined confidentiality constraints lead to separating as fragments objects that will be managed by separate instance managers in the implementation. *Topic, venue* and *time/date* objects are assumed to be object-fragments. The *P-list* object may still be kept in the *meeting* objects since it contains only pointers (references) to *persons* managed by an instance manager of class *person* in the implementation. *Person* is thus another object-fragment. As a consequence, the *meeting* object is then relatively empty since *meeting* sub-objects are scattered in separate fragments.

## 8    Conclusions and future work

The electronic diary system is the first sizeable experiment we have undertaken in implementing an application using Object-Oriented Fragmentation-Redundancy-Scattering techniques. As such the experiment has greatly assisted us in formulating a methodical approach to the use of the techniques, and helped to motivate the development of the scheme for expressing confidentiality constraints that we have described in Section 4. More complex processing could be added to actual object-fragments even in this simple example without introducing any confidentiality problem.

The granularity of objects-fragments obtained in the example to solve the confidentiality problem might appear relatively small. However, this technique can also be used to solve some problems using a very coarse granularity; for instance, let us consider a medical record system where the information is classified into two parts, administrative and properly medical. In this quite simple example, there is no need to go further in the fragmentation process as soon as the link between these two large fragments (some references) is retained at the trusted site. Access to one or both parts of the information (if necessary) then needs appropriate user authentication (medical or administrative staff) to properly grant related authorization.

The performance of FRS mainly depends on the granularity of the fragmentation. Nevertheless, FRS need not introduce any significant information and processing overhead (reassembly is negligible); it obviously introduces communication overhead with respect to a pure processing replication, e.g., in an application that does not attempt to tolerate intentional faults. Although parallelism is not the aim of our fragmentation process, the additional opportunities it provides for the use of parallelism can be of significant benefit with regard to application performance in suitable circumstances. In particular they could reduce the impact of such communication overheads.

From a programming viewpoint, given the awkwardness of the manual translation involved in the final stages of implementation down onto the Delta-4 platform, more extensive trials of further applications will probably best await the provision of means for automatically installing applications onto a suitable object-oriented distributed runtime layer. We are at present just starting to investigate the suitability for this purpose of COOL [91], which runs on the Chorus micro-kernel operating system [135], in the hope that this will provide us with a good basis for using FRS in connection with C++. Other topics on which more work is needed include naming facilities for reference management, algorithms to compute references, and access control mechanisms for fine grain object invocation. By such work we hope to develop the object-oriented FRS scheme to the point where experiments can enable realistic cost/effectiveness assessment of the scheme on a variety of applications. However in parallel we also plan to continue recent closely-related work on object-oriented language concepts, not just inheritance but also in particular delegation and reflection [158], which we believe will facilitate the structuring and implementation of applications using various dependability-related mechanisms in combination, including of course FRS. The OpenC++ language [34] is currently our favoured candidate for experimenting reflection in the implementation of FRS application (see paper III.G).

# Implementing Fault-Tolerant Applications Using Reflective Object-Oriented Programming[*]

Jean-Charles Fabre  Vincent Nicomette  Tanguy Pérennou [1]
Robert Stroud  Zhixue Wu[2]

[1]LAAS-CNRS  [2]University of Newcastle upon Tyne

**Abstract:** This paper shows how reflection and object-oriented programming can be used to ease the implementation of classical fault tolerance mechanisms in distributed applications. When the underlying runtime system does not provide fault tolerance transparently, classical approaches to implementing fault tolerance mechanisms often imply mixing functional programming with non-functional programming (e.g. error processing mechanisms). This means that application programmers must be aware of which fault tolerance mechanism is used and how it should be used. An alternative approach based on reflective object-oriented programming is presented. The use of reflection improves the transparency of fault tolerance mechanisms to the programmer and more generally provides a cleaner separation between functional and non-functional programming.

The implementations of some classical replication techniques using a reflective approach are presented in detail and illustrated by several examples that have been prototyped on a network of Unix workstations. Lessons learnt from our experiments are drawn and future work is discussed.

## 1    Introduction

The implementation of fault-tolerant distributed applications largely depends on the computing environment that is available. The ideal case is when the underlying operating system provides fully transparent error processing protocols such as in Delta-4 [115, 118]. However, when the operating system does not provide such facilities, the application programmer is forced to integrate in the functional part of the application statements to initialise or invoke appropriate non-functional mechanisms for error-processing. This can be done using library calls to pre-defined mechanisms embedded in a specific environment such as in Isis [23]. Another approach, used by systems like Avalon/C++ [43] and Arjuna [149], consists of using properties of object-oriented languages, such as inheritance, to make objects recoverable. However, even if the object model seems appropriate for introducing fault tolerance into applications, there are significant problems with such an approach for implementing various replication techniques in distributed applications, and we show that the use of reflection is a more promising approach.

Reflection [99] enables functional programming to be separated transparently from non-functional programming, i.e., in the present paper, programming of fault tolerance mechanisms. Reflection allows programmers to observe and manipulate the computational behaviour of a program. In particular, in object-oriented languages, this property enables some operations such as object creation, attribute access and

---

[*]   This paper is a revised version of [51].

method invocations to be intercepted and this ability will be used for implementing fault tolerance mechanisms.

The idea of using a meta-level to hide the implementation of non-functional requirements such as dependability and distribution transparency from the application programmer is not new. For example, various authors have proposed using the CLOS meta-object protocol to add attributes such as persistence and concurrency control to application objects [11, 112, 158] has argued that reflection is an appropriate way to address distribution transparency and [1] has described the implementation of dependability protocols using reflection in an actor-based language.

The main objective of this paper is to show that dependability issues (part of the non-functional requirements of an application) can be addressed separately and implemented independently from functional requirements by using reflective object-oriented programming languages. Dependability can thus be provided transparently from the programmer's point of view and dependability-related facilities can be reused in multiple applications. The contributions of this paper are two-fold: (a) to provide a comparison of different approaches to implementing fault-tolerance with respect to the degree of transparency for the application programmer, and (b) to provide detailed case studies showing how meta-level programming can be used to implement various replication strategies transparently in the reflective object-oriented language Open-C++. The latter is illustrated by presenting the implementation of the following three replication techniques used in our examples: *passive replication, semi-active replication* and *active replication with majority voting.* The reflective object-oriented approach is interesting not only with respect to providing transparency, reusability and flexibility from a programmer's point of view but also with respect to the implementation of fault tolerance mechanisms in particular on system platforms based on micro-kernels. In the current status of our experiments, efficiency is not a prime objective.

Section 2 discusses various ways of using fault tolerance mechanisms in the development and implementation of distributed applications. Programming style is underlined in each case. Section 3 provides a brief overview of reflection in object-oriented languages and introduces the reflective capabilities of Open-C++, the language that was used in our experiments. Section 4 briefly presents the distributed processing model used and details the reflective implementation of the three replication techniques that are under investigation. Section 5 mainly describes implementation issues of meta-objects for further development.

## 2    Approaches to programming fault tolerance

The aim of this section is to describe several approaches and programming styles that have been used in practice to add redundancy to applications for fault tolerance. These approaches will be considered for programming fault tolerance in distributed applications. A distributed application will be seen here as a collection of distributed software components (objects, processes) communicating by messages. Various error processing techniques may be used either when the runtime units (corresponding to design objects) are created or at an early stage during the design of the application in terms of objects. They can be based either on software component replication or on other approaches such as checkpointing to stable storage.

Three approaches can be followed for implementing error processing: (i) in the underlying runtime systems through built-in error processing facilities, for instance, to replicate software components, (ii) in the programming environment through predefined software constructions and libraries, and (iii) in the application design environment through properties of the programming language. These three approaches are discussed and used as a basis for comparing various programming styles and implementation approaches. We will also underline the limits of the role of the application programmer in each case.

## 2.1    System-based fault tolerance

In this approach, the underlying runtime system may offer a set of transparent error processing protocols, for instance based on replication as in Delta-4 [115]. Delta-4 provides several replication strategies: passive, semi-active and active replication [1]. These rely on detection mechanisms and voting protocols implemented by the underlying multicast communication system. The error processing protocol is selected at configuration time according to the failure mode assumptions that can be made about the available nodes of the distributed computing architecture and the coverage of these assumptions [117]. When the fail-silent assumption (only crash failures) can be retained, various strategies can be used depending on several criteria including the architecture of individual sites on the network, the amount of information managed by each replica, and the deterministic behaviour of the replicas. When the fail-silent assumption is not valid, solutions based on active replication are provided.

Passive replication can be supported by the system, in particular for the management of replicas, but often requires the programmer to define checkpoints [21]. Nevertheless, it has been shown, in particular in Delta-4, that checkpoints can be automatically issued by the underlying runtime system [154]. This approach enables non-deterministic behaviour of the software component. Semi-active replication enables several replicas to process input messages concurrently. Input messages are delivered by the underlying multicast communication system, thus providing input consistency. In this model, non-deterministic behaviour is possible but may require the programmer to define synchronisation checkpoints to enforce consistency of replicated processing. In some circumstances, synchronisation can be solved by the

---

[1]   "Passive replication is a technique in which only one of the replicas (the *primary* replica) processes the input messages and provides output messages (in the absence of faults), the other replicas (the *standby* replicas) do not process input messages and do not produce output messages; their internal states are however regularly updated by means of checkpoints from the primary replica".

"Semi-active replication can be viewed as a hybrid of both active and passive replication; only one of the replicas (the *leader* replica) processes the input messages and provides output messages (in the absence of faults), the other replicas (the *follower* replicas) do not produce output messages; their internal state is updated either by direct processing of input messages or, where appropriate, by means of notifications or "mini-checkpoints" from the leader replica".

"Active replication is a technique in which all replicas process all input messages concurrently so that their internal states are closely synchronized (in the absence of faults), outputs can be taken from any replica; several inter-replica protocols are available to synchronise replicas".

communication system [20]. Finally, when deterministic behaviour can be ensured, several active replication techniques can be defined that are transparent to the application programmer. In Delta-4, several inter-replica protocols (IRp) are available as part of the underlying multicast communication system [32]. When the deterministic assumption is valid, then the same component can be used with either a semi-active or an active replication technique without any change in the source code. The distributed application programming environment (Deltase in Delta-4) provides well-structured software components and offers remote procedure call (RPC) style programming that hides replication. The advantage of this approach is that it provides transparency in most cases for the application programmer; the main drawback is that it needs a specific runtime system and support environment.

## 2.2    Libraries of fault tolerance mechanisms

This approach is based on the use of pre-defined library functions and basic primitives (i.e. a *tool-kit*). A good example of this approach is Isis [23, 24]. The prime objective of this environment was not initially the implementation of fault-tolerant applications, but rather the development of distributed applications based on the notion of process groups. With respect to fault tolerance issues, the underlying assumption is that nodes are fail-silent.

In Isis, a specific software construct called a *coordinator-cohort* can be used to implement fault-tolerant applications, in particular based on passive replication. This generic software construct enables the computation to be organised using groups of processes (tasks) according to various objectives: parallel computations, partitioned computations, replicated computations for fault tolerance. In the implementation of passive replication, the updated states of the primary copy (coordinator) must be sent to the standby copies (cohorts). When the coordinator fails a new coordinator is elected and loaded with the current state of the computation [62]. A new member can be inserted in the group of replicas and its state initialised using a state transfer primitive. All this must be taken into account when programming the replicas. Different checkpointing strategies are left open to the application programmer.

Other fault tolerance mechanisms based on active replication can be defined using group management facilities and multicast communication protocols. A group of replicas is created and the client of this group is able to broadcast requests to all members using the atomic broadcast primitives. A *token* mechanism may be used to determine a leader in the group of replicas that is responsible for sending back the reply to the client (similar to semi-active replication in Delta-4). When no leader is defined, then multiple reply messages are sent to the client which is responsible for selecting the final results (using a first, one-out-of-n, re-assembly, or voting-on-replies[2] strategy). This is done by the application programmer, even if it can be hidden in library calls. (Another example of the use of a library for programming fault-tolerant applications can be found in [61].)

The main difference with respect to the system-based approach described in the previous section is that in this case, error processing and application programming is done at the same programming level using specific programming constructs. This means that specific function calls (state transfer, synchronisation, sending results,

---

[2]  Not for node fault-tolerance since nodes are supposed to be fail-silent.

voting) must be introduced into the application programs at appropriate points, for instance for sending updates (passive replication), token management (semi-active replication) or decision routines (active replication). In other words, such an approach provides *visible* error processing, whereas it was *invisible* at the programming level in the previous case. Nevertheless, the advantage of this approach is that the application programmer can tailor and optimise his own fault tolerance mechanisms. The main drawback is that functional and non-functional programming are mixed together, and may contradict reusability. The approach is not transparent to the application programmers and may impose a specific runtime environment.

## 2.3    Inheritance of fault tolerance mechanisms

The previous two approaches do not rely on any particular property of the programming language since they are based on appropriate mechanisms provided either by the underlying operating system or by a specific environment. The approach described in this section and also the reflective approach described in this paper take advantage of object-oriented properties for providing error processing features to applications.

An approach based on inheritance involves defining the fault tolerance technique in pre-defined system classes that are responsible for the implementation of a given solution. The idea is to use the notion of inheritance to derive a fault-tolerant implementation of objects. This solution consists in fact of making non-functional characteristics such as persistence and recoverability inheritable, using appropriate system classes and programming conventions. This type of solution has been successfully used in particular in Avalon/C++ [43] and in the Arjuna project [149].

A class can be declared as *recoverable*; this declaration means that any instance of the class will perform some error processing, provided that some additional definitions are given by the class designer (e.g. virtual function definitions). In Arjuna, for instance, a recoverable class is derived from the pre-defined system class `StateManager` which is responsible for providing persistence and recovery mechanisms; the application programmer must define the virtual functions `save_state` and `restore_state` for a recoverable class [9]. In Arjuna and Avalon, the nodes are supposed to be fail-silent; thus, the error processing technique is based on checkpointing the state of the current objects in a computation to an object store, a stable storage system. If a computation fails, a new computation is started from this checkpointed information. As with a passive replication mechanism, the computation is done by a primary object, unless a failure occurs.

One might also consider using inheritance to implement alternative error processing techniques, based on active replication, for instance. It seems that other system classes, like `StateManager`, could be defined to provide replicated processing. However, there would be significant problems with such an approach. Error processing techniques based on active replication would require a mechanism for providing replicated method invocations and synchronising replicas on method invocation. Overriding the creation of objects can also be useful for creating several object replicas on different sites. These cannot be transparently achieved using inheritance. The essential difficulty with this approach is that inheritance does not allow access to the internal structure of objects and redefinition of the fundamental mechanisms of an object-oriented language (e.g. method invocation).

## 2.4 Summary and conclusions

The systems that we have described do not all use the same fault tolerance techniques. Nevertheless, they illustrate three different approaches for implementing fault-tolerant applications. In each case, the role of the programmer is different, according to the degree of transparency and separation of concerns provided by the approach.

In the first case, the error processing mechanisms are provided by the underlying system, and transparency and separation of concerns can be achieved. However, this approach lacks flexibility. In the second case, the environment provides library functions that enable the programmer to define his own error processing mechanisms. Transparency and separation of concerns are not achieved due to specific function calls that must be introduced in the program. With the last approach, as shown by the examples, inheritance can be used to add fault tolerance properties to object-oriented applications. Separation of concerns can be achieved but transparency is not totally achieved, because some programming conventions are required.

The aim of this paper is to show how an object-oriented approach can enable fault-tolerant distributed applications to be implemented transparently, using various classical replication techniques. Inheritance seems limited from this viewpoint: inheritance does not enable the underlying operations of the object model (creation, invocation) to be redefined. Thus, inheritance cannot be used to take advantage of the object structuring for implementing replicated processing. The reflective approach which is described in this paper solves part of this problem since reflection provides at least access to internal object operations.

## 3 Reflection and object-oriented programming

In this section we introduce the concept of reflection in the context of object-oriented programming, and give a brief description of Open-C++, the language that was used in our experiments.

### 3.1 Reflection in object-oriented programming languages

**Reflection.** *Reflection* is the process by which a system can reason about and act upon itself. A reflective computational system is a computational system that exhibits reflective behaviour. In a conventional system, computation is performed on data that represents entities that are external to the computational system. However, a reflective computational system must contain data that represents the structural and computational aspects of the system itself. Moreover, it must be possible to access and manipulate such data from within the system itself, and more importantly, such data must be causally connected to the actual behaviour of the system: changes in the data must cause changes in the behaviour of the system and vice versa. Unlike a conventional system, a reflective system allows users to perform computation on the system itself in the same manner as in the application, thus providing users with the ability to adjust the behaviour of the system to suit their particular needs.

**The meta-object approach.** B. Smith invested the power of computational reflection in the environment of 3-Lisp [152]. P. Maes proposed a meta-object approach to implementing reflective systems in the framework of object-oriented computing [99]. Each object $x$ is associated with a *meta-object* $^\wedge x$ that represents both the structural and computational aspects of $x$. $^\wedge x$ contains the meta-information of the object $x$: its structure and its way of handling operation invocations. By making an object $x$ causally connected with its meta-object $^\wedge x$, a system can ensure that any change to $^\wedge x$ will automatically be reflected to $x$. Thus the structure and behaviour of $x$ can be adjusted by modifying its meta-object $^\wedge x$. Since a meta-object is just another object, it can be manipulated in the same manner as a normal object. In class-based object-oriented languages, each meta-object is an instance of a meta-level class that defines its structure and behaviour, but in the rest of this paper, we will tend to talk about meta-objects rather than meta-level classes, thus emphasising the run-time aspects of the meta-object approach.

The meta-object approach has been used in many application areas: debugging, concurrent programming [103] and distributed systems [34]. A very successful example is the meta-object protocol in CLOS [69]. This provides a new approach to designing programming languages. By using the technology of reflection and object-oriented programming, CLOS gives programmers the ability to incrementally modify the language's behaviour and implementation to meet their particular requirements.

The relation of reflection to object-oriented programming is crucial to the meta-object approach. Reflection makes it possible to open up a system implementation without revealing unnecessary implementation details, and the techniques and features of object-oriented programming make reflection practical to use. In particular, two aspects of object-oriented programming are important. First, inheritance makes it easy to adjust the behaviour of objects incrementally. Thus, programmers can make changes to the system by merely specifying how the new behaviour differs from the default behaviour. Second, polymorphism makes it possible for multiple implementations of the same function to coexist without any clash.

The use of meta-level programming makes it possible to separate functional components from non-functional components in a system transparently [158]. If non-functional components can be implemented in an application-independent fashion, they are potentially usable across a wide range of possible problem domains. There are three tangible benefits in taking the meta-object approach to implementing fault-tolerant mechanisms. Firstly, the separation of functional and non-functional components makes it possible for the realisation of non-functional requirements to be transparent rather than intrusive as far as the application programmer is concerned, thus solving the problems associated with traditional techniques for implementing fault tolerance mechanisms (assuming that system-based fault tolerance is not available). Secondly, relying on meta-objects to deal with a wide range of user requirements allows the basic implementation of a fault-tolerant application to be simpler and thus easier to analyse with respect to its correctness. Thirdly, permitting each object to have its own meta-object makes it possible for an application to apply different strategies for different objects according to their characteristics. These features will be illustrated in the remainder of the paper.

## 3.2 The example of Open-C++

Reflection was described generally in the last sub-section. In this sub-section, we introduce a reflective object-oriented programming language based on the meta-object approach, Open-C++. Although it provides only limited reflective capabilities, it has been successfully used in our experiments and will be used to describe the examples in the paper.

Open-C++ [34] is a C++ pre-processor that provides the programmer with two levels of abstraction: the base-level, dedicated to traditional C++ object-oriented programming, and the meta-level which allows certain aspects of the C++ programming model to be redefined. For example, at the meta-level, one can redefine the general behaviour of a base-level class: how it handles method calls, how it reads or writes its member variables, what happens at instance creation and deletion time. Each instance of a reflective base-level class is controlled at run-time by its meta-object. The association of a base-level class and a meta-level class is made at compile-time by the Open-C++ pre-processor.

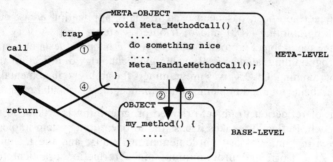

**Fig. 1.** Invocation trapping

Programming the meta-level boils down to programming C++ classes since meta-objects are just instances of traditional C++ classes. Meta-level classes all inherit (directly or indirectly) from the predefined `MetaObj` class. They can redefine the methods describing creation, deletion of an object, method invocation, etc. In Open-C++, the control of base-level object operations is realised via traps to the related meta-object. For example, the handler associated with a base-level method call is a virtual method belonging to the class `MetaObj` called `Meta_MethodCall`, as shown in Fig. 1. It is possible for the application programmer to choose which attributes and methods are reflective. When a reflective method is called at the base-level, the call is trapped and handled at the meta level by `Meta_MethodCall` (①). This meta method makes it possible to redefine the semantics of calling a method at the base-level. Usually, `Meta_MethodCall` invokes the application method from the meta level using another meta operation, `Meta_HandleMethodCall` (②③), but it may also perform some extra processing before or after calling the application method and perhaps not even call the application method directly at all. At the end of `Meta_MethodCall`, any results are returned to the caller as if for a normal method call.(④).

The creation and initialisation of a reflective object is a more complex process but can also be controlled at the meta-level. Other meta-methods are provided to control attribute access for reading and writing, or meta-object cleanup before meta-object deletion.

The reflective attributes and methods of a base-level Open-C++ class are declared using a "`//MOP reflect:`" clause. For example in Fig. 2, the class `MyClass` has a reflective method `g()` and a reflective attribute `x`. These are the only attributes and methods that can be controlled by the meta-object associated with an instance of `MyClass`. The association of a class with a meta-level class is expressed using a

"`//MOP reflect class`" clause. For example, in Fig. 2, the meta-level class for `MyClass` is declared to be `MyMetaObj`. Note that reflection is not completely transparent in Open-C++. Instead, the application programmer is required to use a special reflective version of the original application class that Open-C++ generates automatically. Thus, a reflective object of type `MyClass` is declared to be of type `refl_MyClass` and not `MyClass`.

```
/* Declaration of a class with reflective members */
      class MyClass {
      public:
              f();
      //MOP reflect:
              g();                    /* public reflective method */
      protected:
              int i;
      //MOP reflect:
              float x;        /* protected reflective attribute */
      };
/* Association of a class with a meta-level class */
      //MOP reflect class MyClass : MyMetaObj;
              /* any object of class refl_MyClass (not MyClass!) */
              /* will be controlled by a meta-object of class */
              /* MyMetaObj */
/* Declaration of a reflective object */
      refl_MyClass MyObject;          /* reflective object */
```

**Fig. 2.** An Open-C++ class of a reflective object

Although Open-C++ supports meta-level programming, it only provides a limited model of reflection. First, it does not support structural reflection, i.e., the ability to make changes to the structure of an object by modifying its meta-object. The lack of structural reflection limits the capabilities of the language. For example, it is impossible for users to support debugging or schema evolution by using Open-C++. Second, only limited computational reflection is supported in Open-C++. A meta-object in Open-C++ can control method calls and variable accesses. However, it cannot, for instance, change the way inheritance works in C++. Third, the binding between objects and meta-objects in Open-C++ is made at compile time and cannot be changed subsequently. This means that the behaviour of an object in Open-C++ is determined statically and cannot be changed dynamically. Finally, Open-C++ provides very little meta-information and this limits its reflective power greatly.

Most of the limitations of Open-C++ arise from the fact that it is implemented by a pre-processor. It does not have the full power of a compiler, neither can it access the meta-information produced by the C++ compiler. To solve the above problems, good cooperation between the pre-processor and the compiler must be established.

### 3.3 Summary

The use of reflection and object-oriented programming techniques at the meta-level enables the internal behaviour of an object programming model to be manipulated by defining new kinds of meta-objects. This feature makes it possible to implement non-functional characteristics such as fault tolerance in a way that is transparent to the application programmer but flexible enough to meet the requirements of a wide range of applications. Open-C++ is an example of a reflective object-oriented language whose programming model can be redefined at the meta-level in this way. Although

Open-C++ provides very limited reflection because it is implemented as a pre-processor, its meta-level programming model provides the ability to separate applications into functional and non-functional levels that is most important to our investigations. In Open-C++, programmers are involved in programming meta-level classes that are associated with base-level classes. The usual object/class distinction also applies at the meta-level. However, at run-time meta-objects are associated with objects: this viewpoint will be used to describe the following replication examples and to explain the use of meta-objects. Using the term meta-object simplifies the presentation even if from a strictly object-oriented programming viewpoint, meta-level classes must obviously be defined to implement meta-objects.

# 4    Using meta-objects to support replication

In this section, we present a number of case studies that illustrate how a reflective approach can be used to implement a range of different replication techniques, namely passive, semi-active and active replication. Each replication technique will be implemented by a different meta-object. The run-time association of an object with a meta-object implementing a particular replication strategy enables the application programmer to arrange for application objects to be replicated transparently. The details of how the replication mechanism is implemented are hidden at the meta-level and do not appear in the source code for the application.

The replication mechanisms we consider here follow the principles given in Section 2.1 but have been simplified for our experiments. We will present possible meta-objects for each technique, describing the implementation of passive replication in some detail. We will then discuss how this approach can also be used for semi-active replication, and how meta-objects can be used to support active replication with majority voting. Atomic multicast and failure detection are useful basic system services, but the implementation of the meta-objects described in this section does not rely on such services; we will return to this issue later in Section 5.3.

We consider a distributed application designed as a set of objects. From a distributed point of view we suppose that objects interact following the classic client-server model. For clarity, we will describe the inter-replica protocol implementation with one client and one replicated server. The details of possible inter-replica protocols for the proposed replication techniques are beyond the scope of this paper and can be found for instance in [154, 20, 32].

Distribution can be handled at either the meta-level or the base-level. For our first two replication examples, we chose to implement distribution at the base-level using client and server stubs. A server is composed of a stub that manages communications with the client and a *reflective object* that encapsulates the state of the server. The reflective object is managed by the server and is an instance of a base-level class associated with a meta-level class that implements a particular replication mechanism (e.g. passive replication). The server (a Unix process in the current implementation) encapsulates the object from a run-time viewpoint. When a server receives requests from its client via the stub, it calls the corresponding methods of the reflective object to meet the requests. These methods are intercepted at the meta-level as appropriate and dealt with according to the particular replication mechanism implemented by the meta-object associated with the application object representing the server's state.

For the last replication example distribution is handled at the meta-level. The structure of the client and the server is rather different in this case and communication stubs at the base-level are not used. This aspect of our design will be illustrated in Section 4.3 and discussed later in Section 5.1.

## 4.1   Passive replication

The application is composed of a client, a primary server and one backup replica server. Client requests are processed by the primary server, and upon completion of an operation that updates its state, the server sends the new state to the backup replica. When the primary server crashes, the backup replica takes over the responsibility of providing continued service to the client and a new backup replica is started.

**Base-level.** In order to use passive replication for a particular application object, the application programmer must associate that object's class with the meta-level class `Passive_Repl_MetaObj` which is responsible for implementing the passive replication strategy. The application programmer must also decide which methods of the application class should be reflective - typically those methods that modify the state of the application object.

```
/* Class definition */
        class Medical_Info {
        public:
                void Read_Info(...);
        //MOP reflect:
                void Write_Info(...);            /* reflective method */
        protected:
        //MOP reflect:
                Medical_Record med_rec;          /* reflective attribute */
        };
/* Association with a meta-object */
        //MOP reflect class Medical_Info : Passive_Repl_MetaObj;
/* Definition of object methods */
        void Medical_Info::Read_Info(...) {
                <method statements>
        }
        void Medical_Info::Write_Info(...) {
                <method statements>
        }
/* Declaration of the object */
        refl_Medical_Info My_Info;      /*"refl_" is Open-C++ specific*/
/* Server stub */
        main() {
                server_main_loop();     /* handles client requests */
        }                               /* invokes methods of My_Info */
```

**Fig. 3.** Structure of a server (primary or backup) in Open-C++

In the example (see Fig. 3), the base-level class `Medical_Info` has been associated with the meta-level class `Passive_Repl_MetaObj`. Thus, instances of the class `refl_Medical_Info` such as the object `My_Info` will have a passive replica that is managed at the meta-level by `Passive_Repl_MetaObj`. The details of the passive replication mechanism are implemented by `Passive_Repl_MetaObj` and do not appear in the source code for `Medical_Info`. The communication protocols are managed by the server stub (`server_main_loop`).

In the given example, the state of a `Medical_Info` object corresponds to the `med_rec` protected reflective attribute[3]. Open-C++ requires this state to be reflective so that it can be accessed from the meta-level in order to generate checkpoints[4]. The `Write_Info` method which updates the object state is also declared to be reflective using a `//MOP reflect` declaration. This enables an invocation of `Write_Info` to be trapped at the meta-level in order to checkpoint the updated state of a `Medical_Info` object to the backup server after execution of `Write_Info`. In our example we consider that the `Read_Info` method does not update the state and thus does not need to be reflective. No checkpoint is sent in this case.

**Meta-level.** Reflection is used to control modifications to attributes of the reflective object. As previously mentioned, the methods that modify the data attributes of the primary state are made reflective. The meta-object which controls the primary's reflective object traps all the invocations of its reflective methods; we take advantage of this ability to checkpoint the server state to its backup replica. The inter-replica protocol is handled at the meta-level and includes the following actions:

| Primary actions | Backup actions |
| --- | --- |
| • checkpointing the server state when a client request has been processed | • receiving and storing the primary checkpoints at the base-level |
| • recovery on backup crash | • recovery on primary crash |
| • reconfiguration | • reconfiguration |

The base-level is identical for both replicas, but the actions performed at the meta-level by the primary and the backup replica are different: the primary sends checkpoints to the backup after each reflective method invocation, the backup replica processes these checkpoints. The meta-level also includes mechanisms for error detection and recovery. This protocol is summarised in Fig. 4.

Both sides (primary and backup) presented in this figure are actually implemented by a single meta-level class as shown in Fig. 5. Every reflective method call is trapped (①) at the meta-level. Then the object method is called at the base-level from the meta-level (②). Control returns back to the meta-level (③) and the updated state of the primary replica is then sent in a checkpoint to the backup replica (④). The latter updates its base-level object state directly (⑤) and sends an acknowledgement (⑥) to the primary. The reflective method invocation completes and returns to the client (⑦).

---

[3] Reflective attributes must either be public or protected: the current version of Open-C++ does not allow the declaration of private reflective attributes .

[4] In fact, Open-C++ enables non-reflective attributes to be accessed at the meta-level but this approach is not convenient because it is very intrusive as far as the programmer is concerned. The programmer must define standard methods to pass information from the base-level to the meta-level. When objects are part of the internal state of the reflective object, the programmer must also define marshalling and unmarshalling methods. In our implementation, the internal state of the reflective object is composed of variables defined using standard types of the programming language.

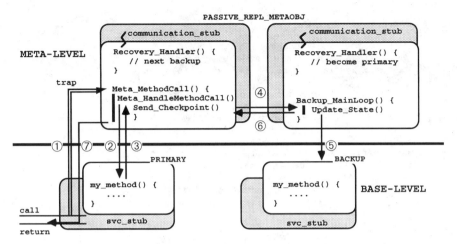

**Fig. 4.** Passive replication protocol

As well as the communication stubs used at the base-level for communication between the client and the primary server, communication stubs are also used at the meta-level mainly for sending/receiving checkpoints and for detecting errors. The detection mechanism is simple but not efficient in the current implementation; this will be discussed later in Section 5.2. When the absence of any peer is detected, either when sending or receiving checkpoints, the `Recovery_Handler` is activated at the meta-level where a recovery procedure is performed. The `Recovery_Handler` can also be activated directly by the meta-level communication stubs. A simple periodic checking of the presence of peers can be implemented in these stubs as well as more sophisticated detection mechanisms with reduced latency that depend on the underlying communication protocols.

For instance, when a primary crashes, the recovery procedure can be briefly described as follows: the backup leaves the main loop, its status is set to primary, a new backup replica is simply selected from a list of pre-created replicas, a connection is established with this new backup and finally the current state of the computation is sent to initialise the new backup. A connection is then established by the new primary with the client at the base level.

The recovery mechanism also involves numbering client calls, possibly including the current reply and a checkpoint number in every checkpoint, etc. Checkpoints are acknowledged in order to detect errors and failures. Not all the related details in the source code are presented here in order to keep it simple and clear.

The source code for the `Passive_Repl_MetaObj` meta-level class used to implement the primary-backup replica is essentially composed of the methods mentioned in Fig. 5.

The notion of reflection is also interesting from a performance point of view. More reflective capabilities in the language would provide a means of minimising checkpointed information. For example, if the meta-level was able to intercept attribute updates during method execution, then only those attributes that were modified by the method would need to be stored in a checkpoint. (In the current version of Open-C++, the whole state of an object must be sent as a checkpoint.)

```
Passive_Repl_MetaObj :: Meta_MethodCall (Id my_method,...){
        /* execution of the method */
                Meta_HandleMethodCall(my_method);
        /* storage of all reflective data in a message */
                Init_Checkpoint(state);
        /* sending a checkpoint to the backup */
                if (Send_Checkpoint(backup,state) == ERROR)
                        Recovery_Handler();
}
Passive_Repl_MetaObj :: Meta_StartUp()           {
/* status initialised by the meta-level class constructor */
                if (status == primary_status) {
                /* selection and connection with a first backup */
                        Replica_Select (backup);
                        Replica_Connect(backup);
                }
                else    {       /* status == backup_status */
                        /* waiting for server connection */
                        Wait_For_Replica_Connect(primary);
                        /* checkpoint receive and store loop */
                        Backup_MainLoop();
                }
        /* begin execution at the base level */
}
Passive_Repl_MetaObj :: Backup_MainLoop()        {
                while (Receive_Checkpoint(primary,state) != ERROR)
                        Update_State(state);
                Recovery_Handler();
}
Passive_Repl_MetaObj :: Recovery_Handler()       {
        /* primary crash: backup becomes primary */
                if (status == backup_status)   {
                        status = primary_status;
                }
        /* selection and connection with a new backup */
                Replica_Select (backup);
                Replica_Connect(backup);
        /* storage of all reflective data in a message */
                Init_Checkpoint(state);
        /* send current state to the new backup */
                if (Send_Checkpoint(backup,state) == ERROR)
                        Recovery_Handler();
}
```

**Fig. 5.** Passive_Repl_MetaObj (pseudo) simplified source code

Finally, the meta-level is also responsible for reconfiguration after the failure of a
peer has been detected. A new replica must be created and initialised with the current
state of the computation. This is why the internal state of the reflective object must
always be made accessible at the meta-level by declaring it reflective. The meta-level
of an operational replica must be able to read the state, and the meta level of the new
replica must be able to write this state down to the base-level. This is true for any
replication protocol.

In summary, the interception of method calls at the meta-level enables fault tolerance
mechanisms embedded within meta-objects to be synchronised transparently with the
application object at the base-level. The accessibility of the state information at the

meta-level enables checkpointing in the case of `Passive_Repl_MetaObj` and initialisation of a new replica during reconfiguration in any case.

## 4.2   Semi-active replication

In this protocol, a client sends its requests to a leader replica which in turn forwards it to its follower replica. Both replicas process the request, but only the leader replies to the client (see Fig. 6). The simple example taken here considers deterministic behaviour of the execution only. One reason for using semi-active replication in this case instead of passive replication is determined by the size of the object state; when it is very large, passive replication would imply large overheads. Multicast protocols are not considered in this example, and therefore the request message received by the leader is forwarded to the follower at the meta-level.

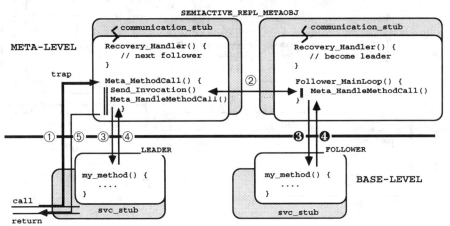

**Fig. 6.** Semi-active replication protocol

The source code of the server is almost identical to the previous case (see Fig. 3), except that the base-level class is associated with a different meta-level class (`Semiactive_Repl_MetaObj` in this case). The object state in this protocol is updated by the concurrent execution of the leader and follower replica.

The implementation of `Semiactive_Repl_MetaObj` is similar to `Passive_Repl_MetaObj`. The main difference is that a method invocation is transmitted instead of a checkpoint. A reflective method call is trapped (①) and transmitted by the leader to the follower (②) and acknowledged. Both the leader and the follower execute the method concurrently. On each side, the method at the base-level is called from the meta-level (③, ❸) and control is returned back to the meta-level when the method execution is completed (④, ❹). Finally, the initial method call returns to the client (⑤). Synchronisation between replicas could be added to this example in order to prevent the follower from getting too far behind the leader. Atomic multicast could also be used to simplify this protocol by broadcasting client requests to both replicas. This could be implemented by a meta-object on the client side (see Section 5); such a solution is mandatory for active replication and voting as described in the next section.

## 4.3   Active replication with majority voting

Several strategies can be defined for active replication. They all involve sophisticated
inter-replica protocols on both the client and the server side. Our objective in this
section is not to investigate these protocols, but briefly underline that they can be
easily implemented using a reflective approach. We consider here a simple example
with one client and a triplicated server: the client sends multiple requests to a group
of servers and handles several reply messages (voting on the replies); all server
replicas process client requests and send replies back to the client (see Fig. 7).

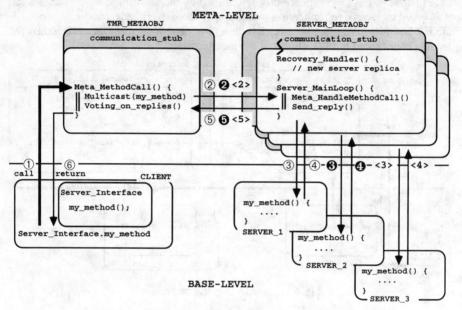

**Fig. 7.**  Active replication with majority voting protocol

A possible implementation using meta-objects can be briefly summarised as follows.
Two meta-objects are required: one for handling the client side, `TMR_MetaObj`, and
one for the server side, `Server_MetaObj`. For the purposes of this example, we are
assuming that the client declares an object representing a remote object located in the
server (just a remote object interface – `Server_Interface` in Fig. 7); the server
encapsulates the remote object. The client invokes the remote object as if it was local
and not replicated.

In the client, the interface object representing the remote object is associated with an
instance of the meta-level class `TMR_MetaObj`; this meta-object traps method
invocations on the remote object (①). The version of `Meta_MethodCall` defined by
`TMR_MetaObj` is responsible for sending a request corresponding to the method
invocation to each server replica (②, ❷, <2>), and then for voting on the replies (⑤,
❺, <5>) before returning the final result to the client base-level (⑥). Two comments
can be made: (i) the protocol used for sending the request in this case should be an
atomic multicast protocol; (ii) `Meta_MethodCall` for `TMR_MetaObj` does not call
`Meta_HandleMethodCall` since the invoked methods will be executed remotely by the
server replicas.

In each server replica, an instance of the meta-level class `Server_MetaObj` is bound to the "reflective object" that encapsulates its state. This meta-object is responsible for handling client remote requests issued by the `TMR_MetaObj` on the client side and for executing the corresponding methods on the server side via the `Meta_HandleMethodCall` (③ -④, ❸-❹, <3>-<4>). The `Server_MetaObj` is also responsible for handling reconfiguration when one of the server replicas in the group fails. Creation of a new server replica is done by the `Server_MetaObj` of the operational replica(s): this operation updates the new replica with the current state of the server (accessible at the meta-level as shown in previous examples) and adds a new member to the group of replicas. The latter action depends on the group management facilities provided by the underlying system (cf. Section 5.3).

Just as in previous examples, the application programmer does not have to be aware of the details of how fault tolerance is implemented. Remote invocation details are also hidden.

## 5      Implementation issues

### 5.1    Handling distribution

In the current implementation, client and server communicate with each other by means of BSD sockets. This simple off-the-shelf communication facility is sufficient to demonstrate the interest of meta-level programming with respect to fault-tolerant computing. Many other communication mechanisms can be used instead, such as C++ RPCs, or micro-kernel IPCs [135], etc.

Meta-level programming could be used to manage distribution. This was illustrated with Object Communities [34], which used Open-C++ facilities. The Object Communities distribution model consists of a unique server collecting and dispatching all messages from all members of a given Object Community. This mechanism is implemented with reflective programming, which improves transparency of distribution for the base-level application programmer. Meta-level programming could help in providing distribution transparency in other ways. For example a local application (client or server) could be implemented in several objects, some of which are object interfaces dedicated to handling communication with remote objects (similar to the notion of proxy implemented with meta-objects). This approach was illustrated in the example given in Section 4.3. The remote object interfaces would be implemented using reflective objects that are rather empty but bound to the meta-object that handles distribution. A client object would invoke remote object methods via local method calls on this object interface which would be reflected at the meta-level. The "distribution" meta-object would trap these local invocations and pass them to the appropriate object(s) on the corresponding site(s). This approach could be used for implementing client-server communications at the meta-level in the other examples given in Section 4.

### 5.2    Handling detection and reconfiguration

The detection mechanism (failure detection) used in our experiments is based on connection abort and is managed at the meta-level, which is not efficient. Other mechanisms could be used according to the communication facilities and basic services provided by the underlying system as described in Section 5.3. For efficiency, detection mechanisms should be put as low as possible in the hierarchy of system layers. For high dependability, error detection must be achieved with low latency and high asymptotic coverage. Only some additional validity checks and complementary error detection mechanisms should be done at the meta-level.

The meta-object approach remains useful for managing the reconfiguration procedure. In any replication model, the operational replicas can use a protocol to determine the location of a new replica and to create it dynamically. The current state of one of the operational replicas can be then captured at the meta-level and used to initialise the new replica. In addition, the election of a new primary (passive replication) or leader (semi-active replication) can be handled by a protocol performed at the meta-level.

## 5.3    System-dependent facilities

Most replication protocols need atomic multicast to deliver input messages to several replicas running concurrently or to send checkpoints to a set of standby replicas, for instance. This service can be implemented at the environment level as in Isis or at the communication level as in Delta-4, the latter providing the better performance.

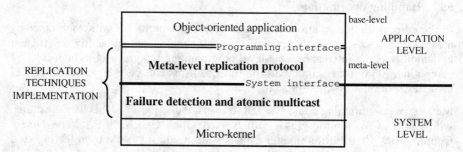

**Fig. 8.** Implementation layers of replication techniques

We discuss here the implementation of replication techniques based on the classic distinction between "application level" (user space) and "system level" (system space). The application level itself involves two programming levels: the base-level and the meta-level. The application meta-level implements the replication techniques (inter-replica protocols) based on the services provided by the system level:

- application meta-level: this level is dedicated to the implementation of the replication protocol, i.e., sending checkpoints from the primary to the standby replicas (passive replication) or various synchronisation protocols between replicas (semi-active and active replication) and voting (active replication); reconfiguration is also handled at this level;

- system level: programming meta-level protocols involves several services that, at least for efficiency, should be provided by the underlying system. Failure detection, atomic multicast and group management protocols are some examples.

The frontier between these two levels may vary according to the underlying run-time system and the hardware architecture of the nodes. Micro-kernel technology provides a good basis for tuning the frontier between application level and system level for implementing meta-level functionalities.

As shown in Fig. 8, this technology provides a good implementation framework for the system dependent services. This approach enables meta-level programmers to define new meta-level classes for various replication protocols, according to several failure assumptions, but also with respect to various hardware architectures and node configurations. The development of meta-level classes can take advantage of inheritance as for the construction of base classes in Arjuna. Solutions proposed in Isis and Delta-4 for failure detection and atomic multicast protocols can be implemented directly on top of the micro-kernel. This approach will be experimented with in the near future using Chorus [135] and the xAMp multicast protocols [134].

# 6    Conclusion

When the underlying system does not provide fully transparent fault tolerance mechanisms, programming fault-tolerant applications is a difficult activity since functional and non-functional programming are often mixed at one level and the programmer needs to know details of the fault-tolerant mechanisms that are used. The approach described in this paper is a step forward in making these mechanisms transparent. The two (or more) levels of programming provided by reflective object-oriented languages enable these two rather different development activities to be done separately using the same language. This approach is obviously not restricted to fault-tolerant mechanisms, but also encompasses distribution and other non-functional aspects such as security, transaction management, configuration management, etc. As a side effect, this approach facilitates testing and debugging.

The simple examples presented in this paper have all been prototyped. Various replication techniques are now being implemented in order to obtain a library of meta-level classes for programming fault-tolerant distributed applications. This activity will also involve the development of other meta-level classes for distribution and security purposes. Meanwhile, original meta-level classes will evolve according to improvements in error processing protocols, error detection mechanisms and communication protocols implemented in user space or at system level. Thanks to the reflective approach, such evolution can occur without any change in the source code of the user applications. Nevertheless, it is clear that a more sophisticated model of reflection would allow better results. For instance, a language with more reflective attributes than Open-C++ would ease the solution of several implementation problems (e.g. minimisation of the amount of information in a checkpoint) that we have encountered using the limited reflective capabilities of Open-C++. It is also important to mention that the ability to bind application-level objects to meta-level objects dynamically could be used to allow the application to adapt dynamically to system evolution either with respect to the underlying operating system services or with respect to new hardware configurations and failure assumptions.

In conclusion, a reflective approach combines the advantages of the object model with the advantages of a system-based approach to fault tolerance (transparency and separation of concerns). Like a system-based approach, a reflective approach provides (i) well defined software component structuring in terms of objects and (ii) access to internal operations of the model. Fault tolerance mechanisms that were supported by the runtime layer can now be implemented as a set of meta-objects, thus making this approach more flexible.

## Acknowledgements

The authors wish to thank our colleagues in the PDCS2 project, especially Brian Randell, who participated in the elaboration of these ideas during the numerous discussions on the subject. We are very grateful to Felicita Di Giandomenico, Alexander Romanovsky and in particular David Powell for their valuable comments on previous versions of this paper.

# The PDCS Implementation of MARS Hardware and Software

Johannes Reisinger   Andreas Steininger   Günther Leber

Technical University of Vienna

**Abstract.** MARS (MAintainable Real-time System) has been developed at the Vienna University of Technology during the last decade with the aim of managing highly critical distributed control applications. It is based on a periodic, time triggered structure and a fail-silent behaviour of the processing nodes. To validate the concept we have designed and implemented hardware components along with an operating system which are both tailored to the specific needs of MARS. This paper presents our solutions to the problems of achieving a deterministic timing behaviour and the fail-silence property of processing nodes. The integral development of hardware and operating system gave us the opportunity to implement specific features either in hardware or in software, allowing a very efficient design which has proved to be good in practice for more than two years.

## 1  Introduction

Distributed computing systems are widely used for control applications, which are most often characterised by the existence of hard deadlines for system reactions. Therefore the computing system has to meet real time requirements. An important group of control applications can further be attributed as critical, because a malfunction of the system can have catastrophic consequences. Since a completely fault-free operation can never be assumed, a computing system for critical applications must be able to tolerate faults, that is continue to provide its service even if it is affected by a fault.

The demand for real time capability on the one hand and fault tolerance on the other hand is a challenge for the design of both, hardware and software. In many approaches much potential is wasted by combining or adapting off-the-shelf-components which are not well suited to each other and to system demands. Often, expensive, sophisticated software is executed on standard hardware, error detection is compromised by the lack of suitable hardware devices and, most of all, timing behaviour of software is determined without a detailed knowledge of the timing behaviour of the underlying hardware.

From this point of view a very straightforward and promising design approach is a kind of top down design for the system. Starting with conceptual ideas on system level, the requirements arising from the system architecture are worked out and satisfied by either hardware or software or both. This not only allows to choose the most efficient solution (no unused hardware features, no software work-around for missing hardware features) but also makes the implementation of some additional features possible. Hardware and operating system are harmonised to fit to the needs of the system philosophy and provide the best possible service.

This paper presents an implementation based on the above ideas. It is organised as follows: Section 2 introduces the system concepts and summarises the resulting requirements. In Section 3 a brief overview of the solution is given. A more detailed explanation and reasoning for the solutions are presented in Sections 4 and 5: While Section 4 deals with the real time aspect of the system, Section 5 concentrates on the fault tolerance behaviour. The paper concludes with Section 6.

## 2    Overall System Structure

A fault-tolerant distributed real-time system can be built of a number of autonomous, fail-silent [119] processing nodes which are interconnected by a real-time network. The MARS System [80] is the realisation of such an approach and was the target system for the design discussed in this paper. In MARS all active and passive components are replicated in order to prevent a single failure from crashing the system. The real-time network consists of two replicated broadcast channels and each processing unit consists of up to three processing nodes (see Fig. 1).

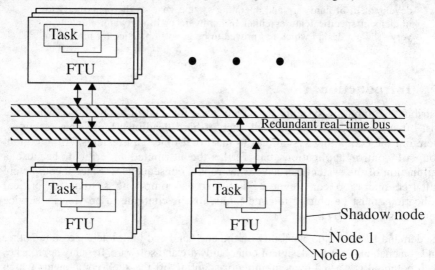

**Fig. 1.** System structure of MARS

To achieve a deterministic timing behaviour even in the presence of faults, the MARS system uses *active redundancy* for all processing and communication activities: each process is executed simultaneously at different nodes and each message is transmitted quasi-simultaneously on each of the broadcast channels. Processing activities are replicated at the *node level*, that is, three processing nodes execute identical software and form a *Fault-Tolerant Unit (FTU)*. Although all three nodes of an FTU work in active redundancy, only two of them actually send their results to other nodes of the system. The third node, the *shadow node*, does not transmit anything on the real-time network as long as all active nodes are operational. After an active node has failed, the shadow node immediately starts to send its results.

In order to be able to *guarantee* the proper timing behaviour of the system already during the design phase of an application, MARS is strictly *time triggered*. Every relevant action of the system is scheduled before operation. The actions to schedule include:

- The points in time when a node is allowed to send a message (consequently, MARS uses a *Time Division Multiple Access (TDMA)* protocol for communication) and the types of messages which may be sent at specific points in time,
- the start times and deadlines of all processes,
- the points in time when sensor values are read and actuator values are written,
- the actions for recovery and reintegration of failed nodes (these actions must be included into the schedule in order to prevent a properly detected fault from affecting the correct timing behaviour of the system).

Error handling at the node level need not be considered in the timing analysis because the *terminate model* is applied instead of the usual *resume model*: After the detection of an error a reset of the processing node is performed.

A precise global time base is the basic requirement for a time triggered system, because this is the only possibility to synchronise the actions within different processing nodes of the system. Global time is maintained by a distributed, fault-tolerant clock synchronisation algorithm (see Section 4.1).

## 2.1 Timeliness

The static structure of MARS forces the system designer to carefully investigate the timing behaviour of all parts of the system; we have to know time bounds for all processing and communication activities in order to assign time slots to them. In particular, the following timing parameters must be known:

- The maximum execution time of each process, considering the architecture and speed of the processor, pipelining, caching, and memory wait states [121],
- the maximum time for communication,
- the operating system overhead,
- the overhead of hardware activities which influence the timing behaviour of the node.

## 2.2 Fault Tolerance

The fault-tolerance of MARS is based on a two-layered mechanism. The bottom layer (node layer) is responsible for error detection and error confinement. These functions are carried out by the processing nodes, which are therefore called *'fail-silent'*. The task of fail-silent nodes is to detect all internal errors and to prevent propagation of the errors by stopping to produce output in case of an error. Therefore the top layer (system layer) need not care about erroneous data, but has to provide enough redundancy to tolerate crash failures of parts of the system. The major functions of the top layer are handling of redundant data and reconfiguration of the system in case of a node failure [56].

## 3  The Processing Node

### 3.1 Hardware

The requirements concerning real-time behaviour and fault tolerance have already been taken into account in the design phase of the hardware [155]. Therefore the processor-board cannot be called "general purpose". Fig. 2 shows the block diagram of the hardware of one processing node.

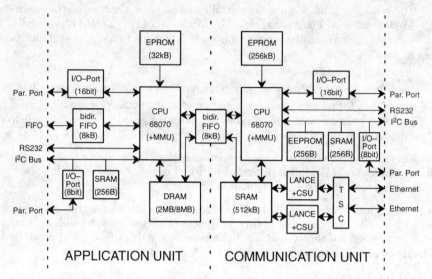

**Fig. 2.** Block diagram of the processor board

The processor-board consists of two complete, independent processing units, an *application unit* and a *communication unit*. The application unit is based on a 68070 CPU clocked with 15MHz. The core of the 68070 is very similar to the 68000, but the chip additionally includes a memory management unit, a two–channel DMA (Direct Memory Access) controller, an interrupt-controller, 3 timer/counters, a UART (Universal Asynchronous Receiver and Transmitter) and an $I^2C$–Interface (Inter-IC Bus). Externally connected are an EPROM, a dynamic RAM, a parallel I/O-Port and two bi-directional FIFOs (First In First Out memory). One FIFO (further called 'internal FIFO') forms the interface to the communication unit, the other one ('external FIFO') is intended to allow a direct connection of process oriented peripheral devices to the application. An additional I/O-Port and a small SRAM (Static RAM) can be addressed via the $I^2C$-Bus.

The communication unit is also based on the 68070, which considerably simplifies development and maintenance of hardware and software. It comprises EPROM, SRAM, parallel I/O-Port, two Ethernet Controllers (LANCE, Local Area Network Controller for Ethernet) which form the main communication system to the other nodes in the system, two CSUs (Clock Synchronisation Unit) for supporting a global time-base (see Section 4.1), and a TSC (Time Slice Controller) for controlling access to the system bus. Via the $I^2C$-Bus an I/O-Port, an SRAM, and an EEPROM for storing system parameters and set-up information are connected. The only interconnection points to the application unit are the internal FIFO, the periodic clock interrupt line, the power supply, and the reset line.

Based on the aspects of predictable timing behaviour and fault tolerance a detailed rationale for the choice of this architecture will be given in the following sections.

## 3.2 The Operating System

The MARS operating system [131] has to deal with the fact, that there are two processors with different fields of activities at a processing node. A microkernel–based operating system [33, 110] allows system designers as well as application programmers to adapt the operating system to their needs in an easy way, since the operating system kernel only slightly depends on the processor's peripherals. By using such an operating system for MARS we are able to execute identical copies of the kernel at both processors of the node. *System processes* running on the microkernel are used to adapt the operating system to the needs of the given environment.

**The Microkernel.** A major goal during the design of the operating system was to keep the microkernel as small as possible to increase its reliability and predictability. Therefore, its functionality is reduced to the absolute minimum, the *execution of context switches* and *maintenance of the global time-base*. Context switches are performed using tables created by the pre-runtime scheduler and in order to increase flexibility run-time data may influence scheduling decisions in a predefined manner. Management of the global time-base is done by the *clock interrupt handler* which maintains the timer and carries out the time-triggered context switches

Only one *system call* is offered to the application tasks by the kernel. This system call *thread_finished()* has to be called by each application thread in order to signal to the kernel, that the calling thread has finished its computations. When a thread fails to call *thread_finished()* before its time quantum expires, the kernel assumes an error has occurred and terminates node operation by resetting the node.

The microkernel communicates with user-level processes by means of system-messages, which are located at fixed positions within a globally readable memory area at each processing unit, the *message base*. This message base is used for communication between processes belonging to different system- or application programs, too. Processes belonging to the *message handler* are allowed to write to the message base, all other processes are only granted read access to the message base.

Additional tasks of the microkernel are: loading of system and application programs, process management, and error handling.

**System Processes.** All other system functions, such as message passing, handling of peripheral devices, clock synchronisation, or redundancy management are performed by system processes running on top of the kernel. In contrast to other microkernel-based operating systems, inter-process communication is handled at user level. This is practicable because the purpose of communication in a time-triggered system is just transmission of data, not data flow control. System threads handling the transmissions can be scheduled by the off-line scheduler at the known points in time when communication has to take place.

In a time triggered system each action a node has to perform is known in advance. Therefore the system processes which are not required for these operations can be removed, thus reducing the size of the system software, which is an important issue in real-time systems, especially if they are considered to be used as embedded systems.

The high adaptability of a microkernel-based operating system is advantageous especially during system design because it allows different groups of designers to design, implement, and test system services without affecting the other groups. The flexibility of the system is increased because the system designers can provide software with distinct properties for one service (without actually increasing the size of the software at the nodes!), respectively application programmers can implement services by themselves, if the provided services do not meet the requirements.

**The Programming Model.** The requirements on a programming language for a time-triggered system differ in two major points from the requirements on a conventional one:

- There are no explicit statements for synchronisation and communication, and
- the worst case execution times of programs must be known before run-time.

Although it may be possible to use a general purpose language like C or Modula-2 and adapt it to the requirements of our system, a new programming language, Modula/R [168] has been developed to meet the specific needs of time-triggered systems.

A Modula/R program does not interact with the operating system or with other programs by means of system calls (except *thread_finished()*). It receives its input messages by reading a *message variable* and transmits its output messages by writing to another *message variable*. The operating system provides the latest instances of the received messages as input message variables and it is responsible for sending the contents of the output message variables to their destinations after the termination of the program.

*Teams.* Each MARS application is structured into *teams*. A team is an object consisting of internal data items and methods which operate on them. Each method may read input message variables and write to output message variables. The different methods of a team may operate on the same internal data items. In this case, they must not be active simultaneously to avoid corruption of data. The internal data items may be used to communicate with other methods of the same team or to store data between two executions of the same method.

There are two different kinds of methods: *Initialisation methods* are executed once at the start time of the system and are used to initialise the internal state of the team. *Cyclic methods* are executed repeatedly during run-time of the system.

The set of internal data items of a team, that have to be preserved between executions of the cyclic methods constitutes its *history-state*. This so-called h-state of teams working in active redundancy must be identical in order to maintain replica determinism. During normal operation the redundant instances of a team start with identical h-states, receive identical input messages, and perform identical operations on them. In case of a node failure and subsequent reintegration of the failed node the identity of the h-states must be re-established. Therefore the h-state is periodically sent to the real-time network and may be received by a failed redundant node during its reintegration phase.

*Access to Global Time.* To give application threads the ability of performing time-dependent computations, access to global time is provided. In order to maintain replica determinism, the access mechanism to the global time has to guarantee that two redundant instances of a thread always read the same value. Passing the *scheduled invocation time*, which is determined during the design phase of an application, meets this requirement.

**Runtime Scheduling.** The smallest schedulable entity in MARS is a *thread*. The thread model in a time-triggered system is quite different from the one in an event-triggered system:

- There are no blocking statements in the programs, and
- all threads (except the initialisation threads) are executed cyclically.

During normal operation, a thread may be in one of the states *active* or *inactive*. At the start of its execution slot, a thread becomes active and remains so until it has finished its work. Afterwards it changes to the inactive state. The active state is partitioned into two sub-states: *running* and *ready*. There is no *blocked* state because there are no blocking statements in the code of a program in a time-triggered system. A thread changes from the running state to the ready state only if it is preempted by another thread. After the termination of the preempting thread it enters the state running again. There is a fourth state, which should never be entered in a correctly functioning system: *deadline missed*. If a thread enters this state, this indicates a node failure and leads to a node shutdown.

*Threads.* A thread is created by executing a method of a team. The start time of a thread and its deadline, as well as team and method to be executed are determined during design. Additionally, resource conflicts between threads belonging to the same team are resolved here. This is done by determining the intersection of the sets of internal data items which are accessed by the threads. If this intersection is empty or it contains only data items which are read by the threads, they may be active simultaneously. If a data item is written by one thread, and read or written by an other thread, the threads must not be active simultaneously.

Each thread is executed within the address-space of the team it belongs to, enabling the thread to access a data- and code segment and possibly some peripherals. In contrast to the data- and text segments, threads of the same team do not share a stack segment, but each thread is provided with its own stack segment. For communication purposes threads may access two additional memory areas:

- The *message base* contains all messages which are read by any thread of a processor unit of a node. To avoid excessive copying of messages, each thread is provided with read access to this memory area. Only the *message handler* may write messages into the message base.
- Some system threads are provided with read-access to the data segment of another team, their so-called *side team*. This mechanism is needed, for example, by the message handler to copy an output message from the data segment of a team into the message base.

*Thread Chains.* In a microkernel based operating system, there are typically a lot of small threads, mainly system threads, with short execution times. If threads can only be started at clock ticks, this would result in poor processor utilisation. Increasing the frequency of the clock interrupt would also increase operating system overhead, thus also resulting in poor processor utilisation. To solve this problem, *thread chains* are introduced, which are sets of threads with a common start time and a fixed execution sequence. After termination of one thread, the next thread in the chain immediately starts executing.

*Mode Change.* For increasing flexibility different application modes, which may be needed to handle different environmental situations, are supported. Each application mode consists of a number of thread chains, which are executed cyclically in a fixed order and with fixed start time offsets within each cycle. To switch to a different application mode, a *mode change* must be performed. The points in time of possible mode changes are determined at design time, because the actions which are needed to change modes must be scheduled by the off-line scheduler. A mode change consists of the following actions:

- An application thread determines, whether the environmental situation has changed or not, and accordingly creates a mode change message containing the number of the mode that can handle the new situation.
- If the mode change concerns more than one node, the mode change request is transmitted over the bus.
- A system thread reads the mode change request at each concerned node and forwards the request to the kernel by means of a system message.
- When a mode change request is pending the mode change is performed by the kernel at the next point in time when it may take place, such that from now on all further scheduling decisions are based on the pre-runtime schedules of the new mode. Threads of the old mode which are already running, are *not* forcibly terminated.

A mode change is therefore no asynchronous, dynamic mechanism, which would violate the principles of a time-triggered system, it solely uses state information to select one of several predefined choices for the further behaviour of the system.

**The Communication Subsystem.** Communication in MARS is based on the exchange of state messages. The term 'state message' refers to the semantics of the message itself, not to the semantics of the contents of the message. That is, the reception of a message itself is not an event, whereas a message may *carry* event information. In this case it must be ensured that the receiver reads each instance of the message in order not to lose event information.

*The Message Base.* The heart of the communication system is the *message base.* It is the only means of communication in the MARS system for application processes as well as for system processes and the kernel. Every thread is granted read access to the message base in order to avoid superfluous message copying. *System messages* located at fixed positions in the message base contain configuration data determined at node start-up and information exchanged between the kernel and system threads which must have an execution time of at most a clock tick in order to have non-interruptible access to the data.

*Local Communication.* Threads of different teams communicate via the message base. The sending team needs the message handler to copy the output message into the message base, from where the receiving thread can read it.

*Remote Communication.* Although local and remote communication are completely transparent to the sending and receiving threads, the operating system has to transfer the message data to the communication unit of the node if necessary. There the data must be included into a bus message, which is then sent onto the real-time network at the node's TDMA slot.

# 4    Supporting Deterministic Timing Behaviour

A processing node of a distributed real-time system, especially of a time triggered system, must offer characteristics which are not required from conventional processing nodes:

- A global time base,
- boundable message transmission times,
- protection of the application software from asynchronous events in the environment,
- predictability of the hardware timing behaviour,
- strictly bounded operating system overhead.

While a global time base is the basic requirement to co-ordinate the activities of processing nodes of a time triggered system, the other features are needed to bound the duration of each action within a node, thus allowing pre-run-time scheduling of application processes.

## 4.1  Global System Time

Clock synchronisation is based on the fault-tolerant average (FTA) algorithm [83] which can synchronise the clocks of all correctly functioning processing nodes of a system even in the presence of $k$ faults. The FTA needs to know the deviation of the local clock of the own processing node from the local clocks of all other nodes of the system. The mean of this set of deviations, excluding the $k$ highest and $k$ lowest deviations, is used to correct the local clock. Because the quality of the clock synchronisation heavily depends on the accuracy of the measured clock deviations, the processing nodes provide a hardware mechanism to determine the deviations of the local clocks of different nodes: Both Ethernet controllers (LANCEs) are coupled to a Clock Synchronisation Unit (CSU) [83] which maintains the global time base, generates the periodic clock interrupt, and provides outgoing and incoming messages with accurate time-stamps. When transmitting a message, the LANCE reads the current time from an internal register of the CSU and appends it to the message. Immediately after reception of the message, the LANCE of the receiver node sends a 'stamp'-signal to the CSU which causes the CSU to latch the current time into a time-stamp register which can be read by the software later. Because all time intervals between reading the current time from the sending node's CSU and generating the 'stamp'-signal at the receiving node are nearly constant, the deviation of each pair of clocks within the system can be determined with a very high accuracy (about 2 µs), which allows the FTA to synchronise the clocks of the system with a precision of about 10 µs.

Tasks on the application processor and on the communication processor are synchronised to the global system time by a periodic interrupt *(clock tick)* provided by the CSU with an adjustable frequency (0.5 to 8 ms).

## 4.2  Message  Passing

The protocol for exchanging messages between processing nodes must allow bounding of communication times even in the case of loss of messages. We use a very simple protocol to achieve this goal: Each message is sent twice at the broadcast network. Experiments have shown [81], that the probability of losing two instances of a message is much lower than the probability of a node failure, therefore the overall system reliability would not benefit considerably from a more reliable communication. On the other hand, sending a message twice is the cheapest way to achieve reliable message transmission, if the worst case timing behaviour must be considered (as in time triggered hard real-time systems). The processing nodes support this message passing mechanism in a number of ways:

- The operating system allows to specify exact points in time when messages are sent. This avoids delays or message losses caused by contention or collision at the communication channel.

- The Ethernet controller is configured to suppress delaying or re-transmission of messages in case the communication channel is blocked. This helps to avoid a single transmission failure from crashing the whole channel by causing excessive retransmissions.

- The processing node is provided with two network interfaces, thus supporting two redundant broadcast channels. Each message is sent on both communication channels.

## 4.3 Protecting Application Software from Asynchronous Events

Real-world events and the corresponding data streams are asynchronous by their nature, and each system that is embedded in a realistic environment has to cope with this fact. A periodic system structure is a very effective but not a complete solution to this problem, because we cannot keep asynchronous events completely away from the system. However, the two–processor architecture provides additional protection against uncertainties in application runtime by preventing external events from affecting the timing behaviour of processes executing on the application unit. Messages arriving at the Ethernet do not require immediate service by the application processor, but they are pre-processed by the communication processor. The extracted information is put into the internal FIFO which is deep enough to provide a reasonable flexibility for the transfer of messages to the application processor's memory. This mechanism allows application processes to handle access to messages like access to main memory; the temporal uncertainties of message transmission (which are present despite the deterministic nature of message transmission) are hidden from the application processes. This also applies to the transmission of results from the application processes to the real-time network.

The overhead for message passing between the communication processor and the application processor is made up by the transfer from and to the FIFO only, the message delay can be kept as low as the transfer delay of one word through the FIFO (not the whole message), since the transfers between FIFO and memory can happen in parallel on both sides.

Another interface is provided for the application processes to allow direct communication with the process environment (e.g., sensors and actuators). Again, its implementation as a FIFO was chosen to shield the application from temporal uncertainties of the environment.

The other communication channels do not influence the timing behaviour significantly: The $I^2C$ bus can be used by the application exclusively and therefore does not affect determinism, and the RS232 interface is intended for auxiliary functions like testing only and not as a main communication path.

As a consequence of that careful architecture design, the application software is embedded in a fully deterministic environment, where all main data streams are buffered by FIFOs and are under full control of the application software. Timing analysis for the application software can be performed in isolation, reducing efforts significantly. This is important because application software often changes, whereas for the communication processor the basic functions stay the same, allowing higher efforts in determining and testing the timing behaviour.

## 4.4 Predictability of Hardware Timing

By its nature the timing behaviour of the processor itself is absolutely predictable. However, predictability is limited by asynchronous events like interrupts (especially if nesting might occur), bus arbitration between multiple bus masters and by refresh cycles for the DRAM.

Therefore our hardware only allows two essential kinds of *interrupts*: One is the *clock tick* which is required for synchronisation and does – by its periodic nature – not result in timing uncertainties. The other interrupt signals that an error has been detected, in which case emergency handling (at the node level!) is activated and real-time constraints become meaningless anyway. In all other cases buffer sizes and polling intervals were matched such that no interrupts were necessary and a questionable [82] complex analysis of a nested interrupt structure can be avoided.

Although it would have been a more consistent approach, bus arbitrations have not been completely avoided for several practical reasons:

The LANCE is only capable of managing its input and output buffers by *Direct Memory Access (DMA)*. The resulting indeterminism in timing behaviour is hidden from the application by the communication processor and therefore does not influence application timing at all. However, the (bounded) timing uncertainty has to be accounted for by the communication software.

The data transfer between FIFO and memory is performed by DMA. This is done because it speeds up the transfer by a factor of approximately two, since the single-address-mode can be used. Time and amount of data to be transferred are known in advance and the transfer is fully controlled by software, so the estimation for the maximum arbitration overhead can be tight and will be outweighed by the reduction of transfer time.

*Refresh cycles* of the DRAM controller are indeterministic from a microscopic point of view, e.g. in comparison with an instruction cycle or a memory access. However, from a more global point of view the refresh happens periodically each 16 microseconds and lasts for 4 clock cycles (267 nanoseconds). Between two clock ticks a maximum of 63 refresh cycles may happen and in the worst case each of them will result in a delay in memory access by the application causing an overhead of 1.68%. The uncertainty induced by DRAM refresh is thus tightly limited and does not impose any problem.

## 4.5  Boundable Operating System Overhead

The microkernel approach allows the operating system to be partitioned into a set of small modules. The methods for determining the maximum execution times of these modules are rather similar to the methods for application processes (see Section 2.1). The maximum execution times of these system modules are rather close to their actual execution times because each of the modules performs only one well-defined function and there are few alternatives and loops with variable execution times. The system modules are treated as ordinary application processes by the pre-run-time scheduler, therefore no special methods are required to bound the overhead caused by these modules.

Apart from the overhead caused by system modules, we must consider the overhead of the microkernel itself. Because there are no interrupts in the system except the periodic clock interrupt, we only have to consider the execution time of the periodic clock interrupt handling routine. The tasks of this routine are handling of local time and process dispatching, which are not time consuming, since handling of local time is supported by the CSU and dispatching is an easy task because of the pre-run-time scheduling of applications. Experiences with the implementation have shown that the execution time of the clock interrupt handler is nearly constant and reasonably low.

# 5    Achieving Fail-Silent Behaviour

In order to be fail-silent, a node must provide comprehensive error detection and proper error handling. Some of the mechanisms used to detect and handle errors do not inhibit the sending of incorrect messages but they provide the messages with enough redundancy to make the error detectable at the receiver side. So, the property of our nodes is to send either correct messages which can be verified as correct by all non-faulty receivers, or to send detectably corrupted messages [150] which are discarded by each non–faulty receiver, or no messages at all.

## 5.1  Error detection

Many error detection mechanisms have been provided and implemented in both, hardware and software, in order to meet the required high self-checking coverage. While the focus of the hardware mechanisms lies on the detection of permanent errors and severe errors (i.e., errors that stop further software execution), software error detection by its nature concentrates on subtle faults like transients causing a slight deviation of the program flow or data errors. Subsequently the mechanisms that have been implemented are presented according to certain error-classes.

**Data and Control Flow Errors.** Experiments ([143, 67]) have shown that a majority of faults affecting a system results in deviations from the correct control flow or in unintended changes of data. Although such errors have a rather high probability of being detected on the behavioural level, the implementation of several simple error detection mechanisms on a lower level improves error detection coverage and latency without compromising availability. The following mechanisms have been chosen:

- Main memory and FIFOs are *parity protected* (one bit per byte). Additionally, pull-up resistors ensure that a high-impedance state on the bus is read as parity error (e.g., in case of reading from an unused address range or an empty FIFO).

- The standard low level protocol of the *Ethernet controller* detects transmission errors by checking, for example, CRC and framing.
- The standard error detection mechanisms of the *MC68000*-family (e.g., illegal op-code, zero divide, bus error, ...) have proved to be very efficient ([41, 143]).

**Behavioural Errors.** Monitoring the abstract behaviour of the processor like memory access behaviour, bus access behaviour, and execution interval of a certain task can provide a very efficient means for error detection [141]. The strictly deterministic, periodic structure of our system allows a convenient implementation of very powerful high level error detection mechanisms:

- The 68070 provides a *memory management unit* which allows efficient error detection on the basis of memory access behaviour. Access to illegal physical addresses is also detected by a *bus time–out logic*.
- A *watchdog-timer* monitors the 'aliveness' of the communication processor. It performs a node-reset unless it is toggled periodically.
- Application unit and communication unit are autonomous and strictly separated. The probability of a simultaneous error in both units is thus kept at a minimum. Consequently *mutual checks* can be used for error detection. The specific way of implementation, however, is left to the system software.
- A *Time Slice Controller (TSC)* monitors the access behaviour of the node to the system bus. During a learning-phase the TSC adapts its internal model of the TDMA protocol by determining position, duration and period of the write accesses. After completion of the learn phase the TSC autonomously monitors all write accesses of the node and activates an error signal, when the node attempts to transmit data outside its legal time slot. The TSC is an autonomous single-chip microcontroller which is only loosely coupled to the communication unit by the $I^2C$ bus in order to avoid correlated errors.
- The high degree of determinism in the MARS system allows some other *checks for illegal system states*: Overflow from the Ethernet receive buffer or the FIFO can be treated as errors, because they must not occur during normal operation.

**Faults Caused by the Environment.** For proper operation the node needs a proper environment. That is why monitoring of environmental conditions appears to be a basic requirement. On the other hand, a rigorous mapping of adverse operating conditions (like over-temperature, radiation, etc.) into system failures leads to an oversensitive system [156] with a highly correlated failure behaviour of the nodes. For this reason only the most essential mechanisms have been chosen for error detection on this level:

- A *power supply monitor* issues a warning in case of low supply voltage. Additionally, the 'power good' signal provided by many power supply units can be monitored, which usually allows an early detection of a power fail leaving some time for emergency measures. An indirect detection of power supply faults on higher levels (e.g., by resulting data errors) cannot rightfully be assumed because of their severe global effects. Additionally, each node is provided with an individual backup battery to reduce the probability of correlated power supply failures.
- For exchange of error information with peripheral devices there is an error input line and an error output line. This allows the inclusion of optional *peripherals* into the error handling concept.

**Errors in Processing and Transmitting Application Data.** The previously described error detection mechanisms focus on the various faults which can occur within a node and try to provide a proper mechanism for each class of these faults. Because it is hardly possible to provide a detection mechanism for each kind of fault, we use a second, completely different strategy to achieve fail-silent behaviour. These mechanisms, which are completely implemented in software, consider only the flow of application data through the system and try to protect both transmission and processing of these data by using redundancy. These mechanisms rely on the existence of the other mechanisms because there are errors which cannot be detected by the software mechanisms (e.g., behavioural errors) or which cannot be detected by them with a sufficient probability (e.g., permanent errors which affect redundant data respectively redundant processing steps in the same way). In principle, two mechanisms are needed to detect errors in processing and transmitting application data (see Fig. 3):

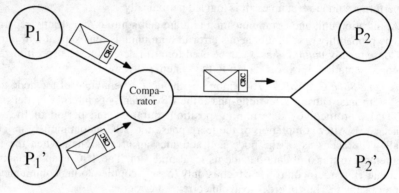

**Fig. 3.** Protecting the path of application data through the system

- Each application message is provided with an end–to–end checksum (CRC) to protect it against any accidental change when being transmitted or when being stored somewhere in memory.
- The processing of messages is done in time redundancy. Each of the redundant processes verifies the checksums of all of its input messages and creates output messages with valid checksums in case of absence of failures. These output messages (respectively their checksums) are compared afterwards and any difference leads to a shutdown of the node.

A valid checksum guarantees the reading process that the message was valid for some process at some time since the start-up of the system, but it does not guarantee that it is the message which the process expects to read. To avoid confusion of (valid) messages, each message is provided with a unique key. This key is not part of the message itself, but the sender and the receiver of the message know the key and incorporate it into the calculation of the message's checksum. Because we can assign a key only to each type but not to each instance of a message (we cannot limit the number of instances!), we have introduced an additional mechanism to be able to distinguish the different instances of a message: Not only the key, but also the creation time of the message is incorporated into the checksum calculation. The scheduled invocation time of the process which creates the message is used as creation time, since the operating system guarantees that this time is equal for both redundant instances of a process. The time triggered nature of MARS allows to determine the difference of the invocation times of sender and receiver, therefore the receiver can determine the creation time of the message out of its own invocation time and therefore calculate the correct checksum.

## 5.2 Error Handling

The layered structure of system fault-tolerance and the fail-silent assumption for the node level allows straightforward error handling. Error propagation to the environment must be prevented *(error confinement)* and acquisition of data about the error cause is required for detecting permanent faults and collecting statistical data about the various error sources *(fault diagnosis)*.

**Error confinement.** Upon detection of an error, provisions must be taken to shut off the erroneous node from the rest of the system instantaneously. Due to the fact that in case of an error, proper execution of software cannot be ensured, a hardware solution appears to be more reliable. Therefore error confinement has been based mainly on hardware and the options of software for handling errors have been strongly restricted. The following mechanisms have been implemented to provide comprehensive error confinement:

- In order to minimise reaction delay, hardware ensures that each activation of an error detection mechanism (maskable by DIP-switches) immediately generates an interrupt. Software configuration is not provided to avoid the risk of accidental misconfiguration in case of an error.
- The Ethernet controller, which forms the only connection to the real-time bus, is locked by hardware as soon as any error is detected *(Error* signal in Fig. 4). Transmission is enabled only after reset of the node.

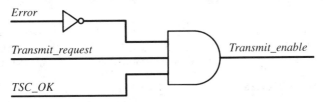

**Fig. 4.** Bus access control

- The Time Slice Controller *(TSC_OK* signal in Fig. 4) blocks all transmissions to the system bus unless they are made in the legal time slot. This ensures that undefined behaviour of the node resulting from undetected errors cannot disturb the TDMA bus protocol.
- Undefined behaviour of the application unit cannot affect the system because the communication unit represents an intelligent interface to the real-time network and detects behavioural errors of the application. The strict hardware separation of application unit and communication unit maximises the probability that the communication unit will work properly in this case and protect the system.

**Fault Diagnosis.** Two levels of fault diagnosis can be distinguished: *System level diagnosis* (which node did fail?) and *node level diagnosis* (why did that node fail?). From the system's point of view, node level diagnosis is important to get information about permanent node failures or frequent occurrences of some type of error in a specific node. For this reason the processor can read the state of the error detection mechanisms to decide which of them has been triggered. In order to provide this function even in case of a severe error, the communication processor can also read the error status of the application side and vice versa. These error signals are preserved until the whole node is reset, regardless of the actual duration of the fault, in order to allow convenient access. This information together with the current system time can be stored in non-volatile memory and forms a base for comparison with succeeding entries. As a result of such a comparison the frequency of error occurrence can be determined and permanent node failures be detected.

Another method which was implemented to detect permanent node failures is the execution of extensive self test routines at start-up time and in the background during run-time of the nodes.

## 6     Conclusions

During the design and implementation of the MARS processing nodes it became evident that the integral development of hardware and operating system was most advantageous in areas where a close co-operation of hardware and software mechanisms is needed to achieve a specific goal. Examples are time stamping of messages, the time slice controller, the deterministic timing behaviour resulting from the joint timing analysis of hardware and software, and the supplementary mechanisms for error detection.

The processing nodes are operating for more than two years at the department of real-time systems in Vienna. Students have developed various real-time applications, which helped us to verify our concepts and to improve the overall system. Hereby it became apparent that time-triggered systems require significant support by development tools, e.g. analysis of the maximum execution time of tasks and scheduling.

Based on results from fault-injection experiments conducted in co-operation with the University of Chalmers in Gothenburg, Sweden [68], and with LAAS in Toulouse, France [10], we will improve the error-detection mechanisms of our nodes.

## Acknowledgements

We want to thank the members of the MARS group for their contributions to the development of the board, especially Leo Mayerhofer for assembling and testing the nodes. We gratefully acknowledge the useful comments on earlier versions of this paper by Hermann Kopetz.

# References for Chapter III

[1]    G. Agha, S. Frolund, R. Panwar and D. Sturman, "A Linguistic Framework for Dynamic Composition of Fault Tolerance Protocols", in *Proc. 3rd IFIP Working Conf. on Dependable Computing for Critical Applications,* (Mondello, Sicily), Dependable Computing and Fault-Tolerant Systems, 8, pp.345-64, 1992.

[2]    N. Ahituv, Y. Lapid and S. Neumann, "Processing Encrypted Data", *Communications of the ACM*, 30 (9), pp.777-80, September 1987.

[3]    P. E. Ammann and J. C. Knight, "Data Diversity: An approach to software fault tolerance", *IEEE Trans. Comput.*, 37 (4), pp.418-25, 1988.

[4]    T. Anderson (Ed.), *Resilient Computing Systems,* Collins Professional and Technical Books, 1985.

[5]    T. Anderson, "A Structured Decision Mechanism for Diverse Software", in *Proc. 6th IEEE Symp. Reliability in Distributed Software and Database Systems,* (Los Angeles, CA), pp.125-9, 1986.

[6]    T. Anderson, P. A. Barrett, D. N. Halliwell and M. R. Moulding, "Software Fault Tolerance: An evaluation", *IEEE Trans. Software Engineering*, SE-11 (12), pp.128-34, 1985.

[7]    T. Anderson and J. C. Knight, "A Framework for Software Fault Tolerance in Real-Time Systems", *IEEE Trans. Soft. Eng.*, SE-9 (3), pp.355-64, 1983.

[8]    T. Anderson and P. A. Lee, *Fault Tolerance: Principles and practice,* Prentice Hall, 1981.

[9]    Arjuna, *The Arjuna System Programmer's Guide*, Department of Computing Science, University of Newcastle upon Tyne, UK, July 1992.

[10]   J. Arlat, M. Aguera, L. Amat, Y. Crouzet, J. C. Fabre, J. C. Laprie, E. Martins and D. Powell, "Fault Injection for Dependability Validation: A methodology and some applications", *IEEE Transactions on Software Engineering*, 16 (2), pp.166-82, February 1990.

[11]   G. Attardi, C. Bonini, M. R. Boscotrecase, T. Flagella and M. Gaspari, "Metalevel Programming in CLOS", in *Proc. 3rd European Conference on Object-Oriented Programming (ECOOP'89),* pp.243-56, 1989.

[12]   A. Avizienis, "The N-version Approach to Fault-Tolerant Systems", *IEEE Transactions on Software Engineering*, 11 (12), pp.1491-501, December 1985.

[13]   A. Avizienis and L. Chen, "On the Implementation of N-Version Programming for Software Fault Tolerance During Execution", in *Int. Conf. Comput. Soft. and Applic.,* (New York), pp.149-55, 1977.

[14]   A. Avizienis and J. P. J. Kelly, "Fault Tolerance by Design Diversity: Concepts and experiments", *IEEE Computer*, 17 (8), pp.67-80, August 1984.

[15]   A. Avizienis and J. C. Laprie, "Dependable Computing: From concepts to design diversity", *Proc. IEEE*, 74 (5), pp.629-38, 1986.

[16]   O. Babaoglu, "On the Reliability of Consensus-Based Fault-Tolerant Distributed Computing Systems", *ACM Trans. on Computer Systems*, 5 (3), pp.394-416, 1987.

[17]   J. P. Banâtre, M. Banâtre and F. Ployette, "The Concept of Multi-Functions: A general structuring tool for distributed operating systems", in *Proc. 6th Int. Conf. Distributed Computing Systems,* pp.478-85, 1986.

[18]   M. Barborak, M. Malek and A. Dahbura, "The Consensus Problem in Fault-Tolerant Computing", *ACM Computing Surveys*, 25 (2), pp.171-220, June 1993.

[19]   G. Barigazzi and L. Strigini, "Application-Transparent Setting of Recovery Points", in *Proc. 13th Int. Symp. on Fault-Tolerant Computing (FTCS-13),* (Milan), IEEE Computer Society Press, 1983.

[20]   P. A. Barrett, A. M. Hilborne, P. G. Bond, D. T. Seaton, P. Veríssimo, L. Rodrigues and N. A. Speirs, "The Delta-4 Extra Performance Architecture (XPA)", in *Proc. 20th Int. Symp. on Fault-Tolerant Computing Systems (FTCS-20),* (Newcastle upon Tyne, UK), pp.481-8, IEEE Computer Society Press, 1990.

[21]   J. F. Bartlett, "A Non-Stop (TM) Kernel", in *Proc. 8th ACM Symp. on Operating Systems Principles,* (Pacific Grove, CA, USA), pp.22-9, 1981.

[22]   E. Best and B. Randell, "A Formal Model of Atomicity in Asynchronous Systems", *Acta Informatica*, 16, pp.93-124, 1981.

[23]   K. P. Birman, "Replication and Fault-Tolerance in the ISIS System", *ACM Operating Systems Review*, 19 (5), pp.79-86, 1985.

[24]   K. P. Birman and T. A. Joseph, "Exploiting Virtual Synchrony in Distributed Systems", *ACM Operating Systems Review*, 21 (5), pp.123-8, 1987.

[25]   D. M. Blough and G. Sullivan, "A Comparison of Voting Strategies for Fault-Tolerant Distributed Systems", in *Proc. 9th Symp. on Reliable Distributed Systems (SRDS-9),* (Huntsville, Alabama), pp.136-45, 1990.

[26]   A. Bondavalli, S. Chiaradonna and F. Di Giandomenico, "Efficient Fault Tolerance: An approach to deal with transient faults in multiprocessor architectures", in *Proc. Int. Conf. on Parallel and Distributed Systems (ICPADS'94),* (Hsinchu, Taiwan), pp.354-9, IEEE Computer Society, 1994.

[27]   A. Bondavalli, F. Di Giandomenico and J. Xu, "A Cost-Effective and Flexible Scheme for Software Fault Tolerance", *J. of Computer Systems Science and Engineering*, 8 (4), pp.234-44, October 1993.

[28]   A. Bondavalli and L. Simoncini, *Failure Classification with respect to Detection*, Esprit Project N°3092 (PDCS: Predictably Dependable Computing Systems), First Year Report, May 1990.

[29]  A. Bondavalli, J. A. Stankovic and L. Strigini, "Adaptable Fault Tolerance for
      Real-Time Systems", in *Proc. 3rd Int. Workshop on Responsive Computer
      Systems,* (New Hampshire), pp.123-32, 1993.

[30]  R. H. Campbell, K. H. Horton and G. G. Belford, "Simulations of a Fault-
      Tolerant Deadline Mechanism", in *Proc. 9th Int. Symp. Fault-Tolerant
      Comput.,* (Madison), pp.95-101, 1979.

[31]  R. H. Campbell and B. Randell, "Error Recovery in Asynchronous Systems",
      *IEEE Trans. Software Engineering,* SE-12 (8), pp.811-26, 1986.

[32]  M. Chérèque, D. Powell, P. Reynier, J.-L. Richier and J. Voiron, "Active
      Replication in Delta-4", in *Proc. 22nd Int. Symp.. on Fault-Tolerant
      Computing (FTCS-22),* (Boston, MA, USA), pp.28-37, IEEE Computer
      Society Press, 1992.

[33]  D. R. Cheriton, "The V Distributed System", *Communications of the ACM,*
      31 (3), pp.314-33, March 1988.

[34]  S. Chiba and T. Masuda, "Designing an Extensible Distributed Language with
      Meta-Level Architecture", in *Proc. 7th European Conference on Object-
      Oriented Programming (ECOOP'93),* (O. Nierstrasz, Ed.), (Kaiserslautern,
      Germany), Lecture Notes in Computer Science, 707, pp.482-501, 1993.

[35]  K. Y. Chwa and S. L. Hakimi, "Schemes for Fault-Tolerant Computing: A
      comparison of modularly redundant and t-diagnosable systems", *Information
      and Control,* 49 (3), pp.212-38, June 1981.

[36]  F. Cristian, "Exception Handling and Software Fault Tolerance", *IEEE Trans.
      on Computers,* C-31 (6), pp.531-40, 1982.

[37]  F. Cristian, "Exception Handling", in *Dependability of Resilient Computers*
      (T. Anderson, Ed.), pp.68-97, Blackwell Scientific Publications, 1989.

[38]  F. Cristian, H. Aghili, R. Strong and D. Dolev, "Atomic Broadcast: From
      simple message diffusion to Byzantine agreement", in *Proc. 15th Int. Symp.
      on Fault-Tolerant Computing (FTCS-15),* (Ann Arbor, Michigan), pp.200-6,
      IEEE Computer Society Press, 1985.

[39]  A. T. Dahbura, K. K. Sabnani and W. J. Hery, "Spare Capacity as a Means of
      Fault Detection and Diagnosis in Multiprocessor Systems", *IEEE
      Transactions on Computers,* C-38 (6), pp.881-91, June 1989.

[40]  A. T. Dahbura, K. K. Sabnani and L. L. King, "The Comparison Approach to
      Multiprocessor Fault Diagnosis", *IEEE Transactions on Computers,* C-36 (3),
      pp.373-8, March 1987.

[41]  A. Damm, "The Effectiveness of Software Error-Detection Mechanisms in
      Real-Time Operating Systems", in *Proc. 16th Int. Symp. on Fault-Tolerant
      Computing (FTCS-16),* (Vienna, Austria), pp.171-6, IEEE Computer Society
      Press, 1986.

[42]  Y. Deswarte, L. Blain and J.-C. Fabre, "Intrusion Tolerance in Distributed
      Computing Systems", in *Proc. 1991 Symp. on Research in Security and*

*Privacy,* (Oakland, California), pp.110-21, IEEE Computer Society Press, 1991.

[43]   D. L. Detlefs, M. P. Herlihy and J. M. Wing, "Inheritance of Synchronization and Recovery Properties in Avalon/C++", *Computer,* pp.57-69, December 1988.

[44]   F. Di Giandomenico and L. Strigini, "Adjudicators for Diverse Redundant Components", in *Proc. 9th Int. Symp. Reliable Distributed Systems,* (Huntsville, Alabama), pp.114-23, IEEE, 1990.

[45]   F. Di Giandomenico, J. Xu and A. Bondavalli, "Software Fault Tolerance: Dynamic combination of dependability and efficiency", in *1st PDCS2 Open Workshop,* (Toulouse, France), pp.93-116, 1993.

[46]   K. Echtle, "Fault Diagnosis by Combination of Absolute and Relative Tests", in *1st European Workshop on Dependable Computing (no proceedings),* (Toulouse), 1989.

[47]   D. E. Eckhardt, A. K. Caglayan, J. C. Knight, L. D. Lee, D. F. McAllister, M. A. Vouk and J. P. J. Kelly, "An Experimental Evaluation of Software Redundancy as a Strategy for Improving Reliability", *IEEE Trans. Soft. Eng.,* 17 (7), pp.692-702, 1991.

[48]   P. D. Ezhilchelvan and S. K. Shrivastava, "A Characterization of Faults in Systems", in *Proc. 5th IEEE Int. Symp. Reliability in Distributed Software and Database Systems,* (Los Angeles, CA, USA), pp.215-22, IEEE Computer Society Press, 1986.

[49]   P. D. Ezhilchelvan and S. K. Shrivastava, *A Classification of Faults in Systems,* University of Newcastle upon Tyne, UK, Technical Report, 1989.

[50]   J. C. Fabre, Y. Deswarte and B. Randell, "Designing Secure and Reliable Applications using Fragmentation-Redundancy-Scattering: An object-oriented approach", in *Proc. of the First European Dependable Computing Conference (EDCC-1),* (Berlin, Germany), Lecture Notes in Computer Science, 852, (K. Echtle, D. Hammer and D. Powell, Eds.), pp.23-38, Springer-Verlag, 1994.

[51]   J. C. Fabre, V. Nicomette, T. Pérennou, R. J. Stroud and Z. Wu, "Implementing Fault-Tolerant Applications using Reflective Object-Oriented Programming", in *Proc. 25th Int. Symp. on Fault-Tolerant Computing (FTCS-25),* (Pasadena, CA, USA), IEEE Computer Society Press, 1995.

[52]   J. C. Fabre and B. Randell, "An Object-Oriented View of Fragmented Data Processing for Fault and Intrusion Tolerance in Distributed Systems", in *Proc. 2nd European Symp. on Research in Computer Security (ESORICS 92),* (Y. Deswarte, G. Eizenberg and J.-J. Quisquater, Eds.), (Toulouse, France), Lecture Notes on Computer Science, 648, pp.193-208, Berlin: Springer-Verlag, 1992.

[53]   J. Gray, "Why Do Computers Stop And What Can Be Done About It?", in *Proc. 5th Symp. on Reliability in Distributed Software and Database Systems,* (Los Angeles, CA, USA), pp.3-12, IEEE Computer Society Press, 1986.

[54]    J. Gray and A. Reuter, *Transaction Processing: Concepts and techniques,* Morgan Kaufmann, 1993.

[55]    S. T. Gregory and J. C. Knight, "A New Linguistic Approach to Backward Error Recovery", in *Proc. 15th Int. Symp. Fault-Tolerant Computing (FTCS-15),* (Michigan), pp.404-9, IEEE Computer Society Press, 1985.

[56]    G. Grünsteidl and H. Kopetz, "A Reliable Multicast Protocol for Distributed Real-Time Systems", in *Proc. 8th IEEE Workshop on Real-Time Operating Systems and Software,* (Atlanta, GA, USA), pp.19-24, 1991.

[57]    H. Hecht, "Fault-Tolerant Software for Real-Time Applications", *ACM Computing Surveys,* 8 (4), pp.391-407, 1976.

[58]    M. Hecht, J. Agron, H. Hecht and K. H. Kim, "A Distributed Fault-Tolerant Architecture for Nuclear Reactor and Other Critical Process Control Applications", in *Proc. 21st Int. Symp. Fault-Tolerant Computing (FTCS-21),* (Montreal), pp.462-9, IEEE Computer Society Press, 1991.

[59]    M. Herlihy, "Apologizing Versus Asking Permission: Optimistic concurrency control for abstract data types", *ACM Trans. DataBase Systems,* 15 (1), pp.96-124, 1990.

[60]    J. J. Horning, H. C. Lauer, P. M. Melliar-Smith and B. Randell, "A Program Structure for Error Detection and Recovery", *Lecture Notes in Computer Science,* 16, pp.177-93, 1974.

[61]    Y. Huang and C. M. R. Kintala, "Software Implemented Fault Tolerance: Technologies and experience", in *Proc. 23rd Int. Conf. Fault-Tolerant Computing (FTCS-23),* (Toulouse, France), pp.2-9, IEEE Computer Society Press, 1993.

[62]    *The Isis Distributed Toolkit: User reference manual,* Isis Distributed Systems, Inc., 1992.

[63]    V. Issarny, "An Exception Handling Mechanism for Parallel Object-Oriented Programming: Towards reusable, robust distributed software", *Journal of Object-Oriented Programming,* 6 (6), pp.29-40, 1993.

[64]    P. Jalote and R. H. Campbell, "Atomic Actions for Fault Tolerance using CSP", *IEEE Trans. Soft. Eng.,* SE-12 (1), pp.59-68, 1986.

[65]    B. W. Johnson, *Design and Analysis of Fault-Tolerant Digital Systems,* Addison-Wesley Pub. Co., 1989.

[66]    K. Kanekawa, H. Maejima, H. Kato and H. Ihara, "Dependable Onboard Computer Systems with a New Method: Stepwise negotiating voting", in *Proc. 19th Int. Symp. Fault-Tolerant Computing (FTCS-19),* (Chicago), pp.13-9, 1989.

[67]    J. Karlsson, U. Gunneflo and J. Torin, "The Effects of Heavy-Ion Induced Single Event Upsets in the MC6809E Microprocessor", in *Proc 4th Int. Symp. Fault-Tolerant Computing Systems (FTCS-4),* (Baden-Baden, W. Germany), Springer Verlag, 1989.

[68]   J. Karlsson, U. Gunnelfo and J. Torin, "Use of Heavy-Ion Radiation from
       Californium-252 for Fault Injection Experiments", in *Proc. Int. Working
       Conf. on Dependable Computing for Critical Applications,* (Santa Barbara,
       CA, USA), pp.79-84, 1989.

[69]   G. Kiczales, J. d. Rivières and D. G. Bobrow, *The Art of the Metaobject
       Protocol,* MIT Press, 1991.

[70]   K. H. Kim, "An Approach to Programmer-Transparent Coordination of
       Recovering Parallel Processes and its Efficient Implementation Rules", in *Int.
       Conf. Parallel Processing,* pp.58-68, 1978.

[71]   K. H. Kim, "Approaches to Mechanization of the Conversation Scheme Based
       on Monitors", *IEEE Trans. Soft. Eng.,* SE-8 (3), pp.189-97, 1982.

[72]   K. H. Kim, "Distributed Execution of Recovery Blocks: An approach to
       uniform treatment of hardware and software faults", in *Proc. 4th Int. Conf.
       Distributed Comput. Sys.,* pp.526-32, 1984.

[73]   K. H. Kim and H. O. Welch, "Distributed Execution of Recovery Blocks: An
       approach for uniform treatment of hardware and software faults in real-time
       applications", *IEEE Trans. Comput.,* C-38 (5), pp.626-36, May 1989.

[74]   K. H. Kim and J. C. Yoon, "Approaches to Implementation of a Repairable
       Distributed Recovery Block Scheme", in *Proc. 18th Int. Symp. Fault-Tolerant
       Computing (FTCS-18),* (Tokyo), pp.50-5, IEEE Computer Society Press,
       1988.

[75]   K. H. Kim and J. H. You, "A Highly Decentralized Implementation Model for
       the Programmer-Transparent Coordination (PTC) Scheme for Cooperative
       Recovery", in *Proc. 20th Int. Symp. Fault-Tolerant Computing (FTCS-20),*
       (Newcastle), pp.282-9, IEEE Computer Society Press, 1990.

[76]   J. C. Knight and N. G. Leveson, "An Experimental Evaluation of the
       Assumption of Independence in Multiversion Programming", *IEEE Trans.
       Soft. Eng.,* SE-12 (1), pp.96-109, 1986.

[77]   J. C. Knight, N. G. Leveson and L. D. S. Jean, "A Large Scale Experiment in
       N-Version Programming", in *Proc. 15th Int. Symp. Fault-Tolerant
       Computing (FTCS-15),* (Michigan), pp.135-40, IEEE Computer Society
       Press, 1985.

[78]   A. Koenig and B. Stroustrup, "Exception Handling in C++", *Journal of
       Object-Oriented Programming,* 3 (7-8), pp.16-33, 1990.

[79]   R. Koo and S. Toueg, "Checkpointing and Rollback-Recovery for Distributed
       Systems", *IEEE Trans. Soft. Eng.,* SE-13 (1), pp.23-31, 1987.

[80]   H. Kopetz, A. Damm, C. Koza, M. Mulazzani, W. Schwabl, C. Senft and R.
       Zainlinger, "Distributed Fault-Tolerant Real-Time Systems: The MARS
       approach", *IEEE Micro,* 9 (1), pp.25-40, February 1989.

[81]   H. Kopetz, G. Grünsteidl and J. Reisinger, "Fault-Tolerant Membership
       Service in a Synchronous Distributed Real-Time System", in *Dependable*

*Computing for Critical Applications* (A. Avizienis and J. C. Laprie, Eds.), pp.411-29, Springer-Verlag, 1991.

[82] H. Kopetz and K. Kim, "Temporal Uncertainties in Interactions among Real-Time Objects", in *Proc. 9th Symp. on Reliable Distributed Systems,* (Huntsville, AL, USA), pp.165-74, IEEE Computer Society Press, 1990.

[83] H. Kopetz and W. Ochsenreiter, "Clock Synchronisation in Distributed Real-Time Systems", *IEEE Trans. Computers,* 36 (8), pp.933-40, August 1987.

[84] J. H. Lala and L. S. Alger, "Hardware and Software Fault Tolerance: A unified architectural approach", in *Proc. 18th Int. Symp. Fault-Tolerant Computing (FTCS-18),* (Tokyo), pp.240-5, 1988.

[85] L. Lamport, R. Shostak and M. Pease, "The Byzantine Generals Problem", *ACM Trans. on Programming Languages and Systems,* 4 (3), pp.382-401, 1982.

[86] J. C. Laprie (Ed.), *Dependability: Basic concepts and terminology — in English, French, German, German and Japanese,* Dependable Computing and Fault Tolerance, 5, 265p., Springer-Verlag, Vienna, Austria, 1992.

[87] J. C. Laprie, J. Arlat, C. Béounes and K. Kanoun, "Definition and Analysis of Hardware-and-Software Fault-Tolerant Architecture, Appendix: Cost of software fault tolerance", in *1st Workshop Predictably Dependable Computing Systems,* (Toulouse), 1990.

[88] J. C. Laprie, J. Arlat, C. Béounes and K. Kanoun, "Definition and Analysis of Hardware-and-Software Fault-Tolerant Architectures", *IEEE Computer (Special Issue on Fault Tolerant Systems),* 23 (7), pp.39-51, July 1990.

[89] J. C. Laprie, J. Arlat, C. Béounes, K. Kanoun and C. Hourtolle, "Hardware and Software Fault Tolerance: Definition and analysis of architectural solutions", in *Proc. 17th Int. Symp. on Fault-Tolerant Computing (FTCS-17),* (Pittsburgh, PA), pp.116-121, IEEE Computer Society Press, 1987.

[90] J. C. Laprie, K. Kanoun, C. Béounes and M. Kaâniche, "The Transformation Approach to the Modelling and Evaluation of Reliability and Availability Growth", in *Proc. 20th Int. Symp. on Fault-Tolerant Computing (FTCS-20),* (Newcastle upon Tyne), pp.364-71, IEEE Computer Society Press, 1990.

[91] R. Lea, P. Amaral and C. Jacquemot, "COOL-2: An object-oriented support platform built above the Chorus Micro-Kernel", in *Proc. IEEE Int. Symp. on Object Orientation in Operating Systems (IWOOOS'91),* (Palo Alto, CA, USA), pp.68-73, 1991.

[92] P. A. Lee, "A Reconsideration of the Recovery Block Scheme", *Computer Journal,* 21 (4), pp.306-10, 1978.

[93] P. A. Lee and T. Anderson, *Fault Tolerance: Principles and practice,* Dependable Computing and Fault-Tolerant Systems, Springer-Verlag, Vienna, 1990.

[94] B. Liskov, "Distributed Programming in Argus", *Comm. ACM,* 31 (3), pp.300-12, 1988.

[95]   F. Lombardi, "Optimal Redundancy Management of Multiprocessor Systems for Supercomputing Applications", in *Proc. 1st Int. Conf. Supercomputing Systems,* (Petersbourgh), pp.414-22, 1985.

[96]   D. B. Lomet, "Process Structuring, Synchronization, and Recovery Using Atomic Actions", *ACM SIGPLAN Notices,* 12 (3), pp.128-37, 1977.

[97]   P. R. Lorczak, A. K. Caglayan and D. E. Eckhardt, "A Theoretical Investigation of Generalized Voters for Redundant Systems", in *Proc. 19th Int. Symp. Fault-Tolerant Computing (FTCS-19),* (Chicago, Illinois), pp.444-51, 1989.

[98]   J. Losq, "A Highly Efficient Redundancy Scheme: Self-purging redundancy", *IEEE Transactions on Computer,* C-25 (6), pp.569-78, June 1976.

[99]   P. Maes, "Concepts and Experiments in Computational Reflection", in *Proc. Conf. on Object-Oriented Programming Systems, Languages and Applications (OOPSLA'87) (ACM SIGPLAN Notices, 22,10),* pp.147-55, 1987.

[100]  S. V. Makam, *Design Study of Fault-Tolerant Computer to Execute N-Version Software,* Ph. D. Dissertation, UCLA Computer Science Department, 1982.

[101]  S. V. Makam and A. Avizienis, "ARIES 81: A reliability and life-cycle evaluation tool for fault-tolerant systems", in *Proc. 12th IEEE Int. Symp. on Fault-Tolerant Computing (FTCS-12),* (Santa Monica, CA), pp.267-74, 1982.

[102]  M. Malek and J. Maeng, "Partitioning of Large Multicomputer Systems for Efficient Fault Diagnosis", in *Proc. 12nd Int. Symp. Fault-Tolerant Computing (FTCS-12),* (Santa Monica), pp.341-6, 1982.

[103]  S. Matsuoka, T. Watanabe and A. Yonezawa, "Hybrid Group Reflective Architecture for Object-Oriented Concurrent Reflective Programming", in *Proc. ECOOP'91,* pp.213-50, Springer-Verlag, 1991.

[104]  P. M. Melliar-Smith and B. Randell, "Software Reliability: The role of programmed exception handling", in *Proc. Conf. on Language Design For Reliable Software (ACM SIGPLAN Notices, vol. 12, no. 3, March 1977),* (Raleigh), pp.95-100, ACM, 1977.

[105]  P. M. Merlin and B. Randell, "State Restoration in Distributed Systems", in *Proc. 8th Int. Symp. Fault-Tolerant Computing (FTCS-8),* (Toulouse), pp.129-34, IEEE Computer Society Press, 1978.

[106]  B. Meyer, *Object-Oriented Software Construction,* Prentice Hall, 1988.

[107]  M. H. Mills, "Predictably Dependable Military Computer-Based Systems (invited speech)", in *1st Workshop Predictably Dependable Computing Systems 2,* (Toulouse), 1993.

[108]  W. R. Moore and N. A. Haynes, "A Review of Synchronisation and Matching in Fault-Tolerant Systems", *Proc. of the IEE,* E-131 (4), pp.119-24, July 1984.

[109] J. E. B. Moss, *Nested Transactions: An approach to reliable distributed computing,* MIT Press, 1985.

[110] S. J. Mullender, G. v. Rossum, A. S. Tanenbaum, R. v. Renesse and H. v. Staveren, "Amoeba: A distributed operating system for the 1990s", *IEEE Computer*, 23 (5), pp.44-53, May 1990.

[111] *Trusted Network Interpretation of the Trusted Computer System Evaluation Criteria,* National Computer Security Center, Report N°NCSC-TG-005, 1987.

[112] A. Paepcke, "PCLOS: Stress testing CLOS", in *Proc. Conf. on Object-Oriented Programming Systems, Languages and Applications (OOPSLA'90) (ACM SIGPLAN Notices),* pp.194-211, 1990.

[113] A. Pagès and M. Gondran, *System Reliability: Evaluation and prediction in engineering,* Springer-Verlag, New York, USA, 1986.

[114] D. Powell, "Fault-Tolerance in Distributed Systems: Error assumptions and their importance", in *Proc. Franco-Brazilian Seminar on Distributed Computing Systems,* (Florianópolis, SC, Brazil), pp.36-43, Federal University of Santa Catarina, 1989 (In French).

[115] D. Powell, "Delta-4: A generic architecture for dependable distributed computing", in *Research Reports ESPRIT (Vol. 1)* p.484, Springer-Verlag, Berlin, Germany, 1991.

[116] D. Powell, *Fault Assumptions and Assumption Coverage,* Esprit Project N°3092 (PDCS: Predictably Dependable Computing Systems), Second Year Report, May 1991.

[117] D. Powell, "Failure Mode Assumptions and Assumption Coverage", in *Proc. 22nd Int. Symp. on Fault-Tolerant Computing (FTCS-22),* (Boston, MA, USA), pp.386-95, IEEE Computer Society Press, 1992.

[118] D. Powell, "Distributed Fault-Tolerance: Lessons learnt from Delta-4", in *Hardware and Software Architecture for Fault Tolerance: Experiences and Perspectives* (M. Banâtre and P. A. Lee, Eds.), Lecture Notes in Computer Science, 774, pp.199-217, New York: Springer Verlag, 1994.

[119] D. Powell, G. Bonn, D. Seaton, P. Verissimo and F.Waeselynck, "The Delta-4 Approach to Dependability in Open Distributed Computing Systems", in *Proc. of the 18th Int. Symp. on Fault-Tolerant Computing (FTCS-18),* (Tokyo, Japan), pp. 246-51, IEEE Computer Society Press, 1988.

[120] F. P. Preparata, G. Metze and R. T. Chien, "On the Connection Assignment Problem of Diagnosable System", *IEEE Transactions on Electronic Computers*, EC-16, pp.848-54, December 1967.

[121] P. Puschner and C. Koza, "Calculating the Maximum Execution Time of Real-Time Programs", *Real-Time Systems*, 1 (2), pp.159-76, September 1989.

[122] J. P. Queille and J. Sifakis, "Fairness and Related Properties in Transition Systems: A temporal logic to deal with fairness", *Acta Informatica*, 19 (3), pp.195-220, 1983.

[123]  M. O. Rabin, "Efficient Dispersal of Information for Security, Load Balancing and Fault-Tolerance", *Journal of the ACM*, 36 (2), pp.335-48, April 1989.

[124]  P. Ramanathan and K. G. Shin, "Checkpointing and Rollback Recovery in a Distributed System using a Common Time Base", in *Proc. 7th Symp. Rel. Distrib. Syst.,* (Columbus), pp.13-21, 1988.

[125]  B. Randell, "System Structure for Software Fault Tolerance", *IEEE Trans. on Software Engineering*, SE-1 (2), pp.220-32, 1975.

[126]  B. Randell, "Fault Tolerance and System Structuring", in *Proc. 4th Jerusalem Conf. on Information Technology,* (Jerusalem), pp.182-91, 1984.

[127]  B. Randell, "Design Fault Tolerance", in *Proc. IFIP Symp. on The Evolution of Fault-Tolerant Computing,* (A. Avizienis, H. Kopetz and J.-C. Laprie, Eds.), (Baden, Austria), Dependable Computing and Fault-Tolerant Systems, 1, (A. Avizienis, H. Kopetz and J.-C. Laprie, Eds.), pp.251-70, Springer-Verlag, 1986.

[128]  B. Randell and J. Xu, "Object-Oriented Software Fault Tolerance: Framework, reuse and design diversity", in *1st PDCS2 Open Workshop,* (Toulouse, France), pp.165-84, 1993.

[129]  B. Randell and J. Xu, "The Evolution of the Recovery Block Concept", in *Software Fault Tolerance* (M. Lyu, Ed.), Trends in Software, pp.1-22, J. Wiley, 1994.

[130]  S. Rangarajan and D. Fussel, "A Probabilistic Method for Fault Diagnosis of Multiprocessor Systems", in *Proc. 18th Int. Symp. on Fault-Tolerant Computing (FTCS-18),* (Tokyo, Japan), pp.278-83, 1988.

[131]  J. Reisinger, "Time Driven Operating Systems: A case study on the MARS Kernel", in *Proc. 5th ACM SIGOPS European Workshop,* (Le Mont Saint-Michel, France), IRISA/INRIA-Rennes, 1992.

[132]  D. Rennels, "Fault-Tolerant Computing: Concept and examples", *IEEE Transactions on Computers*, C-33 (12), pp.1116-29, December 1984.

[133]  R. L. Rivest, L. Adelman and M. L. Dertouzos, "On Data Banks and Privacy Homomorphisms", in *Foundations of Secure Computations* (R. A. DeMillo, D. D. Dobkin, A. K. Jones and R. J. Lipton, Eds.), pp.169-79, Academic Press, 1978.

[134]  L. Rodrigues and P. Veríssimo, "xAMp: A protocol suite for group communication", in *Proc. 11th IEEE Int. Symp. on Reliable Distributed Systems (SRDS-11),* pp.112-21, 1992.

[135]  M. Rozier, V. Abrossimov, F. Armand, I. Boule, M. Gien, M. Guillemont, F. Herrmann, C. Kaiser, S. Langlois, P. Léonard and W. Neuhauser, *Overview of the CHORUS® Distributed Operating Systems*, Chorus Systèmes, Report, N°CS/TR-90-25, April 1990.

[136]  C. M. F. Rubira-Calsavara and R. J. Stroud, "Forward and Backward Error Recovery in C++", *Object-Oriented Systems*, 1 (1), pp.61-85, 1994.

[137] D. L. Russell, "State Restoration in Systems of Communicating Processes", *IEEE Trans. Soft. Eng.*, SE-6 (2), pp.183-94, 1980.

[138] D. L. Russell and M. J. Tiedeman, "Multiprocess Recovery using Conversations", in *Proc. 9th Int. Symp. Fault-Tolerant Computing (FTCS-9)*, pp.106-9, IEEE Computer Society Press, 1979.

[139] C. H. Sauer, E. A. MacNair and J. F. Kurose, *The Research Queueing Package Version 2: CMS users guide*, IBM Thomas J. Watson Research Center Yorktown Heights, New York, Research Report, N°RA-139, 1982.

[140] R. D. Schlichting and F. B. Schneider, "Fail-Stop Processors: An approach to designing fault-tolerant computing systems", *ACM Trans. on Computing Systems*, 1 (3), pp.222-38, August 1983.

[141] M. E. Schmid, R. L. Trapp, A. E. Davidoff and G. M. Masson, "Upset Exposure by Means of Abstraction Verification", in *Proc. 12th Int. Symp. Fault-Tolerant Computing (FTCS 12)*, (Santa Monica, CA), pp.237-44, IEEE Computer Society Press, 1982.

[142] F. B. Schneider, "Byzantine Generals in Action: Implementing fail-stop processors", *ACM Transactions on Computer Systems*, 2 (2), pp.145-54, May 1984.

[143] M. A. Schuette, J. P. Shen, D. P. Siewiorek and Y. X. Zhu, "Experimental Evaluation of Two Concurrent Error Detection Schemes", in *Proc. 16th Int. Symp. on Fault-Tolerant Computing (FTCS-16)*, (Vienna, Austria), pp.138-43, IEEE Computer Society Press, 1986.

[144] R. K. Scott, J. W. Gault and D. F. Mcallister, "The Consensus Recovery Block", in *Proc. Total Sys. Reli. Symp.*, pp.74-85, 1985.

[145] R. K. Scott, J. W. Gault and D. F. McAllister, "Fault-Tolerant Software Reliability Modeling", *IEEE Trans. Soft. Eng.*, SE-13 (5), pp.582-92, 1987.

[146] A. Shamir, "How to Share a Secret", *Comm. ACM*, 22 (11), pp.612-3, 1979.

[147] K. G. Shin and Y.-H. Lee, "Evaluation of Error Recovery Blocks used for Cooperating Processes", *IEEE Trans. Soft. Eng.*, SE-10 (6), pp.692-700, 1984.

[148] S. K. Shrivastava and J.-P. Banâtre, "Reliable Resource Allocation Between Unreliable Processes", *IEEE Trans. Soft. Eng.*, SE-4 (3), pp.230-41, 1978.

[149] S. K. Shrivastava, G. N. Dixon and G. D. Parrington, "An Overview of the Arjuna Distributed Programming System", *IEEE Software*, 8 (1), pp.66-73, January 1991.

[150] S. K. Shrivastava, P. D. Ezhilchelvan, N. A. Speirs, S. Tao and A. Tully, "Principal Features of the VOLTAN Family of Reliable Node Architectures for Distributed Systems", *IEEE Transactions on Computers*, 41 (5), pp.542-9, May 1992.

[151] D. P. Siewiorek and D. Johnson, "A Design Methodology", in *Reliable Computer Systems — Design and Evaluation* (D. P. Siewiorek and R. S. Swarz, Eds.), pp.739-67, Digital Press, Bedford, MA, USA, 1992.

[152] B. C. Smith, "Reflection and Semantics in Lisp", in *11th Annual ACM Symposium on Principles of Programming Languages,* pp.23-35, 1984.

[153] T. B. Smith, "High Performance Fault-Tolerant Real-Time Computer Architecture", in *Proc. 16th Int. Symp. Fault-Tolerant Computing (FTCS-16),* (Vienna, Austria), pp.14-9, IEEE Computer Society Press, 1986.

[154] N. A. Speirs and P. A. Barrett, "Using Passive Replicates in Delta-4 to Provide Dependable Distributed Computing", in *Proc. 19th Int. Symp. on Fault-Tolerant Computing (FTCS-19),* (Chicago, IL, USA), pp.184-90, IEEE Computer Society Press, 1989.

[155] A. Steininger and J. Reisinger, "Integral Design of Hardware and Operating System for a DCCS", in *Proc. 10th IFAC Workshop on Distributed Computer Control Systems,* (Semmering, Austria), Pergamon Press, 1991.

[156] A. Steininger and H. Schweinzer, "Towards an Optimal Combination of Error Detection Mechanisms", in *Proc. Euromicro 91: Hardware and Software Design Automation,* (Vienna, Austria), pp.253-9, 1991.

[157] J. J. Stiffler, "Fault Coverage and the Point of Diminishing Returns", *Journal of Design Automation and Fault-Tolerant Computing*, 2 (4), pp.289-301, October 1978.

[158] R. J. Stroud, "Transparency and Reflection in Distributed Systems", *ACM Operating Systems Review*, 22 (2), pp.99-103, April 1993.

[159] B. Stroustrup, *The C++ Programming Language,* Addison Wesley, 1991.

[160] G. Sullivan and G. Masson, "Using Certification Trails to Achieve Software Fault Tolerance", in *Proc. 20th Int. Symp. Fault-Tolerant Computing (FTCS-20),* (Newcastle), pp.423-31, IEEE Computer Society Press, 1990.

[161] A. T. Tai, A. Avizienis and J. F. Meyer, "Evaluation of Fault-Tolerant Software: A performability modeling approach", in *Dependable Computing for Critical Applications 3* (C. E. Landwehr, B. Randell and L. Simoncini, Eds.), 8, Dependable Computing and Fault-Tolerant Systems, (A. Avizienis, H. Kopetz and J. C. Laprie, Eds.), pp.113-35, Sprinter-Verlag, 1993.

[162] A. T. Tai, A. Avizienis and J. F. Meyer, "Performability Enhancement of Fault-Tolerant Software", *IEEE Transactions on Reliability, Special Issue on Fault-Tolerant Software*, R-42 (2), pp.227-37, June 1993.

[163] P. Traverse, "AIRBUS and ATR System Architecture and Specification", in *Software Diversity in Computerized Control Systems* (U. Voges, Ed.), Springer Verlag, 1988.

[164] G. Trouessin, J.-C. Fabre and Y. Deswarte, "Reliable Processing of Confidential Information", in *Proc. of the 7th Int. Conf. on Computer Security, IFIP/SEC'91,* (Brighton, UK), pp.210-21, 1991.

[165] P. Veríssimo, "Redundant Media Mechanisms for Dependable Communication in Token-Bus LANs", in *Proc. 13th Local Computer Network Conf.,* (Minneapolis, MN, USA), pp.453-62, IEEE Computer Society Press, 1988.

[166] U. Voges (Ed.), *Proc. IFIP Working Conf. "Design Diversity in Action"*, *Baden, Austria, June, 1986*, 2, 1986.

[167] U. Voges (Ed.), *Software Diversity in Computerized Control Systems*, 2, Springer-Verlag, Wien, 1988.

[168] A. Vrchoticky, *Modula/R Language Definition*, Technische Universität Wien, Research Report, N°2/92, March 1992.

[169] W. E. Weihl and B. Liskov, "Implementation of Resilient, Atomic Data Types", *ACM Trans. Programming Languages and Systems*, 7 (2), pp.244-69, 1985.

[170] P. D. Welch, "The Statistical Analysis of Simulation Results", in *Computer Performance Modeling Handbook* (S. S. Lavenberg, Ed.), Academic Press, New York, 1982.

[171] J. H. Wensley, L. Lamport, J. Goldberg, M. W. Green, K. N. Levitt, P. M. Melliar-Smith, R. E. Shostack and C. B. Weinstock, "SIFT: The design and analysis of a fault-tolerant computer for aircraft control", *Proc. IEEE*, 66 (10), pp.1240-55, 1978.

[172] W. Wood, "A Decentralised Recovery Control Protocol", in *Proc. 11th Int. Symp. Fault-Tolerant Computing (FTCS-11)*, pp.159-64, IEEE Computer Society Press, 1981.

[173] J. Xu, *Fault Tolerance Based on System Diagnosis Techniques*, University of Newcastle upon Tyne, PDCS Technical Report Series, N°69, May 1991.

[174] J. Xu, "The t/(n-1)-Diagnosability and its Applications to Fault Tolerance", in *Proc. 21st Int. Symp. on Fault-Tolerant Computing (FTCS-21)*, (Montreal), pp.496-503, IEEE Computer Society Press, 1991.

[175] J. Xu, A. Bondavalli and F. Di Giandomenico, *Software Fault Tolerance: Dynamic combination of dependability and efficiency*, Univ. of Newcastle upon Tyne, Tech. Report, N°442, 1993.

[176] J. Xu, B. Randell, A. Romanovsky, C. M. F. Rubira, R. J. Stroud and Z. Wu, "Fault Tolerance in Concurrent Object-Oriented Software through Coordinated Error Recovery", in *Proc. 25th Int. Symp. Fault-Tolerant Computing (FTCS-25)*, (Los Angeles), IEEE Computer Society Press, 1995.

[177] J. Xu, B. Randell, C. M. F. Rubira and R. J. Stroud, "Toward an Object-Oriented Approach to Software Fault Tolerance", in *Fault-Tolerant Parallel and Distributed Systems* (D. R. Avresky, Ed.), IEEE Computer Society Press, 1994.

[178] S. S. Yau and R. C. Cheung, "Design of Self-Checking Software", in *Proc. Int. Conf. on Reliable Software*, (Los Angeles, CA, USA), pp.450-7, IEEE Computer Society Press, 1975.

# Chapter IV

# Fault Removal

Fault removal is known as being *the* most costly activity out of all activities which take place during the development of computing systems. Accordingly, PDCS and PDCS2 have devoted significant attention to this topic. It has been addressed according to three viewpoints, which are the topics of the papers of this chapter: (i) identifying the strengths and weaknesses of mathematically formal specification and verification, (ii) devising new approaches to software testing, namely statistical testing and formal testing, and (iii) exploring the problems brought about when testing distributed real-time systems.

The first paper, "Advantages and Limits of Formal Approaches for Ultra-High Dependability", proposes a guided tour of the possibilities and limits of formal methods for the development of systems which require ultra-high dependability, i.e. critical systems. The paper examines critically those activities which can be expressed in a mathematically formal way, and those which cannot, and provides recommendation for verifying both types of activities, through the exploration of the (necessary) complementarities between formal proofs and testing.

In the second paper, "Software Statistical Testing", a new testing method is reported on, which is based on a probabilistic generation of test data: structural or functional criteria serve as guides for defining an input profile and a test size. After having presented the motivation and the theoretical foundation of statistical testing, the feasibility of designing statistical test inputs is exemplified on a safety-critical component from the nuclear industry, and the efficiency of these test inputs is assessed through experiments, in which both structural and functional testing are performed. The results show the high fault-revealing power of statistical testing, and its best efficiency in comparison to deterministic and random testing.

The third paper, "An Experimental Evaluation of Formal Testing and Statistical Testing", is devoted to a comparative evaluation of statistical testing and of formal testing (i.e. deterministic tests derived from a formal specification). The preliminary results obtained clearly show that much is to be gained from their complementarities.

The fourth paper, "Testing Distributed Real-Time Systems: An Overview", specifically identifies the influences on testing of distributedness and of real-time requirements. Those problems, as well as their interrelations, are first presented in a general framework, and then exemplified by devising a test methodology for the distributed real-time system MARS.

# Advantages and Limits of Formal Approaches for Ultra-High Dependability*

Marie-Claude Gaudel

LRI, CNRS et Université de Paris-Sud

**Abstract.** This paper discusses the advantages and limits of formal approaches to software development for achieving ultra-high dependability of critical computer systems. It is a companion paper to Paper VI.G on the validation of ultra-high dependability for software systems. Among the issues to be addressed here, are: what is a formal specification, what can be done with it, what is correctness, what kind of certainty comes from a proof, and from testing? The paper does not claim to answer these questions: rather it is a formulation of the author's reflections in this area.

## 1    Introduction

Formal approaches to software development are sometimes presented as *the* solution for the realization of ultra-high dependable computerized systems. It is clear that these approaches can contribute a lot to fault prevention and fault removal. However, they do not solve the question completely. Thus, it is interesting to discuss both their interests and limits.

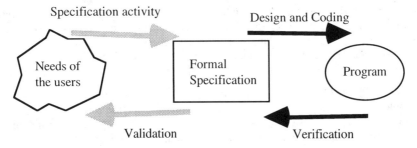

**Fig.   1.**

Let us start with some terminology. Fig. 1 is a somewhat simplified and idealized "view" of the software development process, where boxes stand for documents and arrows stand for activities (we do not aim at proposing a development model: Fig. 1 must be seen as a dependency graph and the way activities or subactivities are organized or iterated is not discussed here; for a discussion on formal methods in safety-critical systems life-cycle, see [60]). Here, we are interested in pointing out what can be formal and what cannot: for instance, the *needs of the users* are by their essence informal since they reflect some aspects of the real world, including some irrational (but quite respectable) feelings or habits. Let us assume that the needs of

---

*   An extended abstract of a preliminary version of this paper was published in [31].

the users are adequately understood; even in this case the *specification activity* can only be empirical, since it aims at stating a description of these aspects of the real world. It is well known that such a description induces some schematisation. However, the resulting *specification document* can be formal: for many years, a lot of work has been carried on formal specifications and formal development methods. Many definitions of the term "formal" have already been proposed.

Formal methods have been introduced in [13] as:

*"mathematically-based techniques, often supported by reasoning tools, that can offer a rigorous and effective way to model, design and analyse computer systems."*

Some variants of this definition can be found (see for instance [8, 74]), but they all agree on the following principles.

A formal method provides a notation for software specification and development with some mathematical meaning: with each specification is associated a mathematical entity. Moreover, there is a formal deduction system that makes it possible to perform some symbolic computations or proofs. This formal system is consistent with the mathematical semantics, i.e. the properties which can be computed from a specification text are properties of its mathematical meaning. The mathematical semantics describe the underlying concepts, the deduction system the mechanisms that can be used. Such methods also provide a way to describe and verify refinements, i.e. passages from an abstract specification to a more detailed specification that must satisfy the former one. We make a distinction between *top-level specifications*, which are the result of an analysis of the users needs, and *detailed specifications*, which are the result of some refinement of another specification.

From the above definitions, it appears that a *program* can be a formal document under the condition that there exists a mathematical semantics, i.e. a formal definition, of the programming language. In such cases, the deduction system is the execution scheme of the programming language and the mathematical understanding is provided by the formal definition (denotational semantics, or weakest preconditions transforms, or any of the numerous existing approaches).

Let us now consider the arrows in Fig. 1. Intuitively, an activity is susceptible of a complete formal treatment only if the relevant documents are formal. Thus, *validation* activity, which consists of checking the top-level specification document against the needs of the users, cannot be completely formal: it is impossible to prove that this specification is correct with respect to some informal needs. However, as soon as the notation is formal, some formal techniques can be used to gain some confidence that the specification is satisfactory[1]. This is discussed in part 2 of this paper.

*Design and coding* activities consist of developing a program from a specification, assuming that the specification is right. Accordingly, the *verification activity* checks the program against the specification. These activities can be completely formal when the specification language and the programming language are formal notations, and if the formal specification covers all the requisite properties of the program. The corresponding formal techniques are discussed in part 3 of this paper.

---

[1]  In this paper, we avoid the use of "correct" to qualify a top-level specification to emphasize our claim that there is no correctness reference and no possibility of correctness proof for a global specification...

This terminology is not completely standard (but it is close to general usage in software engineering). The main underlying motivations for our choice are: (i) to make clear that some activities are of different natures, the criterion being the possibility of using formal methods, and (ii) to make a distinction between the faults which can be introduced/revealed by these activities. For instance the distinction between the specification activity and the design and coding activity naturally induces a distinction between specification faults and design and coding faults. These faults are usually mixed under the same misleading labels: design faults, development faults, etc. Besides, we are aware that the term "validation" is used with different meanings in different contexts, for instance in the first chapter of this book where some distinction is made between checking qualitative or qualitative properties. Similarly, the term "verification" is sometimes understood as implying proof techniques: this is not the case here.

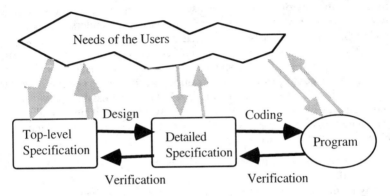

**Fig. 2.**

Another warning is that Fig. 1, which is useful for pointing out some issues such as the distinction between validation and verification, is obviously oversimplified. One omitted aspect that is important for the present discussion is that the needs of the users always include some non-functional requirements [59] or development constraints. A non-exhaustive list of, not necessarily disjoint, categories for these constraints, as stated in [93], is given below:

- quality attributes: performance, reliability, reusability, user comfort,... (most dependability requirements are in this category);
- requirements for system implementation: languages, hardware, interface with existing components;
- requirements for the development process: methods, languages, tools to be used;
- requirements for test, installation and maintenance;
- economic or political considerations: market constraints, costs ...

Even if we assume that all these constraints could be expressed formally, which is rather optimistic, some of them concern just the design and coding activities and must be taken into account during these activities. Consequently, some further validation must be performed at this stage. Fig. 2 is an attempt to represent these validations in the case where the design is made in two steps: the bottom-up fuzzy arrows represent validation.

Another problem is that non-functional requirements may not be kept to by the design and coding activity. An example is security: refinement can add new observation possibilities to a system, through which it may become possible to breach security [59]. Thus security should be validated at the end of each design step.

There is a last point that this paper will address. Ultra high dependability is not an attribute of a program, but of a system. Hardware and software must cooperate to ensure fault tolerance. Figs. 1 and 2 do not take this aspect into account. In some sense, the execution support (i.e. hardware + operating system) is supposed to be perfect. Such an assumption is as rash as claiming that a top-level specification is perfect. We discuss this point in part 3.3.

## 2    Impact of Formal Specifications on the Specification and Validation Activities

Even if it seems obvious, it is always useful to recall that a formal specification can be wrong. It can be wrong for two kinds of reason: misunderstandings of the users needs; errors in the expression of these needs. In both cases, we will speak of *specification faults*. Moreover, the notion of correctness is impossible to formalise in the case of a top-level formal specification since there is no formal correctness reference. As a consequence, it is meaningless to hope to prove that a top-level formal specification is correct. At this level, the only possibility is to use "testing" methods (static or dynamic ones). The great advantage of using formal specifications is that some tools exist to analyse and animate them[2], i.e. to guide and, sometimes, mechanize this testing process.

In presenting evidence of this advantage, it is interesting to attack the problem from the other side, by studying specification faults: is it possible to classify them? are there any methods to prevent them? which verification methods are available in order to remove them?

### 2.1  Classification of Specification Faults

There are a lot of reports and analyses on the various ways a specification can be unsatisfactory. However, work is still needed both on the sources of these problems and on their effects on the specification document, especially when it is formal. The point is that a specification must be *precise but not detailed*. These requirements are not at all antagonistic, as they may look at first sight, but the point is definitely misleading.

Most specification faults come from a misunderstanding of the original problem. This is independent of whether or not the specification is formal. There are three main, non disjoint, classes of specification faults [93]:

- *adequacy faults*: some of the properties expressed in the specification are in contradiction with the required properties.
- *overspecification*: the specification satisfies the required properties, but some feasible solutions are excluded because of the presence of unnecessary properties; the specification is too detailed.

---

[2]  We mean intellectual tools as well as computerized ones.

- *underspecification*: all the properties expressed in the specification are adequate, but some unacceptable solutions are accepted; the specification is not precise enough.

It is not clear how overspecification has an influence on dependability. It may affect for instance feasibility, cost, extensibility: thus it may have an indirect negative influence. It may also affect, in some cases, understandability, but not always in a negative way: there are some well-known examples where the description of a specific solution is simpler than the general description of the problem. The two other classes of faults, i.e. adequacy faults and underspecification, accept forbidden and unexpected behaviours: thus they are an immediate danger for dependability.

When the specification is formal, these faults appear, in some cases, as *inconsistency* or *incompleteness*. Inconsistency is the ultimate form of both overspecification and inadequacy since contradictory properties are required. Incompleteness may (or may not) correspond to some underspecification: some properties, which are expressible in the specification language, cannot be said to be either compatible or contradictory with respect to the specification. Either some cases have been forgotten (underspecification) or it is just that these properties are irrelevant: it does not matter whether or not they are fulfilled by the future system. We discuss in part 2.3 the issue of the detection of inconsistency and incompleteness.

Besides these fundamental faults, there are all the possible "typographic" faults: the cause of these faults is not a misunderstanding of the problem, but a mistake in writing the specification. It can come from a lack of attention (using one identifier in the place of another, ...) or from difficulty in mastering the specification language. Clearly, the resulting specification will be, as above, inadequate, inconsistent or incomplete. However, the origins of these faults are different, and the techniques for preventing or detecting them are probably of different nature.

There are of course other kinds of fault which at first sight seem irrelevant to ultra-high dependability, namely: verbosity, obscurity, inelegance, redundancies, digressions,... However, it appears below that they are relevant in an indirect way.

## 2.2  Prevention of Specification Faults

We discuss here how to avoid specification faults during the specification activity.

Concerning the first kind of specification fault (those coming from a misunderstanding of the problem), obvious criteria are *simplicity* and *conciseness*. For instance, the top-level I/O specification of the SIFT system contains only 8 axioms [63].

In the case of formal specifications, the main concept for achieving both simplicity and conciseness is *abstraction* [59, 66]. A formal specification language must provide a way for writing abstract and structured specifications. Of course, this is not sufficient, just as modules in a programming language do not ensure that programs will be modular. It is clear that a long, complex formal specification of a critical system must be considered as suspect. Thus verbosity, obscurity and similar faults are not as benign with respect to dependability as they look at first sight. More generally, rules for writing good formal specifications are needed, just as there are rules for writing good programs, and these rules probably depend on the underlying formalism. An attempt aimed at the use of algebraic specifications, can be found in [3].

However, the problem is far from being solvable just by stating rules, and SIFT is not a representative example. For expressing the required properties it is often necessary to formalize some aspects of the application domain or of the environment. This is one of the reasons why most case studies in formal specification result in specifications which are neither simple nor concise: it does not come from the formalization but from the number of concepts which are necessary to the expression of the system functionalities. Here, as elsewhere, structuring and reuse will improve the situation. By reuse we mean reuse of theories: mathematicians do not reinvent Peano's axioms each time they use natural numbers. In computer science, a good example is the specification of compilers where accumulated knowledge is sufficient to guide and facilitate any new specification. Another less classical example is discussed in [29]. Reuse of theory is not limited to the reuse of a piece of specification: a theory could be built into the semantics of a specialised, application-oriented, specification language.

Concerning typographic faults, some studies are needed of the syntactic constructs which are prone to errors, similar to those done for programming languages. As formal specification languages are most of the time of an experimental nature, concrete syntax is often the "poor man" in their design. This is quite understandable, but not acceptable if the language is in use for critical system development.

## 2.3 Validation

We discuss here how to detect faults in a specification document. We mainly address the problem of verifying a top-level, formal, specification.

As indicated above, the only possible methods for validation are "testing-like" methods, in the sense that these methods can provide some evidence that the specification is wrong; they only increase confidence in the fact it is satisfactory. However, as the aim of formalism is rigour in reasoning, these methods will consist, most of the time, of proving properties of the specification.

Some formal specification languages, such as VDM [46] , LARCH [30] and to a lesser extent Z [101], associate with each specification some *proof obligations*, i.e. some properties which are necessary for the consistency of the specification and must be proved. These proofs can be performed by hand or supported by a system: for instance [30] shows how to use the LC (Larch Checker) system and the LP theorem prover for LARCH; [101] reports an experiment on Z , using the B theorem prover.

Another, more general, use of a theorem prover for testing formal specifications is reported in [30] for LARCH: it is possible to check, via LP, what the authors call "theory containment", i.e. to try to prove some conjectures (which play the role of "test data") that should be consequences of the formal specification. This technique is also recommended in [74].

For some formal specification languages, there is a possibility of detecting inconsistencies via a specific tool: [27] presents such a tool for algebraic specifications with positive conditional axioms; [30] mentions such a tool for LARCH. It is also possible to give sufficient conditions for (some adapted notion of) completeness, which are mechanizable [55]]. As indicated in part 2.1, the fact that a specification is consistent and complete does not mean that it is adequate. However, inconsistency reveals the presence of a fault, and incompleteness may correspond to some underspecification.

When formal specifications are executable (it is not always the case), rapid prototyping is "for free". An executable specification is just a special case where there is a set of rules and a reasoning tool which make it possible to deduce the output corresponding to some inputs. Besides, executability depends not only on the formalism: it may depend on the specification[3]. If the specification is executable, it can be tested [47] and, since there is a formal notation, some coverage criteria for the text of the specification can be defined: see for instance [7] for algebraic specifications.

From this brief and incomplete tour of validation methods and tools for formal specifications, it appears that there exist a lot of possibilities, even if formality is not the "silver bullet" against specification faults.

## 3     Impact of Formal Specifications on Design and Coding, and Verification

We discuss here the use of formal methods for the activities represented by solid arrows in Figs. 1 and 2, namely *design*, *coding* and *verification*. As usual, we consider that the design and coding activities are performed in one or several steps, the last step resulting in a program. The earlier steps consist in refining a specification document into a more detailed document that is supposed to be closer to a program. As indicated above, each step requires two kinds of check: a *verification* that the resulting document is correct with respect to the original document; some *validation*, that the resulting document satisfies some design constraints or informal requirements that are not expressed or not expressible in the original document.

### 3.1  Design and Coding Faults

These faults are ones introduced during the design and coding activities. The difference with the specification faults discussed in part 2 is that there is a *correctness reference*. (In this part we make the optimistic assumption that the top-level specification is right.)

It would be possible to reuse the same classification as for specification faults, namely adequacy faults, underspecification and overspecification. In a formal framework, adequacy faults will appear as inconsistencies when putting together the original and the more detailed document; underspecifications will appear as incompletenesses; the notion of overspecification remains as unclear as was indicated in 2.1. However, it is not clear that this classification is sufficient or even meaningful for design faults. For instance, some formalisms introduce several "proof obligations" [46] for each refinement step: in VDM, "data reification" and/or "operation decomposition" must be checked. It seems sensible to conjecture that different proof obligations correspond to different classes of faults. However, there is

---

[3]  For instance, algebraic specifications are executable if there exists a rewriting system that is equivalent to the axioms, confluent, and terminating. There are quite respectable specifications, for instance sets with a choice operation of an arbitrary element, that do not fulfill this property.

no obvious correlation with the three classes above. It seems that some research is needed in this area, and it is quite probable that the relevant classification depends on the formalism used.

In the case of the design of ultra-highly dependable systems, the design choices should take into account the possibility of performing verification in a reasonably easy way. This notion is already well-known in circuit design as *design for testability* [100]. Some similar notion is needed for software as well as a notion of *design for provability* as sketched in [19].

## 3.2 Prevention of Design and Coding Faults in the case of Ultra-High Dependability

The best way to prevent human errors in an activity is to automate it, or at least to make it rigourous and systematic. A lot of research has been carried out on the derivation of programs from formal specifications. In some domains, for instance compiler construction, it has been possible to develop true *program generators*. Compiler construction is a successful example of reuse of formalization (cf. part 2.2) and of "design knowledge". This is only possible for a few domains that have been very well studied and formalized. With respect to ultra-high dependability, this solution would be appealing but not completely satisfactory since it must be proved that the generator never introduces faults in the generated program, and this generator may be very complex. Moreover, this approach assumes correlation and commonality between problem domains which can be described and exploited in a systematic way.

A partial solution to this problem is given in the *transformational approach*. The underlying principle is to develop a program from a specification by applications of some transformations that have been proved to preserve the semantics of the specification. In this approach, there is no separation between a specification language and a programming language: the transformation process works on documents in a so-called "wide spectrum language" which contains at the same time specification constructs and programming constructs. Two well-known instances of the transformational approach (among many others) are the CIP project and its continuations by Partsch [70], the Prospectra project [51], the refinement calculus [62], etc. Although this approach has been studied and experimented with a great deal, it seems difficult to use in practice, mainly because: a large number of transformations must be provided; many steps are needed to get a program; and it is difficult to find the right choices among all the possibilities. In the case of ultra-high dependability, these choices should be "driven" by dependability requirements; as far as the author knows, no research has been reported in this area and there is no example of industrial application of this approach.

This approach is a good approximation of *zero-fault design*. However, it must be emphasized that it is not sufficient. There are conditions for applying the transformations, thus it is possible to make mistakes during the design. For instance, in [62], Morgan reports such a mistake and insists on the need to check the design, possibly with the assistance of an automated system[4]. As he says:

*"mathematical rigour cannot eliminate mistakes entirely. All it can do is reduce their likelihood— drastically".*

---

[4]  Checkers are generally simpler than generators, thus less susceptible of faults.

## 3.3  Verification:  proving,  testing

**Proving.** One of the main advantages advocated for formal specifications is the possibility of *proving the correctness of each design step*. It looks very attractive for ultra-high dependability, and this possibility is probably one of the key reasons for the interest in formal methods. More and more examples of correctness proofs in large industrial system developments have been reported. One of the first experiments was the SIFT project discussed in [63]. More recent examples are: [75] reports the formal verification of a fault-tolerant clock synchronization algorithm; [38] describes the development and proof of the SACEM system, which controls the speed of the RER underground in Paris and consists of 21,000 lines of Modula partly embedded; [19] presents the first results in applying formal methods to the verification of the design of a fault-tolerant operating system that schedules and executes the application tasks of a digital flight control system. All these proofs are said to be long[5] and boring, and there is a general agreement on the need for some systems to assist and check this activity. Such systems already exist (Boyer Moore, PVS, Gypsy, HOL,...).

However, the quotation above applies equally to correctness proofs: proofs do not bring certainty, as has been known to and discussed by philosophers for some time [52]. It is true that there may be some mistakes in a proof; but if the proof is formal, i.e. carried out in a formal system, step by step, each step being an application of an inference rule of the formal system, it is possible to develop a *proof checker*[6]. However, the problem is more serious than that: the formal system may be wrong, or to speak more intuitively the definition of correctness may be wrong. The reader probably noticed that we did not define what is the "correctness of a design step". At this stage of the discussion, we are not actually interested in such a definition but rather in the *proof obligation* which is associated with the notion of refinement in the formal specification language. Is this proof obligation right[7]? Fortunately the answer is "yes", very often. But such issues must be assessed in the case of ultra-high dependability. A first version of the design proof of SIFT was severely criticized in [65] for such reasons. In another project [75], the authors report on a formal proof:

*"... we did not find theorem proving to be a bottleneck (discovering the theorems to prove was a bottleneck)".*

Some other points to be addressed carefully are correctness transitivity, and composition of correctness proofs of subsystems.

In conclusion, it seems that correctness proofs are now practicable, and that they can provide high confidence in the absence of design faults.

**Testing.** Testing mainly concerns the verification of the final design step, the one that results in a program, even if as indicated above, some testing can be performed for the intermediate steps, when the specification is executable.

---

[5]  During a panel at the 2nd IFIP Working Conference on Dependable Computing for Critical Applications (Tucson, Feb. 1991), the following numbers were reported for the proof of the ASOS kernel, using Gypsy: 19383 ADA statements, 7604 lines of formal specification, 882,049 lines of proof transcripts...

[6]  See note 5...

[7]  With the same meaning as in: is the global specification right?

Formal specifications also bring new possibilities for defining some so-called black-box dynamic testing strategies. This can be done in a classical way, by definition of some coverage criteria on the text of the formal specification. However, it is possible to go further and to state a link with the notion of correctness. In [7], we have shown how to derive an *exhaustive test data set* associated to a formal specification from the semantic definition of the validity of a property. It is then possible to state a (weak) *hypothesis* on the program, such that, under this hypothesis, the satisfaction of the exhaustive test data set by the program is equivalent to its correctness with respect to the specification. To obtain practicable (i.e. finite) test sets, some hypotheses are added (for instance one can assume uniformity of a property $P$ on a subdomain $SD$, i.e. if $P$ is valid for an arbitrary value $c$ of $SD$, it is valid on all $SD$). Such hypotheses correspond to current testing practices, but are usually left implicit. The operation which adds hypotheses and reduces the test data set accordingly, is called a *testing context refinement*.

In the case of algebraic specifications, we have defined a set of hypotheses which retain the (under-hypothesis) equivalence with correctness. It thus turns out that testing can also be formal, after all [32]. Practical experiments with formal testing are reported in [14] and in tPaper IV.C. Similar approaches has been developed for VDM [18], for LOTOS [11], and other formal methods.

**Testing and proving.** It is generally admitted that testing is not sufficient to ensure ultra-high dependability. This is probably right. However, it would be interesting to study the level of dependability reached after testing a system with as much effort, care, and cleverness as for some of the correctness proofs mentioned above...

Similarly, proving is not sufficient: as was mentioned in the introduction, ultra-high dependability is required for the actual system, not for its description. A proof works on the text of the program, not on the system. It is worth pointing out that when performing a proof, one makes also some strong hypotheses: that the compiler and the execution support are perfect. This difference of nature between programs and systems is pointed out by Parnas in [69]:

*"Strictly speaking we should not consider software as a component in systems at all. The software is simply the initial data in the computer and it is the initialized computer that is the component in question."*

In [38] it is reported how a fault was discovered by testing in the proved SACEM system: it was due to an error in initializing a constant. It seems that the same kind of error (the initialization of a table) is the origin of the recent Pentium bug [72]. Testing and proving are probably complementary, just as proofs and refutations are complementary to prove mathematical conjectures [52]. However, there are some specific characteristics of computer science which must be taken into account: as indicated above, proofs are long, boring, and must be carefully checked. Moreover, they are dependent on the structure of the program and must be redone after every modification. Thus it seems sound to the author to start by some specification-guided testing (looking for as many refutations as possible) and to try to prove programs which have a good chance of being correct. However, Rushby and von Henke in [75] have a different view and conclude from their experience in formal verification that the real benefit comes from failed proof attempts.

# 4    Conclusions

In this paper we have provided a guided tour of the possibilities and limits of formal methods for the development of systems which require ultra-high dependability.

The "caveats" we have recalled have been expressed by all serious proponents of formal methods: the impossibility of being sure that a formal specification expresses the properties required of the system, the difficulty of stating relevant correctness theorems. These problems are far from being inherent to the use of formal methods. Besides, formal methods can help, for instance for the detection of *specification faults*, and we have reviewed several methods and tools.

We have characterized a kind of fault, namely a *design fault*, in our terminology, that can be eliminated by formal verification. We have also pleaded for the use of formal testing as a complement of formal proofs.

In the case of ultra-high-dependable systems, it is clear that one of the goals must be what we have called *zero-fault design*. It is also clear that this is not sufficient and that formal methods alone will not ensure ultra-high dependability: first because we will never be completely sure that the verification is right, second because there are other classes of faults to be prevented, removed and tolerated.

## Acknowledgements

Discussions with the PDCS members, especially Jean-Claude Laprie, John McDermid and Brian Randell, have been very influential. John McDermid deserves special thanks for many helpful suggestions. Thanks are also due to Gilles Bernot, Jean-Pierre Finance, Bruno Marre and Pierre Dauchy.

This paper reflects the personal views of the author.

# Software Statistical Testing[*]

Pascale Thévenod-Fosse  Hélène Waeselynck  Yves Crouzet

LAAS-CNRS

**Abstract.** Statistical testing is based on a probabilistic generation of test data: structural or functional criteria serve as guides for defining an input profile and a test size. The method is intended to compensate for the imperfect connection of criteria with software faults, and should not be confused with random testing, a blind approach that uses a uniform profile over the input domain. First, the motivation and the theoretical foundation of statistical testing are presented. Then the feasibility of designing statistical test patterns is exemplified on a safety-critical component from the nuclear industry, and the fault-revealing power of these patterns is assessed through experiments conducted at two different levels: (i) unit testing of four functions extracted from the industrial component, statistical test data being designed according to classical structural criteria; (ii) testing of the whole component, statistical test data being designed from behaviour models deduced from the component specification. The results show the high fault-revealing power of statistical testing, and its greater efficiency in comparison to deterministic and random testing.

## 1    Introduction

Testing involves exercising software by supplying it with input values. In practice, testing is partial as it is not possible to exercise a piece of software with each possible data item from the input domain. When the focus of testing is *fault removal*, that is, bug-finding rather than reliability assessment, the tester is faced with the problem of selecting a subset of the input domain that is well-suited for revealing the real, but unknown, faults; this issue being further compounded by the increasing complexity of current software systems. Then, the methods for generating test inputs proceed according to one of two principles: either deterministic or probabilistic.

*Deterministic methods* for generating test inputs usually take advantage of information on the target software in order to provide guides for selecting test cases, the information being depicted by means of test criteria. Many test criteria have been proposed (see e.g. [5, 44, 64]): each defines a specific set of elements to be exercised during testing; these elements being parts of either a model of the program structure or a model of its functionality. For example, the program control flow graph is a well-known structural model, and finite state machines are behaviour models that may be used to describe some software functions. State coverage (i.e. instruction testing in the case of a program flow graph) and transition coverage (i.e. branch testing in the case of a program flow graph) are two classical examples of test criteria associated with these models. Given a criterion, the deterministic principle consists in selecting a priori a set of test patterns such that each element defined by the criterion is exercised (at least) once.

---

[*]    This paper is a compendium of [88-90, 95].

On the other hand, the conventional probabilistic method for generating test inputs, called *random testing*, consists in generating random test data based on a uniform distribution over the input domain [21]: this is an extreme case of the black box testing approach, since no information related to the target piece of software is considered, except for the range of its input domain. The argument in favour of random testing is its low cost: large sets of test patterns can be generated cheaply, that is, without requiring any preliminary analysis of the software. Indeed, the fault-revealing power of such a "blind" testing approach is questionable, even if large sets of test data are used, and previous work has shown that its effectiveness can be surprisingly high as well as surprisingly low, depending on both the target software and the particular randomly drawn input values [21].

*Statistical testing* is based on an unusual definition of random testing [86]: it aims at providing a "balanced" coverage of a model of the target software, no part of the model being seldom or never exercised during testing. With this approach, the method for generating statistical test patterns combines information provided by a model of the target software, that is, by a test criterion, with a practical way of producing large sets of patterns, that is, a random generation. The sets of statistical test patterns are then defined by two parameters, which have to be determined according to the test criterion retained:

1.  *the test profile*, or input distribution, from which the patterns are randomly drawn,
2.  *the test size*, or equivalently the number of input patterns (i.e. of program executions) that are generated;

As in the case of deterministic testing, test criteria may be related to a model of either the program structure, which defines *statistical structural testing*, or of its functionality, which defines *statistical functional testing*.

The work reported in the following sections aims first, to show the feasibility of designing statistical testing and second, to assess and compare the efficiency of the three methods for generating test inputs: deterministic, random and statistical. The experiments were conducted with programs taken from a real industrial nuclear reactor safety shutdown system. Although results related to one case study are not sufficient to draw general conclusions on the adequacy of the test methods, they allow us to confirm serious limitations of both the random and the deterministic approaches; the statistical method is likely to be a practical way of compensating for most of these limitations.

This paper proceeds as follows. Section 2 describes the motivation and the principle of statistical testing. Section 3 outlines our experimental framework. Then, in the light of the results obtained from our real case study, Sections 4 and 5 concentrate on the analysis of the strengths and weaknesses of the three methods for generating test patterns, at the unit testing level and at the component testing level respectively.

# 2    Statistical Testing

This section focuses on both the motivation and the theoretical framework of the authors' statistical testing approach.

## 2.1 Statistical Testing: Why?

Test criteria take advantage of information on the program under test in order to provide guides for selecting test inputs. This information, obtained during the software development process, relates either to program structure or its functionality (see e.g. [5, 44, 64]). In both cases, any criterion specifies a set of elements to be exercised during testing. Given a criterion C, let $S_C$ be the corresponding set of elements. To comply with finite test sets, $S_C$ must contain a finite number of elements that can be exercised by at least one input pattern. For example, the structural criterion "All-Branches" requires that each program branch be executed: C = "Branches" $\Rightarrow S_C$ = {executable program edges}.

Given a criterion C, the usual practice for determining test data proceeds according to the *deterministic principle*: the tester selects a priori a set of N patterns such that each element of $S_C$ is exercised at least once; this set is most often built so that each element is exercised *only once*, in order to minimize the test size N. Unfortunately, a major issue still arises from the definition of the test criteria: a main *limitation* is due to the imperfect connection of the criteria with real faults. Because of the (current) lack of an accurate model for software design faults, this problem is not likely to be solved soon. Hence, exercising only once, or very few times, each element defined by such imperfect criteria is far from being enough to ensure that the corresponding set of test patterns possesses a high fault exposure power. And this is the main reason why the efficiency of deterministic testing depends more on the particular test input values chosen than on the given criterion [40].

To make an attempt at improving current testing techniques, two different directions can be investigated:

1. one can *search for more pertinent test criteria* that is, criteria under which, for any faulty program, exercising each element once is very likely to produce a failure, whatever the particular input values chosen [23, 39, 56, 98] (see Paper IV.C);
2. one can cope with current – imperfect – criteria and compensate their weakness by requiring that *each element be exercised several times*.

The *first direction* is arduous since it can be expected that a pertinent criterion depends thoroughly on the residual faults; these faults being specific to the target program, and unknown before testing. For example, as regards current structural criteria, the most stringent criterion, namely "All-Paths", is not pertinent: residual faults tracked down during testing are generally more subtle in the sense that their revealing input data correspond to a small subset of the input subdomain that exercises a given path. Since "All-Paths" testing is feasible for only simple programs, any more refinement should be unrealistic.

The *second direction* involves large sets of test patterns that would be tedious to determine manually; hence the need for an automatic generation of test data. This is the *motivation of statistical testing* designed according to a criterion, which aims to combine the information provided by imperfect (but not irrelevant) criteria with a practical way of producing numerous input patterns, that is, a random generation.

## 2.2 Statistical Testing: How?

When using the probabilistic method for generating test data, the number of times each element k of $S_C$ is exercised is a random variable. Two factors play a part in ensuring that on average each element is exercised several times, whatever the particular test input values generated according to the test profile and within a moderate test duration.

The first factor is the *input probability distribution* which must allow us to increase the probability of exercising the least likely element of $S_C$. Two different methods of deriving such a proper test profile are possible: either *analytical*, or *empirical*. The first supposes that the activation conditions of the elements can be expressed as a function of the input parameters: then their probabilities of occurrence are a function of the input probabilities, facilitating the derivation of a profile that maximises the frequency of the least likely element. The second method consists in instrumenting the software in order to collect statistics on the numbers of activations of the elements: starting from a large number of input data drawn from an initial distribution (e.g. the uniform distribution), the test profile is progressively refined until the frequency of each element is deemed sufficiently high.

The second factor is the *test size N* which must be large enough to ensure that the least likely element is exercised several times under the derived test profile. The notion of test quality with respect to a criterion recalled below [86], provides us with a theoretical framework to assess a test size.

**Definition.** A criterion C is covered with a probability $q_N$ if each element of $S_C$ has a probability of at least $q_N$ of being exercised during N executions with random input patterns. $q_N$ is *the test quality with respect to (wrt) C.*

The quality $q_N$ is a measure of the test coverage wrt C. Let $p_k$ be the probability that a random pattern exercises the element k under the retained test profile, and $P_C = \min \{p_k, k \in S_C\}$ be the occurrence probability per execution of the least likely element. Then the test quality and the test size N are linked by the equation: $(1-P_C)^N = 1-q_N$. The result of this is that on average each element is exercised several times. More precisely, this equation establishes a link between $q_N$ and the expected number of times, denoted n, the least likely element is exercised: $n \cong - \ln(1-q_N)$. For example, $n \cong 7$ for $q_N = 0.999$, and $n \cong 9$ for $q_N = 0.9999$. Thus, knowing the value of $P_C$ for the derived test profile, if a test quality objective $q_N$ is required the *minimum* test size amounts to:

$$N \geq \ln(1-q_N) \,/\, \ln(1-P_C) \tag{1}$$

**Method.** The principle of the *method for designing statistical testing* according to a given criterion C involves two steps, the first of which is the corner stone of the method. These steps are the following:

*Step 1: Search for an input distribution* that is well-suited to exercise each element of $S_C$ rapidly in order to decrease the test size; or equivalently, the distribution must accommodate the highest possible $P_C$ value;

*Step 2: Assessment of the test size N* required to reach a target test quality $q_N$ wrt C, given the value of $P_C$ inferred from the first step; equation (1) yields the test size.

Returning to the imperfect connection of the criteria with real faults, it is worth noting that the criterion does not influence random data generation in the same way as in the deterministic approach: it serves as a guide for defining an input profile and a test size, but does not allow for the a priori selection of a (small) subset of input patterns. Indeed, the efficiency of the probabilistic approach relies mainly on the assumption that the information supplied by the retained criterion is relevant to derive a test profile that enhances the program failure probability. And there is a direct link between fault exposure power and random data: from equation (1), any fault involving a failure probability $p \geq P_C$ per execution according to the test profile has a probability of at least $q_N$ of being revealed by a set of N random patterns[8]. No such link is foreseeable as regards deterministic test data; and this link should carry more weight than a thorough deterministic selection (thus providing in essence a perfect coverage) with respect to *questionable* criteria. The experimental results shown in Section 4 will support this assumption.

# 3    Case Study for Safety Critical Software

## 3.1   Target Programs

The component under study is extracted from a *nuclear reactor safety shutdown system.* It belongs to that part of the system which periodically scans the position of the reactor's control rods. At each operating cycle, 19 rod positions are processed. The information is read through five 32-bit interface cards. Cards 1 to 4 each deliver data about four rod positions; they are all created in the same way and are referred to as *generic cards.* The 5th card delivers data about the three remaining rod positions as well as monitoring data; this card, which is therefore processed differently, is called the *specific card.*

At each operating cycle, one or more interface card may be declared inoperational: the information it supplies is not taken into account. This corresponds to a *degenerated operating mode:* only part of the inputs are processed. A card identified as inoperational remains in that state until the next reset of the system. In the worst situation all cards are inoperational and the component delivers a *minimal service:* no measure is provided, only routine checks are carried out.

After acquisition, the data are checked and filtered. Three checks are carried out: the corresponding rod sensor is connected, the parity bit is correct and the data is stable (several identical values must be read before acceptance). The stringency of the third check (required number of identical values) depends on the outcome of the preceding checks of the same rod. After filtering, the measurements of the rod positions (in Gray code) are converted into a number of mechanical steps. The result of data conversion may be a valid number of mechanical steps or an invalid number or two special limit values.

The *implementation* of the component involves approximately a thousand lines of C language (without comments). It consists of a big controller and four small unit functions FCTi (i = 1, ..., 4): FCT1 and FCT2 perform data acquisition, FCT3 is the filtering unit and FCT4 the conversion unit (Fig. 1). Experimentation was carried out at two levels of integration: first at the *unit level* (functions FCTi); then at the *level of the whole component.* The latter experiments also involved a second version

---

[8]  Since the test profile is derived from the criterion retained, it may have little connection with actual usage (i.e. operational profile): the focus is bug-finding, not reliability assessment.

of the component developed by a student from the same requirements summarised above.

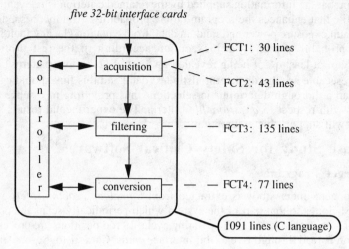

**Fig.1.** General view of the industrial software component

## 3.2  Overview of the Experiments

The whole set of experiments have been designed according to two main investigation goals:

1.  *Comparison of the three methods* for generating test data: deterministic, uniform random and statistical;

2.  *Study of input profiles for statistical testing*; here, the aim is twofold: first, to show the feasibility of designing test profiles from a model of the target software; and second, to analyse the impact of the test profile (uniform or designed) on the effectiveness of the probabilistic approach.

Goal 1 is addressed by the unit testing experiments. Classical structural criteria [73] were used to design both statistical and deterministic test patterns; uniform random patterns were also generated. The comparison of the three types of test data involves 2816 mutation type faults [17] seeded one by one in the source codes.

Goal 2 is addressed at both levels, unit and component: structural profiles were first investigated at the unit level; then functional profiles were designed from graphical behaviour models of the component: finite state machines, decision tables, statecharts [15]. At the component level, the comparison with the uniform profile involves 13 real faults, one minor fault related to the real version and 12 faults residing in the student version.

The next two sections present and comment on the results supplied by each of the testing approaches, at the unit level and at the component level respectively.

## 4     Statistical Structural Testing

The first investigation focuses on the efficiency of test sets designed according to current structural criteria. As structural testing is only applicable to programs that lend themselves to a tractable analysis of their control or data flow graph, the results apply mainly to unit testing.

## 4.1 Design of Statistical Structural Test Patterns

By way of examples, ten well-known criteria have been selected to show the feasibility of designing statistical test data according to structural criteria.

**Structural criteria.** The criteria under study are path selection criteria which means that they select proper sets of paths in the program graph to be executed. They include three criteria related to the control flow graph: *Instructions* (each statement has to be executed), *Branches* (each edge has to be executed) and *All-Paths* (each complete path has to be executed, where complete means that the path begins with a program entry node and ends with an exit node). The seven other criteria, based on data flow analysis, correspond to the criteria family defined in [73]: *All-DU-Paths, All-Uses, All-P-Uses/Some-C-Uses, All-C-Uses/ Some-P-Uses, All-P-Uses, All-C-Uses, All-Defs.* They are constructed so that critical associations between the assignment (definition) of any variable and its use(s), in computations (c-uses) and/or in branch predicates (p-uses), are exercised.

**Design of test patterns.** Given a program and a criterion, the two steps of the general method for designing statistical testing (Section 2.2) were performed. The search for a test profile (step 1) was conducted analytically, as follows. The program flow graph analysis provides the set $S_C$ of (sub)paths, together with the expression of their execution probabilities $p_k$ as functions of the probabilities of input values. Then, an input distribution that lets $P_C = \min\{p_k\}$ be as high as possible is inferred by solving the equation set $\{p_k\}$ (see example below). The structural test profile thus defined ensures that the program structure is soundly probed, the level of probing being an increasing function of the criterion's stringency (from "Instructions" to "All-Paths" level).

**Example: Program FCT2 with respect to "All-Paths" criterion.** FCT2 is the function having the simplest structure. It contains nine complete paths: $C = $"All-Paths" $\Rightarrow S_C = \{9 \text{ paths}\}$.

*Step 1.* The inputs are a boolean value X and a 32-bit data item (one interface card). The probabilities $p_k$ (k = 1, ..., 9) of executing the paths k depend on two boolean values: X, and one bit Y from the interface card. Let x = Prob[X = 1], y = Prob[Y = 1]. One obtains:

$$p_1 = 1\text{-}x; \ p_2 = x.y^3; \ p_3 = p_4 = p_5 = x.y^2.(1\text{-}y);$$
$$p_6 = p_7 = p_8 = x.y.(1\text{-}y)^2; \ p_9 = x.(1\text{-}y)^3.$$

$P_C = \min\{p_k, k = 1, ..., 9\}$ is maximized if the paths are made equally likely, which is possible here by taking x = 8/9 and y = 1/2. Hence:

$$p_k = 1/9 \ \forall \ k \text{ and } P_C = \min\{p_k\} = 1/9 \ .$$

Then the input distribution one chooses to minimize N is: Prob[X = 1] = 8/9, Prob[Y = 1] = 1/2 and the 31 other bits of the interface card, which are not related to the path probabilities, are set to be equiprobable (Prob[bit = 1] = 1/2).

*Step 2.* For this distribution, the minimum test size required to reach $q_N = 0.9999$ wrt the "All-Paths" criterion is, from equation (1): N = 79 (rounded off to 80 in the sets of test patterns described below).

## 4.2 Case Study: Functions FCTi

**Criteria classification.** Classes of criteria were first determined from the analysis of the criteria studied: for a given function FCTi, a class groups the criteria that happen to be equivalent, i.e. that define for this function the same set $S_C$ of (sub)paths to be executed. As a result, criteria group in a class require identical test data. Fig. 2 gives the classes obtained for each FCTi, together with the ordering induced by the criteria stringency: each square defines a class of criteria, and the relation "Class i → Class j" means that the set $S_C$ defined by the criteria in Class j is a strict subset of the one defined by the criteria in Class i. For FCT1, FCT2 and FCT3, the classes are completely ordered; they are only partially ordered in the case of FCT4, the elements of the sets $S_C$ defined by Class 3 and Class 5 being different.

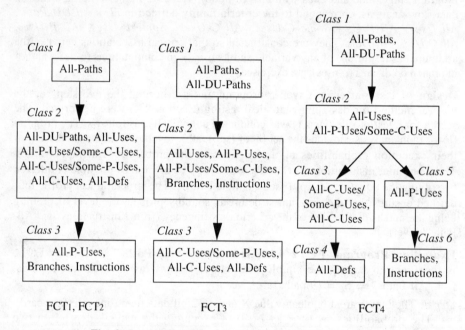

**Fig. 2.** Structural criteria orderings for FCTi (i = 1, ..., 4)

**Deterministic Test Patterns.** For each function and each criteria class, several sets of deterministic test patterns were designed according to the "classical" approach: each set contains the minimum number of patterns selected a priori in order to execute each element defined by the criteria class once. Fig. 3 gives the numbers of test sets, and the numbers N of patterns per set. In the case of FCT1, FCT2 and FCT3, the complete ordering of the classes has led us to select some subsets of the test sets related to Class 1 to be the test sets for Class 2 and other ones for Class 3. In the case of FCT4, the ordering being only partial, the test patterns have been selected independently. Furthermore, FCT4 contains several million complete paths, so that it is not feasible to generate any test set for Class 1.

**Statistical Test Patterns.** The 34 sets of statistical test patterns tabulated in Fig. 4 were designed for the four functions. Su denotes a set of patterns selected randomly from a uniform distribution over the input domain. Si (i = 1, ..., 6) denotes a set of patterns generated from the distribution appropriate to Class i (Fig. 2), that is, the input profile defined so as to obtain the target quality $q_N$ with respect to Class i rapidly. First, the most stringent achievable criteria were adopted: Class 1 for the first three functions, Class 2 for FCT4; and the appropriate input distributions were defined analytically (see the example of the Class 1 distribution for FCT2 in Section 4.1). For $q_N = 0.9999$, the corresponding test sizes N for each FCTi (i = 1, ..., 4) are respectively, from equation (1): 170, 80, 405, 850. For purposes of comparison, each set Su of uniform patterns specific to a function FCTi was the same test size as the structural test set (S1 or S2) related to the same function. As regards FCT1 and FCT2, no other structural distribution derived from least stringent criteria has been investigated, because of the very high simplicity of both functions. As regards FCT3 and FCT4, which are more complex from both a structural and a functional viewpoint, we have experimented with other input distributions derived from the least stringent criteria, namely: those of Class 3 and Class 6, respectively; then, for $q_N = 0.9999$, equation (1) gives N = 152 and N = 42 for the corresponding sets S3 and S6, respectively.

| Function | Class 1 | | Class 2 | | Class 3 | | Class 4 | | Class 5 | | Class 6 | |
|---|---|---|---|---|---|---|---|---|---|---|---|---|
| | # | N | # | N | # | N | # | N | # | N | # | N |
| FCT1 | 5 | 17 | 5 | 3 | 10 | 2 | — | | — | | — | |
| FCT2 | 5 | 9 | 5 | 3 | 10 | 2 | — | | — | | — | |
| FCT3 | 2 | 19 | 8 | 9 | 8 | 9 | — | | — | | — | |
| FCT4 | — | | 3 | 9 | 3 | 9 | 3 | 8 | 3 | 8 | 3 | 2 |

**Fig. 3.** Overview of the 73 sets of deterministic structural test patterns generated
# denotes the number of sets with N input patterns per set

| Function | Input distributions | Sets of test patterns | | |
|---|---|---|---|---|
| | | Notation | # | N |
| FCT1 | Uniform | Su | 1 | 170 |
| | Class 1: *All-Paths* | S1 | 1 | 170 |
| FCT2 | Uniform | Su | 1 | 80 |
| | Class 1: *All-Paths* | S1 | 1 | 80 |
| FCT3 | Uniform | Su | 5 | 405 |
| | Class 1: *All-Paths...* | S1 | 5 | 405 |
| | Class 3: *All-C-Uses...* | S3 | 5 | 152 |
| FCT4 | Uniform | Su | 5 | 850 |
| | Class 2: *All-Uses...* | S2 | 5 | 850 |
| | Class 6: *Branches...* | S6 | 5 | 42 |

**Fig. 4.** Overview of the 34 sets of statistical test patterns generated
# denotes the number of sets with N input patterns per set

Note that, in most cases, several sets of patterns were generated according to each testing approach and for each FCTi (Figs. 3, 4): since it is pointless to define a testing method whose efficiency depends heavily on the particular input values selected, rather than on adequate properties of the test patterns related to the method, they aim to expose eventual disparities.

## 4.3  Experimental  Results

Mutation analysis [17] was used to assess and compare the error detection power of the various sets of test patterns: a total of 2816 mutation faults[9] were seeded one by one in the source codes of the functions FCTi, and the efficiency of the test sets was assessed in terms of the proportion of faults revealed, called the *mutation score*. This score, denoted *ms(P,T)* for a program P and a set T of test patterns, is a number in the interval [0, 1]: a high score indicates that T is very efficient for P with respect to mutation fault exposure.

Indeed, there is no evidence that simple-order mutations correspond to many faults in software; this could deny the representativeness of mutation score with respect to the real fault exposure power of test patterns. But some faulty behaviours observed were typical of "subtle" errors produced by real faults, involving in particular [94]: (i) faults turning a combinational function into a sequential one and, (ii) faults producing intermittent failures under unforeseeable conditions. In both cases, the outcome of an execution does not solely depend on the current input pattern supplied; thus invalidating the usual assertion that the exhaustive testing of all input values yields a correctness proof of the program. The production of such subtle errors leads us to conclude that mutation score is not a meaningless metric to compare the relative efficiency of various sets of test patterns.

**Overview of the mutation scores.** Fig. 5 shows a graphic representation of the mutation scores obtained for each function. A column identifies a family of test data, and the horizontal lines stacked in the column give the scores of the corresponding set(s) of patterns. As an example, for FCT3, the two deterministic sets derived from the Class 1 criteria provide the scores of 0.792 and 0.84, respectively; the five statistical sets S1 provide the same score of 1.

From this comprehensive view, one must notice that the most efficient test data seem to be the statistical structural ones, for which we get the following results.

- As regards the Class 1 distributions (FCT1, FCT2, FCT3), each set S1 allows a perfect score *ms(FCTi, S1) = 1* to be reached.
- As regards the Class 3 distribution (FCT3), each set S3 does not reveal 17 out of 1416 mutations; thereby supplying *ms(FCT3, S3) = 0.988*.
- Both Class 2 and Class 6 distributions (FCT4) provide identical scores: one set S2 and one set S6 leads to *ms(FCT4, Si) = 0.9915* (5 out of 587 mutations are not revealed); while the eight other sets reveal one more mutation, thereby supplying *ms(FCT4, Si) = 0.9898*.

---

[9]  A mutation is a single-point, syntactically correct change introduced in the program to be tested. Three types of change are automatically performed by our mutant generator for C programs: constant replacement, operator replacement, and symbol replacement.

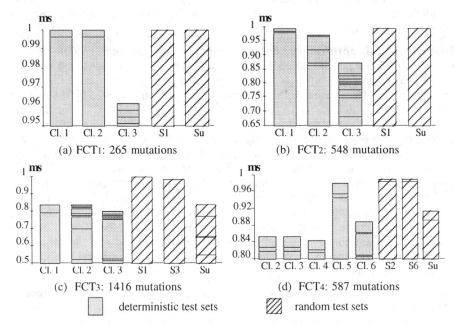

(a) FCT1: 265 mutations

(b) FCT2: 548 mutations

(c) FCT3: 1416 mutations

(d) FCT4: 587 mutations

☐ deterministic test sets       ▨ random test sets

**Fig. 5.** Mutation scores provided by the different sets of test patterns

In cases of the deterministic and uniform patterns, the best test sets never supply a higher score than the statistical structural ones; and the gap seems all the more pronounced as the function is complex. For the simplest functions FCT1 and FCT2, the scores provided by the sets Su and by the deterministic sets related to stringent criteria (Classes 1, 2) are high; for the two other functions, the statistical structural patterns turn out to be significantly superior.

**Limitation of deterministic testing.** The results supplied by the sets of deterministic patterns depend heavily on the particular input values chosen. Given a function and a criteria class, the test sets exhibit mutation scores that may be quite unrelated: for FCT3, the scores of the eight sets of Class 2 range from 0.52 to 0.833. Even when the range is narrower, it does not mean that the test patterns reveal the same faults: for FCT3, both sets of Class 1 provide similar scores (0.79 versus 0.84), but 101 mutations revealed by the least efficient set of patterns are not revealed by the most efficient one. In addition, Fig. 5d shows that the most stringent criteria do not necessarily supply the highest scores. This can be illustrated only by the results related to FCT4 since, for the other functions, the deliberate choice of subsets of the Class 1 test sets to be the Class 2 and Class 3 test sets (Section 4.2) contributes to compliance of the scores with the class ordering. Nevertheless, a surprising result is observed for FCT3: one mutation was revealed by two sets of Class 2 and by two sets of Class 3, but not by the embracing sets of Class 1. The reason is that the mutation corrupts the processing of a global variable, so that the behaviour of FCT3 becomes sequential (instead of combinational): revealing this fault depends on the order the paths are executed. These results support our presumption that deterministic testing suffers from the fact that it involves the selective choice of a small number of test patterns, which may or may not turn out to be adequate. No guarantee is provided in regard to fault exposure, even if a stringent criterion is adopted.

**Inadequacy of uniform random testing.** In [67], uniform random testing experiments were performed on five programs. The author noticed that uniform testing was surprisingly effective for some programs but very ineffective for others, and related the effectiveness to the degree of code coverage achieved by the random patterns. Our results corroborate his observations. For FCT1 and FCT2, the uniform distributions are close to the Class 1 distributions, thereby providing good structural coverage of the programs: all the mutations are revealed, which can be deemed very cost-effective. Yet, the performance of uniform testing falls off heavily as soon as the program's structure no longer lends itself to a uniform stimulation. This appears strikingly in the case of FCT3: the uniform profile being quite different from the two structural ones, the five sets Su exercise the programs poorly, either from a structural or from a functional viewpoint, and fail in revealing hundreds of mutations; besides, as in the deterministic case, the scores vary from one set to the other (from 229 up to 626 mutations are not revealed depending on the set Su), and real disparities are observed between the subsets of mutations revealed (66 mutations revealed by the least efficient set are not revealed by the most efficient one).

**Analysis of statistical testing.** To investigate the behaviour of statistical patterns, emphasis is put on the growth of the mutation score as a function of the number of test patterns, or equivalently of the number of program executions.

For FCT1 and FCT2, the perfect scores ms(FCTi, S1) = ms(FCTi, Su) = 1 are reached between the first 8 executions and the first 25 executions; such steep increases of the scores are probably due to the comparative simplicity of both programs. Moreover, each mutation is revealed tens of times by each set of patterns so that this high fault-revealing power is expected to be repeatedly observed, whatever the particular input patterns generated according to the defined input distributions.

The evolution observed for the two other programs is less steep, but still impressive. Fig. 6 is a good illustration of the typical behaviour of random patterns one has noticed. It plots the score growths provided by four test sets related to FCT3: the sets noted S1 and S3 are "average" sets of the corresponding distributions, that is, they supply neither the slowest nor the fastest growth observed; Su(inf) and Su(sup) are the sets of uniform patterns that reach the lowest and the highest final scores, respectively. Whatever the input distribution, the test patterns rapidly reveal the mutations during a first step: in Fig. 6, the final mutation scores are nearly obtained in the first third of the N = 405 executions. Then, the incremental gain exhibits a sharp slowing down: the scores increase in stages with the occurrence of particular patterns. Actually, given a program and an input distribution, the first phase may be more or less long depending on the patterns generated. But, in any case, the scores are stabilized quite before the test size required for $q_N = 0.9999$, and all concur in a similar value [90]. Fig. 6 also illustrates the fact that little improvement is expected if the uniform test is further pursued since the slopes of the growth associated to the sets Su become almost null during the execution of the second half of the uniform patterns.

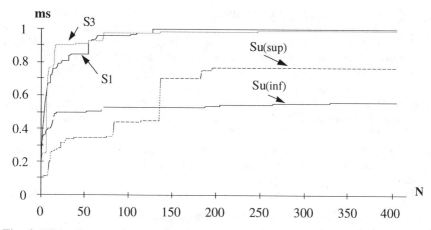

**Fig. 6.** FCT3: Growth of the mutation score as a function of the number of test patterns

## 4.4 Conclusions

Three main conclusions can be drawn from this first experimental work.

1. The comparison between uniform random testing and statistical structural testing showed that *the structural analysis did provide relevant information* to increase the failure probability, even as regards subtle errors loosely connected with the criteria; although derived from the same criteria, the deterministic sets involved too few test patterns to compensate for this imperfect connection.

2. The impact of the criteria stringency was deemed not critical in the case of statistical testing; indeed, the *most cost-effective approach* should be to retain weak criteria (Instructions, Branches) facilitating the search for a test profile, and to require a high test quality (say, 0.9999) wrt them.

3. The efficacy of a *mixed test strategy* combining statistical structural testing and deterministic testing of extremal input values [21, 86] was confirmed: from the total of 2816 mutations, only six faults (seeded in FCT4) were not uncovered after completion of the statistical structural patterns, and they were typical cases for the latter testing approach.

Following these promising results on the probabilistic generation of test patterns, emphasis was placed on testing of larger programs, whose structural complexity prohibits the use of structural criteria. Statistical functional testing was then investigated, based on criteria related to behaviour models of software specifications.

## 5  Statistical Functional Testing

### 5.1  Software Behaviour Models

As regards random generation, relevant functional models and the associated test criteria must facilitate the selection of an input distribution and a test size ensuring that the software functions, and their interactions, are properly scanned. Hence, we opted for *graphical behaviour models deduced from the software specification* for three reasons:

- Functional testing approaches may refer to different levels of software description: external specification [64, 68, 92], internal design [44], program code [44], or a combination of levels [99]. But, modelling of the functions deduced from specification, rather than of the implemented functions deduced from component design, is more in agreement with the goal of functional testing, the test cases being more likely to expose design faults.

- As far as complex components are concerned, a detailed specification analysis is likely to determine a large number of functionalities that may not be described by a single model of reasonable complexity; thus the modelling technique must be suitable to a hierarchical decomposition of the functionalities, thereby involving a sequence of models.

- Keeping in mind that probabilistic generation of test patterns calls for the study of the influence of the input distribution on the coverage of a test criterion, the modelling technique must possess properties that are well-suited for the definition of precise criteria, and for the probabilistic analysis of their coverage.

Different graphical languages meet these three requirements, including the classical SADT technique, based on finite state machines and decision tables, and a more recent technique based on statecharts; these two techniques being used in current specification methods [15]. Whether or not efficient statistical test patterns can be derived from them is the issue we investigate.

The practical benefits of a positive answer to this question are noteworthy: no specific model of the software is required for the design of test patterns, and the facilities offered by current Computer-Aided Software Engineering (CASE) tools supporting these techniques should be of great interest from a test designer perspective. In particular, since most of these tools offer prototyping or simulation facilities, they provide us with an automatic solution to the problem of generating the correct test outputs, thus solving the major oracle problem [97].

## 5.2 Design of Statistical Functional Test Patterns

Given a multi-level specification, the design of statistical test inputs must induce an analysis of reasonable complexity. The general guidelines outlined below aim at managing this complexity, whatever the language(s) involved in the modelling approach.

**Guidelines.** For a sequence of models associated with a multi-level specification, the detailed analysis of the models according to stringent criteria (e.g. sequence of transitions coverage in cases of graph) is presumably intractable, thus compelling us to use only weak criteria (e.g. state coverage in cases of graph). Furthermore, even if weak criteria are adopted, it would not be realistic to attempt intensive coverage of all the models at the same time. This is because of:

1. *the component complexity*, which makes the assessment of the element probabilities difficult as numerous correlated factors are involved;

2. *the explosion of the test size;* even if these assessments are feasible in order to derive an input distribution, a prohibitive test size will probably be required to reach a high test quality, as the probability of the least likely element remains very low due to the large number of elements.

To address this issue several distinct sets of test patterns may be designed, each one focusing on the coverage of a subset of models. Then, a partition of the models into disjoint subsets must be defined, each subset gathering one or several models describing functions of the same or consecutive levels in the specification. For each subset of models, a specific test profile can reasonably be derived, that maximises the probability of the least likely element related to the models grouped. Retaining weak criteria and deriving several test profiles is the general approach that allows us to manage the complexity in cases of multi-level specification. Hence, both steps of the method for designing statistical testing (Section 2.2) must be done for each subset of models.

As regards *step 1*, only a part of the component specification is taken into account to determine the test profile specific to a subset of models. As a result, some input variables may not be involved so that no probability is obtained for them, and information deduced from other partition subsets may be included to define a complete test profile. For this, the inputs that are not involved are classified according to three types:

1. *upper level inputs*, conditioning the activation of the described functions from the upper level models; their probabilities must provide the most likely activations;

2. *lower level inputs*, taken into account in lower level models; their probabilities are set as defined from the corresponding lower level models;

3. *unrelated inputs*, for which a uniform distribution may be used.

It is worth noting that the determination of the test profiles has to proceed according to a bottom-up approach since the input distribution specific to a given partition subset may be partly defined at lower levels (point 2 above).

As regards *step 2*, a proper test size $N_j$ is assessed for each partition subset j (i.e. for each test profile derived in step 1), in order to reach a target test quality wrt the coverage criteria related to the models grouped in subset j. Hence, if the whole specification has been partitioned into s subsets, a complete set of functional test patterns is composed of s suites of test patterns, and it amounts to $N = N_1 + \ldots + N_s$ patterns.

**Finite State Machines (FSMs) and Decision Tables (DTs).** FSMs and DTs are complementary modelling tools, FSMs being appropriate to describe sequential behaviours, and combinational functions being easier to translate into DTs. The application of the above guidelines in cases of multi-level specification based on FSMs and DTs has been detailed in [88]. Here, we briefly recall how the corresponding probabilistic analysis is processed.

An *FSM* can be depicted by a graph having a finite number of states and of transitions. The principle consists in associating one state with each mode of behaviour, and in weighting each transition with the input conditions that trigger it and eventually with the action caused when the transition is made. Different criteria may be defined from an FSM depending on the stringency of the graph coverage [12, 24, 92], state coverage being the weakest criterion. Then, *state coverage in steady state conditions* (i.e. after a number of initial executions large enough to ensure that the transients die down) is the criterion retained. For each state k, the expression $p_k$ of its asymptotic probability as function of the input probabilities is got from the stochastic graph obtained by replacing the input conditions that weight the transitions with their occurrence probabilities in the distribution.

A *DT* defines a finite set of rules, each rule specifying the actions that take place when a specific combination of input conditions is met. Then, a natural criterion is the *rule coverage*. For a rule k, the replacement of the specified combination of conditions with its occurrence probability provides the expression $p_k$ of its activation probability.

For a given subset of models, the *search for a proper test profile* is conducted analytically from the set of expressions $p_k$ related to the states and rules of the FSMs and DTs gathered in the subset, by determining an input distribution which maximises the value $P_C = \min\{p_k\}$. Then, the assessment of the test size involves two factors: first, equation (1) yields the test size in steady-state conditions and second, this test size must be augmented with the number of initial state transitions needed to ensure that the transients die down (if any).

**Statecharts.** Statecharts are extensions of FSM and their visual counterpart, state-transition diagrams: they add the notions of depth, orthogonality and broadcast communication [41]. Their inherent complexity makes it impossible to proceed analytically; hence, the empirical process summarised below (see [89] for a detailed description).

Due to the expressive power of statecharts, even a model involving a small number of states may be very complex. Then, the criterion requiring the coverage of all the states of the finite state machine equivalent to a given statechart is likely to necessitate a tricky analysis in the general case. Indeed, it would imply that every possible configuration, i.e. every possible combination of basic states (that is, states having no offspring) in orthogonal components, be considered. As a result, a weaker and more realistic criterion is adopted, namely the *coverage of the basic states*. Another consequence of the statechart complexity is that, in the present state of the art, it is not possible to draw from their analysis the set of equations relating the basic state probabilities to the input distribution. Given a subset of models, the *search for a proper test profile* has thus to proceed empirically: starting from an initial input distribution, e.g. the uniform one, generate several large sets of input patterns; execute the models with the patterns and count the number of times each basic state is entered; determine the activation conditions of the least exercised basic states in order to improve the input profile. This iterative process is stopped when the frequency of each basic state is deemed sufficiently high. In practice, the feasibility of such an empirical procedure requires the use of a tool that provides facilities to program model execution and to instrument the model in order to collect statistics about coverage measures during execution. Here, the CASE tool STATEMATE$^{TM}$ [42] which uses the language of statecharts to depict the behavioural view of reactive systems, is quite appropriate. Finally, the *test size* cannot be directly assessed from equation (1), the actual value of $P_C$ being not drawn from the empirical process. Then, the relation between $q_N$ (the test quality wrt the criterion) and n (the expecting number of times the least likely element is exercised) given in Section 2.2, provides an empirical stopping rule: for example, requiring that each basic state be activated at least 9 times during testing should correspond to $q_N = 0.9999$; the number of times each basic sate is entered being directly got from the instrumented model.

---

$^{TM}$ STATEMATE is a registered trademark of i-Logix, Inc.

## 5.3  Case Study at the Component Level

As mentioned in Section 3.1, the experimental investigation at the component level was conducted on two versions, called REAL and STU, of the program under study: REAL is the industrial version whose internal design is shown in Fig. 1; STU was developped by a student from the high-level informal specification of the component (summarized in Section 3.1), using a different internal design.

The experimentation with statistical functional testing has been first based on a multi-level description combining finite state machines and decision tables; then, we have studied behaviour models produced in the STATEMATE environment. For purposes of comparison, we have also experimented with two other input distributions: a structural test profile derived from the STU version, and the uniform distribution over the input domain. A total of 16 sets of test patterns, described below, were generated and each of them have been applied to both REAL and STU.

**Statistical functional patterns designed from FSMs and DTs.** Three levels of decomposition were defined from the informal specification of the component. The high-level functionalities were described by an FSM $M_0$ and then refined through two other models, an FSM $M_1$ a DT $M_2$:

- $M_0$ (12 states, 88 transitions) identifies the current operating mode from full to minimal service. Each mode determines a number of measures to be processed;
- $M_1$ (12 states, 54 transitions) models the checks and filtering performed on one measure. Each transition induces the acceptance or rejection of the measure;
- $M_2$ (8 rules) describes the rod position to deliver for each accepted measure.

For the design of statistical test patterns, the three models were partitioned into two subsets, $M_1$ and $M_2$ being grouped together since both relate to the processing of one measure. Hence, two test profiles were analytically determined:

1. the first one aims to ensure the coverage of the low level models ($M_1$ states and $M_2$ rules); under this profile, 85 input patterns are required for $q_N = 0.9999$;
2. the second one aims to ensure a rapid coverage of the high level model ($M_0$ states); under this profile 356 input patterns are required for $q_N = 0.9999$.

Then, a complete functional test set is composed of *441 patterns*: 85 drawn from the first profile, followed by 356 drawn from the second one. Five different test sets of 441 patterns have been experimented with, in order to expose eventual disparities. These are denoted *F-Sets*.

**Statistical functional patterns designed from statecharts.** Based on the informal specification of the component, a new specification was developed in the STATEMATE environment. It involves two levels of hierarchy, the *top level function* and *six subfunctions*, one for each of the five interface cards (checks and filtering of the data acquired), and one for the conversion of the data into rod positions:

- the statechart of the top level view has *33 basic states*;
- the six statecharts of the low level involve a total amount of *299 basic states*.

Two test profiles were empirically determined, one for each level of hierarchy:

1. the first one ensures the coverage of the 299 basic states of the low level;
2. the second one ensures the coverage of the 6 basic states of the top level.

Five test sets have been generated under the new profiles. Their size has been kept the same as previously, that is: 85 patterns from the new first profile + 356 patterns from the second one. It turned out that each of the five sets met the requirement that the basic states be entered at least 9 times (empirical stopping rule associated with $q_N = 0.9999$). As a result, the experiments have been conducted using these five test sets, denoted *STM-Sets*.

**Statistical structural patterns.** A structural input distribution was derived from the structure of the STU version. The complexity of the source code forced us to adopt the weakest criterion, namely *instruction testing*, and to proceed empirically to derive a test profile under which the frequency of each instruction is sufficiently high. Given the requirement that each instruction be executed at least 9 times, an upper bound on the test size was fixed on $N = 500$. Five different structural test sets denoted S-Set were generated, each one being composed of 500 input patterns.

**Uniform patterns.** Finally, conventional random patterns were generated according to a uniform distribution over the valid input domain. The corresponding test set, denoted *U-Set*, contains 5300 input patterns, the test size being arbitrarily chosen without any preliminary analysis of the software: this is in conformity with the foundation of uniform testing, that is, large test sets generated cheaply.

## 5.4  Experimental Results

**Overview.** The thirteen real faults tabulated in Fig. 7 have been identified during our experiments. Twelve faults, denoted A, B, ..., L, were found in STU. The last one, Z, is a minor fault in REAL: it would never lead to failure in operational life due to systematic hardware compensation. Faults A, G and J are structural faults, linked to the coding of STU. Faults B to F, and I, result from the misunderstanding of the filtering check requirements by the student. The others are initialization faults: either an improper initial value is assigned (K, L) or the initialization is missing (H, Z). The initialization faults are subtle since their activation depends on the states that follow the wrong initialization. For example, revealing H requires that G be removed and that the specific card be inoperational immediately after a reset; as regards L, its revealing data depends on input conditions related to the first five acquisitions of rod positions after a reset. Fig. 8 summarizes the results supplied by the 16 test sets.

| | |
|---|---|
| A | wrong operator used in the processing of an output value |
| B, C, D, E, F, I | the filtering checks, as implemented, do not comply with the specification |
| G | wrong control flow when the specific card is inoperational |
| H | initialization missing for variables related to the specific card |
| J | a variable in a loop is initialized out of loop instead of at each iteration |
| K, L | wrong initial states for the filtering process |
| Z | initialization missing |

**Fig. 7.** List of the thirteen real faults uncovered

|  | A | B | C | D | E | F | G | H | I | J | K | L | Z |
|---|---|---|---|---|---|---|---|---|---|---|---|---|---|
| U-Set N = 5300 | ✔ | — | — | ✔ | — | ✔ | ✔ | ✔ | — | — | — | — | — |
| S-Sets N = 500 | ✔ | ✔ | ✔ | ✔ | ✔ | ✔ | 2/5 | 1/5 | ✔ | ✔ | ✔ | — | 3/5 |
| F-Sets N = 441 | ✔ | ✔ | ✔ | ✔ | ✔ | ✔ | ✔ | ✔ | ✔ | ✔ | ✔ | — | 4/5 |
| STM-Sets N = 441 | ✔ | ✔ | ✔ | ✔ | ✔ | ✔ | ✔ | ✔ | ✔ | ✔ | ✔ | ✔ | ✔ |

**Fig. 8.** Results supplied by the sets of test patterns

✔ always revealed
i/j revealed by i sets out of j
— not revealed

**Uniform profile.** Once again, uniform testing provides the *poorest results*, since it reveals only five of the thirteen faults. The U-Set poorly probes STU and REAL, from both a structural and a functional viewpoint. With respect to the structural coverage, four blocks of instructions of STU and one of REAL are never exercised; some are seldom executed (less than three times). As regards the functional coverage, some states of the FSM $M_1$ and some basic states in the low level statecharts are seldom or never reached: most faults related to the filtering checks are not revealed. The five faults uncovered are found within the first 633 executions; the remaining 4667 executions being garbage. Hence, little improvement is expected if the tests are further pursued, unless a very large number of extra test patterns is generated.

**Structural profile.** Nine faults are repeatedly revealed by the five S-Sets; other faults (G, H, and Z) are occasionally revealed, usually late in the test experiment. L is never revealed. Some major features of the component are not identified by the structural profile: most of the time the system delivers a full service, and poor probe is provided as regards the high level functions (degeneration of the operating modes). This accounts for the poor results for G and H, since G is linked to degenerated operating modes with the specific card inoperational, and the exposure of H requires that G be fixed. Hence, structural testing was well-suited in unit testing, but its *effectiveness diminishes as the source code under test grows*. The functions supported by the software move away from the instruction level, while finer examination of the structure becomes intractable. Indeed, here, the size of the component under test is a limit above which instruction testing itself is no longer tractable.

**Functional profiles.** The use of behaviour models as guides for designing statistical testing was relevant to fault exposure: the five F-Sets and the five STM-Sets perform repeatedly better than the S-Sets despite the fact that they involve a smaller number of inputs (441 versus 500). The two input distribution involved in each type of functional patterns provide complementary results: the subsets of 85 and 356 patterns do not reveal the same faults. Moreover, each complete set of functional patterns exercises 100% instructions of the two program versions.

The fault Z was not revealed by one F-Set: Z is linked to the initialization of the filtering checks and its exposure depends on conditions involving states of both FSM $M_0$ (describing the operating modes) and FSM $M_1$ (describing the filtering checks). This points out a weakness of the F-Sets which do not provide a sound probe of interactions between high and low level functions. Finally, although they have been derived empirically, the STM-Sets exhibit the best fault-revealing power: Z is repeatedly revealed, and a new fault, L, is uncovered by the STM-Sets. Remember that the fault L is rather subtle, because its exposure depends on specific conditions involving *five* successive acquisitions of data after a reset.

# 6    Summary and Conclusions

Because the probabilistic method for generating test inputs is generally related to uniform test patterns, it is often deemed a poor methodology: our experimental studies remove this preconceived idea.

Applied to the verification of a non trivial software component from the nuclear field, statistical testing designed from structural or functional models supplied repeatedly a high fault exposure power within a realistic test duration. At the unit level, the efficiency of the method was assessed referring to 2816 faults of mutation type. The experiments at the whole component level involved a sample of real faults that were a priori unknown. A limitation of the statistical test patterns experimented on is their lack of adequacy with respect to faults related to extremal/special cases. Such faults induce, in essence, a very low probability of failure under the profiles defined to ensure a *global* probe of the target programs: they require test data specifically aimed at them. Hence, we support the adoption of a mixed testing strategy involving both statistical and deterministic test patterns; such a mixed strategy having recently been successfully experimented on at the unit testing level [87], as well as at the integration testing level [58].

The results on unit testing presented in Section 4 support the insufficiency of deterministic test patterns derived from current – imperfect – criteria. For larger scale programs, this limitation is expected to get worse. However, the medium size of the component experimented on does not yet allow us to come to a conclusion about the feasibility of statistical testing for complex software. Two problems arise:

- The oracle problem, namely that of how to determine the correct output results a (complex) program should return in response to given input patterns. This problem arises with any dynamic verification technique; but it becomes crucial when numerous responses to probabilistic patterns are concerned.
- The complexity of the probabilistic analysis required by statistical testing.

Fortunately, an answer to these problems is likely to reside in the recent emergence of CASE tools that assist software development by supporting formal models for the specification of behaviour, and offering facilities to computerised simulation. Such tools provide us with an oracle; the possibility of instrumenting the models facilitates the empirical derivation of test profiles proper to ensure a rapid coverage of the software functionalities. In Section 5, the benefit of using CASE tools for the design of statistical testing has been exemplified on the STATEMATE environment. The promising results obtained for the medium-scale component experimented on may constitute a first step along the road.

# An Experimental Evaluation of Formal Testing and Statistical Testing[*]

Bruno Marre[1]   Pascale Thévenod-Fosse[2]   Hélène Waeselynck[2]
Pascale Le Gall[1]   Yves Crouzet[2]

[1]LRI   [2]LAAS-CNRS

**Abstract.** Functional testing from formal specification (or formal testing, for short) and statistical testing are the concern of quite different processes of designing test data sets. These differences are outlined, and their complementary features are analysed. Then, the paper reports on unit testing experiments performed on a program which is a piece of a software from the nuclear industry. Five test sets of each type have been automatically generated, and mutation analysis is used to assess their efficiency with respect to error detection. The 1345 mutants of the target program are killed by each of the five statistical test sets and by three formal test sets, the two other ones leaving alive only one and two mutants. These promising results encourage further investigation of integration testing, where both methods are expected to exhibit complementary efficiency with respect to actual faults.

## 1   Introduction

In the present state of the art, the question of how to select a test input set well-suited for revealing faults still arises, due to the lack of an accurate software design fault model. Many test criteria, related to either the function or the structure of the software, have been proposed in the literature as guides for determining test cases (see e.g. [5]). Each of them defines a proper set of subdomains of the input domain to be exercised during testing. Given a criterion, the most current type of test input generation is deterministic: input test sets are built by selecting one element from each subdomain involved in the set proper to the adopted criterion. Unfortunately, exercising only once each subdomain defined from such criteria is far from being enough to ensure that the corresponding test set is relevant to expose faults, since a real limitation of current criteria is their imperfect connection with faults.

This paper reports on two different methods for designing more relevant test cases. First, *functional testing from formal specification* – called *formal testing* in this paper, for short – aims at defining pertinent functional criteria under which exercising once each subdomain is sufficient. Test data are automatically selected from a formal specification of the software via selection strategies derived from hypotheses tuned by the user of the system [7, 56] The second approach, called *statistical testing*, is intended to deal with imperfect criteria that is, to derive test sets with a high fault-revealing power, in spite of a tricky link between the adopted criterion and the faults. It consists in a probabilistic generation of test data: inputs are randomly generated according to a defined probability distribution on the input domain; both the distribution and the number of input data items being determined according to the adopted criterion [86, 90].

---

[*] This paper is a revised version of [57]

The next section outlines both testing methods, and examines their main complementary features. Then, the paper presents an experimental work performed on a program which is a piece of a software from the *nuclear industry*. Five test sets of each type have been experimented with, using mutation analysis [17] to assess their efficiency with respect to error detection. The experimental results involve a total of 1345 mutation faults, seeded one by one in the original program source code. In the light of the results reported, both testing methods exhibit promising fault-revealing powers. Because of their distinct underlying theoretical background, they should provide complementary test data sets: combining them becomes all the more interesting as there is no trusted design fault model.

# 2     Comparison of Formal and Statistical Testing

As outlined below, the two methods are the concern of quite different processes for designing test data.

## 2.1   Formal Testing

The motivation of this approach is that, providing that a formal specification of the program to be tested is available, it is possible to use the specification *to define black-box test criteria in a formal framework*. Such strategies allow us to test whether all the properties specified in the specification are actually dealt by the program. Test data selection is only guided by the structure of the specification: for each property expressed by a formula of the specification, test data are selected via strategies derived from hypotheses chosen by the user. Referring to these hypotheses offers the advantage to make explicit the relationship between testing and correctness.

General theoretical results are presented in [6, 7]. We will only focus on the points which are relevant to the hereafter case study: the specifications are positive conditional algebraic specifications [34]. A specification is a pair $SP = (\Sigma, Ax)$; the signature $\Sigma$ is a finite set S of *sort* (i.e. type) names plus a finite set of *operation* names with arity in S; the properties of the operations of $\Sigma$ are defined by the set Ax of axioms of the form: $(v_1 = w_1 \& ... \& v_n = w_n) \Rightarrow v = w$, where $v_i$, $w_i$, v and w are $\Sigma$-terms with typed variables.

Let P be the program to be tested which is supposed to implement a specification $SP = (\Sigma, Ax)$. Testing P with respect to (wrt) SP is only possible if the semantics of P and SP are expressible in a common framework. As we are interested in dynamic testing, we have to execute P on a finite subset of its input domain and to interpret outputs wrt SP. In order to consider P compatible with SP, we need first, to be able to compute the values of $\Sigma$-terms from P and secondly, to forbid that P handles "junk" values according to the operations. Indeed, if "junk" values existed, no test derived from SP could detect an error involving such a value. These two conditions mean that P implements all operations in $\Sigma$ and exports only them, and will constitute the minimal hypothesis we do on a program to be tested: we say then that P defines a *finitely generated $\Sigma$-algebra*.

Let Exhaust be the set of all ground instances of the axioms obtained by replacing each variable by all ground terms of the same sort built from the operations in the signature. Each formula $\phi$ in Exhaust is a test which becomes *executable* when it is possible to check from P that $\phi$ is satisfied in P or not (in the first case, we have then successp($\phi$)). In practice, to decide if successp($t_1 = t_1'$ & ...& $t_n = t_n' \Rightarrow t = t'$), we need:

1.  first, to compute in P the values $t_i^P$, $t_i'^P$, $t^P$ and $t'^P$ denoted by the terms $t_i$, $t_i'$, t and t';
2.  then, to verify that whenever ($t_1^P =_p t_1'^P$) and ... and ($t_n^P =_p t_n'^P$), we have also ($t^P =_p t'^P$), where $=_p$ denotes a decision procedure of the equality in P.

Intuitively, we would say that assuming that P defines a finitely generated $\Sigma$-algebra, successp(Exhaust) is equivalent to the correction of P but, in general, the existence of the decision procedure $=_p$ is not guaranteed. In [6], the author proposes a solution based on the notion of *observability*: for each observable sort s, P provides a correct procedure which decides if two terms of sort s are equal or not in P. Moreover, it is shown that it is useless to verify the conditional tests of Exhaust with a false precondition: this result precisely meets our intuition of the definition of successp. Thus, we can define an exhaustive observational equational test data set EqExhaust as the set of all observational ground instances built on the *conclusions of the axioms* that validate the preconditions in the specification. Assuming that P satisfies some observational hypotheses, the success of EqExhaust is then equivalent to the correctness of P wrt SP.

Unfortunately, EqExhaust is often infinite and we can only consider a finite subset of it. More precisely, in order to cover all properties of SP, we select, for each axiom ax of SP, a finite subset $T_{ax}$ of the subset $EqExhaust_{ax}$ of EqExhaust corresponding to ax. When we select $T_{ax}$, we make the following selection hypothesis: successp($T_{ax}$) $\Rightarrow$ successp($EqExhaust_{ax}$). Such hypotheses are usually left implicit. We prefer to bring them up since it seems sound first, to state hypotheses H and only after, to select a test set corresponding to them. We require both following properties for a relevant pair (H,$T_{ax}$) (such a pair is said *practicable*):

1.  under H, the test data set $T_{ax}$ rejects all programs not validating ax ($T_{ax}$ is *valid*), i.e. (H & (successp($T_{ax}$))) $\Rightarrow$ successp($EqExhaust_{ax}$);
2.  under H, the test data set $T_{ax}$ does not reject programs validating ax ($T_{ax}$ is *unbiased*), i.e. (H & (successp($EqExhaust_{ax}$))) $\Rightarrow$ successp($T_{ax}$).

If (H,$T_{ax}$) is practicable and $T_{ax}$ is finite, the success of $T_{ax}$ is equivalent to the correctness of P wrt ax. In order to exhibit relevant hypotheses, we do a decomposition based on a case analysis of the validity domain of ax (i.e. the domain where the preconditions of ax are satisfied in the specification). This case analysis is guided by the structure of the specification. This process of decomposition of subdomains may be refined wrt the specification structure until the size of each subdomain may be considered as sufficiently small in order to only take one element per subdomain (uniformity hypothesis). The tool described in [7, 56] allows the user to find automatically an element of each subdomain of validity: it uses unfolding methods based on equational logic programming with constraints. Decomposition by case analysis ensures that the user gets finite practicable pairs (H,T) where H combines the minimal hypotheses with uniformity hypotheses on each subdomain.

## 2.2  Statistical  Testing

The motivation of statistical testing is *to deal with imperfect test criteria*, that is, to provide a method for determining test data sets with a high fault-revealing power, in spite of a tricky link between the adopted criterion and the actual faults [90]. Since exercising only once each subdomain defined from an imperfect criterion is far from being enough to provide an efficient test set, an obvious improvement consists in exercising each subdomain several times. And for this, the probabilistic method for generating test inputs is a practical automatic means, the key to its effectiveness being the derivation of an appropriate probability distribution over the input domain. In particular, the generation of random test data based on a uniform distribution over the whole input domain [21, 39], is not expected to be an efficient way to design test sets: revealing input data are unlikely to be uniformly distributed over the input domain. Actually, structural or functional criteria in current use do provide a relevant information on the product under test, and it can be expected that they are not strongly inadequate wrt fault exposure [91]. Hence, the idea is to take advantage of this information and to compensate its imperfection by increasing the test size. Statistical testing is based on the theoretical framework recalled below [86], that induces a rigourous method for determining both an input distribution and a number of random test data items according to a given criterion.

**Theoretical background.** Given a criterion C, let $S_C$ be the corresponding set of subdomains to be exercised. For example, the structural criterion "All-branches" requires that each program branch $b_k$ be executed: this defines one subdomain k for each $b_k$, that gathers the input items executing $b_k$; then, C = "branches" $\Rightarrow S_C = \{k, \forall b_k \in B\}$, where B is the set of all the program branches.

*Definition.* A set T of N input data items covers a test criterion C with a probability $q_N$ if each subdomain $\in S_C$ has a probability of at least $q_N$ of being exercised during the N executions supplied by T. $q_N$ *is the test quality wrt C.*

*Theorem.* In the case of statistical testing, the test quality $q_N$ and the number N of input cases are linked by the equation:

$$(1-P_C)^N = 1-q_N \text{ with } P_C = \min \{p_k, k \in S_C\} \tag{1}$$

$p_k$ being the probability that a random input item exercises the subdomain k.

Equation (1) is easy to justify: since $P_C$ is the probability per input case of exercising the least likely subdomain, each subdomain has a probability of at least $1 - (1-P_C)^N$ of being exercised by a test set of N random input cases. A practical consequence is that each subdomain $\in S_C$ is exercised several times on average. More precisely, equation (1) sets a link between the test quality and the expected number of times, denoted n, the least likely subdomain is exercised: $n \cong - \ln(1-q_N)$. For example, $n \cong 7$ for $q_N = 0.999$, and $n \cong 9$ for $q_N = 0.9999$.

**Design of statistical testing.** The method for determining a statistical test set T (input distribution and number N of random input data items) according to a given criterion C is based on the above theorem. Since the values $p_k$, and thus $P_C$, depend on the input distribution, it involves two steps [90]:

1. *search for an input distribution* well-suited to rapidly exercise each subdomain $\in S_C$ in order to reduce the test size; or equivalently the distribution must let the value of $P_C$ be as high as possible;

2. *assessment of the test size N* required to reach a target test quality $q_N$ wrt C, using the distribution previously defined and thus, the value $P_C$ inferred from it; equation (2), deduced from equation (1), gives the minimum test size:

$$N = \ln(1-q_N) \,/\, \ln(1-P_C) \qquad\qquad (2)$$

It is worth noting that the adopted criterion is used only for determining an input distribution and a test size, but not for selecting a priori a subset of input data items. Hence, one can reasonably think that the criterion adequacy wrt actual faults should set a less acute problem in the case of random data generation. Actually, a meaningful link exists between fault exposure and statistical test data: from equation (1), any fault involving a failure probability $p \geq P_C$ per execution (according to the chosen input distribution) has a probability of at least $q_N$ of being revealed by a set of N random inputs.

**Structural and functional criteria.** The above method has already been applied and experimented with, in both unit and module testing (Paper IV.B). At unit level, the adopted criteria were structural, based on the coverage of the control and data flow graph of the programs [90]. At module level, structural criteria being no more tractable due to the program sizes, the adopted criteria were functional, based on the coverage of graphical behaviour models deduced from informal specifications [88, 89].

## 2.3  Complementary Features

Because of their distinct underlying theoretical background, one can expect that the two testing methods, formal and statistical, provide complementary – rather than competing – test data sets, that is, well-suited to expose faults of different kind. Hence, combining them becomes all the more interesting as there is no trusted design fault model. Indeed, although they begin both with a decomposition of the input domain into several subdomains, they differ from one another in the three main following points.

- *Subdomains originate from unrelated criteria*, since based on different software models, namely: in the case of formal testing, an algebraic specification; in the case of statistical testing, either behaviour models deduced from informal specifications, or program flow graphs, depending on the software complexity.

- *Provided with a set of subdomains, the methods support two distinct uses:*
  - For *formal testing*, decomposition may be as fine as wished wrt the specification; applying uniformity hypotheses (and thus exercising only one element per subdomain) suffices when the specification is not too far from the program design. If it is not the case (i.e. unrelated structures), decomposition into subdomains can induce too strong uniformity hypotheses. On the other hand, faults connected to the program limits (special input items) must coincide with an explicit specification property, and consequently, they must normally appear as particular cases of the decomposition.
  - For *statistical testing*, a criterion is not considered as reliable enough; exercising only one element per subdomain is far too weak. So, increasing

the test size by a probabilistic choice of several items from each subdomain aims to improve a non sufficiently sharp decomposition of the input domain. Yet, the risk of leaving extremal/special input values out is the main weakness of the approach, since these values remain, by essence, poorly catered with a random input generation, within reasonable testing time.

- *The oracle problem*, i.e. that of how to determine the correct outputs which a program should return in responses to given input data [97], arises with any testing method, and it becomes crucial when numerous input data are concerned. Formal testing provides an oracle procedure as soon as the selected inputs/outputs are observable, while statistical testing does not.

# 3    Experimental Framework

The whole experimental environment has already been presented in [90], so that we only outline its main features.

## 3.1  Target Program

The target program, written in C language, is extracted from a nuclear reactor safety shutdown system. The whole module periodically scans the position of the reactor's control rods, and is composed of several functional units. The target program is the function called $FCT_3$ in Paper IV.B: it implements the filtering unit, that aims to check the validity of the measures acquired in order to eliminate doubtful ones. Its output results depend on both current and past values filtered. The size of the object code (separately compiled source code) amounts to 1133 bytes.

## 3.2  Target Fault Set

The target faults are *mutations* introduced in the source code [17]. Three types of change are automatically performed by our mutant generator: 1) constant replacement; 2) symbol – scalar variable, array and structure reference, etc. – replacement; 3) operator replacement; leading to an amount of 1345 mutants for the target program. A mutant is "killed" by a test data set if its output history differs from that of the original program. A *mutation score*, denoted MS(T) for a test set T, is defined to be the fraction of non-equivalent mutants which are killed by T. MS(T) is a number in the interval [0, 1]: a high score indicates that T is very efficient wrt mutation fault exposure.

An acute question concerns the representativeness of a mutation score wrt the *actual fault exposure power* of a test set, i.e. the representativeness of the mutations wrt actual faults. The question is still an open issue. In the current state of the art, mutation analysis provides the only practical way to assess and compare the efficiency of various test sets on a large number of fault patterns. Assuming the *competent programmer hypothesis*, the changes introduced correspond to faults likely to be made during the coding phase. Hence, the mutation scores should provide a meaningful experimental metric, at least at the unit testing level addressed here (see also Paper IV.B).

## 3.3  Test Data Sets

Five test sets have been designed from each approach, in order to study eventual disparities within a category of sets. Both test sizes, although rather large for the (small) target program, are particularly justified in the case of safety-critical software.

**Formal test sets.** Five different test sets – denoted $F_1$, ..., $F_5$ – have been designed from a specification of the filtering unit defined with respect to the input data flow. A data flow of at least six inputs is needed to cover all the specified cases. The decomposition into subdomains is done by a case analysis on 30 axioms and applied only on the two last inputs of a data flow. This leads to 47 uniform subdomains (47 flows of six inputs, thus 282 input data). A two level decomposition seems to be a good compromise between the test size and the efficiency of the selected test data. The inputs and the expected corresponding outputs have been automatically generated by the tool [56].

**Statistical test sets.** Five different test sets – denoted $S_1$, ..., $S_5$ – have been designed from a structural analysis of the target program. The internal state of the filtering process is an explicit parameter of the program, in addition to the inputs and outputs defined for the functional unit, so that white box testing breaks the loop provided by the feedback. Hence, compared to the sets $F_i$, the sets $S_i$ involve supplementary input and output data. The input distribution is suited to cover the All-Paths criterion, and for a required test quality of $q_N = 0.9999$ the number of test data generated per set $S_i$ is $N = 405$ from equation (2).

## 4   Experimental Results

Fig. 1 displays the mutation scores supplied by each test set. Note that two scores are provided for the sets $F_i$, depending on whether the internal state of the filtering process is observed, or not.

These results must be compared with the previous ones related to the same program FCT$_3$ (Paper IV.B). Neither structural deterministic testing, nor uniform statistical testing were so efficient: two deterministic sets ensuring the coverage of "All-Paths" provided scores of 0.79 and 0.84; five uniform sets (of size $N = 405$) supplied scores ranging from 0.56 to 0.84.

| | 1 | 2 | 3 | 4 | 5 | controllability & observability |
|---|---|---|---|---|---|---|
| Formal Sets $F_i$ | 0.9703 | 0.9651 | 0.9688 | 0.9784 | 0.9703 | 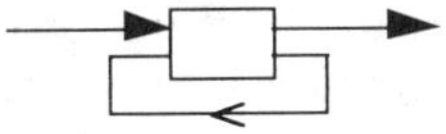 |
| | 1.0 | 1.0 | 0.9993 | 0.9985 | 1.0 | 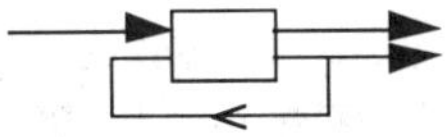 |
| Statistical Sets $S_i$ | 1.0    $\forall S_i$ | | | | | 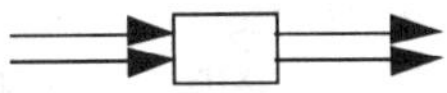 |

**Fig. 1.** Mutation scores

## 4.1 Efficiency of Formal Testing

Mutations altering the internal state may need more than six consecutive inputs to be observable through the data flow outputs. This justifies the differences between the scores reached with and without observation of the internal state. This fact could be predicted since the size of six consecutive inputs is a lower bound to reach all the specified cases.

Additional observations on the internal state allow formal testing to kill almost every mutant still alive: only one mutant is not killed by the test data set $F_3$, and one more by $F_4$. Thus, formal testing provides almost perfect criteria (wrt mutations). This is a very satisfactory result since there was a priori no reason for a functional test data set to reach a better coverage of structural faults than the "All-Paths" deterministic testing.

The single (resp. two) mutant(s) remaining alive for the set $F_3$ (resp. $F_4$) show(s) that the subdomain decomposition is not acute enough to ensure their exposure. Whether the internal state is observed or not, the five mutation scores reached by the sets $F_i$ exhibit some disparity, which proves that uniformity hypotheses on subdomains are too strong in the present case. Hence the decomposition should be pushed further. However, this decomposition is intrinsically pertinent since one input item per subdomain suffices to kill almost every mutant. By comparison, the strongest structural criterion "All-Paths" clearly provides an insufficient partition.

## 4.2 Efficiency of Structural Statistical Testing

The perfect scores $MS(S_i) = 1.0$ are repeatedly observed for the five statistical sets $S_i$, suggesting that the high fault-revealing power is really due to the adequacy of the input distribution, and is not dependent of the particular values generated for the sets. All mutants are *rapidly killed*, far before the completion of the tests: actually, the final scores are practically obtained in the first third of each $S_i$. On the contrary, a blind test based on a uniform sampling of the input domain is far from being adequate, as stated by the previous experiments involving uniform sets: poor final scores are supplied and great disparities are observed from one set to another. This provides evidence that the input distribution has a significant impact on the efficiency of random test data.

An input distribution ensuring a suitable probe of the source code of the program seems very adequate at the unit testing level addressed here. The information brought by the structural analysis is meaningful wrt fault exposure, although not sufficient since the "All-Paths" deterministic sets fail to kill all the mutants and exhibit disparate mutation scores. During statistical testing, the imperfection of the criterion is compensated by the large number of test cases that the probabilistic approach allows to generate.

Actually, the whole experimental study on structural statistical testing involved four functional units of the software module and a total amount of 2816 mutants: only six were not killed by the structural statistical sets (Paper IV.B). These six mutants were changes affecting an array index, that can be revealed only by applying specific input patterns. Extremal/special values are, by essence, poorly catered for by statistical testing within reasonable testing times, and are more efficiently covered by deterministic test data specifically aimed at them.

# 5    Conclusions and Future Work

The efficiency of two testing methods has been exemplified by an experimental work conducted on a real program from the nuclear field. High mutation scores were observed: actually, formal test sets left alive only two of the entire set of 1345 mutants, and structural statistical test sets killed all of them. Neither "All-Paths" deterministic testing, nor uniform statistical testing achieved such a level of success. Hence, these first results clearly provide evidence that both formal testing and statistical testing can drastically enhance test stringency. Yet, this is at the expense of larger test sizes, but testing times remain reasonable at the unit level, and in any case are quite justified for safety-critical programs. They do not set a practical problem since: (i) in both methods, the generation of input data is automatically performed by tools; and (ii) formal testing provides an oracle procedure (as soon as the inputs/outputs are observable), that can also be used to solve the oracle problem remaining in the probabilistic approach.

This comparative experimental study will be extended to *larger programs*. It is worth noting that the required test sizes will not be an increasing function of the software size and complexity: both methods consider adapted criteria for the module testing level [7, 88, 89]

In our mind, the ability of formal testing to cover extremal/special values, and the ability of statistical testing to compensate criteria imperfection (wrt faults), justify a *simultaneous use of both techniques*. And even better, a promising approach could be a more elaborate testing method that merges both approaches. Indeed, a statistical testing strategy based on a decomposition built by selection according to formal testing would surely have the following advantages:

- the extremal input values are covered;
- any remaining imperfection of the functional decomposition is compensated by the statistical selection of input data.

## Acknowledgements

It is a pleasure to acknowledge Marie-Claude Gaudel and Gilles Bernot for their constant help during the elaboration of the algebraic specification used here. In addition to PDCS2, this work has been partially supported by the PRC "Programmation et Outils pour l'Intelligence Artificielle".

# Testing Distributed Real-Time Systems: An Overview[*]

Werner Schütz[**]

Technische Universität Wien

**Abstract.** This paper summarizes our work on testing distributed, hard real-time systems. It first examines the fundamental problems that one faces when testing a distributed, hard real-time system. It specifically identifies the influences of the distributedness and of the real-time requirements of the systems considered. We show how the usual problems of testing become more difficult, and which additional problems are introduced, because of these additional system characteristics.

We identify six such fundamental problems: Organization, Observability, Reproducibility, Host/Target Approach, Environment Simulation, and Representativity. These, as well as their interrelations, are presented in a general framework that is independent of a particular system architecture or application. This framework could serve as a starting point for all activities geared towards a particular system architecture or a specific application.

As an example, we illustrate how these test problems have been handled when developing a test methodology for the distributed real-time system MARS.

## 1    Introduction

During the past years real-time systems have been applied in increasingly complex and safety-critical applications. Examples of application areas include control of automobile engines, nuclear power plants, industrial process control systems, aircraft avionics, and robotics [84]. Both these trends often lead to the decision to implement a real-time system as a *distributed* system [84]: Complex applications require more computing resources which are frequently most easily provided by using several processors. Critical applications usually have more stringent dependability [54] requirements which can be fulfilled by employing suitable fault tolerance mechanisms [48]. Fault tolerance requires redundancy, which may be achieved by using additional processors. Moreover, a distributed architecture often suits the physical distribution of the controlled process or environment, e.g. on a factory floor.

As a consequence of these stringent dependability requirements, also more stringent demands are placed on the verification and validation procedures [83] used during system development, than for "normal", non-critical, systems. While we realize that any successful real-world validation strategy must employ a mix of verification techniques, we concentrate on testing for the following reasons:

1.  Testing is one of the most widely known and most widely applied verification techniques, and is thus of large practical importance. On the other hand it has not

---

[*]    This paper is a condensed and revised version of [82].

[**]   The author is now with Alcatel Austria, Wien.

been very thoroughly investigated in the context of real-time systems. Not much has changed since 1980, when Glass [33] considered this field a "lost world". Recently, however, this topic has received increased interest in the Safety community, both in academia [69] and in industry, e.g. in avionics [20], automobile industry [37], or for railway systems [77]. In industry, further work must have been done, resulting in a lot of practical experience; unfortunately, such work is seldom published.

2. Testing is also one of the most widely applicable techniques; systems of all sizes can in principle be tested, whereas proof-of-correctness techniques [4, 36], for example, do not scale so well in the present state-of-the-art.

3. Testing becomes more complex and expensive with increasing system complexity and size. It has been repeatedly reported that testing typically consumes in the order of 50% of the total project costs [5, 43, 64]. Because of the more stringent dependability demands, as discussed above, this figure is likely to be even higher in the context of safety-critical applications. Thus, better testing techniques can potentially result in considerable savings.

This paper summarizes our work on the testing of distributed, hard real-time systems, to be more exact, on the testing of *application software* for such systems. In this work, we have specifically focused on the test execution aspect because we believe that this is the source of the most significant differences in comparison with testing non-real-time software, partly because of the real-time nature, and partly because of the distributed nature of the systems considered.

The work reported here contributes in at least three areas:

1. It provides an analysis of the fundamental test problems and their interrelations that one has to deal with when testing a distributed, hard real-time system.

2. It compares the properties of two types of system architectures, event-triggered and time-triggered real-time systems, with respect to some of these problems.

3. On this basis, it develops a test methodology for the distributed real-time system MARS.

This paper proceeds as follows: In Section 2 we give the background and the scope of this work by defining what we mean by "real-time system" and "distributed system". We also briefly summarize the definitions of validation, verification, and testing, which are adopted from recent work performed within the IFIP Working Group 10.4 "Dependable Computing and Fault Tolerance" [54](see also chapter 1 of this book). Section 3 discusses the basic problems that one has to consider and solve when testing a distributed, hard real-time system. Section 4 describes the benefits a time-triggered architecture presents with respect to the test problems discussed before. Section 5 shows how these fundamental problems have been handled when developing a test methodology for the distributed real-time system MARS. Section 6 concludes the paper.

## 2    Definitions

### 2.1   Real-Time  System

A *real-time system* is a (computer) system which is required by its specification to adhere not only to functional requirements, but also to temporal requirements, also called "timing constraints" or "deadlines". These requirements are typically of the form "react to this event within x seconds". As a consequence, a real-time system can be defined as follows [84, 85, 96]:

**Definition**: A *real-time system* is a system whose correctness depends not only on the logical result(s) of a computation, but also on the time at which the result(s) are produced.

The *criticality* of a system is a criterion to classify systems with respect to the severity (consequences) of a system failure. We distinguish between *benign* and *catastrophic* failures [53, 54]. The cost of a benign system failure is in the same order of magnitude as the benefits of the system during its normal operation, i.e. the consequence is basically a loss of the benefits of system service. In contrast, if the consequences of a system failure can exceed the benefits of the system by several orders of magnitude, then the failure is catastrophic. Examples are loss of human life (accidents), huge financial losses, or other unacceptable consequences (e.g. environmental pollution).

The criticality allows to distinguish between hard and soft real-time systems.

**Definition**: A *hard real-time system* is a real-time system in which it is absolutely imperative that responses occur within the specified deadline [96], because otherwise severe consequences [85] or possibly catastrophic failures [50] will result.

All other systems, i.e. where all system failures are benign, are called *soft real-time systems*. In the following, we will refer to hard real-time systems simply as "real-time systems", if no confusion is possible.

## 2.2 Distributed System

Distributed systems are characterized by the existence of several loci of control (processors, nodes) which are interconnected by a network. Each node is a self-contained computer, consisting of a CPU, local memory, access to the network, a local clock, and other (optional) peripheral devices. Each node executes a set of (parallel) processes (tasks) concurrently with (i.e. at the same time as) the other nodes. Processors (or processes) may communicate or synchronize themselves in order to achieve their common mission. We assume that processes do not have access to the internals of other processes, regardless of whether these processes execute on the same node or not. Instead, processes communicate by message passing.

## 2.3. Validation, Verification, and Testing

In this section we briefly recapitulate the definitions of validation, verification, and testing (see also chapter 1 of this book).

**Definition**: *Validation* refers to all methods and techniques intended to reach confidence in a system's ability to deliver a service in accordance with an agreed-upon system specification [2, 54].

Validation is concerned with two aspects [54]: *Fault Removal* addresses the reduction of the number or the seriousness of faults present in the system, i.e. it is concerned with system validity at a particular point in time or in a certain state of development. *Fault Forecasting* addresses the estimation of the present number, future occurrences, and the consequences of faults; it is thus concerned with the question of how long a system will be (will remain) valid, i.e. will deliver the expected service.

The first step in Fault Removal is *Verification*, followed by diagnosis and correction, if necessary [54].

**Definition**: *Verification* is the process of checking whether a system satisfies certain properties or conditions which may be either general (e.g. absence of deadlock) or specific to the particular system, directly derived from its specification [54].

If a verification condition is not fulfilled, the reason (fault(s)) must be diagnosed, and the necessary corrections must be performed.

There are a number of different verification techniques [2, 16, 43], among them *testing*.

**Definition**: *Testing* is characterized by execution of the system (dynamic verification) while supplying it with valued inputs [2, 54].

In the context of testing, diagnosis and correction are often summarized in the term *debugging* [2, 5, 28, 64, 83].

## 3    The Fundamental Test Problems

In this section we derive and identify the pertinent facts, principles, and problems that one has to consider and solve when testing a distributed real-time system. These considerations may subsequently be used for the development of a suitable test methodology for any particular system architecture, as well as for the design of support tools for this methodology.

In order to derive these fundamental problems it is necessary to consider three main areas, namely Software Engineering and Testing Principles, Distributed System Characteristics, and Real-Time Computing Principles. We have identified six different fundamental problems, which are called Organization, Observability, Reproducibility, Host/Target Approach, Environment Simulation, and Representativity.

These problems, as well as their interrelations, are briefly discussed in the following sections. More details and background information (e.g. examples how a particular problem has been actually solved) can be found in [81, 82].

### 3.1  Organization

The *Organization* requirement can be stated as follows: All testing activities should be organized into distinct test phases so that they both harmonize with the design phases of the development methodology and are compatible with the system structure. It is derived from general software engineering principles.

The way software engineering methodologies deal with the increasing complexity of modern applications and systems is through step-wise development in well-defined development *phases* [2, 22] (decomposition and refinement). These phases are organized into a consistent and coherent software (system) development *methodology* [43]. Each phase produces a set of products which can be evaluated (verified) by various techniques. Upon successful verification they are used as inputs to subsequent phases. This is true for all software development models, for the (primitive) waterfall model [9], as well as for more advanced ones, such as the spiral model [10] or prototyping models [1].

In these development methodologies the testing activities are (or should be) organized into phases as well, which together comprise a *test methodology* which itself is part of the development methodology [43]. The exact nature, definition, and purpose of the test phases depend of course both on the design phases present in the development methodology and on the particular system structure. In general, both the physical (hardware) and logical structure (e.g. layers of abstraction) have to be considered. For instance, if a system is decomposed into subsystems which are themselves organized in modules, then one might have module (unit) tests for each individual module, followed by subsystem tests for each subsystem, and finally a system or system integration test [22].

*Distributed systems* are usually more complex than centralized ones. System requirements now translate into functional requirements for each individual process (or node) plus requirements for process (or node) interaction or synchronization. This adds (at least) one more layer to the software architecture and has a number of consequences [28]: A distributed system is often much harder to understand because of these interaction and synchronization requirements. There are additional opportunities for errors to occur or to be made (i.e. not only in each sequential process, but also in process interaction or synchronization). Finally, distributed systems tend to be larger in size than sequential ones.

The obvious solution to handle this complexity is again to separate concerns and to organize testing activities into several well-defined phases. Garcia-Molina [28] advocates a bottom-up approach to testing distributed systems: First, each (sequential) process is tested individually, using standard test and debugging tools. Only afterwards is the system tested in its entirety, with the help of distributed debugging tools. This leads again to what we have already said about Organization, but we note that the need to handle the additional complexity introduced by the distributedness will influence (and complicate) the Organization by increasing the number of test phases needed.

## 3.2  Observability

When a system is tested, it is necessary to evaluate the correctness or "appropriateness" of the system behaviour. In order to do this, one must *observe* or *monitor* for each test execution what the system does, how it does it, and perhaps when it does it. The system must facilitate such observation, i.e. it must be *observable* (another name for this concept is "measurability" [2]). The same applies to the system's environment because the correctness of the system behaviour can often only be evaluated with respect to what is or has been happening in its environment. This *Observability* requirement sounds trivial, but it is not for distributed or real-time systems.

The problem begins when one needs to observe intermediate values or variables. For example, a state change that is required in response to a particular input is usually not or not immediately reflected in an output. Frequently, such observations help to determine exactly *why* a program behaved the way it did, or to find the location of an error which has caused a previously observed program failure.

The most straightforward technique to allow the observation of intermediate variables is to insert additional output statements into the source code (*auxiliary outputs*) which output exactly the desired values. A disadvantage is that frequent recompilation is necessary. Another technique is to execute the program with the help of an *interactive debugger* which allows the user to control the execution of the program, to interrupt its execution at predefined points (breakpoints), and then to examine its internal variables.

Clearly, techniques such as these are not suitable for distributed systems. They require modifications which, in the presence of multiple loci of control, may change the behaviour of the system by attempting to observe this behaviour. This phenomenon has been termed the "Probe Effect" [25, 26, 61]. The main concern is possible interference with the relative timing between processes, which may either prevent certain timing or synchronization related errors from occurring, or may introduce new errors which would not occur without the probe.

For example, if one process is delayed by having to execute auxiliary output statements and therefore sends a message to another process a bit later, the receiver may in the meantime have received a message from a third process, and may thus experience a reversal of the order of messages received. This could cause a behaviour different from the one in the other case, and this can ultimately also affect the first process. Similar examples arise with interactive debugging where control of program execution is delegated to the user. Furthermore, interactive debugging cannot be extended easily to distributed systems. Due to communication delays and the (usual) lack of a synchronized global clock, it is very difficult to stop the execution of all processes "immediately" or at least in a consistent state.

Finally, the need to observe the system's adherence to its temporal requirements as well further aggravates the Observability problem. Let us illustrate this with a few examples: In order to evaluate the temporal correctness of the system behaviour we must observe and monitor when events of interest (e.g. inputs, outputs, communication) occur in the system, in addition to the values we are interested in and to the order of events. Thus, much more information needs to be presented and/or recorded which will make the Probe Effect much harder to deal with. In addition, the Probe Effect might now also affect the behaviour of a single, sequential process: If the results of an application algorithm depend on the time of its execution, then a delay (caused by the Probe Effect) changes the time perceived by the software (e.g. because a call to access a timer is delayed) and, subsequently, rather different results could be computed based on this perceived time. Therefore, it will, in general, be necessary to avoid the occurrence of any Probe Effect. An overview of ways to deal with the Probe Effect can be found in [81, 82].

## 3.3  Reproducibility

Another established practice in software engineering is to retest a program after errors have been corrected or after the software has been changed due to enhancements, optimizations, or for other reasons. This is called *regression testing* [2]. It is intended to ensure that (i) the errors have been truly corrected, and/or (ii) that modifications did not introduce new, undesired effects or errors. Usually, already available test data are reused for regression testing. (Depending on the modifications to the system that have been carried out, the test data may have to be updated as well.)

Regression testing is greatly facilitated if test executions are *reproducible*, i.e. if a program computes the same results when repeatedly executed with the same input (test) data. (This is called "test repeatability" in [45].) Otherwise it is not assured that another execution activates the same error, and it would be inconclusive whether any corrective action performed for this error really did achieve its goal. The cost-effectiveness of regression testing can be enhanced if the expected results are also available and comparison of actual and expected results is automated. Again, automatic comparison is much more difficult (if not impossible) when execution is not reproducible, i.e. when there is possibly more than one "correct" result for a given input.

In non-real-time, sequential programs Reproducibility is only very seldom of concern (e.g. when a random number generator is used). The general "SW-Engineering and Testing Principles" are still the primary reason for the existence of the Reproducibility problem. In distributed and/or real-time systems, however, the Reproducibility problem cannot, in general, be neglected.

With *distributed systems*, this problem becomes much harder because the behaviour of a distributed system may be non-reproducible due to nondeterminism in its hardware, software, or operating system. Possible reasons are [61]:

- the presence of nondeterministic statements in the application software, e.g. the use of random numbers; these would pose similar problems in sequential systems.

- the presence of concurrent activities leading to *races*, whose outcome is determined by the CPU load, the network traffic, nondeterminism in the communication protocol, the presence or absence of observations subject to the Probe Effect (see Section 3.2), and possibly other factors. The source of nondeterminism is thus the lack of *sufficient a-priori knowledge* about the type and timing of events which would determine the outcome of such a race and, as a consequence, the behaviour of the system. The most important examples of such events are:

  - Synchronization of processes, given by the order of synchronization events or the order of executing synchronization constructs.

  - Access to the system's notion of "time", e.g. by accessing a clock or a timer.

  - Asynchronous interrupts.

We call these or similar events the "significant events" since it is important to know their order and/or timing in order to be able to completely determine the system behaviour and, consequently, the outcome of a test run. The exact type, appearance, and characteristics of such events depend of course on one or more of: the specific hardware, the operating system, the communication primitives (e.g. synchronous versus asynchronous message passing), and programming language constructs. In principle they must be identified for each application since it is possible that in one application knowledge of their order is sufficient, while in another application knowledge of their timing is required to be able to reproduce test runs. In practice, performing such an analysis for the particular target system (refer to Section 3.5) will often be sufficient.

Finally, with the additional need to respect and reproduce also the temporal behaviour of the system, it is in general not sufficient to recreate a particular sequence of tasks or of significant events to achieve Reproducibility, but it is also necessary to recreate the *time of occurrence* of such significant events. This implies that on the one hand considerably more information must be recorded for replaying, such as external input/output and asynchronous interrupts, and that on the other hand simulated, i.e. recorded, time instead of "real" time must often be used for replay. This is because one cannot, in general, rely on a deterministic behaviour in time of the underlying hardware (and real-time operating system), even if the Probe Effect is avoided.

In order to achieve reproducible behaviour, it is necessary to first select or define a particular execution scenario in terms of the significant events. This can be done either based on the specification (statically), or through an initial execution of the system during which all significant events are monitored and information about them logged. (The latter is the basic idea of all trace-based re-execution or replay mechanisms.) Subsequently (on re-execution) it is necessary to exercise control over the execution in such a way as to re-create or reproduce this same scenario deterministically. More details as well as a survey of existing or proposed re-execution control mechanisms can be found in [81, 82].

## 3.4 Interdependence of Observability and Reproducibility

The situation is further complicated by the fact that the Observability and the Reproducibility problem are *not independent*. The concern here is that, on the one hand, the observations necessary to collect information about the significant events in the first place (which is then used to reproduce the observed execution scenario) may introduce Probe Effects. As a result, the scenario actually tested may be different from the one originally intended or selected. On the other hand, we also need to observe the re-executed test runs – normally we even want to observe more details. Occurrences of Probe Effects may change these observations, even if the original execution scenario is correctly reproduced.

Luckily, this interdependence is not as severe as it seems. Even though the Probe Effect must normally be expected to occur nondeterministically, it is in most cases safe to assume that it will change the order of and/or the temporal distance between the significant events, but that it will not introduce new types of events. Then, any Probe Effect occurring during the initial monitoring of an execution scenario will be reproduced subsequently. If this assumption does not hold, one must either avoid any Probe Effect during initial monitoring or include these new events in the set of significant events while enhancing the re-execution control mechanism to deal with this new set of significant events. To be sure that one tests what one intended to test, however, only the first of these possibilities remains, i.e. avoiding the occurrence of any Probe Effect.

When observing re-executed test runs, one must ensure that these observations do not introduce Probe Effects which interfere with the re-execution control mechanism. That is, such observations must be based on events different from all the significant events. As a simple example, a signal that suspends the execution of a process (breakpoint) is typically never seen by the process concerned; it is instead handled by the operating system, and therefore there is no need to include it in the set of significant events. In other words, once Reproducibility of test runs has been achieved, there might then be a certain freedom in choosing observation mechanisms. For instance, if a unique sequence of computation is all that is needed for reproducible test runs, it does not matter if observations introduce delays.

## 3.5  The Host/Target Approach

Another important factor affecting real-time system development stems from the fact that real-time systems are increasingly being deployed as *embedded systems*. They are built into some larger system or machinery which they are intended to control. Examples range from on-board satellite control to washing machines. They might also be deployed in an environment which is dangerous for humans to access, e.g. production process control in a chemical plant.

Therefore, there are usually two types of computer systems involved in real-time software development, the host system and the target system [16, 33, 35, 45]. The *host system* is a conventional computer system which is used to develop and construct the real-time software. It includes a standard operating system to support time sharing, multiple users, a file system, interconnections to individual systems if the host system is itself distributed, and possibly other features. Interaction with the user is typically based on terminals, possibly with graphical capabilities. To develop real-time software, it allows the execution of a software engineering environment or any other desired tools for software development and testing. It will also have to include a (cross) compiler or (cross) assembler to generate executable machine code for the target system.

The *target system* is the system which the real-time software is eventually executed on. It is often subject to stringent space, weight, and/or cost requirements. It is thus specifically tailored to be small so that as many of the system resources as possible are available for the application, and to efficiently execute the real-time software. Therefore, no software development tools are available. Its operating system provides only the most essential functions for timely execution of hard real-time tasks, task interaction and synchronization, and interaction with the environment. It must often support I/O via special I/O-devices, e.g. analog-digital converters.

This *Host/Target Approach* is therefore derived from Real-Time Computing Principles and has some important consequences on the Organization. First, some of the phases into which we want to structure the test process (see Section 3.1) will be conducted on the host system, and some of them on the target system. It must be clearly defined which test phases are conducted on which system, and what aspects of the software each test phase is particularly suited to test. All test phases taken together must allow, in the end, thorough testing and checking of all aspects of the software system. A crude distinction that is often made is the following [16, 33, 35]:

1. *Testing on the host system* is used for (functional) unit testing and preliminary integration testing.

2. *Testing on the target system* involves completing the integration test and performing the system test. In addition to testing the logical correctness of the software it is also possible to test its performance and timing characteristics at this stage.

In comparison with the case of only one system being involved in software development, where the test phases are usually derived from the levels of abstractions introduced during software design, it is possible that additional test phases must be introduced. For example, system integration tests in DARTS (Design Approach for Real-Time Systems) [35] are performed partly on the host, and partly on the target system. In conventional software development, this would be a single test phase.

Of course, testing on the host system is much more comfortable because of the possibility to use a large variety of different tools. Therefore, it is frequently recommended that as much testing as possible be conducted on the host system [33, 35]. Thus, we need to execute software written for the target system on the host system. One way to do this is to generate machine code for the target system and execute it on the host system with the help of an *instruction-level simulator* [33] which emulates the target system's machine instructions. Gomaa [35] observes that a program interacts with the operating system and suggests an emulation of the target operating system functions (services) on the host operating system. This second approach has the advantage that emulation of the target system is done on a higher level of abstraction, is therefore probably easier to implement, and offers a greater degree of independence of the target hardware architecture. It can also handle certain hardware-specific constructs, such as memory-mapped I/O, which can (and should!) be hidden in an appropriate operating system service (system call). One limitation of this approach is that differences in the representation of basic data types (integers, floating point numbers) between target and host system may become significant when performing numeric computations.

On the other hand, tests on the target system cannot be made completely superfluous. Any performance tests and tests intended to evaluate the temporal behaviour of the system yield only meaningful results if they are conducted on the target system. In this area, however, lie the most important and most wide-spread shortcomings [33] of real-time system testing. On the target system, there is often virtually no test support available, and even for the existing support the interaction between tester and system in most cases takes place at the machine language level, which severely affects productivity.

## 3.6 Environment Simulation

The available literature reveals, however, that there is one well-accepted and (almost) universally used test tool, especially for target system tests, namely the *Environment Simulator* [16, 33, 83]; it is, therefore, derived from Real-Time Computing Principles. An Environment Simulator, however, is often the only support available for target system testing and it can be employed only relatively late in the system life-cycle.

An Environment Simulator is a device or a system that mimics the behaviour of the real-time system's (physical) environment, by providing inputs to and accepting outputs from the system during test runs. Based on these outputs, a new set of inputs is then computed by the Environment Simulator. It therefore implements a model of the system's environment. An Environment Simulator is itself a real-time system, since the temporal properties of the system environment cannot be neglected when testing a real-time system.

There are two types of arguments for using a simulated environment for testing purposes. The first one addresses the use of a simulated vs. the use of the real environment:

• In most cases it is not permissible to use the real environment during testing because of safety and/or cost considerations, especially since confidence in the correctness of the real-time system is still low. Sometimes, using the real environment is not possible simply because it is not yet available; it is developed concurrently with the system controlling it (embedded systems).

- Simulation provides the only possibility to test system behaviour in "rare event situations" which occur only rarely in the real world. Often it is either difficult or unsafe to obtain these situations from the real environment. Frequently, system dependability is of utmost importance if such a "rare event" occurs (e.g. emergency handling of a chemical process).

- Generally, the tester has more control over the simulated environment than over the real one. Test execution is thus easier, and flexibility is enhanced. Evaluating system behaviour under invalid environmental behaviour (either in the value, or the time domain, or both) becomes feasible.

- It is often much easier to obtain system responses and other intermediate test results from a simulated environment than from the real one because the simulated environment is easier to instrument (measurement, observation problem).

The other line of arguments concerns on-line (by the Environment Simulator) vs. off-line test data generation:

- In many real-time applications (e.g. a control problem) the correctness of the system cannot be evaluated based on a single output, but must rather be judged from a sequence of outputs and their temporal relations observed over some time interval (a "trajectory" [69]). In such applications small "errors" or deviations in a single output can be compensated by later outputs within some time interval, thus it is not practical (and may even be impossible) to determine the "correctness" of each single output. Consequently, test runs must be extended over a longer period of time before the results of the test run can be evaluated. An Environment Simulator could help considerably because the need to generate large amounts of input (test) data before test execution is significantly reduced; instead, new inputs are calculated on-line by the Environment Simulator.

- When we want to conduct *realistic* test runs, i.e. using test data which may be typically or possibly encountered during the system's operational deployment, then each test input in a sequence of test data must take into account the (expected) reaction of the system's environment on the previous test inputs of this sequence. Due to the usually tight coupling between a real-time system and its environment, realistic test input sequences may be difficult to derive off-line, i.e. before test execution. Therefore, an Environment Simulator can potentially help to improve the Test Coverage because it facilitates running representative test runs cost-effectively (see also the previous item).

An Environment Simulator must be developed on a project-by-project basis since it is, by necessity, an application-specific tool; this must be accommodated in the development methodology. The need to decide if and in which test phases an Environment Simulator will be used influences the Organization.

The behaviour of the Environment Simulator must match that of the real environment as closely as possible in order to achieve its goals. Note that Environment Simulation does not directly address the Representativity problem. For our purposes we assume that it is possible to construct an Environment Simulator that models the real environment accurately enough and that the test runs performed with the Environment Simulator are, therefore, realistic or representative.

Justification of this assumption is, however, the subject of a different field of Computer Science, i.e. model validation (see e.g. [76] or any other text book on Simulation and Modelling), and is beyond the scope of this paper. One possibility to validate an Environment Simulator is to compare it with the real environment, but that might not always be possible. In general, this has to be handled within the specific application context.

## 3.7 Representativity

Another principle related to good software engineering and testing practices is that a system should, in certain test phases, be at least partially tested with *representative* or *realistic* inputs. It is, therefore, derived from general principles. For example, during the Customer Acceptance Test inputs are drawn according to an (expected) operational profile. As another example, random testing with inputs being sampled according to their expected operational distribution can be used to estimate the operational dependability [16].

The problem arises, at least to a large extent, from the fact that exhaustive testing of a system is impossible in all but the most trivial cases. In general, this is due to the following reasons:

1. Only a fraction of all possible real-world scenarios can be anticipated and taken into account, either because of *incomplete or insufficient knowledge* of the system's environment, or because a number of possible real-world scenarios falls outside the design assumptions and hypotheses that are inevitably made during system development – either consciously or unconsciously. In other words, the model of the system's environment excludes some possible real-world scenarios; this model may of course be incorrect and/or inappropriate.

2. Only a fraction of those anticipated real-world scenarios can be tested, due to the *combinatorial explosion* of possible event and input combinations which rise with the system complexity. It is thus prohibitively expensive (both in cost and in time) to test all anticipated real-world scenarios.

While the first type of limitation is normally unknown and cannot be measured, it is in theory possible to measure or derive the second type of limitation. Therefore, we introduce the *Test Coverage* which indicates how many of the anticipated real-world scenarios can be or have been covered by corresponding test scenarios. Although it is impossible to state something general about the *absolute* value of the Test Coverage, it is possible to say something about its *relative* change over different system architectures (see [80, 81]). It appears, however, that the principle of Environment Simulation (see Section 3.6) is at least partially helpful to achieve representative test runs.

# 4   Advantages of Time-Triggered over Event-Triggered Systems

Based on the implementation of a real-time system we distinguish between event-triggered (ET) and time-triggered (TT) systems. *ET systems* are characterized by the fact that all their actions (task execution, communication) are initiated by the observation of some event (e.g. receiving an external input, receiving a message from another process, interrupt, etc.). Usually, an ET system does not provide a global time to the application processes, i.e. the clocks in different nodes of the system are not synchronized. *TT systems*, on the other hand, are driven by the periodic observation of the state of their environment and start all their actions to process the observed environmental state at predefined, periodic points in time. In this section we describe the benefits a time-triggered architecture presents with respect to the test problems discussed above.

First, no additional mechanisms are needed to ensure Reproducibility. This is because all system activities start at predefined points in time which cannot be influenced by events either in the environment or the system itself (provided the fault and load hypotheses are not violated). Therefore, it is sufficient to re-create the same input scenarios (both in value and in time) at the interfaces with the environment to repeat a test run. This property has been experimentally verified on a MARS system [80, 81].

Second, there are potentially many environmental states that a time-triggered system perceives as equivalent. This is due to the fact that the system periodically inputs the state of its environment. At each of these points in time it is unable to determine the order in which events in the environment occurred since the last observation. (Actually, the "events" can only be inferred by comparing the new and the last environmental state, they are not observed directly.) This property increases the Test Coverage (see Section 3.7) since the number of discernible input scenarios is reduced. Of course, system design has to etermine an appropriate input rate to ensure that ordering information that is actually needed by the application is indeed obtained. More details on this property can be found in [80, 81].

# 5    A Test Methodology for MARS

This section shows how the test problems discussed above have been taken into account when developing a suitable test methodology for the distributed real-time system MARS (MAintainable Real-time System) [49, 50]. The test methodology [79, 81] takes advantage of the architectural properties of time-triggered systems. It has been integrated with the (existing) design methodology for MARS [50].

The MARS hardware and operating system are designed to predictably execute hard real-time tasks and to guarantee that all timing constraints are met under all anticipated fault and load conditions (fault and load hypotheses). MARS is a time-triggered (synchronous) system.

A MARS system consists of a set of *clusters* that may be interconnected in an arbitrary topology depending on application requirements. Those parts of the application which are assigned to a given cluster should be highly related; it is the designers' responsibility to make reasonable choices. Each cluster consists of a set of *nodes* interconnected by an Ethernet-type real-time local area network (*MARS bus*). A node is a self-contained computer consisting of processing, storage, and communication elements. Each node executes an identical copy of the MARS Operating System and a set of system and application *tasks*. Tasks are activated periodically by the operating system and receive, process, and produce messages. Tasks interact with other tasks solely by message passing.

We assume a bottom-up approach to testing, so the Task Test is the first test phase. The goal is to test the functional correctness of each individual task. Since a task is a sequential piece of code that upon invocation receives a message, processes it, and sends a message, and since the timing constraints are handled at the system rather than the task level, the task test is the same as testing a non-real-time sequential program. Determining the worst-case task execution time is not handled by testing, but by static analysis of the task code [71].

The Task Test may be conducted either on the host or on the target system. Execution on the host system requires an emulation of the real-time operating system. Because of the time-triggered nature of MARS, this would be relatively easy to implement (see [81]). As another consequence, no special observation mechanisms are necessary for the Task Test. On the host system, any suitable interactive debugger may be used.

All the following test phases are conducted on the target system. The Cluster Test jointly tests several or all tasks of a cluster, while in the System Test the complete system is tested. Here, the emphasis is on testing the cooperation of tasks and clusters and to verify the temporal behaviour of the system. Finally, the Field Test is conducted with the real operational environment.

The test beds to run such tests are identical to the operational cluster or system configuration, except that a number of monitor nodes are added that allow to monitor the messages exchanged between tasks of a cluster. Messages may be stored on the monitor node and/or sent to the host system for later analysis. Special monitoring functions, e.g. saving only some specified messages, can be implemented on a monitor node. Since a monitor node does not send any messages to other nodes and just receives messages broadcast on the MARS bus, its presence is transparent to all the other nodes. Thus the Probe Effect is avoided. As an advantage, no special hardware is needed for monitoring, on the other hand all intra-task observations must be done during Task Test.

Both the Cluster and the System Test may be conducted in open-loop or in closed-loop mode, i.e. test data are generated off-line or on-line by an Environment Simulator, respectively. The MARS development methodology has been extended to allow the development and implementation of an Environment Simulator [78, 81]. An Environment Simulator is implemented as a MARS cluster and interacts with the cluster (system) under test. Thus it is possible to adhere to the timing constraints of the system environment (since the Simulator is implemented as a real-time system) and to "reuse" parts of the MARS development methodology and the associated tools for the development of the Environment Simulator. As noted before, however, we do not consider model validation, i.e. the adequacy of the behaviour of the Environment Simulator with respect to the behaviour of the real environment; this must be handled within each particular application context.

## 6  Conclusions

In this paper we have derived and identified all the pertinent facts and problems that one has to deal with when testing a distributed real-time system. These facts then serve as requirements or "boundary conditions" which are imposed on any effort undertaken to conduct successful test runs. Such requirements are derived from (1) sound software engineering (including testing) principles and practice, (2) the distributed nature of the systems considered, and (3) the real-time requirements of these systems. Six different basic test problems have been identified which were labeled Organization, Reproducibility, Representativity (Test Coverage),

Observability, Host/Target Approach, and Environment Simulation. These, and their interrelations, are discussed in detail.

The Organization requirement effectively represents the general necessity to integrate all system design, development, and evaluation activities into one coherent methodology. The Host/Target Approach and Environment Simulation are derived from observations of the current state-of-the-practice of real-time system development. Concerning Observability and Reproducibility, one can reasonably conclude that these problems are generally the most important ones. They are also the most complex ones to solve since they are influenced both by the distributed nature and by the real-time requirements of the intended target systems, and since they cannot be considered independently of each other.

We present these fundamental problems, as well as their interrelations, in a general framework which is independent of a particular system architecture or application software. It might be useful to evaluate test methodologies, test techniques, and test tools that have been (or will be) proposed, either in general or for particular systems.

As an example, we then shortly describe how this framework has already been used in the context of our work on the distributed real-time system MARS. In a first step, we summarize the distinct advantages that this system architecture offers with respect to testability because of its design principle of executing all tasks deterministically, both in the logical and the temporal sense. These advantages concern the Reproducibility and the Test Coverage. Based on the results of this first step, we have developed a test methodology for MARS which takes into account all the other fundamental test problems.

# References for Chapter IV

[1]    ACM, "Working Papers from the ACM SIGSOFT Rapid Prototyping Workshop", *ACM SIGSOFT Software Engineering Notes*, 7 Dec. 1982.

[2]    W. R. Adrion, M. A. Branstad and J. C. Cherniavsky, "Validation, Verification, and Testing of Computer Software", *ACM Computing Surveys*, 14 (2), pp.159-92, June 1982.

[3]    S. Antoy, "Systematic Design of Algebraic Specifications", in *5th IEEE International Workshop on Software Specification and Design (IWSSD 89)*, pp.278-80, 1989.

[4]    R. L. Baber, *The Spine of Software*, John Wiley and Sons, New York, 1987.

[5]    B. Beizer, *Software Testing Techniques*, 2nd Edition, Van Nostrand Reinhold, New York, 1990.

[6]    G. Bernot, "Testing Against Formal Specifications: a Theoretical View", in *TAPSOFT CCPSD* Lecture Notes in Computer Science, 494, pp.99-119, Springer Verlag, 1991.

[7]    G. Bernot, M.-C. Gaudel and B. Marre, "Software Testing Based on Formal Specifications: a Theory and a Tool", *Software Engineering Journal*, 6 (6), pp.387-405, 1991.

[8]    D. Bjorner and L. Druffel, "Position Statement: ICSE-12 Workshop on Industrial Experience using Formal Methods", in *12th IEEE-ACM International Conference on Software Engineering (ICSE-12)*, pp.264-7, 1990.

[9]    B. W. Boehm, *Software Engineering Economics*, Prentice Hall, Inc., Englewood Cliffs, NJ, USA, 1981.

[10]   B. W. Boehm, "A Spiral Model of Software Development and Enhancement", *ACM SIGSOFT Software Engineering Notes*, 11 (4), pp.22-42, Aug. 1986.

[11]   E. Brinksma, "A Theory for the Derivation of Tests", in *8th International Conference on Protocol Specification, Testing and Verification*, (Atlantic City), North-Holland, 1988.

[12]   T. S. Chow, "Testing Software Design Modeled by Finite-State Machines", *IEEE Transactions on Software Engineering*, SE-4 (3), pp.178-87, March 1978.

[13]   D. Craigen, S. Gerhart and T. Ralston, *On the Use of Formal Methods in Industry—An Authoritative Assessment of the Efficacy, Utility, and Applicability of Formal Methods to Systems Design and Engineering by the Analysis of Real Industrial Cases*, National Institute of Standards and Technology, Report, March 1993.

[14]   P. Dauchy, M.-C. Gaudel and B. Marre, "Using Algebraic Specifications in Software Testing: A Case Study on the Software of an Automatic Subway", *Journal of Systems and Software*, 21 (3), pp.229-44, 1993.

[15]  A. M. Davis, "A Comparison of Techniques for the Specification of External System Behavior", *Communications of the ACM*, 31 (9), pp.1098-115, September 1988.

[16]  R. A. DeMillo, W. M. McCracken, R. J. Martin and J. F. Passafiume, *Software Testing and Evaluation*, Benjamin/Cummings Publ. Co., Menlo Park, CA, USA, 1987.

[17]  R. A. DeMillo, R.J. Lipton and F. G. Sayward, "Hints on Test Data Selection: Help for the Practicing Programmer", *IEEE Computer Magazine*, 11 (4), pp.34-41, April 1978.

[18]  J. Dick and A. Faivre, "Automating the Generation and Sequencing of Test Cases from Model-based Specifications", in *FME'93 Symposium*, Lecture Notes on Computer Science, 670, pp.268-684, Springer-Verlag, 1993.

[19]  B. L. DiVito, R. W. Butler and J. L. Caldwell, "High Level Design Proof of a Reliable Computing Platform", in *2nd IFIP Int. Working Conf. on Dependable Computing for Critical Applications (DCCA-2)*, (J. F. Meyer and R. D. Schlichting, Eds.), (Tucson, AZ, USA), Tucson, AZ, USA,, 6, pp.279-306, 1991.

[20]  E. L. Duke, "V&V of Flight and Mission-Critical Software", *IEEE Software*, 6 (3), pp.39-45, May 1989.

[21]  J. W. Duran and S. C. Ntafos, "An Evaluation of Random Testing", *IEEE Transactions on Software Engineering*, SE-10 (4), pp.438-44, July 1984.

[22]  R. E. Fairley, "Tutorial: Static Analysis and Dynamic Testing of Computer Software", *IEEE Computer*, 11 (4), pp.14-23, April 1978.

[23]  P. G. Frankl and E. J. Weyuker, "Assessing the Fault-Dectability Ability of Testing Methods", *ACM Software Engineering Notes*, 16 (5), pp.77-91, December 1991.

[24]  S. Fujiwara, G. v. Bochman, F. Khendek, M. Amalou and A. Ghedamsi, "Test Selection Based on Finite State Models", *IEEE Transactions on Software Engineering*, 17 (6), pp.591-603, June 1991.

[25]  J. Gait, "A Debugger for Concurrent Programs", *Software — Practice and Experience*, 15 (6), pp.539-54, June 1985.

[26]  J. Gait, "A Probe Effect in Concurrent Programs", *Software — Practice and Experience*, 16 (3), pp.225-33, March 1986.

[27]  H. Ganzinger and R. Schäfers, "System Support for Modular Order-sorted Horn-Clause Specifications", in *12th IEEE-ACM International Conference on Software Engineering (ICSE-12)*, pp.150-9, 1990.

[28]  H. Garcia-Molina, F. Germano and W. H. Kohler, "Debugging a Distributed Computing System", *IEEE Transactions on Software Engineering*, SE-10 (2), pp.210-9, March 1984.

[29]  D. Garlan and N. Delisle, "Formal Specifications as Reusable Framework", in *VDM'90 Symposium*, Lecture Notes on Computer Science, 428, pp.150-63, Springer-Verlag, 1990.

[30]    S. J. Garland and J. V. Guttag, "Using LP to Debug Specifications", in *IFIP TC2 Working Conference on Programming Concepts and Methods,* (Sea of Gallilee, Israel), North-Holland, 1990.

[31]    M.-C. Gaudel, "Advantages and Limits of Formal Approaches for Ultra-High Dependability", in *6th IEEE International Workshop on Software Specification and Design (IWSSD 91),* pp.237-41, 1991.

[32]    M.-C. Gaudel, "Testing can be Formal too", in *TAPSOFT'95,* Lecture Notes on Computer Science, 915, pp.82-96, Springer-Verlag, 1995.

[33]    R. L. Glass, "Real-Time: The 'Lost World' of Software Debugging and Testing", *Communications of the ACM,* 23 (5), pp.264-71, May 1980.

[34]    J. Goguen, J. Tatcher and E. Wagner, *An Initial Algebra Approach to the Specification, Correctness, and Implementation of Abstract Data Types,* Current Trends in Programming Methodology, 4, Prenctice Hall, 1978.

[35]    H. Gomaa, "Software Development of Real-Time Systems", *Communications of the ACM,* 29 (7), pp.657-68, July 1986.

[36]    D. Gries, *The Science of Programming,* Springer-Verlag, 1981.

[37]    K. Grimm, "An Effective Strategy and Automation Concepts for Systematic Testing of Safety Related Software", in *Proc. IFAC SAFECOMP 89,* (Vienna, Austria), pp.71-9, 1989.

[38]    G. Guiho and C. Hennebert, "SACEM Software Validation", in *12th IEEE-ACM International Conference on Software Engineering (ICSE-12),* pp.186-91, 1990.

[39]    D. Hamlet and R. Taylor, "Partition Testing does not Inspire Confidence", *IEEE Transactions on Software Engineering,* SE-16 (12), pp.1402-11, December 1990.

[40]    R. Hamlet, "Theorical Comparison of Testing Methods", in *3rd IEEE Symposium on Software Testing, Analysis and Verification (TAV-3),* (Key West, USA), pp.28-37, 1989.

[41]    D. Harel, "Statecharts: a Visual Formalism for Complex Systems", *Science of Computer Programming,* 8 (3), pp.231-74, 1987.

[42]    D. Harel, H. Lachover, A. Naamad, A. Pnueli, M. Politi, R. Sherman, A. Shtull-Trauring and M. Trakhtenbrot, "STATEMATE: A Working Environment for the Development of Complex Reactive Systems", *IEEE Transactions on Software Engineering,* SE-16 (4), pp.403-14, April 1990.

[43]    B. Hetzel, *The Complete Guide to Software Testing,* QED Information Sciences, Wellesley, MA, USA, 1988.

[44]    W. E. Howden, *Functional Program Testing and Analysis,* McGraw-Hill, 1987.

[45]    *IEEE Standard Glossary of Software Engineering Terminology,* ANSI/IEEE Standard N°729-1983, 1983.

[46]   C. B. Jones, *Systematic Software Development Using VDM*, 2nd Edition, Prentice Hall International, 1990.

[47]   R. A. Kemmerer, "Testing Formal Specifications to Detect Design errors", *IEEE Transactions on Software Engineering*, SE-11 (1), pp.32-43, 1985.

[48]   H. Kopetz, "Fault Tolerance in Real-Time Systems", in *Proc. IFAC World Congress,* (Tallinn, USSR), pp.Vol. 7, 111-7, 1990.

[49]   H. Kopetz, A. Damm, C. Koza, M. Mulazzani, W. Schwabl, C. Senft and R. Zainlinger, "Distributed Fault-Tolerant Real-Time Systems: The MARS Approach", *IEEE Micro*, 9 (1), pp.25-40, Feb. 1989.

[50]   H. Kopetz, R. Zainlinger, G. Fohler, H. Kantz, P. Puschner and W. Schütz, "An Engineering Approach to Hard Real-Time System Design", in *Proc. Third European Software Engineering Conference (ESEC 91),* (Milano, Italy), pp.166-88, 1991.

[51]   B. Krieg-Brückner, "Algebraic Specifications and Functionals for Transformational Program and Meta Program Development", in *TAPSOFT'89,* Lecture Notes on Computer Science, 352, pp.36-59, Springer-Verlag, 1989.

[52]   I. Lakatos, *Proofs and Refutations, the Logic of Mathematical Discovery,* Cambridge University Press, 1976.

[53]   J.-C. Laprie, "Dependability: A Unifying Concept for Reliable Computing and Fault Tolerance", in *Dependability of Resilient Computers* (T. Anderson, Ed.), pp.1-28, BSP Professional Books, Oxford, U.K., 1989.

[54]   J.-C. Laprie (Ed.), *Dependability: Basic Concepts and Terminology,* Dependable Computing and Fault Tolerance, 5, Springer-Verlag, 1992.

[55]   B. Liskov and J. Guttag, "Chapter 10: Writing Formal Specifications", in *Abstraction and Specification in Program Development* MIT Press, Mc Graw-Hill, 1986.

[56]   B. Marre, "Toward Automatic Test Data Set Selection Using Algebraic Specifications and Logic Programming", in *8th Int. Conference on Logic Programming,* (Paris, France), pp.202-19, M.I.T. Press, 1991.

[57]   B. Marre, P. Thévenod-Fosse, H. Waeselynck, P. Le Gall and Y. Crouzet, "An Experimental Evaluation of Formal Testing and Statistical Testing", in *Proc. SAFECOMP'92,* (Zürich, Switzerland), pp.311-6, 1992.

[58]   C. Mazuet, *Stratégies de Test pour des Programmes Synchrones Application au Langage Lustre,* Doctoral Dissertation, Institut National Polytechnique de Toulouse, France, December 1994.

[59]   J. Mc Dermid, *On the Nature of Specification*, Unpublished paper, 1990.

[60]   J. Mc Dermid, "Formal Methods: Use and Relevance for the Development of Safety Critical Systems", in *Safety Aspects of Computer Control* (P. Bennet, Ed.), Butterworth/Heineman, 1991.

[61]   C. E. McDowell and D. P. Helmbold, "Debugging Concurrent Programs", *ACM Computing Surveys*, 21 (4), pp.593-622, Dec. 1989.

[62]   C. Morgan, *Programming from Specifications,* Prentice-Hall, 1990.

[63]   L. E. Moser and P. M. Melliar-Smith, "Formal Verification of Safety-Critical Systems", *Software Practice and Experience*, 20 (8), pp.799-821, 1990.

[64]   G. J. Myers, *The Art of Software Testing,* John Wiley and Sons, New York, 1979.

[65]   NASA, *Peer Review of a Formal Verification/design Proof Methodology*, NASA Conference Publication 2377, 1985.

[66]   P. G. Newmann, "Flaws in Specifications and what to do About them", in *IEEE International Workshop on Software Specification and Design (IWSSD-89)*, 1989.

[67]   S. C. Ntafos, "On Testing with Required Elements", in *Proc. COMPSAC'81*, pp.132-9, 1981.

[68]   T. J. Ostrand and M. J. Balcer, "The Category-Partition Method for Specifying and Generating Functional Tests", *Communications of the ACM*, 31 (6), pp.676-86, June 1988.

[69]   D. L. Parnas, A. J. v. Schouwen and S. P. Kwan, "Evaluation of Safety-Critical Software", *Communications of the ACM*, 33 (6), pp.636-48, June 1990.

[70]   H. Partsch, "From Informal Requirements to a Running Program: A Case Study in Algebraic Specification and Transformational Programming", *Science of Computer Programming*, 11 (3) 1989.

[71]   G. Pospischil, P. Puschner, A. Vrchoticky and R. Zainlinger, "Developing Real-Time Tasks with Predictable Timing", *IEEE Software*, 9 (5), pp.35-44, Sep. 1992.

[72]   V. Pratt, "Anatomy of the Pentium Bug", in *TAPSOFT'95*, Lecture Notes on Computer Science, 915, pp.97-107, Springer-Verlag, 1995.

[73]   S. Rapps and E. J. Weyuker, "Selecting Software Test Data Using Data Flow Information", *IEEE Transactions on Software Engineering*, SE-11 (4), pp.367-75, April 1985.

[74]   J. Rushby, *Formal Methods and the Certification of Critical Systems*, SRI International, CSL Technical Report, N°SRI-CS-93-07, November 1993.

[75]   J. Rushby and F. Von Henke, *Formal Verification of a Fault-Tolerant Clock Synchronization Algorithm*, NASA, Contractor Report, N°4239, June 1989.

[76]   R. G. Sargent, "Verification and Validation of Simulation Models", in *Progress in Modelling and Simulation* (F. E. Cellier, Ed.), pp.159-69, Academic Press, London, U.K., 1982.

[77]   E. Schoitsch, E. Dittrich, S. Grasegger, D. Kropfitsch, A. Erb, P. Fritz and H. Kopp, "The ELEKTRA Testbed: Architecture of a Real-Time Test

Environment for High Safety and Reliability Requirements", in *Proc. IFAC SAFECOMP 90,* (Gatwick, U.K.), pp.59-65, 1990.

[78]  W. Schütz, "Real-Time Simulation in the Distributed Real-Time System MARS", in *Proc. 1990 European Simulation Multiconference,* (Nürnberg, Germany), pp.51-7, 1990.

[79]  W. Schütz, "A Test Strategy for the Distributed Real-Time System MARS", in *Proc. IEEE CompEuro 90: Computer Systems and Software Engineering,* (Tel Aviv, Israel), pp.20-7, 1990.

[80]  W. Schütz, "On the Testability of Distributed Real-Time Systems", in *Proc. 10th Symposium on Reliable Distributed Systems,* (Pisa, Italy), pp.52-61, 1991.

[81]  W. Schütz, *The Testability of Distributed Real-Time Systems,* Kluwer Academic Publishers, Boston, MA, USA, 1993.

[82]  W. Schütz, "Fundamental Issues in Testing Distributed Real-Time Systems", *Real-Time Systems Journal,* 7 (2), pp.129-57, Sep. 1994.

[83]  I. Sommerville, *Software Engineering,* Addison-Wesley Publishing Co., Wokingham, England, U.K., 1989.

[84]  J. A. Stankovic, "Misconceptions about Real-Time Computing: A Serious Problem for Next-Generation Systems", *IEEE Computer,* 21 (10), pp.10-9, Oct. 1988.

[85]  J. A. Stankovic and K. Ramamritham, *IEEE Tutorial: Hard Real-Time Systems,* IEEE Computer Society Press, Washington, DC, USA, 1988.

[86]  P. Thévenod-Fosse, "Software Validation by Means of Statistical Testing: Retrospect and Future Direction", in *Dependable Computing for Critical Applications (Proc. 1st IFIP Int. Working Conference on Dependable Computing for Critical Applications: DCCA-1, Santa Barbara, CA, USA, August 1989)* (A. Avizienis and J.-C. Laprie, Eds.), Dependable Computing and Fault-Tolerant Systems, 4, (A. Avizienis, H. Kopetz and J.-C. Laprie, Eds.), pp.23-50, Springer-Verlag, Vienna, Austria, 1991.

[87]  P. Thévenod-Fosse, C. Mazuet and Y. Crouzet, "On Statistical Testing of Synchronous Data Flow Programs", in *Proc. 1st European Dependable Computing Conf. (EDCC-1),* (Berlin, Germany), pp.250-67, 1994.

[88]  P. Thévenod-Fosse and H. Waeselynck, "On Functional Statistical Testing Designed from Software Behavior Models", in *Dependable Computing for Critical Applications 3 (Proc. 3rd IFIP Int. Working Conference on Dependable Computing for Critical Applications: DCCA-3, Palermo, Italy, September 1993)* (C. E. Landwehr, B. Randell and L. Simoncini, Eds.), Dependable Computing and Fault-Tolerant Systems, 8, (A. Avizienis, H. Kopetz and J.-C. Laprie, Eds.), pp.3-28, Springer-Verlag, Vienna, Austria, 1993.

[89]  P. Thévenod-Fosse and H. Waeselynck, "Statemate Applied to Statistical Testing", in *Proc. Int. Symposium on Software Testing and Analysis (ISSTA'93),* (Cambridge, MA, USA), pp.99-109, 1993.

[90]   P. Thévenod-Fosse, H. Waeselynck and Y. Crouzet, "An Experimental Study of Software Structural Testing: Deterministic versus Random Input Generation", in *21st IEEE Symposium on Fault-Tolerant Computing (FTCS-21)*, (Montréal, Québec, Canada), pp.410-7, IEEE Computer Society Press, 1991.

[91]   P. Thévenod-Fosse, H. Waeselynck and Y. Crouzet, *Software Structural Testing: an Evaluation of the Efficiency of Deterministic and Random Test Data*, LAAS-CNRS, LAAS Report, N°91-389, 1991.

[92]   H. Ural, "Formal Methods for Test Sequence Generation", *Computer Communications*, 15 (5), pp.311-25, 1992.

[93]   N. Van Diepen and H. Partsch, "Formalizing Informal Requirements: some Aspects", in *METEOR Workshop: Algebraic Methods II,* Lecture Notes on Computer Science, 490, Springer-Verlag, 1989.

[94]   H. Waeselynck, *Vérification de Logiciels Critiques par le Test Statistique,* Doctoral Dissertation, Institut National Polytechnique de Toulouse, France, January 1993.

[95]   H. Waeselynck and P. Thévenod-Fosse, "An Experimentation with Statistical Testing", in *2nd European Int. Conference on Software Testing, Analysis and Review (EuroSTAR'94),* (Bruxelles, Belgium), p.10/1-10/14, 1994.

[96]   A. Wellings, "Editorial: Real-Time Software", *IEE Software Engineering Journal*, 6 (3), pp.66-7, May 1991.

[97]   E. J. Weyuker, "On Testing Non-Testable Programs", *The Computer Journal*, 25 (4), pp.465-70, 1982.

[98]   E. J. Weyuker and B. Jeng, "Analyzing Partition Testing Strategies", *IEEE Transactions on Software Engineering*, 17 (7), pp.703-11, July 1991.

[99]   E. J. Weyuker and T. J. Ostrand, "Theories of Program Testing and the Application of Revealing Subdomains", *IEEE Transactions on Software Engineering*, SE-9 (3), pp.236-46, May 1980.

[100]  T. Williams and K. Parker, "Design for Testability: A Survey", *IEEE Transactions on Computers*, 31 (1) 1982.

[101]  J. C. Woodcock, "Calculating Properties of Z Specifications", *ACM SIGSoft Software Engineering Notes*, 14 (5) 1989.

# Chapter V

# Fault Forecasting -
# Fault Injection

Fault injection is a method for testing the fault tolerance of a mechanism with respect to its own specific inputs: the faults. Fault injection is needed for two different purposes: to test the correct operation of the fault tolerance algorithms/mechanisms and to predict the dependability of the system in a realistic scenario where faults are expected to occur and have to be handled properly.

Fault injection can be applied either on a simulation model of the target fault-tolerant system or on the physical instantiation of the system. Simulation based fault injection can provide valuable early feedback about the proper operation of the planned fault tolerance mechanisms during the design process. However, as with any experiment on an abstract model of the real world, the difficult question to answer is whether the simulation model and the profile of the injected fault types are characteristic for the physical environment the system will have to operate in. Part of this problem even remains if fault injection is carried out on a physical prototype for the purpose of reliability prediction. What are the types of fault and what is their typical distribution in the intended application environment?

The first paper in this chapter "Integration and Comparison of Three Physical Fault Injection Techniques" presents the results of three different fault injection techniques on the same hardware/software target architecture. The three fault injection techniques are: heavy-ion radiation, pin-level injection, and electromagnetic interference (EMI). The target architecture is the MARS hardware/software implementation that has been developed in the context of the PDCS project at the Technical University of Vienna and which is described in chapter III of this book. The main goals of these experiments are the comparison of the three fault injection techniques by identifying the similarities and the differences in the error sets generated by each technique, and the evaluation of the error detection coverage provided by the MARS architecture. In addition, the fault injections carried out made it possible to study experimentally the respective effectiveness of the different hardware/software mechanisms implemented in a MARS node to support its fail-silent behaviour.

The second paper "Fault-Injection into VHDL Models: The MEFISTO Tool" presents the results of research aimed at (i) providing an integrated environment — called MEFISTO (Multi-level Error/Fault Injection Simulation Tool) — for applying fault injection into simulation models encompassing various levels of abstraction and thus (ii) helping to identify and validate an abstraction hierarchy of fault/error models. These goals and its wide use in the industrial and scientific community motivated the selection of VHDL as the simulation language to conduct this study. MEFISTO supports two classes of techniques (sabotaging and mutation) for injecting faults into VHDL models. A functional overview describing MEFISTO and the various functional phases of the realisation of a fault injection campaign are given. As an application, the results of a case study where MEFISTO is used to inject faults in two VHDL models (structural and behavioral) of a simplified 32-bit processor are presented. Abstract error models are extracted from the resulting data and compared.

The third paper "Estimators for Fault Tolerance Coverage Evaluation" investigates the problem of obtaining accurate and useful estimations of coverage through the statistical processing of observations collected during fault injection experiments in which physical faults are directly applied to the pins of the integrated circuits. The complexity of current VLSI chips and the need to take into account temporary faults, that represent the majority of the faults that could occur in a computer system, makes exhaustive testing intractable. As a consequence, coverage evaluation is a problem of statistical estimation, where inferences about a population are based on sample observation. Coverage is formally expressed as the weighted sum of the coverages of each point in the sample space, where the weight of a point is given by its relative probability of occurrence. Several sampling techniques are compared from the viewpoints of the precision that they procure in the estimation of overall system coverage and the testing effort required to obtain sufficiently precise results. Finally, by taking into account available structural information about the target system, it is shown that an *a posteriori* stratification technique based on equipotential groups can considerably improve the precision of the overall coverage estimation.

# Integration and Comparison of Three Physical Fault Injection Techniques

Johan Karlsson[1]     Peter Folkesson[1]     Jean Arlat[2]
Yves Crouzet[2]     Günther Leber[3]

[1]Chalmers University of Technology     [2]LAAS-CNRS
[3]Technical University of Vienna

**Abstract.** This paper describes and compares three physical fault injection techniques — heavy-ion radiation, pin-level injection, and electromagnetic interference — and their use in the validation of MARS, a fault-tolerant distributed real-time system. The main features of the injection techniques are first summarised and analysed, and then the MARS error detection mechanisms are described. The distributed testbed set-up and the common test scenario implemented to perform a coherent set of experiments by applying the three fault injection techniques are also described. The results are presented and discussed; special emphasis is put on the comparison of the specific impact of each technique.

## 1    Introduction

The dependability assessment of a fault-tolerant system is a complex task that requires the use of different levels of evaluation and related tools. Besides and in complement to other possible approaches such as proving or analytical modelling whose applicability and accuracy are significantly restricted in the case of complex fault-tolerant systems, *fault-injection* has been recognised to be particularly attractive and valuable. Indeed, by speeding up the occurrence of errors and failures, fault injection is in fact a method for *testing* the fault tolerance algorithms/mechanisms with respect to their own specific inputs: *the faults.*

Fault injection can be applied either on a simulation model of the target fault-tolerant system (e.g. [20, 28]) or on a hardware-and-software implementation (e.g. [3, 53]).

Clearly simulation-based fault injection is desirable as it can provide early checks in the design process of fault tolerance algorithms/mechanisms. Nevertheless, it is worth noting that fault injection on a prototype featuring the actual interactions between the hardware and software dimensions of the fault tolerance algorithms/mechanisms supplies a more realistic and necessary complement to validate their implementation in a fault-tolerant system. Until recently, most studies related to the application of fault injection on a prototype of a fault-tolerant system relied on physical fault injection, i.e. the introduction of faults through the hardware layer of the target system [48, 22, 3]. A trend favouring the injection of errors through the software layer for simulating physical faults (i.e. software-implemented fault injection) has recently emerged (e.g. see [49, 31]). Although such an approach facilitates the application of fault injection, the correspondence between the types of errors that can be injected this way, and the actual faults is not yet confidently established. In spite of the difficulties in developing support environments and realising experiments, physical fault injection enables real faults to be injected in a very close representation of the target system without any alteration to the software being executed.

Among the large number of experiments reported concerning physical fault injection, all used widely different techniques and/or were applied to distinct target systems. This significantly hampers the possibility to identify the difficulties/benefits associated to each fault injection technique and to analyse the results obtained.

This study relies on two major objectives. The first one is to get a better understanding of the impact and features of the three physical fault injection techniques that are considered and in which the sites have gained expertise in developing and applying dedicated experimental tools or in using standard support environments, respectively: heavy-ion radiation, pin-level injection and electromagnetic interferences (EMI). The distributed fault-tolerant system architecture MARS (see paper III.H) developed by TU-Vienna is being used as the target system to carry out these experiments. Thus, the other driving objective is to evaluate the coverage of the built-in fault-tolerance features of the MARS system. A distributed testbed architecture featuring five MARS nodes and a common test scenario have been implemented at all three sites to perform a coherent set of experiments.

The remaining part of this paper is decomposed into six sections. Section 2 presents and compares the main features of the fault injection techniques considered. The error detection mechanisms of the target system MARS, are described in Section 3. Section 4 defines the approach considered for the experimental evaluation and the predicates characterising the behaviour of the target system in the presence of injected faults. Section 5 depicts the common testbed set-up being used by all sites to carry out the experiments. The results are presented and discussed in Section 6. Finally, concluding remarks are provided in Section 7.

## 2    The Fault Injection Techniques

In this section, we first briefly describe the three fault injection techniques, and then provide a comparison of the main features of these techniques. Note that the pin-level and heavy-ion techniques have been largely reported in the literature, while the EMI technique has not previously been used for evaluation of error detection mechanisms.

### 2.1 Heavy-Ion Radiation

Heavy-ion radiation from a Californium-252 source can be used to inject *single event upsets*, i.e. bit flips at internal locations in integrated circuits. The heavy-ion method has been used to evaluate several hardware- and software-implemented error detection mechanisms for the MC6809E microprocessor [22, 40]. The irradiation of the target circuit must be performed in a vacuum as heavy-ions are attenuated by air molecules and other materials. Consequently, the packaging material that cover the target chip must also be removed. In these experiments, a miniature vacuum chamber containing the target circuit and the Cf-252 source was used. A comprehensive description of the heavy-ion fault injection technique and of the supporting tools is given in [32].

A major feature of the heavy-ion fault injection technique is that faults can be injected into VLSI circuits at locations which are impossible to reach by other techniques such as pin-level and software-implemented fault injection. The faults are also reasonably well spread within a circuit, as there are many sensitive memory elements in most VLSI circuits. Thereby, the injected faults generate a variety of error patterns which allows a thorough testing of fault handling mechanisms.

## 2.2 Pin-Level Injection

Pin-level fault injection, i.e. the injection of faults directly on the pins of the ICs of a prototype was until now the most widely applied physical fault injection technique. It has been used for (i) the evaluation of the coverage of specific mechanisms (in particular for error detection by means of signature analysis [48], and (ii) the validation of fault-tolerant distributed systems (e.g. [15, 53]). Flexible tools supporting some general features have been developed (e.g. the test facility used on the FTMP [36], MESSALINE at LAAS-CNRS [3] or RIFLE [37] at the University of Coimbra). The tool MESSALINE that will be used in these experiments is a flexible tool capable of adapting easily to various target systems and to different measures. It supports two implementations of pin-level fault injection:

- *forcing*, where the fault is directly applied by means of multi-pin probes on IC(s) pin(s) and associated equipotential line(s),
- *insertion*, where the IC(s) under test is(are) removed from the target system and inserted on a specific box where transistor switches ensure the proper isolation of the IC(s) under test from the system.

The fault models supported are stuck-at (0 or 1). Temporary faults can be injected on the pins of the ICs to simulate the consequences of such faults on the pins of the faulted IC(s).

## 2.3 EMI

An important class of computer failures are those caused by electro-magnetic interference (EMI). Such disturbances are common, for example, in motor cars, trains and industrial plants. Consequently, we decided to investigate the use of EMI for the evaluation of the MARS system. The fault injector used in the experiments generates bursts conforming to IEC 801-4 standard (CEI/IEC), i.e. the duration of the bursts is 15 ms, the period is 300 ms, the frequency is 1.25, 2.5, 5, or 10 kHz, and the voltage may be selected from 225 V to 4400 V (see Fig.1). These bursts are similar to those, which arise when switching inductive loads with relays or mechanical circuit-breakers.

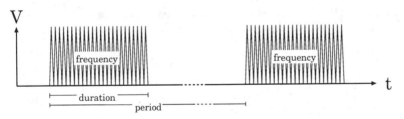

**Fig. 1.** Electro-magnetic bursts

The faults were injected into the target system, which consisted of a single computer board, in two different ways (see Fig.2). In the first way, the computer board was placed between two conducting plates connected to the burst generator. The second way was to use a special probe that could expose a smaller part of the board to the disturbances. In order to direct the faults to specific parts of the computer board, such a the CPU buses, small pieces of wire functioning as antennas were connected to the pins of specific ICs. The antennas were used with both the probe and the plates. In addition, experiments were also conducted using the probe without the antennas.

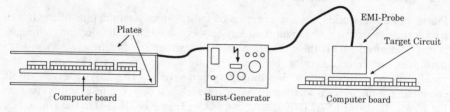

**Fig. 2.** Coupling of EMIs

## 2.4 Comparison of the Fault Injection Techniques

This section presents a comparison of the three fault injection techniques taking into account their fundamental and practical limitations. The comparison is based on five attributes describing the characteristics of the fault injection techniques: *controllability*, with respect to *space* and *time*, *flexibility*, *repeatability* and *physical reachability* and the possibility for *timing measurement* (e.g. error detection latency).

A characterisation of the fault injection techniques based on these attributes is shown in Table 1 and explained below. For each attribute, the fault injection techniques are graded on the scale *none*, *low*, *medium* and *high*. Note that this comparison does not consider the actual impact of the injected faults, i.e. the type of errors that are produced.

**Table 1.** Characterisation of fault injection methods

| Attributes | Heavy-ion | Pin-level | EMI |
|---|---|---|---|
| Controllability, space | low | high | low |
| Controllability, time | none | high/medium | low |
| Flexibility | low | medium | high |
| Reproducibility | medium | high | low |
| Physical reachability | high | medium | medium |
| Timing measurement | medium | high | low |

**Controllability.** We consider controllability with respect to both the *space* and *time* domains. (The space domain corresponds to controlling *where* faults are injected, while the time domain corresponds to controlling *when* faults are injected.)

*Heavy-ion radiation* has low controllability for the space domain. Faults are confined to the irradiated circuit. Faults can also be confined to specific blocks of a circuit, if the rest of the circuit is shielded. However, shielding will not be used in this study. The time of the injection of a fault cannot be controlled as the decay of the Cf-252 source is governed by a random process.

*Pin-level fault injection* has high controllability in both the space and time domain. However, timing controllability may be hampered by the problem of synchronising the fault injection with the activity of the system, especially when the clock frequency of the target system is high.

*EMI fault injection* has low controllability in the space domain because faults may be injected in circuits surrounding the target circuit. The time of injection can be synchronised with system activity, but it is difficult to determine exactly when a fault is injected.

**Flexibility.** Flexibility here refers to the possibility and ease of changing the target circuit in an experimental set-up.

*Heavy-ion radiation* has rather low flexibility as the preparation for each IC type involves several steps including mechanical and electrical adaptation between the target system and the miniature vacuum chamber, and opening of the circuit package. Because of the effort involved in the preparations, heavy-ion experiments are typically conducted only for a few highly integrated key components in a system.

*Pin-level fault injection* can achieve a high degree of flexibility provided a comprehensive fault injection tool, such as MESSALINE, is used. However, flexibility may be restricted by the difficulty to physically access the pins of modern IC packages, and problems caused by the extra load capacitances introduced by the connection probes.

*EMI fault injection* has high flexibility as there is no physical connection between the target circuit and the EMI fault injector.

**Reproducibility.** Reproducibility refers to the ability to reproduce results statistically for a given set-up and/or repeat individual fault injections exactly. Statistical reproducibility of results is an absolute requirement to ensure the credibility of fault injection experiments. The possibility to repeat experiments exactly, or at least with a very high degree of accuracy, is highly desirable, particularly when the aim of the experiments is to remove potential design/implementations faults in the fault tolerance mechanisms.

*Heavy-ion radiation* experiments cannot be repeated exactly due to the lack of controllability. The experiments conducted in this study showed that results are statistically reproducible among different specimens of the target circuits.

For *pin-level fault injection* it is possible to accurately reproduce the injection of a selected fault with MESSALINE. However, although reproducing an experiment is not a major problem for a centralised control automaton, this is not always achievable in the case of a distributed architecture.

The experiments carried out in this study show that statistical reproducibility is difficult to obtain for *EMI fault injection* experiments (see Section 6.3).

**Physical reachability.** Physical reachability is the ability to reach possible fault locations (nodes) in a system.

*Heavy-ion radiation* has high physical reachability as faults are injected at internal locations of ICs.

*Pin-level fault injection* has varying physical reachability depending on the level of integration for the target system. Physical reachability is low for highly integrated systems consisting only of a few VLSI circuits. For the MARS system, which uses a mixture of VLSI, LSI, MSI and SSI circuits, physical reachability is rather high.

*EMI fault injection* has similar physical reachability as pin-level injection as most faults probably are injected via digital input/output signals. However, faults may also occur internally in ICs as a result of disturbances propagated through the power supply lines.

**Timing measurement.** The acquisition of timing information associated to the monitored events (e.g. measurement of error detection latency) is an important outcome from fault injection experiments.

For *heavy-ion radiation* such measurements rely on the use of the golden chip technique. This requires that the target IC is operated synchronously with a reference IC. However, this may not be possible for ICs with non-deterministic external behaviour (caused, for example, by a varying number of wait states cycles inserted during memory accesses).

For *pin-level injection*, the time of the injection of a fault is explicitly known, thus, latency measurements does not pose a problem.

For *EMI fault injection*, latency measurements are difficult. In principle, the golden chip techniques could be used also in this case. However, a major problem is to confine the disturbances to the target circuit.

# 3   Error Detection Mechanisms of the MARS System

Three levels of error detection mechanisms (EDMs) are implemented in the MARS nodes: (i) the hardware EDMs, (ii) the system software EDMs implemented in the operating system [33, 45, 46] and support software (i.e. the Modula/R compiler [52]), and (iii) the application level EDMs at the highest level. The MARS nodes consist of two computers: the communication unit and the application unit. Both units use the 68070 CPU from Philips [42]. The error detection mechanisms provide the fail-silence property of the MARS nodes (see paper III.H). These mechanisms are described in the following subsections.

## 3.1   Hardware EDMs

Whenever an error is detected by one of the hardware EDMs, in general, an exception is raised and the CPU will then wait for a reset issued by a watchdog timer. This watchdog timer is the only device, which may cause a reset of all devices including the CPU.

Two categories of hardware EDMs can be distinguished: the mechanisms provided by the CPU and those provided by special hardware on the processing board. In addition, faults can also trigger unexpected exceptions (UEE) (i.e. neither the EDMs built into the CPU nor the mechanisms provided by special hardware are mapped to these exceptions).

The EDMs built into the CPU are: bus error, address error, illegal op-code, privilege violation, division by zero, stack format error, uninitialized vector interrupt and spurious interrupt. These errors cause the processor to jump to the appropriate exception handling routines, which save the error state to a non volatile memory and then restart the node. Upon restart, a detailed error description is written to a serial port.

The following errors are detected by mechanisms implemented by special hardware on the node: silent shutdown of the CPU of the communication unit, power failure, parity error, FIFO over/underflow, access to physically non-existing memory, write access to the real-time network at an illegal point in time, error of an external device and error of the other unit. We call these mechanisms NMI mechanisms, as they raise a Non-Maskable Interrupt when an error is detected.

An NMI leads to the same exception handling as the error detection mechanisms built into the CPU and can only be cleared by resetting the node, which is done by the watchdog timer.

## 3.2  System Software EDMs

The EDMs implemented by system software include mechanisms produced by the compiler (i.e. Compiler Generated Run-Time Assertions, CGRTA): value range overflow of a variable and loop iteration bound overflow.

The others are built into the operating system as assertions or as integrity checks on data: processing time overflow; various checks on data, done by the operating system; and various assertions coded into the operating system.

When an error is detected by any of these mechanisms, a trap instruction is executed, which leads to a node restart.

## 3.3  Application Level EDMs

The application level EDMs include end-to-end checksums for message data and double execution of tasks. The end-to-end checksums are used to detect mutilation of message data and is therefore used for implementing the *extended fail-silence property* of the nodes, i.e. the node is also considered to be fail-silent even when a corrupted message is sent, if the receiver detects the error and discards the message. Double execution of tasks in time redundancy can detect errors caused by transient faults that cause different output data of the two instances of the task. Combined with the concept of message checksums, task execution in time redundancy forms the highest level in the hierarchy of the error detection mechanisms. These mechanisms also trigger the execution of a trap instruction, which causes a reset of the node.

## 4    Measurements

The fail silence property of a MARS node when subjected to faults will be assessed by means of fault injection campaigns using each of the techniques described in Section 2. In this section, we first provide an overview of the method supporting the experimental assessment, then we precisely define the predicates considered to perform the analyses. The common testbed set-up implemented for carrying out the fault injection experiments with the three techniques will be described in Section 5.

## 4.1  Experimental Assessment

Each campaign consists of several experiment runs. During each experiment a fault is injected into one node (node under test), another node (golden node) will serve as a reference and a third node (comparator node) is used to compare the messages sent by the two previous nodes. Fault injection takes place until the node is declared to be failed by the comparator node. Then this node is shut down by the comparator node to clear all error conditions for the new experiment run. After some time, power is reinstalled and the node under test is reloaded for the next experiment run.

The assessment of the fail-silence property of a MARS node included in the MARS architecture is obtained by monitoring the error detection information provided by EDMs of the injected node or by means of message checksums at a receiving node. Several combinations of enabled/disabled EDMs will be analysed to study selectively their impact on the fail silence property.

Although these measurements provide very valuable inputs for assessing the fail silence coverage of a MARS node, it is worth noting that estimating the 'real' coverage of the EDMs is a much more difficult task. The reason is that the real fault set usually is not known in detail, and even less is known about the probability of occurrence of the individual faults. In principle, an estimate of the 'real' coverage can be calculated as a weighted mean of the coverage factors obtained by different fault injection methods (e.g. see paper V.C). However, the lack of knowledge about the 'real' faults makes it very difficult—and in many practical cases impossible—to calculate the weight factors.

Each fault injection technique used here should therefore be considered strictly as a 'benchmark' method that can be used to evaluate the relative effectiveness of different EDMs. Combining several fault injection techniques improves the possibility to investigate coverage sensitivity with respect to changes in the error set.

## 4.2  Predicates

Four failure types can be distinguished for the node under test:
1)  The node's EDMs detect an error and the node stops sending messages on the MARS bus; in this case the node stores the error condition into a non-volatile memory and resets itself by means of the watchdog timer.
2)  The node fails to deliver the expected application message(s) for one or several application cycles, but no error is detected by the node's EDMs.
3)  The node delivers a syntactically correct message with erroneous content. This is a fail-silence violation in the value domain, which is recognised as a mismatch between the messages sent by the node under test and the golden node.
4)  The node sends a message at an illegal point in time, and thus disturbs the traffic on the MARS bus. This is a fail-silence violation in the time domain.

On every restart the node under test writes its previously saved error data, if available (i.e. if an error was detected by the node's EDMs), and data about its state to two serial ports, where it can be read and stored for further processing. From these data, the following predicates (events) can be derived:

Coldstart (*CS*): Coldstart (power on) of the node under test is made after every experiment run, except when a system failure occurred.

Warmstart (*WS*): Warmstart (reset) of the node under test caused by the detection of (i) an error by the node's EDMs (*Internal WS*) or, (ii) an incoming or outgoing link failure by means of the top layer of the fault-tolerance mechanism, i.e. the membership protocol [34] (*External WS*).

Message loss (*ML*): One message (or more) from the node under test was lost (i.e. not received by the comparator node).

Message mismatch (*MM*): Reception by the comparator node of differing messages from golden node and tested node.

System Failure (*SF*): Failure of either the golden, data generation, or comparator nodes.

A *CS* predicate characterises the end of each data set. The next four predicates characterise four failure types. The assertion (occurrence) of the *WS* predicate in the data corresponds to the normal case when the node under test detects the error (failure type 1). The assertion of *ML* corresponds to a message loss failure (failure type 2); this behaviour is not a fail-silence violation, because no erroneous data is sent, but it cannot be regarded as normal operation. Irrespective of the other events, the assertion of *MM* (failure type 3) corresponds to a fail silence violation (in the data domain). There are two ways in which an *SF* failure may occur: (i) a fail silence violation in the time domain (failure type 4) affect the operation of the other nodes, or (ii) another node than the node under test experience a real hardware failure during the experiments. (Although, no *SF* failures were observed in the experiments, this failure type is described for the sake of completeness.)

Given the above failure types, the number of fail-silence violations can be counted as:

$$\# \ FS \ Viol. = \# \ Exp. \supseteq MM + \# \ Exp. \supseteq SF$$

where $\# \ Exp. \supseteq X$ counts the number of experiments where a $X$-type failure was diagnosed (i.e. predicate $X$ was asserted).

# 5    Common Experimental Set-up

The experimental set-up used by all sites consists of five MARS nodes and is similar to the one used in [16]. The workload is a realistic control application.

## 5.1  Test Application

As error detection coverage is highly dependent on the system activity, it is important to use a realistic workload in fault injection experiments. We selected a typical real-time application—a control problem—as workload in the MARS experiments. The control problem was taken from the rolling ball experiment [35] in which a ball is kept rolling along a circular path on a tiltable plane by controlling the two horizontal axes of the plane by servo motors and observing the position of the ball with a video camera. The tiltable plane and the camera are not present in our set-up; instead, the data from the camera is simulated by a data generation task. An additional task was provided, which compares the results of the two actively redundant computing nodes, both of which execute the control task.

The application executed during the fault injection experiments basically consists of three tasks (see also Fig.3):
1) The *data generation task* generates the input data for the control task. The input data include the nominal and actual values of the position, speed and acceleration of the ball.
2) The *control task*, which does not preserve any data or state information between its periodic executions, receives the emulated data from the data generation task and performs calculations on these data, i.e. calculates the desired acceleration for the ball.
3) The *comparator task* receives the results delivered by the two nodes that run the control-task in active redundancy, and compares them. This task also gives status information about the experiment, and assists in controlling a fault injection

device (i.e. it indicates when fault injection may take place) and the power supply
of the node under test.

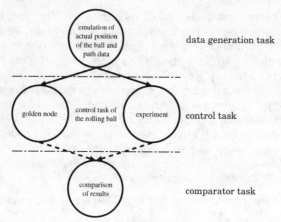

data generation task

control task

comparator task

**Fig. 3.** Tasks and message flow

The entire application has a period of 40 ms, i.e. all application tasks are started
every 40 ms and hence produce a result in the same time interval. The application
software is written in Modula/R [52] a Modula-2 like programming language with
real-time support for MARS.

## 5.2  Hardware Configuration

For the experiments five MARS nodes are needed (see Fig. 4). One serves as a
gateway between the department's local area network and the MARS-bus and is
required for loading the entire application and for reloading the node under test.
Another node is used for emulating input data (i.e. running the data generation task)
for the control task. This task is performed on two actively working redundant nodes,
one of which serves as a *golden node*, the other one is subjected to fault injection.
The fifth node is used for checking the output of the two nodes performing the test
task (i.e. running the comparator task). Further a host computer is used, which is
controlling the experiments, i.e. reloading failed nodes and collecting data from the
experiment for further analysis.

This experimental set-up is based on the assumption that the nodes are *replica
determinate*, i.e. two replicated nodes produce always the same results if provided with
the same input data. The MARS architecture supports this property.

## 5.3  Detailed Operation of the Experimental Set-up

Fig. 4 describes the detailed set-up architecture and identifies the interactions with the
fault injector devices. In the case of heavy-ion (HI), the target circuit is inserted in a
miniature vacuum chamber containing a Cf-252 source; radiation can be controlled by
an electrically manoeuvred shutter [32]. For pin-level injection, the pin-forcing (PF)
technique is used; thus, the injection probe is directly connected to the pins of the
target IC [3]. For EMI, both the technique using the two plates and the probe was
used for the injections.

The experiments are controlled by the comparator MARS node and a UNIX workstation. The workstation is also responsible for data collection. When the comparator node detects an error (error type ML or MM, see Section 4.2), it reports the error type to the workstation and turns off the power to the node under test with the signal AL 6. Signal AL 7 is used to discontinue fault injection (e.g. by closing the shutter mechanism of the vacuum chamber in the case of HI). Then the node under test is powered-up again and restarted. Upon restart, the application unit and the communication unit in the node under test send error data to the workstation via two serial lines. (If the error is not detected by the node under test itself, then the node has no error information available and sends only a status message). Once the node under test has been restarted, the workstation immediately starts to download the application. When the application has been restarted, the comparator node enables fault injection (signal AL 7) and a new experiment begins.

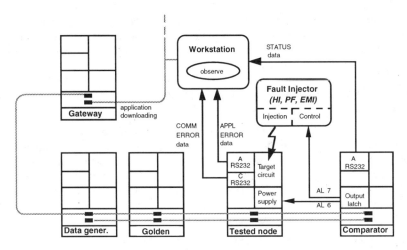

**Fig. 4.** Detailed set-up architecture

# 6 Results

The goal for the comparison of the fault injection techniques is to identify similarities and differences in the error sets generated by the three techniques. If the error sets are found to be disjoint, the fault injection techniques can be judged as fully complementary. In this case, applying all three techniques in the validation of a fault-tolerant system would improve the confidence of the validation results. In our case, the error sets were observed indirectly via the distribution of error detections among the various EDMs. To achieve as much similarity as possible among the error sets, faults were only injected inside, on the pins, or in the vicinity of either the application CPU or the communication CPU of the node under test.

Three different combinations of the application level EDMs have been evaluated for the three fault injection techniques considered. We use the following acronyms for these combinations: NOAM (no application level mechanisms, i.e. single execution and no checksums), SEMC (single execution, message checksums), DEMC (double execution, message checksums), see also Table 2. In addition a fourth combination,

TEMC (triple execution, message checksums), was used in the heavy-ion experiments (see Section 6.1).

**Table 2.** Experimental combinations

| Comb. no. | Execution | Message Checksum | Acronym |
|-----------|-----------|------------------|---------|
| 1 | Single | No | NOAM |
| 2 | Single | Yes | SEMC |
| 3 | Double | Yes | DEMC |
| 4 | Triple | Yes | TEMC |

In the following paragraphs, we present in sequence the results obtained by the application of each technique. Then, these results are analysed and compared in a subsequent paragraph.

## 6.1  Heavy-Ion Radiation

Two circuits in the node under test were irradiated in separate experiments: the CPU of the application unit and the CPU of the communication unit. The irradiation was performed using a miniature vacuum chamber containing the irradiated circuit and a Cf-252 source (nominal activity 37 kBq); the distance between the source and the IC was approximately 35 mm. The IC's pin connections extended through the bottom plate of the miniature vacuum chamber, so that the chamber could be plugged directly into the socket of the irradiated IC in the MARS system.

Because the irradiated ICs were CMOS circuits, they had to be protected from heavy-ion induced latch-up. A latch-up is the triggering of a parasitic four layer switch (npnp or pnpn) acting as a silicon controlled rectifier (SCR), which may destroy the circuit due to excessive heat dissipation. The triggering of a latch-up is indicated by a drastic increase in the current drawn by the circuit. To prevent latch-ups from causing permanent damage to the ICs, a special device was used to turn off the power to the ICs when the current exceeded a threshold value.

Table 3 shows the distribution of error detections among the various EDMs for each of the irradiated CPUs, and the four combinations given in Table 2. The "Other" category in Table 3-a shows those errors for which no error information was given by the unit which contained the fault injected circuit. Error information was instead given by the other (fault free) unit of the tested node for some of these errors ("Other unit" category). This error information is detailed in Table 3-b. The "No error info." category gives the number of errors for which none of the two units produced error information.

The hardware EDMs, in particular the CPU mechanisms, detected most of the errors. This is not surprising since the faults were injected into the CPU. The proportion of errors detected by the hardware EDMs is larger for faults injected into the communication CPU than for faults injected into the application CPU. In particular, the coverage of the NMI EDMs is higher in the former case. Unexpected exceptions occur with a frequency of about 15% in all combinations.

Errors detected by the OS EDMs dominate for the software EDMs, and for Level 3 EDMs, the message checksum EDMs dominate.

The percentage of fail silence violations was between 2.4% and 0.5% for the NOAM, SEMC and DEMC combinations when faults were injected into the application CPU.

As expected, the number of fail silence violations is lower for SEMC than for NOAM, and even lower for DEMC. When faults were injected into the communication CPU, only one fail silence violation was observed (for NOAM).

**Table 3.** Results for heavy-ion radiation

| Error Detection Mechanisms | | application unit CPU irradiated | | | | | | | | communication unit CPU irradiated | | | | | |
|---|---|---|---|---|---|---|---|---|---|---|---|---|---|---|---|
| | | NOAM | | SEMC | | DEMC | | TEMC | | NOAM | | SEMC | | DEMC | |
| | | Errors | % | Errors | % | Errors | % | Errors | % | Errors | % | Errors | % | Errors | % |
| Level 1 Hardware | CPU | 3735 | 47.7% | 1410 | 49.0% | 4280 | 47.4% | 2573 | 51.3% | 1113 | 44.9% | 1270 | 43.2% | 1056 | 43.3% |
| | UEE | 1173 | 15.0% | 459 | 16.0% | 1373 | 15.2% | 736 | 14.7% | 361 | 14.6% | 416 | 14.1% | 326 | 13.4% |
| | NMI | 549 | 7.0% | 173 | 6.0% | 570 | 6.3% | 286 | 5.7% | 500 | 20.2% | 578 | 19.6% | 484 | 19.9% |
| | *Subtotal* | *5457* | *69.7%* | *2042* | *71.0%* | *6223* | *68.9%* | *3595* | *71.7%* | *1974* | *79.6%* | *2264* | *76.9%* | *1866* | *76.6%* |
| Level 2 Software | OS | 610 | 7.8% | 222 | 7.7% | 687 | 7.6% | 273 | 5.4% | 90 | 3.6% | 144 | 4.9% | 128 | 5.3% |
| | CGRTA | 75 | 1.0% | 3 | 0.1% | 30 | 0.3% | 37 | 0.7% | 10 | 0.4% | 7 | 0.2% | 13 | 0.5% |
| | *Subtotal* | *685* | *8.8%* | *225* | *7.8%* | *717* | *7.9%* | *310* | *6.2%* | *100* | *4.0%* | *151* | *5.1%* | *141* | *5.8%* |
| Level 3 Appl. level | Double exec. | — | — | — | — | 75 | 0.8% | 56 | 1.1% | — | — | — | — | 11 | 0.5% |
| | Checksum | — | — | 70 | 2.4% | 247 | 2.7% | 231 | 4.6% | — | — | 48 | 1.6% | 75 | 3.1% |
| | *Subtotal* | *—* | *—* | *70* | *2.4%* | *322* | *3.6%* | *287* | *5.7%* | *—* | *—* | *48* | *1.6%* | *86* | *3.5%* |
| Other | Other unit | 1095 | 14.0% | 381 | 13.2% | 1295 | 14.3% | 566 | 11.3% | 342 | 13.8% | 407 | 13.8% | 293 | 12.0% |
| | No error info. | 402 | 5.1% | 122 | 4.2% | 431 | 4.8% | 216 | 4.3% | 62 | 2.5% | 73 | 2.5% | 51 | 2.1% |
| | *Subtotal* | *1497* | *19.1%* | *503* | *17.5%* | *1726* | *19.1%* | *782* | *15.6%* | *404* | *16.3%* | *480* | *16.3%* | *344* | *14.1%* |
| Triple execution | | — | — | — | — | — | — | 42 | 0.8% | — | — | — | — | — | — |
| Fail silence violations | | 186 | 2.4% | 37 | 1.3% | 48 | 0.5% | 0 | 0% | 1 | <0.1% | 0 | 0% | 0 | 0% |
| *Total no. of errors* | | *7825* | *100%* | *2877* | *100%* | *9036* | *100%* | *5016* | *100%* | *2479* | *100%* | *2943* | *100%* | *2437* | *100%* |

(a) Detection by the EDMs of the unit to which the faulted ICs belong

| Error Detection Mechanisms | | application unit CPU irradiated | | | | | | | | communication unit CPU irradiated | | | | | |
|---|---|---|---|---|---|---|---|---|---|---|---|---|---|---|---|
| | | NOAM | | SEMC | | DEMC | | TEMC | | NOAM | | SEMC | | DEMC | |
| | | Errors | % | Errors | % | Errors | % | Errors | % | Errors | % | Errors | % | Errors | % |
| Level 1 Hardware | CPU | 0 | 0% | 0 | 0% | 0 | 0% | 0 | 0% | 0 | 0% | 0 | 0% | 0 | 0% |
| | UEE | 3 | <0.1% | 2 | 0.1% | 0 | 0% | 3 | 0.1% | 0 | 0% | 0 | 0% | 1 | <0.1% |
| | NMI | 199 | 2.5% | 58 | 2.0% | 243 | 2.7% | 103 | 2.1% | 118 | 4.7% | 147 | 5.0% | 103 | 4.2% |
| | *Subtotal* | *202* | *2.6%* | *60* | *2.1%* | *243* | *2.7%* | *106* | *2.1%* | *118* | *4.7%* | *147* | *5.0%* | *104* | *4.3%* |
| Level 2 Software | OS | 893 | 11.4% | 321 | 11.2% | 1052 | 11.6% | 460 | 9.2% | 224 | 8.9% | 260 | 8.8% | 189 | 7.8% |
| | CGRTA | 0 | 0% | 0 | 0% | 0 | 0% | 0 | 0% | 0 | 0% | 0 | 0% | 0 | 0% |
| | *Subtotal* | *893* | *11.4%* | *321* | *11.2%* | *1052* | *11.6%* | *460* | *0.2%* | *224* | *8.9%* | *260* | *8.8%* | *189* | *7.8%* |
| Level 3 Appl. level | Double exec. | — | — | — | — | 0 | 0% | 0 | 0% | — | — | — | — | 0 | 0% |
| | Checksum | — | — | 0 | 0% | 0 | 0% | 0 | 0% | — | — | 0 | 0% | 0 | 0% |
| | *Subtotal* | *—* | *—* | *0* | *0%* | *0* | *0%* | *0* | *0%* | *—* | *—* | *0* | *0%* | *0* | *0%* |

(b) Detection by the EDMs of the other unit (detail of "Other unit" entry in Table (a) above)

The observation of fail-silence violations for the DEMC combination was unexpected. In principle, all effects of transient faults should be masked by the double execution of tasks. One hypothesis for explaining these violations is that an undetected latch-up caused the same incorrect result to be produced by both executions of the control task.

To further investigate this hypothesis, experiments were carried out with the TEMC combination that used a third time redundant execution of the control task which was provided with fixed input data for which the results were known. This made it possible to detect errors by comparing the produced results with the correct results. This mechanism, which can be viewed as an on-line test program, would detect any semi-permanent fault such as the one suggested by the latch-up hypothesis.

The results show that no fail-silence violations occurred for the TEMC combination. As Table 3-a shows, 0.8% of the errors were detected by the third execution of the control task. This result supports the latch-up hypothesis. However, our experimental set-up does not provide sufficient observability to fully prove the latch-up hypothesis. In principle, the absence of fail-silence violations may merely be an effect of the change of the software configuration caused by the switch from DEMC to TEMC, and the errors detected by the third execution may have been caused by regular transients. Verification of the latch-up hypothesis, would require the use of a logic analyser so that the program flow and behaviour of the microprocessor could be studied in detail.

The OS and NMI EDMs dominate the detections made by the other unit of the tested node. The communication between the two units are done via two FIFO buffers, and nearly all of these detections are made by EDMs signalling empty FIFO. (An empty FIFO can be detected both by the operating system and the special NMI mechanism.)

## 6.2 Pin-Level Injection

The forcing technique was used for the fault injection experiments carried out on the MARS system. The main characteristics of the injected faults are listed hereafter:

- one single IC was fault injected at a time (the maximum number of pins faulted simultaneously — i.e. the multiplicity of the fault — being limited to $mx = 3$),
- uniform distribution over all combination of $mx$ pins was used to select the $mx$ faulted pins,
- stuck-at-0 and -1 fault models (all 0-1 combinations of $mx$ pins considered equally probable),
- to facilitate the comparison with the other techniques, both transient and intermittent (series of transients) faults were injected.

As the pin-forcing technique is being used, it can be confidently considered that all pins of the ICs connected to an injected pin are tested as well. Accordingly, in the set of experiments conducted to date, to simplify the accessibility to the pins of the microprocessors of the application and communication units, the target ICs were mainly buffer ICs connected to them. Seven ICs (5 on the application unit and 2 on the communication unit) were tested. These tests resulted in a total of 3,266 error reports.

Table 4 shows the distribution of the errors detected by the various EDMs for the tested ICs of the tested node for three combinations of the application-level EDMs, together with their percentage of the total number of errors observed in each combination.

**Table 4.** Results for pin-level injection

| Error Detection Mechanisms | | ICs belonging to the application unit | | | | | | ICs belonging to the communication unit | | | | | |
|---|---|---|---|---|---|---|---|---|---|---|---|---|---|
| | | NOAM | | SEMC | | DEMC | | NOAM | | SEMC | | DEMC | |
| | | Errors | % | Errors | % | Errors | % | Errors | % | Errors | % | Errors | % |
| Level 1 Hardware | CPU | 71 | 11.2% | 53 | 9.0% | 38 | 7.0% | 37 | 6.9% | 37 | 8.2% | 20 | 3.9% |
| | UEE | 48 | 7.6% | 59 | 10.0% | 41 | 7.6% | 113 | 21.2% | 73 | 16.2% | 103 | 19.8% |
| | NMI | 474 | 75.0% | 430 | 73.0% | 423 | 78.2% | 265 | 49.7% | 260 | 57.5% | 263 | 50.7% |
| | *Subtotal* | *593* | *93.8%* | *542* | *92.0%* | *502* | *92.8%* | *415* | *77.9%* | *370* | *81.9%* | *386* | *74.4%* |
| Level 2 Software | OS | 6 | 0.9% | 6 | 1.0% | 7 | 1.3% | 35 | 6.6% | 21 | 4.6% | 30 | 5.8% |
| | CGRTA | 0 | 0% | 1 | 0.2% | 0 | 0% | 0 | 0% | 0 | 0% | 0 | 0% |
| | *Subtotal* | *6* | *0.9%* | *7* | *1.2%* | *7* | *1.3%* | *35* | *6.6%* | *21* | *4.6%* | *30* | *5.8%* |
| Level 3 Appl. level | Double exec. | — | — | — | — | 0 | 0% | — | — | — | — | 0 | 0% |
| | Checksum | — | — | 0 | 0% | 0 | 0% | — | — | 1 | 0.2% | 5 | 1.0% |
| | *Subtotal* | *—* | *—* | *0* | *0%* | *0* | *0%* | *—* | *—* | *1* | *0.2%* | *5* | *1.0%* |
| Other | Other unit | 1 | 0.2% | 8 | 1.4% | 2 | 0.4% | 23 | 4.3% | 17 | 3.8% | 26 | 5.0% |
| | No error info. | 32 | 5.1% | 30 | 5.1% | 30 | 5.5% | 59 | 11.1% | 43 | 9.5% | 72 | 13.9% |
| | *Subtotal* | *33* | *5.2%* | *38* | *6.5%* | *32* | *5.9%* | *82* | *15.4%* | *60* | *13.3%* | *98* | *18.9%* |
| Fail silence violations | | 0 | 0% | 2 | 0.3% | 0 | 0% | 1 | 0.2% | 0 | 0% | 0 | 0% |
| *Total no. of errors* | | *632* | *100%* | *589* | *100%* | *541* | *100%* | *533* | *100%* | *452* | *100%* | *519* | *100%* |

(a) Detection by the EDMs of the unit to which the faulted ICs belong

| Error Detection Mechanisms | | ICs belonging to the application unit | | | | | | ICs belonging to the communication unit | | | | | |
|---|---|---|---|---|---|---|---|---|---|---|---|---|---|
| | | NOAM | | SEMC | | DEMC | | NOAM | | SEMC | | DEMC | |
| | | Errors | % | Errors | % | Errors | % | Errors | % | Errors | % | Errors | % |
| Level 1 Hardware | CPU | 0 | 0% | 0 | 0% | 0 | 0% | 0 | 0% | 0 | 0% | 0 | 0% |
| | UEE | 0 | 0% | 0 | 0% | 0 | 0% | 0 | 0% | 0 | 0% | 2 | 0.4% |
| | NMI | 1 | 0.2% | 7 | 1.2% | 2 | 0.4% | 23 | 4.3% | 17 | 3.8% | 24 | 4.6% |
| | *Subtotal* | *1* | *0.2%* | *7* | *1.2%* | *2* | *0.4%* | *23* | *4.3%* | *17* | *3.8%* | *26* | *5.0%* |
| Level 2 Software | OS | 0 | 0% | 1 | 0.2% | 0 | 0% | 0 | 0% | 0 | 0% | 0 | 0% |
| | CGRTA | 0 | 0% | 0 | 0% | 0 | 0% | 0 | 0% | 0 | 0% | 0 | 0% |
| | *Subtotal* | *0* | *0%* | *1* | *0.2%* | *0* | *0%* | *0* | *0%* | *0* | *0%* | *0* | *0%* |
| Level 3 Appl. level | Double exec. | — | — | — | — | 0 | 0% | — | — | — | — | 0 | 0% |
| | Checksum | — | — | 0 | 0% | 0 | 0% | — | — | 0 | 0% | 0 | 0% |
| | *Subtotal* | *—* | *—* | *0* | *0%* | *0* | *0%* | *—* | *—* | *0* | *0%* | *0* | *0%* |

(b) Detection by the EDMs of the other unit (detail of "Other unit" entry in Table (a) above)

The results in Table 4-a indicate a dominant proportion of detections by the hardware EDMs (more than 90% on application unit side and 75% on communication unit side). NMI clearly dominates; however, in addition to CPU exceptions a significant number of UEEs were also triggered. The difference between UEE and NMI for the application and communication units can be explained by the fact that not all ICs tested on the application unit are directly connected to the processor. For software EDMs, detections by the OS significantly dominate. Concerning the application level EDMs, the "Checksum" EDMs are dominating; no detections were triggered by the

"Double execution" EDM when this option was enabled. Only a limited number of fail silence violations were observed: two occurrences for the SEMC combination when faults were injected on the application unit side.

Table 4-b shows that NMI error detection types are also dominating the supplementary detections observed on the other unit. Here also, a significant difference is observed between the results concerning the fault injections affecting the application unit side and the communication unit side; this may indicate that a larger proportion of errors is propagated to the application unit.

## 6.3  EMI

Various fault-injection campaigns were carried out with a variety of voltage levels, with negative or positive polarity of the bursts, and with a burst-frequency of 2.5 kHz and 10 kHz. A total number of more than 17,000 errors were observed during all campaigns conducted with the first method, i.e. when the computer board of the node under test was mounted between two plates, and more than 30,000 errors were observed using the special probe (see Section 2.3). Most of the campaigns were conducted with all application level EDMs enabled.

In the first campaign shown in Table 5 (NOAM(1)) faults were injected into the communication unit using the two plates. Antenna wires were attached to the so-called LO-EPROM, in order to disturb the address bus and the eight low order bits of the data bus. Bursts characterised by a frequency of 2.5 kHz, negative polarity, and a voltage of 230 V were injected. The second campaign (SEMC(2)) was conducted using the special probe with the wires connected to the corresponding LO-EPROM in the application unit. In this case the burst were characterised by a frequency of 10 kHz, negative polarity, and a voltage of 300 V. Campaign number three (DEMC(3)) used the two plates, the bursts had a frequency of 2.5 kHz, negative polarity, and voltage of 230 V. The wires were attached to the LO-EPROM of the application unit.

Campaigns 4 to 6 were only using the special probe for coupling faults into the CPU of the application unit, i.e. the probe was mounted on top of the CPU, and no wires were attached to any chip. The chosen frequency for the bursts was 10 kHz and negative polarity was used for all these experiments. We used a voltage of 290 V for campaign 4 and 6, while a slightly higher voltage, 300 V, was used for campaign 5.

Due to the large number of campaigns made, only selected campaigns are presented in Table 5, which shows the distribution of the errors detected by the various EDMs as total numbers and as percentage. Table 5-a shows the errors detected by the unit, where fault-injection was focused to; errors detected by the other unit of the node are detailed in Table 5-b.

Campaign one and two show similar results, although focus of fault-injection was on different units of the processing node, the communication unit for campaign one and the application unit for campaign two. Most of the errors were detected by the hardware EDMs, where the CPU EDMs clearly dominate. For the software EDMs, which only detected a small fraction of the errors, the OS EDMs dominate. The relatively high amount of no error information for campaign one partly results from the fact that for this campaign no information about the errors detected by the application unit is available, because this is a result from early experiments, where only the outputs of the unit under test was recorded, and therefore all errors which were detected by the application unit are also counted as 'no-error-info'.

**Table 5.** Results for EMI

| Error Detection Mechanisms | | fault-injection with antennas | | | | | | fault-injection with probe only | | | | | |
|---|---|---|---|---|---|---|---|---|---|---|---|---|---|
| | | NOAM(1) | | SEMC(2) | | DEMC(3) | | NOAM(4) | | SEMC(5) | | DEMC(6) | |
| | | Errors | % | Errors | % | Errors | % | Errors | % | Errors | % | Errors | % |
| Level 1 | CPU | 1195 | 72.0% | 193 | 76.6% | 137 | 2.2% | 4933 | 99.4% | 1692 | 98.1% | 1911 | 99.2% |
| Hardware | UEE | 11 | 0.7% | 8 | 3.2% | 9 | 0.2% | 31 | 0.6% | 17 | 1.0% | 15 | 0.8% |
| | NMI | 48 | 2.9% | 18 | 7.1% | 695 | 11.4% | 0 | 0% | 3 | 0.2% | 0 | 0% |
| | *Subtotal* | *1254* | *75.6%* | *219* | *86.9%* | *841* | *13.8%* | *4964* | *100%* | *1712* | *99.3%* | *1926* | *100%* |
| Level 2 | OS | 110 | 6.6% | 5 | 2.0% | 5215 | 85.6% | 0 | 0% | 3 | 0.2% | 0 | 0% |
| Software | CGRTA | 5 | 0.3% | 0 | 0% | 1 | <0.1% | 0 | 0% | 0 | 0% | 0 | 0% |
| | *Subtotal* | *115* | *6.9%* | *5* | *2.0%* | *5216* | *85.6%* | *0* | *0%* | *3* | *0.2%* | *0* | *0%* |
| Level 3 | Double exec. | – | – | – | – | 9 | 0.2% | – | – | – | – | 0 | 0% |
| Appl. | Checksum | – | – | 1 | 0.4% | 8 | 0.1% | – | – | 1 | <0.1% | 0 | 0% |
| level | *Subtotal* | *–* | *–* | *1* | *0.4%* | *17* | *0.3%* | *–* | *–* | *1* | *<0.1%* | *0* | *0%* |
| Other | Other unit | – | – | 24 | 9.5% | 6 | 0.1% | 0 | 0% | 6 | 0.3% | 0 | 0% |
| | No error info. | 271 | 16.3% | 0 | 0% | 13 | 0.2% | 0 | 0% | 2 | 0.1% | 0 | 0% |
| | *Subtotal* | *271* | *16.3%* | *24* | *9.5%* | *19* | *0.3%* | *0* | *0%* | *8* | *0.4%* | *0* | *0%* |
| Fail silence violations | | 20 | 1.2% | 3 | 1.2% | 0 | 0% | 0 | 0% | 0 | 0% | 0 | 0% |
| *Total number of errors* | | *1660* | *100%* | *252* | *100%* | *6093* | *100%* | *4964* | *100%* | *1724* | *100%* | *1926* | *100%* |

(a) Detection by the EDMs of the unit to which the faulted ICs belong

| Error Detection Mechanisms | | fault-injection with antennas | | | | | | fault-injection with probe only | | | | | |
|---|---|---|---|---|---|---|---|---|---|---|---|---|---|
| | | NOAM(1) | | SEMC(2) | | DEMC(3) | | NOAM(4) | | SEMC(5) | | DEMC(6) | |
| | | Errors | % | Errors | % | Errors | % | Errors | % | Errors | % | Errors | % |
| Level 1 | CPU | – | – | 0 | 0% | 0 | 0% | 0 | 0% | 0 | 0% | 0 | 0% |
| Hardware | UEE | – | – | 0 | 0% | 0 | 0% | 0 | 0% | 0 | 0% | 0 | 0% |
| | NMI | – | – | 0 | 0% | 6 | 0.1% | 0 | 0% | 0 | 0% | 0 | 0% |
| | *Subtotal* | *–* | *–* | *0* | *0%* | *6* | *0.1%* | *0* | *0%* | *0* | *0%* | *0* | *0%* |
| Level 2 | OS | – | – | 24 | 9.5% | 0 | 0% | 0 | 0% | 6 | 0.3% | 0 | 0% |
| Software | CGRTA | – | – | 0 | 0% | 0 | 0% | 0 | 0% | 0 | 0% | 0 | 0% |
| | *Subtotal* | *–* | *–* | *24* | *9.5%* | *0* | *0%* | *0* | *0%* | *6* | *0.3%* | *0* | *0%* |
| Level 3 | Double exec. | – | – | – | – | 0 | 0% | – | – | – | – | 0 | 0% |
| Appl. | Checksum | – | – | 0 | 0% | 0 | 0% | – | – | 0 | 0% | 0 | 0% |
| level | *Subtotal* | *–* | *–* | *0* | *0%* | *0* | *0%* | *–* | *–* | *0* | *0%* | *0* | *0%* |

(b) Detection by the EDMs of the other unit (detail of "Other unit" entry in Table (a) above)

A different distribution of errors was observed for campaign three. There the software EDMs detected most of the errors, where error detection by OS EDMs dominates. Most of the errors detected by the OS EDMs were indicating that a message, that was required by the application, was lost. Note that campaign one and three both used the two plates, but the observed results are quite different. Campaign one and two had different EMI conditions but here the results are very similar to each other. In general very different results were observed for similar conditions, e.g. slight changes in voltage levels. Thus, reproducibility appears to be problematic for EMI fault-injection.

In Campaign 4 to 6 almost all of the errors were detected by the CPU EDMs. Only Campaign 5 shows a small amount of errors detected by other EDMs than hardware EDMs. When looking at the results of experiments 4 to 6 in more detail, which is not shown in Table 5 for brevity, we discovered that almost all of the detected errors were spurious interrupts detected by the processor. Spurious interrupts are interrupts signalled to the processor, but the processor cannot find the source of the interrupt, i.e. the device having raised the interrupt. This shows that the interrupt lines of a processor are highly sensitive to EMI.

Errors detected by the other unit were only detected by the NMI EDMs and by the OS EDMs for all campaigns.

## 6.4  Discussion

Almost all of the fault injection campaigns show that the hardware EDMs detect most of the errors. However, one campaign, EMI DEMC(3), shows results which are drastically different from the other campaigns. In order to simplify the discussion, we neglect the results from this campaign, when we compare the different results.

The main difference between the fault injection techniques, when looking at the *hardware EDMs*, is the number of errors detected by the CPU and the NMI mechanisms, respectively; the CPU EDMs dominate for heavy-ion radiation and EMI, while the NMI EDMs dominate for pin-forcing. A closer examination of the results showed that heavy-ion radiation exercised seven of the eight CPU EDMs, while EMI exercised five and pin-level exercised four of the CPU EDMs.

For EMI, when using the probe without antennas, the detection of spurious interrupts strongly dominated. Consequently, this method generates a very restricted error set, which clearly demonstrate that the method is not suitable for evaluation of error detection mechanisms. However, the variation in the error set was much larger when the antennas were used.

The proportion of unexpected exceptions is fairly large for pin-forcing and heavy-ion radiation, but quite low for the EMI technique.

Pin-forcing exercised 34 different combinations of NMI detections; the corresponding numbers for the heavy-ion and EMI techniques were 26 and 16, respectively. This indicates that pin-forcing may be more effective than the other techniques in exercising hardware EDMs located outside of the CPU chip.

One NMI mechanism of particular interest is the time-slice controller, which prevents access to the MARS bus at an illegal point in time. The results show that 5.0%, 11.6% and 1.9% of the errors were detected by the time-slice controller for heavy-ion, pin-forcing and EMI, respectively. Without this mechanism, the fail-silence property would have been violated in the time domain, which could lead to system failure (see Section 4.2). No fail-silence violations in the time domain were observed during the experiments.

The *software EDMs* detected the second largest amount of errors for all techniques. The unbalance observed in the case of heavy-ion radiation between the OS and CGRTA EDMs, is amplified when using pin-forcing and EMI: almost no detections by the CGRTAs were observed for the two latter techniques.

The *application level EDMs* detected the smallest amount of errors for all techniques, but when these were disabled, the fail-silence coverage was reduced (particularly for heavy-ion radiation) which shows the necessity of using these mechanisms as well.

The heavy-ion radiation stresses the system the most (i.e. the largest amount of fail-silence violations was observed for this technique). This technique also generates the largest error set, as indicated by the spread of the error detections among the EDMs. The spread of the detections is approximately the same for pin-forcing and EMI injections using antennas.

# 7   Conclusion

This paper reported on a unique study devoted to the comparison of physical fault injection techniques. The paper described three techniques—heavy-ion radiation, pin-level fault injection, and EMI—and how they were used to validate the MARS system.

The comparison of the fundamental and practical features of the three fault injection techniques showed that (i) pin-level and EMI injection are more flexible than the heavy-ion radiation technique, and that (ii) pin-forcing provides higher controllability than both the EMI and heavy-ion radiation techniques. On the other hand, the unique feature of the heavy-ion technique, that faults can be injected internally in integrated circuits, was shown to have a significant impact on the spread of the detections among the EDMs and thus, in the context of this common experimental set-up, of the error sets generated.

The results show that the fault injection techniques are rather complementary. The pin-forcing technique exercised the hardware EDMs located outside the CPU more effectively than the other techniques, while the heavy-ion and EMI techniques appear to be more suitable for exercising software and application level EDMs. The largest error set was generated by the heavy-ion radiation technique, this technique also generated the largest number of fail-silence violations.

Concerning the adequacy of the EDMs it is shown that although the application level EDMs detect the smallest amount of errors for all techniques, they are nevertheless necessary for improving fail-silence coverage. It was also shown that the time-slice controller of the MARS system effectively prevents fail-silence violations in the time domain.

# Fault Injection into VHDL Models:
# The MEFISTO Tool[*]

Eric Jenn[1]    Jean Arlat[1]    Marcus Rimén[2]    Joakim Ohlsson[2]    Johan Karlsson[2]

[1]LAAS-CNRS        [2]Chalmers University of Technology

**Abstract.** This paper focuses on the integration of the fault injection methodology within the design process of fault-tolerant systems. Due to its wide spectrum of application and hierarchical features, VHDL has been selected as the simulation language to support such an integration. Suitable techniques for injecting faults into VHDL models are identified and depicted. Then, the main features of the MEFISTO environment aimed at supporting these techniques are described. Finally, some preliminary results obtained with MEFISTO are presented and analyzed.

# 1    Introduction

In the last decade, fault injection has emerged as an invaluable means to support the dependability validation of fault-tolerant systems (e.g. see [2, 54, 26]).

Two main trends characterize recent work on fault injection: (i) apply fault injection as early as possible in the design process of fault-tolerant systems, i.e. into simulation models of the target system [41, 13, 19, 54] and (ii) when dealing with the implementation of the target system, favor *software-implemented fault injection* (SWIFI), i.e. based on the mutation of the executing software or of the data [49, 12, 31, 51].

Classically, simulation-based fault injection approaches address different abstraction levels by using distinct description languages. Clearly, a coherent environment should be provided: (i) to favor interoperability between the successive abstraction levels and (ii) to integrate the validation in the design process. SWIFI is primarily motivated to avoid the difficulties and cost inherent to the implementation of physical fault injection approaches (e.g. pin-level [4]or heavy-ion [32]; see also paper V.A in this book). It is also intended to cover errors that can be generated by both software and hardware faults. However, this is only achieved to some extent. Still, further work is needed to validate such abstract error models before it can be confidently considered that SWIFI alone can adequately embrace the consequences of hardware faults.

The paper presents the main objectives and the preliminary results of a research aimed at (i) providing an integrated environment — called MEFISTO (Multi-level Error/Fault Injection Simulation Tool) — for applying fault injection into simulation models encompassing various levels of abstraction and thus (ii) helping to identify and validate an abstraction hierarchy of fault/error models.

The development of an integrated and coherent design environment for fault-tolerant systems based on a single language seems to be achievable when considering the

---

[*]  This paper is a revised version of [28].

emergence of hardware description languages. With this respect, VHDL has been recognized as a suitable language as it presents many useful features:

- ability to describe both the structure and behaviour of a system in a unique syntactical framework,
- widespread use in digital design and inherent hierarchical abstraction description capabilities [30],
- recognition as a viable framework (i) for developing high-level models of digital systems (block diagrams, Petri nets), even before the decision between hardware or software decomposition of the functions takes place, and (ii) for supporting hybrid (i.e. mixed abstraction levels) simulation models [9],
- capability to support test activities [39].

MEFISTO can be used: (i) to estimate the coverage of fault tolerance mechanisms, (ii) to investigate different mechanisms for mapping results from one level of abstraction to another and (iii) to validate fault and error models applied during fault injection experiments carried out on the implementation of a fault-tolerant system (e.g. SWIFI or pin-level fault injection).

The remainder of this paper is made up of six sections. Section 2 presents a critical analysis of four techniques for injecting faults into VHDL models. Section 3 describes the architecture and the main features of the MEFISTO system that supports these techniques. Section 4 details the user interactions necessary to set up a fault injection campaign. Section 5 presents a case study where MEFISTO is used to inject faults in two VHDL models (structural and behavioural) of a simplified 32-bit processor. Abstract error models are extracted from the resulting data and compared. Section 6 concludes the paper with a summary and some remarks.

# 2    Fault injection into VHDL models

Two categories of fault injection techniques are identified: the first one covers two techniques that require *modification of the VHDL model* and the second one covers two other techniques that instead *use the built-in commands* of the simulator. Before describing these two categories, we provide a summary of the characteristics of the VHDL language used in the subsequent sections [24].

## 2.1   Characteristics of the VHDL language

A system modeled in VHDL is made up of *components* linked by *signals*. VHDL allows a signal to have many *drivers* (signal sources), provided that a *resolution function* is supplied to resolve the values generated by the multiple sources into a single value for the signal. Such a signal is called a *resolved signal*; it can be used to model buses and wired-and logic.

A component can have many implementations. In VHDL, each implementation is expressed by a separate component description. To allow simulation of the system, a *configuration* mechanism assigns a single component description to each component. A component description is represented by both an entity declaration and an architecture. The entity declaration specifies the interface, i.e. the set of inputs and outputs, while the architecture describes the internal organization of the component. A component description can be *structural or behavioural* (or a mixture of both). A structural description is a composition hierarchy consisting of subcomponents and signals, while a behavioural description is an algorithmic model of the component's function expressed by means of *processes*. A VHDL process is a set of sequential statements. The process can communicate with other processes by reading and assigning values to *signals*. *Variables* are used inside processes and are not accessible from the outside. Processes are executed repeatedly in a loop fashion, and stopped only at synchronization statements, called *wait statements*.

## 2.2 Modification of the VHDL Model

In this category, two techniques can be distinguished. The first one is based on the addition of dedicated fault injection components, called saboteurs, to the VHDL model. The second one is based on the mutation of existing component descriptions in the VHDL model, which generates modified component descriptions called mutants. In this paper, any change made to an existing component description is regarded as a mutation.

A *saboteur* is a VHDL component that alters the value or timing characteristics of one or several signals when activated. It is usually inactive during normal system operation and activated only to inject a fault. A serial saboteur breaks up the signal path between a driver (output) and its corresponding receiver (input) (Fig. 1-a) or a set of drivers and its corresponding set of receivers (Fig. 1-b). A parallel saboteur is simply added as an additional driver for a resolved signal, as shown by Fig. 1-c. Another way to achieve the same effect is to assign a modified resolution function to signals that are potential fault targets.

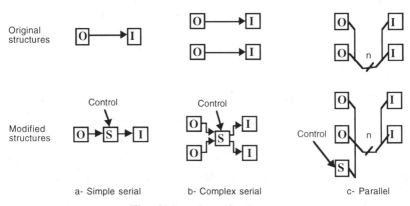

a- Simple serial          b- Complex serial          c- Parallel

**Fig. 1.** Insertion of saboteurs

A *mutant* is a component description that replaces another component description. When inactive, it behaves as the component description it replaces and, when activated, it imitates the component's behaviour in presence of faults. It is easy to implement this replacement technique in VHDL using the configuration mechanism.

Mutation may be accomplished in several ways by:
- adding saboteur(s) to structural or behavioural component descriptions,
- mutating structural component descriptions by replacing subcomponents (e.g. a NAND-gate replaced by a NOR-gate),

- automatically mutating statements in behavioural component descriptions, e.g. by generating wrong operators or exchanging variable identifiers; this is similar to the mutation techniques used by the software testing community,

- manually mutating behavioural component descriptions to achieve complex and detailed fault models.

Both signal and variable manipulations can be used for controlling, i.e. activating and deactivating, saboteurs and mutants. In this way, the injection of faults can be controlled by the built-in commands of the simulator also when mutants and saboteurs are used. This can be achieved by means of global signals or shared global variables. The latter is a new capability introduced in the latest version of VHDL, called VHDL'93 [25].

## 2.3  Use of Built-in Commands of the Simulator

The main reason for using the built-in commands of the simulator for fault injection is that this does not require the modification of the VHDL code; however, the applicability of these techniques depends strongly on the functionnalities offered by the command languages of the simulators.

Two techniques based on the use of simulator commands can be identified: *signal* and *variable* manipulation. For each technique, the required sequence of simulator pseudo-commands is described in Fig. 2 and is explained in the subsequent paragraphs.

```
[1]  SimulateUntil <fault            [1]  SimulateUntil <fault
     injection time>                      injection time>
[2]  FreezeSignal <signal name>      [2]  AssignVariable <variable
     <signal value>                       name>
                                          <variable value>
[3]  SimulateFor <fault duration>
                                     [3]  SimulateFor <observation
[4]  UnFreezeSignal <signal name>         time>
[5]  SimulateFor <observation
     time>
```

    a- Signal: temporary stuck at fault          b: Variable: temporal variable

**Fig. 2.** Fault injection using simulator commands

**Signal Manipulation.** In this technique, faults are injected by altering the value of signals in the VHDL model. This is done by simulating the system until the time of injection is reached and all processes have stopped on a WAIT statement (Fig. 2-a, step 1), then the signal is disconnected from its driver(s) and forced to a new value (step 2); the system is simulated for the duration of the fault (step 3); finally, the signal's driver(s) is (are) reconnected when the fault injection is completed (step 4) and the simulation is continued until the end of the observation time (step 5). For a permanent fault, steps 3 and 4 are skipped. Intermittent faults can be injected using a more complex command sequence.

**Variable  Manipulation.** This technique allows injection of faults into behavioural models by altering values of variables defined in VHDL processes. In the simulation phase, the execution of the sequential code in a process takes no time as viewed by the simulator since time is incremented only when a process stops at a WAIT statement.

A variable is termed *atemporal* when it holds valid information over a number of sequential statements in the process, but never over any WAIT statements. Thus, the variable will not be susceptible to changes made to its contents when the process has stopped. A variable is termed *temporal* if it always holds valid information over WAIT statements. As a result, the variable will be susceptible to changes made to its contents when the process has stopped. In other words, a variable is temporal or atemporal depending whether it is used to transfer information through simulation time space or code space, respectively. Furthermore, a variable is termed *mixed-mode* if it is sometimes temporal and sometimes atemporal.

In the case of temporal variables, faults are injected by the same means as signals, i.e. when all processes are stopped on a WAIT statement (see Fig. 2.b). By definition, this technique cannot be used for atemporal variables since they are only used between two WAIT statements, therefore some extra fine-grained synchronization is required. Fig. 3 shows the simulator controls required to manipulate an atemporal variable. The main idea is to (i) simulate the system until one of the statements where the target variable is assigned a value is reached (steps 1-3) and (ii) then assign a faulty value to it (steps 4-7).

```
[1]  SimulateUntil <fault injection time>
[2]  SetSrcBreakOnLine <LineNo> <Library> <Entity> <Architecture>
     .../...
[2]  SetSrcBreakOnLine <LineNo> <Library> <Entity> <Architecture>
[3]  SimulateFor <time window>
[4]  If (AtSrcBreak) {
[5]  AssignVariable <variable name> <variable value>
[6]  DeleteAllSrcBreaks
[7]  SimulateUntil <fault injection time+observation time> }
```

**Fig. 3.** Variable manipulation of atemporal variables

Step 1 in Fig. 3 is the same as step 1 in Fig. 2. In step 2, breakpoints are set on all VHDL source code lines that follow an assignment to the target variable. Then the simulation is started in step 3 and continues until a breakpoint is reached. However, as the execution can follow paths in the VHDL code where no assignments are made to the target variable from one WAIT statement to the next one, it cannot be ensured that a source line breakpoint will be reached. Therefore it is necessary to specify a maximum time for the simulation, which is defined by the <time window> parameter in step 3. If a breakpoint is reached (step 4), a fault is injected (step 5), then all source line breakpoints are removed (step 6) and the simulation is continued until the end of the observation time (step 7). If a breakpoint is not reached within the time window (step 4) then steps 5-7 are skipped, i.e. no fault is injected.

The injection of faults into mixed-mode variables is achieved by a combination of the above methods; the sequence is the same as the one given in Fig. 3, with an "AssignVariable <variable name> <variable value>" step inserted between the first and the second steps.

## 2.4 Comparison of the Fault Injection Techniques

The fault injection techniques considered are compared in terms of fault modeling capacity, effort required for setting up an experiment and simulation time overhead.

Considering the *fault modeling capacity*, mutants can be designed using the full strength of the VHDL language, and are thus well suited for implementing any behavioural and structural fault models provided they can be expressed within the VHDL semantics. This is also the case for the saboteurs, although they have a very restricted view of the system due to their limited number of input and output ports. Signal manipulation is suited for implementing simple fault models (e.g. permanent or temporary stuck-at faults). Variable manipulation offers a simple way for injecting behavioural faults.

Considering the *effort required for setting up an experiment*, the signal and variable manipulations do not require any modification of the VHDL code, whereas much effort is needed for mutants and saboteurs, as they require (i) creation/generation of saboteurs/mutants, (ii) inclusion of saboteurs/mutants in the model and (iii) recompilation of the VHDL model. The creation of saboteurs and the automatic generation of mutants are relatively easy tasks, provided that simple fault models are considered. It is also worth noting that a saboteur is a reusable component, while a mutant has to be specifically generated for each target component; on the other hand, the inclusion of saboteurs requires the modification of the component description while mutants are easily included in the model by means of the VHDL configuration mechanism.

Considering the *simulation time overhead* induced by the injection mechanisms, signal and variable manipulations impose a model-independent overhead due to the fact that the simulation has to be stopped and started again for each fault injected. The simulation time overhead imposed by saboteurs and mutants depends on several factors such as (i) the amount of additional generated events (signal changes), (ii) the amount of code to execute per event (e.g. a complex behavioural mutant may require many statements to be executed per event), and (iii) the complexity of the injection control.

# 3 Overview of MEFISTO

Fig. 4 gives an overview of MEFISTO and of the main user interactions for defining and executing a *fault injection campaign* (i.e. a *series* of *fault injection experiments*). The fault injection campaign consists of three phases [47, 27]a Setup Phase, a Simulation Phase, and a Data Processing Phase.

## 3.1 The Setup Phase

The two main objectives of the setup phase are to generate:

- an *Executable Model* of the system including mutants, if any;
- an *Experiment Control List* containing the commands necessary to control the simulator for each experiment in the campaign.

For a given VHDL description of the target system, the user specifies during the Setup Phase (i) the fault set to be used, (ii) the readouts to be saved (e.g. signal traces) in the campaign, (iii) how to select faults from the fault set for each experiment, (iv) when to inject the selected fault(s), and (v) when to terminate each experiment.

In the first part of the Setup Phase, the tool analyzes the VHDL target model and provides a list of fault targets to the user. The user specifies the fault set to be used in

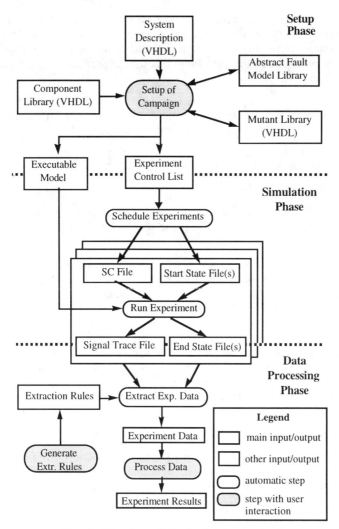

**Fig. 4.** Overview of the fault injection tool

the campaign by selecting targets from the list. Each target belongs to a target group which corresponds to a certain class of VHDL objects, e.g. signal, variable or component. Each target group has at least one attribute such as a type (BOOLEAN, INTEGER, etc.) for a signal or an implementation (VHDL entity declarations and architectures) for a component. For each fault target, a user-definable fault type can be selected. This fault type is called an Abstract Fault Model, or AFM. The act of selecting a fault target and a fault type (AFM) specifies a fault.

AFMs can be applied to any of the target groups described above. It is also possible to restrict the application of an AFM to targets with a specific attribute, e.g. signal of type BIT. Thus, for each target there exists a set of selectable AFMs from which the user can chose.

When mutants are used, after the fault set is specified by the user, a final VHDL configuration for the target system is created and then the Executable Model can be generated. Once the final configuration is decided, all signals, variables etc., are identified and presented to the user. From this list the user selects the readouts to be saved for each experiment.

Finally, the user must specify for each experiment how to select faults from the fault set, when to inject them and when to terminate the experiment. This information is needed by the tool to generate the Experiment Control List.

The main user interactions in the Setup Phase are further described in Section 4. A more comprehensive description can be found in .[47, 28]

## 3.2 The Simulation Phase

In the Simulation Phase, the simulation model created in the Setup Phase together with the Experiment Control List are used to schedule the execution of the injection experiments.

The simulations are executed on a set of simulators running on a network of computers. An experiment scheduler reads the Experiment Control List and schedules simulations on the available simulators. For each simulation, the scheduler reads an entry with simulation control commands from the Experiment Control List and creates a simulation control file (*SC File*) for controlling the simulator, and a start state file. The *Start State File* specifies from which simulation state a simulation should start. The final simulation state (*End State File*) of each simulation can be saved; this makes it possible to use the final simulation state of a previous simulation as a start state for a new simulation. Moreover, the readouts (*Signal Trace File*) from each simulation are saved for further processing in the Data Processing Phase.

## 3.3 The Data Processing Phase

The Data Processing Phase involves two steps: (i) extraction of *Experiment Data* from the raw data produced by the simulations, and (ii) processing of the Experiment Data into *Experiment Results*.

The purpose of the extraction process, which is guided by Extraction Rules generated by the user, is to extract and convert to a convenient format the data needed to generate the experimental results (e.g. error detection coverage and latency measures).

The actual processing of the Experiment Data into Experiment Results is application-dependent and must be tailored for each fault injection campaign. For instance, in one campaign the user may want to compute coverage figures for a fault tolerance mechanism, while in another campaign he may want to obtain enough data to study the error propagation in the system.

## 4    Main User Interactions in the Setup Phase

Section 4.1 and Section 4.2 describe the generation of AFMs and mutants, respectively. Then, Section 4.3 describes the selection of the fault set. Finally, Section 4.4 presents the selection of experiment parameters.

## 4.1  Generation of AFMs

MEFISTO includes an AFM database containing predefined AFMs. The user can expand the database by generating and adding new AFMs to it. By default, certain target groups and attributes are recognized by the tool (such as signals of the type BIT), and associated simple AFMs (e.g. stuck signal of type BIT to 0) for injecting faults are stored in the database.

In addition to the predefined AFMs, the user can add both simple and complex AFMs, such as those supporting the saboteur and mutant-based techniques, to the database. Those techniques require the generation of a mutant. The mutant is stored in a database (the mutant library) and a complex AFM is associated with the mutant, containing a reference to the mutant and also a "description" of how to activate it.

## 4.2  Generation of Mutants

A *mutation* of a component description can be carried out in several ways by (i) manually mutating it, (ii) inserting saboteurs into it and (iii) manually selecting mutation rules for the automatic mutation. A mutation rule states where the mutation must occur, and what modification to make. The only rules available in MEFISTO are those that map one VHDL grammar rule to another one. A mutation rule can make calls to other mutation rules, in a recursive manner. Indeed, the mutation of an entity containing instances (i.e. components) of other entities may be obtained by the mutation of any of these components.

Examples of fault models possible to describe as mutation rules are found in [5] that divides behavioural-level fault models into eight fault classes: Stuck-Then, Stuck-Else, Assignment Control, Dead Process, Dead Clause, Micro-operation, Local Stuck-data and Global Stuck-data.

## 4.3  Selection of the Fault Set

The first step in the process of selecting a fault set consists in the analysis of the VHDL description to get information on potential targets for fault injection: *target group* (e.g. signal, variable, component etc.), *attribute* (e.g. boolean, integer, etc.), etc. As mentioned earlier, because of its group belonging and attribute, each target implicitly defines one or more selectable AFMs.

After analyzing the VHDL description, the faults to be injected are determined interactively and added to a fault set. This is done by selecting targets and AFMs.

The fault injection tool provides three main categories of target selection mechanisms:

- explicit target selection,
- selection of targets that satisfy a given property,
- random target selection.

The properties for the second category concern (i) the entity-instances relationship in the model (e.g. select mutated architectures for components that are instances of a specific entity), (ii) the composition structure of the model (e.g. all signals in a specific architecture, or all variables in a specific process), (iii) the VHDL semantics (e.g. all variables, all signals, all processes, all variables or all signals that carry values of a specific type) and (iv) a given topological property (e.g. all signals connected to a given component).

The selection criteria may be composed; for instance, it is possible to select "all signals that are of a given type and are connected to a given component".

## 4.4 Selection of Experiment Parameters

The experiment parameters include preconditions, fault activation conditions and termination conditions.

The *preconditions* specify the starting state of each experiment. It can be (i) the zero state, i.e. the state corresponding to a reset of the target system, or (ii) the final state of a previous experiment. The preconditions also define the functional activation of the simulation model for each experiment. In particular, the functional activation of a microprocessor is also called the workload.

The *activation* of the injected faults (i.e. AFMs associated with targets) can be triggered according to any mix of the following conditions provided by the simulation environment:

- a given period of simulation time has elapsed,
- a signal has changed (to a given value),
- a given line of code has been executed, or
- one of the above conditions has occurred for the nth time.

All values in these definitions may be chosen at random.

The *termination conditions* state when an individual experiment should complete. The completion of the experiment is characterized by a predicate $P$ on the system's state. Depending on its complexity, the assessment of the $P$ predicate can be performed on-line or off-line with respect to a running simulation within an experiment.

When computed on-line, the $P$ predicate is expressed by means of simulation tool expressions or VHDL code. The simulation environment provides the same means to terminate a simulation as for detecting the time for activating a fault as described above. Expressing the predicate in VHDL is a matter of embedding specific expressions, processes or even components in the original model. Their activation may create events that satisfy one of the conditions that can be monitored by the simulation environment to stop the simulation. When computed off-line, the same means as those cited above are used to assess a first predicate $P1$. However, once $P1$ has been satisfied, the current simulation state is saved, the simulation is stopped and a second, more thorough, analysis is performed to test a second predicate $P2$. If $P2$ is not satisfied, the simulation continues from the saved state.

## 5    A Case Study: The DP32 Processor

This section presents some preliminary results of fault injection experiments carried out with MEFISTO on two models of a simple 32-bit processor. The main goals of the experiment consist in the analysis of the impact of the choice of the injection method and the model description level on the error outcome. More specifically, the differences observed when using (i) signal or variable manipulation methods, and (ii) a structural model or a behavioural model of the target system are studied. The next paragraphs present the design and the realization of the campaign. Finally, the experimental results are given and analyzed.

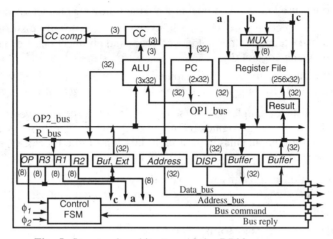

**Fig. 5.** Structural architecture of the DP32 processor

## 5.1  Design of the Campaign

The target system is a model of a very simple 32-bit processor, the DP32 described in [7], for which two architectures, one behavioural and one structural, are available. The structural model, on the register-transfer level, is depicted in Fig. 5; it is mainly composed of a finite state control machine (Control FSM), an ALU, a program counter (PC), a register file and several buffers and latches. The behavioural model, on the procedural description level, mainly consists of a VHDL process containing a large "CASE" statement that initiates the appropriate bus cycles with respect to the operation code of the fetched instruction.

All external operations are synchronized on two non-overlapping clocks $\Phi_1$ and $\Phi_2$ (a cycle is 40 ns); F1 is the main clock which synchronize all bus accesses.

Fig. 6 rates the "simulation efficiency", the "complexity" and the "average simulation duration" for the two models.

| Model | Structural | Behavioural |
|---|---|---|
| Number of simulated events per sec | 4636 | 7927 |
| Number of generated events per nsec | 2.06 | 1.07 |
| Average execution time (3600 clock cycles) | 80 s | 25 s |

**Fig. 6.** Efficiency and complexity of the models

This table shows that for the processor used in the experiments, less events are needed to complete the execution of the same workload on the behavioural model than on the structural model, indicating that the structural model is more complex than the behavioural model. Furthermore, the simulator can simulate the events generated by the behavioural model faster, i.e. more efficiently, than those generated by the structural one. This clearly illustrates the trade-off between speed and accuracy.

The fault models used in the experiments share the following characteristics:

- the time of injection — expressed in cycles — is uniformly distributed in the range [0, the execution time of the workload] and all injections are synchronized with the raising edge of $\Phi_1$,

- the fault values are uniformly distributed in the range of permitted values for the target (e.g. [0,1] for targets of type BIT, [0,255] for targets of type BYTE, etc.).

At the structural level, single random temporary stuck-at faults have been injected systematically on all atomic signals (compound signals, such as buses, were splitted into their basic bit components), with a fault duration of one F1 clock cycle. At the behavioural level, single random bit-flips were injected into variables.

Two fault injection campaigns with two different workloads — a Bubblesort (22 bytes) and a Heapsort (63 bytes) sorting programs applied to a set of 16 values — were run on each model.

## 5.2  Realization of the Campaign

In the following paragraphs, the implementation of the experiments is described in terms of the two main phases that have been identified in Section 3, i.e. setup and data processing. The completion of the simulation phase took about one week on two Sun IPC workstations.

**The Setup Phase.** In this case, it was not necessary to generate new AFMs as predefined AFMs corresponding to signal and variables manipulation techniques could be used.

The analysis of both VHDL models resulted in a set of target signals and variables. The selection mechanism described in Section 4.3 was used to reduce the initial set of (signal) targets resulting from the analysis of the structural model to a set of signals strictly internal to the processor. A manual selection was used to exclude variables that were not used during the execution of the activations from the (variable) targets of the behavioural model. All output ports of the DP32 processor (i.e. *address bus*, *data bus*, *read*, *write*, *fetch*) were chosen as readouts for the fault injection experiments.

**The Data Processing Phase.** The final results were extracted from the experiment data by means of a two-step procedure consisting of (i) the determination of the time and location of the error manifestation on the output ports of the processor and (ii) the classification of these observations with respect to a set of error classes integrating information on latency, location and instruction cycle.

Each injected fault belongs to one of the fault classes listed in Fig. 7. Each fault class corresponds to the function of the target signal/variable.

The first step of the data processing was achieved by comparing the readouts of each fault injection simulation with the readouts of a reference simulation. In the second step, error classification predicates were used to classify the readouts of each experiment. The errors classes derive from an *a priori* knowledge of the processor structure and behaviour.

| Structural fault class | Target | Behavioural fault class | Target |
|---|---|---|---|
| Buses | Internal buses | PC | Program counter |
| Xfer | Buffer control lines | CR | Control register (flags) |
| Latch | Latch control lines | IR | Instruction register |
| Select | Mux control lines | AR | Address register |
| Func | ALU control lines | DR | Data register |
| Misc | Other | UR | User register |

**Fig. 7.** Fault classes

Fig. 8 defines the predicates that characterize the considered error classes.

| Error class | Predicates |
|---|---|
| Direct Execution | PDE = an error on any output port during the execution of instruction(i) |
| Direct Flow | PDF = an address bus error in the fetch phase of instruction(i+1) |
| Indirect Flow | PIF = an address bus error in the fetch phase of instruction($\geq$i+2) |
| Indirect Data | PID = an address bus error in the read or write phase of instruction($\geq$i+1), or a data bus error in the write phase of instruction($\geq$i+1) |

Notes:
(1) "indirect" refers to the fact that the error propagated from one instruction to the other through a storage device such as a user register or a condition code bit, and stayed latent until the storage element was used;
(2) Instruction(i) refers to the instruction executed when the fault is injected;
(3) All predicate values equal 1 when they are asserted and 0 otherwise.

**Fig. 8.** Error classes

## 5.3 Results

**Error behaviour outcome.** Fig. 9 and 10 show the error outcomes of both models for the two activations used in the experiments. In the structural model (Fig. 9), about 80% of all errors manifest as direct Flow or Execution errors. Furthermore, the workload dependency for these errors appears to be low. For the behavioural model (Fig. 10), only 30-43% of all errors manifest directly, and a workload dependency is observed for these errors. For the indirect errors, both models exhibit a workload dependency. The major fault classes contributing to the indirect errors are for the structural model, the fault classes Buses and Misc, while the UR fault class is the major contributor to indirect errors in the behavioural model.

**Error manifestation latency.** We focus our analysis on the indirect error classes, i.e. errors which propagate through the user register file, as the latency for direct errors is by definition smaller than 2. Fig. 11 shows the latency due to indirect errors of both models and activations used in the experiments. Latency is defined here as the time from the injection of a fault to the manifestation of an error on any output port, and is measured by the number of instructions executed between the two events.

| Class | Total | | Buses | | Misc | | Xfer | | Latch | | Select | | Func | |
|---|---|---|---|---|---|---|---|---|---|---|---|---|---|---|
| | % | # | % | # | % | # | % | # | % | # | % | # | % | # |
| Injected | 100 | 3433 | 47.5 | 1632 | 41.6 | 1428 | 5.0 | 172 | 4.5 | 155 | 0.7 | 23 | 0.7 | 23 |
| Effective | 16.6 | 568 | 22.8 | 372 | 8.2 | 117 | 23.3 | 40 | 18.7 | 29 | 8.7 | 2 | 34.8 | 8 |
| Direct Flow | 28.7 | 163 | 31.5 | 117 | 15.4 | 18 | 37.5 | 15 | 31.0 | 9 | 0 | 0 | 50.0 | 4 |
| Direct Execution | 49.5 | 281 | 53.2 | 198 | 35 | 41 | 45.0 | 18 | 65.5 | 19 | 100 | 2 | 37.5 | 3 |
| Indirect Flow | 9.1 | 52 | 6.2 | 23 | 21.4 | 25 | 7.5 | 3 | 3.5 | 1 | 0 | 0 | 0.0 | 0 |
| Indirect Data | 12.7 | 72 | 9.1 | 34 | 28.2 | 33 | 10.0 | 4 | 0.0 | 0 | 0 | 0 | 12.5 | 1 |

a- Heapsort

| Class | Total | | Buses | | Misc | | Xfer | | Latch | | Select | | Func | |
|---|---|---|---|---|---|---|---|---|---|---|---|---|---|---|
| | % | # | % | # | % | # | % | # | % | # | % | # | % | # |
| Injected | 100 | 3820 | 50.3 | 1920 | 40.8 | 1560 | 4.2 | 160 | 3.7 | 140 | 0.5 | 20 | 0.5 | 20 |
| Effective | 14.4 | 550 | 20.1 | 386 | 6.3 | 98 | 20.6 | 33 | 19.3 | 27 | 10.0 | 2 | 20.0 | 4 |
| Direct Flow | 29.8 | 164 | 32.9 | 127 | 22.5 | 22 | 15.1 | 5 | 37.0 | 10 | 0 | 0 | 0 | 0 |
| Direct Execution | 51.5 | 283 | 54.4 | 210 | 33.7 | 33 | 54.5 | 18 | 59.3 | 16 | 100 | 2 | 100 | 4 |
| Indirect Flow | 8.0 | 44 | 7.5 | 29 | 12.2 | 12 | 6.1 | 2 | 3.7 | 1 | 0 | 0 | 0 | 0 |
| Indirect Data | 10.7 | 59 | 5.2 | 20 | 31.6 | 31 | 24.2 | 8 | 0.0 | 0 | 0 | 0 | 0 | 0 |

b- Bubblesort

**Fig. 9.** Structural model

For the structural model, the mean latency is rather short (approx. 3 instructions), while for the behavioural model the latency is much longer. In the following paragraphs, we provide an explanation for this observation.

The latency means shown in Fig. 11 are estimates of the mathematical expectation $E[l] = \sum_i i \times p(e(o^i))$ , where $p(e(o^i))$ represents the probability that an error occurs on an output port when instruction number $i$ is being executed, given that a fault was injected during execution of instruction $i=0$. The differences in the values of the latency obtained for the two models originate from differences in the values of $p(e(o^i))$ .

Now, let $r$ represent a register in the user register file, and let $r^i$ and $r_i$ denote a user register used as a destination and source register, respectively, during instruction $i$. Furthermore, let $e(r)$ denote that $r$ is erroneous. Then, $p(e(o^i))$ can be characterized by:

$$p(e(o^i)) = p\big[e(o^i)\big|e(r_i)\big] \times p[e(r_i)]$$

$$(1)$$

| Class | Total | | Buses | | Misc | | Xfer | | Latch | | Select | | Func | |
|---|---|---|---|---|---|---|---|---|---|---|---|---|---|---|
| | % | # | % | # | % | # | % | # | % | # | % | # | % | # |
| Injected | 100 | 3664 | 8.5 | 313 | 0.8 | 28 | 11.0 | 403 | 18.2 | 665 | 0.3 | 11 | 61.2 | 2244 |
| Effective | 21.9 | 803 | 45.7 | 143 | 3.6 | 1 | 7.2 | 29 | 2.9 | 19 | 0 | 0 | 27.2 | 611 |
| Direct Flow | 11.7 | 94 | 56.6 | 81 | 100 | 1 | 24.1 | 7 | 0 | 0 | | | 0.8 | 5 |
| Direct Execution | 18.9 | 152 | 43.4 | 62 | 0 | 0 | 51.7 | 15 | 100 | 19 | | | 9.2 | 56 |
| Indirect Flow | 33.2 | 267 | 0.0 | 0 | 0 | 0 | 3.4 | 1 | 0 | 0 | | | 43.5 | 266 |
| Indirect Data | 36.1 | 290 | 0.0 | 0 | 0 | 0 | 20.7 | 6 | 0 | 0 | | | 46.9 | 284 |

a- Heapsort

| Class | Total | | Buses | | Misc | | Xfer | | Latch | | Select | | Func | |
|---|---|---|---|---|---|---|---|---|---|---|---|---|---|---|
| | % | # | % | # | % | # | % | # | % | # | % | # | % | # |
| Injected | 100 | 3626 | 11.6 | 421 | 0.8 | 28 | 12.8 | 466 | 21.0 | 763 | 0.6 | 20 | 53.2 | 1928 |
| Effective | 20.6 | 746 | 47.7 | 201 | 0.0 | 0 | 5.2 | 24 | 3.9 | 30 | 10 | 2 | 25.4 | 489 |
| Direct Flow | 19.2 | 143 | 65.7 | 132 | | | 12.5 | 3 | 0 | 0 | 0 | 0 | 1.6 | 8 |
| Direct Execution | 24.3 | 181 | 34.3 | 69 | | | 50.0 | 12 | 100 | 30 | 0 | 0 | 14.3 | 70 |
| Indirect Flow | 33.9 | 253 | 0.0 | 0 | | | 4.2 | 1 | 0 | 0 | 0 | 0 | 51.5 | 252 |
| Indirect Data | 22.6 | 169 | 0.0 | 0 | | | 33.3 | 8 | 0 | 0 | 100 | 2 | 32.5 | 159 |

b- Bubblesort

**Fig. 10.** Behavioural model

The first term is completely determined by the workload and characterizes the propagation of the error from a user register to an output port. The second term combines two phenomena: (i) the propagation of the errors among the registers, and (ii) the potential overwrite of errors. This term depends on both the workload and the fault injection method.

For the structural model we assume that the effect of the injected fault during execution of instruction 0 is one of four possible events. The terms $p_1 \cdots p_4$ represent the probabilities of occurrence of each of these events:

- $p_1$ corresponds to the occurrence of an error in registers $r^0$ and $r$ ($r^0 \neq r$) due to incorrect register selection;

- $p_2$ corresponds to $P_1$ the occurrence of an error in $r^0$ due to a fault on the data lines;

- $p_3$ corresponds to the occurrence of an error in $r^0$ due to a fault on the control line (no latch);

- $p_4$ corresponds to the occurrence of an error in $r$ ($r \neq r^0$) due to a fault on the control line (unexpected latch).

| Class | Error Latency (# instructions) | Structural Model | | Behavioural Model | |
|-------|-------------------------------|------------------|---------|-------------------|---------|
| | | Heap. | Bubble. | Heap. | Bubble. |
| Indirect Flow | min | 2 | 2 | 2 | 2 |
| | max | 13 | 20 | 63 | 129 |
| | median | 2 | 2 | 8 | 39 |
| | mean | 3.42 | 2.93 | 10.96 | 41.21 |
| | std | 2.79 | 3.37 | 9.58 | 31.26 |
| | # of errors | 52 | 42 | 267 | 253 |
| Indirect Data | min | 1 | 1 | 1 | 1 |
| | max | 18 | 5 | 105 | 6 |
| | median | 3 | 3 | 5 | 2 |
| | mean | 3.17 | 2.85 | 8.02 | 2.27 |
| | std | 2.70 | 0.55 | 11.25 | 1.49 |
| | # of errors | 72 | 59 | 290 | 169 |

**Fig. 11.** Indirect errors manifestation latencies

As the fault can affect at most two user registers during instruction 0, it can be easily verified that:

$$p[e(r^0)] + \sum_{r^0 \neq r} p[e(r)] - \sum_{r^0 \neq r} p[e(r^0) \wedge e(r)] = 1$$

The three terms can be respectively developed as: $p[e(r^0)] = p_1 + p_2 + p_3$, $\sum_{r^0 \neq r} p[e(r)] = p_1 + p_4$ and $\sum_{r^0 \neq r} p[e(r^0) \wedge e(r)] = p_1$.

As the fault locations are uniformly distributed among the set of signals and since the data and register selection lines are much more numerous than the control lines (32+24 vs. 1), it can be stated that both $p_3$ and $p_4$ are much smaller than $p_1$ and $p_2$. More specifically, if an error propagates into the user register file, it is very likely that it will propagate into the destination register of instruction 0 (i.e. $r^0$). In other words, at the end of the execution of instruction 0:

$$\forall r0 \neq r, \ p[e(r^0)] \gg p[e(r)] \tag{2}$$

For the behavioural model, the fault locations are also uniformly distributed. In this case, almost all indirect errors are caused by bit-flips injected into the user registers. For these errors, the error occurrences are totally decoupled from the activity of the system, i.e. there is an equal probability to hit any of the user registers. Therefore,

$$\forall r^0 \neq r \ \ p[e(r^0)] = p[e(r)] \tag{3}$$

Expression (2) implies that faults injected by means of signal manipulation are likely to affect a register ($r^0$) which is, by application of the temporal locality principle [23], *likely* to be used soon. Thus, the mean time until the next access of the affected register will be short.

On the other hand, expression (3) implies that faults injected by variable manipulation affect arbitrary user registers, which leads to a longer access delay as temporal locality does not shorten it.

In our case, since the sorting workloads perform mainly indexed transfers between registers and memory, there is a high probability for the content of an erroneous register to appear either on the data or address buses. Consequently, the first term of expression (1) can be expected to be close to 1 and thus:

$$p(e(o^i)) \approx p[e(r_i)] \qquad (4)$$

As a result, the error latency for both workloads is mainly determined by the access delay, which has been demonstrated to be shorter for errors caused by signal manipulation faults than variable manipulation faults. This explains why the error latency is much shorter for the structural model compared to the behavioural one.

## 6    Summary and Concluding Remarks

This paper presents (i) a description of methods to inject faults in VHDL models, (ii) an overview of a simulation-based fault injection tool, called MEFISTO and (iii) a case study where signal and variable-related faults are injected into a structural and behavioural model of a 32-bit processor, respectively.

The case study has proven the capability of both the signal and variable manipulation methods to inject faults in VHDL models. Signal manipulation can be used on a VHDL model, in a similar way as pin-level fault injection is used on physical systems. Using the former technique, it is possible to inject a fault on any signal, not just on the IC pins. The variable manipulation technique also makes it possible to inject faults that are injectable on physical systems; it can be used to simulate the effect of bit-flips in registers, as caused by heavy-ion fault injection. Simulation-based fault injection provides perfect controllability over where and when a fault is injected, in contrast to the heavy-ion technique.

In the case study, the fault effects are classified into two error classes: direct errors, which manifest directly on the output ports, and indirect errors which stay dormant for some time in the user registers before manifesting. The signal-related faults injected into the structural model are shown to result in direct errors in 80% of the cases, while the variable-related faults injected into the behavioural model only result in direct errors in less than 45% of the cases. Furthermore, the error manifestation latency for indirect errors is much shorter for faults related to signals than variables.

The variation in error latency with respect to the fault type is analyzed in detail. It is argued that the faults related to signals will spread inside the processor, as well as to its output ports, more rapidly than those related to variables. It is interesting to note that this line of reasoning most likely can be extended to include a comparison between pin-level (signal) and heavy-ion (variable) induced errors.

Simulation speed and accuracy are important factors to account for when considering fault injection for error propagation studies. The execution times of the sorting programs are much smaller using an instruction-level simulator, as in the experiments (cf. Fig. 6), than using a more accurate gate-level simulator, thus making it possible to simulate much longer instruction sequences. Furthermore, it can be noted that the behavioural model is more efficient (faster) than the structural one.

Both the structural and behavioural models are abstractions of the same processor at an abstraction level significantly above the gate and circuit level. It is possible to inject only a subset of all possible bit-flip faults using the behavioural model, as it only includes a subset of all "real" registers (variables) that would be present in a physical implementation of the DP32. Likewise, it is possible to inject temporary stuck-at faults on only a subset of all "real" signals using the structural model. This limits the use of simulation models on these abstraction levels for validation of fault tolerance mechanisms.

It should be noted that all faults which are injectable using software-implemented fault injection (SWIFI) on a physical system, also are injectable using instruction-level simulation models, such as the structural and behavioural models used here. Clearly, more research is needed to investigate the accuracy of fault injection experiments at these levels (and using SWIFI), with respect to more detailed ones. Such an investigation could possibly identify classes of faults that can be injected at these higher levels without loss of accuracy; MEFISTO is well suited for this type of experiments.

An important point demonstrated by this study is the relative ease in performing fault injection campaigns using VHDL models. This is due to the ability of the used fault injection techniques to take advantage of available VHDL models, without requiring any model modifications.

Further work with MEFISTO will address the early test of fault tolerance mechanisms imbedded in fault-tolerant systems. In particular, the favorable error tracing capabilities depicted in this paper will be used to monitor the fault activation/error propagation processes in order to:

- monitor the sensitization of the fault tolerance mechanisms, when the fault injection experiments are aimed at *removing potential fault tolerance deficiency faults*,

- study the mapping between the set of faults in the fault-tolerant system and the error models used to test the fault tolerance mechanisms, in order to *evaluate their coverage*.

## Acknowledgements

This work was partially supported by the *Midi-Pyrénées* Regional Authority under contract RECH/90078306, as well as PDCS.

# Estimators for Fault Tolerance Coverage Evaluation*

David Powell  Eliane Martins  Jean Arlat  Yves Crouzet

LAAS-CNRS

**Abstract.** This paper addresses the problem of estimating the coverage of a fault tolerance mechanism through statistical processing of observations collected in fault injection experiments. A formal definition of coverage is given in terms of the fault and system activity sets that characterize the input space. Two categories of sampling techniques are considered for coverage estimation: sampling in the whole space and sampling in a space partitioned into classes. Techniques for unbiassed "early" estimations of coverage are also studied. Then, the "no-reply" problem that hampers most practical fault-injection experiments is discussed and an a posteriori stratification technique is proposed that allows the scope of incomplete tests to be widened by accounting for available structural information about the target system.

## 1   Introduction

A central problem in the validation of fault-tolerant systems is the evaluation of the efficiency of their fault tolerance mechanisms. One parameter used to quantify this efficiency is the *coverage factor* defined as the probability of system recovery given that a fault exists [11]. The sensitivity of dependability measures (such as reliability and availability) to small variations in the coverage factor is well known [11, 6]. Consequently, it is very important to determine coverage as accurately as possible. This paper addresses the problem of obtaining accurate and useful estimations of coverage through the statistical processing of observations collected in *fault injection* experiments.

Fault injection can take various forms according to the level of abstraction used to represent the system (from empirical models to physical prototypes) and the level of application of the faults [3]. We consider in this paper the *physical fault injection* approach, where physical faults (stuck-at-0, stuck-at-1, etc.) are directly applied to the pins of the integrated circuits (ICs) that compose a prototype of the system.

A fault injection experiment is performed on a physical system by corrupting the digital signal values of an IC contained in the system via a fault injection module. This fault injection module places the desired fault condition over one or more IC pins at the appropriate point in time. The behaviour of the system is observed to determine whether or not the injected fault has been properly handled by the system's fault tolerance mechanisms. This may be done in various ways, for example: by monitoring specific hardware signals in the system, by assessing the truth of application-level predicates that define "correct operation" or by comparing the system outputs with the fault free case (via a duplicate system or by reprocessing the same inputs with the fault injection module deactivated).

---

* This is a condensed version of [44].

One of the difficulties of the approach is the selection of the faults to be injected, since it is not always possible to physically inject all faults that could occur during the system operational life. The determination of these possible faults is another difficulty: the complexity of current VLSI chips and the need to account for temporary faults, which represent the majority of the faults that actually occur in computer systems [50], makes exhaustive testing intractable. As a consequence, coverage evaluation is a problem of statistical estimation, where inferences about a population are based on sample observation.

Since the effect of a fault is dependent on system activity at the moment of its occurrence, we consider a sample space consisting of the combination of the set of faults and the set of system "activities" at the moment of fault occurrence. As recommended in [8], a *weighted coverage* is calculated: weights are assigned to each point in the sample space based on their relative probability of occurrence.

The paper is organized as follows. Section 2 gives the basic system definitions and formalizes the notion of a coverage factor. Section 3 presents and compares two categories of sampling techniques for coverage factor estimation: sampling in the whole input space and sampling in a space partitioned into *classes*. Several estimators are analyzed and compared by applying them to data relative to three hypothetical systems. Section 4 proposes further sampling techniques that allow unbiased estimations of coverage to be made before all classes of the sample space have been tested. Section 5 is devoted to the "no-reply" problem that hampers most practical fault-injection experiments. This problem occurs if some parts of the target system cannot be tested by the fault injection tool due to inaccessibility or parasitic mutations. An *a posteriori* stratification technique is proposed that allows the scope of incomplete tests to be widened by accounting for available structural information about the target system. Finally, Section 6 concludes the paper.

## 2    Definitions

In this section, we give a formal definition of the coverage *factor* of a fault tolerance mechanism and relate it to the often-used notion of the coverage *proportion*.

### 2.1  Coverage Factor

We consider a fault tolerance mechanism or fault-tolerant system subjected to faults $f$ in a given fault space $F$. Let $Y$ be a variable characterizing the coverage of a particular fault, such that $Y = 1$ if the mechanism correctly handles the fault (0 otherwise).

The effect of a given fault is dependent on system activity at the moment of, and following, the occurrence of the fault. This system activity can be modelled as a trajectory in the system state space starting from the system state at the moment of fault occurrence and evolving in function of the sequence of system inputs (including the passage of time). Here, we call such a trajectory a system *activity* and let $A$ represent the set of all possible activities in the considered operational profile of the system. The input space of a fault tolerance mechanism can thus be considered in two parts: (a) the *activity set* $A$ due to the system's functional inputs, and (b) the *fault set* $F$ which the mechanism should handle. The complete input space of a fault tolerance mechanism is then defined as the Cartesian product $G = F \times A$. The "output" of the mechanism from the viewpoint of fault tolerance is the predicate $Y$.

For a given fault/activity space $G$, coverage is defined as the *cumulative distribution* of the time interval between the occurrence of a fault and its correct handling by a fault tolerance mechanism [18, 3]. In this paper, we focus on the *asymptotic* value of this distribution, which is called the *coverage factor*, defined formally as:

$$c(G) = \Pr\{Y = 1 \mid G\} \qquad (1)$$

i.e. the conditional probability of correct fault handling, given the occurrence of a fault/activity pair $g \in G$.

$Y$ is a random variable that can take the values 0 or 1 for each element of the fault/activity space $G$, the coverage factor $c(G)$ can be viewed as $E\{Y|G\}$, the expected value of $Y$ for the population $G$. In terms of each fault/activity pair $g \in G$, let $y(g) = 1$ if $Y = 1$ when the system is submitted to $g$ (0 otherwise), and let $p(g|G)$ be the *relative probability of occurrence* of $g$. Expression (1) can then be rewritten as:

$$c(G) = \sum_{g \in G} y(g)p(g|G) \qquad (2)$$

## 2.2  Coverage Proportion

Using the same notation as before, the efficiency of a fault tolerance mechanism can alternatively be characterized by the *proportion* of fault/activity pairs in the population $G$ which are correctly handled, i.e. the arithmetic mean of the $y(g)$ in $G$:

$$\tilde{y} = \frac{1}{|G|} \sum_{g \in G} y(g) \qquad (3)$$

The relationship between $c(G)$ and $\tilde{y}$ can be clarified by introducing a variable $P$, representing the fault/activity occurrence process in $G$, i.e. $P$ has the values $p(g|G)$. The *covariance* between $Y$ and $P$, $S_{YP}$ is, by definition:

$$S_{YP} = \frac{1}{|G|} \sum_{g \in G} (y(g) - \tilde{y})(p(g|G) - \tilde{p}) \text{ where } \tilde{p} = \frac{1}{|G|} \sum_{g \in G} p(g|G) = \frac{1}{|G|} \qquad (4)$$

From (2-4), it is easy to show that: $\tilde{y} = c(G) - |G|S_{YP}$ $\qquad (5)$

From (5), it can be seen that the coverage proportion $\tilde{y}$ is less (resp. greater) than the coverage factor $c(G)$ as defined in (2) if $S_{YP}$ is positive (resp. negative). A positive correlation ($S_{YP} > 0$) between $Y$ and $P$ could be expected, for example, if a system designer took account of the relative occurrence probabilities, $p(g|G)$, to implement mechanisms that "cover" the most probable fault/activity pairs [10].

## 3  Coverage Estimation

The most accurate way to determine $c(G)$ as defined in (2) would be to submit the system to all $g \in G$ and to observe all values of $y(g)$. However, such exhaustive testing is only possible under very restrictive hypotheses (for example, the consideration of permanent stuck-at faults only, or when testing only a small part of the system). For this reason, coverage evaluation is in practice carried out by submitting the system to a *subset* of fault/activity occurrences $G^* \subset G$. The selection of the sub-set $G^*$ can be done either (i) deterministically, or (ii) by random sampling in the space $G$. This paper focuses on the latter approach, which allows statistical inferences to be made about the complete space $G$. The important questions that must be addressed are: (i) how to estimate the value of $c(G)$ and to obtain inferences about the error committed in the estimation; (ii) how to select samples, and (iii) how to obtain a sufficiently accurate estimation in a reasonable time.

In this section, we successively consider two approaches for estimating coverage factors based on techniques that carry out the sampling (a) directly in the complete space $G$, and (b) in sub-spaces defined by a partition of $G$. For each technique, the coverage estimator and the variance of the coverage estimator are defined[1].

## 3.1 Sampling in a Non-Partitioned Space

We first consider the theory of coverage factor estimation by sampling in a non-partitioned sample space and then discuss practical implementation aspects.

**Representative Sampling.** We consider sampling with replacement of a sub-set $G^*$ of $n$ fault/activity pairs in $G$. To each element of $G$ is assigned a *selection probability*, $t(g|G)$, such that $\forall g \in G$, $t(g|G) > 0$ and $\sum_{g \in G} t(g|G) = 1$.

To obtain the estimation of $c(G)$, we recall that $c(G)$ is the expected value of the variable $Y$ in the space $G$. We are therefore faced with a problem of estimation of a population mean. It can be shown that an unbiased estimator $\hat{c}'(G)$ of this mean and its variance $V\{\hat{c}'(G)\}$ are given by:

$$\hat{c}'(G) = \frac{1}{n} \sum_{i=1}^{n} y(g_i) \frac{p(g_i|G)}{t(g_i|G)} \tag{6}$$

$$V\{\hat{c}'(G)\} = \frac{1}{n}\left( \sum_{g \in G}\left[ y(g) \frac{p^2(g|G)}{t(g|G)} \right] - c^2(G) \right) \tag{7}$$

If the sample selection distribution is chosen such that $\forall g \in G$, $t(g|G) = p(g|G)$, then (6) and (7) may be rewritten as:

$$\hat{c}(G) = \frac{d}{n} \text{ with } d = \sum_{i=1}^{n} y(g_i) \tag{8}$$

$$V\{\hat{c}(G)\} = \frac{c(G) - c^2(G)}{n} \tag{9}$$

---

[1] For space limitations, we do not give the expressions for the *estimators* of the variances of the estimators studied in this paper. The interested reader may refer to [44].

The reader will recognize the well-known formulas for estimating a binomial *proportion*. However, this sampling technique does indeed give an unbiased estimation of the coverage *factor* $c(G)$. The sampling experiments are Bernoulli trials with outcome $Y = 1$ with probability $\pi$ and $Y = 0$ with probability $1 - \pi$ where $\pi = \sum_{g \in G} y(g) t(g|G)$. If the sampling distribution were uniform (i.e.

$\forall g \in G$, $t(g|G) = 1/|G|$) then we would have $\pi = \tilde{y}$, the coverage *proportion* (cf. (3)). However, by setting the sample selection distribution equal to the fault/activity occurrence distribution, we obtain $\pi = c(G)$, the coverage *factor* (cf. (2)). A sample obtained in this way will henceforth be termed a *representative sample*.

**Practical Implementation.** By definition, a fault/activity pair $g \in G$ corresponds to an activity $a \in A$ and a fault $f \in F$. The representative sampling technique described above therefore requires the random selection of $n$ pairs $\langle a, f \rangle$ such that $a$ and $f$ are selected independently with probabilities $t(a|A) = p(a|A)$ and $t(f|F) = p(f|F)$, where $p(a|A)$ represents the distribution of activities over the considered activity space $A$ at the instant the fault occurs and $p(f|F)$ is the distribution of fault occurrences over the considered fault space $F$, such that $p(g|G) = p(a|A) \times p(f|F)$.

The condition $t(a|A) = p(a|A)$ can be satisfied without having to explicitly define the activity distribution $p(a|A)$. The activity space $A$ depends on the considered target system and its functional input profile. A real fault can occur at any random point in time, so the probability $p(a|A)$ of it occurring in coincidence with a particular activity $a$ (or system state trajectory, cf. Section 2.1) is dependent only on the frequency at which that activity recurs, given the system's functional input profile. Therefore, to ensure that an injected fault "chooses" $a$ with a probability $t(a|A) = p(a|A)$, it suffices to simulate this independence between system activity and the instant of occurrence of a real fault. This can be achieved as follows:

a)  the target system is reset (to remove the effects of previous experiments) and is then activated with the considered functional input profile;

b)  selection of a fault $f \in F$ according to the fault occurrence distribution $p(f|F)$;

c)  the selected fault $f$ is injected at some random delay after initiating the system activation.

The definition of $p(f|F)$ can be simplified by characterizing the set of faults $F$ according to different attributes whose distributions are defined independently. One possible set of attributes suitable for IC-based systems, inspired from [1], consists of: (a) the *location* of the fault in the target system (i.e. the affected IC), (b) the *multiplicity* of the fault (number of IC pins affected, noted $mx$), (c) the affected *pins* of the faulted IC, (d) the fault *value model* (stuck-at-0, stuck-at-1, etc.) for each affected IC pin, and (e) the fault *timing model* (transient, intermittent, permanent, etc.) of each affected IC pin. The fault occurrence probability $p(f|F)$ can then be expressed as the product of a set of conditional probabilities defining the distributions of the attributes of the given fault in each attribute category [44]. Given a definition of $F$ in terms of fault attributes, a representative sample of $n$ faults, noted $F_n$, can be characterized by a set of $n$ vectors, where the elements of each vector define the fault attributes that are selected randomly according to the different attribute distributions:

$$F_n = \begin{cases} f(1) = \{location_1, \ multiplicity_1, \ pins_1, \ value\_model_1, \ timing\_model_1\} \\ f(2) = \{location_2, \ multiplicity_2, \ pins_2, \ value\_model_2, \ timing\_model_2\} \\ \quad \cdots \\ f(n) = \{location_n, \ multiplicity_n, \ pins_n, \ value\_model_n, \ timing\_model_n\} \end{cases}$$

A practical fault injection tool, such as the *MESSALINE* injector developed at LAAS [3], can automatically carry out several fault injection experiments at a single location (IC) of the target system. However, moving the injector probe from one location to another requires manual intervention so it is more practical to sort the set of selected faults by the attribute *location* before carrying out the experiments. Furthermore, the selection of the other attributes can be carried out dynamically for each location to avoid having to store all the $n$ vectors of $F_n$.

In a target system with $N_c$ ICs, a practical representative fault injection campaign thus consists of $N_c$ subsets of experiments. A random number of experiments are carried out on each IC of the target system according to the number of occurrences of the given *location* value in $F_n$. These subsets of the set of possible fault locations effectively partition the fault space $F$ and thus the fault/activity space $G$ into $N_c$ disjoint subsets. We will now consider other techniques for estimating the coverage factor that rely on such a partitioning.

## 3.2  Sampling in a Partitioned Space

For the sampling techniques that follow, the sample space $G$ is considered as partitioned into *classes*. Each class will be referenced by a subscript, according to the following convention: subscripts in Greek letters are used to refer to classes in the sample space $G$ and subscripts in Latin letters are used to refer to classes in the sample (the reason for this convention will only become apparent in the presentation of the 2-stage sampling techniques described in Section 4.2).

By definition of a partition, the classes form $M$ disjoint subsets:

$$G = \bigcup_{\alpha=1}^{M} G_\alpha \text{ such that } \forall \alpha,\beta, \ \alpha \neq \beta, \ G_\alpha \cap G_\beta = \emptyset$$

We can rewrite the coverage factor definition (2) as follows:

$$c(G) = \sum_{\alpha=1}^{M} \sum_{g \in G_\alpha} y(g)p(g|G) = \sum_{\alpha=1}^{M} p(G_\alpha|G) \sum_{g \in G_\alpha} y(g)p(g|G_\alpha) = \sum_{\alpha=1}^{M} p(G_\alpha|G)c(G_\alpha)$$

where $c(G_\alpha) = \sum_{g \in G_\alpha} y(g)p(g|G_\alpha)$ is the coverage factor for fault/activity class $G_\alpha$.

We will now consider two sampling techniques based on the above definitions of a partitioned sample space.

**A Naive Estimator.** The first sampling technique that can be considered in a partitioned sample space is to take an equal number of *representative samples* $n_i = n/M$ in each class $G_i, \forall i \in [1, M]$, to count the number of successfully covered faults for each class, $d_i$, and to apply an estimator derived directly from that given in (8) for sampling in a non-partitioned space:

$$\hat{c}_{na}(G) = \frac{1}{n} \sum_{i=1}^{M} d_i = \frac{d}{n}$$

We call this a *naive* estimator since it is *biased* if the fault occurrences in each class are not equally probable — it can be easily shown that:

$$E\{\hat{c}_{na}(G)\} = \tilde{c}(G_\alpha) = \frac{1}{M} \sum_{\alpha=1}^{M} c(G_\alpha)$$

Reasoning in the same way as in Section 2, the covariance $S_{CP}$ between the coverage $c(G_\alpha)$ and the occurrence probability $p(G_\alpha|G)$ of each class is given by:

$$S_{CP} = \frac{1}{M} \sum_{\alpha=1}^{M} \left( c(G_\alpha) - \tilde{c}(G_\alpha) \right) \left( p(G_\alpha|G) - \frac{1}{M} \right)$$

from which it can be shown that: $\tilde{c}(G_\alpha) = c(G) - M \, S_{CP}$.

The estimator $\hat{c}_{na}(G)$ can therefore provide pessimistic or optimistic estimations of the system coverage depending on whether the covariance $S_{CP}$ is positive or negative. This will be illustrated by the examples presented in Section 3.3.

**Stratified Sampling.** In a stratified sampling, a number of samples $n_\alpha$ is predetermined[2] for each class or *stratum* $G_\alpha, \forall \alpha \in [1, M]$. For each class, a *representative* sample of size $n_i = n_\alpha$ is taken and the class coverage factor is estimated using (8) applied to the class instead of the complete sample space:

$$\hat{c}(G_i) = \frac{d_i}{n_i} \tag{10}$$

where $d_i$ is the number of covered faults in class $G_i$. The system coverage factor is then estimated by:

$$\hat{c}_{st}(G) = \sum_{i=1}^{M} p(G_i|G)\hat{c}(G_i) \tag{11}$$

The variance of this estimator is:

2 The term "*a priori* stratification" is used to underline this fact and to distinguish this approach from "*a posteriori* stratification" considered in Section 5.1.

$$V\{\hat{c}_{st}(G)\} = \sum_{\alpha=1}^{M} p^2(G_\alpha|G) V\{\hat{c}(G_\alpha)\} \qquad (12)$$

where the variance of the estimator $\hat{c}(G_\alpha)$ is given by (9) applied to the class $G_\alpha$:

$$V\{\hat{c}(G_\alpha)\} = \frac{1}{n_\alpha}\left(c(G_\alpha) - c^2(G_\alpha)\right) \qquad (13)$$

From (12) and (13) it can be seen that the variance of the estimator of the system coverage depends on the allocation of the sample size in each class, $n_\alpha$. After the total sample size $n$ is chosen, there are many ways to divide $n$ into the individual classes. Here we consider two possible allocations: a *representative* allocation $\forall \alpha, \ n_\alpha = p(G_\alpha|G)n$, which can be shown to be optimal [21, 44], and a *homogeneous* allocation $\forall \alpha, \ n_\alpha = n/M$.

The estimator corresponding to a representative allocation is denoted $\hat{c}_{stR}(G)$ and, by substituting the value of $n_\alpha$ in (10) and using (11), is expressed by:

$$\hat{c}_{stR}(G) = \sum_{i=1}^{M} p(G_i|G)\frac{d_i}{n\,p(G_i|G)} = \frac{1}{n}\sum_{i=1}^{M} d_i = \frac{d}{n}$$

which is analogous to the estimator of a representative sample in the whole space presented in (8). However, since a *pre-determined* number of samples is taken in each class, the variance of this estimator is different to that given in (9) — by substituting $n_\alpha$ in (13) and using (12), we obtain (after a little algebraic manipulation):

$$V\{\hat{c}_{stR}\} = \frac{1}{n}c(G) - \frac{1}{n}\sum_{\alpha=1}^{M} p(G_\alpha|G) c^2(G_\alpha)$$

The estimator, noted $\hat{c}_{stH}(G)$, and corresponding variance for a *homogeneous allocation* are obtained in a similar way to above:

$$\hat{c}_{stH}(G) = \frac{M}{n}\sum_{i=1}^{M} p(G_i|G) d_i \qquad (14)$$

$$V\{\hat{c}_{stH}(G)\} = \frac{M}{n}\sum_{\alpha=1}^{M} p^2(G_\alpha|G)\left(c(G_\alpha) - c^2(G_\alpha)\right)$$

## 3.3  Comparative Examples

In this Section, the various estimators defined in sections 3.1 and 3.2 are compared by way of three hypothetical systems whose characteristics are defined in Fig. 1. Each system is partitioned into $M = 50$ classes; the distribution of the coverage, $c(G_\alpha)$, and the relative fault/activity occurrence probability $p(G_\alpha|G)$ of each class are presented, as well as the values of the system coverage, $c(G)$, and the mean coverage per class, $\tilde{c}(G_\alpha)$. The values of $c(G)$ for each example are given in Table

1, together with that of the "normalized" covariance (the *correlation factor* ) between $p(G_\alpha|G)$ and $c(G_\alpha)$ defined as:

$$\rho_{CP} = \frac{S_{CP}}{\sqrt{V(C).V(P)}} \times 100\%$$

with: $V(C) = \dfrac{1}{M} \displaystyle\sum_{\alpha=1}^{M} \left(c(G_\alpha) - \bar{c}(G)\right)^2$ and $V(P) = \dfrac{1}{M} \displaystyle\sum_{\alpha=1}^{M} \left(P(G_\alpha|G) - \dfrac{1}{M}\right)^2$

**Table 1.** Coverage and correlation figures

| Overall coverage $c(G)$ | Class correlation $\rho_{CP}$ |
|:---:|:---:|
| 0.978 | -13.5 % |
| 0.9379 | +41.5 % |
| 0.9999963 | -89.1 % |

We assume that, due to the central limit theorem, all the estimators are normally distributed around their expected value. Fig. 2 compares the various estimators in terms of the expected 99% confidence interval defined by:

$$E\{\hat{X}\} - 2.58\sqrt{V\{\hat{X}\}} < h(\hat{X}) < E\{\hat{X}\} + 2.58\sqrt{V\{\hat{X}\}} \qquad (15)$$

The expected confidence intervals are plotted as a function of $n$, the sample size.

From Fig. 1 (top), it can be noted that system A features: a relative homogeneity among the classes with respect to the coverage, a low variability of the relative occurrence probabilities and a slight (negative) correlation $\rho_{CP}$ with the consequence that $c(G)$ and $\tilde{c}(G_\alpha)$ are close to one another, with $\tilde{c}(G_\alpha)$ slightly greater than $c(G)$. For this system, the gain in precision provided by stratification is negligible — Fig. 2 (top) shows that the theoretical confidence intervals are almost the same.

For system B (Fig. 1, middle) there is a greater variability for the coverage and the relative occurrence probability in each class than for system A. Furthermore, the correlation factor $\rho_{CP}$ is positive and greater than 40%. Consequently, $c(G)$ is quite different from $\tilde{c}(G_\alpha)$. The estimator $\hat{c}_{na}(G)$, which converges to $\tilde{c}(G_\alpha)$, provides a very pessimistic value of the system coverage (Fig. 2, middle). Concerning the other estimators, it can be noticed that stratified sampling with representative allocation, $\hat{c}_{stR}(G)$, provides better precision in the estimations, especially for small $n$.

System C (Fig. 1, bottom) has a very high coverage with a high variability over the classes and a large negative correlation with respect to the fault/activity occurrence probabilities. Consequently, $\tilde{c}(G_\alpha)$ is an optimistic evaluation for the system coverage — the same is therefore true for the estimations provided by $\hat{c}_{na}(G)$ (Fig. 2, bottom). It can also be noted that stratification with representative allocation is equivalent to representative sampling in a non partitioned population. However the gain in precision over a stratification with homogeneous allocation is appreciable.

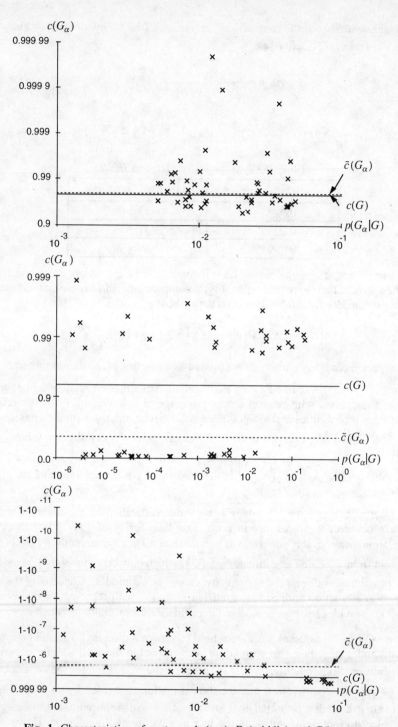

**Fig. 1.** Characteristics of systems A (top), B (middle) and C(bottom)

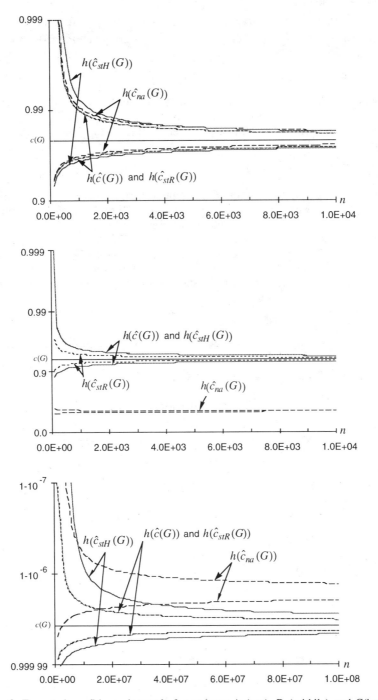

**Fig. 2.** Expected confidence intervals for systems A (top), B (middle) and C(bottom)

In summary, these three examples illustrate that:

1)  a naive estimation of coverage by $\hat{c}_{na}(G)$ can be very pessimistic (system B) or optimistic (system C) depending on the sign of the correlation factor $\rho_{CP}$;

2)  representative stratification allows an appreciable gain in precision when the classes have very different values of $c(G_\alpha)$ (system B).

Concerning the last point, it can be shown [21] that stratification with a representative allocation of samples is in fact never worse than an equivalent sample in the whole space. However, as illustrated by system A (Fig. 2, top), the gain in precision is negligible when the classes are homogeneous.

## 4    Early Estimations

When validating a prototype of a fault-tolerant system, it is of real practical interest to obtain estimations of coverage as soon as possible to provide rapid feedback to the design process. However, fault injection experiments can be very time-consuming. In this section, we consider two techniques that enable unbiased estimations of coverage to be obtained as soon as possible. We first consider what early conclusions can be drawn when a stratified sampling approach has been followed but not yet completed. Second, we introduce another method, called *two-stage* sampling. A comparison of these techniques is then given.

### 4.1  Incomplete Stratified Sampling

When a stratified sampling technique has been followed but not yet completed, the sample space $G$ can be decomposed in two parts:

*   the subset $G'$ containing the $m$ tested classes, with $m \in [1, M]$, with a corresponding probability of fault/activity occurrences: $p(G'|G) = \sum_{\alpha=1}^{m} p(G_\alpha|G)$

*   the subset $\overline{G'} = G - G'$, containing the classes not yet covered by the tests, with a corresponding probability of fault/activity occurrences: $p(\overline{G'}|G) = 1 - p(G'|G)$

The system coverage $c(G)$ can then be expressed as:

$$c(G) = p(G'|G)c(G') + p(\overline{G'}|G)c(\overline{G'}) \tag{16}$$

Letting $p(G_i|G') = p(G_i|G)/p(G'|G)$, the coverage relative to the part tested, $c(G')$, can be estimated according to (11) for the sub population $G'$ by:

$$\hat{c}_{st}(G') = \sum_{i=1}^{m} p(G_i|G').\hat{c}(G_i)$$

Since classes are selected deterministically, we cannot make any statistical inference about $c(\overline{G'})$ the coverage for the sub-population not yet covered by the tests. The only thing we can say about $c(\overline{G'})$ is that it is some value between zero and one! This means that we can only estimate *bounds* on the *system* coverage $c(G)$ taking into account the lack of knowledge about $c(\overline{G'})$. If, for a given confidence level, we have: $\hat{c}_{st}(G') - \delta_{G'} \le c(G') \le \hat{c}_{st}(G') + \delta_{G'}$, then, applying this relation to (16), we can write with the same confidence level:

$$p(G'|G).[\hat{c}_{st}(G') - \delta_{G'}] \le c(G) \le p(G'|G).[\hat{c}_{st}(G') + \delta_{G'}] + p(\overline{G'}|G) \qquad (17)$$

From relation (17), it can be concluded that in incomplete stratified sampling, the error in extending the estimation to the complete system space is minimized if $p(G'|G)$ is maximized for a given $m$. This occurs if classes are tested by decreasing order of $p(G_\alpha|G)$.

## 4.2  Two-Stage  Sampling

Another way to obtain unbiased early estimations of system coverage is to use *two-stage* sampling. In this technique, the sample space is again divided into $M$ classes but the sampling process is carried out in two steps:

1)  selection of a *random* sample of $m$ classes among $M$ ;
2)  selection of a representative random sample of *predetermined* size $n_\alpha$, $\alpha \in [1, M]$ in each of the $m$ classes.

Three different two-stage sampling procedures are considered. They differ by the sampling technique used in the first stage and the type of estimator used:

- sampling without replacement, with an equal probability of choosing each class — a *linear* and a *quotient* estimator are considered, noted $\hat{c}_{2epL}(G)$ and $\hat{c}_{2epQ}(G)$;

- sampling with replacement, with different probabilities $A_\alpha$ of choosing each class $G_\alpha$ — the corresponding estimator is noted $\hat{c}_{2dp}(G)$.

The theory behind these two-stage sampling techniques is not detailed here — we use results presented in [17] by adapting the notation. The expressions for the different estimators and variances are presented in Table 2. In this table, $\hat{c}(G_i)$ and $V\{\hat{c}(G_\alpha)\}$ are given by equations (10) and (13) respectively. Note that, since the first stage sampling is carried out *without* replacement, $\hat{c}_{epL}(G)$ and $\hat{c}_{epQ}(G)$ both become equal to the stratified sampling estimator $\hat{c}_{st}(G)$ (cf. (11)) when $m = M$.

## 4.3  Comparative  Examples

The same three systems that were presented in Fig. 1 are used to compare the estimators obtained from an *incomplete stratified sampling* (with classes selected by decreasing probability) and *two-stage sampling*. In all methods, a representative sample size in each class is fixed in advance: $n_\alpha = p(G_\alpha|G)n$. For the estimator $\hat{c}_{2dp}(G)$, the 1st-stage class sampling probabilities are given by: $A_\alpha = p(G_\alpha|G)$.

Fig. 3 compares the various two-stage estimators in terms of the expected range of variation of coverage estimates as defined by (15).

**Table 2.** Expressions for two-stage sampling techniques

| **1st-stage: equal probabilities w/o replacement — linear estimator** |
|---|

$$\hat{c}_{2epL}(G) = \frac{M}{m} \sum_{i=1}^{m} p(G_i|G)\, \hat{c}(G_i)$$

$$V\{\hat{c}_{2epL}(G)\} = \frac{M}{m} \left(\frac{M-m}{M-1}\right) \sum_{\alpha=1}^{M} \left[ p(G_\alpha|G)\, c(G_\alpha) - \frac{c(G)}{M} \right]^2 + \frac{M}{m} \sum_{\alpha=1}^{M} p^2(G_\alpha|G)\, V\{\hat{c}(G_\alpha)\}$$

| **1st-stage: equal probabilities w/o replacement — quotient estimator** |
|---|

$$\hat{c}_{2epQ}(G) = \sum_{i=1}^{m} p(G_i|G)\, \hat{c}(G_i) \Big/ \sum_{i=1}^{m} p(G_i|G)$$

$$V\{\hat{c}_{2epQ}(G)\} = \frac{M}{m}\left(\frac{M-m}{M-1}\right) \sum_{\alpha=1}^{M} p^2(G_\alpha|G)\, [c(G_\alpha) - c(G)]^2 + \frac{M}{m} \sum_{\alpha=1}^{M} p^2(G_\alpha|G)\, V\{\hat{c}(G_\alpha)\}$$

| **1st-stage: different probabilities with replacement** |
|---|

$$\hat{c}_{2dp}(G) = \frac{1}{m} \sum_{i=1}^{m} \frac{p(G_i|G)}{A_i}\, \hat{c}(G_i)$$

$$V\{\hat{c}_{2dp}(G)\} = \frac{1}{m} \sum_{\alpha=1}^{M} A_\alpha \left[ \frac{p(G_\alpha|G)}{A_\alpha}\, c(G_\alpha) - c(G) \right]^2 + \frac{1}{m} \sum_{\alpha=1}^{M} \frac{p^2(G_\alpha|G)}{A_\alpha}\, V\{\hat{c}(G_\alpha)\}$$

The figures give the bounds of the system coverage estimation as a function of $m$, the number of classes tested. For incomplete (representative) stratified sampling, the expected value of the partial estimate $E\{\hat{c}_{stR}(G')\}$ is shown, together with the lower and upper limits of the overall coverage, noted $\underline{\hat{c}_{stR}(G')}$ and $\overline{\hat{c}_{stR}(G')}$, obtained from relation (17) with $\hat{c}_{st}(G') = \hat{c}_{stR}(G')$ and $\delta_{G'} = K_\gamma \sqrt{V\{\hat{c}_{stR}(G')\}}$.

For all three systems, the estimator $\hat{c}_{2epL}(G)$ gives the worst results, since the estimations obtained are subject to great variability.

The incomplete stratified sample shows better precision for system B only, especially for $m \geq 13$. This is because class 13 — i.e. the class with the 13th highest value of $p(G_\alpha|G)$, (cf. Fig. 1, middle) has a very low coverage value and its inclusion in the sample has a significant effect on the global coverage estimate.

The estimator $\hat{c}_{2dp}(G)$ displays a good precision for systems A and C, but not for system B. This is due to the fact that system B has a greater variability of the coverage values than the other two. Moreover, the estimations provided do not converge to $\overline{c}(G)$ when $m \to M$, because the first stage samples are selected with replacement.

Finally, the estimator that provides quite good results for the three systems considered is $\hat{c}_{2epQ}(G)$. This estimator provides relatively good precision for small values of $m$. Only for system B is it necessary to wait till $m \approx 30$. This is due to the heter-

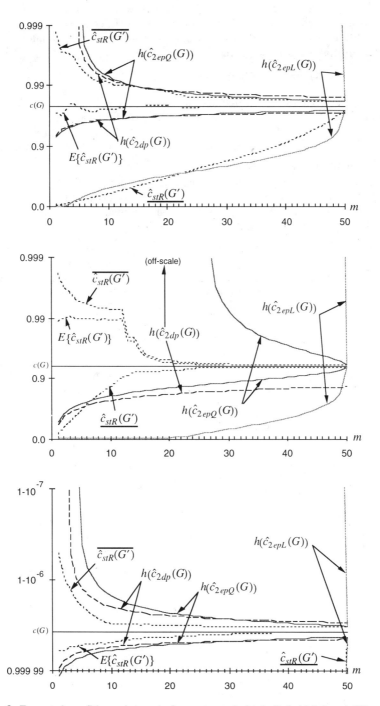

**Fig. 3.** Expected confidence intervals for systems A (top), B (middle) and C(bottom)

ogeneity of the class coverage values of system B, which means that more classes must be tested to reduce the variance of the estimator. In conclusion, this estimator provides the best overall early estimations — moreover, the estimator becomes equivalent to stratified sampling when $m = M$.

# 5    The No-Reply Problem

One source of estimation errors that is quite common in opinion polls is the "no-reply" problem that occurs when it is not possible to obtain measures from some elements in the sample [14]. In physical fault injection, a similar problem occurs because of non-significant experiments, which can occur for at least two reasons:

1) Some injected faults may not be activated[3].
2) Some experiments foreseen in the sample set may not be feasible due to physical problems such as injection probes not adapted to certain circuits or parasitic mutations (e.g. capacitive loading effects) that prevent the target system from working even though no faults are explicitly injected.

In case (1) above, it is sometimes possible to carry out further experiments to increase the effective sample size and restore the level of precision. In case (2), however, it is not usually possible to carry out further experiments. Whatever sampling technique was adopted at the outset, as soon as a circuit is chosen that cannot be sampled, then — from a circuit-only viewpoint — it will be impossible to sample the whole system and the only way to make an inference about the overall coverage is to extend a partial estimate to the bounds expressed by relation (17) for incomplete stratified sampling.

In this section, we study an "*a posteriori* stratification" technique that enables better estimations to be obtained if structural information about the target system is available.

## 5.1  A Posteriori Stratification

*A posteriori* stratification is based on the definition of "strata" or classes *after* having sampled the fault/activity space. We consider the case where an attempt is made to test the target system using the homogeneous (*a priori*) stratification technique (estimator $\hat{c}_{stH}(G)$, cf. (14)). The classes are defined here by the integrated circuits that compose the target system.

When a fault is injected directly onto a single pin of an IC (i.e. a fault of multiplicity 1, cf. Section 3.1), for instance, by forcing a particular voltage pattern on it, the fault that is injected simulates a fault that could have occurred in that IC or, indeed, in any IC that has a pin connected to the same equipotential line (wire). In the general case of faults of multiplicity $mx \geq 1$, the same can be said for the *group* of affected equipotentials[4].

---

[3]   Fault activation can be observed if the fault injector is equipped with a current-sensing device at the level of the injection probe. If this is not the case, then experiments with non-activated faults cannot be discarded, with pessimistic or optimistic consequences on the coverage estimation, depending on the observed fault-handling predicate $Y$.

[4]   Note that for $mx>1$, the group of equipotentials could have less than $mx$ members if the faulted circuit has more than one pin on the same equipotential.

This suggests a different way of "counting" the fault injection experiments — instead of counting the experiments for each circuit, they can be counted by groups of equipotentials. This can be done if the detailed wiring diagram of the target system is available. If the target system has $Q$ equipotentials and faults of multiplicity $mx \leq MX$ are taken into account during the fault injection experiments, the sample space can be partitioned according to the $\Theta = \sum\limits_{mx=1}^{MX} \theta(mx)$ equipotential groups that can be affected, where $\theta(1) = Q$ and $\theta(mx) \leq \begin{pmatrix} Q \\ mx \end{pmatrix}$ for $mx \in [2, MX]$.

The estimator, noted $\hat{c}''_{st}(G)$, that applies to *a posteriori* stratification is the same as that for *a priori* stratification with a representative sample in each class, i.e. from (10) and (11), and letting $G''_i$ represent a class in the sample space partitioned according to equipotential groups:

$$\hat{c}''_{st}(G) = \sum_{i=1}^{\Theta} p(G''_i|G) \frac{d_i}{n_i}$$

where $n_i$ is the number of injected faults that affect equipotential group $G''_i$, $d_i$ the number of covered faults and $p(G''_i|G)$ is the probability of fault/activity occurrence affecting that equipotential group. The probabilities $p(G''_i|G)$ are calculated from the distributions of the various fault attributes as defined in Section 3.1, together with the connectivity information derived from a description of the target system, which enables the probability of faults at the IC pin level to mapped onto the corresponding equipotential group [38].

The variance of this estimator cannot be determined in advance however, since the number of faults affecting each equipotential group is no longer fixed but is in fact itself a random variable. Nevertheless, once a set of experiments has been carried out, the number of faults $n_\alpha$, $\alpha = 1..\Theta$ affecting each equipotential group is known, so the variance of the estimator $\hat{c}''_{st}(G)$, given the actual sample distribution $[n_1, n_2, ..., n_\Theta]$, can be calculated in exactly the same way as for *a priori* stratification:

$$V\left\{\hat{c}''_{st}(G)\middle|\langle n_1, n_2, ..., n_\Theta\rangle\right\} = \sum_{\alpha=1}^{\Theta} \frac{p^2(G''_\alpha|G)}{n_\alpha}\left(c(G''_\alpha) - c^2(G''_\alpha)\right) \qquad (18)$$

Now, if the original sample selection distribution was chosen such that the probability of an injected fault/activity occurring in equipotential group $G''_\alpha$ is equal to $p(G''_\alpha|G)$ and, given that all equipotential groups are sampled at least once, then the random variables $n_\alpha$, $\alpha = 1..\Theta$ are distributed according to a positive binomial distribution with parameters $n$ (the total sample size) and $p(G''_\alpha|G)$. Therefore, we can write [29 page 73]:

$$E\left\{\frac{1}{n_\alpha}\right\} \approx \frac{1}{np(G_\alpha|G) - (1 - p(G_\alpha|G))}$$

Taking expectations of expression (18), and approximating for large $n$, we can thus show that the expected estimator variance is given by:

$$E\left\{V\{\hat{c}_{st}''(G)\}\right\} \approx \sum_{\alpha=1}^{\Theta} \frac{p(G_\alpha''|G)}{n}\left(c(G_\alpha'') - c^2(G_\alpha'')\right)$$

It should be noted that the number of equipotential groups to be considered is usually much greater than the number of integrated circuits — this means that the number of injected faults that affect a given equipotential group can be quite small. This can lead to an overall *decrease* in precision due to the higher variance of the estimations of the equipotential group coverage. This will be illustrated by the example given in the next section.

## 5.2 Comparative Example

The gain in precision obtained using *a posteriori* stratification based on equipotentials is again illustrated by means of a hypothetical example. Since structural information about the target system is necessary to map the fault counts and the fault occurrence probabilities from circuit pins to equipotential groups, structural information from a real target system is considered. The considered system is composed of a card with 111 integrated circuits and 597 equipotential lines. The considered fault-injector (*MESSALINE*) only has adequate test-probes for 64 of the 111 integrated circuits. The "no-reply" problem therefore occurs for the 47 non-testable circuits. Values for the relative probabilities of fault occurrences at the circuit level were calculated based on IC failure rate data. Coverage values were randomly assigned to each equipotential (and thereby to the target system ICs) on a purely hypothetical basis — they do not in any way represent the real coverage values of the target system and serve only as an illustration of the proposed technique. The theoretical coverage of this hypothetical system is 0.99.

The results presented correspond to a fault injection campaign in which the initial plan was to inject 150 faults on each IC of the target system (homogeneous *a priori* circuit-level stratification). For simplicity, we only consider faults of multiplicity $mx = 1$. The comparison is based on the upper and lower limits of the overall system coverage obtained from an incomplete stratified sample as expressed by relation (17). The probability of fault/activity occurrences in the tested part of the system, $p(G'|G)$, is obtained by summing the fault/activity probabilities corresponding to classes that have been tested either from the circuit level *a priori* stratification viewpoint or from the equipotential-level *a posteriori* stratification viewpoint. The estimation of the coverage of the tested part of the system $\hat{c}_{st}(G')$, and the associated two-sided 99% confidence half-interval $\delta_{G'}$, are obtained from the *a priori* and *a posteriori* estimators $\hat{c}_{stH}(G')$ and $\hat{c}_{st}''(G')$, and their corresponding variances (in the latter case, the *expected* variance).

Fig. 4 shows the results obtained when the circuits are tested in an order corresponding to decreasing fault/activity occurrence probabilities, discounting the non-testable
circuits. The curves are plotted in function of the number of tested circuits $m$.

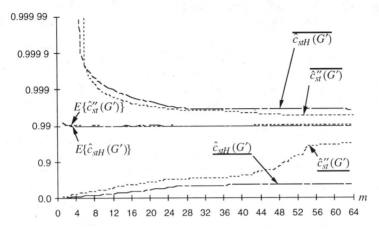

**Fig. 4.** Reduction of "no-reply" problem with *a posteriori* stratification

It can be seen that as soon as 7 circuits have been tested, the *a posteriori* stratification
by equipotential gives better results than the estimation with *a priori* circuit-level
stratification. Also, the final result with *a priori* circuit-level stratification is very
poor: the 64 testable circuits have a total relative fault/activity occurrence probability
of only 58% — the consequent uncertainty on the overall coverage means that it can
only be bounded by $0.57 < c(G) < 0.996$. When the additional information concerning
the target system structure is taken into account, the *a posteriori* stratification technique gives an appreciable improvement since now the 99%-confidence interval on
overall coverage becomes $0.968 < c(G) < 0.994$.

## 6   Discussion and Conclusions

In this paper, various sampling methods have been presented that can be applied
when estimating coverage based on physical fault injection. A formal definition of
coverage has been given in terms of the relative probabilities of points in the complete input space of a fault-tolerant system that includes both system activities and
fault occurrences. The considered sampling techniques have been compared from the
viewpoints of the precision that they procure in the estimation of overall system
coverage and the testing effort required to obtain sufficiently precise results.

When all the circuits in the complete system can be tested, *a priori* circuit-level stratification with a representative sample allocation enables an unbiased estimation of
system coverage that is never worse than representative sampling in the complete
space and is sometimes appreciably better.

Two-stage sampling techniques allow unbiased early estimations of overall coverage
to be obtained that are usually better than the bounds on coverage that can be deduced
from incomplete stratified sampling. Of the three two-stage sampling techniques considered, a quotient estimator based on first-stage sampling with equal probabilities

(without replacement) gives the best results. Moreover, the technique is equivalent to *a priori* stratification when all classes have been tested.

The "no reply" problem that unfortunately affects most practical fault-injection experiments means however that little can be gained from two-stage circuit-level sampling and one must often resort to the poor bounds obtained from incomplete stratified sampling.

By taking into account available structural information about the target system, we were able to consider an alternative stratification technique based on equipotential groups. This stratification technique was used in an *a posteriori* fashion to improve the results obtained after a set of experiments initially carried out with circuit-level stratification in mind.

We are currently carrying a set of fault injection experiments on a real system in which equipotential groups are used as a basis for *a priori* stratification with the aim of avoiding, rather than correcting, the "no-reply" problems posed by inadequate injection probes and parasitic mutations.

Further research on coverage estimation techniques is being considered in two directions. First, we are investigating estimation techniques that allow stratification to be used to estimate coverage confidence limits for systems with very high coverage, i.e. so high that very few (or even zero) fault-tolerance deficiencies are observed during fault injection experiments. Under such extreme conditions, the normal approximation for confidence interval calculation is no longer valid and other techniques must be developed [43]. Second, since the definition of a coverage factor as a conditional probability must involve the distributions of fault and system activity occurrences, it is essential to assess the impact on the estimations of inaccuracies in our assumptions about these distributions. It would thus be of very real interest to study the sensitivity of the results to variations in the distributions. Note however, that if new evidence about the distributions is obtained after carrying out the fault injection experiments then *a posteriori* stratification can often be used to correct the estimations.

# References for Chapter V

[1]     J. Arlat, *Dependability Validation by Fault Injection: Method, Implementation, Application,* State Doctoral Dissertation, National Polytechnic Institute of Toulouse, France, December 1990 (in French).

[2]     J. Arlat, "Fault Injection for the Experimental Validation of Fault-Tolerant Systems (Invited paper)", in *Proc. Workshop Fault-Tolerant Systems,* (IEICE, Tokyo, Japan), pp.33-40, 1992.

[3]     J. Arlat, M. Aguera, L. Amat, Y. Crouzet, J. C. Fabre, J. C. Laprie, E. Martins and D. Powell, "Fault Injection for Dependability Validation — A Methodology and Some Applications", *IEEE Transactions on Software Engineering,* 16 (2), pp.166-82, February 1990.

[4]     J. Arlat, M. Aguera, L. Amat, Y. Crouzet, J. C. Fabre, J. C. Laprie, E. Martins and D. Powell, "Fault Injection for Dependability Validation: A methodology and some applications", *IEEE Transactions on Software Engineering,* 16 (2), pp.166-82, February 1990.

[5]     J. R. Armstrong, F.-S. Lam and P. C. Ward, "Test Generation and Fault Simulation for Behavioral Models", in *Performance and Fault Modelling with VHDL* (J. M. Schoen, Ed.), pp.240-303, Prentice-Hall, Englewood Cliffs, NJ, USA, 1992.

[6]     T. F. Arnold, "The Concept of Coverage and its Effect on the Reliability Model of Repairable Systems", *IEEE Transactions on Computers,* C-22 (3), pp.251-4, March 1973.

[7]     P. J. Ashenden, *The VHDL Cookbook,* University of Adelaide, South Australia, Tech. Report, 1990.

[8]     A. Avizienis and D. Rennels, "Fault-Tolerance Experiments with the JPL-STAR Computer", in *Proc. 6th Ann. IEEE Computer Society Conference,* (San Francisco, CA, USA), pp.321-4, 1972.

[9]     J. H. Aylor, R. Waxman, B. W. Johnson and R. D. Williams, "The Integration of Performance and Functional Modeling in VHDL", in *Performance and Fault Modelling with VHDL* (J. M. Schoen, Ed.), pp.22-145, Prentice-Hall, Englewood Cliffs, NJ, USA, 1992.

[10]    B. Bjurman, G. M. Jenkins, C. J. Masreliez and J. E. Templeman, *Airborne Advanced Reconfigurable Computer System,* NASA, Report, N°CR-145024, 1976.

[11]    W. G. Bouricius, W. C. Carter and P. R. Schneider, "Reliability Modeling Techniques for Self-Repairing Computer Systems", in *Proc. 24th National Conference,* pp.295-309, ACM, 1969.

[12]    R. Chillarege and N. S. Bowen, "Understanding Large System Failures — A Fault Injection Experiment", in *Proc. 19th. Int. Symp. on Fault-Tolerant Computing (FTCS-19),* (Chicago, IL, USA), pp.356-63, IEEE Computer Society Press, 1989.

[13]  J. A. Clark and D. K. Pradhan, "REACT: A Synthesis and Evaluation Tool for Fault-Tolerant Microprocessor Architectures", in *Proc. Annual Reliability & Maintainability Symp.,* pp.428-35, IEEE, 1993.

[14]  W. G. Cochran, *Sampling Techniques,* John Wiley & Sons, New York, 1977.

[15]  A. Damm, "The Effectiveness of Software Error-Detection Mechanisms in Real-Time Operating Systems", in *Proc. 16th Int. Symp. on Fault-Tolerant Computing (FTCS-16),* (Vienna, Austria), pp.171-6, IEEE Computer Society, 1986.

[16]  A. Damm, *Experimental Evaluation of Error-detection and Self-Checking Coverage of Components of a Distributed Real-time System,* Doctoral Dissertation, Technical University, Vienna, Austria, October 1988.

[17]  J. Desbadie, *Theory and Practice of Sample Surveys,* Statistique et Programmes Economiques, 10, Dunod, Paris, 1966 (In French).

[18]  J. B. Dugan and K. S. Trivedi, "Coverage Modeling for Dependability Analysis of Fault-Tolerant Systems", *IEEE Transactions on Computers,* 38 (6), pp.775-87, June 1989.

[19]  K. K. Goswami, *Design for Dependability: A Simulation-Based Approach,* Ph.D. Dissertation, Univ. of Illinois at Urbana-Champaign, USA, 1993.

[20]  K. K. Goswami and R. K. Iyer, *DEPEND: A Simulation-Based Environment for System Level Dependability Analysis,* Univ. of Illinois at Urbana-Champaign, Tech. Report, N°CHRC-92-11, June 1992.

[21]  B. Grais, *Statistical Methods,* Dunod, Paris, 1991 (In French).

[22]  U. Gunneflo, J. Karlsson and J. Torin, "Evaluation of Error Detection Schemes Using Fault Injection by Heavy-ion Radiation", in *Proc. 19th Int. Symp. Fault-Tolerant Computing (FTCS-19),* (Chicago, IL, USA), pp.340-7, IEEE Computer Society Press, 1989.

[23]  J. L. Hennessy and D. A. Patterson, *Computer Architecture — A Quantitative Approach,* Morgan Kaufmann, 1990.

[24]  *IEEE Standard VHDL Language Reference Manual,* IEEE Std. N°1076-1987, 1988.

[25]  *IEEE Standard VHDL Language Reference Manual,* IEEE Std. N°1076-1993, 1993.

[26]  R. K. Iycr and D. Tang, "Experimental Analysis of Computer System Dependability", in *Fault-Tolerant Computing* (D. K. Pradhan, Ed.), Second Edition, Prentice-Hall, Englewood Cliffs, NJ, USA, 1994.

[27]  E. Jenn, *On the Validation of Fault-Tolerant Systems: Fault Injection in VHDL Simulation Models,* Doctoral Dissertation, INP, Toulouse, France, July 1994 (in French).

[28]  E. Jenn, J. Arlat, M. Rimén, J. Ohlsson and J. Karlsson, "Fault Injection into VHDL Models: The MEFISTO Tool", in *Proc. 24th Int. Symp. Fault-*

*Tolerant Computing (FTCS-24),* (Austin, TX, USA), pp.66-75, IEEE Computer Society Press, 1994.

[29]  N. L. Johnson and S. Kotz, *Distributions in Statistics — Discrete Distributions,* John Wiley & Sons, New York, 1969.

[30]  H.-P. Juan, N. D. Holmes, S. Bakshi and D. P. Gajski, "Top-Down Modeling of RISC Processors in VHDL", in *Proc. EURO-VHDL'93,* (Paris, France), pp.454-9, 1993.

[31]  G. A. Kanawati, N. A. Kanawati and J. A. Abraham, "FERRARI: A Tool for the Validation of System Dependability Properties", in *Proc. 22nd Int. Symp. on Fault-Tolerant Computing (FTCS-22),* (Boston, MA, USA), pp.336-44, IEEE Computer Society Press, 1992.

[32]  J. Karlsson, P. Lidén, P. Dahlgren and R. Johansson, "Using Heavy-Ion Radiation to Validate Fault-Handling Mechanisms", *IEEE Micro,* 14 (1), pp.8-23, February 1994.

[33]  H. Kopetz, G. Fohler, G. Grünsteidl, H. Kantz, G. Pospischil, P. Puschner, J. Reisinger, R. Schlatterbeck, W. Schütz, A. Vrchoticky and R. Zainlinger, *"The Distributed Fault-Tolerant Real-Time Operating System MARS",* IEEE Operating Systems Newsletter, 6 (1), 1992.

[34]  H. Kopetz, G. Grünsteidl and J. Reisinger, "Fault-Tolerant Membership in a Synchronous Distributed Real-Time System", in *Dependable Computing for Critical Applications* (A. Avizienis and J.-C. Laprie, Eds.), Dependable Computing and Fault-Tolerant Systems, 4, pp.411-29, Springer-Verlag, Vienna, Austria, 1991.

[35]  H. Kopetz, P. Holzer, G. Leber and M. Schindler, *The Rolling Ball on MARS,* Institut für Technische Informatik, Technische Universität Wien, Tech. Report, N°13/91, 1991.

[36]  J. H. Lala, "Fault Detection, Isolation, and Reconfiguration in FTMP: Methods and Experimental Results", in *Fifth AIAA/IEEE Digital Avionics Sys. Conf.,* pp.21.3.1-.3.9, 1983.

[37]  H. Madeira, M. Rela, F. Moreira and J. G. Silva, "A General Purpose Pin-level Fault Injector", in *Proc. 1st European Dependable Computing Conf. (EDCC-1),* (Berlin, Germany), pp.199-216, Springer-Verlag, 1994.

[38]  E. Martins, *Validation of Distributed Systems by Fault Injection,* Doctoral Dissertation, Ecole Nationale Supérieure de l'Aéronautique et de l'Espace, Toulouse, France, June 1992 (in French).

[39]  A. Miczo, "VHDL as a Modeling-for-Testability Tool", in *Proc. COMPCON'90,* pp.403-9, IEEE Computer Society Press, 1990.

[40]  G. Miremadi, J. Karlsson, U. Gunneflo and J. Torin, "Two Software Techniques for On-line Error Detection", in *Proc. 22nd Int. Symp. on Fault-Tolerant Computing (FTCS-22),* (Boston, MA, USA), pp.328-44, IEEE Computer Society Press, 1992.

[41]  J. Ohlsson, M. Rimén and U. Gunneflo, "A Study of the Effects of Transient Fault Injection into a 32-bit RISC with Built-in Watchdog", in *Proc. 22th Int. Symp. Fault-Tolerant Computing (FTCS-22),* (Boston, MA, USA), pp.316-25, IEEE Computer Society Press, 1992.

[42]  Philips Semiconductors, *SCC68070 User Manual 1991, Part 1 - Hardware,* 1992.

[43]  D. Powell, M. Cukier and J. Arlat, *On the Confidence of Very High Coverage Estimations,* LAAS-CNRS, Research Report, N°94506, December 1994.

[44]  D. Powell, E. Martins, J. Arlat and Y. Crouzet, "Estimators for Fault Tolerance Coverage Evaluation", *IEEE Transactions on Computers,* 44 (2), pp.261-74, February 1995.

[45]  J. Reisinger, "Time Driven Operating Systems - A Case Study on the MARS Kernel", in *5th ACM SIGOPS European Workshop,* (Le Mont Saint Michel, France), 1992.

[46]  J. Reisinger, *Konzeption und Analyze eines zeitgesteuerten Betriebssystems für Echtzeitsanwendungen,* Technische Universität Wien, 1993.

[47]  M. Rimén, J. Ohlsson, J. Karlsson, E. Jenn and J. Arlat, "Design Guidelines of a VHDL-based Simulation Tool for the Validation of Fault Tolerance", in *Proc. 1st Open Workshop ESPRIT Basic Research Project 6362: PDCS-2,* (Toulouse, France), pp.461-83, LAAS-CNRS, 1993.

[48]  M. A. Schuette, J. P. Shen, D. P. Siewiorek and Y. X. Zhu, "Experimental Evaluation of Two Concurrent Error Detection Schemes", in *Proc. 16th Int. Symp. Fault-Tolerant Computing (FTCS-16),* (Vienna, Austria), pp.138-43, IEEE Computer Society Press, 1986.

[49]  Z. Segall, D. Vrsalovic, D. Siewiorek, D. Yaskin, J. Kownacki, J. Barton, D. Rancey, A. Robinson and T. Lin, "FIAT — Fault Injection-based Automated Testing Environment", in *Proc. 18th Int. Symp. on Fault-Tolerant Computing (FTCS-18),* (Tokyo, Japan), pp.102-7, IEEE Computer Society Press, 1988.

[50]  D. P. Siewiorek and R. S. Swarz, *Reliable Computer Systems — Design and Evaluation,* Digital Press, Burlington, MA, USA, 1992.

[51]  J. M. Voas, "PIE: A Dynamic Failure-Based Technique", *IEEE Transactions on Software Engineering,* 18 (8), pp.717-27, August 1992.

[52]  A. Vrchoticky, *Modula/R Language Definition,* Institut für Technische Informatik, Technische Universität Wien, Tech. Report, N°2/92, 1992.

[53]  C. J. Walter, "Evaluation and Design of an Ultra-Reliable Distributed Architecture for Fault Tolerance", *IEEE Transactions on Reliability,* 39 (4), pp.492-9, October 1990.

[54]  C. R. Yount, *The Automatic Generation of Instruction-Level Error Manifestation of Hardware Faults: A New Fault Injection Model,* Ph.D. Dissertation, Carnegie-Mellon Univ., Pittsburgh, PA, USA, May 1993.

# Chapter VI

# Fault Forecasting -
# Software Reliability

The issue of how to assess and predict the dependability of systems in the presence of design faults has been an important theme of both PDCS and PDCS2. Inevitably, much of this work has concentrated upon the effects on system dependability of *software* faults.

The first four papers consider the important problem of modelling the reliability growth that takes place when fault removal takes place. In "Software Reliability Trend Analyses - From Theoretical to Practical Considerations" it is shown how reliability trend analyses can help the project manager in controlling the progress of development activities: in particular identifying undesirable changes such as slowing down of testing effectiveness. "The Transformation Approach to the Modelling and Evaluation of the Reliability and Availability Growth" extends reliability growth modeling from black box systems (to which the many published reliability growth models are restricted) to multi-component systems. The results presented constitute a significant step toward the evaluation of reliability and availability of systems with respect to both physical and design faults, as they enable (i) reliability growth phenomena to be incorporated into hardware models, and (ii) system structure to be accounted for in software models. Whilst there are now many software reliability growth models in the literature, their accuracy is variable: some models give good results some of the time, but no model can be guaranteed to give accurate results. In "New Ways to get Accurate Reliability Measures", techniques are described for evaluating accuracy on a particular data source, and it is shown how a new recalibration technique can often improve accuracy dramatically. These ideas are taken a step further in "Combination of Predictions Obtained from Different Software Reliability Growth Models", which shows how the combination of predictions from different, disagreeing, models can bring useful improvement in accuracy.

The next two papers address the problem of evaluating the dependability of fault-tolerant systems. A detailed reliability and safety analysis of the two major software fault-tolerance approaches, Recovery Blocks and N-Version Programming, is presented in "Dependability Modelling and Evaluation of Software Fault Tolerance"; the unified modeling carried out enables the most failure-prone characteristics of both approaches to be identified and compared. It is known that many physical systems can tolerate isolated failures of their control systems but not longer bursts of failures; in "Dependability Analysis of Iterative Fault-Tolerant Software Considering Correlation", the important question of sequences of consecutive failures arising from correlation among successive inputs is addressed.

Finally, "Validation of Ultra-High Dependability for Software-Based Systems" examines the limits to the levels of dependability that can be evaluated quantitatively within a probabilistic framework. Different sources of evidence for assessment are examined critically to determine how much they could contribute to claims for high dependability.

# Software Reliability Trend Analyses: From Theoretical to Practical Considerations*

Karama Kanoun   Jean-Claude Laprie

CNRS-LAAS

**Abstract.** This paper addresses the problem of reliability growth characterization and analysis. It is intended to show how reliability trend analyses can help the project manager in controlling the progress of the development activities and in appreciating the efficiency of the test programs. Reliability trend change may result from various reasons, some of them are desirable and expected (such as reliability growth due to fault removal) and some of them are undesirable (such as slowing down of the testing effectiveness). Identification in time of the latter allows the project manager to take the appropriate decisions very quickly in order to avoid problems which may manifest later. The notions of reliability growth over a given interval and local reliability trend change are introduced through the subadditive property, allowing better definition and understanding of the reliability growth phenomena; the already existing trend tests are then revisited using these concepts. Emphasis is put on the way trend tests can be used to help the management of the testing and validation process and on practical results that can be derived from their use; it is shown that, for several circumstances, trend analyses give information of prime importance to the developer.

## 1   Introduction

Generally, software reliability studies are based on reliability growth models application in order to evaluate the reliability measures. When performed for a large base of deployed software systems, the results are usually of high relevance (see e.g. [2],[66] for examples of such studies). However, utilization of reliability growth models during early stages of development and validation is much less convincing: when the observed times to failure are of the order of magnitude of minutes or hours, the predictions performed from such data can hardly predict mean times to failure different from minutes or hours ... which is so distant of any expected reasonable reliability. In addition, when a program under validation becomes reliable enough, the times to failure may simply be large enough in order to make impractical the application of reliability growth models to data belonging to the end of validation only, due to the (hoped for) scarcity of failure data. On the other hand, in order to become a true engineering exercise, software validation should be guided by quantified considerations relating to its reliability. Statistical trend tests for trend analysis provide such guides. It is worth noting that trend analyses are generally carried out by most of the companies during software testing [52, 119, 106]. However they are usually applied in an intuitive and empirical way rather than in a quantified and well defined method.

---

* This paper is a revised version of [65].

The work presented in this paper is an elaboration on the study carried out in [64], which focused on experimental data. In this paper, the discussion of these experimental data is more detailed, it is preceded by developments on the very notion of reliability growth. Emphasis is first put on the characterization of reliability growth via the subadditive property and its graphical interpretation. Then, the already existing reliability growth tests (mainly the Laplace test) are briefly presented and their relationship with the subadditive property outlined. The way trend tests can be used to help the management of the validation process is then addressed before illustration on three data sets issued from real-life systems.

The paper is composed of five sections. Section 2 is devoted to formal and practical definitions of reliability growth. In Section 3, some trend tests are presented and discussed; the type of results which can be drawn from trend analysis are stated. Section 4 is devoted to exemplifying the results from Sections 2 and 3 on failure data collected on real-life systems.

## 2    Reliability Growth Characterization

Software lack of reliability stems from the presence of faults, and is manifested by failures which are consecutive to fault sensitization. Removing faults should result in reliability growth. However, it is not always so, due to the complexity of the relation between faults and failures, thus between faults and reliability, which has been noticed a long time ago (see e.g. [80]). Basically, complexity arises from a double uncertainty: the presence of faults and the fault sensitization via the trajectory in the input space of a program[1]. As a consequence, one usually observes reliability trend changes, which may result from a great variety of phenomena, such as (i) the variation in the utilization environment (variation in the testing effort during debugging, change in test sets, addition of new users during the operational life, etc.) or (ii) the dependency between faults (some faults can be masked by others, they cannot be activated as long as the latter are not removed [100]).

Reliability decrease may not, and usually does not, mean that the software has more and more faults; it does just tell that the software exercises more and more failures per unit of time under the corresponding conditions of use. Corrections may reduce the failure input domain but more faults are activated or faults are activated more frequently. However, during fault correction, new faults may be also introduced — regression faults — which can deteriorate or not software reliability depending on the conditions of use. Last but not least, reliability decrease may be consecutive to specification changes, as exemplified by the experimental data reported in [70].

### 2.1  Definitions of Reliability Growth

A natural definition of reliability growth is that the successive inter-failure times tend to become larger, i.e., denoting $T_1$, $T_2$,... the sequence of random variables corresponding to inter-failure times:

$$T_i \underset{st}{\leq} T_j, \text{ for all } i < j \tag{1}$$

---

[1] As an example, data published in [2] concerning nine large software products show that for a program with a mean lifetime of fifteen years, only 5% of the faults will be activated during this period.

where $\underset{st}{\leq}$ means stochastically smaller than (i.e., $P\{T_i <v\} \geq P\{T_j <v\}$ for all $v > 0$).

Under the stochastic independency assumption, relation (1) is equivalent to, letting $F_{Ti}(x)$ denote the cumulative distribution function of $T_i$:

$$F_{Ti}(x) \geq F_{Tj}(x) \qquad \text{for all } i < j \text{ and } x > 0 \qquad (2)$$

An alternative to the (restrictive) assumption of stochastic independency is to consider that the successive failures obey a non-homogeneous Poisson process (NHPP). Let $N(t)$ be the cumulative number of failures observed during time interval $[0, t]$, $H(t) = E[N(t)]$ its mean value, and $h(t) = dH(t)/dt$ its intensity, i.e. the failure intensity. A natural definition of reliability growth is then that the increase in the expected number of failures tends to become lower, i.e. that $H(t)$ is concave, or, equivalently, that $h(t)$ is non-increasing. There are however several situations where even though the failure intensity fluctuates locally, reliability growth may take place on average on the considered time interval[2]. An alternative definition allowing for such local fluctuations is then that the expected number of failures in any initial interval (i.e. of the form $[0, t]$) is no lower than the expected number of failures in any interval of the same length occurring later (i.e. of the form $[x, x+t]$). The independent increment property of an NHPP enables to write this later definition as:

$$H(t_1) + H(t_2) \geq H(t_1+t_2) \quad \text{for all } t_1,t_2 \geq 0 \text{ and } 0 \leq t_1+t_2 \leq T \qquad (3)$$

inequality is presumed strict for at least one couple $(t_1,t_2)$. When relation (3) holds, the function is said to be *subadditive* over $[0,T]$ (see e.g. [57]). When relation (3) is reversed for all $t_1,t_2 \geq 0$ and $0 \leq t_1+t_2 \leq T$, the function is said to be *superadditive* indicating reliability decrease on average over $[0,T]$. This relation is very interesting since it allows for local fluctuations: locally sub-intervals of reliability decrease may take place without affecting the nature of the trend on average (over the considered time interval). For instance, when $h(t)$ is strictly decreasing over $[0, T]$ relation (3) is verified but the converse is not true. This is detailed in the next sub-section.

## 2.2 Graphical Interpretation of the Subadditive Property

In this section, we will derive a graphical interpretation of the subadditive property and show the link between this property and several situations of reliability growth and reliability decrease.

Let $C_t$ denote the portion of the curve representing the cumulative number of failures in $[0, t]$ as indicated in Fig. 1 and $L_t$ the line joining the two ending points of $C_t$ (i.e., the chord from the origin to point $(t, H(t))$ of $C_t$). Let $A[C_t]$ denote the area delimited by $C_t$ and the coordinate axis, $A[L_t]$ denote the area delimited by $L_t$ and the coordinate axis and $aH(t)$ the difference between these two areas, i.e., $a_H(t) = (A[Ct] - A[Lt])$. With these notations, relation (3) becomes:

$$a_H(t) = (A[Ct] - A[Lt]) \geq 0 \text{ for all } t \in [0, T] \qquad (4)$$

---

2   The NHPP assumption (more precisely the property of independent increments) is fundamental since a stationary process which is a non-Poisson process may undergo transient oscillations that are impossible to be distinguished from a trend in a non-stationary Poisson process (see for instance [8], p. 25, or [48], p. 99, for renewal processes).

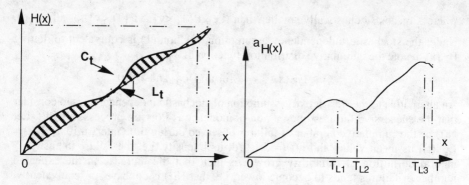

**Fig. 1.** Graphical interpretation of the subadditive property

❑ Proof

Let us divide the interval $[0, t]$ in K small time intervals of length dt, i.e., $t = K$ dt. K may be either even or odd. Let us consider the even case. In relation (3), let $t_1$ take successively the values $\{0, dt, 2dt, 3dt, \ldots K/2 \ dt \}$ and $t_2 = t - t_1$. Relation (3) becomes successively:

$$H(0) + H(Kdt) \geq H(t)$$

$$H(dt) + H((K-1)dt) \geq H(t)$$

$$\ldots$$

$$H(\frac{K}{2}dt) + H(\frac{K}{2}dt) \geq H(t)$$

Summing over the $\frac{K}{2} + 1$ inequalities gives:

$$\sum_{j=0}^{K} H(jdt) + H(\frac{K}{2}dt) \geq ( \frac{K}{2} + 1 )H(t)$$

Replacing K by t/dt and taking the limit when dt approaches zero lead to:

$$\int_0^t H(x) \ dx \geq \frac{t}{2} H(t).$$

The left term corresponds to the area of the region delimited by $C_t$ and the coordinate axis and the right term to the area of the region between $L_t$ and the coordinate axis. Relation (3) is thus equivalent to:

$$\int_0^t H(x) \ dx - \frac{t}{2} H(t) \geq 0.$$

That is: $a_H(t) \geq 0$.

When K is odd derivation can be handled in a similar manner.

❑ End of proof

With this graphical representation, the identification of the subadditive property becomes very easy. For instance, the function considered in Fig. 1 is subadditive over [0, T]: there is reliability growth over the whole time interval even though local fluctuations take place in the meantime.

It is worth noting that, given a subadditive function, when t varies from 0 to T the difference between the two areas, $a_H(t)$, may increase, decrease or become null without being negative in any case. It is positive increasing at the beginning and:

- without local reliability fluctuation, the cumulative number of failures curve is concave leading to a positive increasing $a_H(t)$ (see Fig. 2, case A),

- in case of local reliability fluctuation, the difference between the two areas takes its first maximum when the chord from the origin to point (t, H(t)) of $C_t$ is tangent to $C_t$; let $T_L$ denote this point; from $T_L$, $a_H(t)$ is decreasing until the next point where the chord is tangent to $C_t$ and so on.

Considering again the case of local reliability fluctuation of Fig. 1, the existence of point $T_L$ is due to the change in the concavity of the curve giving the cumulative number of failures, more precisely, it takes place after the point of concavity change. Taking $T_L$ as the time origin, would lead to a superadditive function from $T_L$ to the following point of local trend change (since the curve giving the cumulative number of failures is convex over this time interval). This is illustrated on Fig. 1 where the function considered has two sub-intervals of local reliability decrease (namely, intervals $[T_{L1}, T_{L2}]$ and $[T_{L3}, T]$) in spite of reliability growth on the whole interval [0, T] since the function is subadditive over [0, T].

What precedes is true for a superadditive function also:

- without local reliability fluctuation, the cumulative number of failures curve is convex leading to a negative $a_H(t)$ (Fig. 2, case B),

- in case of local reliability fluctuation, $a_H(t)$ takes its first minimum at $T_L$ where the chord is tangent to $C_t$; from $T_L$, $a_H(t)$ is increasing until the next point of local trend change and so on.

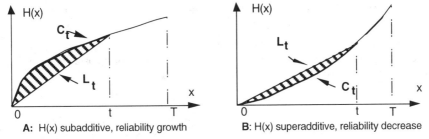

A: H(x) subadditive, reliability growth     B: H(x) superadditive, reliability decrease

**Fig. 2.** Subadditivity / superadditivity without local trend variation

There are however more complicated situations where the cumulative number of failures is neither subadditive nor superadditive over the considered interval. For these cases, a change in the time origin is thus needed. Two such situations are illustrated in Fig. 3.

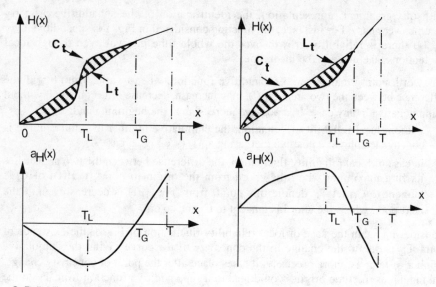

**C**: Reliability decrease then reliability growth      **D**: Reliability growth then reliability decrease

**Fig. 3.** Subadditivity / superadditivity and local trend variation

For situation C, before $T_G$ the function is superadditive denoting reliability decrease over $[0, T_G]$. $T_G$ corresponds to the point where the sign of $a_H(t)$ changes: the function is no more superadditive. $T_L$ corresponds to the region where $a_H(t)$ is no more decreasing denoting local trend change, however the function continues to be superadditive until point $T_G$. On the sub-interval of time between $T_L$ and $T$ the curve is concave indicating reliability growth over $[T_L, T]$. Situation D is the converse of situation C: until point $T_G$ the cumulative number of failures is subadditive denoting reliability growth over $[0, T_G]$; from $T_G$, it is no more subadditive. On $[T_L, T]$ the function is superadditive corresponding to reliability decrease over this time interval. Combining situations C and D leads to interesting situations where the trend changes more than once.

What precedes shows that the notion of reliability growth as defined by the subadditive property is related to the whole interval of time considered and is, as thus, strongly connected with the origin of the time interval.

Finally, it is worth while to point out an interesting situation which may be encountered for real systems: the case where the difference between the two areas, $aH(t)$, is constant (or null) over a given interval, say $[t_1, t_2]$. This is characterized by the fact that the derivative of $a_H(t)$ given by relation (5) is null over $[t_1, t_2]$.

$$\frac{d}{dt} a_H(t) = \frac{d}{dt} \left[ \int_0^t H(x) \, dx - \frac{t}{2} H(t) \right] = \frac{1}{2} \left[ \int_0^t h(x) \, dx - t \, h(t) \right] = 0 \qquad (5)$$

Integration of (5) leads to a linear cumulative number of failures function, i.e., a constant failure intensity over $[t_1, t_2]$. The constancy of $a_H(t)$ over a given time interval indicates thus stable reliability over this time interval.

# 3 Trend Analysis

Reliability growth can be analyzed through the use of trend tests. We will present only the most used and significant trend tests in this section and put emphasis on the relationship between the Laplace test (the most popular one) and the subadditive property. The presentation of the tests is followed by a discussion on how they can be used to follow up software reliability.

Failure data can be collected under two forms: *inter-failure times* or *number of failures per unit of time*. These two forms are related: knowing the inter-failure times it is possible to obtain the number of failures per unit of time (the second form needs less precise data collection). The choice between one form or the other may be guided by the following elements: (i) the objective of the reliability study (development follow up, maintenance planning or reliability evaluation), (ii) the way data are collected (data collection in the form of inter-failure times may be tedious mainly during earlier phases of the development, in which case it is more suitable and less time consuming to collect data in the form of number of failures per unit of time) and (iii) the life cycle phase concerned by the study. Using data in the form of "number of failures per unit of time" reduces the impact of very local fluctuations on reliability evaluation. The unit of time is a function of the type of system usage as well as the number of failures occurring during the considered units of time and it may be different for different phases.

## 3.1 Trend Tests

There are a number of trend tests which can be used to help determine whether the system undergoes reliability growth or reliability decrease. These tests can be grouped into two categories: graphical and analytical tests [8]. Graphical tests consist of plotting some observed failure data such as the inter-failure times or the number of failure per unit of time versus time in order to deduce visually the trend displayed by the data: they are as such informal. Analytical tests correspond to more rigorous tests since they are statistical tests: the raw data are processed in order to derive trend factors. Trend tests may be carried out using either inter-failure times data or failure intensity data.

Several publications have been devoted to the theoretical definition and comparison of analytical trend tests [32, 8, 46]. In the latter reference very interesting and detailed presentation, analysis and comparison of some analytical tests (e.g. Laplace, MIL-HDBK 187, Gnedenko, Spearman and Kendall tests) are carried out. It is shown that (i) from a practical point of view, all these tests give similar results in their ability to detect reliability trend variation, (ii) the tests of Spearman and Kendall have the advantage that they are based on less restrictive assumptions and (iii) the Gnedenko test is interesting since it uses exact distributions. From the optimality point of view, it is shown in this reference that the Laplace test is superior and it is recommended to use it when the NHPP assumption is used (even though its significance level is not exact and it is not possible to estimate its power). These results confirm our experience on processing real failure data: we have observed the equivalence of the results from these various tests and the superiority of the Laplace test.

**Inter-failure Times.** Two trend tests are of usual practice: the arithmetical mean and the Laplace tests. The **arithmetical mean test** consists of calculating $\tau(i)$ the arithmetical mean of the first i observed inter-failure times $\theta_j$ (which are the realizations of $T_j$, j = 1, 2, ..., i):

$$\tau(i) = \frac{1}{i} \sum_{j=1}^{i} \theta_j.$$

When $\tau(i)$ form an increasing series, reliability growth is deduced. This test is very simple and is directly related to the observed data. A variant of this test consists of evaluating the mean of inter-failures times over periods of time of the same length to put emphasis on the local trend variation.

The **Laplace test** [32] consists of calculating the Laplace factor, u(T), for the observation period [0, T]. This factor is derived in the following manner. The occurrence of the events is assumed to follow an NHPP whose failure intensity is decreasing and is given by: $h(t) = e^{a+bt}$, $b \le 0$. When b=0 the Poisson process becomes homogeneous and the occurrence rate is time independent. Under this hypothesis (b=0, i.e., homogeneous Poisson process, HPP), the statistics:

$$u(T) = \frac{\frac{1}{N(T)} \sum_{i=1}^{N(T)} \sum_{j=1}^{i} \theta_j - \frac{T}{2}}{T \sqrt{\frac{1}{12\, N(T)}}} \qquad (6)$$

have an asymptotic normal distribution with mean zero and unit variance.

The practical use of the Laplace test in the context of reliability growth is:
- negative values of u(T) indicate a decreasing failure intensity (b < 0),
- positive values suggest an increasing failure intensity (b > 0),
- values oscillating between -2 and +2 indicate stable reliability.

These practical considerations are deduced from the significance levels associated with the statistics; for a significance level of 5%:
- the null hypothesis "no reliability growth against reliability growth" is rejected for u(T) < -1.645,
- the null hypothesis "no reliability decrease against reliability decrease" is rejected for u(T) > 1.645.
- the null hypothesis "no trend against trend" is rejected for $|u(T)| > 1.96$,

The Laplace test has the following simple interpretation:

- $\frac{T}{2}$ is the midpoint of the observation interval,

- $\frac{1}{N(T)} \sum_{i=1}^{N(T)} \sum_{j=1}^{i} \theta_j$ corresponds to the statistical center of the inter-failure times.

under the reliability growth (decrease) assumption, the inter-failure times $\theta_j$ will tend to occur before (after) the midpoint of the observation interval, hence the statistical center tends to be small (large).

**Failure Intensity and Cumulative Number of Failures.** Two very simple graphical tests can be used: the plots giving the evolution of the observed cumulative number of failures and the failure intensity (i.e. the number of failures per unit of time) versus time respectively. The inevitable local fluctuations exhibited by experimental data make smoothing necessary before reliability trend determination, and favor the cumulative number of failures rather than failure intensity. Reliability trend is then related to the subadditive property of the smoothed plot as we have seen in Section 2.

The formulation of the **Laplace test** for failure intensity (or the cumulative number of failures) is as follows. Let the time interval [0, t] be divided into k units of time of length 1, and let n(i) be the number of failures observed during time unit i. Following the method outlined in [32] the expression of the **Laplace factor** is given by (detailed derivation has been published in [61]):

$$u(k) = \frac{\sum\limits_{i=1}^{k} (i-1)n(i) - \frac{(k-1)}{2} \sum\limits_{i=1}^{k} n(i)}{\sqrt{\frac{k^2-1}{12} \sum\limits_{i=1}^{k} n(i)}} \tag{7}$$

The same results as previously apply: negative values of u(k) indicate reliability growth whereas positive values indicate reliability decrease.

### 3.2 Relationship Between the Laplace Test and the Subadditivity Factor

In Section 2, we have presented some features related to the subadditive property mainly the notions of trend on average over a given period of time and local trend change. In section 3, we presented one of the well known trend test, the Laplace test which, when used in the same way as any statistical test with significance levels as indicated above, does not allow to detect local trend changes. We derive hereafter a relationship between the Laplace factor and the subadditive property allowing extension of the former. Let N(k) denote the cumulative number of failures,

$N(k) = \sum\limits_{i=1}^{k} n(i)$; the numerator of (7) can be written as:

$$\sum\limits_{i=1}^{k} (i-1)[N(i)-N(i-1)] - \frac{k-1}{2} N(k).$$

Which is equal to: $\left[ k\,N(k) - \sum\limits_{i=1}^{k} N(i) \right] - \frac{k-1}{2} N(k) = \frac{k+1}{2} N(k) - \sum\limits_{i=1}^{k} N(i)$

Relation (7) becomes thus:

$$u(k) = - \frac{\sum\limits_{i=1}^{k} N(i) - \frac{k+1}{2} N(k)}{\sqrt{\frac{k^2-1}{12} N(k)}} = - \frac{a_H(k)}{\sqrt{\frac{k^2-1}{12} N(k)}} \qquad (8)$$

The numerator of u(k) is thus equal to $[- a_H(k)]$. Therefore, testing for the sign of u(k) is testing for the sign of difference of areas between the curve plotting the cumulative number of failures and the chord joining the origin and the current cumulative number of failures. This shows that the Laplace factor (fortunately) integrates the unavoidable local trend changes which are typical of experimental data, as the numerator of this factor is directly related to the subadditive property.

We use hereafter a simple example to illustrate the relationship between these features and the Laplace factor. Fig. 4-a gives the failure intensity, the cumulative number of failures, N(k), the curve corresponding to the difference of areas between the chord joining the origin and the current cumulative number of failures and the curve plotting N(k), $-a_H(k)$, and the Laplace factor, u(k).

Considering the whole data set (Fig. 4-a) leads to the following comments: (i) $a_H(t)$ is negative until point 9 indicating superadditivity and hence reliability decrease until this point, and (ii) the sign of the Laplace factor follows the sign of $-a_H(t)$. If we consider now the data set from a point where the function is still superadditive and the Laplace factor is positive, point 6 for example, and plot the same measures in Fig. 4-b, the results of this time origin change are: (i) $a_H(t)$ is positive for each point showing reliability growth over [6, 19], and (ii) the Laplace factor becomes negative.

In conclusion, and more generally, changes of the time origin affect in the same manner the subadditive property and the Laplace factor. However, the change in the origin does not result in a simple translation of the curve representing the Laplace factor in all situations: removal of a sub-set of failure data usually amplifies the variations of the Laplace factor due to the presence of the denominator (relation (8)).

What precedes is illustrated in Fig. 5 on a real situation corresponding to experimental data, where the data are relative to the TROPICO-R switching system studied in [61].

Fig. 5-a gives the Laplace factor for the whole data set from validation to operation. At the beginning of the validation, reliability decrease took place, as a result of the occurrence of 28 failures during the third unit of time whereas only 8 failures occurred during the first two time units and 24 during the next two time units. This situation is usual during validation: reliability decrease is due to the activation of a great number of faults at the beginning. Applying the Laplace test without the data belonging to the two first units of time leads to reliability growth on average from unit time 3 (Fig. 5-b). Even though we have removed only two data items, comparison of Fig. 5-a and 5-b confirms the previous points: (i) amplification of the variation of the Laplace factor and (ii) conservation of the trend change.

From a pragmatic viewpoint, i.e. using the Laplace factor as a trend indicator rather than a conventional statistical test, the above considerations and the link derived between the Laplace factor and the subadditive property enable reliability growth on average and local trend change to be defined. The denominator of the Laplace factor acts as a norming factor allowing reduction of the range of variation of $a_H(k)$. From what precedes — and due to the fact that the Laplace test is already well known and quite used [32, 7] — in real situations, we will use mainly the Laplace test to analyze the trend considering the sign of its factor as well as the evolution of this factor with time as it enables both local trend change and trend on average to be identified "at a glance".

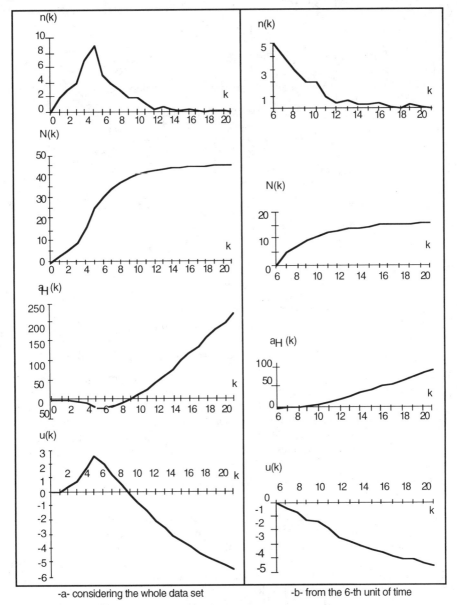

-a- considering the whole data set          -b- from the 6-th unit of time

**Fig. 4.** Subadditive property and Laplace factor

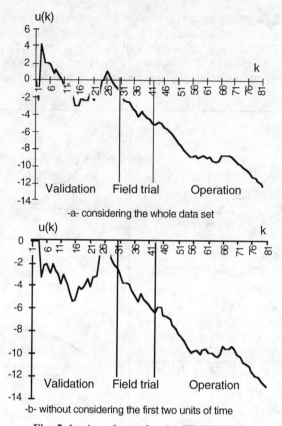

-a- considering the whole data set

-b- without considering the first two units of time

**Fig. 5.** Laplace factor for the TROPICO-R

## 3.3 Typical Results that Can Be Drawn From Trend Analyses

Trend analyses are of great help in appreciating the efficiency of test activities and controlling their progress. They help considerably the software development follow up. Indeed graphical tests are very often used in the industrial field [51, 52, 119, 106] even though they are called differently, such as descriptive statistics or control charts). It is worth noting that the role of trend tests is only to **draw attention** to problems that might otherwise not be noticed until too late, and to accelerate finding of a solution. Trend tests cannot replace the interpretation of someone who knows the software that the data is issued from, as well as the development process and the user environment. In the following, three typical situations are outlined.

**Reliability decrease** at the beginning of a new activity like (i) new life cycle phase, (ii) change in the test sets within the same phase, (iii) adding of new users or (iv) activating the system in a different profile of use, etc., is generally expected and is considered as a normal situation. Reliability decrease may also result from regression faults. Trend tests allow this kind of behavior to be noticed. If the duration of the period of decrease seems long, one has to pay attention and, in some situations, if it keeps decreasing this can point out some problems within the software: the analysis of the reasons of this decrease as well as the nature of the activated faults is of prime importance in such situations. This type of analysis may help in the decision to re-examine the corresponding piece of software.

**Reliability growth** after reliability decrease is usually welcomed since it indicates that, after first faults removal, the corresponding activity reveals less and less faults. When calendar time is used, mainly in operational life, sudden reliability growth may result from a period of time during which the system is less used or is not used at all; it may also result from the fact that some failures are not recorded. When such a situation is noticed, one has to be very careful and, more important, an examination of the reasons of this sudden increase is essential.

**Stable reliability** with almost no failures indicates that the corresponding activity has reached a "saturation": application of the corresponding tests set does not reveal new faults, or the corrective actions performed are of no perceptible effect on reliability. One has either to stop testing or to introduce new sets of tests or to proceed to the next phase. More generally, it is recommended to continue to apply a test set as long as it exhibits reliability growth and to stop its application when stable reliability is reached. As a consequence, in real situations, the fact that stable reliability is not reached may lead the validation team (as well as the manager) to take the decision to continue testing before software delivery since it will be more efficient to continue testing and removing faults.

Finally, trend analyses may be of **great help** for reliability growth models to give better estimations since they can be applied to data displaying trend in accordance with their assumptions rather than blindly. Applying blindly reliability growth models may lead to non realistic results when the trend displayed by the data differs from the one assumed by the model. Failure data can be partitioned according to the trend:

*   in case of reliability growth, most of the existing reliability growth models can be applied,
*   in case of reliability decrease, only models with an increasing failure intensity can be applied,
*   when the failure data exhibit reliability decrease followed by reliability growth, an S-Shaped model [100, 123] can be applied,
*   when stable reliability is noticed, a constant failure intensity model can be applied (HPP model): reliability growth models are in fact not needed.

# 4    Application to Real-life Systems

This section is intended to illustrate the type of results that can be issued from trend analysis during the development and operational phase, as well as for reliability growth models application. Since the previous section showed how the relationship between the subadditive property and the Laplace factor allows the identification of local trend changes by the Laplace factor, we will use mainly the latter. The aim of this section is just to illustrate some of the points introduced in the previous section and not to make detailed analyses of the considered data sets.

Three different systems are considered: (i) the first one corresponds to system SS4 published in [98], called system A hereafter, (ii) the second, corresponds to system S27 (referred to as system B) published also in [98], and (iii) the last one corresponds to an electronic switching system (referred to as system C) which has been observed during validation and a part of operational life [62]. For each of them, we will give the results of trend analysis and comment on the kind of reliability growth models that could be used.

## 4.1 System A

Failure data gathered on System A correspond to operational life. Application of the arithmetical mean test in Fig. 6-a shows that the mean time to failure is almost constant: it is about 230 000 units of time.

The corresponding Laplace factor displayed in Fig. 6-b oscillates between -2 and +2 indicating also stable reliability for a significance level of 5%.In this case, a constant failure rate (i.e., HPP model) is well adapted to model the software behavior and is of simpler application than a reliability growth model. This result is not surprising since the software was not maintained (no fault correction). This is an example of a situation where the classical Laplace test is applicable and sufficient to analyze the trend at a glance (since there are no local trend changes).

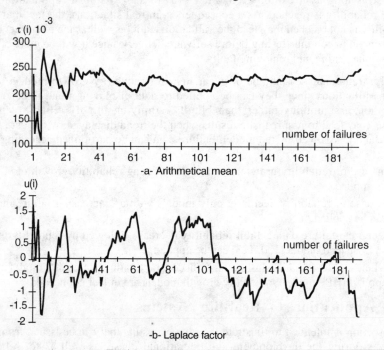

-a- Arithmetical mean

-b- Laplace factor

**Fig. 6.** Trend tests for system A

## 4.2 System B

System B is an example of systems which exhibit two phases of stable reliability; transition between them took place about failures 23-24 (Fig. 7). This system was under test and one has to look for the reasons of this sudden change and to see why no reliability growth took place. It was not possible from the published data to identify the reasons of this behavior. In this case, data may be partitioned into two subsets each of them being modeled by a constant failure rate.

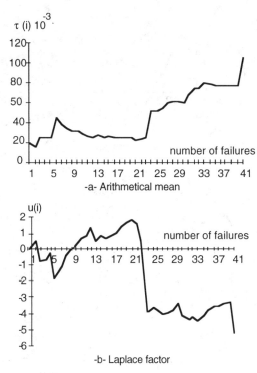

**Fig. 7.** Trend tests for system B

Figs. 7-a and 7-b illustrate the link between a graphical test (the mean of the inter-failure times) and the Laplace factor: the discontinuity in software behavior is pointed out by both of them.

### 4.3 System C

System C displayed reliability decrease during the validation, reliability growth took place only during operational life as indicated in Fig. 8-a. This is confirmed by Fig. 8-b where the Laplace test for operational life is applied to the data collected during operation only. It can also be seen that some reliability fluctuations took place around unit time 15, this fluctuation is due to the introduction of new users. Clearly, not any reliability growth model is applicable during validation. However, an S-Shaped model can be applied to the whole data set and any reliability growth model to operational data (from unit time 9) as carried out in [62]. This is an example of situation where the classical Laplace test does not help in detecting the local trend change around point 9. The only information available from the classical test is that reliability growth took place from point 18 which is indeed so far from the real situation.

## 5    Conclusions

In this paper, we have characterized reliability growth and derived a graphical interpretation of the subadditive property and we have shown the equivalence between

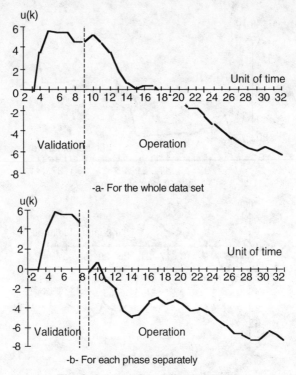

**Fig. 8.** Laplace factor for System C

this property and the Laplace factor allowing thus the Laplace factor to identify local trend changes as well. We have shown (i) that trend analyses constitute a major tool during the software development process and (ii) how the results can guide the project manager to control the progress of the development activities and even to take the decision to re-examine the software for specific situations. Trend analyses are also really helpful when reliability evaluation is needed. They allow periods of times of reliability growth and reliability decrease to be identified in order to apply reliability growth models to data exhibiting trend in accordance with their modelling assumptions. Trend tests and reliability growth models are part of a global method for software reliability analysis and evaluation which is presented in [62] and which has been applied successfully to data collected on real systems [66, 61, 62].

# Acknowledgements

We wish to thank Mohamed Kaâniche and Sylvain Metge from LAAS-CNRS for their helpful comments when reading earlier versions of the paper.

# The Transformation Approach to the Modelling and Evaluation of Reliability and Availability Growth*

Jean-Claude Laprie  Christian Béounes[†]  Mohamed Kaâniche  Karama Kanoun

## LAAS-CNRS

**Abstract.** Reliability growth phenomena are not usually taken into account when performing dependability evaluations of hardware and/or software systems during their operational life. However, such phenomena are significantly important. In this paper, an approach is presented which is aimed at the modelling and evaluation of reliability and availability of systems from the knowledge of the reliability growth of their components. Section 2 is devoted to the characterization of system behavior with respect to reliability and availability. The hyperexponential model for reliability and availability growth modelling is introduced in the third section, which is then applied to multi-component systems in the fourth section. The results presented constitute a significant step towards the evaluation of reliability and availability of systems, with respect to both physical and design faults, as they enable 1) *reliability growth* phenomena to be incorporated in *hardware models*, and 2) *system structure* to be accounted for in *software models*. These results are thus a contribution to a solution to the (unfortunate) current separation between hardware models and software models.

## 1   Introduction

When dealing with the assessment of dependability the *users* of computing systems are interested in obtaining figures resulting from modelling and evaluation of *systems,* composed of *hardware and software*, with respect to both *physical and design faults.* Faced with these user requirements, hardware-and-software evaluations are far from being current practice, with a few exceptions (e.g. [31, 111, 104]). An explanation to this state of affairs lies in the fact that hardware evaluation and software evaluation have followed courses which can hardly be more separated [76].

Hardware evaluation has concentrated on operational life, focusing on the influence on dependability of the system structure; however, in spite of early work [39], it has largely been ignored that the reliability of hardware parts is significantly growing during the whole system's life, as shown, for instance, by the experimental data displayed in [14].

Software evaluation has mainly concentrated on the development-validation phase, focusing on the reliability growth of single-component ("black box") systems. Many models have been proposed (see surveys such as [124, 95]). Less attention has been paid to accounting for the structure of software systems, and has been restricted to the

---

*   This paper is a revised version of [77].

†   Christian Béounes passed away on April 23, 1993.

failure process, either for non-fault tolerant [81, 73] or for fault-tolerant software systems (e.g. [56, 73]).

In this paper, an approach is presented which is aimed at filling the gaps identified above. The results we have obtained enable both reliability and availability of hardware and/or software systems to be evaluated, from the knowledge of the reliability growth of their components. Section 2 is devoted to the characterization of system behavior with respect to reliability and availability. The hyperexponential model is introduced in Section 3, which is then applied to multi-component systems in Section 4.

## 2     Characterization of System Behavior

The reliability of a system is conveniently illustrated by the failure intensity, as it is a measure of the frequency of the system failures as noticed by its user(s). Failure intensity is typically first decreasing (reliability growth), due to the removal of residual design faults, either in the software or in the hardware. It may become stable (stable reliability) after a certain period of operation; the failures due to internal faults occurring in this period are due to either physical faults, or to design faults which are admitted not to be removed. Failure intensity generally exhibits an increase (reliability decrease) upon the introduction of new versions incorporating modified functionalities; it then tends towards an asymptote again, and so on. It is noteworthy that such a behavior is not restricted to the operational life of a system, but also applies to situations occurring during the development-validation phases of a system, e.g. a) during incremental development, or b) during system integration.

Typical variations of the failure intensity may be represented as indicated on Fig. 1, curve a. Such a curve depends on the granularity of the observations, and may be felt as resulting from the smoothing of more noticeable variations (curve b); it may in turn be smoothed into a continuously decreasing curve (c). Although such a representation is very general and covers many practical situations, there are situations which exhibit discontinuities important enough such that the smoothing process cannot be considered as reasonable (e.g. upon introduction of a new system generation).

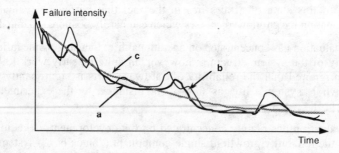

**Fig. 1.** Typical variations of a system's failure intensity

We have above identified three classes of behavior: stable reliability, reliability growth, and reliability decrease. They may be defined as follows:

- *stable reliability:* the system's ability to deliver proper service is *preserved* (stochastic identity of the successive times to failure);

- *reliability growth:* the system's ability to deliver proper service is *improved* (stochastic increase of the successive times to failure);
- *reliability decrease:* the system's ability to deliver proper service is *degraded* (stochastic decrease of the successive times to failure).

Practical interpretations of stable reliability and of reliability growth are as follows:

- stable reliability: at a given restoration, the system is identical to what it was at the previous restoration; this corresponds to the following situations:
  - in the case of a hardware failure, the failed part is changed for another one, identical and non failed,
  - in the case of a software failure, the system is restarted with an input pattern different from the one having led to failure;
- reliability growth: the fault whose activation has led to failure is diagnosed as a design fault (in software or in hardware) and is removed.

*Reliability decrease* is theoretically, and practically, possible. In such a case, it has to be hoped that the decrease is limited in time, and that reliability is globally growing over a long observation period of time. Reliability decrease may originate from:

- introduction of new faults during corrective actions, whose probability of activation is greater than for the removed fault(s);
- introduction of a new version, with modified functionalities;
- dependencies between faults: some software faults can be masked by others, i.e. they cannot be activated as long as the latter are not removed [100]; removal of the masking faults will have as a consequence an increase in the failure intensity.

In order to formalize the above mentioned properties, our approach [63, 75, 60, 76] has been to generalize the renewal theory to the non-stationary case, i.e. when the successive times to failures are not stochastically identical. This generalization of the renewal theory leads to the knowledge model which enables various operation resumption and maintenance policies to be considered from a) restoration after correction only to b) restart with off-line correction(s) performed either one-at-a-time or batch (after several failures have occurred). Detailed derivations for the knowledge model are given in [78] and the main results are summarized below when the inter-failure times constitute a piecewise Poisson process converging towards a Poisson process after r corrections have taken place. Let $\{\lambda_1, \lambda_2,...,\lambda_r\}$ be the sequence of the failure rates. The failure intensity h(t) is then shown to have the following properties:

- h(t) is a continuous function of time, with $h(0) = \lambda_1$, $h(\infty) = \lambda_r$;
- a condition for h(t) to be a non increasing function of time, i.e. a condition for *reliability growth*, is: $\lambda_1 \geq \lambda_2 \geq ... \geq \lambda_r$
- h(t) is a continuous function of time, with $h(0) = \lambda_1$, $h(\infty) = \lambda_r$;
- when no correction takes place, we are in the case of a classical renewal process (stable reliability); then $h(t) = \lambda_1$;
- if a (local) increase in the failure rates occurs, then the failure intensity correspondingly (locally) increases.

These properties hold whatever maintenance policy is considered: no assumption is made on the relation between the failure instants and the instants when a corrected system is put into operation (several failures can occur between two fault removal actions, and the instants when a corrected system is put into operation may not coincide with failure instants, e.g. in the case of preventive maintenance).

These results are illustrated by Fig. 2 in the case of a reliability growth phase followed by a stable reliability phase. Since we have up to now considered reliability, the times to restoration are assumed to be equal to zero on this figure.

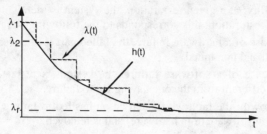

**Fig. 2.** Failure rate and failure intensity

A measure of major interest for a wide variety of systems in operational use is availability, denoted hereafter A(t). Availability is generally growing significantly during the whole operational life of a system (see e.g. the field data displayed in [121, 104]). It was shown in [31] that the unavailability $\overline{A}$ (t) = 1 - A(t) has the shape displayed by Fig. 3: assuming a system initially working, unavailability raises sharply to a maximum, and then slowly decreases as the design faults are progressively removed.

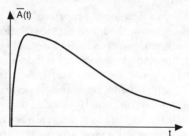

**Fig. 3.** Typical system unavailability

The same approach of generalizing the renewal theory (under the various service restoration policies mentioned above) has been applied to availability in [60]; the corresponding derivations are not displayed due to space limitation. The results confirm and generalize what was previously established in [31, 73] through modelling via multi-state Markov and semi-Markov chains — assuming a more restrictive service restoration policy, namely operation restart after correction only. A summary is as follows:

P1) there is a single unavailability maximum (availability minimum) if reliability is growing; in the converse, local maxima (minima) occur as failure intensity increases;

P2) when reliability becomes stable, unavailability (availability) becomes constant;

P3) the changes in availability are significantly more influenced by the stochastic changes in the times to failure than in the times to restoration, which can be assumed as stochastically identical over the system's life;

P4) the time to reach the maximum unavailability (minimum availability) is of the order of magnitude of the mean time to restoration;

P5) the distribution of the time to restoration is of negligible influence;

P6) if the inter-failure occurrence times constitute a piecewise Poisson process, continuously non increasing from $\lambda_1$ to $\lambda_r$, and if the times to restoration are assumed exponentially distributed with rate $\mu \gg \lambda_1$, then:

$$\overline{A}_{max} \approx \frac{\lambda_1}{\mu} \quad , \quad \overline{A}(\infty) \approx \frac{\lambda_r}{\mu}$$

The results summarized in this section are — although still suffering from some limitations such as the assumed independency between the times to failure necessary for performing the renewal theory derivations (see [95, 76] for a discussion about this assumption)— more general than what was previously published in the literature, especially with respect to:

- their ability to consider reliability and availability measures for both hardware and software,
- the maintenance policies considered,
- their ability to cover stable reliability, reliability growth and reliability decrease.

However, the results derived are too complex[1] (see [78] for more details) in order to be directly applied in real life for performing predictions, hence the need for simplified models for practical purposes, which can be termed *action models*.

# 3   The Hyperexponential Model for Reliability and Availability Growth

## 3.1   The Model and its Properties

Our willingness to focus on the operational life rather than on the development-validation phase can be expressed through the following requirements:

R1) ability to restitute stable reliability occurring after reliability growth,

R2) derivation of both reliability and availability,

R3) applicability to hardware and/or software multi-component systems.

None of the other models which appeared previously in the literature — which can be considered as action models with respect to what has been summarized in the previous section — satisfies this set of requirements. Especially, requirement R2 has not been

---

[1]  The Laplace transform of the failure intensity obtained through the generalization of the renewal theory is, assuming that the jth correction is undertaken after $a_j$ failures have occurred since the j-1th correction, and denoting by $v$ the service restoration rate:

$$\tilde{h}(s) = \sum_{i=1}^{r-1} \left(\frac{v}{v+s}\right)^{i-1} \prod_{m=1}^{i-1} \left(\frac{\lambda_m}{\lambda_m + s}\right)^{a_m} \sum_{j=1}^{a_i} \left(\frac{\lambda_i}{\lambda_i+s}\right)^j + \frac{\lambda_r}{s} \left(\frac{v}{v+s}\right)^{r-1} \prod_{m=1}^{r-1} \left(\frac{\lambda_m}{\lambda_m+s}\right)^{a_m}$$

previously paid attention. It is however worth mentioning that some models bring solutions for R1 or for R3, e.g.:

- requirement R1 is satisfied by the extension of the Duane's model presented in [44]; the S-shaped [100, 124] model restitutes reliability decrease followed by reliability growth (although on the number of uncovered faults rather than on reliability per se), whereas the other models restitute reliability growth only with a failure intensity tending asymptotically towards zero;

- with respect to requirement R3, the Duane's model has been applied to single-component software in [1], multi-component software has been examined in [100], and the Littlewood's model has been applied to single-component systems either software or hardware in [82].

In this section, we examine compliance to requirements R1 and R2. Requirement R3 will be dealt with in the next section.

We define the hyperexponential model [74, 60] as a non-homogeneous Poisson process (NHPP) of failure intensity given by:

$$h(t) = \frac{\omega\, \zeta_{sup}\, e^{-\zeta_{sup}t} + \varpi\, \zeta_{inf}\, e^{-\zeta_{inf}t}}{\omega\, e^{-\zeta_{sup}t} + \varpi\, e^{-\zeta_{inf}t}} \qquad \text{with } 0 \le \omega \le 1,\ \omega + \varpi = 1 \qquad (1)$$

This model admits as special cases:

- the stable reliability situation, with exponential times to failures: a) $\zeta_{sup} = \zeta_{inf}$, or b) $\omega = 0$ or $\varpi = 0$;

- a failure intensity tending asymptotically towards zero: $\zeta_{inf} = 0$.

h(t) is non-increasing with time, from $h(0) = \omega\, \zeta_{sup} + \varpi\, \zeta_{inf}$ to $h(\infty) = \zeta_{inf}$, as indicated on Fig. 4.

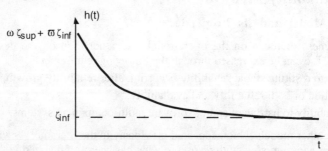

**Fig. 4.** Typical failure intensity for the hyperexponential model

The rate of decrease of h(t) can be adjusted via the values of the 3 parameters $\zeta_{sup}$, $\zeta_{inf}$, $\omega$, as illustrated by Fig. 5.

An important property of NHPPs is as follows: let $s_{i-1}$ denote the instant of occurrence of the (i-1)th failure, and $\tau$ denote the time elapsed since $s_{i-1}$. Then, we have the relation (see e.g. [99]) $\lambda i(\tau \mid s_{i-1}) = h(s_{i-1}+\tau)$: the failure rate for the ith failure cannot be distinguished from the failure intensity. We can thus, from a prediction viewpoint, consider our model as originating from the 2-stage hyperexponential Cox

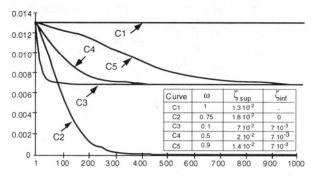

**Fig.5.** Example failure intensity for the hyperexponential model

law (hence its name): it can be interpreted as a Markov model, where, instead of a single UP state, there are two such states, with initial probabilities $\omega$ and $\varpi$. The reliability growth model of a system can then be modeled from the transformation of a traditional Markov model (stable reliability, exponential failure process) into another Markov model, as indicated by Fig. 6.

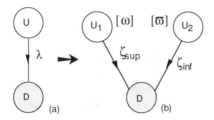

**Fig. 6.** Markov interpretation of the hyperexponential model

When considering availability, the transformation approach just introduced (Fig. 6) leads — when accounting for properties P3 and P5 of Section 2 — to the model of Fig. 7-b, from the classical Markov model of a single-component system (Fig. 7-a). Parameters p and q, $0 \leq p \leq 1$, $0 \leq p \leq 1$, $p+q=1$, are determined hereafter.

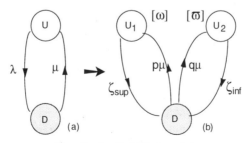

**Fig. 7.** Availability models

Processing model of Fig. 7-b leads, when accounting for the fact that $\mu \gg \zeta_{sup}$, to the following expression for the unavailability $\overline{A}(t)$:

$$\overline{A}(t) = \alpha + \beta \exp\left(-\left(q\,\zeta_{sup}+p\,\zeta_{inf}+o\left(\frac{\zeta_{sup}}{\mu},\frac{\zeta_{inf}}{\mu}\right)\right)t\right)$$

$$+ \gamma \exp\left(-\left(\mu+o\left(\frac{\zeta_{sup}}{\mu},\frac{\zeta_{inf}}{\mu}\right)\right)t\right)$$

with:

$$\alpha = \frac{\zeta_{sup}\,\zeta_{inf}}{\mu\,(q\,\zeta_{sup}+p\,\zeta_{inf})} + o\left(\frac{\zeta_{sup}}{\mu},\frac{\zeta_{inf}}{\mu}\right)$$

$$\beta = \frac{(\omega\,\zeta_{sup}+\varpi\,\zeta_{inf})(q\,\zeta_{sup}+p\,\zeta_{inf})-\zeta_{sup}\,\zeta_{inf}}{\mu\,(q\,\zeta_{sup}+p\,\zeta_{inf})} + o\left(\frac{\zeta_{sup}}{\mu},\frac{\zeta_{inf}}{\mu}\right)$$

$$\gamma = -\frac{\omega\,\zeta_{sup}+\varpi\,\zeta_{inf}}{\mu} + o\left(\frac{\zeta_{sup}}{\mu},\frac{\zeta_{inf}}{\mu}\right)$$

$o(x)$ denotes quantities such that $\displaystyle\lim_{x\to 0}\frac{o(x)}{x}=0$

The maximum of unavailability is given by:

$$\overline{A}_{max} = \frac{\omega\,\zeta_{sup}+\varpi\,\zeta_{inf}}{\mu} + o\left(\frac{\zeta_{sup}}{\mu},\frac{\zeta_{inf}}{\mu}\right)$$

This relation is in accordance with the result recalled in Section 2 (property P6); since $\omega\,\zeta_{sup}+\varpi\,\zeta_{inf}=h(0)$.

The asymptotic value $\overline{A}_\infty$ of $\overline{A}(t)$ is $\overline{A}_\infty = \alpha$. We wish (property P6 of Section 2) $\overline{A}_\infty = \zeta_{inf}/\mu$; which is obtained for q=1 and p=0 (another solution would be $\zeta_{sup}=\zeta_{inf}$; thus contrary to the assumption $\zeta_{sup}\neq\zeta_{inf}$ which is necessary for representing reliability growth).

The availability model for a single-component system with reliability growth is then given by Fig. 8.

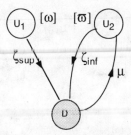

**Fig. 8.** Availability model for a single-component system

Processing the model of Fig. 8 leads to the following expression for the unavailability $\overline{A}(t)$:

$$\overline{A}(t) = \frac{\zeta_{inf}}{\mu + \zeta_{inf}} + \frac{\omega\,(\zeta_{sup} - \zeta_{inf})}{\mu - (\zeta_{sup} - \zeta_{inf})}\, e^{-\zeta_{sup}t}$$
$$- \frac{\mu\,(\omega\,\zeta_{sup} + \varpi\,\zeta_{inf}) - \varpi\,\zeta_{inf}\,(\zeta_{sup} - \zeta_{inf})}{(\mu + \zeta_{inf})\,(\mu - \zeta_{sup} + \zeta_{inf})}\, e^{-(\mu+\zeta_{inf})t}$$

This expression becomes, when accounting for $\mu \gg \zeta_{sup}$:

$$\overline{A}(t) \approx \frac{\zeta_{inf}}{\mu} + \frac{\omega(\zeta_{sup} - \zeta_{inf})}{\mu}\, e^{-\zeta_{sup}t} - \frac{\omega\zeta_{sup} + \varpi\,\zeta_{inf}}{\mu}\, e^{-\mu t} \qquad (2)$$

The corresponding unavailability curve is given by Fig. 9, curve a; curves b and c are relative to stable reliability, either pessimistic before reliability growth took place (b) or optimistic after (c).

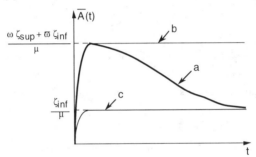

**Fig. 9.** Unavailability curves

Interpretation of the model of Fig. 8 as representing a behavior such as reaching stationarity after having left the transient state U1 would be misleading since such an interpretation does not account for the fact that initial probabilities of states U1 and U2 are both different from 0 or 1. Space limits prevent from giving a detailed physical interpretation of the model, and it can thus be considered as a mathematical artifact satisfying physical properties (P1, P3, P4, and P6 stated in Section 2).

### 3.2 Application to Field Data

The utilization of the hyperexponential model to reliability prediction has been published elsewhere, and we shall restrict ourselves to summarize the corresponding results. We shall then present an application of the model to availability.

**Reliability.** In [63], the hyperexponential model was applied to the data reported in [98] and compared to other models: the Jelinski-Moranda, the Duane, the Littlewood-Verral and the Keiller-Littlewood models. Comparison showed that it gives results comparable to the other models, in that sense that it is better than other models on some sets of data, whereas other models are better on other sets; this is a usual situation when comparing several reliability growth models (see e.g. [1]).

The system considered in [66] is a sub-system of the E-10 switching system from ALCATEL installed on an increasing number of sites, with more than 1400 sites at the end of the observation period. Data were collected during 3 years including the end of the validation phase and a part of operational life. The software size is about 100 Kbytes. The ability of the hyperexponential model to predict the software behavior has been compared to the Jelinski-Moranda and the Keiller-Littlewood models, and it revealed to give predictions as good as these two models. In addition, the ability of the hyperexponential to cover stable reliability enabled the asymptotic failure rate to be evaluated, and thus to perform an evaluation of the system (hardware and software).

**Availability.** Statistical estimation of the availability for a set of systems is given by the ratio of non-failed systems at time t to the total number of systems in the set. When the field data are relative to times to failure and to times to restoration, considering average availability instead of availability eases the estimation process, as average availability is the expected proportion of time a system is non-failed [12]. The average availability over [0,t] is defined by:

$$A_{av}(t) = \frac{1}{t} \int_0^t A(\tau) \, d\tau.$$

Denoting respectively by $UT_i$ and $DT_i$ the observed times to failure and times to restoration, a statistical estimator of $A_{av}(t)$ is: $\hat{A}_{av}(t) = \frac{1}{t} \sum_{i=1}^{n_t} UT_i$ , where $n_t$ is the number of failures which occurred in [0,t].

The expression of the average unavailability for the hyperexponential model (Fig. 8) obtained from relation (2) is:

$$\overline{A}_{av}(t) \approx \frac{\zeta_{inf}}{\mu} + \frac{\omega(\zeta_{sup}-\zeta_{inf})}{\mu} \frac{1-e^{-\zeta_{sup}t}}{\zeta_{sup}\,t} - \frac{\omega\,\zeta_{sup}+\varpi\,\zeta_{inf}}{\mu} \frac{1-e^{-\mu t}}{\mu\,t} \quad (3)$$

The data considered which we used in the estimation are relative to the software of the TROPICO-R switching system, developed by TELEBRAS, the Brazilian telecommunication company. The software is about 330 Kbytes. The data collection extended over the validation phase and the beginning of operational life. A total of 211 failure reports have been issued, over a period of 32 months; we have conducted the estimation of the average availability on the last 15 months of the observation period concerning operational life of the system, during which the number of systems in service went progressively from 4 to 42 and 50 failures have been reported. The failure reports do not give any information on the time to restoration subsequent to the reported failure. Since the corrections are performed off-line, restoration corresponds to system restart or software reloading. A data collection conducted on the times to restoration showed that they vary between 1 and 5 minutes. In order to complement the information given by the failure reports, we have performed a random sampling according to a uniform distribution with values between 1 and 5.

The results are displayed on Fig. 10, which gives the observed average unavailability (C2) and the average unavailability evaluated via the hyperexponential model (C1);

the observed instantaneous unavailability is also given as an indication (C3). The parameters $(\omega, \zeta_{sup}, \zeta_{inf})$ of the latter have been determined by a least square optimization. The results displayed on Fig. 10 are evidently satisfactory. It is noteworthy that criteria for reliability growth models validation (and comparison) are either based on the distribution of the considered random variable (e.g., the Kolmogorov-Smirnov distance or the prequential approach) or the residue (which corresponds to the sum of the differences between the observed and the evaluated measure). Criteria of the first kind are not suited for availability, and the residue criterion is useful only when comparing predictions achieved by different models.

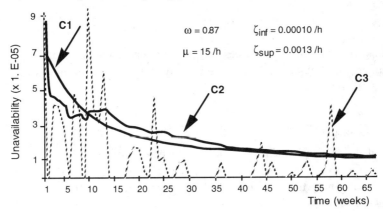

Fig. 10. Unavailability of the TROPICO-R software.

# 4    Modelling of Reliability and Availability Growth of Multi-Component Systems

Owing to the Markov interpretation of the hyperexponential model, a natural approach to modelling multi-component systems is to build a Markov model for the system from models of its components which incorporate reliability growth (Fig. 8). We introduce this approach through two — deliberately — simple examples. We then propose a general approach, based on stochastic Petri nets, and we apply it to a more realistic example. We finally give the interest and limits of the transformation approach.

## 4.1  Two  Simple  Examples

Let us consider first a two-component hardware redundant system, with perfect coverage and unrestricted repair facilities. The classical — stable reliability — Markov model of such a system is recalled on Fig. 11.

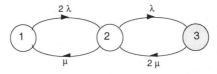

Fig. 11. Markov model of a two-component redundant system in stable reliability

As the two components are stochastically independent, the model of Fig. 11 can be formally derived from the transition matrices of its components through the Kronecker algebra [3].

The Kronecker product of two matrices $\mathbb{A} = [a_{ij}]$, of dimensions (p,q), and $\mathbb{B} = [b_{ij}]$, of dimensions (m,n), is given by:

$$\mathbb{A} \otimes \mathbb{B} = \begin{pmatrix} a_{11}\,\mathbb{B} & a_{12}\,\mathbb{B} & \cdots & a_{1q}\,\mathbb{B} \\ a_{21}\,\mathbb{B} & a_{22}\,\mathbb{B} & \cdots & a_{2q}\,\mathbb{B} \\ \vdots & \vdots & & \vdots \\ a_{p1}\,\mathbb{B} & a_{p2}\,\mathbb{B} & \cdots & a_{pq}\,\mathbb{B} \end{pmatrix}$$

The Kronecker sum of two matrices $\mathbb{C} = [c_{ij}]$, of dimensions (n,n), and $\mathbb{D} = [d_{ij}]$, of dimensions (m,m), with $\mathbb{I}_x$ denoting the identity matrix of dimensions (x,x), is given by: $\mathbb{C} \oplus \mathbb{D} = \mathbb{C} \otimes \mathbb{I}_m + \mathbb{I}_n \otimes \mathbb{D}$.

Let $\Lambda_c = \begin{pmatrix} -\lambda & \lambda \\ \mu & -\mu \end{pmatrix}$ denote the transition matrix of each component. The transition matrix of the system is then $\Lambda_s = \Lambda_c \oplus \Lambda_c$, where $\oplus$ denotes the Kronecker sum. The transition matrix corresponding to the model of Fig. 11 is derived from $\Lambda_s$ by the Kemeny-Snell theorem for Markov chain reduction [69] since the two components are identical.

When reliability growth of the components is accounted for, the transition matrix $\Lambda_c$ of each component becomes (Fig. 8):

$$\Lambda_c = \begin{pmatrix} -\zeta_{sup} & 0 & \zeta_{sup} \\ 0 & -\zeta_{inf} & \zeta_{inf} \\ 0 & \mu & -\mu \end{pmatrix}$$

Let $\mathbb{P}_c(0) = (\,\omega \quad \varpi \quad 0\,)$ be the initial probability vector of each component. The initial probability vector of the system is then given by: $\mathbb{P}_s(0) = \mathbb{P}_c(0) \otimes \mathbb{P}_c(0)$, where $\otimes$ denotes the Kronecker product.

The Markov chain so generated, reduced in the Kemeny-Snell sense, is given by Fig.12. This model is simple enough in order to derive analytical expressions. We get for instance for unavailability, accounting for $\mu \gg \zeta_{sup} > \zeta_{inf}$:

$$\overline{A}(t) = \frac{\zeta_{inf}^2}{\mu^2} + 2\,\frac{\omega\zeta_{inf}(\zeta_{sup}-\zeta_{inf})}{\mu^2}\,e^{-\zeta_{sup}t} + \frac{\omega^2\,(\zeta_{sup}-\zeta_{inf})^2}{\mu^2}\,e^{-2\zeta_{sup}t}$$
$$- 2\,\frac{(\omega\zeta_{sup} + \varpi\,\zeta_{inf})^2}{\mu^2}\,e^{-\mu t}$$

The approach obviously applies to the case when components are not identical. Let us consider for instance a two-component hardware-and-software non-redundant system. Let $\lambda_S$, $\mu_S$, and $\lambda_H$, $\mu_H$, denote the failure and restoration rates of the software and of the hardware components, respectively. Going through the same steps

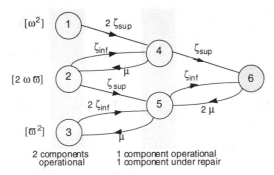

**Fig. 12.** Markov model of a two-component redundant system in reliability growth

as in the previous example (except the reduction step a la Kemeny-Snell as the two components are here different), leads to the models of Fig. 13, where the (a) model is the stable reliability model, and the (b) model is the reliability growth model.

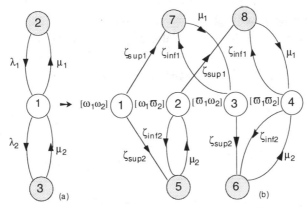

**Fig. 13.** The transformation approach for a hardware-and-software system

## 4.2    General Approach

In most realistic systems, there exist stochastic dependencies among components, which are conveniently modeled by stochastic Petri nets (SPN) [15] under the form of synchronization and cooperation among concurrent processes. The introduction of instantaneous transitions led to the generalized stochastic Petri nets (GSPN) [92].

Considering the hyperexponential model of a single-component introduced in the section 3, the GSPN modelling approach leads to the models of Fig. 14 where the white ovals represent instantaneous transitions and the black rectangles represent timed transitions.

The Markov models corresponding to the GSPNs of Figs. 14-a and -b are, respectively, the Markov models of Figs 7-a and 8. In the GSPN of Figs. 14-b, the instantaneous transitions enable the assignment of initial probabilities distinct from 1 or 0 to the initial states of the associated Markov chain to be modeled (this is in fact a relaxation of the implicit assumption in classical GSPNs about the equivalence of

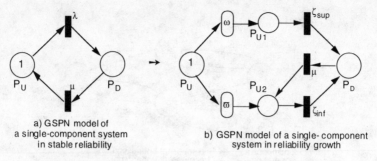

a) GSPN model of
a single-component system
in stable reliability

b) GSPN model of a single- component
system in reliability growth

**Fig. 14.** GSPN models for single-components systems

the initial marking and a probability equal to 1 assigned to the initial state of the associated Markov chain).

The transformation approach when using GSPNs then consists in the following steps:

S1)   Construction of the GSPN of the system assuming stable reliability.

S2)   Transformation of the GSPN according to Fig. 14.

S3)   Derive the reachability graph of the transformed GSPN, which is the Markov chain accounting for reliability growth.

We illustrate this approach on a two-component system with imperfect coverage and single repair facility. Let:

•   $\lambda_c$ and $\lambda_{\bar{c}}$ denote the failure rates corresponding to covered and non-covered errors, respectively,

•   $\mu1$, $\mu2$, and $\mu3$ denote the restoration rates after a) the first covered failure, b) the first non-covered failure and c) a second covered failure, respectively.

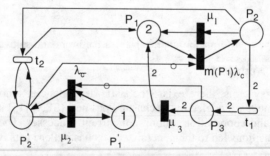

**Fig. 15.** GSPN of the system in stable reliability

The stable reliability GSPN is given by Fig. 15. The transformed GSPN in order to account for reliability growth via the hyperexponential model is given by Fig. 16, where $\zeta_{c;sup}$, and $\zeta_{c;inf}$ result from the transformation of $\lambda_c$, and $\zeta_{\bar{c};sup}$, and $\zeta_{\bar{c};inf}$ result from the transformation of $\lambda_{\bar{c}}$. The Markov chains corresponding to the GSPNs of Figs 15 and 16 are given by Figs 17 and 18, respectively.

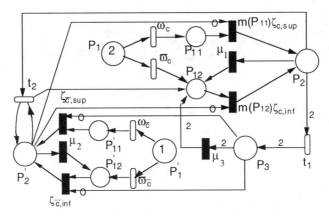

**Fig. 16.** GSPN of the system in reliability growth

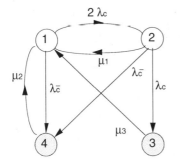

| State | Marking |
|-------|---------|
| 1 | {2p1,p'1} |
| 2 | {p1,p2,p'1} |
| 3 | {2p3,p'1} |
| 4 | {2p1,p'2} |

**Fig. 17.** Markov chain of the system in stable reliability

Processing the Markov chain of Fig. 18 by the SURF program [30] leads to the results plotted on Fig. 19, where:

- the covered failure rate and the non-covered failure rate after reliability growth ($\zeta_{c;inf}$ and $\zeta_{\bar{c};inf}$), have been taken as equal to $10^{-4}$/h and $5 \cdot 10^{-7}$/h, respectively (thus $\zeta_{\bar{c};inf} / \zeta_{c;inf} = 5 \cdot 10^{-3}$);

- the extent of reliability growth for both sources of failures is equal to 10, we have thus $10^{-4} \le \lambda_c \le 10^{-3}$ and $5 \cdot 10^{-7} \le \lambda_{\bar{c}} \le 5 \cdot 10^{-6}$;

- the restoration rates are such that: $\zeta_{c;inf}/\mu_1 = 5 \cdot 10^{-3}$ ; $\zeta_{c;inf}/\mu_2 = \zeta_{c;inf}/\mu_3 = 10^{-3}$ (restoration is considered easier when one of the components is still operating than when the system is totally down);

- curve C1 (respectively C5) corresponds to stable reliability conditions, with $\lambda_c$ and $\lambda_{\bar{c}}$ taking their minimal values (respectively maximal values);

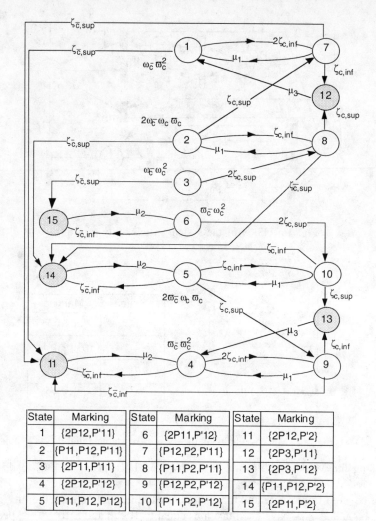

**Fig. 18.** Markov chain of the system in reliability growth

- C4 corresponds to reliability growth, with $\lambda_c$ and $\lambda_{\bar{c}}$ decreasing from their maximal values to their minimal values respectively and $\omega_c = \omega_{\bar{c}} = 0.5$;

- Curves C2 and C3 are displayed in order to show the influence of the reliability growth of the covered failure rate and of the uncovered failure rate taken in isolation, respectively.

## 4.3  Interest and Limitations of the Transformation Approach

The transformation approach when applied to multi-component systems satisfies requirement R3 of Section 3.1: we can model the dependability growth of a system from the dependability growth of its components. In addition, this is performed in re-utilizing all the body of results which have been derived for building and processing Markov models.

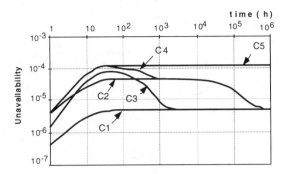

**Fig. 19.** Unavailability curves for model of Fig. 18

The main limitation of the approach clearly lies in the increase in the state space with respect to the stable reliability models. The cardinality of the state space for an n-component system in stable reliability with 2-state components is comprised between $n+1$ (all components identical) and $2^n$ (all the components different), and it ranges from $(n+1)(n+2)/2$ to $3^n$ in the case of reliability growth. However, this limitation is not so drastic as it would have been a few years ago, thanks to the powerful current methods for processing Markov models [55], which have been reported to have the capability of processing models of several tens of thousand states [50]. These cardinalities assume stochastic independence. However, stochastic dependencies generally have more impact on the interstate transitions than on the state space cardinality. It is noteworthy that the model of Fig. 18 is relative to a system whose components have more than two states, and are stochastically dependent.

## 5    Conclusions

Incorporating reliability growth into dependability predictions performed for systems in operational use is actually extremely worthwhile: the field data displayed in [121] show that unavailability is decreased by a factor of 250 during 3 and half years of operation. Stable reliability, as usually assumed in the dependability evaluations currently performed for systems in their operational life, is in fact a — very — special case.

A step further than estimating dependability growth for a system from field data collected for this system, would be accounting for future reliability growth when performing evaluations during the design of the considered system. This is potentially possible with our approach, as reliability growth of subsystems can be estimated from the data collected by manufacturers. This is examplified on Fig. 20, where we have conducted an estimation of reliability growth on data displayed in [14] (the parameters of the hyperexponential model estimation have been determined through a least square estimation).

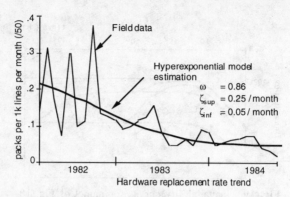

**Fig. 20.** Reliability growth estimation from [14]

We wrote "potentially": indeed, such estimations have to be completed by an estimation of the variations in dependability growth over successive products, which would mean performing an estimation of the parameters of reliability growth for a future product from the same parameters for previous products.

## Acknowledgements

The data relative to the TROPICO-R system have been provided by Jorge Moreira de Souza and Marta Bastos Martini, in the framework of a cooperation program between TELEBRAS-CPqD and LAAS-CNRS.

# New Ways to Get Accurate Reliability Measures*

Sarah Brocklehurst  Bev Littlewood

City University

**Abstract** A plethora of software reliability models have been developed over the years but, in spite of extravagant claims for their efficacy, none can be trusted to give accurate results in all circumstances. This presents potential users with a serious difficulty, and has probably been the main reason why there has been such a poor take-up of these techniques. The work described here has largely overcome this problem, and it is now possible in most cases to obtain reliability measures and predictions that can be trusted. This position arises *not* because of the creation of better models, but of techniques for analysing *predictive accuracy*. Essentially, it is now possible to apply *many* models to a particular source of software failure data, and decide which (if any) is giving results of acceptable accuracy. The techniques which have brought about this new perspective on software reliability modelling also bring with them a bonus: they enable even more accurate predictions to be made from the available models by a process of *recalibration*. In this paper we show how these techniques work when applied to some real data sets.

## 1    Introduction

Over the years, many software reliability models have appeared in the literature, with quite a few emanating from the Centre for Software Reliability (CSR). Unfortunately, it must be admitted that no single model has emerged that can be universally recommended to a potential user. In fact, the accuracy of the reliability measures arising from the models tends to vary quite dramatically: some models sometimes give good results, some models are almost universally awful, but no model can be trusted to be accurate at all times. Worse than this, it does not seem possible to identify a priori those data sets for which a particular model will be appropriate [1].

This unsatisfactory position has undoubtedly been the major factor in the poor take-up of these techniques: users who have experienced poor results adopt a 'once bitten, twice shy' approach, and are unwilling to try new techniques. It is with some trepidation that we claim that our approach to be presented here has largely eliminated these difficulties. It might be as well, therefore, before giving some details of the techniques and examples of their use, to declare our *credo*. We believe that it *is* now possible *in most cases* to obtain *reasonably accurate* reliability measures for software, and *to have reasonable confidence that this is the case* in a particular situation, so long as the reliability levels required are *relatively modest*. The italicised *caveats* here are important, because there are some limitations to what can currently be achieved, but they should not be so restrictive as to deter readers from attempting to measure and predict software reliability in industrial contexts.

---

* This paper is a condensed version of [23].

We begin by recalling briefly the nature of the software reliability problem. In the form in which it has been most studied, this is a problem of dynamic assessment and prediction of reliability in the presence of the reliability growth which stems from fault-removal. A program is executing in a test (or real) operating environment, and attempts are made to fix faults when these are found as a result of the observation of software failures. There is therefore reliability growth, at least in the long term, although there may be local reversals as a result of poor fixes causing the introduction of new faults. The reliability growth models attempt to use the data collected here, usually in the form of successive execution times between failures (or, sometimes, numbers of failures in successive fixed time intervals), to estimate the current reliability and predict the future development of the growth in reliability.

It is important to realize that all questions of practical interest involve *prediction*. Thus even if we want to know the *current reliability* at a particular point in this process, we are asking a question about *the future*: in this case about the random variable, $T$, representing the time to the next failure. However we care to express our questions concerning the current reliability - as a rate of occurrence of failures, as a probability of surviving a specified mission time without failure, as a mean time to next failure, or in any other convenient way - we are attempting to predict the future. Longer term prediction might involve attempting to estimate the (distribution of) time needed to achieve some target reliability, or the reliability that might be expected to be achieved after a certain duration of further testing.

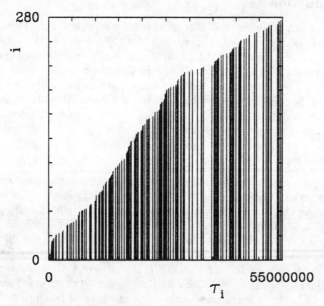

**Fig. 1.** Cumulative number of failures plotted against total elapsed time for data set SS3.

The important point here is that when we ask, rather informally, whether a model is giving accurate reliability measures, we are really asking whether it is *predicting* accurately. This is something which is sometimes overlooked even in the technical literature: there are several examples of authors 'validating' a model by showing that it can accurately explain past failure behaviour and claiming thereby that it is 'accurate'. It is a simple matter to demonstrate that such ability to capture accurately the past does not necessarily imply an ability to predict accurately. The point is nicely expressed in a quotation of Niels Bohr: "Prediction is difficult, especially of the future."

We shall now briefly describe our own approach to the problem of evaluating predictive accuracy, before going on to give some examples of its use on some real data.

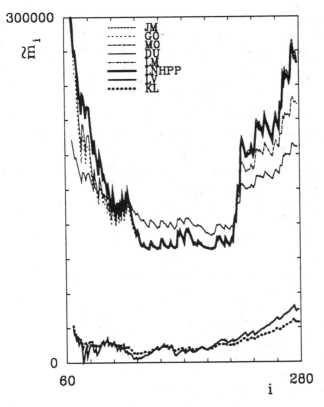

**Fig. 2.** Raw median predictions for data set SS3.

## 2   The New Approach

Consider, for simplicity, the simplest prediction problem of all: that of estimating the current reliability. Let us assume that we have observed the successive inter-failure times $t_1, t_2, \ldots, t_{i-1}$, and we want to predict the next time to failure $T_i$. We shall do this by using one of the models to obtain an estimate, $\tilde{F}_i(t)$ of the true (but unknown) distribution function $F_i(t) \equiv P(T_i < t)$. Notice that, if we knew the true distribution function, we could calculate any of the measures of current reliability that may be appropriate for a particular application.

We now start the program running again, and wait until it next fails; this allows us to observe a realisation $t_i$ of the random variable $T_i$. We shall repeat this operation of *prediction* and *observation* for some range of values of $i$. We would say, informally, that the model was giving good results if what we *observed* tended to be in close agreement with what we had earlier *predicted*. Our approach is based upon formal ways of comparing prediction with observation.

Of course, our problem would be easier if we could observe the true $F_i(t)$ so as to compare it with the prediction, $\tilde{F}_i(t)$. Since this is not available, we must somehow use the $t_i$, which is all we have. Clearly this is not a simple problem, and it is compounded by its being non-stationary: we are interested in the accuracy of a sequence of *different* distributions, for each of which we see only one observation. However it is possible to think of simple comparisons we can make. Let us imagine, for example, that we are only interested in having an accurate estimate of the *median*, $m_i$, of $T_i$. Remember that the median is the value of $T_i$ that is exceeded with probability $1/2$. We could count what proportion of the actual $t_i$ exceeded their predicted medians, $\tilde{m}_i$, and if this proportion were very different from $1/2$ we would conclude that the median predictions were poor.

Such an analysis does not tell us a great deal. Even if a series of predictions passed this test, we would only acquire confidence in the medians. It would not tell us whether other measures, such as the mean time to failure or the failure rate function, were accurate. What we really need is to be able to detect *any* kind of departure between prediction, $\tilde{F}_i(t)$, and truth, $F_i(t)$.

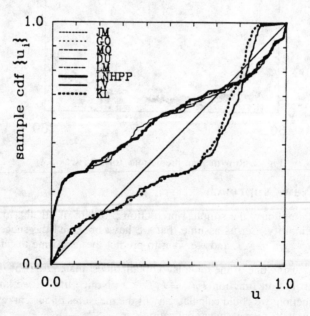

**Fig. 3.** Raw $u$-plots for data set SS3.

Our first general technique for detecting systematic differences between predicted and observed failure behaviour is called the *u-plot* and it is based on a generalisation of the simple median check described above. Details of this are given in Appendix 1. The *u*-plot can be thought of as detecting a *systematic* difference between the predictions and the truth. This is very similar to the notion of *bias* in statistics: there we use the data to calculate an *estimator* of a population parameter, and this estimator is called unbiased if its average value is equal to the (unknown) parameter. Of course, our case is more complex since at each stage we wish to estimate a *function*, rather than merely a number, and we can only detect prediction error over a *sequence* of *different* predictions because of the inherent non-stationarity of the problem.

In the unlikely event that the prediction errors are completely stationary, i.e. that the nature of the error is the same at all stages, there will be a constant (functional) relationship between $\tilde{F}_i(t)$ and $F_i(t)$. The *u*-plot is an estimate of this functional relationship. It turns out, in fact, that there is often *approximate* stationarity of errors of this kind. We shall show later that in such cases it is possible to 'recalibrate' the model - essentially allowing it to 'learn' from past mistakes - and obtain more accurate predictions.

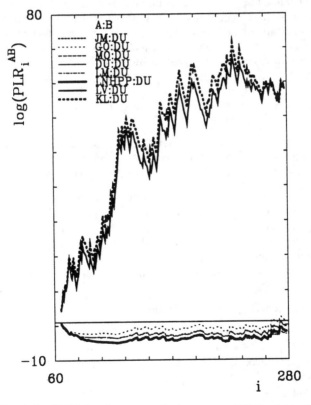

**Fig. 4.** *Log(PLR)* for the raw predictions versus DU for data set SS3.

If for a particular data set a model gives predictions which have a good *u*-plot, this does not guarantee that they are accurate in all possible ways. Returning to the analogy of estimating a population parameter in statistics, even if we have an estimator that is unbiased we may still prefer on other grounds to use a biased one. For example, the unbiased estimator may have a large variance, so that although its expected value is equal to the unknown parameter, any particular calculated value of the estimator may be very far from this. This is the difference between what happens *on average* and what happens at *a particular instance*. Similar arguments apply to a good *u*-plot, which also tells us something about average behaviour, but which can also mask large inaccuracies on particular predictions.

Such considerations bring us to our next technique for analysing predictive accuracy, the *prequential likelihood function*, and the prequential likelihood ratio (*PLR*): see Appendix 2 for details. The *PLR* allows us to compare the ability of two models to predict a particular data source, and select the one that has been most accurate over a sequence of predictions. Unlike the *u*-plot, which is specific for a particular type of inaccuracy, the *PLR* is quite general [36]: the model that it selects as the 'best' is objectively so in a general way. Thus, for example, it can detect those circumstances when the predictions are 'too noisy', and so are individually inaccurate, even when the *u*-plot is good and the predictions are 'unbiased'.

It must be admitted that these ways of examining the accuracy of predictions are non-trivial, and users may find them at first quite unfamiliar. This is not surprising, since traditional statistical methods have tended to neglect the problem of prediction in favour of estimation. It is only recently that techniques such as *PLR* analysis have become available. However, the *use* of the techniques is really quite straightforward, involving nothing more than simple graphical analysis as we shall see in the following examples. But before showing some analysis of real software failure data via this new approach, we shall describe briefly how the *u*-plot can be used to *improve* the accuracy of predictions.

The basic idea here is to exploit the fact that it is sometimes the case that the prediction errors are approximately stationary. More formally, there is clearly always an (unknown) function, $G_i$, that will transform the predicted distribution into the true distribution, i.e., for which $F_i(t) = G_i[\tilde{F}_i(t)]$, but it is only sometimes the case that this function is approximately the same, i.e., $G_i \approx G$, say, for all $i$. When this occurs, we have the opportunity of *estimating* this function, $G$, via the comparison of earlier predictions we have made against their corresponding observations, and using our estimate to adjust future predictions, thus improving their accuracy. In fact, it can be shown that the *u*-plot based upon these earlier predictions is a suitable estimator of $G$ [22].

The recalibration procedure is therefore as follows

1   Obtain the *u*-plot, say $G_i^*$, based upon the raw predictions that have been made before stage $i$. (For technical reasons, which do not detract from the general explanation given here, it is desirable for $G_i^*$ to be a *smoothed* version of the joined-up step-function *u*-plot; a spline-smoothed version has been used in the following examples).

2   Obtain $\tilde{F}_i(t)$ from the 'raw model' for prediction at stage $i$.

3   Calculate the recalibrated prediction $\tilde{F}_i^*(t) \equiv G_i^*[\tilde{F}_i(t)]$.

4   Repeat at each stage $i$.

The most important point to note about this procedure is that it is truly predictive, inasmuch as only the past is used to predict the future. This means that it is not necessary to believe *a priori* that the recalibrated predictions will be better than the raw ones, or that the prediction errors, $G_i$, are approximately stationary, since the various techniques for comparing and analysing predictive accuracy can be used. In particular, the *PLR* will tell us whether recalibration has produced better results than a simple use of the raw model.

We now consider an example where these various techniques are applied to some real software failure data.

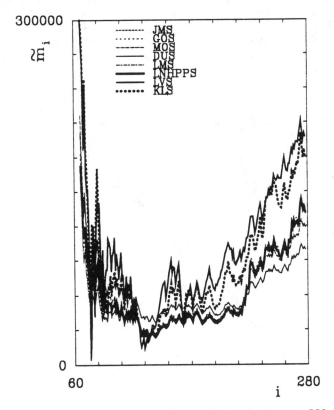

Fig. 5. Recalibrated median predictions for data set SS3.

# 3   Example

Our example concerns a data set, SS3 , collected several years ago by John Musa [98]. This data set is unusual inasmuch as we shall show that *all* models seem to give extremely poor results as determined by the $u$-plot criterion, but the effect of recalibration is to bring about a dramatic improvement in this poor performance. Fig. 1 shows the raw data, plotted as cumulative number of failures, $i$, against total elapsed execution time, $\tau_i$. Fig. 2 shows predictions from eight models: JM [59], GO [49], MO [99], DU [33], LM [82], LNHPP [96], LV [88] and KL [67]. The predictions being made here are of the *median*, $\tilde{m}_i$, of the next time to failure at each stage, $i$. There is extraordinary disagreement between the different models. LV and KL give results that are far more pessimistic than the other six. Although these remarks only apply to the predicted medians, it is clear that if these are inaccurate then other measures of reliability such as rate of occurrence of failures, mean time to failure, etc, will also be inaccurate. In fact, the $u$-plot (Fig. 3) shows that *all* predictions *are* extremely inaccurate, with plots that differ from the line of unit slope with very high statistical significance. It can be seen that the six models giving approximate agreement in Fig. 2, with the larger medians, are in fact generally much too optimistic since their $u$-plots are almost everywhere above the line of unit slope. LV and KL, on the other hand, are (with the exception of the extreme ends of the plots) below the line of unit slope, and are thus generally too pessimistic in their predictions. These results would suggest that the truth lies somewhere between the two clusters of results shown in Fig. 2. Fig. 4 shows the *log(PLR)* plotted for each model against a reference model, here DU. This analysis reveals that LV and KL are significantly superior to the other six models for this data set, even though, of course, we know these two to be poor.

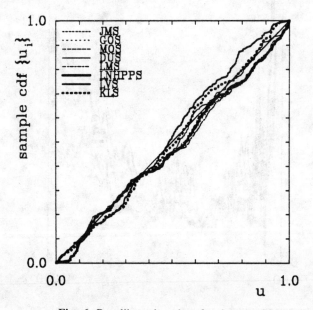

**Fig. 6.** Recalibrated $u$-plots for data set SS3.

Since all models give poor $u$-plots, we have no reliability predictions for this data source that can be trusted. It is therefore a candidate for application of recalibration to all models. Fig. 5 shows the effect of recalibration on the predicted medians. There is now much closer agreement than there was from the raw models in Fig. 2. The $u$-plots of the recalibrated predictions, Fig. 6, are an enormous improvement over those of the raw predictions. We find in this case that none of the plots now have $KS$ distances that are statistically significant at the 5% level. The improvement in general predictive performance of all models arising from recalibration can be seen from the *log(PLR)* plots of recalibrated versus raw predictions given in Fig. 7. This is dramatic in all cases, but slightly less so for LV and KL. This is largely because these were originally the best performing pair of models of the eight - since they were less bad than the other six, they had less room for improvement. After recalibration, all eight models perform roughly comparably; this is shown by Fig. 8 where there is no single plot that shows consistent trend, compared with the equivalent plot for the raw predictions (note the scale change).

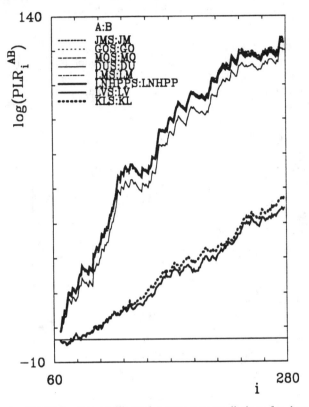

**Fig. 7.** *Log(PLR)* for the recalibrated versus raw predictions for data set SS3.

Clearly, recalibration has had a dramatic effect on the accuracy of the predictions we can make about this data source. Faced with these results, a user would clearly make future predictions using one of the recalibrated versions of the models: possibly GOS, although there is little to choose between this and JMS, LMS on the *PL* and *u*-plot criteria (the letter S added to the abbreviated labels of the various models indicates their having been recalibrated via our spline smoothing technique). As more data becomes available, of course, this whole analysis will be up-dated and a decision as to which, if any, predictions are to be trusted will be made at each stage.

The most important point about this procedure is that it 'allows the data to speak for themselves', and does not require the user to have an *a priori* belief that a particular model will give accurate predictions. Since such beliefs are highly questionable, this is an important new way of acquiring confidence in the accuracy of reliability predictions.

## 4    Discussion

The techniques we have described here are important because they largely resolve a basic dilemma of software reliability modelling: a user is now faced with a plethora of models, but no one of them can be recommended for universal use, nor are there any means by which the user might select *a priori* the most appropriate for his/her own application.

It cannot be stated too strongly that a user should never believe claims for the universal validity of a particular software reliability model; indeed it is our belief that the relatively poor take-up of software reliability modelling techniques has been a result of certain models being sold as universal panaceas. Users rightly adopt an attitude of 'once bitten, twice shy' when they see these models occasionally giving ludicrous results.

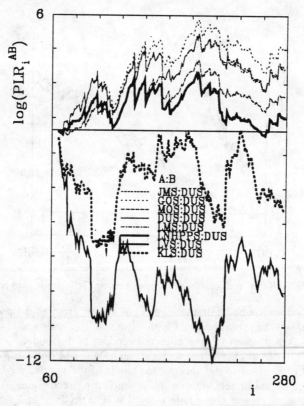

**Fig. 8.** *Log(PLR)* for the recalibrated predictions versus DUS for data set SS3.

We think that the techniques we have developed provide a means to overcome these difficulties and that it is now possible to measure and predict software reliability for the relatively modest levels that are needed in the vast majority of applications. Most importantly, the techniques provide a means whereby the user can be *confident* that the results are sufficiently accurate for the particular program under examination. There is thus no need to subscribe to dubious claims about the inherent 'plausibility' of a particular model in order to have some assurance that the reliability figures can be trusted.

The example we chose for this paper is one in which the raw models perform rather badly (but see [23] for a fuller version with analyses of further data sets that support the conclusions drawn here). We did this deliberately to show the power of the recalibration technique, but it is often the case that some individual raw models will perform reasonably well even before recalibration. From a user's point of view, however, this is immaterial. The recalibration procedure is easy to use and is genuinely predictive, so it should be applied as a matter of course; then it is easy to use the analytical methods to find which of the many different (raw and recalibrated) versions is performing best for the data of interest.

Although the techniques we have described depend upon rather novel and subtle statistical methods, we think that their actual use and interpretation from the graphical presentations is comparatively straightforward. This is aided by software developed within CSR to carry out the analyses we have presented here.

Our advice to anyone contemplating measuring and predicting software reliability is to go ahead and try our approach. Most times you will get results you can trust. In those rare cases where none of the models or recalibration work, our techniques will provide a warning.

Finally, a word of caution. Software is increasingly being used in safety-critical applications where a very high reliability is demanded. We believe that this poses enormous, and possibly insurmountable problems for those responsible for system validation. It should be emphasized that all the discussion in this paper relates, as we have said, to fairly modest reliability levels. The techniques which depend upon reliability growth data cannot be used to assure very high reliability without the need for infeasibly large periods of observation of the system. It has been argued elsewhere that this problem of assuring ultra-high software reliability is even harder than these comments suggest: essentially that it is impossible [84].

# Appendix 1

The purpose of the $u$-plot is to determine whether the predictions, $\widetilde{F}_i(t)$, are 'on average' close to the true distributions, $F_i(t)$. It can be shown that, if the random variable $T_i$ truly had the distribution $\widetilde{F}_i(t)$, in other words if the prediction and the truth were *identical*, then the random variable $U_i = \widetilde{F}_i(T_i)$ will be uniformly distributed on (0,1). This is called the *probability integral transform* in statistics [38].

If we were to observe the realisation $t_i$ of $T_i$, and calculate $u_i = \widetilde{F}_i(t_i)$, the number $u_i$ will be a realisation of a uniform random variable. When we do this for a sequence of predictions, we get a sequence $\{u_i\}$ which should look like a random sample from a uniform distribution. Any departure from such 'uniformity' will indicate some kind of deviation between the sequence of predictions, $\{\widetilde{F}_i(t)\}$, and the truth $\{F_i(t)\}$.

We look for departure from uniformity by plotting the *sample distribution function* of the $\{u_i\}$ sequence. This is a step function constructed as follows: on the interval $(0,1)$ place the points $u_1, u_2, \ldots u_n$ (each of these is a number between 0 and 1), then from left to right plot an increasing step function, with each step of height $1/(n+1)$ at each $u$ on the abscissa. The range of the resulting monotonically increasing function is $(0,1)$, and we call it the $u$-plot.

If the $\{u_i\}$ sequence were truly uniform, this plot should be close to the line on unit slope. Any serious departure of the plot from this line is indicative of non-uniformity, and thus of a certain type of inaccuracy in the predictions. A common way of testing whether the departure is significant is via the Kolmogorov-Smirnov (*KS*) distance, which is the maximum vertical deviation between the plot and the line [38], for which there are tables. However, a formal test is often unnecessary: for many of the examples in this paper it is clear merely from an informal perusal of the plots that the predictions are poor.

More importantly, such informal inspections of $u$-plots can tell us quite a lot about the *nature* of the prediction errors. For example, if the predictions were consistently too *optimistic* we would be underestimating the chance of the next failure occurring before $t$ (for all $t$). The number $u_i$, in particular, is the estimate we would have made, before the event, of the probability that the next failure will occur before $t_i$, the time when it *actually does* eventually occur. This number would therefore tend to be smaller than it should be in the case of consistently too optimistic predictions. That means the $u$s will tend to bunch too far to the left in the $(0,1)$ interval, and the resulting $u$-plot will tend to be *above* the line of unit slope. A similar argument shows that a $u$-plot which is entirely below the line of unit slope indicates that the predictions are too pessimistic. More complex $u$-plot shapes can sometimes be interpreted in terms of the nature of the inaccuracy of prediction that they represent.

## Appendix 2

The *PLR* is a means of deciding which of a pair of prediction systems is giving most accurate results on a particular data source. Consider Fig. 9, where there are shown two ways, $A$ and $B$, of making a prediction at stage $j$. Here we see the true distribution (in fact the probability density function, *pdf*) of the next time to failure, $T_j$, together with estimates of this (i.e. predictions) coming from two different models, $A$ and $B$. Clearly here $A$ is better than $B$. After making these predictions, we wait and eventually see the failure occur after a time $t_j$. Obviously, we would expect $t_j$ to lie in the main body of the true distribution, as it does here: i.e. it is more likely to occur where $f_j(t)$ is larger. If we evaluate the two predictive *pdf*s at this value of $t$,

there will be a tendency for $\tilde{f}_j^A(t_j)$ to be larger than $\tilde{f}_j^B(t_j)$. This is because the $A$ *pdf* tends to have more large values close to the large values of the true distribution than does the $B$ *pdf*: this is what we mean when we say 'the $A$ predictions are closer to the truth than the $B$ predictions'.

Thus if the predictions from $A$ are more accurate than those from $B$, $\tilde{f}_j^A(t_j)/\tilde{f}_j^B(t_j)$ will tend to be larger than 1. The *PLR* is merely a running product of such terms over many successive predictions:

$$PLR_i^{AB} = \prod_{j=k}^{j=i} \frac{\tilde{f}_j^A(t_j)}{\tilde{f}_j^B(t_j)}$$

and this should tend to increase with $i$ if the $A$ predictions are better than the $B$ predictions. Conversely, superiority of $B$ over $A$ will be indicated if this product shows a consistent decrease.

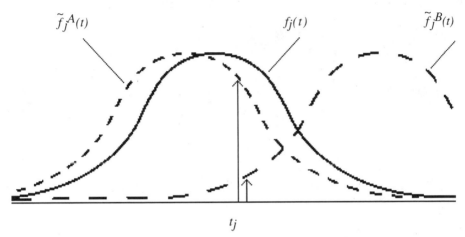

$\tilde{f}_j^A(t)$        $f_j(t)$        $\tilde{f}_j^B(t)$

$t_j$

**Fig. 9.** True *pdf* of the time to next failure, $T_j$, together with estimates of this (i.e. predictions) coming from two different models, $A$ and $B$.

Of course, even if $A$ is performing consistently more accurately than $B$, we cannot guarantee that $\tilde{f}_j^A(t_j)/\tilde{f}_j^B(t_j)$ will always be greater than one. Thus typically in a case where $A$ is better than $B$, we would expect the plot of *PLR* (or more usually, for convenience, the *log* of this) to exhibit overall increase but with some local random fluctuations. See, for example, Figs. 4 and 7.

We are usually interested in comparing the accuracy of more than two sequences of predictions. To do this we select one, quite arbitrarily, as a reference and conduct pairwise comparisons of all others against this, as above.

*PLR* is a completely general procedure for identifying the better of a pair of sequences of predictions. Apart from the intuitive plausibility of *PLR* as a means of selecting between many competing prediction methods on a particular data source, support for this technique comes from a more formal asymptotic theory [36].

# Combination of Predictions Obtained from Different Software Reliability Growth Models*

Minyan Lu   Sarah Brocklehurst   Bev Littlewood

Centre for Software Reliability

**Abstract** In the development of techniques for software reliability measurement and prediction, many software reliability growth models have been proposed. Application of these models to real data sources has shown that there is commonly great disagreement in predictions, while none of them has been shown to be more trustworthy than others in terms of predictive quality in all applications. Recent work has largely overcome this problem through the development of specialized techniques which analyse the accuracy of predictions from reliability models. Such techniques allow the user to choose, for future predictions for a particular data source, those models which gave the best predictions in the past, for this data.

In this paper, various methods are used to get new predictions by *combining* the predictions obtained from different models. For each data set, the weights used in the combination of the models for each prediction of future data are based on the accuracy of the past predictions from the different models on this data. The resulting predictive quality of the combined predictions is investigated by application of these techniques to some real failure data. By using the combined prediction method it is demonstrated that improved predictions, or automatic selection of the "best" prediction system from all available prediction systems, can be achieved. An important benefit of the combination method presented in this paper is that there are no specific requirements on the nature of the initial prediction systems being combined.

## 1   Introduction

It is a well-known fact that the problem of estimating and predicting software reliability has not yet been solved in a satisfactory way. The predictive accuracy varies from one model to another in one application (i.e., when applied to one data source) and from one application to another for a single model. No single model yet available has been shown to be sufficiently trustworthy in most or all applications.

Some effort has been made for improving the accuracy of predictions made by each model. For example, a *recalibration* technique [22] has been shown to be remarkably effective in some applications for improving predictive accuracy. The recalibration idea essentially allows a model to "learn" from its past errors.

What we are going to present in this paper is another kind of "learning" technique from past predictions. Instead of looking at previous predictions given by one model, we learn from all or more recent previous predictions obtained from *all available models*. We then *combine* the predictions emanating from these models in order to

---

* This paper is a condensed version of [90].

predict the future failure behaviour of the software. The contribution that each of the original models makes to our final combined predictor is based on its *past predictive performance*.

The combined prediction method has no limitation on the prediction systems being combined. They could be either parametric, non-parametric, recalibrated or not, or a mixture of these.

In the following sections we shall briefly talk about the raw (i.e., not recalibrated) software reliability growth models (section 2), the analysis techniques used in order to compare the predictive accuracy and the recalibration procedure (section 3). The Bayesian inference weighted decision approach and window systems used for the combination of the resulting raw and recalibrated predictions will be discussed in section 4. We apply the above methods to one data set (application to more data sets can be found in [90] by combining eight raw parametric models, their corresponding recalibrated ones and the raw plus the recalibrated ones together. The performance of the resulting combined predictions, according to the analysis techniques (described in section 3) is discussed in section 5. We conclude with a summary of the performance (with respect to predictive accuracy) of these new combination techniques.

## 2    Raw  Reliability  Growth  Models

The data we are considering are times $t_1$, $t_2$, $t_3$,... (which can be C.P.U. execution time, calendar time, or any other applicable measure) between successive failures resulting when a system (in test or operation) is undergoing *debugging*.

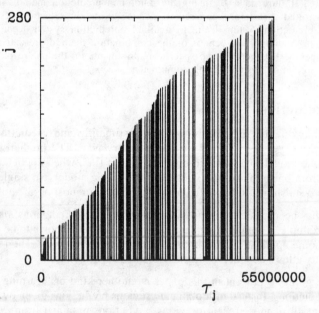

**Fig. 1.** Cumulative failure plot for data set *SS3*.

Fig. 1 shows some inter-failure time data, *SS3* [98], plotted as the cumulative number of failures, $j$, against the total elapsed time, $\tau_j = \sum_{r=1}^{j} t_r$. This data is inter-failure times, measured in seconds of running clock time, of a word processor in operation. We shall be using this data set to illustrate the techniques discussed in this paper.

For simplicity we shall be considering one-step-ahead predictions. Using the previous inter-failure times, $t_1, t_2, ..., t_{j-1}$, the raw models provide a prediction of the current (and as yet unobserved) inter-failure time, $T_j$, in the form of a predictive cumulative distribution function (*cdf*),

$$\hat{F}_j(t) = \hat{Pr}(T_j \leq t) \tag{2.1}$$

From *(2.1)* we also have a predictive probability density function (*pdf*) for $T_j$,

$$\hat{f}_j(t) = \hat{F}_j'(t) \tag{2.2}$$

These can be thought of as estimates of the true *cdf* and *pdf*, $F_j(t)$ and $f_j(t)$.

The models which are applied in this paper are the Jelinski-Moranda *(JM)* [59], Goel Okumoto *(GO)* [49], Musa Okumoto *(MO)* [99], Duane *(DU)* [39, 33], Littlewood *(LM)* [82], Littlewood non-homogeneous Poisson process *(LNHPP)* [96], Littlewood Verrall *(LV)* [88] and Keiller Littlewood *(KL)* [67] models. These models assume a form for the *pdf* (*cdf*) which depends on some unknown parameter(s) and on the observed data. Estimates for these parameters are made at each stage, $j$, by using the previous failure data, $t_1, t_2, ..., t_{j-1}$, and the method of maximum likelihood (*ML*). These parameters are then plugged back into the *pdf* (*cdf*) in order to make one-step-ahead predictions about $T_j$. The resulting predictive performance of these models will depend not only on their precise mathematical structure, but on the *ML* inference technique and the substitution rule for prediction. It should be noted that these two approaches to statistical inference and prediction are chosen here for convenience: other techniques, such as Bayesian inference, tend to be computationally intensive. Since most of the models are well known further details are omitted from this paper.

## 3    Techniques for Analysing Predictive Quality and Recalibration

In this section the methods for assessing and comparing the performance of the various predictors (including those resulting from recalibration or from the combination techniques) are briefly described. They all depend on a comparison between the estimated *cdf* or *pdf* (see *(2.1)* and *(2.2)* at stage $j$, and the (later observed) realization, $t_j$, of the next inter-failure time, $T_j$. Suppose we have $q$ inter-failure times altogether. Then we can apply the raw models summarized in section 2 (or the recalibration or combination techniques described later in sections 3.3 and 4) to the data, $t_1, ..., t_{j-1}$, to obtain our predictions for $T_j$, for $j = s, ..., q$, say, where $s$ is a number sufficiently large for making the first prediction. We then have what we shall refer to as our "prediction system" for each of the predictors, i.e.,

$$\{\hat{F}_j(t), \hat{f}_j(t); \, j = s, \, ..., \, q\} \tag{3.1}$$

## 3.1  The u-plot

$$\text{Let} \quad u_j = \hat{F}_j(t_j) \qquad\qquad j = s, \, ..., \, q \tag{3.2}$$

If our prediction system is identical to truth, i.e., $\hat{F}_j \equiv F_j \circledR j$, then the $u$'s should behave as if they come from a $U(0,1)$ distribution [1].

The first measure we shall discuss is the *u-plot* which is the sample *cdf* of the $u$'s defined in *(3.2)*. This is a step function with step-size $1/(q-s+2)$ as shown in Fig. 2. Departures of the $u$-plot from the $45°$ line, which is the $U(0,1)$ *cdf*, indicate that our prediction system is biased in some way. To test whether such departures are significant the Kolmogorov-distance (K-distance), which is the maximum vertical distance of the plot from the $45°$ line, may be compared against tables.

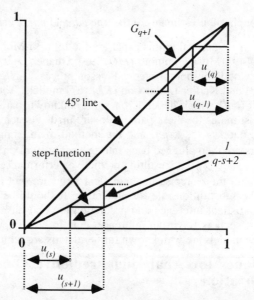

**Fig. 2.** The $u$-plot. Here $\{u(j); \, j = s, \, ..., \, q\}$ are the $u_j$ in *(3.2)* re-ordered in ascending magnitude.

Informally, the $u$-plot is a powerful means of detecting various kinds of *consistent bias* in predictions in those situations where the prediction errors are in some sense *stationary*.

## 3.2  The Prequential Likelihood Ratio

It should be noted that it is possible for a prediction system to give a good $u$-plot and yet still be inaccurate, for example it could be very noisy, so that individual predictions emanating from it are inaccurate even though on average there is no bias. For this reason we use a further measure called the *prequential likelihood ratio* (*PLR*) which is intended as a global comparison of goodness of prediction for one prediction system versus another.

Suppose we have two prediction systems, $A$ and $B$, say. Then the $PLR$ is defined to be

$$PLR_{sq}^{AB} = \frac{\prod\limits_{j=s}^{q} \hat{f}_j^A(t_j)}{\prod\limits_{j=s}^{q} \hat{f}_j^B(t_j)} = \frac{PL_{sq}^A}{PL_{sq}^B} \qquad (3.3)$$

where $PL$ is the prequential likelihood of a single predictor. Notice that, unlike the $u$-plots, this measure depends upon the *pdf*s rather than the *cdf*s.

If $PLR \to \infty$ as $q \to \infty$ then we would choose predictor $A$ as being the better of the two predictors. Conversely, if $PLR \to 0$ as $q \to \infty$, we would favour predictor $B$ over predictor $A$. As we clearly never have $q \to \infty$ in practice, the best we can do is to look for steady increases and decreases in our $PLR$ plots of one prediction system versus another over the whole data set. In the analysis that follows we actually plot the $log(PLR)$ at stage $j$ against $j$.

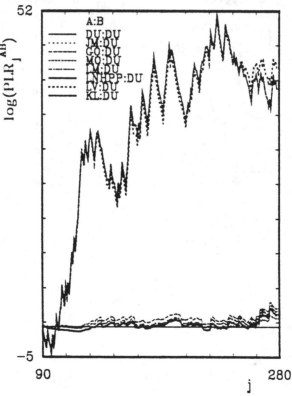

**Fig. 3.** *Log(PLR)* for the raw predictors versus *DU* for data set *SS3*.

Fig. 3 shows the *PLR* analysis for the *8* raw reliability models referred to in section 2 when they are applied to data set *SS3* (see Fig. 1). The *DU* model has been chosen arbitrarily as the reference model against which to compare the other *7* models. From Fig. 3 we can see that the *LV* and *KL* models (very close to one another in this plot) are much better than the other six raw models (also very close) for this data although there is some local fluctuation.

For a more detailed explanation of the use of these methods for analysis of predictive accuracy in the context of software reliability modelling see [1].

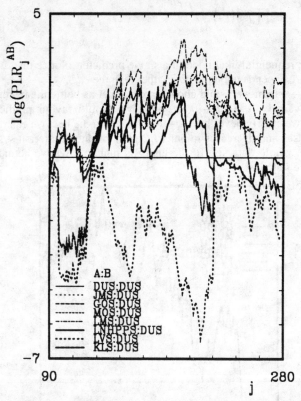

**Fig. 4.** *Log(PLR)* for the recalibrated predictors versus *DUS* for data set *SS3*.

## 3.3  The Recalibration Technique

If we have captured the trend in the data but the predictions are biased (i.e., the prediction errors are stationary) then the (approximately) consistent departure of the prediction system from the truth is represented by the departure of the $u$-plot from the $45°$ line. This is where the *recalibration* technique can be applied; this consists of using the $u$-plot to eliminate this bias from the raw prediction system and thus construct a new improved prediction system. This technique uses the joined up $u$-plot (see Fig. 2), $G_i$, based on *previous* predictions of $t_S, ..., t_{i-1}$, in order to adjust the current raw prediction,

$$\hat{F}_i^*(t) = G_i(\hat{F}_i(t)) \tag{3.4}$$

More details on this technique can be found in [22]. We can repeat this recalibration procedure over $i = p, ..., q$, where $p\text{-}s$ is suitably large and we then have a recalibrated prediction system,

$$\{\hat{F}_i^*(t), \hat{f}_i^*(t); \ i = p, ..., q\} \tag{3.5}$$

We can then use the $u$-plots and the $PLR$ as outlined above in exactly the same manner as with the raw prediction system to assess our new recalibrated prediction system. Since we are using the $PLR$ to compare our prediction systems we will use the *spline* recalibration technique [25] which consists of smoothing each $G_i$ using a spline smoothing technique before recalibration.

All the raw prediction systems from the parametric models referred to in section 2 are spline-recalibrated. An $S$ added onto the end of the model names will be used to denote the recalibrated prediction system (eg. *MOS, LVS* etc.). This results in a number of different prediction systems for the data and from these we can form our new combined predictions.

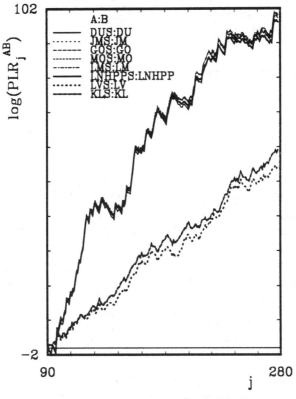

**Fig. 5.** *Log(PLR)* for the recalibrated versus raw predictors for data set *SS3*.

Fig. 4 shows the *log(PLR)* plots for the recalibrated predictors for data set *SS3*. Here the *DUS* model is used as the reference model against which to compare the other recalibrated predictors. In contrast to the raw predictors (see Fig. 3) this *PLR* analysis suggests that the recalibrated predictors are very similar in performance (notice the large change in the scale in Fig. 4).

Fig. 5 shows the *log(PLR)* plots for the recalibrated versus raw predictors, for example *JMS* versus *JM* and so on. This analysis suggests that the recalibrated predictors are giving much more accurate predictions than the raw models. The least improvement via recalibration is shown for the *LV* and *KL* models because the raw predictions from these models where initially much better than those from the other six raw models. It is clear from Figs. 3 and 5 that, although the *LV* and *KL* models were initially much better than the other raw models, all the raw models are in error for this data set.

## 4     Combined Prediction Methods

In this paper our new combined predictors are constructed by taking a general linear combination of the initial predictors, i.e.,

$$\hat{F}_j^0(t) = \sum_{r=1}^{m} w_j^r \hat{F}_j^r(t) \tag{4.1}$$

or     $$\hat{f}_j^0(t) = \sum_{r=1}^{m} w_j^r \hat{f}_j^r(t) \tag{4.2}$$

where     $$\sum_{r=1}^{m} w_j^r = 1 \tag{4.3}$$

and $\left\{ \hat{F}_j^r(t), \hat{f}_j^r(t); r = 1, \ldots, m \right\}$ are $m$ initial predictions of $T_j$ which we are going to combine. Note that these initial predictions may have emanated from the raw models referred to in section 2 or from the recalibrated predictors as described in section 3.3 (or both).

Similar weighted decision making methods have been introduced in [83] and [41]. We are going to present the Bayesian inference weighted decision method where in order to optimize predictive accuracy, the weights in *(4.3)* are based on the past predictive accuracy of the initial set of predictors. In this way, from *(4.1)* and *(4.2)*, it can be seen that our new combined prediction for $T_j$ is truly predictive (i.e., is only based on past data, $t_1, \ldots, t_{j-1}$). Thus we can assess the quality of the predictions from our combination methods by using the techniques previously described in section 3.

Since deciding on the value of the weights $w$ for each prediction system is a learning process from the previous predictions, it seems clear that the numbers of previous predictions used to get corresponding weights would affect the combined prediction results. And intuitively, it seems likely that the current prediction should rely more on the recent predictions than on the whole predictions in history, if the length of predictions is long enough. Taking this view into account, we are going to apply some window systems to the combined prediction method.

## 4.1 Bayesian Inference Weighted Decision Approach

In this approach, the weight for prediction system $r$, at prediction stage $j$ is :

$$w_j^r = \frac{PL_{1\ j-1}^r}{\sum_{k=1}^{m} PL_{1\ j-1}^k} \tag{4.4}$$

Obviously $w_j^r$ satisfies (4.3). Examining (4.4) it can be seen that to construct these weights it would be necessary to have predictions of $t_1$, $t_2$, ... from the initial predictors which are going to be combined. Strictly speaking it would be possible to have such predictions using a Bayesian approach. Since we are using the $ML$ method to construct the raw predictors (see section 2), and also due to the recalibration method (see section 3.3), such predictions are not available until a number of inter-failure times have been observed. Thus, this combined prediction method will be applied by constructing the weights in (4.4) starting from the first initial prediction available.

The weights in (4.4) can be interpreted as Bayesian posterior probabilities for the models, as the following shows.

Suppose $M_r$ is a prediction system numbered $r$ (i.e., the series of one-step-ahead predictions from model $r$); $t_1$, ..., $t_{j-1}$ are known inter-failure times; $T_j$ is the inter-failure time at stage $j$, the behaviour of which we are going to predict. Then the cumulative probability distribution function (cdf) of $T_j$ conditioned on $t_1$, ..., $t_{j-1}$ is:

$$P(T_j \leq t | t_{j-1}, ..., t_1)$$

$$= \sum_{r=1}^{m} P(M_r | t_{j-1},...,t_1) \cdot P(T_j \leq t | t_{j-1}, ..., t_1, M_r) = \sum_{r=1}^{m} w_j^r \hat{F}_j^r(t) \tag{4.5}$$

where $\quad w_j^r = P(M_r | t_{j-1},...,t_1) = \dfrac{P(M_r) \cdot p(t_{j-1},...,t_1 | M_r)}{\sum_{k=1}^{m} P(M_k) \cdot p(t_{j-1},...,t_1 | M_k)} \tag{4.6}$

In the case of prior ignorance, a rational way would be to assign an equal prior probability to each prediction system, i.e., $P(M_r) = 1/m$, $r=1,...,m$. Then equation (4.6) can be written as:

$$w_j^r = \frac{p(t_{j-1},...,t_1|M_r)}{\sum\limits_{k=1}^{m} p(t_{j-1},...,t_1|M_k)} = \frac{\prod\limits_{l=1}^{j-1} \hat{f}_l^r(t_l)}{\sum\limits_{k=1}^{m} \prod\limits_{l=1}^{j-1} \hat{f}_l^k(t_l)} = \frac{PL_{1\ j-1}^r}{\sum\limits_{k=1}^{m} PL_{1\ j-1}^k} \qquad (4.7)$$

which is identical to *(4.4)*.

In [90], we have also presented another weighted decision approach called Switching which can be seen as subsumed in the Bayesian approach. Instead of giving weights to all initial predictors like the Bayesian method does, this method selects the predictor with the highest weight in the Bayesian method as the one used to predict the failure behaviour at the next stage. Application in [90] on three data sets showed that the Bayesian method is sometimes much better than the Switching method and never significantly worse, which is not surprising since the latter method is a cruder version of the former one.

## 4.2 Weighted Decision with One-window System

As discussed earlier in this section, when we learn from the previous predictions coming from each of the prediction systems, it seems likely that more recent previous predictions may give a clearer indication of current predictive accuracy than earlier predictions. Here we are going to use a window as a filter with a fixed size *a* to dynamically eliminate some of the early predictions; in other words we shall only take account of the last *a* predictions for deciding on the weights in the combined predictions.

Applying the one-window system to the Bayesian inference weighted decision method *(4.4)* we get

$$w_j^{ra} = \frac{PL_{j-a\ j-1}^r}{\sum\limits_{k=1}^{m} PL_{j-a\ j-1}^k} \qquad (4.8)$$

where $\qquad PL_{j-a\ j-1}^r = \prod\limits_{l=j-a}^{j-1} \hat{f}_l^r(t_l) \qquad (4.9)$

It is natural to raise the question of how to choose the fixed window size *a*. In this paper we will choose quite arbitrarily, *a = 1, 5, 10, 20, 30, 40* and *50* for showing the effect of the combined prediction methods applied with one fixed-size window system.

## 4.3 Weighted Decision with Two-window System

The purpose of introducing the one-window system is to eliminate the impact of information about earlier predictive accuracy on the current combined prediction.

Clearly the application of the combined predictor with a small window size will tend to capture more recent *local* predictive behaviour while a larger window size will tend to capture the *global* predictive performance. Thus a small window size may be too sensitive to local fluctuations that do not truly represent the performance of the predictor. A large window, on the other hand, may give too much prominence to predictions in the distant past when these are no longer representative.

Here we are faced with a trade-off in deciding which window size, $a$, will result in the best predictive accuracy of the combined predictor. As the data evolves, predictive accuracy of each predictor varies locally and/or globally and so it is highly probable that the optimum window size, $a_j^*$, say, will change as we move through the data (i.e., with $j$). It was decided, therefore, to apply a technique which results in a dynamically changing window size for each combined prediction. Since we require *true predictions* the window size for the current combined predictor, $\hat{a}_j^*$, is chosen based on the *past* predictive accuracy of (previous) combined predictions obtained from *all possible* window sizes, $a$. In other words we choose for our next one-step-ahead combined prediction to use that window size which resulted in the "best" one-step-ahead combined predictions in the past.

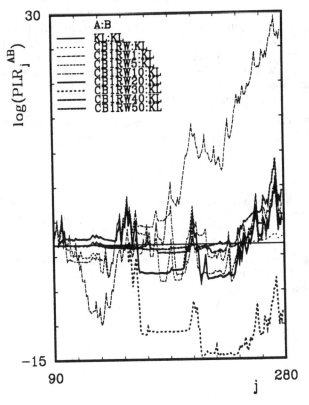

**Fig. 6.** *Log(PLR)* for the *CB1R* predictors versus *KL* for data set *SS3*.

As before we shall use the Prequential Likelihood as the criterion for judging the past predictive performance coming from the different window sizes, $a$. The optimum value for $a$ is thus chosen as that which gives maximum Prequential Likelihood for the past predictions. Once again we have the problem of deciding the length of past predictions used for deciding on the "best" window size for combining the current prediction. As previously we just set the second window size, $b$, say, with some arbitrary values to see their effects on predictive performance. The values chosen are again $b = 1, 5, 10, 20, 30, 40$ and $50$.

We could apply the same idea to try to find the "best" second windows, $b_j^*$, then the third and so on. Here we shall limit our analysis to investigation of this *Two-window System*. The precise mathematical details on this two-fold windowing can be found in [90].

### 4.4  Notation for Combined Prediction Systems

Below we show the structure of the notation used to identify the various combined prediction systems introduced in this paper.

$$C B [x] [y] W [z]$$

where $CB$ stands for the Bayesian inference weighted decision combination method; $[x]$ the window system which could be $1$ for the one-window system and $2$ for the two-window system; $[y]$ the initial predictor type which could be $R$ for the raw predictors, $S$ for the spline-recalibrated and $RS$ for combination over $R$ and $S$ together; $[z]$ the window size, which is a positive integer. In the case of the one-window system, when $[z]$ is left blank this means that instead of using a fixed window size, the weights in $(4.4)$ are constructed always from the first available prediction. For the two-window system, due to computational intensity, a fixed window size was always applied.

Therefore we have, for example, $CB1RW10$ meaning the combined prediction method using the Bayesian inference weighted decision approach over the raw initial predictors with the one-window system, size $10$.

## 5    Analysis of Combined Predictions

In [90] we applied the methods to three data sets - $AAA$, $SYS1$ and $SS3$ [98, 25]. Since there are no great differences in predictive accuracy between the initial prediction systems on data sets $AAA$ and $SYS1$, insignificant differences between the various combined prediction systems result. They are nearly all comparable with the "best" of the initial prediction systems and never significantly worse. Here the judgement as to which initial predictor is "best" is based on the $log(PLR)$ plots. Clearly this is an over-simplification of the situation; the best performing model will vary as the data evolves; we have chosen that model which is best on average over the whole data set based on observation of the initial $log(PLR)$ plots. This is a retrospective judgement.

Here, due to space constraints, we shall only show data set $SS3$ in detail since there are large differences in predictive accuracy between the initial prediction systems and so the results of the combined predictors are more interesting than for the other two data sets.

Fig. 6 shows that $CB1RW1$ gives dramatic improvement over the raw $KL$ model from the $130^{th}$ failure onwards. But this improvement (about 40 in scale), compared with Fig. 5, is marginally worse than that given by recalibration (about 50) in this region. The *u*-plot (Fig. 7) shows that this combined predictor has indeed less bias than the raw model predictions although this plot still remains significant at the *1%* level. Prior to *130* Fig. 6 shows that *CB1RW1* is steadily *worse* than the *KL* model. With the exception of the large jump downwards at the $160^{th}$ failure for *CB1RW30* the remaining combined predictors are about the same in performance as the *KL* model.

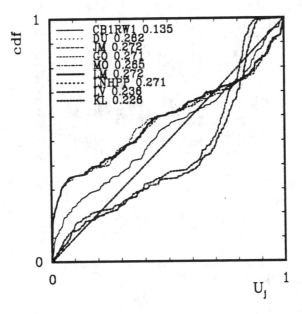

**Fig. 7.** *u*-plots from the *CB1RW1* and raw predictors for data set *SS3*. The numbers shown are the *K*-distances for each *u*-plot.

For this data set it can be seen from Fig. 3 that there are two groups of raw predictors identified by their performance. The *LV* and *KL* predictors, from Fig. 7 we can see are similar in predictive accuracy and giving pessimistic predictions whereas the remaining six models, also close, are giving very optimistic predictions. This grouping of models in performance is also reflected in the resulting weights for the combined predictors. Fig. 8 shows the weight assigned to the most heavily weighted model (i.e., the maximum weight) within each of these two identified groups of models against the prediction stage, *j*. On further examination of Fig. 3 it can be seen that the (locally) best performing group of models switches between these two identified groups quite rapidly, as seen by changes in slope, as the data evolves and from Fig. 8 we can see that this behaviour is reflected in the weights by rapid switching between the two groups of models. Since some of the larger jumps upward and downward in Fig. 3 last for just a few predictions, it can be seen how window size *1* captures many of these local changes, while larger window sizes do not. From Fig. 9, which shows the equivalent weight plot for *CB1RW40*, we can see that for a larger window size, large weights are more consistently given to the models which are globally better for this data set (i.e., *LV* and *KL*).

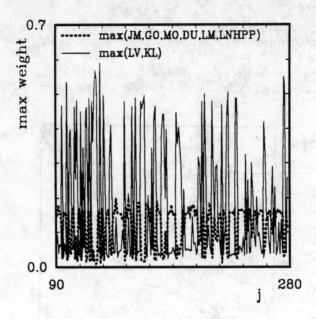

**Fig. 8.** Maximum weight plots for the initial predictors used in *CB1RW1* for data set *SS3*.

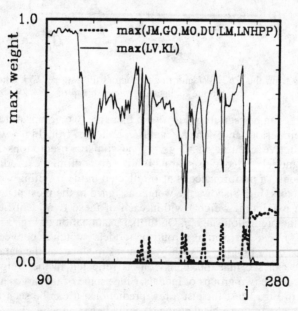

**Fig. 9.** Maximum weight plots for the initial predictors used in *CB1RW40* for data set

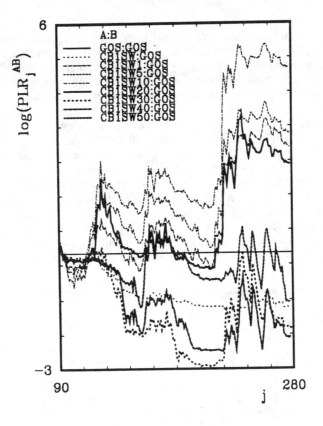

**Fig. 10.** *Log(PLR)* for the *CB1S* predictors versus *GOS* for data set *SS3*.

Fig. 10 shows some minor improvements in predictive accuracy of the combined predictor *CB1S* when applied with window sizes of *1, 5, 10* and *20*, although this is mainly due to some jumps in the plot. These jumps are due to the occurrence of extreme values in the data; for example, $t_{224} = 2039460$, which is much larger than the previous inter-failure times. From Fig. 4 we can see that at stage *224* the *pdfs* for the *LVS* and *KLS* models have larger right-hand tails than the remaining models. The combined predictors with jumps at this stage in Fig. 10 are clearly giving larger weights to these two models. Apart from these jumps the combined predictors are about the same as *GOS*. Fig. 11 shows that this is also the case when both the raw and recalibrated prediction systems are combined with the exception of window size *5* for which the combined predictions are slightly worse than the *GOS* predictor (selected as "best" from among all the initial prediction systems) over much of the data set. Comparing Fig. 11 with the previous one shows that including the initially very bad predictors (i.e., the raw models) in the combination gives slightly worse results than just limiting the combination to the better initial predictors (i.e., the recalibrated).

Fig. 12 shows that again there are improvements in predictive accuracy over the raw models (although, again, not as good as that given by recalibration (see Fig. 5)) in the latter part of the data for many of the *CB2R* predictors while prior to this there is little or no improvement. Comparison of Fig. 12 with Fig. 6 shows that applying a

secondary windowing system has resulted in more consistent predictive accuracy for
the varying window sizes. Note that the differences in scale resulting for the two-
window system are caused by differences early on, while in the second half of the data
they follow a similar pattern. For the one-window system, however, differences for
some window sizes are present throughout the data although for other sizes there is
close similarity. Similar consistency is shown for combination over the recalibrated
predictors (compare Fig. 13 with 10). Here we have slight improvements over *GOS*
for the two-windowing system similar to the better of the combined predictors when
only one window is applied although this slight improvement is, again, due to jumps
coincident with single extreme data points. Comparison of Fig. 14 with 13 again
indicates that including the initially inaccurate raw models in the combination has
resulted in worse results than limiting the combination to the recalibrated models,
particularly for window size *1* which is steadily worse than *GOS* in the former part of
the data. For the remaining window sizes the performance is comparable with *GOS*
and comparison with Fig. 11 shows that for these window sizes, again performance is
more consistent over the varying window sizes for the two-window system than for
the one-window system.

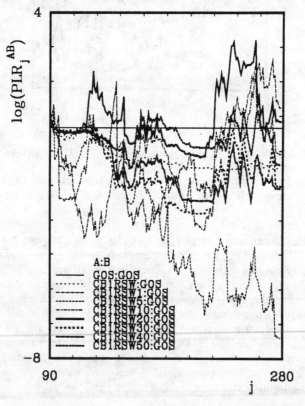

**Fig. 11.** *Log(PLR)* for the *CB1RS* predictors versus *GOS* for data set *SS3*.

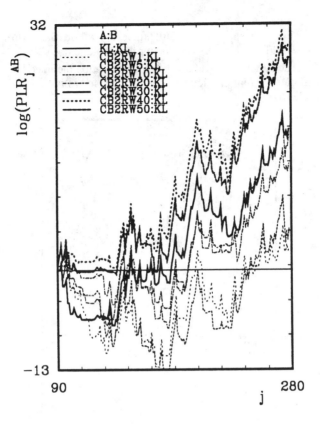

**Fig. 12.** *Log(PLR)* for the *CB2R* predictors versus *KL* for data set *SS3*.

For this data set there is a great variation in predictive performance of the initial predictors to be combined (apart from the recalibrated predictions). This has resulted in obvious disparity between the resulting combined prediction systems. In particular, in some cases, the window size has a marked impact on the predictive accuracy, especially for the one-window system. We have also seen that there is little to be gained by including the initially bad predictors (in this case the raw models) in our combination (i.e., *RS*).

## 6   Conclusions

From the analysis of the data set presented in this paper and the other two data sets in [90] we draw the following conclusions.

a. Dramatic improvement can be achieved by applying the combination method over the initial raw predictions alone but this was not as great or consistent as the improvement given by the recalibration technique.

b. The combination method always gives predictions that are comparable with the best of the initial predictions that are being combined.

c. The two-window system generally, but not always, gives more consistent accuracy over the various window sizes than the one-window system. Sometimes the two-window system can give better predictions than the one-window and sometimes vice versa. This is a surprising result since a method that allows dynamic optimization would be expected to be better than a static one.

d. Better predictive accuracy was obtained when combination included the better of the raw or recalibrated initial predictors alone, as opposed to including both the raw and recalibrated together.

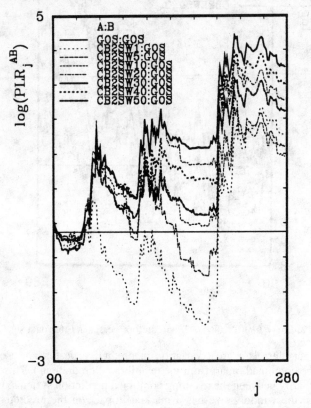

**Fig. 13.** *Log(PLR)* for the *CB2S* predictors versus *GOS* for data set *SS3*.

Overall, the Bayesian together with the two-window system combined prediction method seems to be the best strategy for getting improved predictive accuracy over raw initial predictors or as good as the best given by all initial predictors. It should be noted that the combined prediction method used in this paper is truly predictive and that it can be applied to any set of initial predictors; this means that a user who has the dilemma of a number of initial prediction systems from which to choose may use such a method to select automatically a prediction system with reasonable assurance that the resulting predictions will be as good as the best of the initial predictors. Clearly we need to apply these combination methods to additional data sets in order to support more strongly the conclusions we have made.

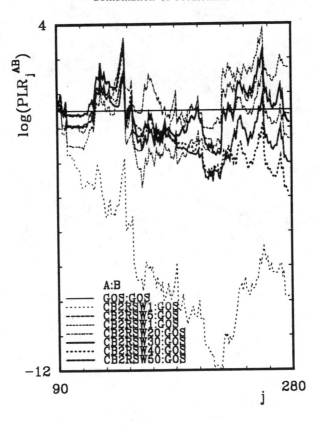

**Fig. 14.** *Log(PLR)* for the *CB2RS* predictors versus *GOS* for data set *SS3*.

# Dependability Modelling and Evaluation of Software Fault-Tolerant Systems*

Jean Arlat    Karama Kanoun    Jean-Claude Laprie

LAAS-CNRS

**Abstract.** The paper provides dependability modelling and evaluation (encompassing reliability and safety issues) of the two major fault tolerance software approaches: recovery blocks (RB) and N-version programming (NVP). The study is based on the detailed analysis of software architectures able to tolerate a single fault (RB: two alternates and an acceptance test, NVP: three versions and a decider).

## 1    Introduction

A number of papers devoted to the dependability analysis of software fault-tolerance approaches have appeared in the literature, for which two major goals can be identified: (i) modelling and evaluation of the dependability measures [56, 54, 73, 97, 24, 118, 110, 34], (ii) detailed analysis of the dependencies in diversified software [40, 109, 85, 18].

This paper belongs to the first class and analyzes the two most documented approaches to software fault-tolerance: RB [105] and NVP [26] (see also papers III.A and III.B). The major features concern: i) the definition of a unified modelling framework based on the identification of the possible types of faults through the analysis of the software production process [73], ii) the evaluation of both reliability and safety measures, and iii) the consideration of two specific characteristics of the architectures that have received little treatment up to now: the discarding of a failed version, for NVP, and the nesting of the blocks, for RB.

Two classes of faults are considered: *independent faults* and *related faults*. Related faults result either from a fault in the common specification, or from dependencies in the separate designs and implementations. Two types of related faults may be distinguished: (i) among several variants (alternates for RB or versions for NVP) and (ii) among one or several variants and the decider (the acceptance test of the RB or the voting algorithm of NVP). Related faults manifest under the form of *similar errors*, whereas we shall assume that independent faults cause *distinct errors*.

Since the faults considered are design faults that are introduced in the software, either during its specification or during its implementation, we shall start the analysis of each approach by relating the various types of faults to the production process [73].

When a failure occurs, the detection of the inability to deliver acceptable results may be an important consideration, in that sense that an undetected failure may have, and generally has, catastrophic consequences. Although the notion of safety strongly depends on the considered application, in practice, the detection of the inability to deliver proper service is a prerequisite to initiate the specific safety procedures. A detected failure (no acceptable result is identified by the decider and no output result

---

* This paper is a condensed version of [6].

is delivered) will thus be termed as a benign failure, whereas an undetected failure (an erroneous result is delivered) will be termed as a catastrophic failure.

As usual, we shall consider reliability as a measure of the time to failure and safety as a measure of the time to catastrophic failure.

Software faults can manifest only when it is executed. We shall thus consider the execution process and the fault manifestation process.

The general behavior model is given in Fig. 1. Transition from B to I stands only for safety, in which case it is assumed that it is possible to restore service delivery by means of procedures carried out at an upper level, i.e. supplying input data different from those having led to benign failure. State class C is absorbing for safety whereas both state classes B and C are absorbing for reliability.

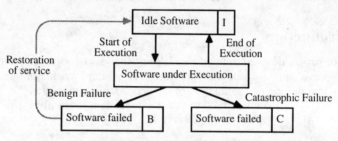

**Fig.1.** General behavior model

We shall assume that the behavior of the systems under consideration can be modeled as a Markov chain; for a discussion of this assumption, see e.g. [81, 73, 27]. The execution process will be modeled through execution rates and the fault manifestation process will be modeled through probabilities conditioned on the execution of the various components of the software: the variants and the decider. The transition rates outputting from the non-absorbing states are of the form:

$$\lambda_{ij} = p_{ij}\ \lambda_i \text{ with } \textstyle\sum_j p_{ij} = 1 \tag{1}$$

where, for each non-absorbing state i, $\lambda_i$ is the rate associated to the tasks executed in state i and $p_{ij}$ is the transition probability from state i to state j of the model.

When the non-absorbing states (non-failed states for reliability, non-failed and benign failure states for safety) constitute an irreducible set [43] (i.e., the graph associated to the non-absorbing states is strongly connected), it is shown in [101] that the absorption process is asymptotically a Homogeneous Poisson Process (HPP), whose failure rate $\Gamma$ is given by:

$$\Gamma = \sum_{\substack{\text{paths from}\\ \text{initial state (I) to}\\ \text{absorbing state (s)}}} \frac{\Pi \text{ (transition rates of the considered path )}}{\Pi \{\sum \text{ (output rates of the considered state) }\}} \tag{2}$$
$$\substack{\text{states in}\\\text{path}\\\text{(I excepted)}}$$

The rate of convergence of the absorption process towards the asymptotic HPP is directly related to the execution rates; it is thus reached very rapidly (say, after three executions). We shall adopt this approach in the following whenever possible, and we shall denote as equivalent rate, the rate of the asymptotic HPP. $\Gamma_R$ (resp. $\Gamma_S$) will denote the *equivalent failure rate* for reliability (resp. the *equivalent catastrophic failure rate* for safety).

From relations (1) and (2), it can be easily verified that the equivalent failure rates can be expressed simply using: (i) the departure rate σ from state I of Fig. 1 and (ii) the probability of failure of the software obtained from the embedded discrete chain. Let $Q_R$ (resp. $Q_S$) be the probability of failure (resp. catastrophic failure), thus:

$$\Gamma_R = \sigma\, Q_R, \Gamma_S = \sigma\, Q_S \tag{3}$$

Accordingly, reliability (R(t)) and safety (S(t)) are given by:

$$R(t) = \exp(-\Gamma_R\, t), S(t) = \exp(-\Gamma_S\, t) \tag{4}$$

As $Q_R$ and $Q_S$ are evaluated directly from the discrete Markov chain, in the sequel we focus essentially in the presentation of the discrete Markov chains describing the fault manifestation process of the fault-tolerant softwares.

Finally, it is worth noting that we focus on the fault-tolerant software itself, i.e. the underlying mechanisms are not considered: (i) recovery point establishment and restoration for RB, and (ii) synchronisation of the versions, cross-check points establishment for NVP.

The sequel of the paper is organized into four sections. Sections 2 and 3 present respectively the analyses of RB and NVP: for each approach a detailed model based on the production process of the fault tolerant software is first established and then it is simplified through the assumptions that only a single fault type may manifest during execution of the fault tolerant software and that no error compensation may take place within the software. Section 4 introduces some elements for RB and NVP comparison. Finally, Section 5 concludes the paper.

## 2    Recovery Blocks

Fig. 2-a shows the production process of a RB with two alternates (a primary (P) and a secondary (S)), and one acceptance test (AT). During the diversified designs and implementations of P & S and of AT, *independent faults* may be created. However, due to dependencies, some *related faults* between P and S or between P & S and the AT may be introduced. Faults committed during common specification (path $1 \rightarrow 2$, $1 \rightarrow 3$, $1 \rightarrow 2 \rightarrow 3$) are likely to be related faults and, as such, the cause of *similar errors*. Faults created during the implementation can also lead to related faults between P & S and AT (channels a, b, c); all these faults are summarized in Fig. 2-b. It is worth noting that the probabilities listed could be obtained from controlled experiments such as the one reported in [5].

For deriving the fault manifestation model, a question immediately arises: what types of faults are considered as possibly manifesting as the consequence of their activation? This leads to consider successively the following assumptions:

**A1:** Only a single fault type (either independent or related) may manifest during the execution of an alternate and the AT and no error *compensation* may take place within an alternate and the AT during an execution, i.e. an error is either detected and processed or leads to a catastrophic failure.

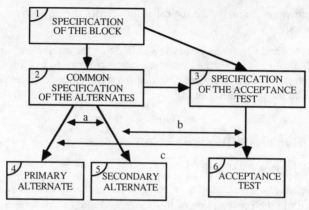

a- Fault Sources in production process

| Path where fault(s) is (are) created or dependency channel(s) | Fault type(s) | Probability of activation |
|---|---|---|
| 1 → 2 or (a) | Related fault in P and S | $q_{PS}$ |
| 1 → 3, (c) or 1 → 2 → 3 | Related fault in P and AT (or P, S and AT) | $q_{PT}$* |
| (b) | Related fault in S and AT | $q_{ST}$ |
| 2 → 4 or 2 → 5 | Independent fault in P or S | $q_P$ or $q_S$ |
| 3 → 6 | Independent fault in AT | $q_T$ |

\* Since the activation of a related fault between P and AT leads to RB failure, no further decomposition with respect to the faults of S is necessary.

b- Fault types and notation

**Fig. 2.** RB analysis

**A2:** Only a single fault type may manifest during the execution of the whole RB and no error *compensation* may take place within the RB.

The detailed model will be based on assumption A1, which enables some singular behaviors of the decider to be characterized. Assumption A2 will serve as a basis for the simplified model.

## 2.1  Detailed RB Model

Fig. 3 describes the MI model based on the notation of Fig. 2-b. P, TP, S and TS form the Software under Execution class from Fig. 1, respectively: execution of P, execution of AT after P, execution of S, execution of AT after S.

Different states are considered for TP to account for the various types of faults that may be activated in P:

TP1) no fault activated [pp],

TP2) activation of an independent fault [$q_P$],

TP3) activation of a related fault between P and S [$q_{PS}$],

TP4) activation of a related fault between P and the AT [$q_{PT}$].

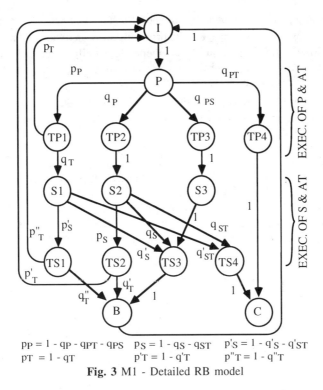

$$p_P = 1 - q_P - q_{PT} - q_{PS} \qquad p_S = 1 - q_S - q_{ST} \qquad p'_S = 1 - q'_S - q'_{ST}$$
$$p_T = 1 - q_T \qquad\qquad p'_T = 1 - q'_T \qquad\qquad p''_T = 1 - q''_T$$

**Fig. 3** M1 - Detailed RB model

This partition leads to a subsequent decomposition of states S and TS. It is assumed that no fault can be activated in AT after activation of an independent fault in P (unity transition from state TP2): these faults are considered as consisting essentially of related faults and, as such, are accounted for in probability $q_{PT}$ leading to state TP4. Activation of a related fault between P and S (state TP3) corresponds to a detected failure and leads through S3 and TS3 to state B. The activation of a related fault between P and AT (state TP4) corresponds to a catastrophic failure and leads to state C.

Due to the fact that S is executed only when an independent fault has been activated either in P or in AT, conditional probabilities were introduced in the model; in particular:

$q_S$  = Prob { activation of an independent fault in S | S is executed after activation of a fault in P }

$q'_S$  = Prob { activation of an independent fault in S | S is executed after activation of a fault in AT }

The same differences in the conditions apply for $q_{ST}$ and $q'_{ST}$ and also for the probabilities of activation of an independent fault in the AT following the execution of S: $q'_T$ and $q''_T$.

The path $\pi = \{P, TP1, S1, TS1, I\}$ corresponds to an error compensation identifying a singular behavior of the AT: the AT *rejects* an acceptable result provided by P and subsequently *accepts* the result given by S.

It is worth noting that M1 can be reduced when considering that:

- $q_T \approx q'_T$ , $q_S \approx q'_S$ , $q_{ST} \approx q'_{ST}$: the probabilities of activation of a fault in S (or AT) following the activation of an independent fault either in P or in AT are equivalent, since in any case their execution is a consequence of the application of error-prone input data,
- $p"_T \ll 1$: error compensation (path $\pi$) is unlikely to occur,
- each state belonging to the Software under Execution class with an outgoing transition equal to 1 can be merged with the next state,

## 2.2 Simplified RB Model

In this case, since assumption A2 applies, a single fault type can be activated in the whole RB; thus transitions from S1 and S2 to TS4 of model M1 (resp. S1 to C for M'1) must be deleted. This is equivalent to make $q_{ST} = 0$ and to merge the related faults between S and AT with the related faults between P and AT; it follows that $q_{PT}$ becomes $q_{PST}$. The corresponding model (M2) is given in Fig. 4.

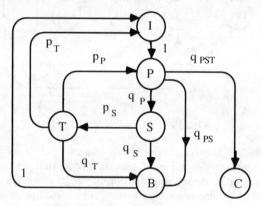

**Fig. 4.** M2 - Simplified RB model

## 2.3 Processing of the Models

Assuming that $p_P \approx 1-q_P$ and $p_S \approx 1-q_S$, we obtain for models M1 and M'1:

for reliability: $\quad \Gamma_R = \sigma \{ q_{PS} + q_{PT} + q_T + q_P [q_{ST} + q_S (1 - q_T)] \}$        (5)

for safety: $\quad\quad \Gamma_S = \sigma \{ q_T q_{ST} + q_{PT} + q_P q_{ST} (1 - q_T) \}$        (6)

For model M2, we obtain:

$$\Gamma_R = \sigma \{ q_{PS} + q_{PST} + q_T + q_P q_S (1 - q_T) \}$$        (7)

$$\Gamma_S = \sigma q_{PST}$$        (8)

## 2.4 Comparison with a Non Fault-Tolerant Software

The comparison with a non fault-tolerant software leads to consider a software with no internal fault detection mechanism whose failure rate is equal to the sum of the elementary failure rates of an alternate:

$$\Gamma'_R = \sigma \{ q_P + q_{PS} + q_{PT} \}$$        (9)

where $q_{PT}$ must be replaced by $q_{PST}$ when considering assumption A2.

Comparison is presented for reliability only, since the notion of safety as defined here does not apply to a software with no internal detection mechanisms. Let define r as: $r = \Gamma_R / \Gamma'_R$; the RB provides a reliability improvement if $r < 1$. This leads to:

For model M'1:     $q_T < q_P (1 - q_P - q_{ST}) / (1 - q_P q_S)$     (10)

For model M2:     $q_T < q_P (1 - q_S) / (1 - q_P q_S)$     (11)

Since the AT is usually less complex than P or S and assuming that complexity and probability of failure are related, we have $q_T \ll q_P$, which enables relations (10) and (11) to be verified. However, the quantification of the improvement must be studied for each specific case.

# 3    N-Version Programming

The potential sources of faults in the production process of a NVP software with three versions and one decider are shown on Fig. 5-a.

As the versions correspond to operational software of good quality, it can be assumed that they are of equivalent reliability, and thus:

A3: The probability of fault activation is the same for the three versions.

This leads to the following notation:

$q_{IV}$ = Prob { activation of an independent fault in one version }

$q_{2V}$ = Prob { activation of a related fault between 2 specific versions }

$q_{3V}$ = Prob { activation of a related fault between the 3 versions }

Two other probabilities are defined in order to account for the faults of the decider:

$q_D$ = Prob { activation of an independent fault in the decider }

$q_{VD}$ = Prob { activation of a related fault between the 3 versions and the decider }

The probabilities concerning the versions could be evaluated from controlled experiments such as [5, 72]. However, these experiments do not account for the analysis of the faults in the decider. The presented models and decider-associated probabilities enables the performance of various voters under failure conditions shuch as the ones theoretically investigated in [89] to be accounted for and may constitute a framework for conducting more comprehensive and more adapted experiments. Fig. 5-b summarizes this notation and relates the considered types of faults with the production process of Fig. 5-a.

Further notation will be introduced when required; in particular, let $q_V$ denote the probability of activation of a fault in any version, thus from assumption A3 we have:

$$q_V = q_{3V} + 2 q_{2V} + q_{VD} + q_{IV}$$     (12)

An important characteristic to account for is related to the fact that besides *error processing* procedures (majority vote based on cross-checks [26], selection of the median result [10] or other voters identified in [89], etc.), the decider implements or not specific *fault treatment* mechanisms to make a disagreeing version passive.

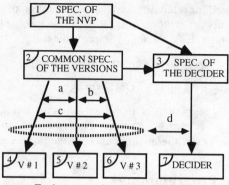

a- Fault sources in production process

| Paths where fault(s) is(are) created or dependency channel(s) | Fault type(s) | Probability of activation |
|---|---|---|
| $1 \rightarrow 2$ | Related fault in the 3 versions | $q_{3V}$ |
| (a), (b) or (c) | Related fault in 2 versions | $q_{2V}$ |
| $1 \rightarrow 2 \rightarrow 3$, $1 \rightarrow 3$ or (d) | Related fault in versions and decider | $q_{VD}$ |
| $2 \rightarrow 4$, $2 \rightarrow 5$ or $2 \rightarrow 6$ | Independent fault in a version, | $q_{IV}$ |
| $3 \rightarrow 7$ | Independent fault in the decider | $q_D$ |

b- Major fault types and notation

**Fig. 5.** NVP analysis

Accordingly, the following assumptions will be considered successively:

**A4**: No fault treatment is carried out after error processing: should a version disagree with the result selected by the decider, the version is kept in the NVP architecture and supplied with the new input data. This applies when faults exhibit a *soft* behavior [53] (see also paper III.B), i.e. when it is likely that the error will not recur in next execution.

**A5**: Fault treatment is carried out: it consists in the identification of a disagreeing version and its elimination from the NVP architecture.

### 3.1 NVP Model Without Fault Treatment

In this case, the major specification of the decision algorithm is only to provide an acceptable output result when the versions provide at least two acceptable results.

Due to the fact that, (i) the versions are executed in parallel and (ii) the decision of acceptance of the current execution and selection of the "best" result is made on a relative basis, the dependability analysis of NVP requires that the interactions between the faults in the versions and the faults in the decider, as well as their consequences, be precisely identified. Thus, as for RB, we consider the following assumptions:

**A6**: Only a single fault type may manifest during the execution of the versions.

**A7:** Only a single fault type may manifest during the whole NVP software execution (versions and decider) and no compensation may take place between the errors of the versions and of the decider.

**Detailed NVP Model.** The behavior of NVP when considering assumption A6 is described by model M3 shown in Fig. 6.

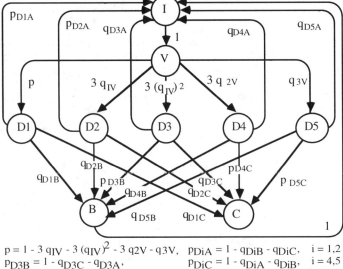

$$p = 1 - 3\,q_{IV} - 3\,(q_{IV})^2 - 3\,q2V - q3V, \quad PDiA = 1 - q_{DiB} - q_{DiC}, \quad i = 1,2$$
$$PD3B = 1 - q_{D3C} - q_{D3A}, \quad\quad PDiC = 1 - q_{DiA} - q_{DiB}, \quad i = 4,5$$

**Fig. 6.** M3 - Detailed NVP model without fault treatment

State V is the state when the versions are executed. States Di, correspond to the execution of the decider. Based on A3 and on the impact of the evaluation of acceptable, distinct or similar erroneous results on dependability, five cases are distinguished:

**D1**: no fault activation [p]; the versions provide 3 acceptable results,

**D2**: activation of an independent fault in 1 version [$3\,q_{IV}\,(1 - q_V)^2 \approx 3\,q_{IV}$]; the versions provide 2 acceptable results,

**D3**: activation of independent faults in 2 or 3 versions [$3\,(q_{IV})^2\,(1 - q_V) + (q_{IV})^3 \approx 3\,(q_{IV})^2$]; the versions give 3 distinct results,

**D4**: activation of related faults in 2 versions [$3\,q2V$]; the versions provide 2 similar erroneous results,

**D5**: activation of related faults in the 3 versions [$q3V$]; the versions provide 3 similar erroneous results.

From these states, the nominal (fault free) behavior [$p_{DiA}$] resulting from the execution of the decider, leads to a transition from:
- D1 & D2 to I, since the decider evaluates 3 or 2 acceptable results,
- D3 to B, since the decider evaluates 3 distinct results,
- D4 & D5 to C: the decider evaluates 2 or 3 similar erroneous results.

Considering decider faults, leads to the following singular events:

- *error compensation*, the decider delivers an acceptable result when evaluating, at least two distinct results (state D3)[1], two (state D4) or three (state D5) similar erroneous results, which leads to state I; the associated probabilities are denoted $q_{DiA}$,

- *rejection of an execution* although at least two similar results are provided by the versions (states D1, D2, D4 and D5)[2], which leads to state B; the associated probabilities are denoted $q_{DiB}$,

- *delivery of an erroneous output result* when evaluating, either at least two acceptable, or at least two distinct erroneous results; (states D1, D2, D4 and D5)[3] leading to state C, the associated probabilities are denoted $q_{DiC}$.

As the decision made by the decider is essentially relative, its efficiency depends rather on the *similar/distinct* than on the *acceptable/erroneous* aspects of the results to be evaluated; thus, the following assumptions can be considered in practice to simplify model M3:

**A8**: The decider is not able to discriminate similar acceptable results from similar erroneous results, thus: $q_{D1B} \approx q_{D5B}$ and $q_{D2B} \approx q_{D4B}$.

**A9**: The decider has the same nominal behavior (it provides a common output result) when evaluating either 2 (majority) or 3 similar results; accordingly:

$$PD1A \approx PD2A, \; q_{D1B} \approx q_{D2B}, \text{ and thus } q_{D1C} \approx q_{D2C},$$

$$PD4A \approx PD5A, \; q_{D4B} \approx q_{D5B}, \text{ and thus } q_{D4C} \approx q_{D5C}.$$

**Simplified NVP Model.** The corresponding model (M4) can be directly derived from the analysis of the NVP production process (Fig. 5-a) and is shown on Fig. 7.

States D1, D2 and D3 are equivalent to related states of M3. State D4/5' corresponds to the activation of related faults either a) among the versions (merging of states D4 and D5 from M3 [$q_{RV} = 3\, q_{2V} + q_{3V}$]), or b) between the 3 versions and the decider [$q_{VD}$] (cf. Fig. 6). In this case, $q_{VD}$ includes all the interactions between the faults of the versions and of the decider.

Thus, the impact of the activation of an independent fault in the decider is considered only for state D1 with probability $q_D = q_{D1B} + q_{D1C}$. For states D2, D3 and D4/5', the description is limited to the nominal (fault free) behavior of the decider.

---

[1]  This would take place, for example, in the case of a median-based decision when the erroneous results are placed on each side of the acceptable result.

[2]  The decider is too "tight"; this results in a reliability penalty, in the case when the similar results correspond to acceptable results.

[3]  This case does not correspond to the usual case when the decider is evaluating at least two similar erroneous results. The singularities correspond here to the cases — hopefully rare! — when the decider outvotes acceptable results or when the decider is too "loose".

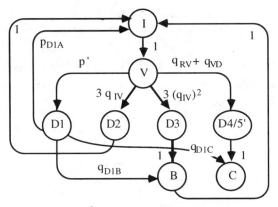

$$p' = 1 - 3\,q_{IV} - 3\,q_{IV}^2 - q_{RV} - q_{VD}, \quad PD1A = 1 - q_{D1B} - q_{D1C}$$

**Fig. 7.** M4 - Simplified NVP model without fault treatment

**Processing of the Models.** For model M3:

$$\Gamma_R = \sigma\,\{\,(p + 3\,q_{IV})\,(q_{D1B} + q_{D1C}) + q_{RV}\,(PD4C + q_{D1B}) \\ + 3\,(q_{IV})^2\,(PD3B + q_{D3C})\,\} \tag{13}$$

$$\Gamma_S = \sigma\,\{\,(p + 3\,q_{IV})\,q_{D1C} + q_{RV}\,PD4C + 3\,(q_{IV})^2\,q_{D3C}\,\} \tag{14}$$

For model M4, we have:

$$\Gamma_R = \sigma\,\{\,p'\,q_D + q_{RV} + q_{VD} + 3\,(q_{IV})^2\,\} \tag{15}$$

$$\Gamma_S = \sigma\,\{\,p'\,q_{D1C} + q_{RV} + q_{VD}\,\} \tag{16}$$

for which the expressions below are close pessimistic approximations:

$$\Gamma_R = \sigma\,\{\,q_D + q_{RV} + q_{VD} + 3\,(q_{IV})^2\,\} \tag{15'}$$

$$\Gamma_S = \sigma\,\{\,q_{D1C} + q_{RV} + q_{VD}\,\} \tag{16'}$$

It is worth noting that the same expressions can be obtained from M3, (i) when there is no compensation [$q_{D3A} = q_{D4A} = 0$] and (ii) noting that expression [$3\,q_{IV}\,q_{D1C} + 3\,(q_{IV})^2\,q_{D3C}$] obtained in (13) and (14) can be identified to the probability of activation of a related fault in the versions and in the decider [$q_{VD}$] from (15) and (16). Indeed, (13) and (14) write as:

$$\Gamma_R = \sigma\,\{\,(p + 3\,q_{IV} + q_{RV})\,q_{D1B} + p\,q_{D1C} + q_{RV}\,PD4C + q_{VD} \\ + 3\,(q_{IV})^2\,PD3B\,\} \tag{13'}$$

$$\Gamma_S = \sigma\,\{\,p\,q_{D1C} + q_{RV}\,PD3C + q_{VD}\,\} \tag{14'}$$

for which it can be verified that (15') and (16') constitute valid approximations.

Accordingly, further analyses will be carried out considering essentially these approximate expressions.

**Comparison with a Non Fault-Tolerant Software.** From (12) the failure rate of the non fault-tolerant software corresponding to the selection of any version is expressed as:

$$\Gamma'_R = s \, q_V = s \, \{q_{3V} + 2 \, q_{2V} + q_{VD} + q_{IV}\} = s \, \{q'_{RV} + q_{VD} + q_{IV}\} \qquad (17)$$

where $q'_{RV}$ corresponds to the probability of activation of the faults in the selected version that could be mapped to related faults in the other two versions in the NVP software.

The ratio $r = \Gamma_R / \Gamma'_R$ is then:

$$r = \frac{q_D + q_{RV} + q_{VD} + 3 \, (q_{IV})^2}{q'_{RV} + q_{VD} + q_{IV}} \qquad (18)$$

For the comparison, we introduce the ratio i identifying the proportion of independent faults in the selected version:

$$q_{IV} = i \, q_V = i \, (q'_{RV} + q_{VD} + q_{IV}) \qquad (19)$$

It follows that:

$$r = \frac{q_D}{q_V} + \frac{q_{RV} + q_{VD}}{q_V} + 3 \, (i)^2 \, q_V \qquad (20)$$

As $q_{RV} = q_{3V} + 3 \, q_{2V}$ and $q'_{RV} = q_{3V} + 2 \, q_{2V}$, we have $q_{RV} \approx q'_{RV}$, when related faults in 3 versions dominate (specification), and $q_{RV} \approx (3/2) \, q'_{RV}$, when related faults in 2 versions dominate (implementations). Thus, r is comprised into domain determined by the lower (r') and upper (r") bounds:

$$r' = \quad q_D/q_V + (1 - i) + 3 \, (i)^2 \, q_V \qquad (21)$$

$$r" = \quad q_D/q_V + (3/2) \, (1 - i) + 3 \, (i)^2 \, q_V \qquad (22)$$

These expressions enable to quantify the following qualitative (and intuitive) results:
- the decider must be far more reliable than the versions,
- if related faults dominate ($i \approx 0$) no improvement has to be expected, which confirms the results obtained in a large number of previous studies, e.g. see [71, 85],

## 3.2 NVP Model with Fault Treatment

In this case (since assumption A5 applies), a supplementary specification of the decider is to correctly diagnose a disagreeing version when two versions provide acceptable results.

**Description of the Model.** The corresponding model (M5) is shown on Fig. 8.

Submodel SM1 is equivalent to model M4, the only differences concern:
- the elimination of the states Di with an output transition equal to 1 by merging them with the next state,

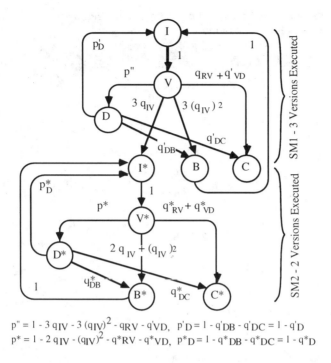

$p'' = 1 - 3 q_{IV} - 3 (q_{IV})^2 - q_{RV} - q'_{VD}, \quad p'_D = 1 - q'_{DB} - q'_{DC} = 1 - q'_D$

$p^* = 1 - 2 q_{IV} - (q_{IV})^2 - q^*_{RV} - q^*_{VD}, \quad p^*_D = 1 - q^*_{DB} - q^*_{DC} = 1 - q^*_D$

- the modification of the probabilities of activation of a fault in the decider to account for the change in its specification, (i) change of $q_{VD}$ into $q'_{VD}$[4] and (ii) change of $q_{D1i}$ into $q'_{Di}$ ($i \in \{B,C\}$),
- when an independent fault has been activated in a single version, this version is discarded and thus SM2 is entered.

**Fig. 8.** M5 - NVP model with fault treatment

Submodel SM2 has the same structure as SM1; however, as only 2 versions are used, the probabilities of fault activation in the versions and in the decider are modified in accordance; in particular, $q^*_{RV} = q_{2V}$.

**Processing of the Model.** As in model M5 the non-failed states do not constitute an irreducible Markov chain, it is not possible to obtain equivalent failure rates. However, equivalent failure rates may be derived for each submodel in isolation:

for SM1:    $\Gamma_{R1} = \sigma \{ q'_D + q_{RV} + q'_{VD} + 3 (q_{IV})^2 \}$  (23)

$\Gamma_{S1} = \sigma \{ q'_{DC} + q_{RV} + q'_{VD} \}$  (24)

for SM2:    $\Gamma_{R2} = \sigma \{ q^*_D + q^*_{RV} + q^*_{VD} + 2 q_{IV} + (q_{IV})^2 \}$  (25)

$\Gamma_{S2} = \sigma \{ q^*_{DC} + q^*_{RV} + q^*_{VD} \}$  (26)

---

[4] In particular $q'_{VD}$ includes the risk of failure of the diagnosis of the decider: discarding a version providing an acceptable result.

Reliability and safety of the model can then be analyzed by processing model M6 of Fig. 9, where X = R for reliability and X = S for safety.

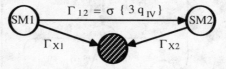

**Fig. 9.** M6 - Model for reliability and safety analysis

Reliability and safety and the associated mean times to failure express as:

$$R(t) = \exp\left[-(\Gamma_{12}+\Gamma_{R1})t\right]+\frac{\Gamma_{12}}{\Gamma_{12} + \Gamma_{R1} - \Gamma_{R2}}\left\{\exp\left[-\Gamma_{R2}\,t\right]- \exp\left[-(\Gamma_{12}+\Gamma_{R1})t\right]\right\}$$

$$S(t) = \exp\left[-(\Gamma_{12}+\Gamma_{S1})t\right]+\frac{\Gamma_{12}}{\Gamma_{12} + \Gamma_{S1} - \Gamma_{S2}}\left\{\exp\left[-\Gamma_{S2}\,t\right]- \exp\left[-(\Gamma_{12}+\Gamma_{S1})t\right]\right\}$$

$$(27)$$

$$MTTF_R = \frac{\Gamma_{12}}{\Gamma_{12} + \Gamma_{R1}}\left(\frac{1}{\Gamma_{R2}}-\frac{1}{\Gamma_{R1}}\right)+\frac{1}{\Gamma_{R1}}$$

$$MTTF_S = \frac{\Gamma_{12}}{\Gamma_{12} + \Gamma_{S1}}\left(\frac{1}{\Gamma_{S2}}-\frac{1}{\Gamma_{S1}}\right)+\frac{1}{\Gamma_{S1}}$$

$$(28)$$

Analysis of these expressions requires that the rates be precisely evaluated which is a rather difficult task due to the uncertainty in the values of the probabilities from which they are derived. Nevertheless, interesting results can be obtained with the following assumptions:

**A10:** The decider has the same behavior when evaluating either three versions (SM1) or two versions (SM2), i.e., $q'_{Di} \approx q*_{Di}$ and $q'_{VD} \approx q*_{VD}$,

**A11:** Due to the intrinsic simplicity of the algorithm involved, the behavior of the decider is not significantly altered when its specifications are modified from assumption A4 (model M4) to assumption A5 (model M5), i.e., $q_{D1i} \approx q'_{Di}$ and $q_{VD} \approx q'_{VD}$.

According to A10, it can be verified from relations (23) to (26), that:

$$\Gamma_{R1} = \sigma\{q'_D + q_{3V} + 3\,q_{2V} + q'_{VD} + 3\,(q_{IV})^2\} \tag{29}$$

$$\Gamma_{S1} = \sigma\{q'_{DC} + q_{3V} + 3\,q_{2V} + q'_{VD}\} \tag{30}$$

$$\Gamma_{R2} = \sigma\{q'_D + q_{2V} + q'_{VD} + 2\,q_{IV} + (q_{IV})^2\} \tag{31}$$

$$\Gamma_{S2} = \sigma\{q'_{DC} + q_{2V} + q'_{VD}\} \tag{32}$$

These relations show that $\Gamma_{S1} > \Gamma_{S2}$ and that:

• $\Gamma_{R1} < \Gamma_{R2}$, when independent faults in the versions dominate,

• $\Gamma_{R1} > \Gamma_{R2}$, when related faults among the versions dominate.

Expressions (28) show that the decision to discard the disagreeing version improves $MTTF_S$, which is not always the case for $MTTF_R$[5]. Analogous conclusions can be derived from expressions (27) for S(t) and R(t).

More generally, the expressions confirm a general system reliability result, i.e. it is better to use two versions than three versions, when emphasis is put on safety rather than on reliability. Furthermore, in the case of reliability, the impact of related faults is clearly indicated by the fact that no improvement has to be expected when using 3 versions instead of two if related faults among the versions dominate significantly over independent faults [85].

# 4    RB and NVP Comparison

In order to be homogeneous, the comparison is carried out only when:

- assumptions A2 and A7 hold (a single fault type activation and no error compensation within the whole software),
- no specific fault treatment is considered for NVP.

For each architecture, specific notations have been used. However, similar expressions can be derived for $\Gamma_R$ and $\Gamma_S$, based on the following notation:

$$q_I = \text{Prob \{independent failure of one variant I execution\}, thus: } q_{I,RB} = q_P \approx q_S$$
$$\text{and } q_{I,NVP} = q_{IV}$$

$$q_{CM} = \text{Prob \{common-mode failure I execution\}, thus: } q_{CM,RB} = q_{PST} + q_{PS} + q_T$$
$$\text{and } q_{CM,NVP} = q_{VD} + q_{RV} + q_D$$

Accordingly, relations (7) with $q_T \ll 1$ and (15') become respectively:

for RB:    $$\Gamma_R = \sigma \{ q_{CM,RB} + (q_{I,RB})^2 \} \qquad (33)$$

for NVP:    $$\Gamma_R = \sigma \{ q_{CM,NVP} + 3 (q_{I,NVP})^2 \} \qquad (34)$$

Although the form of these expressions would suggest that RB is better than NVP, it has to be noted that the influence of the various terms may be different. Indeed, if the probabilities of activation of (i) an independent fault in one variant [$q_P$ (or $q_S$) and $q_{IV}$] and (ii) of related faults between variants [$q_{PS}$ and $q_{RV}$], are of the same order of magnitude, however, the probabilities of activation of (i) an independent fault in the decider [$q_T$ and $q_D$] and (ii) of related faults between the variants and the decider [$q_{PST}$ and $q_{VD}$] are likely to be greater for RB than for NVP; this is mainly due to the fact that the AT is specific to each application, whereas the decider in NVP is generic to a large extent.

It follows that independent failures of the variants have more impact for the NVP, whereas the impact of the decider is lower for this architecture. However, a precise knowledge of these probabilities would be needed in order to perform a more detailed comparison.

Considering safety analysis, we have obtained:

---

[5]    Indeed, $1/\Gamma_{R1}$ (resp. $1/\Gamma_{S1}$) can be interpreted as the $MTTF_R$ (resp. $MTTF_S$) of the NVP software when no fault treatment is carried out (Model M4).

for RB:          $\Gamma_S = \sigma\ q_{PST}$                                                    (35)

for NVP:         $\Gamma_S = \sigma\ \{\ q_{RV} + q_{VD} + q_{D1C}\ \}$                           (36)

Related faults among variants have no influence for RB, but are of prime importance for NVP. This is a consequence of the fact that for RB an absolute decision is taken for each alternate against the specification and that for NVP the decision is made on a relative basis among the results provided by the versions.

Due to the very nature of the NVP decider, $q_{D1C}$ may be made very low, thus $q_{VD} \ll q_{RV}$ and $q_{RV}$ has to be compared with $q_{PST}$.

Finally it is worth noting that only partial conclusions can be drawn from this analysis. Additional features need to be taken into account, such as the fact that, for RB, service delivery is suspended during error recovery, i.e., when the secondary is invoked.

# 5    Conclusions

This paper presented a detailed *reliability and safety analysis* of the two major software fault-tolerance approaches: RB and NVP.

The methodology used for *modelling* is based on (i) the identification of the possible types of faults introduced during the specification and the implementation, (ii) the analysis of the behavior following fault activation.

An important comment concerns the *fault assumption* used in the modelling. The most significant issue for evaluation of diversified software in operation concerns the types of errors (distinct or similar) that result from the activation of faults. We considered a direct mapping of these errors with two distinct fault classes: independent and related faults. Such a mapping is pessimistic as it enables to incorporate only positive correlation in the manifestation of related faults. As evidenced in [18], another form of correlation (negative correlation) does exist among related faults which has a beneficial consequence on the execution of multi-variant software in forcing the delivery of distinct errors. However, although they could be traced to (negatively correlated) related faults, faults leading to distinct errors are not distinguishable at the execution level from independent faults and thus they both can be merged into a single category: the independent faults. A dual discussion applies also to similar errors since in some — very rare (e.g. see [11])— cases they also could be traced to independent faults. It is worth noting that the detailed analysis of the relationship between classes of errors and faults would result in a further increase in the — already large — number of parameters of the models. In addition, owing to the prominent influence of the deciders in the failure process of a fault-tolerant software, such an analysis should not be limited to examining the inter-variant correlations, but should cover the positive and negative correlations between the variants and the deciders, as well.

The main outcome of the *evaluation* carried concerns the derivation of analytical results enabling (i) to identify the conditions of improvement, when compared to a non fault-tolerant software, that could result from the use of RB (the acceptance test has to be more reliable than the alternates) and NVP (related faults among the versions and the decider have to be minimized) and (ii) to reveal the most critical types of related faults. In particular, for safety, the related faults between the variants have a significant impact for NVP, whereas only related faults between the alternates and the acceptance test, have to be considered for RB.

The specific study of the *discarding of a failed version in NVP* showed that this strategy is always worthwhile for safety, whereas, for reliability, it is all the more beneficial as independent faults dominate.

# Dependability Analysis of Iterative Fault-Tolerant Software Considering Correlation[*]

Andrea Bondavalli[1]   Silvano Chiaradonna[1]
Felicita Di Giandomenico[2]   Lorenzo Strigini[2]

[1] CNUCE-CNR     [2] IEI-CNR

**Abstract.** We consider the dependability of fault tolerant software executed iteratively, as e.g. in process control applications. We recall the models usually adopted for evaluating the probability of mission survival (reliability at a certain time) and performability, and show the results obtained by applying these models to the adaptive scheme for software fault-tolerance SCOP, "Self-Configuring Optimal Programming" and to the more popular schemes, recovery blocks and multiple version programming. In the case considered, SCOP is equivalent to N-version programming in terms of the probability of delivering correct results, but achieves better performance by delaying the execution of some of the variants until it is made necessary by an error. A discussion follows highlighting the limits in the realism of these analyses, due to the assumptions made to obtain mathematically tractable models and to the lack of experimental data. As a contribution to overcoming these limitations, we present a simple black-box model of an iterative software component which takes into account dependencies among input values of successive iterations and the possibility that repeated, non fatal failures may together cause mission failure. Using this model we show the effects of different distributions of the correlations among inputs on the dependability indicators selected.

## 1   Introduction

The effectiveness of software fault tolerance, in the sense of diverse redundancy in software design, for tolerating residual design faults in operational software products is the topic of numerous papers (see paper VI.E in this volume and [58]). In the fault-tolerant techniques we consider, a (fault-tolerant) software component consists of a set of diversely implemented, functionally equivalent *variants*, plus *adjudication* subcomponents. At each execution of the component, a subset of these subcomponents is executed, in such a way that they may check and correct each other's results. The best known such techniques are Recovery Blocks (RB) [105] and N-version programming (NVP) [9]. In the simplest form of NVP, the N variants are executed in parallel, and the adjudication is a more or less complex vote on their results (see paper III.D in this volume). In RB, only one variant is executed, at first; if its result does not pass an *acceptance test*, other variants are invoked, in turn, until one passes or the available variants are used up. Clearly, these are two extremes in a range of trade-offs between consumption of "space" (level of parallelism) and "time" (elapsed time), and between the goals of low average resource consumption and low worst-case response time [11]. Many other combinations are possible [112, 113]. We

---

[*] This paper is a compendium of [29, 20].

shall consider the scheme called "Self-Configuring Optimistic Programming", which includes a useful family of such execution schemes and is described in detail in paper III.E of this volume.

This article deals with the *evaluation* of software (including software fault tolerance schemes), in terms of either simple reliability evaluation or assessment of the utility (or cost) derived from operating a system (*performability* evaluation [93]). [115, 116] contain performability evaluations of schemes for software fault tolerance. We use very similar models and extend that work to cover the SCOP scheme, and discuss the application of modelling to realistic problems in fault-tolerant design. We compare recovery blocks with two variants, N-version programming with three variants, and SCOP with three variants executed in 2 rounds. Our evaluations (like those by most other authors) are derived assuming unlimited resources. As such, they are independent of any individual application, and can be considered as limiting results useful in the early dimensioning of a design, like, for instance, figures of throughput of a communication channel with permanently full input queues.

However, the realism of the models proposed and therefore their practical utility are limited by the large number of assumptions made to obtain mathematically tractable models and by the lack of experimental data. Among the limiting factors, which are quite similar in all the models proposed so far, we chose to address the correlation among successive inputs of the software and the effects of sequences of consecutive failures: many physical systems can tolerate failures of their control systems if isolated or in short bursts, but not a sequence of even "benign" failures leaving the system without feed-back control for a while. We present a more realistic evaluation model which, although it considers the software component as a black box without taking into account its internal structure, does take into account both correlation among successive inputs and sequences of consecutive failures.

In Section 2, we describe the class of systems we evaluate, with the assumptions that affect our models and the reward structure used. Models for evaluating NVP, RB and intermediate schemes such as SCOP are recalled and applied and the resulting figures compared in Section 3. Section 4 contains a discussion of the limits of such eva- luations, and of how these could be overcome. In addition we describe new hypotheses we make about correlated inputs and sequences of failures. In Section 5, we describe our new model and show how different probabilistic hypotheses about the correlation among successive iterations affect the dependability indicators derived previously. Section 6 summarises our conclusions.

## 2    System and Hypotheses

We assume an application of an iterative nature, where a *mission* (of duration t) is composed of a series of iterations of the execution of the fault-tolerant software component. At each iteration, the component accepts an input and produces an output. If the execution lasts beyond a pre-set maximum duration, it is aborted by a watchdog timer (which is assumed never to fail). Unlimited resources and an "infinite" load are assumed: the redundant component always executes with the maximum degree of parallelism allowed by its design, and as soon as an iteration is over the next iteration is started. The outcomes of an individual iteration may be: i) *success*, i.e., the delivery of a correct result, ii) a *benign failure* of the program, i.e., an output that is not correct but does not, by itself, cause the entire mission to fail, or iii) a *catastrophic failure*, i.e., an output that causes the immediate failure of the mission. Whether a failure is benign or catastrophic is determined by the characteristics of the controlled system. For simplicity's sake, we assume that errors detected (by comparison of redundant results, by an acceptance test or by the watchdog timer) inside the fault-tolerant component cause benign failures, and that undetected errors cause catastrophic failures.

We consider two dependability measures: the probability of surviving a mission (reliability at time t) and a performability measure [93, 116, 29, 114]. A low probability of mission failure is the typical main requirement for critical applications. An alternative scenario is that of comparatively non-critical applications such as somewhat complex transaction-processing or scientific applications, where more complex reward measures (performability) become appropriate. We call $M_t$ the total reward accumulated over a mission, and evaluate the expected total reward $E[M_t]$ (which we will simply call the "performability"). Our reward model is: successful executions add 1 to the value of $M_t$; benign failures add zero; a catastrophic failure reduces the value of $M_t$ to zero. Different reward functions could be used, e.g., attributing large negative rewards to failed missions.

Additional assumptions, similar to those used by other authors (see Paper VI.E of this volume, [91, 116, 115]) are:

1.  the behaviour of each variant at an iteration is statistically independent of its behaviour at other (previous or later) iterations;
2.  the execution times of the variants are independently and exponentially distributed and, without the watchdog timer, are independent of their value outcome;
3.  all the outcomes (of an execution) which include errors of subcomponents (variants and adjudicators) can be subdivided into two classes: those where there are *catastrophic* (i.e., undetected) failures and those where only *benign* failures occur; in this latter case, the errors of the subcomponents are statistically independent events;
4.  "compensation" among errors never happens: e.g., if a majority of erroneous results exists, it never happens that the adjudicator errs in such a way as to choose a correct result instead;
5.  a certain degree of symmetry is assumed in the probabilistic behaviour of the system: the probabilities of most events are assumed invariant under permutation among the variants; this has obvious mathematical convenience;
6.  correct results are always seen as consistent by the adjudicator.

Of course, these assumptions limit the realism of the results obtained. We shall discuss this aspect in more detail in Section 4.

# 3    Models with Independence Among Successive Inputs

## 3.1  Modelling Approach

As in the previously quoted papers, we first use a "dependability submodel" to obtain the probabilities of the different outcomes at each execution of the redundant component: success, benign failure, or catastrophic failure, without considering deadlines and the watchdog timer. Then, we use a "performance submodel" to determine the probability of violating the deadlines and the number of iterations in the time interval of interest. Our dependability submodels are similar to those in paper VI.E of this volume, as well as in [115, 116], with slight corrections (discussed in [28]), which do not significantly change the results obtained, if parameters with similar meanings are given similar values. The relevant events for the dependability submodels are defined in the following tables.

**Table 1.** Error types and notation for NVP and SCOP

| Error Types | Probabilities |
|---|---|
| 3 variants err with consistent results | $q_{3v}$ |
| 2 variants err with consistent results (the 3rd result is inconsistent with them, and may be correct or erroneous) | $q_{2v}$ |
| The adjudicator errs by selecting an erroneous, non-majority result; for SCOP this has been divided in two subcases to distinguish if execution terminates in phase 1 or phase 2; with probabilities $q_{vd1} = 2\,q_{vd}$ and $q_{vd2} = q_{vd}$ | $q_{vd}$ |
| A variant errs, conditioned on none of the above events happening (i.e., there are one or more *detected* errors; their statistical independence is assumed) | $q_{iv}$ |
| The adjudicator errs by not recognising a majority (hence causing a detected failure), conditioned on the existence of a majority | $q_d$ |

**Table 2.** Error types and notation for RB

| Error Types | Probabilities |
|---|---|
| The secondary variant errs and the adjudicator accepts its result, conditional on the secondary being executed | $q_{sa}$ |
| Common mode error of P and AT, or P, S and AT (the primary variant errs and the adjudicator accepts its result) | $q_{pa}, q_{psa}$ |
| Common mode error of P and S (the primary and the secondary variant err with consistent results) | $q_{ps}$ |
| Detectable error of the primary or secondary variant (assumed independent) | $q_p, q_s$ |
| Error of the acceptance test AT causing it to reject a result, given that the result is correct | $q_a$ |

The same "performance submodel" as in [115] is then used. The maximum execution time allowed by the watchdog timer is called $\tau$. The probabilities of benign failure, $p_b$, and catastrophic failure, $p_c$, are determined considering that the intervention of the watchdog-timer turns into benign failures some execution which would otherwise produce either success or catastrophic failure. Last, the probability of mission failure $P[C_t]$ and the performability $E[M_t]$ are obtained according to these equations:

$$P[C_t] = 1 - (1 - p_c)^\mu \int_{-\hat{\mu}/\hat{\sigma}}^{\infty} (1 - p_c)^{\hat{\sigma}x} \varphi(x)dx$$

$$E[M_t] = \frac{1 - p_b - p_c}{1 - p_c} \; (1 - p_c)^{\hat\mu} \left( \hat\sigma \int\limits_{-\hat\mu/\hat\sigma}^{\infty} x \, (1 - p_c)^{\hat\sigma x} \varphi(x)dx + \hat\mu \int\limits_{-\hat\mu/\hat\sigma}^{\infty} (1 - p_c)^{\hat\sigma x} \varphi(x)dx \right)$$

where $\hat\mu = t / \mu$ and $\hat\sigma = \sqrt{t\sigma^2/\mu^3}$. $\mu$ and $\sigma^2$ are the mean and variance of the duration of an execution of the redundant component, respectively. These models are described and solved in [29, 28]. We will now show their results.

### 3.2 Evaluation Results

Figs. 1 and 2 show the results obtained from these models with parameter values as in Tables 3 and 4. The independent variable is the probability of consistent errors of more than one variant, the main factor in determining the outcome of the individual executions.

**Table 3.** Values of the "dependability" parameters used for Figs. 1 and 2

| Recovery Blocks | N-Version Programming | SCOP |
|---|---|---|
| $q_{ps} = q_{pa} = q_{sa}$: from 0 to $1.8 \cdot 10^{-7}$ | $q_{2v}$ : from 0 to $1.8 \cdot 10^{-7}$ | $q_{2v}$ : from 0 to $1.8 \cdot 10^{-7}$ |
| $q_{psa} = 10^{-10}$ | $q_{3v} = 10^{-10}$ | $q_{3v} = 10^{-10}$ |
| $q_p = 10^{-4}$ | $q_{iv} = 10^{-4}$ | $q_{iv} = 10^{-4}$ |
| $q_s = 10^{-4}$ | $q_{vd} = 10^{-10}$ | $q_{vd1} = 2 \cdot 10^{-10}$ |
| $q_a = 10^{-4}$ | $q_d = 10^{-9}$ | $q_{vd2} = 10^{-10}$ |
| | | $q_d = 10^{-9}$ |

**Table 4.** Values of the timing parameters $(\text{msec}^{-1})$ used for Figs. 1 and 2

| | Equal execution rates | Strongly different execution rates |
|---|---|---|
| RB | $\lambda_p = \lambda_s = \lambda_a = 1/20$ <br> $\tau = 250$ msecs | $\lambda_p = \lambda_a = 1/20, \lambda_s = 1/72$ <br> $\tau = 250$ msecs |
| NVP and SCOP | $\lambda_1 = \lambda_2 = \lambda_3 = 1/20$ <br> $\lambda_d = 1/2$ <br> $\tau = 250$ msecs | $\lambda_1 = 1/20, \lambda_2 = 1/24, \lambda_3 = 1/72$ <br> $\lambda_d = 1/2$ <br> $\tau = 250$ msecs |

Our choice of parameter values deserves some discussion. The mission duration is 10 hours, a reasonable order of magnitude for e.g. a workday in non-continuous process factory operation, or flight duration for civil avionics. The values assigned to the other parameters reflect plausible assumptions: the adjudicator (acceptance test for RBs) has a much lower error probability than the variants in an NVP or SCOP system, and a comparable probability for recovery blocks; the probabilities of coincident errors of three subcomponents are much lower than those of two independent (and detectable) errors, but higher than those of three independent errors. The limits of using "plausible" values will again be discussed later on. For the execution times, two situations are chosen: similar distributions for the three variants and strongly different distributions. For RBs and SCOP, we assume that the slower variants are designated for conditional execution when errors are detected.

Figs. 1.a and 1.b show, for each scheme, the probability of having at least one undetected error in a mission, which increases towards the right in the figures. As shown, this choice of parameter ranges extends to unrealistically low probabilities of success of a mission. However, the curves do show the important factors in the behaviour of the models.

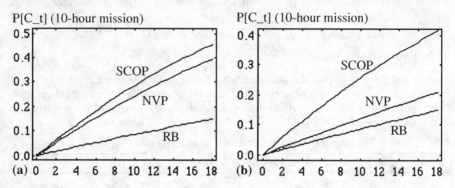

**Fig. 1.** Probability of failure of a 10-hour mission for RB, NVP and SCOP. The execution rates of the variants ($\lambda_i$) are equal in (a) and strongly different in (b) . The abscissae represent the probability of two consistent errors: $q_{ps}$, $q_{pa}$, $q_{sa}$ and $q_{2v}$ (times $10^{-8}$)

The performability $E[M_t]$ (Figs. 2.a, 2.b) is approximately equal to the product of:

1. the expected number of executions in a mission. From this point of view, having to wait for the slowest variants (SCOP, NVP) is a disadvantage. So, RB performs the best. However, adjudication has been assumed to be faster for SCOP and NVP than for RB, and this explains the high values shown for SCOP for abscissae close to zero. In RB and SCOP the number of executions is also affected by the fact that some execution may last for two phases instead of one. However, these are realistically very few, so that the number of executions per mission is practically constant, for any given scheme, once the distributions of execution times for the subcomponents are assigned;

2. the probability of completing a mission without a catastrophic failure, determined by the probability $p_c$, practically equal to the probability of two variants delivering consistent erroneous results (for NVP and SCOP), or, in the recovery block scheme, of the primary variant producing an erroneous result accepted by the acceptance test. This determines how many of the missions yield a non-zero reward;

3. the probability of benign failures, which in these plots is practically constant (for each scheme), and determines the fraction of the executions in a mission which contribute to the utility of the mission.

These considerations explain the shape of the plots shown. Towards the left in these figures, as the probability of catastrophic failure approaches zero, the utility of a mission tends to the mean number of executions in a mission, decreased by the (constant) fraction of benign failures. The advantages of SCOP and RB described in point 1 above predominate. Moving to the right, the probability of catastrophic failures, and hence missions with zero utility, increases. SCOP and RB, being able to pack more execution in the same mission time, suffer more than NVP. The differences between

Figs. 2.a and 2.b are explained by considering that differences among the mean execution times of the variants increase the performance disadvantage of NVP compared to SCOP, and of SCOP compared to RBs. With our parameters, while the number of executions per mission is maximum in SCOP, which explains SCOP having the highest E[M$_t$] for the lower values of the abscissae, the slope of the curves is lowest for RB, as its probability of undetected failure per execution has been set to roughly one third of that of the others. An interesting consideration is that in the left-hand part of these plots, SCOP yields the best performability values, but the worst probability of surviving a mission.

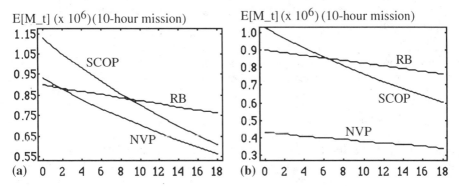

**Fig. 2.** Performability comparisons of RB, NVP and SCOP. The execution rates of the variants are equal in (a) and strongly different in (b). The abscissae represent the probability of two consistent errors: $q_{ps}$, $q_{pa}$, $q_{sa}$ and $q_{2v}$ (times $10^{-8}$)

## 4    Limits of These Models and Possible Improvements

We now discuss in some more detail the scope of applicability and the loss of realism implied by the assumptions used. Then we describe some new hypotheses and the background necessary for considering correlation among inputs and taking into account the possibility that a sequence of benign failures causes mission failure.

### 4.1  Discussion

The models used assume that the executions of the redundant software are contiguous in time: each execution is triggered by the end of the previous one. Currently, software fault tolerance is mostly used in control or safety systems with static periodic scheduling. Our model would apply in special cases, e.g., a surveillance system which performs elaborate processing on each image captured, so that the end of the processing of one image is the trigger for capturing the next one. In practice, the evaluation results (in our range of parameter values) depend only on the mean execution times, so that models with constant execution times (as we will use in the following sections) yield similar results.

The performability measure adopted here has two uses. First, to model specific scenarios where its reward model applies (changing the reward model for a different scenario would be simple). In addition, this particular performability measure describes the amount of processing obtainable from a redundant software component in a given amount of time, with sufficient resources and no overhead (e.g. for scheduling). So, it gives an optimistic assessment useful in the preliminary design stage. This should be coupled with an indicator of run-time cost, to account for the different uses of resources by fault-tolerant schemes that score comparably on the performability scale.

The "dependability submodel" includes many assumptions which are not supported by experimental evidence [68, 17, 21]: for instance, no compensation between errors, independence between inconsistent errors by the variants, "symmetry" in the values of the dependability parameters. These, together, simplify the solution of the model and allow one to predict "plausible" behaviours of a system. One could build a more complete model, with more parameters, to explore the whole space of possible behaviours. A user would, however, need some assistance to understand the thought experiments thus generated.

We concentrate instead on two problems in modelling *sequences* of executions. One is the assumption of independence between the outcomes of successive executions, which is often false, especially because of the effect of "input trajectories". We represent the data on which programs operate as discrete, finite, multi-dimensional spaces. For example, a program may read a set of 20 numbers and have another set of 30 internal variables: we then say that it has an *input space* with 50 dimensions, in which the consecutive inputs to the program describe a trajectory. In process control applications, typically, any two consecutive input values are close together in the input space. A program would produce bursts of errors when this trajectory intersects a "failure region" (defined as a region of points where the software normally fails). So, an error at one execution would be an indication of a high probability (i.e., higher than the marginal probability) of an error at the next execution. Other causes for positive correlation exist: periods of peak load in time-shared computers or in communication links, or imperfect recovery from corruption of the program state. A realistic reward model should thus consider *sequences* of failures: many physical systems can tolerate failures of their control systems, if isolated or in short bursts, but a sequence of even benign failures such that the system is effectively without feed-back control for a while will often cause damage. Predicting the distribution of burst lengths is trivial with the independence assumption, but optimistic. We address this problem in the following sections in the general context of programs seen as black boxes, without considering their internal structure.

## 4.2 Background and Assumptions for Considering Sequences of Failures

The effects of correlation among successive iterations have been modelled in [34, 117]. [34] models a RB structure with two variants and a perfect acceptance test. Successive input values are close together. Two kinds of failure events of the primary variant are distinguished:

i)   *point failure,* when the input sequence of the primary enters a failure region,

ii)  *serial failures*: one or more consecutive failures, following a point failure, until the input trajectory exits the failure region. The number of serial failures after a point failure is a random variable.

[117] uses the same model but also considers other forms of correlation (viz between the two variants). Both papers deal with reliability (MTTF).

We briefly describe our new modelling context; more details can be found in [19, 20].

*Failure Regions*: Failure regions are subsets of the program input space, consisting of contiguous points. "A priori", all points in the input space have the same probability of belonging to a failure region (this "ignorance" assumptions need not always be necessary: in some cases, one may know that some parts of the input space are more prone to failures than others). We have no reason for assuming specific shape and size distributions for failure regions (see [16] for some examples from experiments). Our choice will be guided by considerations of simplicity, plausibility and robustness of the models.

*Input Sequence*: Successive inputs form a "trajectory", a random or deterministic walk with a step length that is small, compared to the size of the input space [17].

*Consecutive Benign Failures* : We assume that any sequence of $n_c$ or more benign failures ($n_c > 0$) causes the failure of the entire mission.

In modelling sequences of correlated failures, we assume that one success, after any series of less than $n_c$ benign failures, brings the system into a stable state, i.e. the memory of the previous failure sequence is immediately lost. This is a plausible assumption if failure regions are small and widely dispersed in the input space, and the probability that the trajectory rc-cnters a failure region it just left is small. For instance, this is true in the case of convex failure regions and trajectories that change direction only slightly between any two consecutive inputs.

As previously mentioned, we consider missions of a fixed number of iterations with fixed duration, as we saw before that we could obtain a satisfactory approximation from our more complex distributions by using the mean execution duration as if it were a constant duration.

# 5   Correlation Between Successive Iterations, Allowing Mission Failures from Repeated Benign Failures

## 5.1   The Model

Our new model (Fig 3) assumes that after an iteration with success (state S), there is a probability $p_{sb}$ that the next execution will produce a benign failure (i.e., that the input trajectory has entered a failure region). However, once in a failure region, the probabilities of staying there for one, two or more iterations are given by the parameters $p_1$, $p_2$, etc. The parameter $p_{nn}$ designates the probability of staying for $n_c$ iterations or more, i. e. $p_{nn} = 1 - \sum_{i=1}^{n_c - 1} p_i$ .

For instance, with probability $p_{sb}p_2$ the program enters a failure region, represented by state $B_2$ in our model, from which, unless a catastrophic failure occurs (arc from $B_2$ to C labelled $p_{bc}$) it will be compelled to move to $B_1$, after which it exits the failure region. This explains the role of states $B_1$, $B_2$, etc., all designating a benign failure of the last execution. If the sequence of failures were longer than $n_c$-1, a mission failure would occur, described by adding the term $p_{sb} p_{nn}$ to the probability of the transition from S to C. Notice that once in $B_1$ (the last benign failure in the crossing of a failure region), the program may move to another success, or it may enter another failure region: this is modelled by the series of downward arcs issuing from $B_1$, labelled $p_{sb}p_1$, $p_{sb}p_2$, $p_{sb}p_3$, etc. The probabilities on these arcs are the same as those on the downward arcs issuing from S on the left: the probabilities of the trajectory entering a new failure region is independent of how long ago it left another failure region. This seems appropriate for a situation of sparse, small failure regions.

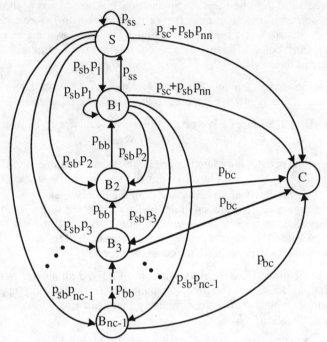

**Fig. 3.** The model for iterative executions with failure clustering

We point out that state C models a mission failure due either to staying in a failure region for at least $n_C$ iterations, or to a catastrophic failure. A third cause for mission failure is crossing two or more failure regions without interruption, so that the *total* number of consecutive benign failures exceeds $n_C$-1. In solving the models we neglected this kind of events but developed an analysis (detailed in [19]) to verify whether this simplification is acceptable with given values of the parameters.

**Probability of completing a mission.** The positive correlation between successive iterations affects the probability of completing a mission in two ways: through the probability of having $n_C$ consecutive benign failures, and through the longer stays in failure regions. Inside failure regions we also assume an increased probability of catastrophic failures. Assuming that the random variables $X_i$ represent the state of the system at time steps $i = 0,1,2,...$, and the initial state of the system is S, i.e. $P(X_0 = S) = 1$, we can use the expression:

$$P(\text{mission success}) = \prod_{i=1}^{n} P(X_i \neq C \mid X_{i-1} \neq C).$$

Where each term in the product has the form: $P(X_i \neq C \mid X_{i-1} \neq C) =$

$$= (1 - p_{sc}) + (p_{sc} - p_{bc}) * P(X_{i-1} = B_2 \text{ or..or } X_{i-1} = B_{n_c-1}|X_{i-1} \neq C) -$$

$$-p_{nn} * p_{sb} * (1 - P(X_{i-1} = B_2 \text{ or..or } X_{i-1} = B_{n_c-1}|X_{i-1} \neq C)).$$

We observe that the first term in this sum represents the case that series of benign failures do not affect the probability of mission failure. The second term is the contribution of the higher (or lower, as the case might be) probability of catastrophic failure after a benign failure, compared to that after a successful iteration. The third term is the probability of mission failure due to series of $n_c$ or more failures.

**Performability.** The expected total reward is affected by: 1) the number of benign failures, 2) the increased probability of catastrophic failure, if $p_{bc} > p_{sc}$, and 3) mission failures due to series of $n_c$ or more benign failures.

Our model is not tied to any specific distribution of the length of stays in failure regions. There is no basis for choosing one distribution function as generally valid, so we show the effects of four plausible distributions, plus two distributions $f$ and $g$ representing extreme cases (a more complete discussion is in [20]):

- geometric distribution, $p_i = q * (1-q)^{i-1}, i = 1,2,3,..., q \in (0,1]$;

- modified Poisson distribution, $p_i = \dfrac{e^{-\alpha} * \alpha^{i-1}}{(i-1)!}, i = 1,2,3,....,  \alpha > 0$ ;

- modified negative binomial, $p_i = \binom{i+r-2}{r-1} * q^r * (1-q)^{i-1}, i = 1,2,3,...,$ with $q \in (0,1]$ and r=1,2,3,.. (we use r=5);

- an *ad-hoc* distribution for square-shaped failure regions defined as: $p_i = \dfrac{i+1}{3i-1} * p_L(i) + \sum_{j=i+1}^{maxL} \dfrac{2}{3j-1} * p_L(j)$, with i=1,2,3,.., where: the truncated-geometric distributed variable $p_L(j)$ is the probability that a failure region has side length equal to j, $2 \leq j \leq maxL$, and maxL is set to 30;

- distribution function $g$, defined as $\sum_{i=1}^{n_c-2} g(i) = 0$, with $g(n_c - 1) = 1 - p_{nn}$ and $\sum_{i>n_c-1} g(i) = p_{nn}$: the input trajectory, once in a failure region, stays in it for at least $(n_c - 1)$ iterations;

- $f$, defined as $f(1) = 1 - p_{nn}$, with $\sum_{i=2}^{n_c-1} f(i) = 0$, and $\sum_{i>n_c-1} f(i) = p_{nn}$: once in a failure region, the trajectory may either exit immediately (after one benign failure) or else stay in it for at least $n_c$ iterations.

## 5.2 Evaluation and Discussion

We show the results for the probability of mission failure $P[C_n]$ and the performability $E[M_n]$ with the distributions described above for the length of stays in failure regions. The other parameters (Table 5) are set consistently with the analysis of SCOP in Section 3.

**Table 5.** Parameter values as derived from the previous evaluation of SCOP

| Parameters | values | |
|---|---|---|
| $p_{sb} = 5 \cdot 10^{-5}$ | $p_{bc} = 10^{-4}$ | **(notice that** |
| $p_{sc} = 3 \cdot 10^{-9}$ | $p_{bb} = 1 - p_{bc}$ | **$p_{bc} \gg p_{sc}$)** |
| $p_{ss} = 1 - p_{sb} - p_{sc}$ | $n_c = 10$ | |
| | $n = 1025523$ | |

The two main factors affecting the probability of mission failure and the per-formability are 1) the probability $p_{nn}$ of series of $n_c$ or more failures, and 2) the mean length of stay in a failure region, once the input trajectory enters it. We plot our results as a function of these two factors, keeping all the others constant.

Figs. 4.a and 4.b show our dependability measures as functions of $p_{nn}$, in the range $[0, 10^{-3}]$. Higher values would imply excessive probabilities of mission failure. In the case of independence, $p_{nn}=1.36 \cdot 10^{-39}$ and $P[C_t]=0.00336$. A few remarks follow:

1) $f$ shows better figures than $g$ because we set $p_{bc} > p_{sc}$. Moreover, increasing $n_c$ increases the difference between their probabilities of mission failure;

2) as expected, the curves for the four "plausible" distributions are all enclosed between those of $f$ and $g$; their distance from $f$ depends on the mean duration of stay in the failure regions (and on the difference $p_{bc} - p_{sc}$);

3) the value of $p_{sb}$ determines the slope of the curves; increasing $p_{sb}$ increases the probability of entering a failure region and hence probability of mission failure;

4) $f$ and $g$ give bounds on the probability of mission failure and the performability, allowing simple tests on the viability of a specific design, given only an esti-mate of $p_{nn}$.

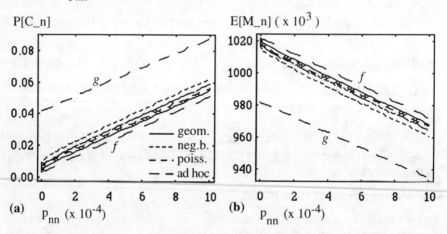

**Fig. 4.** Probability of mission failure (a) and performability (b) as a function of $p_{nn}$, the probability of $n_c$ or more consecutive failures once in a failure region

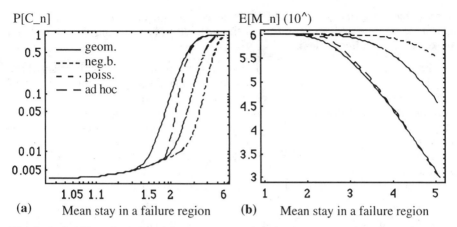

**Fig. 5.** Probability of mission failure (a) and performability (b) as a function of the mean duration of stay in a failure region

Figs. 5.a and 5.b show our dependability measures as functions of the mean stay in a failure region. We observe that, for a given mean, distributions with higher variance cause worse behaviour. The range of parameter values shown extends to unrealistic situations: with such values, our plots show that, to obtain probabilities of mission failure up to $10^{-1}$, the mean stay in failure regions must be limited to 2-3 steps.

## 6    Conclusions

We have applied an evaluation method, previously proposed by other authors, to the SCOP adaptive software fault tolerance scheme. SCOP, by delaying the execution of some variants until it is made necessary by errors, has not only a lower run-time cost than N-version programming with the same number of variants, but also a shorter response time due to a lower synchronisation overhead. The probabilities of failure per execution are the same as in NVP. With respect to RBs, SCOP allows good error detection in applications where satisfactory acceptance tests are not available, while keeping the advantage of delaying redundant executions whenever possible, which gives it a performance and performability edge over NVP. This kind of modelling can indicate bounds on the usability of the different schemes for software fault tolerance, subject to assumptions about the model parameters. Rough estimates of the probability of failure per execution, performability measures, response time, run-time cost can together help a designer in a first choice of schemes for a design. The reward model for performability is easily changed as appropriate for different applications.

All applications of mathematical modelling have the problem that attempting to describe in more detail the behaviour of a system increases the number of parameters to be estimated, the difficulty of estimating them, and the difficulty of validating the model; assumptions that make a model mathematically tractable make it less realistic. We have discussed these limits in our context, considering the diverse problems in modelling fault-tolerant software. A more complete model than used here, with more degrees of freedom, would be useful, with appropriate computer support, for exploring how different, non-intuitive assumptions affect the probabilities of the different outcomes. For estimating reliability or performability as done here, however, the parameters needed regarding each execution are just the probabilities of success and detected or undetected failure: the imprecision introduced to keep a tractable model of repeated executions, and the difficulty of estimating the parameters, make further detailing useless.

We have then explored issues related to *sequences* of failures of iterative software. We have proposed a model in which both dependencies among input values of successive iterations and the effects of sequences of consecutive failures are taken into account. The proposed model can accommodate different distributions of the length of stays in failure regions. We have considered a few such distributions and shown their effects on the dependability figures analysed. The main factors are the probability of exceeding a given number of consecutive failures and the mean length of stay in failure regions. We have defined two extreme distributions, which produce upper and lower bounds for the figures derived from all the other distributions.

A further step would be a white-box model of the execution (i.e., a model showing the interplay of variants and adjudicators in each execution, as we used in the first part of this paper), incorporating the aspects of failure clustering modelled in our black-box model. Such a model would describe the effects of assumptions about rather subtle phenomena, like the relative positions and sizes of the failure regions (of the different variants) with respect to their common input trajectories. We are now studying the possibility of building useful models with these characteristics.

# Validation of Ultra-High Dependability for Software-based Systems*

Bev Littlewood[1]  Lorenzo Strigini[2]

[1]City University        [2]IEI-CNR

**Abstract** Modern society depends on computers for a number of critical tasks in which failure can have very high costs. As a consequence, high levels of dependability (reliability, safety, etc.) are required from such computers, including their software. Whenever a quantitative approach to risk is adopted, these requirements must be stated in quantitative terms, and a rigorous demonstration of their being attained is necessary. For software used in the most critical roles, such demonstrations are not usually supplied. The fact is that the dependability requirements often lie near the limit of the current state of the art, or beyond, in terms not only of the ability to satisfy them, but also, and more often, of the ability to demonstrate that they are satisfied in the individual operational products (validation). We discuss reasons why such demonstrations *cannot* usually be provided with the means available: reliability growth models, testing with stable reliability, structural dependability modelling, as well as more informal arguments based on good engineering practice. We state some rigorous arguments about the limits of what can be validated with each of such means. Combining evidence from these different sources would seem to raise the levels that can be validated; yet this improvement is not such as to solve the problem. It appears that engineering practice must take into account the fact that no solution exists, at present, for the validation of ultra-high dependability in systems relying on complex software.

## 1    Introduction

Computers are used in an increasing number of applications where their failure may be very costly, in terms of monetary loss and/or human suffering. Examples include control of aircraft, industrial plants, railway and air traffic, weapons and military units, banking and commercial transactions. To reduce the cost to society of operating these computer-controlled systems, dependability requirements for their essential computers are often very high. The most frequently quoted requirement is probably that of less than $10^{-9}$ "catastrophic failure conditions" per hour of operation (excluding software faults) in civil transport airplanes [42]; in the U.S. Federal Aviation Administration's Advanced Automation System (for air traffic control), one of the key computer systems has a required total unavailability of less than $10^{-7}$, or 3 seconds per year; a safety-critical processor for urban trains must fail with a probability of less than $10^{-12}$ per hour. We shall call these levels of dependability 'ultra-high', for brevity: we are talking about levels that are unusually high, and obviously very difficult to achieve.

The main problem with achieving such levels of dependability is the possibility of subtle design faults. This problem is common to all complex systems, but the

---

* This paper is a condensed version of [87].

prevalence of software technology for the production of very complex, digital systems has made it predominantly felt in the software field. Most of the following discussion, therefore, refers directly to 'software', although it is applicable in a more general scope.

Software dependability is well known to be a serious problem. Whereas a mechanical engineer can to some degree decide the reliability of a part whilst designing it (within a certain range of technologically feasible values) by setting design and manufacturing parameters, a software designer (and therefore any designer of computer-based systems) has very little ability to plan the dependability of a product. Among the reasons for this are: i) software failures are due to design faults, which are difficult both to avoid and to tolerate; ii) software is often used to implement radically new systems, which cannot benefit much from knowledge acquired from previous, successful designs; and iii) digital systems in general implement discontinuous input-to-output mappings intractable by simple mathematical modelling. This last point is particularly important: continuity assumptions cannot be used in validating software, and failures are caused by the occurrence of specific, non-obvious *combinations* of events, rather than from excessive levels of some identifiable stress factor.

Given this common unsatisfactory state of the art, adding the requirement of dependability levels that are at the boundary of what is known to be attainable, or beyond, evidently creates a very serious problem.

These ultra-high levels of dependability would also be difficult to attain in a system built purely in hardware. It is true that we now have means of capturing the statistical properties of component life-times, and the effect that component unreliability has on overall system reliability. We know how to employ simple redundancy schemes to obtain high overall system reliability from relatively unreliable components. However, these methods ignore the effects of design faults. Thus the 'solution' we sometimes hear to the software problem - 'build it in hardware instead' - is usually no solution at all. The problem of design dependability arises because the *complexity* of the systems is so great that we cannot simply postulate the absence of design faults, and concentrate on the conventional hardware reliability evaluation. Apart from the increased complexity that may arise from *implementing* functions in software (think of a software-based thermostat switch vs a mechanical one using a bi-metallic strip), if the *functionality* required implies a similar complexity in both cases, a 'purely hardware' system version may be as difficult to validate as a software-based version.

It could be argued here, in favour of the 'hardware solution', that the discipline of building a system purely in hardware might serve as a constraint upon complexity and thus contribute to greater design dependability. The price paid, of course, would be a reduction in functionality. However, the tendency seems to be to move in the opposite direction: to implement as much as possible of the functionality in software, sometimes with an intent to reduce the 'hardware' unreliability (besides producing other benefits, such as ease of modification). Ideally such trade-offs would be made quantitatively, but this is rare. Even when it is reasonable to use software to overcome the reliability limitations of a hardware solution, a decision often follows to take advantage of the use of software to build a *more* complex product, providing more desirable functionality but at the risk of lower design dependability. This tendency to exploit the versatility of software-based systems, at the expense of greater complexity, is understandable in many routine, low-risk applications, but questionable in the safety-critical area.

The problems posed by the procurement of computers with ultra-high dependability requirements are of three kinds:

- *specifying* the dependability requirements: selecting the dependability goals (requirements) that have to be pursued in building the computing system, based on known or assumed goals for the part of the world that is directly affected by the computing system;

- designing and implementing the computing system so as to *achieve* the dependability required. This can be very difficult, as we shall see later;

- *validating*: gaining confidence that a certain dependability goal (requirement) has been attained. This is a problem of *evaluation*.

This paper is mainly about this final problem. More particularly, we want to investigate the limits to the levels of dependability that can currently be validated. Our premise is that it is unreasonable to exempt software from quantitative reliability requirements, whenever dependability and risk are otherwise treated in a quantitative fashion; then, there should be an obligation to convincingly and rigorously demonstrate that such requirements are satisfied. For complex software, there is an often voiced fear that we are now building systems with such high dependability requirements that, even if they were satisfied, they cannot be validated with present methods, or even with all foreseeable methods. Without pretending to give a definitive view, we review the current situation, presenting some rigorous arguments about the limits of current methods.

## 2      Specification of Dependability Requirements

The goal of very high dependability in a computer that is a part of a larger system is to help attain some dependability goal for that larger system. Requirements for the computer are then derived from a dependability analysis for the larger system. For instance, to assess the safety of a new industrial plant, we would ideally build a model where the dependability figures for the computers are parameters. Then, to estimate the effect of the dependability of the computer on the safety of the plant, we need an understanding both of the internal operation of the computer (to assess the probabilities of different failure modes) and of the interactions between the computer and the rest of the plant (to know the probabilities that different computer failures will cause failures or accidents). The latter analysis, done before the computer is designed, yields the dependability requirements for the computer system.

Not all critical computing systems have explicit numerical requirements of very high dependability. In some cases, the application of computers started before the attendant risks were clearly perceived, so that no need was felt for special requirements. Military systems often have lower safety requirements than similar, civil applications, since there is a trade-off between safety from enemy action, which is largely based on technological sophistication, and safety against faults of the system itself, which would instead require simple, conservative designs. In certain proposed applications, such as robotic surgery, the human activity that the computer system is replacing is known to be quite failure-prone, so that a moderately dependable robot would often reduce the current level of risk, by among other things allowing intervention in situations where human surgeons could not act.

How exactly it is appropriate to express dependability requirements will vary from one application to another. Some examples are:

- *Rate of occurrence of failures* (ROCOF): appropriate in a system which actively controls some potentially dangerous process;
- *Probability of failure on demand*: suitable for a 'safety' system, which is only called upon to act when *another* system gets into a potentially unsafe condition. An example is an emergency shut-down system for a nuclear reactor;
- *Probability of failure-free survival of mission*. This makes sense in circumstances where there is a 'natural' mission time;
- *Availability*. This could be used in circumstances where the amount of loss incurred as a result of system failure depends on the length of time the system is unavailable. An airline reservation system, or a telephone switch, would clearly have availability requirements.

These examples are by no means exhaustive: for example, the *mean time to failure* (or *between failures*) is still widely used. They are meant to show that selecting an appropriate way of expressing a dependability requirement is a non-trivial task. The measures above are obviously interdependent, and the selection of a particular one, or more, is a matter of judgment. For example, in the case of an air traffic control system, it would be wise to consider the precise way in which unavailability might show itself: infrequent long outages are probably less dangerous than frequent short ones, or simply than certain kinds of incorrect output. It might be better to be also concerned, therefore, with the *rate* of incidents rather than just their contribution to total down time. In the case of flight-control avionics, the probability of safety-related failure is highest at take-off and landing, so that it may be sensible to express the requirement in terms of a probability of a failure-free flight: i.e. as a rate per flight rather than a rate per hour.

In what follows we shall be less concerned with the way in which dependability requirements should be expressed than with the actual numerical levels, and whether we can reasonably expect to be able to say that a certain level has been achieved in a particular case.

Clearly, validating some of the required reliability levels presents formidable problems: some are several orders of magnitude beyond the state of the art. However, that should not be taken to mean that such numbers for required dependability are *meaningless*. The aforementioned requirement for critical avionic systems of $10^{-9}$ failures per hour represents a probability of about 0.1 that at least one such failure will occur in a fleet of 1000 aircraft over a 30 year lifetime [94]; since this safety-critical system is likely to be one of many on the aircraft, such a probability does not seem an unreasonable requirement.

# 3    Reliability Growth Modelling

The most mature techniques for software dependability assessment are those for modelling the growth in software reliability that takes place as a result of fault removal. There is now an extensive body of literature together with some considerable experience of these techniques in industrial practice, and it is now often possible to obtain measures of the operational reliability of a program.

We shall consider here the direct evaluation of the reliability of a software product from observation of its actual failure process during operation. This is the problem of *reliability growth*: in its simplest form it is assumed that when a failure occurs there is an attempt to remove the design fault which caused the failure, whereupon the software is set running again, eventually to fail once again. The successive times of failure-free working are the input to probabilistic reliability growth models, which use these data to estimate the current reliability of the program under study, and to predict how the reliability will change in the future.

Many detailed models exist, purporting to represent the stochastic failure process. Unfortunately, no single model can be trusted to give accurate results in all circumstances, nor is there any way for choosing *a priori* the most suitable model for a particular situation. Recent work, however, has largely resolved this difficulty [1]. We can now apply many of the available models to the failure data coming from a particular product, analyse the predictive accuracy of different models, and gradually learn which (if any) of the different predictions can be trusted.

Some warnings apply here:
- successful predictions depend upon the observed failure process being similar to that which it is desired to predict: the techniques are essentially sophisticated forms of extrapolation. In particular, if we wish to predict the operational reliability of a program from failure data obtained during testing, the selected test cases must be representative (statistically) of the inputs during operational use. This is not always easy, but there is some experience of it being carried out in realistic industrial conditions, with the test-based predictions validated in later operational use [35].
- although we often speak loosely of the reliability of a software product, we really mean the reliability of the product working in a particular environment: the perceived reliability will vary considerably from one user to another. It is a truism, for example, that operating system reliability differs greatly from one site to another. It is not currently possible to test a program in one environment (i.e., with a given selection of test cases) and use the reliability growth modelling techniques to predict how reliable it will be in another. This may be possible in the future but we currently do not even know how to characterize the 'stress' of a software system's environment so that we could relate one to another.

With these reservations, it is now possible to obtain accurate reliability predictions for software in many cases and, perhaps equally importantly, to know when particular predictions can be trusted. Unfortunately, such methods are really only suitable for the assurance of relatively modest reliability goals. The following example, although it refers to modest reliability levels, will serve to illustrate the difficulties related to ultra-high levels.

Table 1 shows a simple analysis of some failure data from the testing of a command and control system, using a software reliability growth model. The question 'how reliable is the program now?' is answered immediately following the 40th, 50th, . . , 130th failures, in the form, (in this case) of a *mean time to next failure*. Alongside the mttf in the table is the total execution time on test that was needed to achieve that estimated mttf. Clearly, the mttf of this system (and hence its reliability) improves as the testing progresses. However, the final column shows a clear *law of diminishing returns*: later improvements in the mttf require proportionally longer testing.

**Table 1** An illustration of the law of diminishing returns in heroic debugging. Here the total execution time required to reach a particular mean time to failure is compared with the mean itself.

| sample size, $i$ | elapsed time, $t_i$ | achieved mttf, $m_i$ | $t_i/m_i$ |
|---|---|---|---|
| 40 | 6380 | 288.8 | 22.1 |
| 50 | 10089 | 375.0 | 26.9 |
| 60 | 12560 | 392.5 | 32.0 |
| 70 | 16186 | 437.5 | 37.0 |
| 80 | 20567 | 490.4 | 41.9 |
| 90 | 29361 | 617.3 | 47.7 |
| 100 | 42015 | 776.3 | 54.1 |
| 110 | 49416 | 841.6 | 58.7 |
| 120 | 56485 | 896.4 | 63.0 |
| 130 | 74364 | 1054.1 | 70.1 |

Of course, this is only a single piece of evidence, involving a particular measure of reliability, the use of a particular model to perform the calculations, and a particular program under study. However, this law of diminishing returns has been observed consistently in our own work, and the reasons are not hard to see.

A plausible conceptual model of the software failure process is as follows. A program starts life with a finite number of faults, and these are encountered in a purely unpredictable fashion. Different faults contribute differently to the overall unreliability of the program: some are 'larger' than others, i.e., they would show themselves (if not removed) at a larger *rate*. Thus different faults have different rates of occurrence.

Suppose we adopt a policy of carrying out fixes at each failure, and assume for simplicity that each fix attempt is successful. As debugging progresses, a fault with a larger rate will tend to show itself before a fault with a smaller rate: large faults get removed earlier than small ones. Hence the law of diminishing returns. As debugging progresses and the program becomes more reliable, it becomes harder to find faults (because the rate at which the *program* is failing is becoming smaller), and the improvements to the reliability resulting from these fault-removals are also becoming smaller and smaller. Some dramatic evidence for this interpretation was found in data about some large systems [2], where about one third of the faults only caused errors at the rate of about once every *5000 years* of execution.

It should be noted that these limits to the confidence we can gain from a reliability growth study are not due to inadequacies of the models. Rather they are a consequence of the relative paucity of the information available. If we want to have an assurance of high dependability, using only information obtained from the failure process, then we need to observe the system for a very long time. No improvement in the predictive accuracy of reliability growth modelling will be able to overcome this inherent difficulty.

Let us now return to the assumption that it is possible to fix a fault when it has been revealed during the test, *and to know that the fix is successful*. In fact, there has been no serious attempt to model the fault-fixing operation and most reliability growth models simply assume that fixes are perfect, or average out any short-term reversals to give the longer term trend. It is fairly easy to incorporate the possibility of a purely ineffectual fix (simply introduce an extra parameter representing the probability that an attempted fix leaves the reliability unchanged), but the more realistic situation in which an attempted fix introduces a *novel* fault seems much harder and has not been studied to any great extent. For a safety-critical application, this source of inaccuracy cannot be ignored, as the potential increase in unreliability due to a bad fix is unbounded. In order to have high confidence that the reliability after a fix was even as high as it was immediately prior to the last failure, it would be necessary to have high confidence that no new fault had been introduced. The only way to obtain this confidence seems to be to exercise the software for a long time and never see a failure arise from the fix. Eventually, of course, as the software runs failure-free after this fix, one would acquire confidence in the efficacy of the fix, and thus (taken with the earlier evidence) of the program as a whole. The question of what can be concluded from a period of failure-free working since the last fix is one we shall now consider in some detail.

## 4    Inferences to be Drawn from Perfect Working

For safety-critical software, it could be argued that acceptance of a product should only be based on the evidence gathered during testing. For the purposes of this analysis, let us ignore possible reservations about whether this testing is representative of operational use. If the software was tested without failure (the 'best news' it is possible to obtain from operational testing alone) for, let us say, 1000 hours, how confident can one be about its future performance, and therefore its suitability for use in a safety-critical application?

Let the random variable $T$ represent the time to next failure of the program under examination, and let us assume that this program has been on test for a period $t_O$, during which no failures have occurred. Let us assume that the distribution of $T$ is exponential with rate $\lambda$, and so has mean time to failure $\theta = \lambda^{-1}$. These assumptions are plausible, since we are interested only in the time to the first failure, and so do not need to be concerned about problems such as possible dependence between faults, one fault 'hiding' another, etc. In fact it is useful to think of the sequence of failures as a Poisson process, even though we shall only be interested in the first event.

There are classical approaches to this problem giving, for example, confidence bounds on parameters such as the probability of failure on demand [102]. However, we believe that the Bayesian approach is more satisfactory since it provides a single subjective probability figure about the *event* of interest, not merely a parameter. Details are in the Appendix, where it is shown that the posterior reliability function is

$$R(t \mid \text{no failures in time } t_o) \equiv P(T > t \mid \text{data}) = \left( \frac{b + t_0}{b + t_0 + t} \right)^a ,$$

where $a$ and $b$ are parameters that represent the 'prior belief' of the observer about the parameter $\lambda$. Clearly, $a$ and $b$ will depend upon the nature of the knowledge this observer has, so it is not possible to say anything specific here about the values they take. However, in the Appendix we see how it is possible to model an observer who comes to this problem with a special kind of 'complete ignorance'. In this case

$$R(t \mid \text{no failures in time } t_o) = t_o / (t + t_o)$$

When we have seen a period $t_o$ of failure-free working there is a 50:50 chance that we shall wait a further period exceeding $t_o$ until the first failure, since $R(t_o \mid 0, t_o) = {}^1/_2$. It follows that if we want the posterior median time to failure to be, e.g., $10^9$ hours, and we do not bring any prior belief to the problem, we would need to see $10^9$ hours of failure-free working!

The full Bayesian analysis shows clearly the two sources of final confidence in the system dependability: i) the prior belief of the observer (represented by the prior distribution, Gam(a, b)); and ii) the likelihood function representing what was actually observed of the system failure behaviour. The relative paucity of information we can gain from the latter suggests that, to obtain an assurance of very high dependability, an observer must start with very strong *a priori* beliefs. In the Appendix we give an example where, if we require a median time to failure of $10^6$, and are only prepared to test for $10^3$, we essentially need to *start* with the belief in the $10^6$ median.

We have treated this example in some detail because it shows the great gap that exists between the levels of dependability that are often required for a safety-critical system, and that which can feasibly be learned from observation of system behaviour. Certainly it is possible to quibble about the details of how we represent prior ignorance, but such quibbles cannot remove this gap of *several orders of magnitude*.

It is also worth noting that, although we have preferred a Bayesian approach, the conclusions of this section remain the same if a classical view of probability is adopted. Unless the Bayesian brings *extremely* strong prior beliefs to the problem (and these must, of course, have a scientific foundation), both approaches will generally give results that agree to within an order of magnitude. We shall now discuss how sufficiently strong prior beliefs could be justified.

# 5   Other Sources of Evidence for Validation

Products with very high design reliability do exist, as demonstrated by the statistics collected during the operational use of very many copies. These include some products containing complex software. For example, the Bell system telephone switches in the U.S. reportedly satisfied (before the large outage on the 15th of January, 1990) the requirement of 3 minutes maximum down-time per year [47].

Is it possible to have justified confidence in such extremely successful operation *before* observing it in real use? More precisely, can we identify factors that increase our confidence in a system beyond that which we can realistically gain just from direct testing?

For non-software engineering, there are such factors that help build confidence in this way. First, the design methods used are well tested *and* based on a well understood theory for predicting system behaviour. Following this accepted practice in the design of a novel system makes it more credible that design errors are avoided. However, additional sources of trust are needed and in fact exist.

For example, systems can be over-engineered to cope with circumstances that are more stressful than will occur in operation. Such systems can then be expected to have high dependability in an environment that is merely normally stressful. Of course, arguments of this kind depend upon a basic continuity of the system model, and identifiable stress factors, which are both normally lacking in software. Another example is the common practice of building prototypes which can be debugged extensively. When the operational testing of the prototype is over, there is increased confidence that all relevant design flaws have been exposed. When very high reliability is required, additional design principles can be applied, to guarantee better understanding of the product's behaviour. Among these are:

- step-wise evolution: new designs contain as little change as possible with respect to previous, trusted designs;
- simple design, to avoid errors born of complexity. Although designs cannot be simplified arbitrarily (some minimum level of complexity is dictated by each application's requirements), a general attitude of privileging simplicity in all design decisions improves confidence in the resulting design.

These aids can also be used to obtain confidence in software designs, though usually to a lower extent, as we shall argue in the rest of this section.

## 5.1 Past Experience with Similar Products, or Products of the Same Process

A new product is usually considered more trustworthy if based on 'proven' technologies or design method. This can be stated more rigorously as a statistical argument. The product is considered as an element of a larger population, whose statistical properties are reasonably well-known: this population may be that

- of 'similar' products for which sufficient operational experience exists;
- of products developed by the same organization, or using similar methods (process-based arguments).

We may be interested in forecasting the dependability of a new design, or of a new instance of a design (say an individual installation of a computer system). In the former case, we can use experience with samples of products built using other, similar designs; in the latter, we can use experience with other instances of the same design. Two separate sources of error are present in such forecasts: i) inaccuracy caused by inference from the sample rather than the whole population; ii) uncertainty as to whether the population from which the sample has been drawn actually includes the new product that is being evaluated: there may be some important aspect of the new product which has not been seen before. Such statistical arguments can only be applied, therefore, when there is a high degree of similarity between the old products and the new one.

It is thus a commonly accepted belief that the risk that a new product will behave in ways unforeseen by the designer increases with the degree of novelty of the design.

Unfortunately, for software we do not have a clear understanding of how perceived differences between two products should affect our expectations.There are obvious *factors* of similarity (application, developing organization, methods and tools used), but for evaluation we would need a convincing *measure* of similarity. No such measure exists. In our case, we would like to be able to measure the degree of similarity of software development processes, of the resulting software products, and even of the underlying problems that the products are being created to solve. Would it be reasonable to assume, for example, that building an auto-land system is similar to building a fly-by-wire system? And if so, what is the degree of similarity?

Even if we can resolve these difficulties so that the statistical model can be used, we still face the problem of the amount of evidence available, and the results are rather disappointing. Consider, for example, the question: how much can we trust a particular product if it is the output of a methodology that has *always* been 'successful' in the past? can we assume that the present application of the methodology has been successful?

The problem is formally stated, with some loss of realism, as follows. The applications of the methodology to each new development are independent trials, with the same probability $p$ of success (i.e., compliance of the product with our ultra-high reliability requirements, whatever they are). Then, if we start with prior ignorance about $p$, our posterior expectation about $p$, after observing $n$ successes out of $n$ trials, would be [84]:

$$E(p \mid n \text{ successes in n trials}) = (n+1)/(n+2).$$

With the usual small values of $n$, there is a significant probability that the next application of the methodology will not be 'successful', i.e., it will not achieve ultra-high operational reliability.

If, on the other hand, we could bring to the problem a prior belief that $p$ were very small, the posterior belief would be correspondingly strong. However, in such a case the additional confidence to be gained from an additional, successful trial would not be significant.

The assumptions that go into this result can, of course, be challenged in detail. However, this formal analysis at least captures the magnitude of the difficulty facing us. In fact, the assumptions are probably optimistic. For example the 'similarity' assumption is likely to be violated. Also, it must be admitted that, for most software development methodologies, there is little quantitative evidence of 'success' in the sense indicated: hence the 'prior ignorance' analysis seems the most appropriate one. The history of Software Engineering is strewn with very strong claims for the efficacy of particular methodologies, which, in the formalism used here, would be represented by large prior probabilities of success. However, these claims are not usually supported by much evidence, and we do not believe that such strong prior beliefs can usually be justified. In conclusion, claims about the dependability of a product, based solely upon the efficacy of the development methodology used, must be justified by formal analysis of statistical evidence: at this stage, only modest claims can be supported.

## 5.2 Structural Reliability Modelling

Structural reliability models allow one to deduce the overall dependability of a product from the dependability figures of its parts. This method has given good results as a design aid to obtain high dependability in mechanical and electronic systems . A model is built to describe the effects of the behaviours of individual parts on the whole product, and reliability data for the individual parts (obtained at lower cost than would be needed for the whole system, possibly from use of the same modules in previous products) can be used to estimate the parameters of the model. Thus it can be argued that the reliability goal has been attained, without a statistical test of the product.

Structural modelling has obvious limitations with respect to design faults, and software in particular. It relies on the correctness of the model used, which is often directly derived from the design itself. Thus a Markov model of software execution will typically assume transitions among executions of different modules to be as planned by the designer, so neglecting certain categories of typical errors, e.g., upsets in the flow of control, or omissions in the specification. In addition, the probabilities to be used as parameters are difficult to estimate.

In the context of ultra-high reliability, one important aspect of structural modelling is its application to modelling fault tolerance obtained through design diversity [11]. Here, two or more versions are developed by different teams in the hope that faults will tend to be different and so failures can be masked by a suitable adjudication mechanism at run time. The concept owes much to the hardware redundancy idea, where several similar components are in parallel. In the hardware analogy, it is sometimes reasonable to assume that the stochastic failure processes of the different components in a parallel configuration are *independent*. It is then easy to show that a system of arbitrarily high reliability can be constructed from unreliable components.

In practice, of course, the independence assumption is often unreasonable: components tend to fail together as a result of common environmental factors, for example. In the case of design diversity, the independence assumption is unwarranted: recent experiments [4, 71, 17] suggest that design diversity does bring an increase in reliability compared with single versions, but this increase is much less than what completely independent failure behaviour would imply. One reason for this is the similarity of errors in the construction of more than one version. Another reason [86] is that, even if the different versions really are independent objects (defined in a plausible, precise fashion), they will still fail dependently as a result of variation of the 'intrinsic hardness' of the problem over the input space. Put simply, the failure of version A on a particular input suggests that this is a 'difficult' input, and thus the probability that version B will also fail on the same input is greater than it otherwise would be. The greater this variation of 'difficulty' over the input space, the greater will be the dependence in the observed failure behaviour of versions.

Since we cannot *assume* independence of failure behaviour for component versions, reliability models for fault-tolerant software must take into account failure dependency between diverse software variants. The degree of dependence must be estimated for each particular case. Trying to measure it directly from the operational behaviour of the system would lead us back to the 'black-box' estimation problem that has already defeated us [94]. If we wish to estimate it indirectly, via evidence of the degrees of version dependence obtained from previous projects, we are once more in the same difficulties we have seen earlier: past experience of successfully achieving low version dependence does not allow us to conclude that we shall be almost certain to succeed in the present instance.

## 5.3  Proofs and Formal Methods

There are many roles that formal methods may play in the implementation and validation of highly dependable software. Some of the techniques that have been labelled 'formal methods' are merely particular examples of software development process, such as we have considered earlier: formal specification techniques are an example. Perhaps the most important aspect of formal methods for ultra-high dependability concerns the notion of proof.

There are at least two important applications of proofs. One can prove that a design has certain properties: a protocol is deadlock-free, for example, or a given output will only be produced if there is consensus between two modules. Such properties can be used to simplify the task of dependability evaluation. Secondly, it is possible to prove that there is consistency between different stages in the evolution of the product from (formal) specification to final implementation.

There are two problems with proofs [13]. Firstly, proofs are subject to error: direct human error, in proofs by hand or with the aid of semiautomatic tools, and/or error by the proof-producing software in machine proof. In principle, one could assign a failure probability to proofs, and use this in a probabilistic analysis. In practice, such probabilities would be quite difficult to assign, and to incorporate into a dependability evaluation. Even if we knew that a given proof were erroneous, we would not know anything about the true state of things, which might range from a very high to a very low failure rate.

We believe that this problem of error in proof can be greatly reduced by improvements in techniques. However, a more fundamental second problem would remain. Proofs apply to some formal description of the product (a design at some stage of refinement, typically) and its environment rather than to the product itself in the real world. This is well known in non-software engineering, where design margins can be employed to guard against inadequacies of the formal model: all the uncertainties in the mapping of the design into reality are lumped into an additional stress. The difficulty with trying to do something similar for software-based systems is, of course, that the notion of stress is less well defined, and may sometimes not be definable. Indeed, for those macroscopic phenomena that are known to behave as 'stress' (load in operating systems, for example), there is no clear understanding of the exact nature of their impact on the behaviour of computers. Thus, the so-called 'stress testing' of software is at best seen much more as an aid in debugging than as a means of dependability evaluation. This problem of possible mismatch between the model and reality is not helped by formal methods (although they can help in clarifying the implications of the top-level specifications), and will remain as a source of uncertainty. We believe that proofs may eventually give "practically complete" assurance about software developed for small, well-understood application problems, but the set of these problems is now empty and there is no way of foreseeing whether it will grow to be of some significance.

The issue of when a design is simple enough that it can be trusted to be fault-free based only on logical arguments about the design itself can be treated, again, as a peculiar kind of process-based argument. Convincing statistics about large populations of small, *similar* programs could be used to substantiate such claims, but this approach presents the difficulties discussed in Section 4.1.

## 5.4  Combination of Different Kinds of Evidence

We have seen how we can draw only quite weak conclusions from even extensive evidence of a product working without failure, or of a development process demonstrating its ability to produce highly dependable products. It is often the case that many such sources of evidence are available: for example, if a software product has been tested for a given time without failures, has been produced by a company with a long, successful experience in the same field, and uses design diversity in some critical parts, what can be concluded about its dependability? A problem with most attempts to argue that a product satisfies very strict dependability requirements is that information gained from different sources is combined in an informal, non rigorous, and often unconvincing manner.

This problem surfaces in many forms. It arises when discussing how to allocate resources between static analysis of software and dynamic testing. It arises when deciding whether to use new or older, more proven technology. For example, in some space applications, relatively old computers with low throughput and small memory are used. The limitation to old technology is not due solely to the small market available, but also to the slow certification process, meant to assure the dependability of these components. Arguably, faster CPUs and larger memories would allow more use of modern programming concepts, which do not emphasize thrifty use of memory and CPU cycles. Another example is the debate about using low-level or high-level languages in small, safety-critical systems. High-level languages offer the potential for fewer coding errors, but more dependence on compiler technology.

In all these cases, a project manager can control many variables known to affect the dependability of the final product, but varying one of them to improve the product's dependability also affects other variables so as to possibly, indirectly, *decrease* dependability. Without a clear, quantitative model of how all these variables contribute to the final result, it is difficult to make rational decisions to improve dependability (let alone to optimize it).

In principle, once again, a Bayesian approach can be applied to this problem. Assume that we know that a product was developed using a process that has shown itself to be successful on previous similar products, and a long operational test of the product shows no failures. Clearly, we would be more confident here than we would have been if we had only one of the two pieces of evidence. Moreover, we would have a clear, verifiable representation of how we gained this higher confidence. However, we would not be *very* much more confident. We have seen earlier that if we start with a reasonable prior belief and observe evidence for the efficacy of a process, our posterior belief will not be very strong. Now the latter is the belief we shall use as our prior before observing the test results on the particular product we have built. Such a prior, followed by evidence of failure-free working for a long time, will result in a posterior belief about the system dependability that is better than we obtained in an earlier section with the 'ignorance' prior, but it will not be a dramatic improvement.

## 5.5 Validation by Stepwise Improvement of a Product

In *conventional*, non-software, systems trust can often be built up by considering their history, if they are the product of a series of stepwise improvements. The designers of each new generation of product make only small improvements to the previous design. The small improvement typically implies the redesign of some part, in such a way that the overall system dependability is almost certainly not reduced and is likely to be improved. For example, if the motivation for the new design is to improve on the reliability of the previous one, the candidates for change are those parts that proved to be 'weak links' in the old design. The redesigned parts can be proven to be better than the old ones by normal testing techniques (including stress or accelerated testing, where considered trustworthy). Then a simple structural reliability model of the system allows one to conclude that improving the parts did improve the whole. A series of small improvements, each left in operation long enough to yield a convincing statistical record, *could* lead to trustworthy ultra-high dependability starting from a product with ordinary dependability.

Even for non-software systems, however, this conclusion is not always well-founded. For the above argument to be convincing, we need to be sure that the system behaviour can be described by well-behaved models, and there are reasons why this may not be the case. Reinforcing one part of a mechanical structure can sometimes redirect the strain to some other part that has not been designed to accept it. If the non-software system is sufficiently complex that there is a significant chance of the introduction of design faults during the stepwise 'improvements', we cannot assume increasing dependability. These remarks apply *a fortiori* to software itself, where there is evidence that for some large systems the reliability approaches an asymptote as the history of fixes becomes very long. There is uncertainty whether a particular fix will make things better or worse, and eventually a stage is reached where the expected reliability improvement from a fix is zero: we are as likely to reduce the reliability of the software as to improve it [2].

If the policy of stepwise improvement is to be convincing, at the very least designs must be kept such that the interactions among parts, and the effect of each part on global dependability, are simple and well-understood. Only then can validation by analysis and modelling of individual products be trusted. Two common applications of this principle are avoiding non-obvious error propagation paths (e.g. by physical separation of different software-implemented functions into separated hardware units, and, in multiprogrammed computers, by hardware protection of process memory); and building safety (or security) monitors as independent as possible of the main control systems.

In conclusion, evolutionary design practice is clearly desirable (when feasible), but it does not provide a *general* answer to the problem of assuring ultra-high dependability.

## 6    Discussion

A common theme underlying much of our discussion is that of the limitations of formal, mathematically tractable models. We describe reality by simplified models, suitable for the application of some rigorous (possibly probabilistic) reasoning technique. The validity of our results then depends on the validity of the modelling assumptions. There is always a chance that reality will violate some of these assumptions: we need to form an idea of the probability of this happening. Examples of such assumptions are:

- in reliability growth modelling: regularity of the growth process, and in particular, realism of the test data with respect to the intended operational environment;
- in process-based statistical arguments: representativeness of the new product with respect to the known population from which statistical extrapolations are made;
- in structural reliability modelling: correctness of the parameters, completeness of the model (e.g., independence assumptions, transitions in a Markov model, branches in a fault tree);
- in proofs of correctness: conformance of the specification to the informal engineering model.

Powell describes this issue (see III.C in this volume), as it arises normally in the design of fault-tolerant systems, in terms of *assumption coverage*. In a typical example, a designer can assume that only certain component failure modes are possible, such that they are provably (or with some known probability) tolerated by the fault-tolerance mechanisms in the system. By thus neglecting the possibility of some failures a simpler design becomes sufficient, requiring less computing time and less hardware, which of course tends to improve reliability. In evaluation, one can separately evaluate the probability of such an assumption actually holding, $P(A)$, and use it as a parameter in the expression of failure probability for the system. At the very least, one can obtain a conservative estimate by assuming that the system will fail whenever the assumption is violated.

In this example, the 'coverage' of the restrictive fault assumption, $P(A)$, can probably be estimated by tests on the individual components. Using the assumption in design is a 'divide and conquer' approach to attaining and proving the required dependability. This may prove more effective than designing to tolerate arbitrary, even very unlikely, faults. The important consideration here is that a rigorous mathematical argument can be used to choose one or the other approach. Of course, other assumptions underlie such an argument, e.g. a correct implementation of the design, so this way of reasoning does not by itself simplify the validation of ultra-high dependability. Its use is, rather, in providing a clear description of some sources of uncertainty in the evaluation. In the probabilistic terminology that we have used widely, we are expressing the high-level probability statements of dependability in terms of lower level probabilities: *conditional* probability statements about the system behaviour *assuming that* certain fault hypotheses are true, together with probability statements about the truth of these hypotheses.

The approach just outlined shows how considerations of validation can be taken into account rationally in the design process. Indeed, there *are* well-known principles of good design that can aid the system validation process. Absence of unnecessary complexity, reuse of tried and trusted designs with known dependability, an evolutionary rather than revolutionary approach to the creation of new products, separation of safety concerns, are all examples of known good practice not only for attaining high dependability levels, but for validating them as well. In particular, the separation of safety concerns has an important role: isolating safety-critical functions in (as near as possible) separate, simple subsystems simplifies safety evaluation; directing the analysis of a design specifically to look for dangerous failure modes (rather than for every deviation from the nominal required behaviour) may make the analysis less arduous and hence more trustworthy [79]. Such general principles are already part of many standards and of normal practice, although there are trends to the contrary, like the plans to integrate all avionic software in a few large computers per aircraft.

However, these methods do not solve the problem of obtaining *quantitative*, probabilistic statements about dangerous failures. The main point of our paper has been to try to show that here lies the main difficulty when we want to build a system with an ultra-high dependability requirement. Even if, by the adoption of the best design practices, we were to succeed in achieving such a dependability goal, it is our view that *we would not know of our achievement* at least until the product proved itself after a very great deal of operational use. Nor can we expect to overcome this problem with improved mathematical and statistical techniques. Rather, the problem is in the paucity of evidence: informally, in order to believe in these very high dependability levels we need more evidence than could reasonably be expected to be available. Work on the formalization of the combination of evidence obtained from different sources could help to certify slightly higher levels of dependability than currently possible. However, it is fraught with difficulties, and it does not seem likely to move us much closer to the levels of dependability that we call 'ultra-high'.

Is there a way out of this impasse? One approach would be to acknowledge that it is not possible to confirm that a sufficiently high, numerically expressed dependability had been achieved, and instead make a decision about whether the delivered system is 'good enough' on different grounds. This is the approach currently adopted for the certification of software in safety-critical avionics for civil airliners [107, 108]:

> ' . . techniques for estimating the post-verification probabilities of
> software errors were examined. The objective was to develop
> numerical requirements for such probabilities for digital computer-
> based equipment and systems certification. The conclusion reached,
> however, was that currently available methods do not yield results
> in which confidence can be placed to the level required for this
> purpose. Accordingly, this document does not state post-
> verification software error requirements in these terms.'

This seems to mean that a very low failure probability is *required* but that, since its achievement cannot be proven in practice, some other, *insufficient* method of certification will be adopted. Indeed, the remainder of the document only gives guidelines to 'good practice' and documentation, which as we have seen fall far short of providing the assurance needed. In other words, directives are given to support *qualitative* evaluation only. This approach is not new. The *design* reliability of hardware systems has traditionally not been evaluated as part of certification procedures: reliability estimation has referred only to physical failures. Sometimes such a view was reasonable, since the complexity of the design was low and it could be plausibly argued that it was 'almost certainly' correct. In addition, evolutionary design was the rule. Similar considerations apply for the design of *environments* containing computers, like industrial plants or space systems: actually, probabilistic risk assessment techniques are not yet widely applied in some high-risk industries [45]. Rather, qualitative techniques, such as Failure Mode and Effect Analysis, are trusted to find 'weak links' in designs and cause adequate corrective actions. There is probably a need for further research for improving the practice of Probabilistic Risk Assessment: conventional 'hardware' reliability or safety evaluation does not consider design faults, and yet many accidents in complex systems, not involving software, appear to be caused by the design, either of the physical system or of the procedures for its use [103].

In support of the qualitative approach, it might be argued that stating requirements so high that they cannot be used in the acceptance or the certification of a product serves more to pave the way for future litigation than to safeguard current users. However, ultra-high dependability requirements for a computer typically result from a probabilistic risk assessment of the environment where the computer has to be deployed: if the computer does not satisfy its requirements, some requirement for the environment itself cannot be proven to be satisfied. As a very minimum, it would seem necessary to perform sensitivity and worst-case analyses on the models used for risk assessment, with respect to the uncertainty on the computer dependability figures. For instance, if the requirement of a $10^{-9}$ probability of catastrophic failures for systems in civilian aircraft were derived from such a risk analysis, it would have to apply to all failures, including those caused by design. The problem with placing complex software in a position where this requirement applies would then be, of course, that there would be no way to demonstrate achievement of this requirement.

This leads to another way to avoid the problem, that is, to designing environments in such a way that ultra-high dependability is *not* required of software. For instance, guidelines for the U.K. nuclear power industry are that the assumed probability of failure on demand for safety-critical software can never be better than $10^{-4}$ [120]. This leads back to the accepted practice of separate and redundant safety mechanisms. Of course, probabilistic risk assessment and requirement specification are complex issues. It is difficult to model the effects of computer failure on complex environments, and there may be no explicit statement of desirable levels of risk. Even the seemingly obvious requirement that the introduction of a new computer must not make the risk level any worse is often ambiguous. Consider for instance an alarm system, intended to signal some dangerous situation to a human operator. Its contribution to the global risk level is a function of the probabilities of its different failure modes (false alarms vs missed alarms), its human interface and the training of operators, etc. If one were to procure a new model of alarm system, risk assessment would be relatively easy only if the new model mimicked the old one almost perfectly. In other words, whenever computers are introduced with new functions, specification of their requirements is subject to difficulties and uncertainties in the analysis of the environment, not unlike those in the dependability analysis of the computer itself. Obviously, a prudent solution is to overstate dependability requirements for the computer, but this leads us back to the very problem from which we started.

Uncertainty is an unavoidable consequence of having computers (or any very complex design) as parts of hazardous but reasonably safe environments. In view of this, one may question the policy of using computers in such environments. A few distinctions may be useful here. In the first place, there are those existing environments that are known to be within the required risk level in their current configuration. The substitution of components of that configuration with new computers may or may not imply ultra-high dependability requirements for the latter.

In view of the considerations which we have presented, these kinds of requirements should be seen with scepticism. A different case presents itself when the introduction of a new computer is meant to obtain a substantially new and better environment. As an example, computers are introduced in "fly-by-wire" aircraft not merely to reproduce the somewhat limited functionality of conventional control systems, but also to provide extra functions (such as some degree of protection against pilot error). Then, there is usually no question of avoiding the use of the new computer, but a proper risk analysis should take into account the difficulties discussed in this paper. An attempt should usually be made to design for validation, as outlined above. However, the comparatively low levels of dependability that can be validated should always be taken into account in evaluating the costs and benefits of the new environment proposed.

# Appendix

The Bayesian approach to statistics takes the view that probabilities are subjective; they represent the strength of belief of an observer about whether certain events will take place. It is assumed that this observer will have some prior beliefs which will change as a result of seeing the outcome of the 'experiment' (i.e. the collection of data). Bayesian theory provides a formalism for this transformation from prior to posterior belief. For our own purposes, the major advantage of the theory is the idea that prior belief can be quantified and incorporated with experimental evidence into a final probability assessment..

Suppose that we have, in the example in the main text, seen $x$ failures of the program during the period of testing $t_O$. Bayes theorem states

$$p(\lambda \mid data) \propto p(\lambda) . p(data \mid \lambda)$$

where the distribution $p(\lambda)$ represents the prior belief about the rate of occurrence of failures, $\lambda$, and $p(\lambda \mid data)$ represents the posterior belief after seeing the data.

This use of Bayes theorem shows how our *a priori* belief changes into our *a posteriori* belief via use of the *likelihood function*, $p(data \mid \lambda)$, for the evidence we have obtained from the experiment: here proportional to $\lambda^x \exp(-\lambda t_O)$ because of the assumption of a Poisson process.

Notice the natural way in which we can here express confidence statements about $\lambda$ in the form of probability statements in which $\lambda$ itself is a random variable. This contrasts with the rather contrived interpretation of a confidence statement in the classical context, which must invoke a set of experiments which *could hypothetically* have been performed, and which treats the quantity calculated from the data as the sole random variable about which confidence is being expressed. This advantage of the Bayesian approach becomes even more clear as we go on to obtain probability statements about $T$, the residual time to next failure.

To proceed further, we need to formalize the representation of our prior belief about $\lambda$, i.e. we need to decide on a form for $p(\lambda)$ above. There are good arguments [37] that this should be chosen from the *conjugate family* of distributions for our particular likelihood function: this is the (unique) *parametric family* of distributions which has the property that both posterior distribution and prior will be a member of the same family. The informal idea is that there should be a certain homogeneity in the way in which our beliefs change as we acquire more evidence about the unknown rate parameter $\lambda$. Under conjugacy, such homogeneous change is represented by changes solely in the values of the hyper-parameters of the conjugate family.

The conjugate family here is the gamma, $\mathrm{Gam}(\alpha, \beta)$, which has probability density function $\beta^\alpha \lambda^{\alpha-1} e^{-\beta\lambda} / \Gamma(\alpha)$, where the hyper-parameters $\alpha, \beta$ are both positive. If we let $\mathrm{Gam}(a, b)$ represent our prior belief (for some suitable choice of $a$ and $b$), our posterior belief about $\lambda$, $p(\lambda \mid x, t_0)$, is represented by $\mathrm{Gam}(a + x, b + t_0)$. This fits in well with intuition: for example the expected value, $E(\lambda)$, changes from $a/b$ to $(a + x)/(b + t_0)$, so that observing a small number of failures, $x$, in a long time $t_0$, will cause the posterior expected value to be smaller than the prior.

We can now make probability statements about $\lambda$, and about $T$ itself:

$$p(t \mid x, t_0) \quad = \int p(t \mid \lambda)\, p(\lambda \mid x, t_0)\, d\lambda$$

$$= \frac{(a + x)(b + t_0)^{a + x}}{(b + t_0 + t)^{a + x + 1}}$$

It follows that the reliability function is

$$R(t \mid x, t_0) \quad = \quad P(T > t \mid x, t_0)$$

$$= \left( \frac{b + t_0}{b + t_0 + t} \right)^{a + x}$$

and in our case, when $x = 0$,

$$= \left( \frac{b + t_0}{b + t_0 + t} \right)^{a}$$

The naturalness of the Bayesian method is bought at some price. Its subjective nature forces the users to describe formally their prior belief about the parameter(s): in our case, to choose the hyper-parameters $a$ and $b$. However, it is rarely the case that we do not have *some* prior belief, and in this example it is possible to think of various sources for such belief: experience of developing similar software systems in the past, previous experience of the efficacy of the software development methodology used, etc. Eliciting such subjective prior belief from people in order to arrive at values for $a$ and $b$ is a non-trivial exercise, although there has been some recent progress in semi-automatic elicitation procedures [122].

It is often tempting to avoid the difficulty of selecting values of hyper-parameters of the prior distribution to represent 'your' beliefs, by devising instead a prior distribution which represents 'total ignorance'. Unfortunately this is difficult. One argument here runs as follows. Since $\mathrm{Gam}(a + x, b + t_0)$ represents our posterior belief about the rate, *large* parameter values represent beliefs based on considerable data (i.e. large $x$, $t_0$). To represent initial ignorance, therefore, we should take $a$ and $b$ as small as possible. Now $\mathrm{Gam}(a, b)$ exists for all $a, b > 0$. If we take $a$ and $b$ both very small, the posterior distribution for the rate is approximately Gam($x$, $t_o$), with the approximation improving as $a$, $b \to 0$. We could therefore informally think of Gam($x$, $t_O$) as the posterior in which the data 'speak for themselves'.

This argument is fairly convincing if we are to see a reasonable amount of data when we conduct the data-gathering experiment. Unfortunately it breaks down precisely in the case in which we are interested here: when $x = 0$ the posterior distribution for the rate is proportional to $\lambda^{-1}$ and is thus improper (i.e., it yields a total probability mass greater than 1). Worse, the predictive distribution for $T$ is also improper, and is thus useless for prediction.

Here is a possible way forward. Choose the improper prior

$$p(\lambda) \quad \equiv \quad 1$$

giving the posterior

$$p(\lambda \mid 0, t_o) \quad = \quad t_0 \exp(-\lambda t_o)$$

which is a proper distribution. More importantly, the predictive distribution for $T$ is also proper:

$$p(t \mid 0, t_o) \quad = \quad \int p(t \mid \lambda) \, p(\lambda \mid 0, t_o) \, d\lambda$$

$$= \quad t_o / (t_o + t)^2$$

The reliability function is

$$R(t \mid 0, t_o) \quad \equiv \quad P(T > t \mid 0, t_o)$$

$$= \quad t_o / (t + t_o)$$

and in particular, $R(t_o \mid 0, t_o) = {}^1/_2$: i.e. we have a 50:50 chance of seeing a further period of failure-free working as has already been observed.

The conclusion here is that observing a long period of failure-free working does not *in itself* allow us to conclude that a system is ultra-reliable. However, it must be admitted that the prior distribution here is rather unrealistic. Therefore, let us consider the case where the observer has genuine prior beliefs about $\lambda$, perhaps arising from his or her faith in the efficacy of the methods used to develop the software. Consider the following example: the reliability requirement is that the median time to failure is $10^6$ hours, and the test has shown failure-free working for $10^3$ hours, what prior belief would the observer have needed in order to conclude that the requirement had been met?

From above, $(a, b)$ must satisfy

$$^1/_2 \quad = \quad \left( \frac{b + 10^3}{b + 10^3 + 10^6} \right)^a$$

which implies, since $b > 0$, that $a > 0.1003288$. It is instructive to examine what is implied by prior beliefs in this solution set. Consider, for example, $a = 0.11$, $b = 837.2$. Is this a 'reasonable' prior belief? We think not, since the *prior* probability that $T > 10^6$ is 0.458; in other words, the observer must believe *a priori* that there is almost a 50:50 chance of surviving for $10^6$ hours. If $a = 0.50$, $b = 332333$, the prior $P(T > 10^6)$ is 0.499. As $a$ increases this problem becomes worse.

In other words, to believe that 'this is a $10^6$ system' after seeing only $10^3$ hours of failure-free working, we must *initially* believe it was a $10^6$ system. To end up with a very high confidence in a system, when we can see only a modest amount of testing, we must *bring to the problem* the relevant degree of belief.

## Acknowledgments

This paper owes much to discussions with other members of the PDCS projects, in particular during a project workshop held on the topic in October 1990 at LRI-University of Paris Sud in Orsay. We are also grateful to John Rushby for some valuable comments and suggestions on an earlier version of this paper.

# References for Chapter VI

[1]  A. A. Abdel-Ghaly, P. Y. Chan and B. Littlewood, "Evaluation of Competing Software Reliability Predictions", *IEEE Trans. on Software Engineering*, 12 (9), pp.950-67, 1986.

[2]  E. N. Adams, "Optimizing Preventive Service of Software Products", *IBM J. of Research and Development*, 28 (1), pp.2-14, January 1984.

[3]  V. Amoia, G. De Micheli and M. Santomauro, "Computer-Oriented Formulation of Transition-Rate Matrices via Kronecker Algebra", *IEEE Trans. on Reliability*, 30 (2), pp.123-32, June 1981.

[4]  T. Anderson, P. A. Barrett, D. N. Halliwell and M. R. Moulding, "An Evaluation of Software Fault Tolerance in a Practical System", in *Proc. 15th Int. Symp. on Fault-Tolerant Computing (FTCS-15)*, (Ann Arbor, Mich.), pp.140-5, 1985.

[5]  T. Anderson, P. A. Barrett, D. N. Halliwell and M. R. Moulding, "Software Fault Tolerance: An Evaluation", *IEEE Trans. on Software Engineering*, 11 (12), pp.1502-10, December 1985.

[6]  J. Arlat, K. Kanoun and J.-C. Laprie, "Dependability Modeling and Evaluation of Software Fault-Tolerant Systems", *IEEE Trans. on Computers*, 39 (4), pp.504-13, April 1990.

[7]  H. Ascher and H. Feingold, "Application of Laplace's Test to Repairable Systems Reliability", in *1st International Conference on Reliability and Maintainability*, (Paris), pp.254-8, 1978.

[8]  H. Ascher and H. Feingold, *Repairable Systems Reliability: Modeling, Inference, Misconceptions and Their Causes*, Vol. 7, 1984.

[9]  A. Avizienis and L. Chen, "On the Implementation of N-Version Programming for Software Fault Tolerance During Program Execution", in *Proc. 1st Int. Conf. on Computing Software Applications (COMPASAC-77)*, pp.149-55, 1977.

[10]  A. Avizienis, P. Gunningberg, J. P. J. Kelly, L. Strigini, P. J. Traverse, K. S. Tso and U. Voges, "The UCLA DEDIX System: A Distributed Testbed for Multiple-version Software", in *Proc. 15th Int. Symp. on Fault-Tolerant Computing (FTCS-15)*, (Ann Arbor, MI, USA), pp.126-34, IEEE Computer Society Press, 1985.

[11]  A. Avizienis and J. P. J. Kelly, "Fault Tolerance by Design Diversity: Concepts and Experiments", *IEEE Computer*, 17 (8), pp.67-80, August 1984.

[12]  R. E. Barlow and F. Prochan, *Statistical Theory of Reliability and Life Testing*, Holt, New-York, 1975.

[13]  J. Barwise, "Mathematical Proofs of Computer System Correctness", *Notes of the AMS*, 36, pp.844-51, Sept 1989.

[14]    H. A. Bauer, L. M. Croxall and E. A. Davis, "The 5ESS Switching System: System Test, First-Office Application, and Early Field Experience", *AT&T Technical J.*, 64 (6), pp.1503-22, August 1985.

[15]    B. Beyaert, G. Florin and S. Natkin, "Evaluation of Computer Systems Dependability Using Stochastic Petri Nets", in *Proc.11th Int. Symp. on Fault-Tolerant Computing (FTCS-11),* (Portland, ME, USA), pp.79-81, IEEE Computer Society Press, 1981.

[16]    P. G. Bishop, "The Variation of Software Survival Time for Different Operational Input Profiles (or why you Can Wait a long Time for a big Bug to Fail)", in *Proc. 23th Int. Symp. on Fault-Tolerant Computing (FTCS-23),* (Toulouse, France), pp.98-107, 1993.

[17]    P. G. Bishop and F. D. Pullen, "PODS Revisited - A Study of Software Failure Behaviour", in *Proc. 18th Int. Symp. on Fault-Tolerant Computing (FTCS-18),* (Tokyo, Japan), pp.1-8, 1988.

[18]    P. G. Bishop and F. D. Pullen, "Failure Masking: A Source of Failure Dependency in Multi-version Programs", in *Dependable Computing for Critical Applications (Proc. 1st IFIP Int. Working Conference on Dependable Computing for Critical Applications: DCCA-1, Santa Barbara, CA, USA, August 1989)* (A. Avizienis and J.-C. Laprie, Eds.), Dependable Computing and Fault-Tolerant Systems, 4, (A. Avizienis, H. Kopetz and J.-C. Laprie, Eds.), pp.53-73, Springer-Verlag, Vienna, Austria, 1991.

[19]    A. Bondavalli, S. Chiaradonna, F. Di Giandomenico and L. Strigini, *Modelling Correlation Among Successive Inputs in Software Dependability Analyses*, CNUCE-CNR, Pisa, Italy, Technical Report, N°C94-20, 1994.

[20]    A. Bondavalli, S. Chiaradonna, F. Di Giandomenico and L. Strigini, "Dependability Models for Iterative Software Considering Correlation among Successive Inputs", in *Proc. Int. Symp. on Computer Performance and Dependability (IPDS'95),* (Erlangen, Germany), 1995 (to appear).

[21]    S. S. Brilliant, J. C. Knight and N. G. Leveson, "Analysis of Faults in an N-Version Software Experiment", *IEEE Trans. on Software Engineering*, 16 (2), pp.238-47, February 1990.

[22]    S. Brocklehurst, P. Y. Chan, B. Littlewood and J. Snell, "Recalibrating software reliability models", *IEEE Trans Software Engineering*, 16 (4), pp.458-70, 1990.

[23]    S. Brocklehurst and B. Littlewood, "New Ways to get Accurate Reliability Measures", *IEEE Software*, 9 (4), pp.34-42, 1992.

[24]    S. D. Cha, "A Recovery Block Model and its Analysis", in *Proc. 5th IFAC Workshop Safety of Computer Control Systems (SAFECOMP'86),* (W. J. Quirk, Ed.), (Sarlat, France), pp.21-6, Pergamon Press, 1986.

[25]    P. Y. Chan, *Software Reliability Prediction,* PhD, City University, London, UK, 1986.

[26]    L. Chen and A. Avizienis, "N-version Programming: A Fault Tolerance Approach to Reliability of Software Operation", in *Proc. 8th Int. Symp. on*

*Fault Tolerant Computing (FTCS-8),* (Toulouse, France), pp.3-9, IEEE Computer Society Press, 1978.

[27]   R. C. Cheung, "A User-Oriented Software Reliability Model", *IEEE Trans. on Software Engineering,* 6 (2), pp.118-25, March 1985.

[28]   S. Chiaradonna, A. Bondavalli and L. Strigini, *Comparative Performability Evaluation of RB, NVP and SCOP,* CNUCE-CNR, Pisa, Italy, Technical Report, N°C94-02, 1994.

[29]   S. Chiaradonna, A. Bondavalli and L. Strigini, "On Performability Modeling and Evaluation of Software Fault Tolerance Structures", in *Proc. 1st European Dependable Computing Conference (EDCC-1),* (Berlin, Germany), pp.97-114, Springer-Verlag, 1994.

[30]   A. Costes, J. E. Doucet, C. Landrault and J.-C. Laprie, "SURF: a Program for Dependability Evaluation of Complex Fault-Tolerant Computing Systems", in *Proc. 11th Int. Symp. Fault-Tolerant Computing (FTCS-11),* (Portland, Maine, USA), pp.72-8, IEEE Computer Society Press, 1981.

[31]   A. Costes, C. Landrault and J.-C. Laprie, "Reliability and Availability Models for Maintained Systems Featuring Hardware Failures and Design Faults", *IEEE Trans. on Computers,* 27 (6), pp.548-60, June 1978.

[32]   D. R. Cox and P. A. W. Lewis, *The Statistical Analysis of Series of Events,* Monographs on  Applied Probability and Statistics, Chapman and Hall, London, 1966.

[33]   L. H. Crow, *Confidence interval procedures for reliability growth analysis,* US Army Materiel Systems Analysis Activity, Aberdeen, Maryland, Tech Report, N°197, 1977.

[34]   A. Csenski, "Recovery Block Reliability Analysis with Failure Clustering", in *Dependable Computing for Critical Applications (Proc. 1st IFIP Int. Working Conference on Dependable Computing for Critical Applications: DCCA-1, Santa Barbara, CA, USA, August 1989)* (A. Avizienis and J.-C. Laprie, Eds.), Dependable Computing and Fault-Tolerant Systems, 4, (A. Avizienis, H. Kopetz and J.-C. Laprie, Eds.), pp.75-103, Springer-Verlag, Vienna, Austria, 1991.

[35]   P. A. Currit, M. Dyer and H. D. Mills, "Certifying the Reliability of Software", *IEEE Trans. on Software Engineering,* 12 (1), pp.3-11, 1986.

[36]   A. P. Dawid, "Statistical theory: the prequential approach", *J Royal Statist Soc, A,* 147, pp.278-92, 1984.

[37]   M. H. DeGroot, *Optimal Statistical Decisions,* McGraw-Hill, New York, 1970.

[38]   M. H. DeGroot, *Probability and Statistics,* Series in Statistics, Addison-Wesley, Reading, Mass, 1986.

[39]   J. T. Duane, "Learning Curve Approach to Reliability Monitoring", *IEEE Trans. on Aerospace,* 2, pp.563-6, 1964.

[40]    D. E. Eckhardt and L. D. Lee, "A Theoretical Basis for the Analysis of
        Multiversion Software Subject to Coincident Errors", *IEEE Trans. on
        Software Engineering*, 11 (12), pp.1511-7, November 1985.

[41]    G. Edwards, "A Bayesian Procedure for Drawing Inferences from Random
        Data", *Reliability Engineering and System Safety*, 9, pp.1-17, 1984.

[42]    FAA, *Federal Aviation Administration Advisory Circular*, N°AC 25.1309-1A,
        June 1988.

[43]    W. Feller, *An Introduction to Probability Theory and its Application,* 1,
        Wiley, New York, USA, 1968.

[44]    J. M. Finkelstein, "Starting and Limiting Values for Reliability Growth",
        *IEEE Trans. on Reliability*, 28 (2), pp.111-3, June 1979.

[45]    B. J. Garrick, "The Approach to Risk Analysis in Three Industries: Nuclear
        Power, Space Systems, and Chemical Processes", *Reliability Engineering and
        System Safety*, 23 (3), pp.195-205, 1988.

[46]    O. Gaudoin, *Statistical Tools For Software Reliability Evaluation,* Joseph
        Fourier University, Grenoble 1, 1990.

[47]    F. K. Giloth and K. D. Prantzen, "Can the reliability of digital
        telecommunication switching systems be predicted and measured?", in *13th
        International Symposium on Fault-Tolerant Computing,* (Vienna, Austria),
        pp.392-7, 1983.

[48]    B. V. Gnedenko, Y. K. Belyayev and A. D. Slovyev, *Mathematical Methods
        of Reliability Theory,* Academic, New-York, USA, 1969.

[49]    A. L. Goel and K. Okumoto, "Time-Dependent Error-Detection Rate Model
        for Software and Other Performance Measures", *IEEE Trans. on Reliability*,
        28 (3), pp.206-11, 1979.

[50]    A. Goyal, W. C. Carter, E. de Souza e Silva and S. S. Lavenberg, "The
        System Availability Estimator", in *Proc. 16th Int. Symp. on Fault-Tolerant
        Computing (FTCS-16),* (Vienna, Austria), pp.84-9, IEEE Computer Society
        Press, 1986.

[51]    M. E. Graden and P. S. Hosley, "The effects of Software Inspections on a
        Major Telecommunications project", *AT&T Technical J.*, 65 (3), pp.32-40,
        1986.

[52]    R. B. Grady and D. L. Caswell, *Software Metrics: Establishing a Company-
        Wide Program,* Prentice-Hall, Inc., Englewood Cliffs, New Jersey, USA,
        1987.

[53]    J. Gray, "Why Do Computers Stop and What Can Be Done About It?", in
        *Proc. 5th Symp. on Reliability in Distributed Software and Database Systems
        (SRDSDS-5),* (Los Angeles, CA, USA), pp.3-12, IEEE Computer Society
        Press, 1986.

[54]    A. Grnarov, J. Arlat and A. Avizienis, "On the Performance of Software Fault
        Tolerance Strategies", in *Proc. 10th Int. Symp. on Fault-Tolerant Computing
        (FTCS-10),* (Kyoto, Japan), pp.251-3, IEEE Computer Society Press, 1980.

[55] D. Gross and D. R. Miller, "The Randomization Technique as a Modeling Tool and Solution Procedure for Transient Markov Processes", *Operation Research*, 32 (2), pp.343-61, 1984.

[56] H. Hecht, "Fault-Tolerant Software", *IEEE Trans. on Reliability*, 28 (3), pp.227-32, August 1979.

[57] M. Hollander and F. Proschan, "A Test For Superadditivity For the Mean Value Function of a Non Homoneneous Poisson Process", *Stochastic Proc. and Their Appli.*, 2, pp.195-209, 1974.

[58] IEEE-TR, "Special Issue on Fault-Tolerant Sofware", *IEEE Trans. on Reliability*, R-42 (2), pp.177-258, June 1993.

[59] Z. Jelinski and P. B. Moranda, "Software Reliability Research", in *Statistical Computer Performance Evaluation* (W. Freiberger, Ed.), pp.465-84, Academic Press, New York, 1972.

[60] K. Kanoun, *Software Dependability Growth Characterization, Modeling, Evaluation,* State Doctoral Dissertation, National Polytechnic Institute of Toulouse, France, September 1989 (in French).

[61] K. Kanoun, M. Bastos Martini and J. Moreira de Souza, "A Method for Software Reliability Analysis and Prediction—Application to The TROPICO-R Switching System", *IEEE Trans. Software Engineering*, 17 (4), pp.334-44, April 1991.

[62] K. Kanoun, M. Kaâniche and J.-C. Laprie, "Experience in Software Reliability: From Data Collection to Quantitative Evaluation", in *4th Int. Symp. on Software Reliability Engineering (ISSRE'93),* (Denver, CO, USA), pp.234-45, 1993.

[63] K. Kanoun and J.-C. Laprie, *Modeling Software Reliability and Availability from Development Validation up to Operation*, LAAS-CNRS, Toulouse, France, Research Report, N°85042, August 1985.

[64] K. Kanoun and J.-C. Laprie, "The Role of Trend Analysis in Software Development and Validation", in *Safecomp'91,* (Trondheim, Norway), pp.169-74, 1991.

[65] K. Kanoun and J.-C. Laprie, "Software Reliability Trend Analyses: from Theoretical To Practical Considerations", *IEEE Trans. on Software Engineering*, 20 (9), pp.740-7, 1994.

[66] K. Kanoun and T. Sabourin, "Software Dependability of a Telephone Switching System", in *Proc. 17th IEEE Int Symp. on Fault-Tolerant Computing (FTCS-17),* (Pittsburgh, PA, USA), pp.236-41, 1987.

[67] P. A. Keiller, B. Littlewood, D. R. Miller and A. Sofer, "Comparison of Software Reliability Predictions", in *Proc. 13th Int. Symp. on Fault-Tolerant Computing (FTCS-13),* (Milan), pp.128-34, 1983.

[68] J. P. J. Kelly, A. Avizienis, B. T. Ulery, B. J. Swain, R.-T. Lyu, A. Tai and K.-S. Tso, "Multi-Version Software Development", in *Proc. 5th IFAC*

*Workshop Safety of Computer Control System (SAFECOMP-86),* (Sarlat, France), pp.43-9, 1986.

[69]  J. G. Kemeny and J. L. Snell, *Finite Markov Chains,* Princeton, NJ: Van Nostrand, 1959.

[70]  G. Q. Kenney and M. A. Vouk, "Measuring the Field Quality of Wide-Distribution Commercial Software", in *3rd Int. Symp. on Software Reliability Engineering (ISSRE'92),* (Raleigh, NC, USA), pp.351-7, 1992.

[71]  J. C. Knight and N. G. Leveson, "An Empirical Study of Failure Probabilities in Multi-version Software", in *Proc. 16th Int. Symp. on Fault Tolerant Computing (FTCS-16),* (Vienna, Austria), pp.165-70, IEEE Computer Society Press, 1986.

[72]  J. C. Knight, N. G. Leveson and L. D. S. Jean, "A Large Scale Experiment in N-version Programming", in *Proc. 15th Int. Symp. on Fault Tolerant Computing (FTCS-15) ,* (Ann Arbor, MI, USA), pp.135-9, IEEE Computer Society Press, 1985.

[73]  J.-C. Laprie, "Dependability Evaluation of Software Systems in Operation", *IEEE Trans. on Software Engineering,* 10 (6), pp.701-14, November 1984.

[74]  J.-C. Laprie, "Dependability Modeling and Evaluation of Hardware-and-Software Systems", in *2nd GI/NTG/GMR Conf. on Fault-Tolerant Computing,* (Bonn, Germany), pp.202-15, 1984.

[75]  J.-C. Laprie, "Towards an X-ware Reliability Theory", *Technique et Science Informatiques,* 7 (6), pp.315-30, 1988.

[76]  J.-C. Laprie, "Hardware-and-Software Dependability Evaluation", in *IFIP 11th World Computer Congress,* (San Francisco, CA, USA), pp.109-14, North-Holland, 1989.

[77]  J.-C. Laprie, C. Béounes, M. Kaâniche and K. Kanoun, "The Transformation Approach to the Modeling and Evaluation of the Reliability and Availability Growth", in *Proc. 20th Int. Symp. Fault-Tolerant Computing (FTCS-20),* (Newcastle, UK), pp.364-71, IEEE Computer Society Press, 1990.

[78]  J.-C. Laprie, K. Kanoun, C. Béounes and M. Kaâniche, "The KAT (Knowledge-Action-Transformation) Approach to the Modeling and Evaluation of Reliability and Availability Growth", *IEEE Trans. on Software Engineering,* 17 (4), pp.370-82, 1991.

[79]  N. Leveson, "Software Safety in Embedded Computer systems", *Communications ACM,* 34 (2), pp.34-46, 1991.

[80]  B. Littlewood, "How To Measure Software Reliability and How Not to", *IEEE Trans. on Reliability,* 28 (2), pp.103-10, 1979.

[81]  B. Littlewood, "Software Reliability Model for Modular Program Structure", *IEEE Trans. on Reliability,* 28 (3), pp.241-6, 1979.

[82]  B. Littlewood, "Stochastic Reliability Growth: A Model for Fault-Removal in Computer Programs and Hardware Designs", *IEEE Trans. on Reliability,* 30 (4), pp.313-20, October 1981.

[83]   B. Littlewood, "Predicting Software Reliability", *Phil Trans Royal Soc London*, A 327, pp.513-49, 1989.

[84]   B. Littlewood, "Limits to Evaluation of Software Dependability", in *Software Reliability and Metrics (Proceedings of 7th Annual CSR Conference, Garmisch-Partenkirchen)* (B. Littlewood and N. E. Fenton, Eds.), pp.81-110, Elsevier, London, 1991.

[85]   B. Littlewood and D. R. Miller, "A Conceptual Model of Multi-Version Software", in *Proc. 17th. Int. Symp. on Fault-Tolerant Computing (FTCS-17)*, (Pittsburgh, PA, USA), pp.150-5, IEEE Computer Society Press, 1987.

[86]   B. Littlewood and D. R. Miller, "Conceptual Modelling of Coincident Failures in Multi-Version Software", *IEEE Trans on Software Engineering*, 15 (12), pp.1596-614, 1989.

[87]   B. Littlewood and L. Strigini, "Assessment of ultra-high dependability for software-based systems", *CACM*, 36 (11), pp.69-80, 1993.

[88]   B. Littlewood and J. L. Verrall, "A Bayesian Reliability Growth Model for Computer Software", *J. Royal Statist. Soc. C,* 22, pp.332 46, 1973.

[89]   P. R. Lorczak, A. K. Caglayan and D. E. Eckhardt, "A Theoretical Investigation of Generalized Voters for Redundant Systems", in *Proc. 19th Int. Symp. on Fault Tolerant Computing (FTCS-19)*, (Chicago, IL, USA), pp.444-51, IEEE Computer Society, 1989.

[90]   M. Lu, S. Brocklehurst and B. Littlewood, "Combination of predictions obtained from different software reliability growth models", *J. Computer and Software Eng.*, 1 (4), pp.303-24, 1993.

[91]   M. R. Lyu and Y. He, "Improving the N-Version Programming Process Through the Evolution of a Design Paradigm", *IEEE Transation on Reliability, Special Issue on Fault-Tolerant Software*, R-42 (2), pp.179-89, June 1993.

[92]   A. Marsan, G. Balbo and G. Conte, "A Class of Generalized Stochastic Petri Nets for the Performance Analysis of Multiprocessor Systems", *ACM Trans. on Computers*, 2 (2), pp.93-122, May 1984.

[93]   J. F. Meyer, "On Evaluating the Performability of Degradable Computing Systems", *IEEE Trans. on Computers*, 29 (8), pp.720-31, August 1980.

[94]   D. Miller, "The Role of Statistical Modelling and Inference in Software Quality Assurance", in *Software Certification* (B. de Neumann, Ed.), Elsevier Applied Science, Barking, 1989.

[95]   D. R. Miller, "Exponential Order Statistic Models of Software Reliability Growth", *IEEE Trans. on Software Engineering*, 12 (1), pp.12-24, January 1986.

[96]   D. R. Miller and A. Sofer, "A non-parametric approach to software reliability using complete monotonicity", in *Software Reliability: State of the Art Report* (A. Bendell and P. Mellor, Eds.), 14:2, pp.183-95, Pergamon Infotech, London, 1986.

[97]    M. Mulazzani, "Reliability Versus Safety", in *Proc. 4th IFAC Workshop Safety of Computer Control Systems (SAFECOMP'85)*, (W. J. Quirk, Ed.), (Como, Italy), pp.141-6, Como, Italy, 1985.

[98]    J. D. Musa, *Software Reliability Data*, Data and Analysis Center for Software, Rome Air Development Center (RADC), Technical Report, 1979.

[99]    J. D. Musa and K. Okumoto, "A Logarithmic Poisson Execution Time Model for Software Reliability Measurement", in *Proc. Compsac 84*, (Chicago), pp.230-8, 1984.

[100]   M. Ohba, "Software Reliability Analysis Models", *IBM J. of Research and Development*, 21 (4), pp.428-43, July 1984.

[101]   A. Pagès and M. Gondran, *System Reliability: Evaluation and Prediction in Engineering*, Springer-Verlag, New York, USA, 1986.

[102]   D. L. Parnas, A. J. van Schowan and S. P. Kwan, "Evaluation of safety-critical software", *Communications ACM*, 33 (6), pp.636-48, 1990.

[103]   C. Perrow, *Normal Accidents: Living with High Risk Technologies*, Basic Books, New York, 1984.

[104]   P. I. Pignal, "An Analysis of Hardware and Software Availability Exemplified on the IBM-3725 Communication Controller", *IBM J. of Research and Development*, 32 (2), pp.268-78, March 1988.

[105]   B. Randell, "System Structure for Software Fault Tolerance", *IEEE Trans. on Software Engineering*, 1 (2), pp.220-32, June 1975.

[106]   N. Ross, "The Collection and Use of Data for Monitoring Software Projects", in *Measurement for Software Control and Assurance* (B. A. Kitchenham and B. Littlewood, Eds.), pp.125-54, Elsevier Applied Science, London and New York, 1989.

[107]   RTCA, *Software considerations in airborne systems and equipment certification*, Radio-Technical Commission for Aeronautics, N°DO-178A, 1985.

[108]   RTCA, *Software considerations in airborne systems and equipment certification*, REquirements and Technical Concepts for Aeronautics, N°DO-178B, July 1992.

[109]   F. Saglietti and W. Ehrenberger, "Software Diversity - Some Considerations about its Benefits and its Limitations", in *Proc. 5th IFAC Workshop Safety of Computer Control Systems (SAFECOMP'86)*, (Sarlat, France), pp.157-64, Pergamon Press, 1986.

[110]   R. K. Scott, J. W. Gault and D. F. McAllister, "Fault-Tolerant Software Reliability Modeling", *IEEE Trans. on Software Engineering*, 13 (5), pp.582-92, May 1987.

[111]   G. E. Stark, "Dependability Evaluation of Integrated Hardware/Software Systems", *IEEE Trans. on Reliability*, 36 (4), pp.440-4, October 1987.

[112] L. Strigini, *Software Fault Tolerance*, PDCS ESPRIT Basic Research Action, Technical Report, N°23, July 1990.

[113] G. F. Sullivan and G. M. Masson, "Using Certification Trails to Achieve Software Fault Tolerance", in *Proc. 20th Int. Symp. on Fault-Tolerant Computing (FTCS-20)*, (Newcastle-upon-Tyne, U.K.), pp.423-31, 1990.

[114] A. T. Tai, "Performability-Driven Adaptive Fault Tolerance", in *Proc. 24th Int. Symp. on Fault-Tolerant Computing (FTCS-24)*, (Austin, Texas), pp.176-85, 1994.

[115] A. T. Tai, A. Avizienis and J. F. Meyer, "Evaluation of Fault Tolerant Software: a Performability Modeling Approach", in *Dependable Computing for Critical Applications 3* (C. E. Landwher, B. Randell and L. Simoncini, Eds.), 8, Dependable Computing and Fault-Tolerance series, (A. Avizienis, H. Kopetz and J. C. Laprie, Eds.), pp.113-35, Springer-Verlag, 1993.

[116] A. T. Tai, A. Avizienis and J. F. Meyer, "Performability Enhancement of Fault-Tolerant Software", *IEEE Trans. on Reliability, Special Issue on Fault-Tolerant Sofware*, R-42 (2), pp.227-37, June 1993.

[117] L. A. Tomek, J. K. Muppala and K. S. Trivedi, "Modeling Correlation in Software Recovery Blocks", *IEEE Trans. on Software Engineering*, 19 (11), pp.1071-85, November 1993.

[118] K. S. Tso and A. Avizienis, "Error Recovery in Multi-Version Software", in *Proc. 5th IFAC Workshop Safety of Computer Control Systems (SAFECOMP'86)*, (W. J. Quirk, Ed.), (Sarlat, France), pp.35-41, Pergamon Press, 1986.

[119] V. Valette, "An Environment for Software Reliability Evaluation", in *Software Engineering & its Applications*, (Toulouse, France), pp.879-97, 1988.

[120] N. Wainwright, *Software Aspects of Digital Computer Based Protection Systems*, Nuclear Installations Inspectorate, UK, 1991.

[121] J. J. Wallace and W. W. Barnes, "Designing for Ultrahigh Availability: The Unix RTR Operating System", *IEEE Computer*, pp.31-9, August 1984.

[122] G. Wright and P. Ayton, *Judgemental Forecasting,* John Wiley, Chichester, 1987.

[123] S. Yamada, "Software Quality / Reliability Measurement and Assessment: Software Reliability Growth Models and Data Analysis", *J. of Information Processing*, 14 (3), pp.254-66, 1991.

[124] S. Yamada and S. Osaki, "Software Reliability Growth Modeling: Models and Assumptions", *IEEE Trans. on Software Engineering*, 11 (12), pp.1431-7, December 1985.

# Chapter VII

# Fault Forecasting -
# Large State Space Modelling

The general theme of this chapter is the quantitative evaluation of the long-term performance and reliability characteristics of large and complex systems. The methodology employed is that of probabilistic modelling, and in particular the analysis of Markov models. In cases of systems with special structure, that analysis can be exact, leading to closed-form solutions or efficient numerical algorithms. If the state space of the process of interest is too large and intractable to permit either a brute force, or an analytical solution, then suitable approximation and/or bounding techniques have to be applied. Both approaches are represented here.

The paper "Computable Dependability Bounds for Large Markov Chains" presents new results for the analysis of complex computer systems. It describes a new iterative method for bounding the complete steady-state vector solution of a Markov chain.

The method yields tight bounds when the Markov chain presents high locality. Its major practical advantage is that it does not require the generation of the complete state space. Its complexity is basically cubic in the size of the state subspace which is actually generated for the calculation of the bounds. It becomes quadratic or even linear when certain structural properties are satisfied.

These features make the method especially attractive for the calculation of the availability of models of repairable fault-tolerant systems of realistic complexity. To illustrate the method, the model of a system of this kind, with 16 million states, has been considered. There is no hope of computing exactly the steady state vector of a model of that size. Tight bounds on its availability were nevertherless obtained by considering small parts of its state space only.

The second paper, "Fast Numerical Solution for a Class of Markov Models", presents a method for obtaining the exact solution of certain processes whose state space is two-dimensional and infinite in one direction. That class includes systems with unbounded queues, where the arrival, service and availability characteristics are modulated dynamically by a finite-state Markov chain.

That solution method, called *spectral expansion* is readily implementable. It is based on expressing the steady-state probability distribution of the process in terms of the eigenvalues and eigenvectors of a matrix polynomial. This is shown to be more efficient than the alternative, 'matrix-geometric', solution technique. In fact, numerical experiments demonstrate that the former can be orders of magnitude faster than the latter.

It is clear from the results presented in this chapter that Markov processes can be applied successfully to the evaluation of systems that are much more than 'toy examples'. Efficient methods have been developed for the computation of performance and reliability measures, either exactly, or approximately, or by enclosing them within narrow bounds. Moreover, it is certain that the possibilities of this methodology have not been exhausted. Future effort is likely to be directed, on one hand, towards enlarging further the applicability of our models, and on the other, towards providing better and more general software support for the solution methods that have been shown to work.

# Computable Dependability Bounds
# for Large Markov Chains[*]

Pierre-Jacques Courtois[1,2]   Pierre Semal[2]

[1]AV Nucléaire, Belgium   [2]Université Catholique de Louvain

**Abstract**. A new method to bound the steady-state solution of large Markov chains is presented. The method integrates the concepts of eigenvector polyhedron and of aggregation. It is specially suited for Markov chains with high locality and very large state spaces.

A model of a repairable fault-tolerant system with 16 millions states is used as an example. Bounds on its availability are obtained by considering a small part of its state space only. The method is potentially useful to bound other types of dependability requirements.

## 1   Introduction

This paper introduces a new technique which can be used to efficiently compute lower and upper bounds on reliability and availability measures in very large Markovian models of computer fault-tolerant systems. By large models, we mean models that may have millions of states. Only the principles of the method are presented. The interested reader may find additional information in [19].

The technique is based on decomposition and aggregation. The principle of aggregation is simple, but not easy to apply. Subsets of states of the model are replaced by single aggregated states, and the system macroscopic behaviour is modelled by the transitions between these aggregated states only. These transitions between subsets are obtained from the transitions between the individual states of the subsets. The objective is an economy of computation. The difficulty comes from the fact that, except for simple or degenerated cases, the transitions between two subsets are not simply obtained from the superposition or the addition of transitions between their individual states; these transitions depend on, and must be weighted by the relative probabilities of these individual states. These probabilities are unknown, so that, in general, approximations must be used. It is therefore impossible, except for very restricted cases, to obtain exact results by decomposition and aggregation, and the accuracy of the method is an important issue.

In the 70's and 80's, much research work has been done on the estimation of the approximation error for different techniques of aggregation. The approach taken here is different. In [2], we found possible, when each subset is considered in isolation, to determine lower and upper bounds on the relative steady-state values of the variables and probabilities associated with each state of that subset.

---

[*] This paper is in part based on [19].

In this paper we apply this result to the efficient computation of bounds on the (un)availability or reliability of system markovian models that are too large to be generated and analysed in their entirety.

## 2    An Example

We shall explain the technique by applying it on a real system model taken from [15]. The system is a fault-tolerant and repairable data base and is shown on Figures 1 and 2. It is made of 24 components, each component (front end, processor switch, processor, memory, bus, disk unit) being supposed to be in one of two states, failed or operational. The system is assumed to remain operational as long as there exists at least one path made of operational components connecting one front-end to one disk unit.

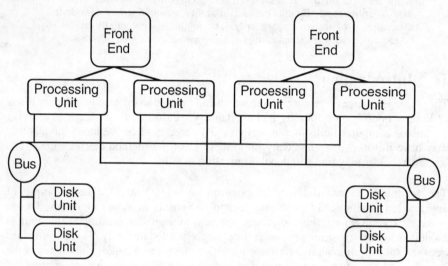

**Fig. 1.** Database Architecture

There is one single repair facility, the components being repaired on a fixed priority scheme in case of simultaneous failures. Repair times and inter-failure times are assumed to be exponential random variables, with rates in the ranges of $[1.0 - 3.0]$ and $[1.125 \ 10^{-4} - 40 \ 10^{-4}]$ respectively.

The total number of distinct states of this model is $2^{24}$ states, i.e. more than 16 millions states. In order to compute the availability of the system, one needs to know the steady state probability of all those states in which the system is operational. The vector $x$ which contains these probabilities is the steady state vector of the transition probability matrix $\mathbf{Q}$ of the system, and is solution of the equation

$$x = x\mathbf{Q} \tag{1}$$

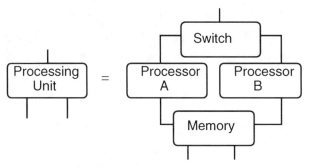

**Fig. 2.** Processing Unit Structure

Grouping together the states with $I$ failed components in block $I$ leads to a block matrix $\mathbf{Q}$ which is block tridiagonal since, all random variables being exponential, the probability of more than one component failing or being repaired in a same transition is negligible:

$$\begin{pmatrix} \mathbf{Q}_{00} & \mathbf{Q}_{01} & \mathbf{0} & \mathbf{0} & \cdots \\ \mathbf{Q}_{10} & \mathbf{Q}_{11} & \mathbf{Q}_{12} & \mathbf{0} & \cdots \\ \mathbf{0} & \mathbf{Q}_{21} & \mathbf{Q}_{22} & \mathbf{Q}_{23} & \cdots \\ \mathbf{0} & \mathbf{0} & \mathbf{Q}_{32} & \mathbf{Q}_{33} & \cdots \\ \mathbf{0} & \mathbf{0} & \cdots & \cdots & \cdots \end{pmatrix} \tag{2}$$

For the same reason, all the elements of each diagonal block $\mathbf{Q}_{II}$ are null except on the diagonal. Transitions between states are non zero between states of different and adjacent blocks only. The vector $x$ is too large to be computed exactly; in double precision, its mere storage would already require 128 Mbytes. To obtain upper and lower bounds on some of its elements is however possible. The diagonal structure of $\mathbf{Q}$ and the differences in magnitude of the failure and repair rates are not indispensable, but will be useful for the computation of these bounds.

## 3   A Useful Polyhedron

A short interlude in matrix algebra is needed because the method is based on a fundamental result in Linear Algebra [Courtois and Semal 1984, 1985]. Suppose that $\mathbf{B}$ is a non-negative and in this case stochastic matrix of which we only know a lower bound matrix $\mathbf{L}$. More precisely:

$$\mathbf{B} = \mathbf{L} + \mathbf{R} \tag{3}$$

where $\mathbf{L} \geq \mathbf{0}$ is known, $\mathbf{R} \geq \mathbf{0}$ is unknown, and both have same size as $\mathbf{B}$. Then, if is the steady state vector of B, we can write:

$$v = v\mathbf{B} = v(\mathbf{L} + \mathbf{R})$$

$$= \beta\,\Sigma^{-1}(\mathbf{I} - \mathbf{L})^{-1}$$

$$= \beta \begin{bmatrix} --\,r_1\,-- \\ --\,r_2\,-- \\ \ldots \\ --\,r_i\,-- \\ \ldots \end{bmatrix} \tag{4}$$

where $\beta$ is a non negative vector whose elements sum up to one, and $\Sigma^{-1}$ is the inverse of a diagonal matrix which simply normalizes the rows of $(\mathbf{I} - \mathbf{L})^{-1}$ so that its resulting normalized rows $r_i$ also sum up to one. This result expresses the fact that the eigenvector of matrix $\mathbf{B}$ is a convex combination of the rows of the known matrix $\Sigma^{-1}(\mathbf{I} - \mathbf{L})^{-1}$. Therefore every element $v_j$ is bounded by:

$$\min_i \{r_{ij}\} \leq v_j \leq \max_i \{r_{ij}\} \tag{5}$$

These bounds have an intuitive significance. If $\mathbf{L}$ is a substochastic matrix, and is a block embedded in a larger stochastic matrix, the element $r_{ij}$ is the rate of visit to state $j$ when the subsystem $\mathbf{L}$ is started in state $i$ before the occurrence of a transition leading outside $\mathbf{L}$. Equation (4) also means that the vector $v$ belongs to the polyhedron defined by the rows $r_i$.

In other words, if we are interested in the steady-state vector $v$ of a matrix $\mathbf{B}$ for which a lower bound matrix $\mathbf{L}$ only is known, then $v$ cannot be exactly determined, but it can be bounded by the space spanned by the convex combinations of the rows $r_i$, i.e. by the polyhedron that we shall note $P[(\mathbf{I}-\mathbf{L})^{-1}]$, and which is defined by these rows. The inequalities (5) are the most practical consequence of this property. Note also that the larger $\mathbf{L}$ is, i.e. the closer to $\mathbf{B}$, the smaller the polyhedron and the tighter the bounds become. Besides, it is proved in [2, 4] that, given $\mathbf{L}$, the polyhedron and the bounds are the tightest ones that can be obtained.

## 4     The Method

How can we apply these results to compute bounds on the availability of a system such as the one described in Section 2 ?

Consider again the matrix $\mathbf{Q}$, defined by equation (2), where $\mathbf{Q}_{II}$ is the block of transitions between states with exactly $I$ failed components. Apply the same partitioning to its steady state vector $x$, and define $\chi_I v_I$ as the steady state vector corresponding to block $\mathbf{Q}_{II}$. $\chi_I$ is the *marginal probability* of being in any state of the set $I$. $v_I$ is the vector of *conditional probabilities* for the individual states of that subset.

First we have to compute the bounds of these conditional probabilities; those of the marginal probabilities will be computed in Section 7.

The vector $V_I$ can be obtained in the following way. Rewrite the matrix $\mathbf{Q}$ as:

$$\mathbf{Q} = \begin{pmatrix} \mathbf{Q}_{II} & \mathbf{E}(I) \\ \mathbf{F}(I) & \mathbf{G}(I) \end{pmatrix} \tag{6}$$

Then, solving Equation (1) for $V_I$ leads to:

$$V_I \left[ \mathbf{Q}_{II} + \mathbf{E}(I)(\mathbf{I}-\mathbf{G}(I))^{-1}\mathbf{F}(I) \right] = V_I \tag{7}$$

where the matrix $\mathbf{E}(I)(\mathbf{I}-\mathbf{G}(I))^{-1}\mathbf{F}(I)$ is called the Schurr complement of $\mathbf{Q}_{II}$, is non-negative, and has the same size as $\mathbf{Q}_{II}$. In practice, the computation of this Schurr complement is prohibitive, since $\mathbf{E}(I)$, $\mathbf{G}(I)$ and $\mathbf{F}(I)$ are almost the same size as the whole state space. However, it is quite possible to bound it from below, and, by application of Equation (4), to obtain the polyhedron which contains $V_I$. For instance, if this bound is taken equal to 0, one would obtain that:

$$V_I \in P\left[ (\mathbf{I}-\mathbf{Q}_{II})^{-1} \right] \tag{8}$$

or, if one can easily compute a lower bound matrix $\mathbf{S}(I)$ such that:

$$0 \leq \mathbf{S}(I) \leq \mathbf{E}(I)(\mathbf{I}-\mathbf{G}(I))^{-1}\mathbf{F}(I) \tag{9}$$

one can obtain a tighter polyhedron:

$$V_I \in P\left[ (\mathbf{I}-\mathbf{Q}_{II}-\mathbf{S}(I))^{-1} \right] \tag{10}$$

and tighter bounds (5).

A lower bound matrix $\mathbf{S}_{\mathbf{p}}(I)$ similar to $\mathbf{S}(I)$ can be obtained at little cost by an iterative procedure which is explained in the following section.

## 5    Iterative Procedure

Suppose for a moment that we already have a first approximation of the conditional probability vectors $V_J$ for all the blocks $J$ others than $I$. Then we can compute the transition probabilities between any pair of blocks not involving $I$; the block transition probability between block $J$ and $K$ is given by the scalar $V_J \mathbf{Q}_{JK} \mathbf{1}'$, where $\mathbf{1}'$ is a column vector of one. If we do not touch to the block $\mathbf{Q}_{II}$, then $\mathbf{Q}$ reduces to a matrix $\mathbf{Q}_{\mathbf{p}}$ where each block except $I$ corresponds to a single state:

$$
Q_p = \begin{pmatrix}
v_0 Q_{00} 1' & \cdots & v_0 Q_{0I} & \cdots & v_0 Q_{0N} 1' \\
\cdots & \cdots & \cdots & \cdots & \cdots \\
Q_{I0} 1' & \cdots & Q_{II} & \cdots & Q_{IN} 1' \\
\cdots & \cdots & \cdots & \cdots & \cdots \\
v_N Q_{N0} 1' & \cdots & v_N Q_{NI} & \cdots & v_N Q_{NN} 1'
\end{pmatrix}
$$

Each block $(K,I)$ in column $I$ is replaced by a row vector $v_K Q_{KI}$ of probabilities out of $K$ to each individual state of $I$. Each block $(I,K)$ in row $I$ is replaced by a vector $Q_{IK} 1'$ of transition probabilities out of each individual state of $I$ to block $K$.

If we rewrite $Q_p$ as

$$
Q_p = \begin{pmatrix}
G_p & F_p & G_p \\
E_p & Q_{II} & E_p \\
G_p & F_p & G_p
\end{pmatrix}
\tag{11}
$$

the reduced steady state vector $X_p$ of $Q_p$ which is equal to

$$
X_p = \begin{pmatrix} \chi_0 & \cdots & \chi_{I-1} & \chi_I v_I & \chi_{I+1} & \cdots & \chi_N \end{pmatrix}
\tag{12}
$$

is solution of the equation

$$
X_p = X_p Q_P
\tag{13}
$$

and the conditional distribution $v_I$ is given by:

$$
v_I = v_I \left( Q_{II} + E_p (I - G_p)^{-1} F_p \right)
\tag{14}
$$

where the Schurr complement involves an inverse $(I - G_p)^{-1}$ of size $(N-1) \times (N-1)$ only.

Now, if we have a first set of lower bounds on the vectors $v_J$, $J \neq I$, we can obtain a lower bound matrix $S_p$ at low cost in terms of these bounds, compute a new polyhedron for $v_I$, new bounds, and then a set of new matrices $S_p$, and so on. This process can be iterated indefinitely, starting with a set of initial values for the vectors $v_J$ obtained for instance by equation (8), the initial matrices $S_p$ being taken equal to 0. The sequence of $S_p$ matrices is non-decreasing, and the sequence of polyhedra non-increasing. The process does not diverge. However, because matrices are at each iteration substituted with lower bounds only, some information is never taken into account, and polyhedra will not eventually reduce to a single point, nor the bounds to the true vector.

An attractive possibility of this process is to restrict the analysis to the conditional distributions of interest, with only the corresponding parts of the Markov chain being needed.

## 6    Tridiagonal Matrices

The computation of the matrices $\mathbf{S_p}$ is further simplified when the matrix $\mathbf{Q}$, as in our example, is block tridiagonal. As shown in [Semal 1992], the Schurr complements involve no inverse. What needs to be added to $\mathbf{Q}_{II}$ to obtain the bounds on $V_I$, are the transitions to the two immediately adjacent blocks only. The equation (14) which defines $V_I$ reduces, in this case, to:

$$V_I = V_I \left( \mathbf{Q}_{II} + \frac{\left(\mathbf{Q}_{I,I-1}\,\mathbf{1}'\right)\,\left(V_{I-1}\mathbf{Q}_{I-1,I}\right)}{V_{I-1}\,\mathbf{Q}_{I-1,I}\,\mathbf{1}'} + \frac{\left(\mathbf{Q}_{I,I+1}\,\mathbf{1}'\right)\,\left(V_{I+1}\mathbf{Q}_{I+1,I}\right)}{V_{I+1}\,\mathbf{Q}_{I+1,I}\,\mathbf{1}'} \right) \quad (15)$$

Therefore, bounds on $V_{I-1}$ and $V_{I+1}$ only are needed to obtain those on $V_I$.

## 7    Bounding The Marginal Distribution

If bounds on elements of the complete vector are needed, one must also obtain bounds on the marginal distribution vector $\chi$. These bounds can be obtained by a procedure similar to the one described above. The marginal distribution is the steady state solution of the matrix $\mathbf{P}$ of transition probabilities between blocks:

$$\mathbf{P}_{IJ} \;=\; V_I\,\mathbf{Q}_{IJ}\,\mathbf{1}' \qquad I,J = 0,...,N \qquad\qquad (16)$$

With lower bounds on the vectors $V_I$, one can construct a lower bound matrix for $\mathbf{P}$. If $\mathbf{L_P}$ ($\leq \mathbf{P}$) is this matrix, then one has that $\chi \in P[(\mathbf{I}\text{-}\mathbf{L_p})^{-1}]$, from which bounds on the elements of $\chi$ are readily obtained.

Moreover, if, as it is typically the case (e.g; our example), the matrix $\mathbf{Q}$ is block tridiagonal, then the matrix $\mathbf{P}$ is tridiagonal., and tighter bounds can be obtained in the following way. A lower bound on $\chi_0$ is obtained by maximising the elements of the upper diagonal of $\mathbf{P}$ (i.e. the transitions away from block 0), and minimising those of the lower diagonal (the return transitions to block 0). This tridiagonal matrix can then be solved analytically. The technique can be repeated for each component of the vector $\chi$.

## 8    Complexity

Thus, when bounds on the complete solution vector $x$ are needed, the general method works as follows. For the conditional distributions $V_I$ of interest, polyhedra are computed iteratively as shown by Box 1 until some criterion of convergence is met.

---

**While** (convergence criterion is not met) **do**:

    **step 1.1** Select $I$

    **step 1.2** Compute the lower bound matrix $\mathbf{Sp}(I)$

    **step 1.3** Compute the polyhedron $P[\,(\mathbf{I} - \mathbf{Q}_{II} - \mathbf{Sp}(I))^{-1}]$


    **step 1.4** Derive bounds on $v_I$ from this polyhedron.

BOX 1

---

**step 2.1** Compute the lower bound matrix $\mathbf{L_p}$

**step 2.2** Compute the polyhedron $P[\,(\mathbf{I} - \mathbf{L_p})^{-1}]$

**step 2.3** Derive bounds on $\chi$ from this polyhedron

BOX 2

---

Polyhedra for the marginal distribution $\chi$ are then computed as shown in Box 2. In [19], the computation aspects of each of these steps are discussed, and simplifications and optimisations are given. Some of the most essential ones concern the polyhedra which are all computed from matrix inverses of the form $(\mathbf{I}\text{-}\mathbf{L})^{-1}$ When the matrix $\mathbf{L}$ tends to a stochastic matrix, the polyhedron tends to a single point, which is the Perron-Frobenius eigenvector of $\mathbf{L}$. However, the computation of the inverse becomes ill-conditioned since an eigenvalue tends to zero. The existence of such a small eigenvalue $(1 - \rho(\mathbf{L}))$ is however a good sign. It means that the polyhedron is *almost* uniquely defined by the eigenvector corresponding to this eigenvalue. The other eigenvalues and their eigenvectors introduce perturbations only, while in fact they are responsible for enlarging the polyhedron from a single point to a set.

Attention must therefore be given to this eigenvalue $(1 - \rho(\mathbf{L}))$ during the computation of the inverse. If it reduces to round-off errors, the best alternative is to consider the lower bound matrix $\mathbf{L}$ as being stochastic, and take its Perron-Frobenius vector as the exact value of the vector to be bounded. In all our numerical experiments, however, this eigenvalue remained away from zero, i.e. between $10^{-6}$ and $10^{-1}$. Note also that the determination of a polyhedron $P[\mathbf{A}]$ requires the computation of the normalized rows of $\mathbf{A}$ only. Normalisation factors can therefore be introduced at any stage of the polyhedron computation.

Note that the brute force computation of an inverse of the form $(\mathbf{I} - \mathbf{Q}_{II} - \mathbf{S})^{-1}$ requires $O(n_I^3)$ operations, where $n_I$ is the size of $\mathbf{Q}_{II}$ and of $\mathbf{S}$. This amount is already prohibitive in many applications. It can be reduced because this inverse can be computed as a rank N update of $(\mathbf{I} - \mathbf{Q}_{II})^{-1}$, where N is the rank of the perturbation matrix $\mathbf{S}$, and because $(\mathbf{I} - \mathbf{Q}_{II})^{-1}$ usually can be obtained cheaply. In many models, indeed, and in availability models in particular, the diagonal blocks $\mathbf{Q}_{II}$ are such that the matrix $(\mathbf{I} - \mathbf{Q}_{II})^{-1}$ remains very sparse. In models of repairable fault-tolerant systems for example, the fill ratio of this inverse is at most equal to the inverse of $\binom{N}{I}$, because system states with distinct failed components do not communicate through $\mathbf{Q}_{II}$, and thus $\mathbf{Q}_{II}$ is diagonal. In those cases, one can use the expression (see [19]):

$$\left(\mathbf{I} - \mathbf{Q}_{II} - \mathbf{S}\right)^{-1} = \left(\mathbf{I} - \mathbf{Q}_{II}\right)^{-1} - \mathbf{UV} \tag{17}$$

where the matrices $\mathbf{U} \in R_{n_I \times N}$, and $\mathbf{V} \ R_{N \times n_I}$ can be computed in $O(N^3 + N^2 n_I + N d_I)$ operations, where $d_I$ is the number of non-null components in $(\mathbf{I} - \mathbf{Q}_{II})^{-1}$. The number of operations remains thus linear in $n_I$. If $(\mathbf{I} - \mathbf{Q}_{II})^{-1}$ is not sparse, $O(N n_I^2)$ operations will be necessary, which represents a substantial saving compared to the initial $O(n_I^3)$. Further reductions in complexity are possible, and discussed in [19].

## 9    The Example Revisited

Our $2^{24}$ state space example of section 2 illustrates very well how the method can yield interesting results at surprising low cost. Because of the size of this state space, our objective is to bound the marginal distribution $\chi$ and a few conditional distributions $V_I$ only.

As said earlier, grouping the states with $I$ failed components in block $I$ leads to a stochastic matrix with diagonal blocks $\mathbf{Q}_{II}$ which are themselves diagonal. The inverses $(\mathbf{I}\text{-}\mathbf{Q}_{II})^{-1}$ are thus also diagonal. The bounds on $V_I$ were obtained using the equation (15). Two procedures were coded. A first procedure is needed for the first iteration and must assume that bounds on $V_{I-1}$ only are available when computing the bounds on $V_I$; the following lower matrix derived from (15) is used for this purpose:

$$S(I) \ \leq \ \frac{\left(\mathbf{Q}_{I,I-1}\ I'\right)\ \left(v_{I-1}\mathbf{Q}_{I-1,I}\right)}{v_{I-1}\mathbf{Q}_{I-1,I}\ \mathbf{1}'}$$

$S(I)$ is a rank one matrix; using (17) the rank one matrices $\mathbf{U}$ and $\mathbf{V}$ are determined in $O(n_I)$ operations. This matrix $S(I)$ is also used to compute the bounds corresponding to the last block which is taken into consideration. Bounds on the elements of $V_I$ are then obtained from (4) and (5).

In the subsequent iterations, values for both the bounds of $V_{I-1}$ and $V_{I+1}$ are available when computing those of $V_I$, and the following lower bound matrix is used:

$$S(I) \leq \frac{\left(\mathbf{Q}_{I,I-1}\,\mathbf{1}'\right)\left(v_{I-1}\,\mathbf{Q}_{I-1,I}\right)}{v_{I-1}\,\mathbf{Q}_{I-1,I}\,\mathbf{1}'} + \frac{\left(\mathbf{Q}_{I,I+1}\,\mathbf{1}'\right)\left(v_{I+1}\,\mathbf{Q}_{I+1,I}\right)}{v_{I+1}\,\mathbf{Q}_{I+1,I}\,\mathbf{1}'}$$

Using (17), the matrices $\mathbf{U}$ and $\mathbf{V}$, which are this time of rank two, are obtained in $O(n_i^2)$ operations.

The conditional distribution $V_0$ corresponding to 0 failed components is degenerated to a single state, and $V_0 = 1$. We have limited ourselves to the calculation of bounds for the conditional distributions $V_1$ to $V_F$ of the first F blocks. Numerical results for F=5 are given in Table 1 for $V_1$ and $V_5$ at ten successive iterations. Because of their lengths, the bound vectors $v^{inf}$ and $v^{sup}$ are given by their sums only; the closer to one these sums are, the tighter the bounds.

Note that increasing the number of iterations will never reduce the polyhedra to single points since the influence of the blocks $I$, $I > F$, is never taken into account. The theory guarantees however that these bounds are the tightest that one can obtain under those circumstances. One can also see from Table 1 that the neglected blocks have a larger influence on $V_5$ than on $V_1$, the bounds on the latter being tighter than those on the former.

**Table 1:** Quality of $V_I$ bounds for $I=1$ and $I=5$

| Iter. | $v_1^{\text{inf}}\,\mathbf{1}'$ | $v_1^{\text{sup}}\,\mathbf{1}'$ | $v_5^{\text{inf}}\,\mathbf{1}'$ | $v_5^{\text{sup}}\,\mathbf{1}'$ |
|---|---|---|---|---|
| 0 | 0.97057296 | 1.51081352 | 0.66085877 | 10747.925 |
| 1 | 0.99590078 | 1.07123235 | 0.88154804 | 3587.743 |
| 2 | 0.99920877 | 1.01375111 | 0.94878869 | 1533.806 |
| 3 | 0.99982092 | 1.00311225 | 0.96859991 | 937.785 |
| 4 | 0.99995537 | 1.00077566 | 0.97425200 | 768.459 |
| 5 | 0.99998807 | 1.00020725 | 0.97582994 | 721.243 |
| 6 | 0.99999653 | 1.00006017 | 0.97626554 | 708.213 |
| 7 | 0.99999879 | 1.00002086 | 0.97638519 | 704.634 |
| 8 | 0.99999941 | 1.00001020 | 0.97641799 | 703.653 |
| 9 | 0.99999958 | 1.00000729 | 0.97642698 | 703.384 |
| 10 | 0.99999962 | 1.00000650 | 0.97642944 | 703.311 |

The computation of bounds for the marginal distribution $\chi$ was done by following the procedure of Section 7. However, this procedure, in principle, assumes that conditional distribution bounds have been computed for *all* blocks, while we have explicitly computed those of the first 5 blocks only. In this example, and in availability models in general, this is feasible because the aggregated matrix is tridiagonal. Non-trivial upper and lower bounds on the repair rate and the failure rate can be determined for each block $I$, $I > F$ , without information on the conditional distributions of these blocks; minimum/maximum repair and failure rates over the states of each block can be used for instance. The bounds obtained for $\chi$ using the procedure of Section 7 are given in Table 2. Unavailability bounds are given in Table 3, with SUN 4 CPU computing times, for three different values of $F$.

The computational complexity of the whole algorithm is dominated by the computation of the bounds of the conditional distributions of the first F blocks, a complexity of $O(n_{F-1}^2)$. These blocks have a size $n_I$ which grows approximately with $N^I$. It is thus imperative to keep F small. The difference in order of magnitude between repair and failure rates induces a strong locality ( or near-decomposability) in the system matrix structure. This is the main factor which allows tight bounds on system availability to be obtained with small F values. For example, the bounds for F=4 were obtained within 6 CPU minutes on a SUN4 workstation. This value of F corresponds to only 12,951 states out of 16,777,216 states. That is, less than 0.1 percent of the total state space is being used by the analysis.

**Table 2.** Bounds on Marginal Distribution $\chi$

| $I$ | $\chi_I^{\text{inf}}$ | $\chi_I^{\text{sup}}$ |
|---|---|---|
| 0 | 9.7524506e-01 | 9.7524508e-01 |
| 1 | 2.4196310e-02 | 2.4196323e-02 |
| 2 | 5.4713023e-04 | 5.4713505e-04 |
| 3 | 1.1261528e-05 | 1.1263011e-05 |
| 4 | 2.1278181e-07 | 2.1323658e-07 |
| 5 | 3.6789961e-09 | 3.8219805e-09 |
| 6 | 2.6455985e-11 | 8.3829687e-11 |
| 7 | 1.2670814e-13 | 2.6554535e-12 |
| 8 | 5.2238309e-16 | 8.3452321e-14 |
| 9 | 1.8370472e-18 | 2.6017736e-15 |
| 10 | 5.6948463e-21 | 7.8513118e-17 |
| 11 | 1.5281171e-23 | 2.2907590e-18 |
| 12 | 3.4637321e-26 | 6.4546184e-20 |
| 13 | 6.4079044e-29 | 1.7541567e-21 |
| 14 | 9.7186549e-32 | 4.5479612e-23 |
| 15 | 1.1500408e-34 | 1.1222898e-24 |
| 16 | 9.7753471e-38 | 2.6291623e-26 |
| 17 | 5.0505960e-41 | 5.8306321e-28 |
| 18 | 2.1885916e-44 | 1.1870343e-29 |
| 19 | 7.6600706e-48 | 2.1792270e-31 |
| 20 | 2.1703533e-51 | 3.5164800e-33 |
| 21 | 4.7024322e-55 | 4.7952000e-35 |
| 22 | 7.0536483e-59 | 5.2601890e-37 |
| 23 | 5.8780403e-63 | 1.3389572e-39 |
| 24 | 2.4491834e-67 | 1.7852763e-42 |

**Table 3.** Bounds on Unavailability

| F | $n_F$ | lower bound | upper bound | CPU(sec.) |
|---|---|---|---|---|
| 4 | 10626 | 4.63e-08 | 6.51e-07 | 325. |
| 5 | 42504 | 4.63e-08 | 8.02e-08 | 4965. |
| 6 | 134596 | 4.63e-08 | 4.98 e-08 | 78280. |

# 10   Conclusions

This new iterative computation method to bound conditional and marginal steady-state distributions in Markov chains dispenses from generating the whole state space, and is specially suited - and may even be indispensable - when the state space is too large to use classical procedures. The bounds are proven to be the tightest ones that can be obtained, given the part of the state space being considered. Locality or near-decomposability are important factors contributing to tightness [3].

The method is limited by the computational requirements of matrix inversions. These requirements are however strongly mitigated when the diagonal blocks $Q_{II}$ of the Markov chain are such that the inverses $(I-Q_{II})^{-1}$ can be economically computed. Fortunately, this is always the case in models of system availability.

Other computational complexity reductions are possible and have been mentioned. Further investigations are needed, however, as it seems that the whole bounding process could remain linear in the part of the state space which is considered.

# Fast Numerical Solution for a Class of Markov Models[*]

Ram Chakka    Isi Mitrani

University of Newcastle upon Tyne

**Abstract.** Many two-dimensional Markov models whose state space is a semi-infinite strip (i.e. finite in one dimension and infinite in the other) can be solved efficiently by means of spectral expansion. This method and its application are described in the context of an M/M/N queue with general breakdowns and repairs. The results of experiments aimed at evaluating the relative merits of the spectral expansion and the matrix-geometric solutions are also presented.

## 1  Introduction

There is a large class of models which involve two-dimensional Markov processes on semi-infinite lattice strips. That is, the system state is described by two integer random variables, $I$ and $J$; one of these has a finite range, and the other can take any non-negative value. Often these models are cast in the framework of a Markov-modulated queue: then the bounded variable, $I$, indicates the state of the Markovian environment, while the unbounded one, $J$, represents the number of jobs in the system (a recent survey can be found in [18]).

We are interested in a sub-class of the above processes, characterized by the following two properties:

(i).    the instantaneous transition rates out of state $(i,j)$ do not depend on $j$ when the latter is sufficiently large;

(ii).   the jumps of the random variable $J$ are limited in size.

When the jumps of $J$ are of size 1, the process is said to be of the *Quasi-Birth-and-Death* type (the term *skip-free* is also used, e.g. in [11]).

There are three known methods for solving such models exactly. The first method is to reduce the infinite-state problem to a linear equation involving a vector generating function and some unknown probabilities. The latter are then determined with the aid of the singularities of the coefficient matrix. A comprehensive treatment of that approach, in the context of a discrete-time process with a more general M/G/1 structure, is presented in [7].

The second method, which is the subject of this paper, is called *spectral expansion*. It is based on expressing the invariant vector of the process in terms of the eigenvalues and left eigenvectors of a certain matrix polynomial. The idea of the spectral expansion method has been known for some time (e.g., see [17, 5]), but there are very few examples of its application in the performance evaluation literature (some recent instances where that solution has proved useful are reported in [6] and

---

[*] This paper is based in part on material in [13].

[14]). The generating function and the spectral expansion methods are closely related. However, the latter produces steady-state probabilities directly, whereas the former provides them through a transform.

The third way of solving these models is by the *matrix-geometric* method [16]. This widely used approach relies on determining the minimal positive solution, $R$, of a non-linear matrix equation; the invariant vector is then expressed in terms of powers of $R$.

The purpose of this paper is two-fold. First, we wish to popularize the spectral expansion method by describing its application in the context of a non-trivial problem. The model in question involves an M/M/N queue where job behaviour and processor availability are governed by a general Markovian environment [12, 17].

The second objective is to compare the effectiveness of the spectral expansion and the matrix-geometric solutions. Such a comparison has not been carried out before. A number of numerical experiments are performed, where the same examples are solved by both methods. Issues of speed, numerical stability and accuracy are considered. The available results are strongly in favour of the spectral expansion method.

The model is described in section 2. To keep the presentation simple, only single arrivals and departures are considered. The spectral expansion solution is presented in section 3. Section 4 is devoted to the comparison between the spectral expansion and the matrix-geometric solutions.

## 2    The Model

Consider a system where $N$ identical parallel processors serve a common, unbounded job queue. The processors break down from time to time, and return to an operative state after being repaired. When operative, each processor serves jobs, one at a time, and each job is allowed to occupy at most one operative processor at a time. The policy concerning services interrupted by breakdowns can be thought of as either *resume*, or *repeat with re-sampling*; however, the precise specification is contained in the process evolution assumptions given below.

Let $I(t)$ and $J(t)$ be the random variables representing the number of operative processors at time $t$, and the number of jobs in the system at time $t$, respectively. We shall sometimes refer to $I(t)$ as the *operative state* of the set of processors. It is assumed that $X = \{[I(t), J(t)] ; t \geq 0\}$ is an irreducible Markov process with state space $\{0, 1, ..., N\} \times \{0, 1, ...\}$. The evolution of that process proceeds according to the following set of possible transitions:

(a) *From state* $(i, j)$ *to state* $(k, j)$ $(0 \leq i, k \leq N ; i \neq k)$;

(b) *From state* $(i, j)$ *to state* $(k, j + 1)$ $(0 \leq i, k \leq N)$;

(c) *From state* $(i, j)$ *to state* $(k, j - 1)$ $(0 \leq i, k \leq N)$.

We assume further that there is a threshold, $M$, $(M \geq 1)$ such that the instantaneous transition rates do not depend on $j$ when $j \geq M$. In other words, if we denote the transition rate matrices associated with (a), (b) and (c) by $A_j$, $B_j$ and $C_j$ respectively (the main diagonal of $A_j$ is zero by definition; also, $C_0 = 0$ by definition), then we have

$$A_j = A \, ; B_j = B \, ; C_j = C \, , j \geq M \, . \tag{1}$$

Transitions (a) correspond to changes in the number of operative processors. For example, if all processors break down and are repaired independently of each other and of the number of jobs present, with rates $\xi$ and $\eta$ per processor respectively, then the matrices $A$ and $A_j$ would be tri-diagonal, given by:

$$A = A_j = \begin{bmatrix} 0 & N\eta & & & \\ \xi & 0 & (N-1)\eta & & \\ & 2\xi & 0 & \ddots & \\ & & \ddots & \ddots & \eta \\ & & & N\xi & 0 \end{bmatrix} . \tag{2}$$

Clearly, a large class of different breakdown and repair patterns can be modelled by choosing $A$ and $A_j$ appropriately.

A transition of type (b) represents a job arrival coinciding with a change in the number of operative processors. If arrivals are not accompanied by such changes, then the matrices $B$ and $B_j$ are diagonal. For example, if jobs arrive according to an independent Poisson process with rate $\sigma_i$ when there are $i$ operative processors, then

$$B = B_j = diag[\sigma_0, \sigma_1, \ldots, \sigma_N] \tag{3}$$

Similarly, a transition of type (c) represents a job departure coinciding with a change in the number of operative processors. Again, if such coincidences do not occur, then the matrices $C$ and $C_j$ are diagonal. In particular, if each operative processor serves jobs at rate $\mu$, then

$$\begin{aligned} C_j &= diag[0, \min(j,1)\mu, \min(j,2)\mu, \ldots, \min(j,N)\mu] \, ; \, j < N, \\ C &= diag[0, \mu, 2\mu, \ldots, N\mu] \, ; \, j \geq N. \end{aligned} \tag{4}$$

The requirement that all transition rates, and in particular those affecting the reliability of the system, cease to depend on the size of the job queue beyond a certain threshold, is not too restrictive. It enables, for example, the consideration of models where the breakdown and repair rates depend on the number of busy processors. On the other hand, it is difficult to think of applications where those rates would depend on the number of jobs waiting to begin execution. Note that we impose no limit on the magnitude of the threshold $M$, although it must be pointed out that the larger $M$ is, the greater may be the complexity of the solution. Of course, if the only dependencies of the various transition rates on $j$ are the ones manifested in equations (4) and/or the ones mentioned in this paragraph, then the threshold is equal to the number of processors: $M = N$.

It is clear that, although we have been talking in terms of $N$ servers subject to breakdowns and repairs, the above is in fact a general Quasi-Birth-and-Death process which can be used to model a large class of queues in Markovian environments.

As well as the matrices $A_j$, $B_j$ and $C_j$, it will be convenient to define the diagonal matrices $D_j^A$, $D_j^B$ and $D_j^C$, whose $i^{th}$ diagonal element is the $i^{th}$ row sum of $A_j$, $B_j$ and $C_j$, respectively. Those row sums are the total rates at which the process $X$

leaves state $(i,j)$ , due to (a) changes in the number of operative servers, (b) job arrivals (perhaps accompanied by such a change) and (c) job departures (ditto), respectively. The $j$-independent versions of these diagonal matrices are denoted by $D^A, D^B$ and $D^C$, respectively.

The object of the analysis is to determine the joint steady-state distribution of the number of operative processors and the number of jobs in the system:

$$p_{i,j} = \lim_{t \to \infty} P(I(t) = i, J(t) = j) ; i = 0,1,...,N ; j = 0,1.... \tag{5}$$

That distribution exists for an irreducible Markov process if, and only if, the corresponding set of balance equations has a unique normalisable solution.

Once the probabilities $p_{i,j}$ are known, various performance measures of interest can be obtained easily.

## 3    Spectral Expansion Solution

Rather than working with the two-dimensional distribution $\{p_{i,j}\}$ , we shall introduce the row vectors,

$$\mathbf{v}_j = (p_{0,j}, p_{1,j}, ..., p_{N,j}) ; j = 0,1.... \tag{6}$$

whose elements represent the states with $j$ jobs in the system.

The balance equations satisfied by the probabilities $p_{i,j}$ can be written in terms of the vectors $\mathbf{v}_j$. They are:

$$\mathbf{v}_j[D_j^A + D_j^B + D_j^C] = \mathbf{v}_{j-1}B_{j-1} + \mathbf{v}_j A_j + \mathbf{v}_{j+1}C_{j+1} ; j = 0,1,...,M \tag{7}$$

(where $\mathbf{v}_{-1} = 0$ by definition), and

$$\mathbf{v}_j[D^A + D^B + D^C] = \mathbf{v}_{j-1}B + \mathbf{v}_j A + \mathbf{v}_{j+1}C ; j = M+1, M+2,... \tag{8}$$

In addition, all probabilities must sum up to 1:

$$\sum_{j=0}^{\infty} \mathbf{v}_j \mathbf{e} = 1, \tag{9}$$

where $\mathbf{e}$ is a column vector with $N+1$ elements, all of which are equal to 1.

We shall start by finding the general solution of equation (8). That equation has the nice property that its coefficients do not depend on $j$. It can be rewritten in the form

$$\mathbf{v}_j Q_0 + \mathbf{v}_{j+1}Q_1 + \mathbf{v}_{j+2}Q_2 = \boldsymbol{0} ; j = M, M+1,..., \tag{10}$$

where $Q_0 = B$, $Q_1 = A - D^A - D^B - D^C$ and $Q_2 = C$. This is a homogeneous vector difference equation of order 2, with constant coefficients. Associated with it is the characteristic matrix polynomial, $Q(\lambda)$ , defined as

$$Q(\lambda) = Q_0 + Q_1\lambda + Q_2\lambda^2. \tag{11}$$

Denote by $\lambda_k$ and $\psi_k$ the eigenvalues and corresponding left eigenvectors of $Q(\lambda)$. In other words, these are quantities which satisfy

$$\psi_k Q(\lambda_k) = \mathbf{0} \; ; \; k = 1, 2, \ldots, d, \tag{12}$$

where $d = degree\{det[Q(\lambda)]\}$.

The eigenvalues do not have to be simple, but we shall assume that if $\lambda_k$ has multiplicity $m$, then it also has $m$ linearly independent left eigenvectors. This is invariably observed to be the case in practice. Some experiments in that direction are mentioned in section 4.

It is readily seen, by direct substitution, that for every eigenvalue $\lambda_k$, and corresponding left eigenvector $\psi_k$, the sequence

$$\{\psi_k \lambda_k^j \; ; \; j = M, M + 1, \ldots\}, \tag{13}$$

is a solution of equation (10). By combining multiple eigenvalues with each of their independent eigenvectors, we thus obtain a total of $d$ linearly independent solutions. On the other hand, it is known (e.g., see [8]), that the dimensionality of the solution space of equation (10) is exactly $d$. Therefore, any solution of (10) can be expressed as a linear combination of the $d$ solutions (13):

$$\mathbf{v}_j = \sum_{k=1}^{d} x_k \psi_k \lambda_k^j \; ; \; j = M, M + 1, \ldots, \tag{14}$$

where $x_k$ $(k = 1, 2, \ldots, d)$, are arbitrary (complex) constants.

However, we are only interested in solutions which are, or can be normalized to become, probability distributions. Hence, we wish to select from the set (14), those sequences for which the series $\sum \mathbf{v}_j \mathbf{e}$ converges. This requirement implies that if $|\lambda_k| \geq 1$, then the corresponding coefficient $x_k$ must be 0. We have thus arrived at the following

**Proposition 1** *Suppose that $c$ of the eigenvalues of $Q(\lambda)$ are strictly inside the unit disk (each counted according to its multiplicity), while the others are on the circumference or outside. Let the numbering be such that $|\lambda_k| < 1$ for $k = 1, 2, \ldots, c$. The corresponding independent eigenvectors are $\psi_1, \psi_2, \ldots, \psi_c$. Then any solution of equation (8) which can be normalized to a probability distribution is of the form*

$$\mathbf{v}_j = \sum_{k=1}^{c} x_k \psi_k \lambda_k^j \; ; \; j = M, M + 1, \ldots, \tag{15}$$

*where $x_k$ $(k = 1, 2, \ldots, c)$, are arbitrary constants.*

Note that if there are non-real eigenvalues in the unit disk, then they appear in complex-conjugate pairs. The corresponding eigenvectors are also complex-conjugate. The same must be true for the appropriate pairs of constants $x_k$ in order that the right-hand side of (15) be real. To ensure that it is also positive, it seems that the real parts of $\lambda_k$, $\psi_k$ and $x_k$ should be positive. Indeed, that is always found to be the case.

Clearly, the powers $\lambda_k^j$ in (15) can be replaced by $\lambda_k^{j+m}$, for any fixed $m$, without altering the validity of the proposition. Such a change has to be made, for instance, when one or more of the eigenvalues are zero. Then the expansion should be of the form

$$\mathbf{v}_j = \sum_{k=1}^{c} x_k \psi_k \lambda_k^{j-M} \; ; j = M, M+1, \ldots,$$

in order to make use of the corresponding eigenvectors.

So far, we have obtained expressions for the vectors $\mathbf{v}_M, \mathbf{v}_{M+1}, \ldots$, which contain $c$ unknown constants. Now it is time to consider equations (7), for $j = 0, 1, \ldots, M$. This is a set of $(M+1) \times (N+1)$ linear equations with $M \times (N+1)$ unknown probabilities (the vectors $\mathbf{v}_j$ for $j = 0, 1, \ldots, M-1$ ) , plus the $c$ constants $x_k$. However, only $(M+1) \times (N+1) - 1$ of these equations are linearly independent, since the generator matrix of the Markov process is singular. On the other hand, an additional independent equation is provided by (9).

Clearly, this set of $(M+1) \times (N+1)$ equations with $M \times (N+1) + c$ unknowns will have a unique solution if, and only if, $c = N+1$. This observation, together with the fact that an irreducible Markov process has a steady-state distribution if, and only if, its balance and normalisation equations have a unique solution, implies

**Proposition 2** *The condition $c = N+1$ (the number of eigenvalues of $Q(\lambda)$ strictly inside the unit disk is equal to the number of operative states of the set of processors), is necessary and sufficient for the ergodicity of the Markov process X.*

If job arrivals and departures do not trigger processor breakdowns or repairs (i.e., the matrices $B$, $B_j$, $C$ and $C_j$ are diagonal), and if the breakdown and repair rates do not depend on the number of jobs in the system (i.e., $A_j = A \; ; j = 0,1,\ldots$), then there is an intuitively appealing probabilistic condition for ergodicity. Denote by $\mathbf{v}$ the marginal distribution of the number of operative processors:

$$\mathbf{v} = (p_{0.}, p_{1.}, \ldots, p_{N.}) = \sum_{j=0}^{\infty} \mathbf{v}_j.$$

This is the stationary probability vector of the matrix $A - D^A$, and can be obtained by solving the equations

$$\mathbf{v}(A - D^A) = \mathbf{0} \quad ; \quad \mathbf{v}\mathbf{e} = 1. \tag{16}$$

It is then possible to assert that the system is stable if, and only if, when the queue is long, the average incoming load is less than the average service capacity [17]:

$$\mathbf{v}B\mathbf{e} < \mathbf{v}C\mathbf{e} . \tag{17}$$

(the matrices $B_j$ *and* $C_j$, which are relevant only for queue sizes below the threshold $M$, play no role here).

Condition (17) is thus equivalent to the requirement in Proposition 2.

In summary, the spectral expansion solution procedure consists of the following steps:

(1)     Compute the eigenvalues, $\lambda_k$, and the corresponding left eigenvectors, $\psi_k$, of $Q(\lambda)$. If $c < N+1$, stop; a steady-state distribution does not exist.

(2)     Solve the finite set of linear equations (7) and (9), with $v_M$ and $v_{M+1}$ given by (15), to determine the constants $x_k$ and the vectors $v_j$ for $j < M$.

(3)     Use the obtained solution for the purpose of determining various moments, marginal probabilities, percentiles and other system performance measures that may be of interest.

Careful attention should be paid to step 1. The `brute force' approach which relies on first evaluating the scalar polynomial $det[Q(\lambda)]$, then finding its roots, may be rather time-consuming for large $N$ and is therefore not recommended. An alternative which is preferable in most cases is to reduce the quadratic eigenvalue-eigenvector problem

$$\psi[Q_0 + Q_1\lambda + Q_2\lambda^2] = 0, \tag{18}$$

to a linear one of the form $yQ - \lambda y$, where $Q$ is a matrix whose dimensions are twice as large as those of $Q_0$, $Q_1$ and $Q_2$. The latter problem is normally solved by applying various transformation techniques. Efficient routines for that purpose are available in most numerical packages.

This linearisation can be achieved quite easily when at least one of the matrices $B$ and $C$ is non-singular. Indeed, suppose that $C^{-1} = Q_2^{-1}$ exists. After multiplying (18) on the right by $C^{-1}$, it becomes

$$\psi[R_0 + R_1\lambda + I\lambda^2] = 0, \tag{19}$$

where $R_0 = Q_0C^{-1}$, $R_1 = Q_1C^{-1}$ and I is the identity matrix of order $N+1$. By introducing the vector $\varphi = \lambda\psi$, equation (19) can be rewritten in the equivalent linear form

$$[\psi \quad \varphi]\begin{bmatrix} 0 & -R_0 \\ I & -R_1 \end{bmatrix} = \lambda[\psi \quad \varphi]. \tag{20}$$

If $C$ is singular but $B$ is not, a similar linearisation is achieved by a multiplication of (18) on the right by $B^{-1}$, and a change of variable $\lambda \rightarrow 1/\lambda$. The relevant eigenvalues are then those outside the unit disk.

If both $B$ and $C$ are singular, then the desired result is achieved by an alternative change of variable: $\lambda \rightarrow (\theta + \lambda)/(\theta - \lambda)$ ( see [10]. The parameter $\theta$ is chosen so that the matrix $S = \theta^2 Q_2 + \theta Q_1 + Q_0$ is non-singular.

Step 2 may be computationally expensive if the threshold $M$ is large. In the present case, because of the block tridiagonal structure of the set of equations, they can be solved efficiently by a block iterative method. Also, if the matrices $B_j$ ($j = 0, 1,...,$ $M-1$) are non-singular (which is usually the case in pactice), then the vectors $v_{M-1}$, $v_{M-2}$, ...,$v_0$ can be expressed in terms of $v_M$ and $v_{M-1}$, with the aid of equations (7) for $j = M, M-1,...,1$. One is then left with equations (7) for $j = 0$, plus (9) (a total of $N+1$ independent linear equations), for the $N+1$ unknowns $x_k$. This is in fact the method adopted in all our implementations.

The spectral expansion solution is illustrated in the following numerical example. A 10-processor system is considered, with a state-independent Poisson arrival process,

$$B = B_j = \sigma I , \tag{21}$$

and a service rate matrix given by (4). Individual servers break down at rate $\xi$ and are repaired at rate $\eta$; in addition, there are `global' simultaneous breakdowns of all currently operative servers, at rate $\xi_0$, and `global' simultaneous repairs of all currently inoperative processors, at rate $\eta_N$. The operative state transition matrix is then given by

$$A = A_j = \begin{bmatrix} 0 & N\eta & & & \eta_N \\ \xi_0 + \xi & 0 & (N-1)\eta & & \eta_N \\ \xi_0 & 2\xi & 0 & \ddots & \vdots \\ \vdots & & \ddots & \ddots & \eta + \eta_N \\ \xi_0 & & & N\xi & 0 \end{bmatrix} . \tag{22}$$

Fig. 1 shows the conditional and unconditional 95-percentiles, together with $E(J)$, as functions of the arrival rate. The unconditional percentile, $J95$, is defined by $P(J \le J95) = 0.95$, while the conditioning is upon the number, $m$, of operative processors. The figure demonstrates that the mean can be a very poor predictor of the percentiles. More extensive performance results on this and related systems are reported in [1].

Before leaving this section, it is worth pointing out that the spectral expansion method can be extended also to (i) processes where the variable $J$ (i.e. the queue size), is bounded, (ii) the case of batch arrivals where the variable $J$ may jump by arbitrary but bounded amounts in either direction, and (iii) the case of non-identical processors. These extensions are reported in [13].

# 4     Comparison with the Matrix-Geometric Solution

The models described in this paper can be solved also by the matrix-geometric method [16]. For the Quasi-Birth-and-Death processes considered in section 3, the vectors $\mathbf{v}_j$, $j \ge M$, are expressed in the form

$$\mathbf{v}_j = \mathbf{v}_M R^{j-M} , \tag{23}$$

where $R$ is the minimal non-negative solution of the quadratic matrix equation corresponding to the difference equation (10):

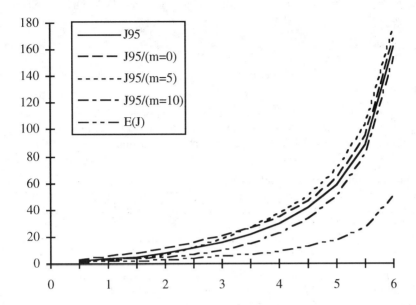

**Fig. 1.** Conditional and unconditional 95-percentiles, and E(J), as functions of the arrival rate for the system: $N=10$, $\mu=1.0$, $\xi=0.05$, $\eta=0.1$, $\xi_0=0.05$, $\eta_N=0.1$; Saturation point: $\sigma_{max} = 6.66667$.

$$Q_0 + RQ_1 + R^2Q_2 = 0 . \tag{24}$$

The remaining unknown probabilities are determined from the balance equations for $j \leq M$, together with the normalizing equation. This part of the solution is very similar to step 2 of the spectral expansion procedure (summary in section 3), and has the same order of complexity.

There is a close relationship between the matrix equation (24) and the eigenvalue-eigenvector equation (12). If a matrix $R$ satisfies (24), and $\psi R = \lambda R$ for some $\psi$ and $\lambda$, then those $\psi$ and $\lambda$ satisfy (12). Conversely, any $N+1$ numbers $\lambda_k$ and independent vectors $\psi_k$ that satisfy (12), determine a matrix $R$ which has them as eigenvalues and eigenvectors, and satisfies (24). For an ergodic system, the minimal solution of (24) is the one whose eigenvalues are the $N+1$ solutions of (12) that are inside the unit disk.

Thus the main operational difference between the two approaches is that spectral expansion involves the computation of eigenvalues and eigenvectors of a given matrix, whereas the matrix-geometric method requires the determination of an unknown matrix by solving a matrix equation. To evaluate the impact of that difference, we have performed a series of experiments where the same models were solved by both methods. The performance measure that is computed is $E(J)$, the average number of jobs in the system. The aim of these experiments is to examine the issues of efficiency, accuracy, numerical stability and limits of application.

There are several iterative procedures for solving equation (24). We have used the so-called *modified SS method* [16, 9],

$$R_{n+1} = \left[ -Q_0 - R_n^2 Q_2 \right] Q_1^{-1}, \tag{25}$$

starting with $R_0 = 0$. The number of iterations depends on the model parameters and on the desired accuracy.

The tasks that are similar in both methods are, whenever possible, carried out by the same piece of software. No attempt is made, in either method, to optimize the code or to exploit particular model features. Double precision arithmetic is used throughout (except inside the NAG routines, which sometimes employ extended precision).

It should be emphasized that both solution methods are exact in principle. That is, if the eigenvalues and eigenvectors on the one hand, and the matrix $R$ on the other, are determined exactly, and if the respective sets of linear equations are solved exactly, then in both cases the values of the resulting probabilities and performance measures would be correct. In practice, the accuracy of the results depends on many factors and varies between the methods.

The overall computational complexity of determining all eigenvalues and eigenvectors is $O(N^3)$. Moreover, that complexity is more or less independent of the parameters of the model. Even when two eigenvalues coincide, or almost coincide, the algorithm finds linearly independent eigenvectors if the latter exist. The accuracy of the spectral expansion solution is limited only by the precision of the numerical operations. When there is no diagnostic about an ill-conditioned set of linear equations, the value of $E(J)$ computed by this method is observed to be correct to about 10 signifficant digits, i.e. it is exact for all practical purposes.

The matrix-geometric solution relies on the matrix $R$, which is computed approximately by the iterative procedure described above. The criterion for terminating that procedure would normally include some trade-off between computation time and accuracy. The situation is illustrated in table 1, where the 10-server model from the example at the end of section 3 is solved by both methods. The iterative procedure (25) is terminated when

$$\max_{i,j} \left| R_{n+1}(i,j) - R_n(i,j) \right| < \varepsilon$$

for a given value of $\varepsilon$. The performance measure that is computed is the average queue size, $E(J)$, for three different values of the arrival rate, $\sigma$. The spectral expansion solution is of course independent of $\varepsilon$. Column 4 gives the percentage relative difference $100 * [\, E(J)(\text{spect.exp.}) - E(J)(\text{mat.geom.}) \,] / E(J)(\text{spect.exp.})$.

The table confirms that when $\varepsilon$ decreases, the matrix-geometric solution approaches the spectral expansion one. However, it is important to observe that the accuracy of $R$ is not related in any obvious way to the accuracy of $E(J)$. Thus, taking $\varepsilon = 10^{-6}$ yields an answer whose relative error is $0.0004$ % when $\sigma = 3$, $0.06$ % when $\sigma = 6$, and $6.3$ % when $\sigma = 6.6$. Another important aspect of the table is that, for a given $\varepsilon$, the number of iterations required to compute $R$ increases with $\sigma$.

**Table. 1.** Trade-off between accuracy and complexity

| $\sigma = 3.0$ ; | $E(J)_{(spect.\ exp.)} = 5.1997104203$ | | |
|---|---|---|---|
| $\varepsilon$ | iterations | $E(J)_{(mat.\ geom.)}$ | % difference |
| $10^{-3}$ | 29 | 5.175072879090 | 0.4738252555 |
| $10^{-6}$ | 93 | 5.199686527032 | 0.0004595110 |
| $10^{-9}$ | 158 | 5.199710396767 | 0.0000004521 |
| $10^{-12}$ | 223 | 5.199710420254 | 0.0000000004 |
| $\sigma = 6.0$ ; | $E(J)_{(spect.\ exp.)} = 50.4058205572$ | | |
| $\varepsilon$ | iterations | $E(J)_{(mat.\ geom.)}$ | % difference |
| $10^{-3}$ | 77 | 35.0382555318 | 30.4876795091 |
| $10^{-6}$ | 670 | 50.3726795846 | 0.0657483051 |
| $10^{-9}$ | 1334 | 50.4057872349 | 0.0000661080 |
| $10^{-12}$ | 1999 | 50.4058205241 | 0.0000000657 |
| $\sigma = 6.6$ ; | $E(J)_{(spect.\ exp.)} = 540.46702456$ | | |
| $\varepsilon$ | iterations | $E(J)_{(mat.\ geom.)}$ | % difference |
| $10^{-3}$ | 77 | 58.19477818 | 89.23250160 |
| $10^{-6}$ | 2636 | 506.34712584 | 6.31303986 |
| $10^{-9}$ | 9174 | 540.42821366 | 0.00718099 |
| $10^{-12}$ | 15836 | 540.46698572 | 0.00000719 |

The computational complexity of the two solutions is compared in Fig. 2. In both cases, the time taken to compute $E(J)$ is plotted against the arrival rate, $\sigma$. For the spectral expansion solution, that time is independent of $\sigma$ and is about *0.6* seconds. The plots for the matrix-geometric solution are obtained as follows: First, the program is run with varying numbers of iterations, in order to establish the exact number of iterations which yields the value of $E(J)$ with the desired accuracy (relative to the spectral expansion result). A run with that fixed number of iterations is then timed. (In the absence of an exact result, one would have to rely on internal accuracy checks for the termination criterion.)

The most notable feature of Fig. 2 is the steep deterioration of the matrix-geometric run time when $\sigma$ increases. For a heavily loaded system, that run time may be many orders of magnitude larger than the spectral expansion one. The extra time is almost entirely taken up by the procedure that calculates the matrix $R$. It seems clear that, even when the accuracy requirements are modest, the computational demands of the iterative procedure have a vertical asymptote at the saturation point.

It can be argued that a different procedure for computing $R$ may yield better results. A number of such procedures have been compared in [9], and improvements have indeed been observed. However, the results reported in [9] indicate that all iterative approaches suffer from the drawbacks exhibited in table 1 and Fig. 1, namely that their accuracy and efficiency decrease when the load increases. Perhaps the fastest existing method for computing $R$ is not by iterations, but via its eigenvalues and eigenvectors (this was done in [5] for a model with real eigenvalues and a non-singular matrix $C$ ). If that method is adopted,

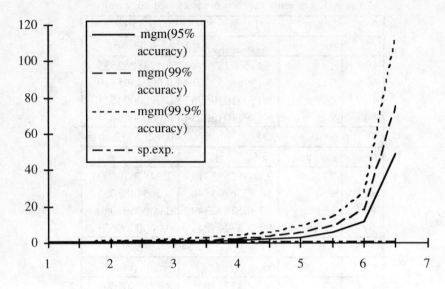

**Fig. 2.** Mean queue length computation times ( in sec.) for different arrival rates for the system: $N=10$, $\mu=1.0$, $\xi=0.05$, $\eta=0.1$, $\xi_0=0.05$, $\eta_N=0.1$; Saturation point: $\sigma_{max} =$ 6.66667.

then ·one might as well use spectral expansion directly, and avoid the matrix $R$ altogether.

In our experience, using different starting points for the iterations (rather than $R_0 = 0$), does not bring significant benefits and may be dangerous. The procedure could diverge or it could, conceivably, converge to a non-minimal solution of (24).

The next set of experiments concerns the behaviour of the two algorithms when the size of the problem, chiefly determined by the number of processors, increases. It is perhaps worth restating the effect of the parameter $N$.

Spectral expansion: The characteristic polynomial is of degree at most $2N+2$ ; finding the eigenvalues and left eigenvectors is a task of complexity $O(N^3)$ . The coefficients of the $N+1$ term expansion are determined by solving a set of $N+1$ simultaneous linear equations, which is also a task of complexity $O(N^3)$ .

Matrix-geometric solution: The matrix $R$ is of dimensions $(N + 1) \times (N + 1)$ ; each step in the iterative procedure is of complexity $O(N^3)$ . An unknown vector with $N+1$ elements is determined by solving a set of $N+1$ simultaneous linear equations (complexity $O(N^3)$ ).

The results of the experiments are displayed in Fig. 3. In all cases, constant load is maintained by increasing the arrival rate in proportion to $N$ . When timing the matrix-geometric runs, the number of iterations for matrix $R$ is chosen so as to achieve $99\%$ accuracy in $E(J)$ , relative to the spectral expansion value. The figure illustrates the big difference in the run times of the two algoritms.

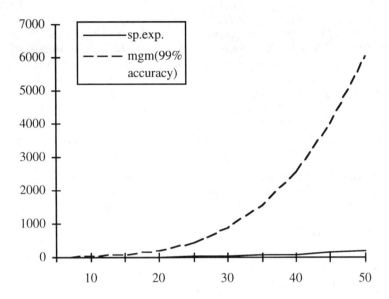

**Fig. 3.** Mean queue length computation times (in sec.) for different N for the system: $\mu=1.0$, $\xi=0.05$, $\eta=0.1$, $\xi_0=0.05$, $\eta_N=0.1$, $\sigma=0.6N$;  Saturation point: $\sigma_{max} = 0.66667N$.

If the number of iterations is considered as a function of $N$, with the load fixed, then the increase has been observed to be approximately linear. If that is a general phenomenon, then the overall computational complexity of the iterative procedure for computing $R$ is $O(N^4)$.

The second step in both algorithms (solving a set of linear equations), is where emerging numerical problems begin to manifest themselves. The observable symptom of such problems is usually an ill-conditioned matrix. It should be emphasized that neither the spectral expansion nor the matrix-geometric algorithm is immune to ill-conditioned matrices. We have observed them generally when the number of processors is large and the system is lightly loaded. For example, taking $N = 50$, $\sigma < 15$ (other parameters as in the figures), leads to ill-conditioned matrices in both algorithms.

In many cases, the problem of ill-conditioning can be alleviated by appropriate scaling (e.g. multiplying certain vectors by suitable constants). We have tried a few scaling techniques in connection with the spectral expansion algorithm, and have had some success. However, it is a reasonable guess that, within the constraint of double precision arithmetic, neither method can handle accurately models with more than about 100 processors. Of course, that range can be extended considerably by using extended precision, but then the choice of programming language and/or compiler would be restricted.

A question of relevance to the spectral expansion solution concerns its application when two or more eigenvalues coincide or are very close to each other. We have attempted to construct some examples of this type. Consider a moderately large system with $N = 30$. By examining the 31 eigenvalues in the unit disk for different values of the arrival rate (other parameters as in Fig. 10) it is noticed that when $\sigma$ changes from *14.6128383* to *14.6128384* , two real eigenvalues, *0.649104533666* and *0.649107441313* , change to a pair of complex conjugate ones: *0.649105990110 - 0.000001630665i* and *0.649105990110 + 0.000001630665i* . Hence, there is a value of $\sigma$ in that interval which would produce a double eigenvalue. The nearest we were able to get to it is the interval $\sigma \in$ *(14.61283834428,14.61283834429)* , where the two real eigenvalues, *0.649105971264* and *0.649106006036* , change to a pair of complex conjugate ones: *0.649105988650-0.000000016211i* and *0.649105988650+0.000000016211i* . Even in this last case, where the distance between two eigenvalues is on the order of *10⁻⁷* , the algorithm works well: the equations are not ill-conditioned and a correct value for *E(J)* is obtained.

Having repeated the above exercise for different models (e.g. giving rise to a double eigenvalue at *0* ), with similar results, we feel justified in saying that multiple eigenvalues present an interesting theoretical problem, but not a practical one.

## 5    Conclusions

We have considered a class of Markov-modulated models, exemplified by the multiprocessor queue subject to general breakdowns and repairs. In that context, spectral expansion is an efficient and readily implementable solution method. It enables various queue length statistics to be computed easily and accurately, over a wide range of parameter values.

When comparing the spectral expansion and the matrix-geometric solutions, a strong case can be made for the former. Spectral expansion offers considerable advantages in efficiency, without undue penalties in terms of numerical stability. The speed gains are especially pronounced, and indeed appear to be unbounded, when the system approaches saturation. However, further comparisons, perhaps with different methods for computing $R$ , or with other methods such as aggregation-disaggregation, would be desirable. It would also be interesting to compare the different methods on problems where the jumps of $J$ are greater than 1.

It should be pointed out that the matrix-geometric approach can be applied to models with block-M/G/1 or block-G/M/1 structure, which are not of the type discussed here. We believe that it would be possible to extend the spectral expansion method to those models too (see [7]).

## Acknowledgements

We wish to thank P.-J. Courtois and P. Semal for some pertinent remarks concerning Proposition 1, and for other helpful comments. This work was carried out in connection with the ESPRIT Basic Research project QMIPS, as well as PDCS.

# References for Chapter VII

[1]  R. Chakka and I. Mitrani, "A Numerical Solution Method for Multiprocessor Systems with General Breakdowns and Repairs", in *6th Int. Conf. on Modelling Techniques and Tools for Computer Performance Evaluation*, (Edinburgh), pp.289-304, Edinburgh University Press, 1992.

[2]  P.-J. Courtois and P. Semal, "Bounds for the Positive Eigenvectors of Non-Negative Matrices and for their Approximations by Decomposition", *J. ACM*, 31 (4), pp.804-25, 1984.

[3]  P. J. Courtois, *Decomposability: Queueing and computer system application*, Academic Press, New York, 1979.

[4]  P. J. Courtois and P. Semal, "On Polyhedra of Perron-Frobenius Eigenvectors", *Linear Algebra and its Appl.*, 65, pp.157-70, 1985.

[5]  J. N. Daigle and D. M. Lucantoni, "Queueing Systems Having Phase-Dependent Arrival and Service Rates", *Numerical Solutions of Markov Chains*, pp.161-202, 1991.

[6]  A. I. Elwalid, D. Mitra and T. E. Stern, "Statistical Multiplexing of Markov Modulated Sources: Theory and computational algorithms", in *Proc. Int. Teletraffic Congress,* 1991.

[7]  H. R. Gail, S. L. Hantler and B. A. Tailor, *Spectral Analysis of M/G/1 Type Markov Chains*, IBM Research Division, 1992.

[8]  I. Goldberg, P. Lancaster and L. Rodman, *Matrix Polynomials,* Academic Press, 1982.

[9]  L. Gun, "Experimental Results on Matrix-Analytical Solution Techniques: Extensions and comparisons", *Stochastic Models*, 5 (4), pp.669-82, 1989.

[10]  A. Jennings, *Matrix Computations for Engineers and Scientists,* Wiley, 1977.

[11]  G. Latouche, P. A. Jacobs and D. P. Gaver, "Finite Markov Chain Models Skip-Free in One Direction", *Naval Research Logistica Quarterly*, 31, pp.571-88, 1984.

[12]  I. Mitrani and B. Avi-Itzhak, "A Many-Server Queue with Service Interruptions", *Operations Research*, 16 (3), pp.628-38, 1968.

[13]  I. Mitrani and R. Chakka, "Spectral Expansion Solution for a Class of Markov Models: Application and comparison with the Matrix-Geometric Method", *Performance Evaluation*, 23 1995.

[14]  I. Mitrani and D. Mitra, "A Spectral Expansion Method for Random Walks on Semi-Infinite Strips", in *Proc. IMACS Int. Symp. on Iterative Methods in Linear Algebra*, (Brussels), 1991.

[15]  R. R. Muntz, E. De Souza Silva and A. Goyal, "Bounding Availability of Repairable Systems", *Performance Evaluation Review*, 17 (1), pp.29-38, 1989.

[16]  M. F. Neuts, *Matrix Geometric Solutions in Stochastic Models: An algorithmic approach,* The Johns Hopkins University Press, Baltimore, 1981.

[17]  M. F. Neuts and D. M. Lucantoni, "A Markovian Queue with N Servers Subject to Breakdowns and Repairs", *Management Science*, 25, pp.849-61, 1979.

[18]  N. U. Prabhu and Y. Zhu, "Markov-Modulated Queueing Systems", *QUESTA*, 5, pp.215-46, 1989.

[19]  P. Semal, *Analysis of Large Markov Models: Bounding techniques and applications,* Ph.D. Dissertation, Faculté des Sciences Appliquées, Université Catholique de Louvain, 1992.

# Chapter VIII

# Fault Forecasting - Security Modelling

Ideally, a measure of the security of a system should capture quantitatively the intuitive notion of 'the ability of the system to resist attack'. That is, it should be *operational*, reflecting the degree to which the system can be expected to remain free of security breaches under particular conditions of operation (including attack). Instead, current security *levels* at best merely reflect the extensiveness of safeguards introduced during the design and development of a system. Whilst we might expect a system developed to a higher level than another to exhibit 'more secure behaviour' in operation, this cannot be guaranteed; more particularly, we cannot infer what the actual security behaviour will be from knowledge of such a level. In PDCS and PSCS2 this problem of operational security measurement has been studied from both theoretical and empirical perspectives.

In the first paper, "Towards Operational Measures of Computer Security: Concepts", some theoretical issues concerning probabilistic modelling of security are considered. The starting point of this work is the recognition of similarity between security and reliability. We wish to be able to say that a system will be able to withstand an attack of a particular kind with a certain probability: in reliability we express this as the probability that the system will experience no failure during a particular *time* of operation. It is argued in this paper that time is not an appropriate parameter for a security model, and instead a more general measure of *effort* needs to be constructed. Another issue of importance is the reward (to an attacker) or cost (to a system owner) of successful breaches: that these differ shows the importance in this modelling of the viewpoint that is adopted. The second paper describes two experiments carried out to examine the feasibility of measuring effort and rewards in real-life settings. A pilot experiment was conducted first. This identified some of the difficulties of execution and data recording that were then addressed in the second experiment. This was successful in capturing the effort expended by the attackers in achieving some 65 security breaches. Analysis of the extensive data collected in this experiment continues, and it is likely that it will be possible to investigate the breach rewards also.

# Towards Operational Measures of Computer Security: Concepts*

Bev Littlewood[1]    Sarah Brocklehurst[1]    Norman Fenton[1]
Peter Mellor[1]    Stella Page[1]    David Wright[1]    John Dobson[2]
John McDermid[3]    Dieter Gollmann[4]

[1]City University    [2]University of Newcastle upon Tyne
[3]University of York    [4]Royal Holloway College

**Abstract.** Ideally, a measure of the security of a system should capture quantitatively the intuitive notion of 'the ability of the system to resist attack'. That is, it should be *operational*, reflecting the degree to which the system can be expected to remain free of security breaches under particular conditions of operation (including attack). Instead, current security *levels* at best merely reflect the extensiveness of safeguards introduced during the design and development of a system. Whilst we might expect a system developed to a higher level than another to exhibit 'more secure behaviour' in operation, this cannot be guaranteed; more particularly, we cannot infer what the actual security behaviour will be from knowledge of such a level. In the paper we discuss similarities between reliability and security with the intention of working towards measures of 'operational security' similar to those that we have for reliability of systems. Very informally, these measures could involve expressions such as the rate of occurrence of security breaches (cf rate of occurrence of failures in reliability), or the probability that a specified 'mission' can be accomplished without a security breach (cf reliability function). This new approach is based on the analogy between *system failure* and *security breach*. A number of other analogies to support this view are introduced. We examine this duality critically, and have identified a number of important open questions that need to be answered before this quantitative approach can be taken further. The work described here is therefore somewhat tentative, and one of our major intentions is to invite discussion about the plausibility and feasibility of this new approach.

## 1    Introduction

Current approaches to measuring and predicting system reliability [13, 17] are based on the definition of reliability in terms of the probability of failure-free operation for a specified length of time. The advantage of this operational approach is that it allows us to obtain measures of the actual *behaviour* of a device, or of a computer program, as seen by a user, rather than merely of some static properties. Thus users are likely to be more interested in knowing the reliability of their system, expressed for example as a rate of occurrence of failures (ROCOF), than in knowing that it possesses certain structural properties or measures, or that it was developed under a particular regime. These static attributes and measures of the system, and its development process, undoubtedly do influence the user-perceived operational reliability, but they are not sufficient in themselves to determine this reliability.

---

\*    This present paper is a concise version of [20].

The present position in security seems to be that current 'measures', or rankings, of security of systems are merely analogous to the static attributes and measures discussed above. The Orange Book [22] levels, for example, are concerned with those factors which are likely to *influence* 'operational security', and may very well be beneficial in producing secure systems, but they do not facilitate quantitative *evaluation* of the actual achieved operational security. Indeed, it is not possible even to know that a particular system that has reached a higher level in this scheme than another system is, in some real operational sense, 'truly more secure'.

Thus the Orange Book levels, in part, represent levels of *trust*, an unquantified belief about security. We shall show that *belief* about operational security is indeed an appropriate approach, but our intention is to find ways in which this can be formally quantified. The first task would be to try to define measures of 'operational security' sufficiently rigorously and realistically to gain the acceptance of the security community. This immediately presents some difficulties which, whilst possibly not insurmountable, seem more serious than is the case for reliability: we shall see that there are several open questions that may need empirical investigation.

There does not seem to be a large literature on probabilistic treatment of system security. Lee [14] proposes to model levels of security in terms of the probability distribution of the 'level of threat' required to achieve a penetration involving information of a given classification. Thus $r_{c_1, c_2}(t)$, denotes the probability that a system at level $c_1$ will allow a breach involving information classified at level $c_2$ when the system is subjected to a level of threat $t$. Hierarchical relationships between security levels can then be represented in the obvious way by inequalities between these functions. He also introduces probability distributions for the amounts of damage resulting from various illegal transfers of information. He claims that various conclusions can be drawn from this kind of model concerning the greatest security risks and the rules of combination for system security levels. However, the independence assumptions are suspect and the analysis seriously flawed in a number of other respects. Denning [7] considers a statistical approach to detecting when the operational environment switches from 'non-threatening' to 'threatening'. Bishop [4], in a popular account of what he calls a 'common sense' security model, suggests that it is possible to assign in an empirical way some of the probabilities discussed here, but gives no details.

In Section 2 we describe the terminological analogies between reliability and security, making clear the scope of our discussion. In Section 3 we discuss in detail some general problems and deficiencies associated with these analogies. In Section 4 we concentrate upon the most basic of these issues, namely the security analogy for the time-to-next-event random variable in reliability and give tentative consideration to some questions which need further investigation.

## 2 Terminological Analogies Between Security and Reliability

In the reliability context, the *input space* is the totality of all inputs that might ever be encountered. Thus for a process-control system it might be a many-dimensional space representing all the possible settings of sensors and controls. We can informally think of a fault as represented by a subset of this space: when an input is selected from the subset a failure will result. In the security context the input space is again the set of all possible inputs to the system, including both those involved in normal operational use *and those which result from intentional attacks upon the system*.

The *usage environment* in reliability determines the mechanism by which the inputs will be selected from the input space. The analogy of usage environment in security is thus the population of attackers and their behaviours together with normal system operation. Although we are not concerned with the detailed nature of the attacks, this population is much wider than, say, the simplistic view of a hacker typing in keyboard 'entries' to the system. Thus, for example, a valid attack in our sense could include

- 'passive' attacks, such as listening to and analysing public traffic,
- illegal use of the system, such as the insertion of trap-doors by privileged system users, or even
- attacks upon personnel, such as bribery or blackmail, that may not require any computing knowledge whatsoever, nor even any interaction with the computer system itself.

In reliability, however, it is common for the system boundary to be drawn quite tightly. Conventional hardware reliability theory tends to treat well defined physical systems; software reliability deals with failures of a well-defined program. Such a narrow view of the 'system' can be misleading [23] even for reliability, when, say, the people interacting with this system form a significant source of failures according to a wider view. It is common to ascribe responsibility for aircraft crashes to the pilot, for example, when more insight would be gained by viewing the pilot as a component in a wider system. The inappropriateness of this narrow view of system boundaries seems even more marked in the case of security, where often it is *precisely* the fact that attackers are interacting with the computer system and its human owners that defines the problem. We are not qualified to discuss in detail how security system boundaries should be defined in practice; suffice it to say that we intend our modelling to apply as widely as possible to practical security problems. This means that, in addition to obvious attacks on the computer system (e.g. entering password guesses), we must consider attacks upon the wider system (e.g. bribery, blackmail of personnel), and attacks which tamper with the system design before the operational system even exists (introduction of intentional vulnerabilities, e.g. Trojan horses, that can be exploited at a later stage).

The concept of system failure is central to the quantitative approach to reliability. The obvious analogy of system failure is *security breach*. By security breach we mean an event where the behaviour of the system deviates from the security requirements. We have chosen to use the word 'requirements' deliberately instead of 'policy': our intention is to capture something analogous to 'informal engineering requirements' in reliability, rather than 'formal specification', since the latter could itself be wrong. These security requirements may be stated or merely 'reasonably expected': certain events that are surprising to the specifier of the system can be considered to be failures and thus classed as breaches after the event. Our notion of security breach is therefore, like that of failure, quite general [13].

System failures are caused by faults in the system. Most importantly, these can be specification and design faults that have arisen as a result of human failures; indeed, in the case of computer software, this is the only source of failure. Analogously, security breaches are caused by *vulnerabilities*, such as the omission of a particular data integrity function, in the system and these are clearly special types of faults. These faults can be *accidental*, or they can be *intentional*, these latter may be malicious (Trojan horses, trap-doors) or non-malicious (resulting, for example, from deliberate trade-offs between security and efficiency). All appear to have reliability analogies except malicious intentional faults.

The notion of intentionality seems to have two meanings here. It can refer to the process whereby a system comes to have vulnerabilities (faults) - that these are inserted deliberately and sometimes maliciously during the system design. Alternatively, it can refer to the way in which those faults that are present are activated during the operational life of the system and so result in security breaches (failures). Thus we can speak of both accidental faults and intentional faults, as well as accidental failures and intentional failures. It seems that all four possible classes could exist. There is an informal, and not rigid, division into the concerns of *reliability* and *security* according to whether there is any intentionality present in the class. Reliability theory is mainly the study of *accidental* faults that result in *accidental* failures, but it must be admitted that the dividing line is not always clear and security practitioners might also concern themselves with some of these. Thus any intentional attempt to cause a breach by exploiting a vulnerability, whether this be an intentional or accidental vulnerability, is a security issue. Similarly, breaches that result from *malicious* intentional vulnerabilities, whether these are triggered by deliberate action or not, are also a security issue.

When we attempt to model these different classes, we find different problems. It seems clear that accidental security breaches, arising from accidental or intentional vulnerabilities, are the easiest to handle since they can be modelled using the techniques developed for reliability, so in this paper we shall instead concentrate on the special problems of those breaches where some intentionality is present in the *failure* process. Perhaps the hardest class is that of intentional breaches arising from intentional malicious vulnerabilities, of which Trojan Horses are an example. It may be possible to model the process of *insertion* of such vulnerabilities, but modelling the process by which they are triggered during system operation looks difficult.

The most difficult analogy is with that of *execution time* in reliability. In the reliability context we are always dealing with a stochastic process, usually of *failures* in *time*. Although in different contexts we would wish to express the reliability differently (e.g. ROCOF, mean time to failure, probability of failure-free mission), a complete description of the underlying stochastic process would be sufficient for all questions that are of interest. Even in the reliability context, care needs to be taken in choosing the time variable to be used. In the case of a nuclear reactor protection system, for example, it might be convenient to express the reliability as a probability of failure upon demand rather than as a rate of occurrence of failures in (calendar) time. Although the latter is of interest as a measure of the reliability of the wider system which incorporates this safety system, it would be unreasonable to allow the frequency of demands to affect our judgement of the reliability of the protection system. Here time is a discrete variable, represented by the individual demands. The important point is that there is always some notion of stress, or load, involved in our choice of time variable, even though this may be done quite informally. Occasionally it may be the case that calendar time itself will be a good representation of this stress, for example in certain types of process control. Usually, however, we need at least to be careful to count only the time that the system is being exercised, so that in the case of software reliability *execution time* has come to be a widely used variable [21].

For the security 'process', where we are trying to model the process that results from intentional attacks, it is not obvious what should play the role of time in order to capture the notion of stress. Clearly a system might be able to continue to deliver its ordinary functionality indefinitely without security breaches, as long as there is no attack present. This contrasts with the case in reliability, where it is usually assumed that a system is always susceptible to failure as a result of accidental faults (even though the extent of the susceptibility, expressed for example as a failure rate, will depend on the nature of the use). It seems that time, however ingeniously defined, will rarely be an appropriate variable in the case of intentional breaches. Instead we think it is necessary to consider the *effort* expended by the attacking agent. This effort *could* sometimes be time itself, perhaps the time expended by the attacking agent, but it will be only rarely the same time as that seen by, say, the system user or owner. More usually, effort will be an indirect measure of a whole range of attributes, including financial cost, elapsed time, experience and ability of attacker, etc. In particular, such an effort measure can take account of such behaviour as learning about a system off-line, or by using an entirely different system from the one that is the subject of the attack. It is interesting that effort has previously been used informally in security. For example it is often suggested that the effectiveness of a cryptographic technique is measured in terms of the cost of accessing the data in comparison with the value of that data to the attacker.

Using effort may also allow us to deal with two situations where the reliability analogy is not helpful. In the first place, there is the case of intentional breaches arising from intentional malicious faults, such as Trojan Horses. Here any notion of time of usage of the system is meaningless: the effort is expended in inserting the intentional fault, before the operational system exists, and any effort involved in triggering such a latent fault to cause the security breach during operational use is likely to be trivial. Secondly, there are circumstances where the expenditure of effort is instantaneous, and any notion of sequence, which seems essential in a time variable, is absent. An example would be the offering of a bribe to exploit human cupidity; here the chance of success would clearly depend upon the magnitude of the bribe (effort), but it is hard to see this as analogous to time.

Finally, if we accept that effort in security can play the same role that a general notion of time plays in reliability, then it is reasonable to consider the *effort-to-breach distribution* as analogous to the *time-to-failure distribution* of reliability. Assuming that we can obtain an appropriate variable to represent effort, operational security could in principle now be expressed in terms of probability statements: for example, mean effort to next security breach, probability of successfully resisting an attack[1] involving a given expenditure of effort, etc.

In practice, of course, from most viewpoints it *is* often desirable to know something about the security of a system expressed in terms of time: a system owner, for example, might like to know the probability that there will be no breaches of the

---

[1] Notice that we now have a broad definition of attack that includes any expenditure of effort with malicious intent.

system during its predicted lifetime. Clearly this requires knowledge of a doubly stochastic process: in the first place we need to understand the process of security breaches as a function of effort, then we need to know the process of effort as a function of time. In this paper we are going to restrict ourselves to the former: in statistical terminology we shall be making probability statements that are *conditional* upon the effort process. Although one justification for this approach is pragmatic, specifically that knowledge of the effort process (in time) is hard to obtain and very much dependent upon the application and the nature of the environment, there is a more important reason. Seeing security *conditionally* as a system attribute (informally its ability to resist attacks involving a specified effort environment) seems more natural than seeing it *marginally*, that is averaging over all the different efforts (environments) that attackers *might* expend.

We have addressed this issue at some length since it seems to be an important departure from the reliability analogy. The departure is not, of course, an absolute one since the two stage approach could also be applied in reliability: the failure process as a function of system load, and the load process as a function of time. Indeed, in some reliability work exactly this structure is adopted. More usually, however, the load process is simply equated with a suitably defined time variable, and this can often be a good approximation to reality. In security, we believe, such an approximation via time alone is rarely valid.

These detailed remarks apply to intentional breaches [13]. As we have seen, accidental breaches will result in a process of security breaches similar in its properties to the failures treated by reliability methods involving *time*. It is clear from the above that we could not model in a single process *all* security breaches, accidental and intentional, without having knowledge of the effort process in time.

It is worth remarking here that security work seems to have concentrated to a large extent on the problems arising in circumstances where *very* high security is demanded. Certainly it appears to be the case that some of the major funding agencies for security research are concerned with issues of national security. Problems of this kind in security are similar to the problems of safety-critical systems in reliability, where very high levels of reliability often need to be assured. The work on ultra-high reliability evaluation, however, has so far been notably unsuccessful, at least for software and design reliability [18], in comparison with the achievements in the modelling and evaluation of more modest levels [5]. This lesson suggests that, in these initial stages of attempting to model operational security, we should restrict ourselves to systems for which the security requirements are also relatively modest. It is only for such systems that sufficient numbers of breaches could be observed for the empirical studies that seem necessary.

## 3     Difficulties and Deficiencies of the Analogies

### 3.1     Failures, Security Breaches and Reward Processes

In reliability we observe a realisation of a *stochastic point process* of failures in time, Fig 1. It is sometimes convenient to show this graphically as the step function representing the cumulative number of failures against time, Fig 2. Such a plot will usually clearly reveal the growth in reliability, due to fault-removal, as the failures tend to become more separated in time and the 'slope' of the plot becomes smaller. In principle, in the case of security, a similar plot could be drawn of the number of security breaches against effort.

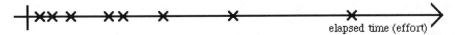

**Fig. 1.** The failure process in reliability (breach process in security).

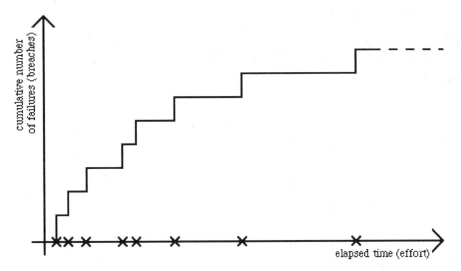

**Fig. 2.** Typical cumulative failure plot for reliability data (security equivalent).

Even in reliability, such a view of the failure process can be too simplistic. A user is interested not only in the process of failures, but also in their (random variable) consequences. In security especially it is likely to be the case that not all security breaches have the same value for the attacker (similar remarks apply to the consequences for the system owner). The reward an attacker would get from breaking into a system determines her[2] motivation and affects whether she is willing to spend the effort that is needed in order to perform the attack. Examples of rewards are personal satisfaction, gain of money, revenge or simply pure curiosity, but it is also possible that the attacker may get negative rewards (losses) such as those due to the consequences of detection. A more general model, then, would describe the stochastic process of *rewards* to the attacker as she incurs effort, Fig 3.

There is a further generalisation in the security context that does not seem to have a parallel in reliability. That is the possibility that an attacker may gain continuous reward even in the absence of security breaches. Consider, for example, the very simple case of a system with a finite number, $n$, of potential passwords, and an

---

[2]   For convenience we adopt the convention that the system owner is male, the attacker female.

attacker trying these at random but not repeating failed attempts. Clearly, when she
has tried $m$ passwords, all of which have failed, she has learned something that is of
value. In a sense, this value is only potential, since she has not actually acquired
whatever benefit will accrue from the actual breach (for example, changing financial
software in order to steal money). But this is value nevertheless: thus, for example,
she could sell this information to another attacker, who might then thereby expect to
be able to gain entry with less expenditure of effort. Indeed, it seems clear that the
(potential) value of these failures approaches the value of a breach as $m \to n$. In cases
such as this we need to consider the possibility that reward may increase essentially
continuously as effort is expended, as well as discretely at particular events (e.g.
security breaches), Fig 4.

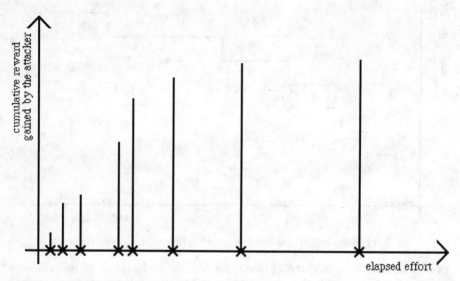

**Fig. 3.** Stochastic process of rewards to the attacker as she incurs effort; reward obtained in
discrete amounts only as the result of a breach.

In summary, there are three levels at which operational security modelling could be
aimed: a simple counting process of breaches versus effort, a reward process of
random variables defined on these events, and the most general random process of
reward as a function of effort expended as well as events observed. These are clearly
in ascending order of realism, as well as of difficulty (particularly with respect to the
availabililty of empirical data) For example, it is clearly easier to recognize the mere
fact of a security event than to estimate the reward associated with such an event, not
least because of its subjective nature.

### 3.2   Usage Environment Analogy

It is well known that the reliability of systems depends upon the nature of their use.
Strictly, therefore, there is no sense in which we can really speak of 'the' reliability
of a system, but instead we ought to specify the exact nature of the operating
environment and a reliability figure will then refer to both the system and this
environment. In other words, we should always be careful in our probability

statements to specify the exact nature of the conditioning events. Thus reliability could be expressed as a mean time to failure *given that* the system is operating in environment $A$, security could be expressed as the mean effort to security breach *given that* the system is operating in threatening environment $B$.

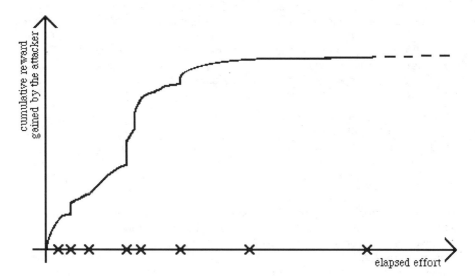

**Fig. 4.** Stochastic process of rewards to the attacker as she incurs effort; here reward may be obtained continuously as effort is expended.

Here we are addressing a slightly different point from our earlier discussion of effort versus time. There we argued that the effort process in time was an attribute of the environment, and we showed that there were advantages in treating this separately from the process of security breaches as a function of effort. However, effort cannot capture all the variation that there will be between different environments. One example, of course, is that variation in the nature of the *legitimate* use of the system may increase its susceptibility to security breaches, for a particular fixed effort expenditure on the part of an attacker. This is similar to the reliability case, but in addition there is variation arising solely from the presence of attackers.

Unfortunately, it seems possible that there is more variability in threatening environments in security than there is in operational environments in reliability, not least because the threatening environments may be deliberately created rather than randomly generated. We are dealing with deliberately malign attackers rather than merely randomly perverse nature[3]. In the software reliability context, for example, we assume that in principle it is possible to identify *a priori* all possible inputs, even though this may be impracticably onerous in a particular case. In the case of security,

---

[3]  Notwithstanding the differing likely variability in environments, it is not clear whether human ingenuity or nature can produce the *greatest* perversity (variability). Inasmuch as we all, as humans, share much of our cultural baggage, one view would be that nature, at its most extreme, will occasionally produce those results that surprise us the most.

it is not clear that even in principle it is possible to identify all possible attacks *a priori*. Sometimes, in fact, the role of the attacker is to *invent* that which has not been thought of. Will such an attacker restrict herself to trying out attacks from an initial repertoire, modelled analogously to some fixed input space? Or is it more realistic to assume some kind of learning process and increased familiarity with the system, until entirely new attacks will be invented which exploit peculiarities of the particular system, and were initially completely outside the imagination of the attacker (and system owner). If this is the case, then it represents a kind of enlargement of the space of potential attacks over time, or at least a drastic shift in the operational profile (probability distribution over the input space) resulting in attacks which were initially unimagined (i.e. 'impossible') acquiring an increasing probability of occurrence as time and effort are expended.

Clearly, one effect of intentionality and learning would be the tendency eventually to give up on a line of attack which had proved unsuccessful once its possibilities appeared exhausted. The probability attached to the corresponding subset of the attack space would in this case decrease over time. This means that we shall never encounter in security the situation that pertains in reliability of a fixed operational profile.

Such considerations seem to have at least two sets of implications for any model of effort-to-breach random variables. In the first place, the properties of the process (against effort) of breaches caused by an individual attacker will be affected, for example the hazard rate of the effort-to-next event distribution. Secondly, the rules of combination for the breaches achieved by different attackers will be affected by considerations such as whether they communicate and learn from each other's experience, and whether, after repertoires of standard attacks have been exhausted, their imaginations tend to diverge in thinking of novel forms of attack.

Having said all this, it is not clear that these considerations are overriding. For example, it does seem a rather subtle distinction that is being made above between the security scenario, where the input space of attacks is expanded by the inventiveness of the attacker, and the reliability scenario, where the 'perverseness of nature' throws up inputs that we *could have* anticipated but *didn't*. In both cases it seems plausible to assume that the view of the system owner, for example, will change in the same way: he merely sees inputs being generated that he had not thought of. This is reminiscent of the discovery of specification faults during operational use. Perhaps such considerations do not detract from the principle of treating security stochastically, but only suggest we should be wary of the details. Once again, empirical investigation may be the best way forward to decide upon some of these open questions.

### 3.3    Viewpoints

In all of the above it is taken for granted that *probability* is a suitable way of expressing our uncertainty about how a system responds to its operating environment, in both the reliability and security contexts. In the case of reliability this is probably more obvious. There we can think of the system receiving a sequence of input cases from some (usually large) input space. Some of the inputs in the space are such that, when they are presented to the system, unacceptable output is produced: we say the system has failed. There is uncertainty about which inputs will be selected in the future, and there is uncertainty about which untried inputs will produce unacceptable output. The first source of uncertainty relates to the aforementioned nature of the operational environment, and it is to be expected that if we inspected streams of inputs from two different environments we would be able to observe differences. It has been argued elsewhere [16, 18] that this uncertainty should be represented by probability, and that Bayesian subjective probability seems most appropriate.

It should be emphasized that the subjective interpretation of probability is not in any way less 'scientific' than the more usual interpretation based on limiting relative frequency. The present paper is not the place to argue this case; interested readers should consult [9, 15].

This approach via the subjective interpretation of probability seems particularly appropriate in the case of security. Here we must contend with the possibility of more than one viewpoint of the system. The system owner, even if he could be regarded as having complete knowledge of the system (i.e. of those inputs that would result in breaches), is uncertain about the sequence of inputs (here attacks) that will arise from the adversary's attempts to breach security. This adversary, on the other hand, is at least partially ignorant about the system and thus does not know the potential effects of her possible choices of inputs (attacks), even though she has complete knowledge and control of these choices. It seems clear that, since they are based upon information which is incomplete in different ways, these two subjective views need not coincide; indeed it would be surprising if they did. In fact, not only will there be different probabilities associated with the same event when seen from the different viewpoints, but some events may not be seen from all viewpoints - for example, some breaches may not be seen by the system owner. In addition to this, *rewards* are also likely to differ from one viewpoint to another, even when the same events are observed. The attacker's reward resulting from a breach will not generally be the same as the system owner's loss[4]: there is no sense in which this is a zero-sum game.

It may be helpful to consider other viewpoints. Thus, for example, in security testing, it may be sensible to consider the viewpoint of an all-knowing, all-seeing oracle, 'God', as well as the owner and attacker. God would see all security breaches, including those not detected during test by the owner (and those not detected by the attacker), and so this viewpoint could be regarded as being in a sense the 'true' security of the system in the testing environment. If the owner could trust the security test to be representative of the operational (threatening) environment, it would be interesting to him to compare his own subjective view of the system's security with God's. Thus if the system owner knew that in *test* he had formed an unreasonably optimistic view of the security of the system, it would be prudent of him to regard his view of the *operational* security as also optimistic. It might even be possible for him to carry out a formal recalibration of his subjective view of the operational security, using this information from testing together with the operational observations.

### 3.4   System Boundaries and Definition

In system reliability we normally have a very clear idea of the boundaries of the system to which we are to attach reliability measures. Usually this is a well-defined

---

4   Information seems to be unique in that you (usually) still own that which you have given away, sold, or had stolen; but its value to you has changed as a result of such a transaction.

system, operating in a well-understood environment, and the important variable upon which the failure process is defined is *time*.

For security evaluation we should ideally view the operational system, which is the overt subject of the security evaluation, in the widest sense. Thus we should include all products associated with the system: that is all documentation (including, for example, requirements specification, designs and test results) and all executable code. We should include all resources associated with the development and operation of the system: for example, personnel, software tools such as compilers, and hardware.

As we have seen earlier, for security it is convenient to define the relevant process instead upon *effort*. Although in many cases it is still valid to use the reliability analogy of inputs to this system being prone to result in security breaches, the use of effort instead of time allows us to generalize the notion of attack. Although we have so far been largely concerned with the modelling of intentional *breaches*, it may also be possible to use effort to model the introduction of intentional *vulnerabilities* during system development, such as Trojan horses. In a case like this, it becomes difficult to argue that it is the operational system that is under attack. On the other hand, the consequences of such an attack can certainly show themselves during operational use of this final product.

One way forward might be to consider this kind of security measure as different in kind from the measures for the operational system that have been the subject of the earlier discussion. Thus we might, for example, try to estimate the probability that the system is free from malicious intentional vulnerabilities; this could be seen as a measure of the 'security' of the development process. Although ideally we would like to know the effect of potential malicious intentional vulnerabilities upon operational security, so as to arrive at a single measure incorporating all possible breaches, this seems a sufficiently hard problem that the foregoing separation of concerns might be the best approach at this stage.

## 4     Probabilistic Requirements for an Operational Security Model

In the remainder of the paper, for simplicity, we shall not consider these malicious intentional vulnerabilities. Neither shall we deal with accidental breaches since, as we have discussed earlier, these seem most easily amenable to the reliability approach. Instead, in this section we shall restrict ourselves to some important questions concerning a probabilistic treatment of intentional attacks upon a system containing accidental (and non-malicious intentional) vulnerabilities. A further simplification here is that we shall not treat reward processes; instead we shall concentrate upon breach event processes since an understanding of these is a necessary precursor to any modelling of rewards.

There are three basic scenarios that we might consider. The first of these concerns a system that has been exposed to security attacks, but has not suffered a breach. The second concerns the case where breaches have occurred and there have been attempts to correct the underlying vulnerabilities. These situations correspond, respectively, to the work on estimating the reliability of a program that has never failed [18], and to the classic reliability growth models [1, 11, 20, 21]. The intermediate case in reliability, where failures occur but faults are not fixed, can also arise in security - for example for economic reasons in a system of only modest security. Unfortunately, whereas in reliability this produces a particularly simple, stationary stochastic process, in security things are more complicated. Some vulnerabilities are of a nature that will allow many breaches to follow the first one with little effort, and a stochastic process of clusters of breaches will result.

These three cases all concern situations where any attempt to remove vulnerabilities arises solely from the discovery of these via detection of security breaches. Clearly it is also possible for vulnerabilities to be discovered before they have been successfully exploited by real attackers. One important example of this is, of course, security testing (although it *may* be possible to use data from such testing to obtain estimates of operational security, and this will be discussed below). Other methods of discovering vulnerabilities, such as design reviews, code inspections, etc, do not readily lend themselves to modelling operational security, as is equally the case for their equivalents in reliability. Similar problems arise in modelling the effects of vulnerabilities which are removed in operational use without their having been revealed by breaches, for example by the system manager noticing unusual patterns of use. It may sometimes be the case that countermeasures are known for certain types of attack but these have not been implemented for economic reasons; if a particular system is found to be operating in an environment which exposes it to this kind of attack, it may be possible to quickly insert protection and avert a breach. We shall not attempt at this stage to address any of these issues. It is worth noting, however, that neither do the classical reliability models address the equivalent reliability problems.

Before considering the complication of treating the whole stochastic process of successive breaches (and consequent evolution in the security), we need to understand the simpler case concerning a snapshot of the security at a single moment in time. This concerns the distribution of the (random variable) effort, E, required for the next breach[5]. We begin with some notation. The *security function*, by analogy with the *reliability function*, is

$$R(e) = P(E > e)$$

with the cumulative distribution function (cdf) and probability density function (pdf), if it exists, of effort to next breach

$$F(e) = 1 - R(e), \quad f(e) = F'(e)$$

respectively, and *security hazard rate* (cf *hazard rate*)

$$h(e) = f(e)/R(e)$$

We shall generally wish to make clear the particular viewpoint, in which case we shall denote attacker's security function $R_a(e) = P(E_a<e)$, owner's $R_o(e) = P(E_o<e)$, etc.

The equivalent problem in reliability concerns the distribution of the time to next failure of a program. The simplest assumption here is that this distribution is as it would be if the failure process were 'purely random'. Then there is a constant probability $\lambda \, \delta t$ of a failure in a short time interval $(t, t + \delta t]$, independently of what has happened in $(0, t]$, i.e. the process is memoryless. Here $\lambda$ is the failure rate of the

---

5   This breach must be the first one associated with a particular vulnerability.

exponential distribution of $T$, the random variable time to next failure. This assumption seems reasonably plausible in the software reliability context, for example, where $T$ represents the time spent in a trajectory through the input space before meeting the next input to precipitate a failure. In practice, of course, the rate $\lambda$ is never known exactly, and so the exponential distribution of $T$ should be seen only as a conditional one; to express our unconditional beliefs about $T$ we need in addition to describe our belief about $\lambda$.

In reliability, the exponentiality can be seen as the limiting case of the number of input cases until the next failure. In the simplest case, there is a constant probability $p$ of failure on each input, independently for successive inputs. The number of inputs until next failure is then geometrically distributed, which is exponential in the limit as $p \to 0$. This limit applies under much wider conditions: the probabilities of failure on the different inputs do not need to be equal, the successive inputs do not need to be independent with respect to failures. We can expect the time to next failure to be approximately exponential as long as there is *stationarity*, i.e. no tendency for the probability of failure on an input to be a function of time, and there is limited dependence between successive inputs: both these conditions seem plausible for real systems.

Can any of these ideas be carried over into the security context? In particular, are there circumstances where it is reasonable to expect the 'effort to next security breach' random variable to be conditionally exponentially distributed? The question arises as to whether similar underlying conditions hold in the security context to make the exponential assumption plausible there. Certainly, it is not clear whether the necessary assumption of stationarity holds in the security context.

Consider the viewpoint of the attacker. If we regard each attempt to carry out a security breach as a series of elementary 'attacks', it seems likely that these attacks will be carried out in such a way as to minimize the perceived likely effort of success. Thus, for example, the attacks may be carried out in a descending order of (perceived) chance of success (per unit outlay of effort). From the attacker viewpoint, then, there is a clear violation of the stationarity condition needed for exponentiality of the attacker's subjective probabilistic distribution of the random variable 'effort', $E_a$, until next breach. We might expect the distribution to be a 'decreasing failure rate' (DFR) one [3]. The system owner's view of such a process of attacks from a single attacker is also likely to be DFR, but less strongly so if he sees a sequence of attacks that differs in its ordering from the optimal ordering that he (the owner) believes to be the case.

The system owner may sometimes see the combined effects of many attackers operating simultaneously, and their *different* rankings of likely successful attacks will again tend to diminish the tendency for DFR-ness. However, the system owner will presumably believe there is some positive correlation between different attackers' views of likely successful attacks, suggesting that this viewpoint *will* also be DFR.

Any tendency for DFR from the owner's viewpoint may also be weakened in the following way. If an owner is to see many attackers, it is most likely that these will not make their attacks simultaneously, but approximately sequentially. Thus at any one time it may be the case that there are a few, but not many, attacks under way. Since it might also be reasonable to assume that most attackers incur the expenditure of a relatively small amount of effort, as a crude approximation we could regard the process as a stationary sequence of many different successive attacks as a function of the total effort incurred by the population of attackers, $E_O$. In a case like this, then, the system owner might be justified in believing the distribution of $E_O$ to be exponential.

The arguments here do not, however, take account of any learning about a system's weaknesses that an attacker could gain from her successive failures to breach the security, or from the failures of other attackers. Presumably such learning will tend to *increase* the success rate, producing, in the absence of any contrary tendency such as mentioned above, an increasing failure rate (IFR) distribution for the effort to next breach. These remarks apply to the attacker's viewpoint, and are probably applicable in a weaker form for the owner viewpoint, using similar reasoning to above.

It may be the case that *both* these tendencies - to DFR-ness and to IFR-ness - are present, and tend to cancel one another out. In that case the exponential may be a reasonable approximation for distribution of the time to next breach. At this stage, the important point is that *we do not know* the answers to questions such as these, and they are thus candidates for empirical investigation.

Indeed, concentration upon exponentiality versus IFR or DFR could involve over-simplification, since the actual distributions here might fit into none of these classes. We now consider some more general questions about these distributions that are prompted by the special circumstances of the security context.

One interesting question concerns what happens as the amount of effort expended becomes large. Clearly $R(e)$ decreases as $e$ increases, but can we assume it approaches 0, i.e. that breach is certain with the expenditure of unlimited resources? If instead it approaches a non-zero limit as $e$ becomes infinite, the distribution of effort to breach is 'improper' - there is a chance that even with infinite expenditure there will be no breach. This seems to be a plausible description of what an attacker would believe and would therefore be an argument against exponentiality.

Another issue concerns the several ways in which 'combination' plays an important role in security. For example, for a single attacker, the $E_a$ random variable is presumably really a sum of the efforts of 'elementary' failed attacks: the implementation of different ideas as early ones are tried and fail, stopping with the first success. What does a sequence of elementary attacks look like? We have already touched on the question of whether the process of attack outcomes against effort is stationary, or monotonically increasing or decreasing. Could there be more complex behaviour here? What, for example, is the nature of the dependence between the outcomes of successive attacks? Independence seems too simplistic, if only because an attack that has failed will not be tried again, but presumably the dependence drops off with distance. Is there a law of large numbers here: *large* number of *small* attacks, each with a *low* probability of success? How should the stopping rule for an attacker operate? Is it too naive to assume she has infinite resources? Or should we assume finite resources? If so, does this affect her allocation and ordering of the elementary attacks? What different kinds of objective function might an attacker employ in identifying one particular ordering as optimal?

Similar issues of combination arise when we consider how the owner would see a *combination of attackers*? This involves us in a generalisation of the univariate distributions considered earlier. Assume that the owner knows that there are $n$ attackers. Let $R_O(e_1, \ldots, e_n)$ represent the probability that the system has not been breached when, for i = 1, .. n, the $i$th attacker has expended $e_i$. What does $R_O(e_1, \ldots e_n)$ look like?

A very naïve approach assumes that attackers are independent, and similar, with successes occurring purely randomly, i.e. $R_O(e_1, \ldots e_n) = \exp(-\lambda \Sigma e_i)$. The likelihood function, when we have seen no breach in many attacks, is then $\exp(-\lambda \Sigma e_i)$, i.e. the same as a single attack of expenditure $\Sigma e_i$. This is not very interesting! It implies that a large number of small attacks is equivalent to a small number of large attacks. Is this reasonable? If not, can we frame the optimality issues formally: if there was a certain amount of effort, $\Sigma e_i$, to be expended, what allocation of this among attackers would the owner fear most? And how would this change with $\Sigma e_i$?

Are there *any* circumstances where the owner might be interested only in the total effort being expended, and not at all on its allocation (this is, in the statistical terminology, a kind of 'sufficient statistic' argument)? Do the hardware shock models [3] have any relevance here: is there a sense in which the system succumbs as a result of the *accumulation* of attacks (for example via accumulation of knowledge), or is it waiting for an attack beyond some suitably defined *threshold*?

If, as seems to be the case, we cannot assume independence between attackers, what is the nature of the dependence? One view might be that the different attackers are selecting their 'elementary attacks' from the same fairly small finite set: is this reasonable?

Is it reasonable, at least, to assume that $R_O(e_1, \ldots e_n)$ is 'exchangeable', i.e. that it remains unchanged under permutation of the subscripts, representing a kind of subjective indifference between different attackers on the part of the system owner?

If we consider the way that a group of cooperating attackers might divide up the effort amongst themselves, there arises the intriguing possibility of modelling something like the 'forced diversity' ideas in Littlewood and Miller [19]. Here the Eckhardt and Lee [8] work on program diversity through separate and 'independent' development was generalized to introduce the idea of 'negatively correlated' development. It can be shown that in principle such forced diversity can give better results in a fault-tolerant system than those achievable under (anyway unattainable) independence. It was also shown that there was a complete duality in this conceptual modelling: for every theorem about many program versions operating in a single operational environment, there is a dual concerning a single program operating in many operational environments. Is it reasonable to think that there are similar results to these in the security context? For example, does it make sense to talk of forced diversity in co-operating attackers?

# 5    Conclusions

In this paper, we have begun to address some quantitative aspects of operational security in a manner analogous to that which has been successful for operational reliability. We have identified some important questions which need to be answered before this quantitative approach can be taken further. We have mainly restricted ourselves to the very simplest problem, analogous to the situation in reliability concerning time to next failure. There are clearly other parallels worth investigating. For example, we have not yet considered any of the interesting parallels with *availability*. We hope to address some of these issues in further work, but we believe that the difficulties posed even by the restricted scenario presented here need to be resolved before we can attempt to model these more difficult cases.

At the very least, we hope that the preceding discussion has made clear the desirability of a probability-based framework for operational security measurement. However, the many unanswered questions that have arisen in the course of the discussion (and we would not claim that those raised here are exhaustive) mean that we are presently far from having a modelling theory that would allow us to allocate quantitative measures of operational security to particular systems, and it is this which will determine whether this new approach is of practical utility. Where do we go from here?

Some of the open questions are suitable for empirical investigation, and one way forward might be to devise controlled experiments in which 'tame' attackers are allowed to try to make security breaches on a designated system. A combination of system instrumentation and attacker interview might allow us to learn about the key notions of effort and reward that have been discussed here. Some of the authors of this paper are presently conducting a pilot experiment along these lines. Another approach would be to collect data on real systems in operation, as is done in the case of reliability studies. This seems fraught with difficulty, but it is a possibility that we do not rule out.

A different approach, and one of our reasons for writing this paper, would be to ask whether there is any consensus within the security community on any of these questions. Since our approach acknowledges the basically subjective nature of many of the questions - it concerns the way in which an individual will construct a quantitative personal viewpoint - it would be valuable to learn what practitioners currently think about these issues. We would therefore welcome comments from members of the security community on the feasibility of this whole approach, as well as answers to the specific questions we have raised.

## Acknowledgements

Earlier versions of the paper were read by Tom Anderson, Chris Dale, Yves Deswarte, Jean-Claude Laprie, David Powell, Michael Roe, Lorenzo Strigini. We are grateful for their comments and suggestions.

# Towards Operational Measures of Computer Security: Experimentation and Modelling

Tomas Olovsson[1]   Erland Jonsson[1]   Sarah Brocklehurst[2]   Bev Littlewood[2]

[1]Chalmers University   [2]City University

**Abstract.** The two experiments described here were intended to investigate the empirical issues that arise from the probabilistic view of security assessment discussed in the previous paper. Specifically, they investigated the problems of measuring *effort* and *reward* associated with security attacks and breaches.

## 1    Background

The aim of the work presented in this paper is to find appropriate methods for collection of data, by means of which the operational security of a system could be measured. Here, an immediate parallel would be that of reliability modelling. Reliability theory can be thought of as the description of processes involving failure events taking place in time. In the case of security, a naïve view would be that the process of security breaches could be modelled likewise. However, it quickly became clear that this would lead to a very restricted view of security. Even if there are some parallels, there are also important distinctions that would require a different approach.

### 1.1    Effort

Thus, in the case of security, time alone is not an appropriate variable. In particular, elapsed time when a system is not under attack is irrelevant for the evaluation of resistance to deliberate attacks. Instead, we need to consider a variable which captures the *effort* expended in attacking the system, and informally we expect a system which requires more effort to be expended until it is successfully breached, to be 'more secure'. We might with these terms define operational security analogous to reliability: the security function would be the probability of surviving without a security breach for the expenditure of a given effort by an attacker; other measures such as the rate of security breaches per unit effort, mean effort to the next security breach, etc, have obvious meanings.

Clearly, different systems will vary in their ability to resist a particular expenditure of effort from an attacker. Factors influencing this resistance include how the system is configured, the presence of security enhancing mechanisms, the quality of the system design and how the system is operated. The idea is that this 'ability to resist attacks' can be estimated by means of measuring the effort expended in order to achieve a breach. A complications is that effort is a variable composed of several factors: the attacker's education, skill and experience as well as time, money and other resources spent by the attacker are important factors. It is important that any differences between the ability of different attackers to break into the system is captured in the effort variable. It should capture the intuitive notion that the more effort is invested in attacking the system, the greater is the chance of achieving a breach. The major motivation for the experimentation described in this paper, is to find out whether it is possible to devise an effort measure with these properties.

## 1.2    Breaches and Rewards

The classical notion of a security breach as a security 'failure event' is sometimes too simplistic for our purposes. Firstly, it is clear that the value of different security breaches to a single attacker may vary enormously and this notion of reward should be incorporated into the measures. Secondly, whilst an attacker of a system may certainly gain something of value from these breach events, they may also acquire reward continuously - for example by gradually learning about the system. For these reasons we believe that, instead of the failure events in time that characterize the reliability process, the most general description of the security process would be in terms of a reward process, involving both discrete and continuous increments, against effort expended.

In our experiments we want to collect empirical data on breach events in order to learn about the nature of the reward process in security. Unfortunately, there are various practical limitations to what we could ever expect to achieve here. Although it would be desirable to include all types of breach events, some cannot be allowed in an experiment in which a real system is used due to the possible consequences for other users of the system.

The reward an attacker would get from breaking into a system determines his/her motivation and affects whether he/she is willing to spend the effort that is needed in order to perform the attack. Examples of such rewards are personal satisfaction, gain of money, revenge or simply pure curiosity. A reward may also be negative. An example of a negative reward could be the consequences of detection.

Considerations about the reward processes suggests that each attacker has a subjective view of his/her rewards, which is in general different from the system owner's view of these same rewards. For example, the loss due to a breach event for a system owner is likely to be different from the reward to the attacker. Thus, the system owner would normally only attach *negative* reward, i.e. actual loss, to (illegal) attacker activity. Furthermore, the subjective view of an attacker may be different from other attackers' views in similar circumstances. However, each attacker may be expected to apportion their effort optimally according to their view of their (potential) rewards, while the owner may be expected to respond to attacker activity in accordance with his view of his potential losses.

Note that the attacker may also attach some reward to legal activity, e.g. activity that allows the attacker to learn something about the system that would be useful in other, illegal, attacks.

## 2      Conditions for the Experimentation

Two experiments have been conducted: a pilot experiment and a first full-scale experiment. This section defines the common conditions under which they were performed: the actors, the system and what we hoped to achieve. The differences between the experiments are referred to under each separate paragraph.

There are three different kinds of actor involved in the experimentation: *the Attackers, the System administrator* and *the Coordinator*. Each of the actors plays a different role in the experiment and with respect to the target *System*. Furthermore, each actor is subject to a set of rules and restrictions, as well as a desirable behaviour. These rules and restrictions are discussed below.

## 2.1   The System

The target system was the same for both experiments: a set of 24 SUN ELC diskless workstations (22 in the pilot) connected to one file-server, all running SunOS 4.1.2. The system was during this time in operational use for laboratory courses taken by undergraduate students at the Department of Computer Engineering at Chalmers. The attackers were legal users of the system and were given normal user privileges and had physical access to all workstations except the file server. The system itself was configured as a 'standard' configuration as specified by the supplier and supervised by an experienced system administrator. No special security improvements were introduced for the experiment, and therefore the system presented only a modest level of security. The system had all standard monitoring and accounting features enabled in order to allow us to monitor the activities on each user account and to measure the resources each attacker spent during the breach process.

It should be emphasized that the choice of system was not the result of any specific preference. It was rather due to the fact that this was the system that was readily available for laboratory use. However, we realized that it was not a disadvantage that the type of system that we had available was rather common, and could therefore be assumed to be quite representative of a 'normal' system. Also, it is our intention to conduct experiments on different systems in the future to avoid general conclusions being drawn from system-specific results.

## 2.2   The Attackers

**Attacker profile.** A non-trivial problem was to find potential attackers. We were aiming for attackers that either already were or at least in the future would become the 'normal' users of the system, i.e. users without any special knowledge of operating system details and security issues. It is important to note that we *did not want professional crackers* who already knew about most weaknesses in the system. Professional crackers would give us information about where and how our particular system needed to be tightened. Such experiments or investigations have indeed been performed [2, 10], but from a modelling point of view, it is essential that the attackers were representative of a more general distribution of users, and using 'security experts' would radically reduce the value and representativeness of data.

A possible and attractive solution turned out to be using university students. Firstly, they were a good approximation of 'normal users' since they would very soon be working as such in industry, and secondly, we believed that it would not be a problem to convince university students to participate in such an experiment.

At the same time, when starting up the pilot experiment we were unsure of to the extent to which the students would really succeed in breaking into the system. An experimental result with no or very few breaches would definitely be an experimental failure. Even if this would be a good result from a system security point of view, it would not give us any data, nor would it give much information of how to perform such experimentation. To reduce this risk we decided to use only members of the Chalmers University Computer Club for the pilot experiment. The rationale for this decision was that since they had a special interest in computers, it was quite probable that they should be successful in this task. And conversely, if they did not succeed, 'regular' students would be unlikely to succeed. In the full-scale experiment we would then, depending on the outcome of the pilot, be prepared to continue with 'regular' students.

**Rules for the Attackers.** The attackers were told (rather informally) that a security breach occurs *whenever they succeed in doing something they were not normally allowed to* do, for example to read or modify a protected file, to use another user's account or to falsify or disturb normal system function. In general, it was our intention to restrict attacker action as little as possible. Despite this it was necessary to pose some restriction on their activity. One obvious restriction was that the attackers (or, in the case of the second experiment, the attacker *teams*) were forbidden to cooperate with others, since this would impair the collected data. Also, for obvious reasons, they were not allowed to cause physical damage to the system or to tamper with the hardware in order to reduce system availability. Finally they were told that activities that could cause disruption of system service to the normal users to the system had to be performed under supervized control, which in general meant that the activity was either performed during evenings or performed with the presence of an experiment coordinator.

It was essential for the attackers to be given a general description of the overall objectives of the experiment so that they had a complete understanding of why the rules should be obeyed, and why and in what way they should report their actions. Afterwards, it turned out that this requirement really motivated the attackers to work and follow the rules, and it become a major factor for the success of these experiments.

### 2.3    The Coordinator

The coordinator's role was to monitor and coordinate all activities during the experiment. In particular he had to make sure that the attackers and the system administrator were complying with the experimental rules. This meant that, as much as possible, the coordinator continually monitored all activity throughout the experiment and that he was normally available for consultation by the attackers and the system administrator. He was also to make sure that the activity of attackers would not interfere with each other.

### 2.4    The System Administrator

The system administrator was supposed to behave as realistically as possible. He was aware of the fact that the experiment was taking place, but he would monitor the system in the usual way and not intensify his search for security violations or other unwanted user behaviour (the extended logging imposed on the system was for data collection use only). Also, whenever he found a security violation on the system, he should contact the Coordinator who recorded the observation. Thus, the system administrator reported all attacking behaviour he observed and all security related actions he performed during the experiment.

### 2.5    Anticipated Results

The ultimate goal for these experiments was to collect data for modelling operational security. Some questions were especially interesting to find answers to:

*   Can we derive our single quantified measure of effort expended by an attacker, unifying the different factors (time, expertise, etc)?

- What is the distribution of the effort that needs to be expended to achieve a breach, for a single attacker?
- What is the nature of the more general stochastic process of reward from the attackers' and owner's views (i.e. when rewards can be continuously accrued as well as being associated with discrete breach events).

It should be noted that some of these problems would require extensive experimentation and innovative new approaches before even an approximate result could be anticipated. A more extensive discussion of modelling issues can be found in the previous chapter of this book.

In addition to the issues related to modelling (i.e., security evaluation) we hope to make some interesting qualitative observations. It is anticipated that answers, or at least partial answers, to these questions should be possible to find:

- How hard is it for regular users to break into their own (Unix) system? Will they be able to break in at all?
- Would it be possible for other users to work on the attacked system during the experiment? (A preferred situation from a modelling point of view, but also preferred since the available system was in operational use.)
- How do regular users approach such a task, i.e., what do they do when they are asked to break into their own system?
- Are only previously known vulnerabilities in the system exploited by these attackers or are new ones found?
- What kind of security breaches occur? Is the first security breach followed by new independent breaches, or is it more likely that the first breach is followed by new breaches where the knowledge collected from earlier breaches is used?
- How many and what types of security breaches were (or could have been) detected by the system owner? How many and what types of breaches could have been detected if we added non-standard hardware or software?
- How many of the attacks and breaches could have been carried out by attackers that were not users on the system?
- Is it an advantage for attackers to cooperate, for example to work in groups of two? Will two cooperating attackers produce more security breaches than two independently working attackers? Cooperation may favour sharing of knowledge and resources at the expense of lack of diversity.

We hoped that if the type of experimentation described here turned out to present a practicable way towards quantitative modelling of security, we would continue with further experiments which would clarify and give even more detailed answers to these questions regarding quantitative modelling. Also, hopefully future such experiments could be the basis for comparing systems with respect to security properties and could give system owners a possible idea, i.e. a measurement, of how secure their systems are.

## 2.6   Reporting

In addition to the automatic logging and recording of data, the attackers were required to perform extensive reporting. The reason for this was twofold: firstly, much of the information of interest was not available for automatic recording and secondly, we wanted to be able to compare results from automatic and manual reporting to be able to estimate the magnitude of mis-reporting, i.e., how erroneous the reporting process was. There were three principal manual reports: the *background report, the attack- and breach report* (which in the full-scale experiment were combined into a single *activity report*), and an *evaluation report*.

The *background report* was submitted before the experiment started. In this the attackers had to document their background (formal education, prior experience with computers and computer security, etc.) together with their interest and motivation for participating in the experiment. They were also asked to estimate their knowledge in computer security compared to all other last year students.

Each *activity report* contained data for one specific activity such as working-time, whether spent at the computer or elsewhere, on-line time, used resources (e.g. books, manuals, other computers, etc) and when the activity took place. Here the attacker would also note the motivations for his activity as well as other observations. If they managed to perform a security breach or gained some other sort of substantial reward, they had to give a full description of this, as well.

When the experiment was completed, the attackers had to fill in another questionnaire anonymously, the *evaluation report*. The goal of this report was to get some cross-checking of the experimental results. For example, they were asked in how many attacks they got help or hints from other attacking groups, which was something that was against the rules.

Also, in the very end, the attackers were asked to write a *final report* where each attacker described his/her activities and results quite freely. This report was delivered a few weeks after finalization of the experiment and served as the attackers' personal evaluation and reporting of their work. The final report turned out to be a very helpful means for checking the contents of the other reports.

## 3 The Pilot Experiment

### 3.1 Goal

The first experiment, the pilot, was conducted during spring 1993. The purpose was to investigate *if* it was at all possible to collect data for quantitative security modelling in the proposed way, and in such a case to find out *how* the data collection experimentation should appropriately be organized. Examples of open issues at this time were that of attacker behaviour and success (*could* they break in?), and their ability and willingness to report correctly.

### 3.2 The Attackers and Their Motivation

In the pilot experiment we decided to use members from Chalmers University Computer Club, i.e. students who were expected to be more skilled than regular students. The reason for this choice was to increase the probability of successful breaches.

In order to encourage the attackers to try to make breaches (and not to spend as much time as possible with the project) and to adhere to the rules of the experiment, two types of reward were given. Firstly, the most successful attacker was to receive a small personal 'medal' type gratitude. We hoped that this would motivate the attackers to work in the 'desired' way, where being successful would not necessarily mean 'performing many breaches', but rather to come up with innovative ideas and to document his actions in a purposeful way. Secondly, a small gift was handed over to the Chalmers Computer Club, a gift that could be used by all members of the Club and which would be our appreciation for the help we received.

## 3.3 Results from the Pilot Experiment

In the beginning of the experiment, we had 13 active attackers working independently. However, during the experiment the number of active attackers decreased, mainly due to lack of motivation. The 13 attackers submitted 37 attack reports showing roughly 50 hours of expended working time. However, later investigations showed that this figure was grossly underestimated and the real working time was more than twice as high. The expended working time was unevenly distributed among the different attackers: the 3 most active attackers accounted for more than 85% of the reported time. The automatic accounting system recorded 73 000 commands which were executed by the attackers, out of a total of 800 000 commands, indicating that the attackers accounted for less than 10% of the total system activity during this time.

The attackers' reports contained 25 successful attacks, showing that it was indeed possible for students to break into a Unix system. Most breaches were 'standard' breaches in the sense that they were already reported in literature or available over Internet. Broadly speaking they go into three different groups (for a further discussion of some of these methods, see the following discussion of the full-scale experiment):

*   achieving root privileges by means of a single-user boot-up, possibly followed by using the SUID-mechanism to transfer root privileges to the server.
*   finding out user passwords using the *Crack* program, i.e., a dictionary attack.
*   using the Xkey snooping program to monitor the key strokes of other users, thus hoping to get passwords or other interesting information.
*   The use of security-enhancing program such as *Cops* to find vulnerabilities.

There were also some less standard attempts made:

*   one attacker found out that the screen devices for some workstations were default readable (and writable), meaning that it was possible to monitor all the output on the screen.
*   one attacker planted a Trojan Horse for other users in a faked 'ls'-command.

A detailed description of breaches and effort expended, can be found in [6]. It should be noted that there are remedies for many of these attacks. However, the system administrator was either not aware of the vulnerability or, in a few cases, a vendor-provided solution was received but had not yet been installed.

## 3.4 Conclusions of the Pilot Experiment

The amount of data received from this pilot experiment was, as expected, too sparse to allow any statistical modelling, but the experiment showed that it should be possible to conduct a full scale experiment that would yield real data. There were several important conclusions drawn from this experiment:

*   students *are indeed able to break into a standard Unix system*, even though they were given such a short time for the task. Several of them performed many different breaches.

- students *can* be used in this kind of experiment. They were quite interested in participating in the experiment and they showed a remarkable understanding of and compliance to the experimental rules.
- the system *will* be operable to other users at the same time.
- However, attackers had a tendency to leave the experiment due to lack of ideas and/or motivation. This emphasized the importance of motivation for the attackers in future experiments.
- Also, the required reporting turned out to be too extensive. Many of the questions, e.g. regarding personal reward of a breach, were answered with insufficient detail or not at all. It also became evident that the understanding of what constituted an 'attack' and 'breach' differed between the attackers, which led to incomplete reporting of attacker activities. Therefore, in the full-scale experiment, we reduced the number of questions and merged the attack report and the breach report into one single *activity report*, containing all information we wanted to know about an activity.

# 4     The Full-scale Experiment

## 4.1     Goal

Since the pilot experiment had showed the potential feasibility of the method as such, a full-scale experiment was performed. The goal of the full-scale experiment was to gather enough data for a quantitative modelling attempt. We hoped that we could use the data to develop a quantitative methodology, by means of which quantitative conclusions could be made. However, it should be emphasized that those conclusions would *not be representative* for a more general class of systems, attackers or environments. The statistical basis would be far too limited for any such generalisations.

Further, we hoped to learn more about the attacking process and system vulnerabilities.

## 4.2     The Attackers and Their Motivation

The full-scale experiment was conducted during a 4 week period in November and December 1993. As a result of the successful outcome, in terms of breaches, of the pilot experiment, we engaged 'regular' last year students as attackers in the second experiment, and offered them to do a project work within a course in Applied Computer Security. The conditions for this experiment were similar to those for the pilot experiment, except that one security improvement had been carried out: the system hardware had been equipped with a password to prevent users performing a single user boot-up sequence. Furthermore, the reporting system was simplified as described above.

This time, the students were grouped into groups of two, with the intention to increase the motivation and the persistence of the attacking process. There were 24 attackers (i.e. 12 groups) participating in the experiment and we expected each group to spend around 40 hours of effective working time during a 4 week calendar period. However, there was no absolute requirement to spend exactly this amount of time. Their goal was to create as many and as valuable security breaches as possible, not to sit down and wait for 40 hours to pass by. The attackers were supposed to meet with the Coordinator twice a week and discuss their progress.

The major motivation of the attackers was that the experiment was a compulsory part of the course they were taking, and that well performed work, including a good final report, could result in a higher mark on the course. We also found that most attackers were genuinely interested in learning more about security by testing and attacking a real system and that they were interested in discussing their results long after the experiment had ended.

### 4.3    Some Numerical Results

During the full-scale experiment we received 181 activity reports describing a total of 65 security breaches of various kinds. The number of breaches is an approximate fig-ure, since the limit of what to consider to be a security breach or not, is a matter of definition (this problem is further discussed below). The groups reported 483 hours of working time, i.e. time where at least one group member was active, and altogether 594 man-hours were spent, which is an average working time of 50 hours per group.

An informal interpretation of these figures are that an 'average' computer science student can perform one security breach every seventh hour, on an average. However, there were great variations between students, and between the breach rates early in their activity and those later on.

Furthermore, 281 hours of on-line time at the target system and 65 hours on other systems was reported. A comparison with the automatic logging shows that the reported numbers are somewhat underestimated (33 hours), but the discrepancy is much lower that in the pilot experiment, a fact that can probably be accredited to the improved reporting system.

### 4.4    Types of Breaches

Table 1. Number of breaches per category

| Category | Attempts | Breaches |
|---|---|---|
| Execution of security enhancing programs | 22 | 20 |
| Spoofing programs with SUID privileges | 14 | 8 |
| OS and administration related problems | 19 | 18 |
| User related problems | 11 | 8 |
| Snooping | 9 | 6 |
| Other | many | 5 |

The experiment resulted in 65 breaches. We have divided these breaches into five categories, mainly depending on what kind of vulnerability they exploited. The definition of each category and examples of breaches are given in the following. The table below shows a summary of breaches and attempted breaches per category. Note that these figures are only valid given the present tentative classification and definition of breach and breach attempt.

**Execution of security enhancing programs.** The intended use of security enhancing programs is to help the system administrator to maintain security in his system, and many of them are freely available over the Internet. These programs look for specific or general (potential) vulnerabilities in the system and output a list of warnings. The administrator is supposed to run those programs on a regular basis and take proper action. However, in many cases this is not done regularly, which means that an intruder has an automatic tool for finding vulnerabilities.

Examples of used programs are *Crack, Cops, Tiger* and *ISS (Internet Security Scanner)*. Crack is a password guessing program performing a so-called dictionary attack. It exploits the fact that users have a tendency not to chose random passwords, but passwords that could be found in a dictionary or encyclopaedia, possibly with minor modifications. Cops and Tiger scans the system searching for a number of different potential problems. ISS does the same thing but from the 'outside' of the system.

These programs revealed several vulnerabilities in the system: a number of accounts with badly selected passwords, files with insufficient protection, incorrect system configuration, etc. In some cases, these programs were modified to exploit some specific characteristic. A good example of this is the modification of the crack program to look especially for passwords with a special distribution of consonants and vowels. In this way the computer generated passwords given to all students working in the laboratory exposed a greater risk to be guessed.

**Spoofing programs with root privileges.** Many Unix programs are executed with root (super-user) privileges, which are often necessary to accomplish the function of the program. This is implemented by using the SUID (Set User ID on execution) facility in Unix, which is a service that permits the user of a program to run it with *the privileges of the owner* of the program, instead of the users' own privileges. If the owner is root (the system administrator), a user can execute the program with the system administrator's rights. Normally, such SUID rights are only given to a few trusted programs. However, in some cases these programs contains bugs so that they can be spoofed to perform an unintended function, and this function may be selected so that a breach occurs.

Since this is a very general methodology for attacking a system, the breaches in this category are quite diverse. One example is a problem with the program Xterm, a virtual terminal program in the X-Windows system, which executes with root privileges. A facility of this program is that it can log all terminal output into a user-specified file. Due to a serialisation error in the procedure for checking this write privilege [12], the output can be diverted to any file in the file system.

Another attack made use of the X-window server to remove a directory, even though it was not empty. The result was a number of 'lost' files and subdirectories that would continue to exist and occupy disk space, but yet could not be referenced. This breach provides a means to fill the available disk space of the system, whilst from a system administrator's view it appears to be almost empty. It can be characterized as an availability breach. It is possible for the system administrator to recover the lost files once he figures out what has happened, something that is not evident. (The administrator of the target system would later have done a restoration of the file-system from a back-up, which apart from a lot of work and making the system unavailable, could have resulted in lost user files.)

**Operating system and administration related problems.** Many problems were found which either correspond to bugs within the operating system or to bad management of the system. The target operating system had several files, directories and devices that by default were readable and writable! Some attackers discovered that a couple of such devices could be a suitable target for compromising system security. For example, one group found out that the system back-up tape for the previous week was installed and readable. In this way all information on the tape was unprotected and available to the attackers.

A couple of attacker groups exploited the insufficient checking of sender that 'send-mail' (the mail delivery program) performs. Thus, it is very simple to send email with a faked sender name. As a consequence, the source of an incoming email could never be trusted based on the contents of the 'From-field' only. A similar bug affects the Internet News service. Still another vulnerability of this kind that was discovered is that a remote copy command (*rcp*) given to a device will crash the system.

Most problems in this category had already been warned about by CERT. However, one vulnerability found by the attackers was that the file /etc/*utmp* was writable. This file contains login records for the current users of the system, and opened a possibility to introduce false information into the system, which could lead to a variety of breaches. This vulnerability was found and reported by CERT about 3 months after the experiment was finished (CERT Advisory CA-94:06, March 21, 1994).

**User related problems.** This category includes all problems that are directly due to user action or lack of action. The target system was in daily use and more than 800 different student accounts existed. Therefore, with a high probability, some students would unintentionally leave files and directories readable and writable, when they should not have been. This opens up many possible attacks, e.g., just changing or deleting the contents of files or reading files that were supposed to be confidential. Another obvious attack is to use the unintended write permission to plant Trojan horses.

A quite unconventional and interesting and successful attack was carried out by one group, who sent a message to all normal users of the system (they got a special permission from the Coordinator to perform this attack.) The message claimed that all passwords had been revealed due to an operating system failure, and required all users to immediately change their passwords, and *to reply back informing about their new password.* The message was signed by something that could be interpreted as 'System administrator'. Two users actually sent their password back (!) but a more important observation was that users begun to change their passwords from the machine generated (random) passwords, into simple, easily guessed passwords. This simple attack clearly shows the key role of the users in determining the security of a system.

**Snooping.** Snooping attacks aim at confidentiality. We have put two types of attacks in this category. The first one exploits the fact that the X-Windows server offers a service that permits other programs to 'listen' to events that occur, unless protected by an authentication file (*.Xauthority*). This makes it possible to use programs to record keystrokes, and thus collect confidential data.

The second one is a pure passive attack against the network connecting the worksta-tions. These attacks are very hard to detect and could have been performed outside the lab as well. On the target system network, messages are sent in clear-text including passwords. Five groups realized that it must be possible to listen to the network and tried this approach. Three groups succeeded to filter out relevant data from the extensive network traffic. For example, one group found the root password, two user passwords and two passwords to external systems. The possible outcome of this attack is much greater than these passwords, since given enough time, they would have recorded all passwords ever sent on this network! Two other groups could listen to the network, but due to the extensive traffic did not manage to extract any sensitive data.

**Other breaches.** Finally, there are a number of breaches that do not naturally go into any of the above categories. The most interesting one, found by one group, is that the command *kbd_mode*, whose intended function is to reset the console keyboard, could be used remotely to (silently) disable another user's keyboard.

### 4.5    The Attacking Process

How do the attackers approach their task? By far, the most common method is to make use of the Internet, which seems to be an almost inexhaustible source of information. In some cases books, manuals and journals were used. Thus, most breaches were 'known' on the Internet. The major exceptions were the *utmp* and the *kbd_mode* attacks, one of which was later reported. Example of information sources on the Internet are BBS's, the News service and World Wide Web (WWW) pages. Furthermore, the Computer Emergency Response Team (CERT) is an organisation that monitors computer security and break-in activities, and sends out alerts and 'fixes' for security vulnerabilities. This experiment clearly stresses the importance of forcing system administrators to follow these recommendations.

### 4.6    Discussion

The experiment shows that there are many ways to enter a standard Unix system even for a regular user. However, since no extended security enhancements had been carried out on the target system, many of the vulnerabilities could have been removed. Some required an extended security 'kit' to be installed, e.g. NIS+ which is available from some vendors. However, not many sites use them. If they had been used here, the number of successful attacks would have been smaller, but many loopholes would still remain. Furthermore, if the system were threatened by 'professional' attackers, they would probably penetrate it much more easily then did the students. Also, for many - even experienced - system administrators, it may not be evident how a vulnerability should indeed be removed. The attempt, before starting the full-scale experiment, to remove the possibility to gain *root* privileges by means of carrying through a single-user boot-up sequence clearly failed.

An overall conclusion from a practical security point of view is that sensitive information should not be stored on this kind of system, unless extensive security-enhancing precautions are taken.

## 5    Lessons for Quantitative Assessment

### 5.1    Measuring Effort

The pilot experiment provided valuable lessons which successfully allowed the second experiment to provide extensive data on 'effort'. More events were observed in the second experiment and the recording of the data was much fuller and more complete. In addition, a flexible data-base structure is being built to allow easy investigation of some of the theoretical issues.

Much of the data collection was concerned with trying to establish the feasibility of identifying a single measure of effort. Most relevant and easily quantifiable was effort represented by three different (but associated) measures of *time*. The first time variable is the *working time* expended by the attacker, for example by learning about the system (on- or off-line), or by manually searching files for vulnerabilities.

Other time variables are associated with those attacks where the attacker executed some software, e.g. *Crack*. Here it was possible to measure the time that the attacker was using a machine, the *on-line time* as well as the *execution time* (or *CPU time*) of that machine on the attack(s). (In some cases the programs were executed on other systems than the target machines, in which case this possibility disappears.) Some attackers, for example, executed software on many machines in parallel and the use of these additional hardware resources can be taken into account by measuring the total execution time across the machines.

The three time measures together form a important component of our intuitive notion of effort. Obtaining a single measure of effort from these poses some difficulties that are currently being addressed as the data from the experiments is analysed. An obvious way forward is to take a simple linear combination of the three different times spent on an attack and treat this as the 'effort' spent. The parameters of the linear combination have to be chosen in some way that 'normalizes' the disparate 'times'. One way of doing this that is under investigation is to try to assess, subjectively, the different values (e.g. in monetary terms) of each different time unit.

These difficulties are compounded, of course, when we take account of aspects of effort other than time. For example, some attackers reported having used external resources (e.g. documentation, friends, ...) off-line in order to learn about possible ways to break into the system, but it is not presently clear how to combine these with time-based effort. However, in many attacks the software used by the attackers was publicly available (e.g. *Crack*, *Xkey*), and could thus be regarded as having zero cost. In that case the times the attackers spent retrieving, learning about and setting up such software and monitoring any results could be sufficient to characterize the effort involved, as described above.

An alternative way out of the difficulty of combination would be to generalize the underlying theoretical model so that effort can be represented as a vector. However, this has the disadvantage of losing the conceptual simplicity of the original approach, where different types of effort could be imagined to be equivalent via some 'common currency' such as cost. Our present view is that a single measure, whilst somewhat idealistic, is the best way forward.

In most cases carrying out a single attack involved the attacker in a combination of different kinds of activity, e.g. some learning and planning, followed by writing some software, followed by executing the software, etc. The reporting in the second experiment was sufficiently complete that it is possible to associate effort measures (i.e. times) to the different activities that constitute an attack. This introduces another type of variation between attackers - how they *apportion* their effort - that seems worthy of further attention.

## 5.2    Breach Events and Rewards

From the accounts of their attacking activity, and from the reports of the breaches they claimed to have made, it was possible to learn something about the nature of the attackers' reward processes. Firstly, it was clear that each attacker generally associated very different rewards with the achievement of different successes. Not surprisingly, attackers associated a very high reward with getting root on the server ('the ultimate goal' for many of them) whilst, for example, associating a lesser reward with getting root on a local machine. Again, fairly obviously, in cases where one (*partial*) breach was used to achieve some further goal - for example local root to achieve root on the server, or discovery of some other vulnerability in the system which later led to getting root on the server - the attackers attached higher reward to the ultimate breach than to the prior partial breach. The main other type of success with which the attackers clearly associated substantial rewards was that of obtaining passwords. Other events with which the attacker associated rewards were generally to do with learning about security issues in the system. In some cases the attackers seemed to attach reward to having proved that a particular attack method would work even though no higher objective was achieved (e.g., proving that their implementation of a Trojan horse could catch passwords, but not subsequently actually getting any passwords from this method).

In the pilot it was sometimes possible to rank different successes in order of the amount of subjective reward they represented to the attacker, but this was generally not the case, particularly when successes were of different types. For example, for ordinary user accounts where an attacker is indifferent between these users, whilst most attackers would rate getting many passwords for different accounts more highly than getting just one, it was not clear how they would value getting many passwords of ordinary users compared with getting the system owner's password. Ranking of even more disparate kinds of successes, e.g. local root versus some users' passwords, seems even more of a problem.

Both the pilot and the second experiment confirmed our conjecture that different attackers *did* seem to have different rewards associated with the occurrence of the same successes (in other words different attackers had different motivation driving their attacking behaviour). For example, it was apparent that some attackers seemed to get more personal satisfaction from being in a position to do something malicious than others, some found learning particularly important and attached more reward to this than other attackers, others seemed to get a lot of intellectual satisfaction from having done something clever. These results confirm the necessity to adopt a subjective approach to the probability modelling.

It was noticeable that the attackers found it much harder to assess continuous accrual of reward even than they did the reward associated with single breach events. Thus it seems particularly difficult to assess the reward associated with gradual learning about a system.

# 6    Conclusions

These experiments have demonstrated the feasibility *in principle* of measuring effort expended in attacking a system, and thus eventually obtaining a quantitative, probabilistic theory of security akin to that which has been available for many years for reliability. The pilot experiment was invaluable in pointing to difficulties such as incomplete reporting, so that these were overcome in the second experiment. The result was that we obtained accurate measures of the different times associated with attacks, and with different activities of attackers that constituted the attacks. Although even the second experiment was quite small, it succeeded in obtaining a considerable amount of data of this kind.

Further work is now needed on ways to combine the different components of 'effort', such as these different times, into single measures of effort as required by the probabilistic theory of security assessment. This work is currently underway.

Measures of reward present even harder problems than effort. Our approach to this was to be as comprehensive as possible in our data collection, so that there exists a data-base containing details of the nature of all reported breaches as well as the constituents of effort discussed earlier. This data-base structure will itself be a valuable resource in future experiments. In the meantime, the results of the second experiment are being analysed using the subjective judgements of the experimenter as the measures of reward.

In conclusion, we recognize that there remain formidable difficulties in this kind of quantitative assessment of security. On the other hand, we have shown that it is possible to come close to defining the required effort-based measures of security, even in the small confines of the experiments that we have conducted. We believe that it is worthwhile to continue with the work in the expectation that the remaining problems can be overcome after further investigation.

# References for Chapter VIII

[1]     A. A. Abdel-Ghaly, P. Y. Chan and B. Littlewood, "Evaluation of Competing Software Reliability Predictions", *IEEE Trans. on Software Engineering*, 12 (9), pp.950-67, 1986.

[2]     C. R. Attanasio, P. Markstein and R. J. Phillips, "Penetrating an Operating System: A Study of VM/370 Integrity", *IBM Systems J.*, 15 (1), pp.102-16, 1974.

[3]     R. E. Barlow and F. Proschan, *Statistical Theory of Reliability and Life Testing*, 290p., Holt, Rinehart and Winston, New York, 1975.

[4]     R. Bishop, "Computer Security - A Common Sense Model", *Computer* (5 October), pp.42-3, 1989.

[5]     S. Brocklehurst and B. Littlewood, "New Ways to get Accurate Reliability Measures", *IEEE Software*, 9 (4), pp.34-42, 1992.

[6]     S. Brocklehurst, B. Littlewood, T. Olovsson and E. Jonsson, "On Measurement of Operational Security", in *COMPASS 94 (9th Annual IEEE Conference on Computer Assurance)*, (Gaithersburg), pp.257-66, IEEE Computer Society, 1994.

[7]     D. E. Denning, "An Intrusion-Detection model", *IEEE Trans Software Engineering*, 12 (2), pp.222-32, 1987.

[8]     D. E. Eckhardt and L. D. Lee, "A Theoretical Basis of Multiversion Software Subject to Coincident Errors", *IEEE Trans. on Software Engineering*, 11, pp.1511-7, 1985.

[9]     B. d. Finetti, *Theory of Probability,* Wiley, Chichester, 1975.

[10]    I. S. Herschberg, "Make the Tigers Hunt for You", *Computers and Security*, 7, pp.197-203, 1988.

[11]    Z. Jelinski and P. B. Moranda, "Software Reliability Research", in *Statistical Computer Performance Evaluation* (W. Freiberger, Ed.), pp.465-84, Academic Press, New York, 1972.

[12]    C. E. Landwehr, A. R. Bull, J. P. McDermott and W. S. Choi, "A Taxonomy of Computer Program Security Flaws", *ACM Computing Surveys*, 26 (3) 1994.

[13]    J.-C. Laprie, "Dependability: A Unifying Concept for Reliable Computing and Fault Tolerance", in *Resilient Computing Systems* (T. Anderson, Ed.), pp.1-28, Blackwell Scientific Publications, Oxford, 1989.

[14]    T. M. P. Lee, "Statistical Models of Trust: TCBs Versus People", in *IEEE Symposium on Security and Privacy,* (Oakland), pp.10-9, IEEE Computer Society Press, 1989.

[15]    D. V. Lindley, *Making Decisions,* Wiley, Chichester, UK, 1985.

[16]    B. Littlewood, "How to Measure Software Reliability, and How Not to ...", *IEEE Trans. on Reliability*, 28 (2), pp.103-10, 1979.

[17]   B. Littlewood, "Predicting Software Reliability", *Phil Trans Royal Soc London*, A 327, pp.513-49, 1989.

[18]   B. Littlewood, "Limits to Evaluation of Software Dependability", in *Software Reliability and Metrics (Proceedings of 7th Annual CSR Conference, Garmisch-Partenkirchen)* (B. Littlewood and N. E. Fenton, Eds.), pp.81-110, Elsevier, London, 1991.

[19]   B. Littlewood and D. R. Miller, "Conceptual Modelling of Coincident Failures in Multi-Version Software", *IEEE Trans on Software Engineering*, 15 (12), pp.1596-614, 1989.

[20]   B. Littlewood and J. L. Verrall, "A Bayesian Reliability Growth Model for Computer Software", *J. Royal Statist. Soc. C*, 22, pp.332-46, 1973.

[21]   J. D. Musa, "A Theory of Software Reliability and its Application", *IEEE Trans. on Software Engineering*, 1, pp.312-27, 1975.

[22]   NCSC, *Department of Defense Trusted Computer System Evaluation*, National Computer Security Center, Department of Defense, N°DOD 5200.28.STD, 1985.

[23]   C. Perrow, *Normal Accidents: Living with High Risk Technologies,* Basic Books, New York, 1984.

# PDCS Publications

The following lists all the papers describing research supported in whole or in part by PDCS that have been published in refereed journals and technical conferences.

[1]  J. Arlat, "Fault Injection for the Experimental Validation of Fault-Tolerant Systems (Invited paper)", in *Proc. Workshop Fault-Tolerant Systems*, (IEICE, Tokyo, Japan), pp.33-40, 1992.

[2]  J. Arlat, A. Costes, Y. Crouzet, J. C. Laprie and D. Powell, "Fault Injection and Dependability Evaluation of Fault-Tolerant Systems", *IEEE Transactions on Computers*, 42 (8), pp.913-23, August 1993.

[3]  J. Arlat, Y. Crouzet and J. C. Laprie, "Fault Injection for the Experimental Validation of Fault Tolerance", in *Proc. 1991 ESPRIT Conf.*, (Brussels), pp.791-805, 1991.

[4]  J. Arlat, K. Kanoun and J. C. Laprie, "Dependability Modelling and Evaluation of Software-Fault Tolerant Systems", *IEEE Trans. Computers (Special Issue on Fault Tolerance)*, 39 (4), pp. 504-13, 1990.

[5]  N. Audsley, A. Burns, M. Richardson, K. Tindell and A. Wellings, "Applying New Scheduling Theory to Static Priority Pre-emptive Scheduling", *Software Engineering Journal*, 8 (5), pp.284-92, September 1993.

[6]  D. R. Avresky and J. Arlat, "Functional Programming for Fault Tolerance in Parallel Computing Systems", in *Proc. 6th ISCA Int. Conf. on Parallel and Distributed Computing Systems (PDCS'93)*, (Louisville, KY, USA), pp.38-45, ISCA, 1993.

[7]  D. R. Avresky, J. Arlat, J. C. Laprie and Y. Crouzet, "Fault Injection for the Formal Testing of Fault Tolerance", in *Proc. 22th Int. Symp. Fault-Tolerant Computing (FTCS-22)*, (Boston, MA, USA), pp.345-54, IEEE Computer Society Press, 1992.

[8]  O. Babaoglu, "Fault-Tolerant Computing Based on Mach", in *Proc. USENIX Mach Workshop*, (Vermont), 1990.

[9]  O. Babaoglu, L. Alvisi, A. Amoroso and R. Davoli, "Mapping Parallel Computations onto Distributed Systems in Paralex", in *Proc. IEEE CompEuro '91*, (Bologna, Italy), 1991.

[10]  A. Baker, J. Bieman, N. E. Fenton, D. Gustafson, A. Melton and R. W. Whitty, "A Philosophy for Software Measurement", *Journal of Systems Software*, 12, pp.277-81, 1990.

[11]  G. Bernot, M.-C. Gaudel and B. Marre, "Software Testing Based on Formal Specifications: A theory and a tool", *Software Engineering Journal*, 9 (6), pp.387-405, 1991.

[12]   J. Bieman, N. E. Fenton, D. Gustafson, A. Melton and R. W. Whitty, "Moving from Philosophy to Practice in Software Measurement", in *Formal Aspects of Software Measurement* (T. Denvir, H. R. and R. W. Whitty, Eds.), pp.38-59, Springer Verlag, 1992.

[13]   A. Bondavalli, S. Chiaradonna and F. Di Giandomenico, "Efficient Fault Tolerance: An approach to deal with transient faults in multiprocessor architectures", in *Proc. Int. Conf. on Parallel and Distributed Systems (ICPADS'94),* (Hsinchu, Taiwan), pp.354-9, IEEE Computer Society, 1994.

[14]   A. Bondavalli, S. Chiaradonna, F. Di Giandomenico and L. Strigini, "Dependability Models for Iterative Software Considering Correlation among Successive Inputs", in *Proc. Int. Symp. on Computer Performance and Dependability (IPDS'95),* (Erlangen, Germany), p.in publication, 1995.

[15]   A. Bondavalli, F. Di Giandomenico and J. Xu, "A Cost-Effective and Flexible Scheme for Software Fault Tolerance", *J. of Computer Systems Science and Engineering*, 8 (4), pp.234-44, October 1993.

[16]   A. Bondavalli, M. Mannocci, F. Tarini, P. Zini, L. Nardone and L. Simoncini, "A Performable BSM Architecture", in *Proc. 5th GI/ITG/GMA Int. Conf. on Fault-Tolerant Computing,* (Nurnberg, Germany), 1991.

[17]   A. Bondavalli and L. Nardone, "Supporto a Tempo di Esecuzione ed Ambiente per un Linguaggio Dataflow Esteso", in *Proc. Congresso Annuale A.I.C.A., Vol. 2,* (Siena), pp.1061-75, 1991.

[18]   A. Bondavalli and L. Simoncini, "Failure Classification with respect to Detection", in *Proc. 2nd Workshop on Future Trends of Distributed Computing Systems in the 90s,* (Cairo), pp.47-53, IEEE, 1990.

[19]   A. Bondavalli and L. Simoncini, "Structured Software Fault Tolerance with BSM", in *Proc. 3rd IEEE Workshop on the Future Trends of Distributed Computing Systems,* (Taipei, Taiwan), 1992.

[20]   A. Bondavalli, J. A. Stankovic and L. Strigini, "Adaptable Fault Tolerance for Real-Time Systems", in *Proc. 3rd Int. Workshop on Responsive Computer Systems,* (New Hampshire), pp.123-32, 1993.

[21]   A. Bondavalli, L. Strigini and L. Simoncini, "Data-Flow like Languages for Real-Time Systems: Issues of computational models and notation", in *Proc. 11th Symp. on Reliable Distributed Systems (SRDS-11),* (Houston, Texas), pp.214-21, 1992.

[22]   S. Brocklehurst, P. Y. Chan, B. Littlewood and J. Snell, "Recalibrating Software Reliability Models", *IEEE Trans. Software Engineering*, 16 (4), pp.458-70, 1990.

[23]   S. Brocklehurst, K. Kanoun, J. C. Laprie, B. Littlewood, S. Metge, P. Mellor and A. Tanner, "Reliability Analyses of Software Failure Data", in *Proc. 1991 ESPRIT Conf.,* (Brussels), pp.806-21, 1991.

[24]   S. Brocklehurst and B. Littlewood, "New Ways to get Accurate Reliability Measures", *IEEE Software (Special Issue on Applications of Software Reliability Models)*, 9 (4), pp.34-42, 1992.

[25]   S. Brocklehurst, B. Littlewood, T. Olovsson and E. Jonsson, "On Measurement of Operational Security", in *Proc. 9th Annual IEEE Conference on Computer Assurance (COMPASS 94),* (Gaithersburg), pp.257-66, IEEE Computer Society, 1994.

[26]   A. Burns, "Scheduling Hard Real-Time Systems: A review", *Software Engineering Journal,* 6 (3), pp.116-28, 1991.

[27]   A. Burns, "Real-Time System Scheduling", *Software Engineering Journal* 1993.

[28]   A. Burns, J. A. McDermid and J. E. Dobson, "On the Meaning of Safety and Security", *Computer Journal,* 34 (1) 1992.

[29]   R. Chakka and I. Mitrani, "Multiprocessor Systems with General Breakdowns and Repairs", in *Proc. Sigmetrics — Performance '92,* (Newport, RI), 1992.

[30]   R. Chakka and I. Mitrani, "A Numerical Solution Method for Multiprocessor Systems with General Breakdowns and Repairs", in *6th Int. Conf. on Modelling Techniques and Tools for Computer Performance Evaluation,* (Edinburgh), pp.289-304, Edinburgh University Press, 1992.

[31]   R. Chakka and I. Mitrani, "Heterogeneous Multiprocessor Systems with Breakdowns: Performance and optimal repair strategies", in *Proc. INRIA/ORSA/TIMS/SMAI Conf. on Applied Probability in Engineering, Computer and Communication Sciences,* (Paris), 1993.

[32]   S. Chiaradonna, A. Bondavalli and L. Strigini, "On Performability Modeling and Evaluation of Software Fault Tolerance Structures", in *First European Dependable Computing Conference (EDCC1),* (Berlin, Germany), pp.pp. 97-114, 1994.

[33]   S. J. Clarke, A. C. Coombes and J. A. McDermid., "Methods for Developing Safe Software", in *Proc. SafetyNet '90,* (Royal Aeronautical Society, London), p.6:1 — 6:8, 1990.

[34]   P. J. Courtois (Ed.), *Software Important to Safety in Nuclear Power Plants,* Technical Reports Series N0367, 169p., International Atomic Energy Agency, Vienna, 1994.

[35]   P. J. Courtois and D. L. Parnas, "Documentation for Safety Critical Software", in *Proc. 15th Int. Conf. on Software Eng. (ICSE 15),* (Baltimore), 1993.

[36]   M. Dacier, "A Petri Net Representation of the Take-Grant Model", in *Proc. of the Computer Security Foundations Workshop VI,* (Franconia, USA), pp.99-108, IEEE Computer Society, 1993.

[37]   M. Dacier and Y. Deswarte, "Privilege graph: an extension to the Typed Access Matrix model", in *Proc. European Symposium on Research in Computer Security (ESORICS 94),* (D. Gollmann, Ed.), (Brighton, UK), Lecture Notes in Computer Science (LNCS), 875, pp.319-34, Springer-Verlag, 1994.

[38] R. de Lemos, A. Saeed and T. Anderson, "Distributed Real-Time Systems: Value Inconsistencies due to time uncertainties", in *Proc. of DCCS-10*, (Semmering, Austria), 1991.

[39] R. de Lemos, A. Saeed and T. Anderson, "Analysis of Timeliness Requirements in Safety-Critical Systems", in *Proc. Symp. on Formal Techniques for Real-Time and Fault-Tolerant Systems*, (Nijmegen. Netherlands), 1992.

[40] R. de Lemos, A. Saeed and T. Anderson, "A Train Set as a Case Study for the Requirements Analysis of Safety-Critical Systems", *The Computer Journal (Special Issue on Security and Safety)*, 34 (2), pp.30-40, February 1992.

[41] R. de Lemos, A. Saeed and A. Waterworth, "Exception Handling in Real-Time Software from Specification to Design", in *Proc. Workshop on Responsive Computer Systems*, (Saitama, Japan), pp.108-21, 1992.

[42] R. de Lemos, A. Saeed and A. Waterworth, "Exception Handling in Real-Time Software from Specification to Design", in *Responsive Computer Systems (Dependable Computing and Fault-Tolerant Systems, Vol. 7)* (H. Kopetz and Y. Kakuda, Eds.), Springer-Verlag, New York, 1993.

[43] Y. Deswarte, L. Blain and J.-C. Fabre, "Intrusion Tolerance in Distributed Computing Systems", in *Proc. 1991 Symp. on Research in Security and Privacy*, (Oakland, California), pp.110-21, IEEE Computer Society Press, 1991.

[44] F. Di Giandomenico and L. Strigini, "Adjudicators for Diverse Redundant Components", in *Proc. 9th Int. Symp. Reliable Distributed Systems*, (Huntsville, Alabama), pp.114-23, IEEE, 1990.

[45] F. Di Giandomenico and L. Strigini, "Implementations and Extensions of the Conversation Concept", in *Proc. 5th GI/ITG/GMA Int. Conf. Fault-Tolerant Computing Systems*, (Nurnberg, Germany), 1991.

[46] J. E. Dobson, "Conversation Structures as an Instrument of Security Policy", in *Database Security: Status and Prospects III* (D. L. Spooner and C. E. Landwehr, Eds.), pp.25-40, North-Holland, Amsterdam, 1990.

[47] J. E. Dobson, "A Methodology for Analysing Human and Computer-Related Issues in Secure Systems", in *Compusec 90 (IFIP Int. Conf. on Computer Security)*, (Helsinki), 1990.

[48] J. E. Dobson, "Elicitation and Representation of a Security Policy for a Telecommunications Application", in *Eighth Int. Conf. on Software Engineering for Telecommunications Systems and Services*, (Florence, Italy), 1992.

[49] J. E. Dobson, J. C. Laprie and B. Randell, "Predictably Dependable Computing systems: An ESPRIT Basic Research Project", *Bulletin of the EATCS (European Association for Theoretical Computing Science)*, 40 1990.

[50] J. E. Dobson, M. J. Martin, C. W. Olphert and S. E. Powrie, "Determining Requirements for Co-operative Working", in *Conf. on Collaborative Work,*

*Social Communications and Information Systems Theories (COSCIS '91),* (Helsinki), 1991.

[51] J. E. Dobson and J. A. McDermid, "Security Models and Enterprise Models", in *Database Security: Status and Prospects II* (C. Landwehr, Ed.), Elsevier Science Publishers, Amsterdam, 1989.

[52] J. C. Fabre, Y. Deswarte and B. Randell, "Designing Secure and Reliable Applications using Fragmentation-Redundancy-Scattering: An object-oriented approach", in *Proc. of the First European Dependable Computing Conference (EDCC-1),* (Berlin, Germany), Lecture Notes in Computer Science, 852, (K. Echtle, D. Hammer and D. Powell, Eds.), pp.23-38, Springer-Verlag, 1994.

[53] J. C. Fabre, V. Nicomette, T. Pérennou, R. J. Stroud and Z. Wu, "Implementing Fault-Tolerant Applications using Reflective Object-Oriented Programming", in *Proc. 25th Int. Symp. on Fault-Tolerant Computing (FTCS-25),* (Pasadena, CA, USA), IEEE Computer Society Press, 1995.

[54] J. C. Fabre and B. Randell, "An Object-Oriented View of Fragmented Data Processing for Fault and Intrusion Tolerance in Distributed Systems", in *Proc. 2nd European Symp. on Research in Computer Security (ESORICS 92),* (Y. Deswarte, G. Eizenberg and J.-J. Quisquater, Eds.), (Toulouse, France), Lecture Notes on Computer Science, 648, pp.193-208, Berlin: Springer-Verlag, 1992.

[55] N. E. Fenton, "Measurement of Complex Systems", in *Computer-Based Systems Engineering Workshop,* (Israel), pp.16-21, IEEE Computer Soc. Press, 1990.

[56] N. E. Fenton, *Software Metrics: A rigorous approach,* Chapman and Hall, London, 1991.

[57] N. E. Fenton, "Software Measurement: Why a formal approach?", in *Formal Aspects of Software Measurement* (T. Denvir, H. R. and R. W. Whitty, Eds.), pp.3-27, Springer Verlag, 1992.

[58] N. E. Fenton, "When a Software Measure is not a Measure", *Software Eng J.,* 7 (5), pp.357-62, 1992.

[59] N. E. Fenton, "How Effective are Software Engineering Methods?", *Journal of Systems & Software,* 20, pp.93-100, 1993.

[60] N. E. Fenton, "Software Measurement: A necessary scientific basis", *IEEE Trans Software Eng,* 20 (3), pp.199-206, 1994.

[61] N. E. Fenton, *Software Quality Assurance and Metrics: A worldwide perspective,* Chapman and Hall, 1995.

[62] N. E. Fenton and B. A. Kitchenham, "Validating Software Measures", *J. Software Testing Verification and Reliability,* 1 (2), pp.27-42, 1991.

[63] N. E. Fenton and B. Littlewood (Eds.), *Software Reliability and Metrics,* Elsevier, 1991.

[64] N. E. Fenton and N. E. Melton, "Deriving Structurally Based Software Measures", *Journal of Systems Software,* 12, pp.177-87, 1990.

[65]    G. Fohler, "Realizing Changes of Operational Modes with Pre Run-Time Scheduled Hard Real-Time Systems.", in *Proc. of the Second Int. Workshop on Responsive Computer Systems,* (Saitama, Japan), 1992.

[66]    D. Gollmann and P. Wichmann, "PC-Security Evaluation", in *Proc. 5th European Conference on Information Systems Security, Control and Audit,* (Copenhagen), 1990.

[67]    A. G. Greenberg, B. D. Lubachevsky and I. Mitrani, "Unboundedly Parallel Simulations Via Recurrence Relations", in *Proc. Sigmetrics,* (Boulder), 1990.

[68]    G. A. Greenberg and I. Mitrani, "Massively Parallel Algorithms for Network Partition Functions", in *Proc. Int. Conf. on Parallel Processing,* (Chicago), 1991.

[69]    G. Gruensteidl, H. Kantz and H. Kopetz, "Communication Reliability in Distributed Real-Time Systems", in *Proc. 10th IFAC Workshop on Distributed Computer Control Systems,* (Semmering, Austria), 1991.

[70]    G. Grünsteidl, H. Kantz and H. Kopetz, "Communication Reliability in Distributed Real-Time Systems", in *Proc. 10th IFAC Workshop on Distributed Computer Control Systems,* (Semmering, Austria), pp.123-9, Pergamon Press, 1991.

[71]    G. Grünsteidl and H. Kopetz, "A Reliable Multicast Protocol for Distributed Real-Time Systems", in *Proc. 8th IEEE Workshop on Real-Time Operating Systems and Software,* (Atlanta, GA, USA), pp.19-24, 1991.

[72]    E. S. Hocking and J. A. McDermid, "Towards an Object-Oriented Development Environment for Secure Systems", in *Proc. European Symp. on Research in Computer Security (ESORICS 90),* (Toulouse, France), pp.191-200, 1990.

[73]    E. Jenn, J. Arlat, M. Rimén, J. Ohlsson and J. Karlsson, "Fault Injection into VHDL Models: The MEFISTO Tool", in *Proc. 24th Int. Symp. on Fault-Tolerant Computing (FTCS-24),* (Austin, TX, USA), pp.66-75, IEEE Computer Society Press, 1994.

[74]    E. Jonsson, M. Andersson and S. Asmussen, "A Practical Dependability Measure for Degradable Computer Systems with Non-Exponential Degradation", in *Proc. IFAC Symp. on Fault Detection, Supervision and Safety for Technical Processes (SAFEPROCESS'94),* (Espoo, Finland), pp.227-33, 1994.

[75]    E. Jonsson and S. Asmussen, "A Practical Dependability Measure for Embedded Computer Systems", in *Proc. IFAC 12th World Congress, Vol. 2,* (Sydney, Australia), pp.647-52, 1993.

[76]    E. Jonsson and T. Olovsson, "On the Integration of Security and Dependability in Computer Systems", in *Proc. IASTED Int. Conf. for Reliability, Quality Control and Risk Assessment,* 1992.

[77]    M. Kaâniche and K. Kanoun, "The Discrete-Time Hyperexponential Model for Software Reliability Growth Evaluation", in *Proc. 3rd Int. Symp. on*

*Software Reliability Engineering (ISSRE'92)*, (Research-Triangle Park, USA), pp.64-75, 1992.

[78] M. Kaâniche and K. Kanoun, "Qualitative and Quantitative Analysis of the Failure Data of Two Switching Systems", in *Proc.12th Int. Conf. on Computer Safety, Reliability and Security (SAFECOMP'93)*, (J. Górski, Ed.), (Poznan-Kiekrz, Poland), pp.230-9, London: Springer-Verlag, 1993.

[79] M. Kaâniche, K. Kanoun, M. Cukier and M. Bastos Martini, "Software Reliability Analysis of Three Successive Generations of a Switching System", in *Proc. First European Conference on Dependable Computing (EDCC-1)*, (Berlin, Germany), Lecture Notes in Computer Science, 852, pp.473-90, Berlin: Springer-Verlag, 1994.

[80] K. Kanoun, "Data Collection for Software Reliability Databases", in *Reliability, Maintainability and Safety (ICRMS'94)*, (Beijing, China), pp.3-9, 1994.

[81] K. Kanoun, M. Kaâniche, C. Béounes, J. C. Laprie and J. Arlat, "Reliability Growth of Fault-Tolerant Software", *IEEE Transactions on Reliability*, 42 (2), pp.205-19, 1993.

[82] K. Kanoun, M. Kaâniche and J. C. Laprie, "Experience in Software Reliability: From data collection to quantitative evaluation", in *Proc. 4th IEEE Int. Symp. on Software Reliability Engineering (ISSRE'93)*, (Denver, USA), 1993.

[83] K. Kanoun, M. Kaâniche, J. C. Laprie and S. Metge, "SoRel: A tool for reliability growth analysis and prediction from statistical failure data", in *Proc. 23rd Int. Symp. Fault-Tolerant Computing (FTCS-23)*, (Toulouse, France), pp.654-9, IEEE Computer Society Press, 1993.

[84] K. Kanoun and J.-C. Laprie, "Software Reliability Trend Analyses: From theoretical to practical considerations", *IEEE Transactions on Software Engineering*, 20 (9), pp.740-7, 1994.

[85] K. Kanoun and J.-C. Laprie, "Trend Analysis", in *Software Reliability Engineering Handbook* (M. Lyu, Ed.), p.Ch. 10, Mc Graw Hill, 1995.

[86] K. Kanoun and J. C. Laprie, "The Role of Trend Analysis in Software Development and Validation", in *Proc. IFAC Symp. on Safety of Computer Control Systems (SAFECOMP'91)*, (Trondheim, Norway), pp.169-74, 1991.

[87] H. Kantz, "Flexible Handling of Diverse Dependability Requirements in MARS", in *Proc. 10th Symp. on Reliable Distributed Systems*, (Pisa, Italy), pp.142-51, IEEE Computer Society Press, 1991.

[88] H. Kantz, "Integrating Dependability Analysis into the Design of Distributed Computer Systems", in *IEEE CompEuro 91*, (Bologna, Italy), 1991.

[89] Kopetz, "A Communication Infrastracture for a Fault-Tolerant Real-Time System", *Control Engineering Practice-- A Journal of IFAC* 1995.

[90] H. Kopetz, "Fault Tolerance in Real-Time Systems", in *Proc. IFAC World Congress*, (Tallinn, USSR), pp.111-8, 1990.

[91]   H. Kopetz, "Event-Triggered versus Time-Triggered Real-Time Systems", in *Proc. Int. Workshop on Operating Systems for the 90s and Beyond (Lecture Notes on Computer Science, Volume 563)* (A. Karshmer and J. Nehmer, Eds.), pp.87-101, Springer-Verlag, Berlin, Germany, 1991.

[92]   H. Kopetz, "Real-Time Systems", in *The Software Engineer's Reference Book* (J. A. McDermid, Ed.), Butterworth Scientific, Ltd., Surrey, UK, 1991.

[93]   H. Kopetz, "Six Difficult Problems in the Design of Responsive Systems", in *Proc. of the Second Int. Workshop on Responsive Computer Systems,* (Saitama, Japan), 1992.

[94]   H. Kopetz, "Software Engineering in Real-Time Systems", in *Shifting Paradigms in Software Engineering* Klagenfurt, Austria, 1992.

[95]   H. Kopetz, "Sparse Time versus Dense Time in Distributed Real-Time Systems", in *Proc. 14th Int. Conf. on Distributed Computing Systems,* (Yokohama, Japan), pp.460-7, IEEE Press, 1992.

[96]   H. Kopetz, "Should Responsive Systems be Event-Triggered or Time-Triggered?", *IEICE Trans. on Information and Systems (Special Issue on Responsive Computer Systems)* 1993.

[97]   H. Kopetz, "The Systematic Design of Large Real-Time Systems or Interface Simplicity", in *Proc. of Workshop Hardware and Software Architectures for Fault Tolerance: Perspectives and Towards a Synthesis,* (P. Lee, Ed.), (Le Mont Saint-Michel, France), Springer Verlag, 1993.

[98]   H. Kopetz, "An Analysis of the Communication Service in Responsive Systems", in *Proc. IEEE Int. Workshop on Object-Oriented Real-Time Dependable Systems,* (Dana Point, Cal.), pp.pp. 50-5, IEEE Press, 1994.

[99]   H. Kopetz, "The Design of Fault-Tolerant Real-Time Systems", in *Proc. Euromicro 1994,* (Liverpool), pp.4-11, IEEE Press, 1994.

[100]  H. Kopetz, "Fault-Management in the Time-Triggered Protocol", in *Proc. SAE World Congress,* pp.77-84, SAE Press, 1994.

[101]  H. Kopetz, "A Solution to an Automotive Control System System Benchmark", in *Proc. 15th IEEE Real-Time Systems Symp.,* (Puerto Rico), IEEE Press, 1994.

[102]  H. Kopetz, "TTP/A - A Time-Triggered Protocol of Body Electronics Using Standard UARTS", in *Proc. SAE World Congress,* 1995.

[103]  H. Kopetz, G. Fohler, G. Grünsteidl, H. Kantz, G. Pospischil, P. Puschner, J. Reisinger, R. Schlatterbeck, W. Schütz, A. Vrchoticky and R. Zainlinger, "The Programmer's View of MARS", in *Proc.13th Real-Time Systems Symp.,* (Phoenix, Arizona), pp.223-6, 1992.

[104]  H. Kopetz, G. Fohler, G. Grünsteidl, H. Kantz, G. Pospischil, P. Puschner, J. Reisinger, R. Schlatterbeck, W. Schütz, A. Vrchoticky and R. Zainlinger, "Real-Time System Development: The programming model of MARS", in *Proc. Int. Symp. on Autonomous Decentralized Systems,* (Kawasaki, Japan), pp.290-9, 1993.

[105] H. Kopetz and G. Grünsteidl, "A Reliable Multicast Protocol for Distributed Real-Time Systems", in *Proc. 8th IEEE Workshop on Real-Time Operating Systems and Software*, (Atlanta, GA, USA), Pergamon Press, 1991.

[106] H. Kopetz and G. Grünsteidl, "TTP-A Time-Triggered Protocol for Automotive Applications", *IEEE Computer*, 24 (1), pp.22-66, 1994.

[107] H. Kopetz, H. Kantz, G. Grünsteidl, P. Puschner and J. Reisinger, "Tolerating Transient Faults in MARS", in *Proc. 20th Int. Symp. on Fault-Tolerant Computing (FTCS-20)*, (Newcastle upon Tyne, UK), pp.466-73, 1990.

[108] H. Kopetz and K. Kim, "Temporal Uncertainties in Interactions among Real-Time Objects", in *Proc. 9th Symp. on Reliable Distributed Systems*, (Huntsville, AL, USA), pp.165-74, IEEE Computer Society Press, 1990.

[109] H. Kopetz and J. Reisinger, "The Non-Blocking Write Protocol NBW: A Solution to a Real-Time Synchronisation Problem", in *Proc. 14th Real-Time Systems Symp.*, (Raleigh-Durham, North Carolina), 1993.

[110] H. Kopetz and W. Schwabl, "Global Time in Distributed Real-Time Systems", in *Advances on Real-Time Computer Systems* JAI Press Inc., Greenwich, Conn., USA, 1991.

[111] H. Kopetz, R. Zainlinger, G. Fohler, H. Kantz, P. Puschner and W. Schütz, "The Design of Real-Time Systems: From specification to implementation and verification", *IEE Software Engineering Journal*, 5 (3) 1991.

[112] H. Kopetz, R. Zainlinger, G. Fohler, H. Kantz, P. Puschner and W. Schütz, "An Engineering Approach to Hard Real-Time System Design", in *Proc. 3rd European Software Engineering Conf.*, (Milano, Italy), 1991.

[113] J.-C. Laprie, "Hardware-and-Software Dependability Evaluation", in *Proc. IFIP 11th World Computer Congress*, (San Francisco, CA), pp.109-14, 1989.

[114] J.-C. Laprie, J. Arlat, C. Beounes and K. Kanoun, "Architectural Issues in Software Fault Tolerance", in *Software Fault Tolerance* (M. Lyu, Ed.), p.Ch. 3, J. Willey & Sons, Ltd, 1995.

[115] J.-C. Laprie and K. Kanoun, "Software Reliability and System Reliability", in *Software Reliability Engineering Handbook* (M. Lyu, Ed.), p.Ch. 2, Mc Graw Hill, 1995.

[116] J. C. Laprie (Ed.), *Dependability: Basic concepts and associated terminology*, Dependable Computing and Fault-Tolerant Systems, Springer-Verlag, 1991.

[117] J. C. Laprie (Ed.), *Dependability: Basic concepts and terminology — in English, French, German, German and Japanese*, Dependable Computing and Fault Tolerance, 5, 265p., Springer-Verlag, Vienna, Austria, 1992.

[118] J. C. Laprie, "For a Product-in-a-Process Approach to Software Reliability Evaluation (Invited paper)", in *Proc. 3rd Int. Symp. on Software Reliability Engineering (ISSRE'92)*, (Research-Triangle Park, USA), pp.134-9, 1992.

[119] J. C. Laprie, "Dependability: From concepts to limits (Invited paper)", in *Proc.12th Int. Conf. on Computer Safety, Reliability and Security*

*(SAFECOMP'93),* (J. Górski, Ed.), (Poznan-Kiekrz, Poland), pp.157-68, Berlin: Springer-Verlag, 1993.

[120]  J. C. Laprie, J. Arlat, C. Béounes and K. Kanoun, "Definition and Analysis of Hardware-and-Software Fault-Tolerant Architectures", *IEEE Computer (Special Issue on Fault Tolerant Systems)*, 23 (7), pp.39-51, July 1990.

[121]  J. C. Laprie, J. Arlat, C. Béounes and K. Kanoun, "Hardware- and Software-Fault Tolerance", in *Proc. ESPRIT'90,* (Brussels, Belgium), pp.786-9, Kluwer Academic Press, Dordrecht, The Netherlands, 1990.

[122]  J. C. Laprie and K. Kanoun, "X-ware Reliability and Availability Modelling", *IEEE Trans. on Soft. Eng.*, 18 (2), pp.130-47, 1992.

[123]  J. C. Laprie, K. Kanoun, C. Béounes and M. Kaâniche, "The Transformation Approach to the Modelling and Evaluation of Reliability and Availability Growth", in *Proc. 20th Int. Symp. on Fault-Tolerant Computing (FTCS-20),* (Newcastle upon Tyne), pp.364-71, IEEE Computer Society Press, 1990.

[124]  J. C. Laprie, K. Kanoun, C. Béounes and M. Kaâniche, "The KAT — Knowledge-Action-Transformation — Approach to the Modeling and Evaluation of Reliability and Availability Growth", *IEEE Transactions on Software Engineering*, 12 (4), pp.370-82, 1991.

[125]  J. C. Laprie and B. Littlewood, "Quantitative Assessment of Safety-Critical Software: Why and how?", *Communications of ACM*, 35 (2), pp.13-21, 1992.

[126]  P. Liden, P. Dahlgren and J. Torin, "Transistor Fault Coverage for Self-Testing CMOS Checkers", in *Proc. Int. Test Conf. 92 (ITC92),* 1992.

[127]  B. Littlewood, *Computer Safety (Edition of Antenna, Channel 2, 24th October, 1990),* BBC Television, 1990.

[128]  B. Littlewood, "Modelling Growth in Software Reliability", in *Software Reliability Handbook* (P. Rook, Ed.), Elsevier, 1990.

[129]  B. Littlewood, "Limits to Evaluation of Software Dependability", in *Software Reliability and Metrics* (B. Littlewood and N. Fenton, Eds.), Elsevier, 1991.

[130]  B. Littlewood, "Reliability", in *Software Metrics: A Rigorous Approach (Chap. 11)* (N. E. Fenton, Ed.), pp.230-49, Chapman and Hall, London, 1991.

[131]  B. Littlewood, "Software Reliability Modelling", in *Software Engineer's Handbook* (J. McDermid, Ed.), Butterworth Scientific, 1991.

[132]  B. Littlewood, "Software Reliability Modelling: Achievements and limitations", in *Proc. IEEE CompEuro 91,* (Bologna), pp.336-44, IEEE Computer Society, 1991.

[133]  B. Littlewood, "Software Reliability Modelling: Achievements and limitations (Invited paper)", in *Proc IEEE CompEuro 91,* (Bologna, Italy), pp.336-44, IEEE Computer Soc. Press, 1991.

[134]  B. Littlewood, "Validation of Ultra-High Dependability for Software-Based Systems", in *Software Reliability and Metrics* Elsevier, 1991.

[135] B. Littlewood, "Why We Should Learn not to Depend too Much on Software", in *Trans. IFIP Congress 94, 13th World Computer Congress*, (Hamburg), pp.254-61, North Holland, 1994.

[136] B. Littlewood, S. Brocklehurst, N. E. Fenton, P. Mellor, S. Page, D. Wright, J. E. Dobson, J. A. McDermid and D. Gollmann, "Towards Operational Measures of Computer Security", *Journal of Computer Security*, 2 (3), pp.211-29, 1993.

[137] B. Littlewood and R. Miller (Eds.), *Software Reliability and Safety*, Elsevier, 1991.

[138] B. Littlewood and L. Strigini, "The Risks of Software", *Scientific American*, 267 (5), pp.38-43, November 1992.

[139] B. Littlewood and L. Strigini, "Validation of Ultra-High Dependability for Software-Based Systems", *Communications of the ACM*, 36 (11), pp.69-80, November 1993.

[140] B. Littlewood and M. Thomas, "Reasons why Safety-Critical Avionics Software Cannot be Adequately Validated", in *Proc. Safety and Reliability Society Spring Conf., "Air Transport Safety"*, (Manchester), pp.77-87, SaRS, 1991.

[141] B. Littlewood and D. Wright, "On a Stopping Rule for the Operational Testing of Safety Critical Software", in *Proc. 25th Inter. Symp. Fault -Tolerant Computing (FTCS-25)*, (Pasadena), IEEE Computer Society Press, 1995.

[142] M. Lu, S. Brocklehurst and B. Littlewood, "Combination of Predictions Obtained from Different Software Reliability Growth Models", in *Proc 10th Annual Software Reliability Symp.*, (Denver, Colorado), 1992.

[143] B. Marre, P. Thévenod-Fosse, H. Waeselynck, P. L. Gall and Y. Crouzet, "An Experimental Evaluation of Formal and Statistical Testing", in *Proc. IFAC Symposium on Safety of Computer Control Systems (SAFECOMP'92)*, (Zurich, Switzerland), pp.311-6, 1992.

[144] J. A. McDermid, "Integrated Project Support Environments: General principles and issues in the development of dependable systems", in *Software Engineering for Large Software Systems (CSR Conf.)*, (B. A. Kitchenham, Ed.), pp.27-83, Elsevier, 1990.

[145] J. A. McDermid, "Safety Arguments, Software and System Reliability", in *Proc. 2nd Int. Symp. on Software Reliability Engineering*, (Austin, Texas), IEEE, 1991.

[146] J. A. McDermid and E. S. Hocking, "Security Policies for Integrated Project Support", in *Security III: Status and Prospects (Proc. IFIP Conf. on Database Security)*, (D. L. Spooner and C. Landwehr, Eds.), pp. 41-74, North Holland, 1990.

[147] J. A. McDermid and E. S. Hocking, "Towards and Object-Oriented Development Environment for Secure Applications", in *Proc. European Symp. on Research in Computer Security (ESORICS 90)*, (Toulouse), pp.191-200, 1991.

[148] P. Mellor, "Software Reliability Modelling", in *Proc. COMPSEC Intl.,* (London), pp.301-24, Elsevier Advanced Technology, 1990.

[149] P. Mellor, "Failures, Faults and Changes in Dependability Measurement", *Information and Software Technology*, 34 (10), pp.640-54, 1992.

[150] P. Mellor, "CAD: Computer-Aided Disaster", *High Integrity Systems Journal*, 1 (2), pp.101-56, 1994.

[151] D. Mitra and I. Mitrani, "Analysis of a Kanban Discipline for Cell Coordination in Production Lines", *Management Science*, 36 (12), pp.1548-66, 1990.

[152] D. Mitra and I. Mitrani, "Asymptotic Optimality of the Go-Back-n Protocol in High Speed Data Networks with Small Buffers", in *Proc. 4th Int. Conf. on Data Communication Systems and Their Performance,* (Barcelona), 1990.

[153] I. Mitrani, "Queueing Theory", in *The Software Engineer's Reference Book* (J. A. McDermid, Ed.), Butterworth Scientific Ltd, 1991.

[154] I. Mitrani and R. Chakka, "Spectral Expansion Solution for a Class of Markov Models: Application and comparison with the Matrix-Geometric Method", *Performance Evaluation*, 23 1995.

[155] I. Mitrani and D. Mitra, "A Spectral Expansion Method for Random Walks on Semi-Infinite Strips", in *Proc. IMACS Int. Symp. on Iterative Methods in Linear Algebra,* (Brussels), 1991.

[156] J. Ohlsson and M. Rimén, "Implicit Signature Checking", in *Proc. 25th Int. Symp. Fault-Tolerant Computing (FTCS-25),* (Los Angeles, CA), IEEE Computer Society Press, 1995.

[157] J. Ohlsson, M. Rimén and U. Gunneflo, "A Study of the Effects of Transient Fault Injection into a 32-bit RISC with Built-in Watchdog", in *Proc. 22th Int. Symp. Fault-Tolerant Computing (FTCS-22),* (Boston, MA, USA), pp.316-25, IEEE Computer Society Press, 1992.

[158] T. Olovsson and E. Jonsson, "Security Forms for Protection against Vulnerabilities in Computer Systems", in *Proc. IASTED Int. Conf. for Reliability, Quality Control and Risk Assessment,* 1992.

[159] G. Pospischil, P. Puschner, A. Vrchoticky and R. Zainlinger, "Developing Real-Time Tasks with Predictable Timing", *IEEE Software*, 9 (5), pp.35-44, 1992.

[160] D. Powell, "Failure Mode Assumptions and Assumption Coverage", in *Proc. 22nd Int. Symp. on Fault-Tolerant Computing (FTCS-22),* (Boston, MA, USA), pp.386-95, IEEE Computer Society Press, 1992.

[161] D. Powell, E. Martins, J. Arlat and Y. Crouzet, "Estimators for Fault Tolerance Coverage Evaluation", in *Proc. 23rd Int. Symp. Fault-Tolerant Computing (FTCS-23),* (Toulouse, France), pp.228-37, IEEE Computer Society Press, 1993.

[162] D. Powell, E. Martins, J. Arlat and Y. Crouzet, "Estimators for Fault Tolerance Coverage Evaluation", *IEEE Transactions on Computers*, 44 (2), pp.261-74, February 1995.

[163] G. Pucci, "On the Modelling and Testing of Recovery Block Structures", in *Proc. 20th IEEE Int. Symp. on Fault-Tolerant Computing (FTCS-20)*, (Newcastle upon Tyne), pp.353-63, 1990.

[164] P. Puschner and A. Vrchoticky, "An Assessment of Task Execution Time Analysis", in *Proc. 10th IFAC Workshop on Distributed Computer Control Systems*, (Semmering, Austria), pp.41-5, Pergamon Press, 1991.

[165] P. Puschner and R. Zainlinger, "Developing Software with Predictable Timing Behavior", in *Proc. 7th IEEE Workshop on Real-Time Operating Systems and Software*, (Charlottesville, VA, USA), pp.70-6, 1990.

[166] Qi Shi and J. A. McDermid, "A Formal Model of Security Dependency for Analysis and Testing of Secure Systems", in *Proc. Computer Security Foundations Workshop IV*, (Franconia, NH), IEEE Computer Society Press, 1991.

[167] Qi Shi and J. A. McDermid, "A Formal Approach for Security Evaluation", in *Proc. Seventh Annual Conference on Computer Assurance*, IEEE and BCS, 1992.

[168] Qi Shi and J. A. McDermid, "Secure Composition of Systems", in *Proc. Eighth Annual Computer Security Applications Conf.*, IEEE Computer Society Press, 1992.

[169] Qi Shi and J. A. McDermid, "Achieving System Security by Testing", in *Proc. Test Technology Transfer Symp.*, International Test and Evaluation Association (ITEA), 1993.

[170] Qi Shi and J. A. McDermid, "Applying Noninterference to Composition of Systems: A more practical approach", in *Proc. 9th Annual Computer Security Applications Conf.*, IEEE Computer Society Press, 1993.

[171] Qi Shi and J. A. McDermid, "Constructing Secure Distributed Systems Using Components", in *Proc. 12th Symp. on Reliable Distributed Systems*, IEEE Computer Society Press, 1993.

[172] Qi Shi and J. A. McDermid, "Designing Secure Systems of Good Quality", in *Proc. 3rd Int. Conf.. on Software Quality*, American Society for Quality Control, 1993.

[173] Qi Shi and J. A. McDermid, "Developing Secure Systems in A Modular Way", in *Proc. Eighth Annual Conf. on Computer Assurance*, IEEE and BCS, 1993.

[174] Qi Shi and J. A. McDermid, "Testing and Evaluating System Security", in *Proc. Test Technology Transfer Symp.*, International Test and Evaluation Association (ITEA), 1993.

[175] B. Randell and J. C. Fabre, "Fault and Intrusion Tolerance in Object-Oriented Systems", in *Proc. Int. Workshop on Object-Orientation in Operating*

*Systems,* (Palo Alto, CA), pp.180-4, IEEE Technical Committee on Operating Systems and Application Environments (TCOS), 1991.

[176] B. Randell and J. C. Laprie, "Predictably Dependable Computing Systems: Second year report", *Bulletin of the EATCS (European Association for Theoretical Computing Science),* 44, pp.61-86, 1991.

[177] B. Randell and J. Xu, "The Evolution of the Recovery Block Concept", in *Software Fault Tolerance* (M. Lyu, Ed.), Trends in Software, pp.1-22, J. Wiley, 1994.

[178] J. Reisinger, "Time Driven Operating Systems: A case study on the MARS Kernel", in *Proc. 5th ACM SIGOPS European Workshop,* (Le Mont Saint-Michel, France), IRISA/INRIA-Rennes, 1992.

[179] J. Reisinger and A. Steininger, "The Design of a Fail-Silent Processing Node for MARS", *Distributed Systems Engineering Journal* 1994.

[180] M. Rimén and J. Ohlsson, "A Study of the Error Behavior of a 32-bit RISC Subjected to Simulated Transient Fault Injection", in *Proc. Int. Test Conf. 92 (ITC92),* 1992.

[181] M. Rimén, J. Ohlsson and J. Torin, "On Microprocessor Error Behavior Modeling", in *Proc. 24th Int. Symp. Fault-Tolerant Computing (FTCS-24),* IEEE Computer Society Press, 1994.

[182] C. M. F. Rubira-Calsavara and R. J. Stroud, "Forward and Backward Error Recovery in C++", *Object-Oriented Systems*, 1 (1), pp.61-85, 1994.

[183] A. Saeed, T. Anderson and M. Koutny, "A Formal Model for Safety-Critical Computing Systems", in *Proc. IFAC Workshop SAFECOMP' 90,* (London), pp.1-6, 1990.

[184] A. Saeed, R. d. Lemos and T. Anderson, "The Role of Formal Methods in the Requirements Analysis of Safety-Critical Systems: A train set example", in *Proc. 21st. IEEE Int. Symp. on Fault-Tolerant Computing (FTCS-21),* (Montreal), 1991.

[185] W. Schütz, "Real-Time Simulation in the Distributed Real-Time System MARS", in *Proc. 1990 European Simulation Multiconference,* (Nuremberg, Germany), pp.51-7, The Society for Computer Simulation International, 1990.

[186] W. Schütz, "A Test Strategy for the Distributed Real-Time System MARS", in *Proc. IEEE CompEuro 90 (Computer Systems and Software Engineering),* (Tel Aviv), pp.20-7, 1990.

[187] W. Schütz, "On the Testability of Distributed Real-Time Systems", in *Proc. 10th Symp. on Reliable Distributed Systems,* (Pisa, Italy), pp.52-61, 1991.

[188] W. Schütz, *The Testability of Distributed Real-Time Systems,* 160p., Kluwer Academic Publishers, Boston, MA, 1993.

[189] P. Semal, "Two Bounding Schemes for the Steady-State Solution of Markov Chains", in *Computation with Markov Chains* (W. J. Stewart, Ed.), Kluwer, 1995.

[190] S. K. Shrivastava, L. V. Mancini and B. Randell, "The Duality of Fault-Tolerant System Structures", *Software Practice and Experience*, 23 (7), pp.773-98, 1993.

[191] A. Steininger and J. Reisinger, "Integral Design of Hardware and Operating System for a DCCS", in *Proc. 10th IFAC Workshop on Distributed Computer Control Systems*, (Semmering, Austria), Pergamon Press, 1991.

[192] L. Strigini, "Considerations on Current Research Issues in Software Safety", *Reliability Engineering and System Safety*, 43 (2), pp.177-88, 1994.

[193] L. Strigini, A. Bondavalli and L. Simoncini, "Data-Flow like Languages for Designing Dependable Real-Time Control Systems", in *Proc. 10th IFAC Workshop on Distributed Computer Control Systems*, (Semmering, Austria), 1991.

[194] L. Strigini and F. Di Giandomenico, "Flexible Schemes for Application-Level Fault Tolerance", in *Proc. 10th Symp. on Reliable Distributed Systems*, (Pisa, Italy), pp.86-95, IEEE Computer Society Press, 1991.

[195] P. Thévenod-Fosse, "On the Efficiency of Statistical Testing with respect to Software Structural Test Criteria", in *Proc. IFIP Working Conference on Approving Software Products*, (Garmisch-Partenkirchen, FRG), pp.29-42, North Holland, 1990.

[196] P. Thévenod-Fosse, "From Random Testing of Hardware to Statistical Testing of Software", in *Proc. COMP-EURO'91*, (Bologna, Italy), pp.200-7, 1991.

[197] P. Thévenod-Fosse, C. Mazuet and Y. Crouzet, "On Statistical Testing of Synchronous Data Flow Programs", in *Proc. 1st European Dependable Computing Conference (EDCC-1)*, (Berlin, Germany), pp.250-67, 1994.

[198] P. Thévenod-Fosse and H. Waeselynck, "An Investigation of Statistical Software Testing", *Journal of Software Testing, Verification and Reliability*, 1 (2), pp.5-25, July-September 1991.

[199] P. Thévenod-Fosse and H. Waeselynck, "On Functional Statistical Testing Designed from Software Behavior Models", in *Dependable Computing for Critical Applications 3 (DCCA-3)* (C. E. Landwehr, B. Randell and L. Simoncini, Eds.), Dependable Computing and Fault-Tolerant Systems, 8, (A. Avizienis, H. Kopetz and J. C. Laprie, Eds.), pp.3-28, Springer-Verlag, Vienna, 1993.

[200] P. Thévenod-Fosse and H. Waeselynck, "Statemate Applied to Statistical Software Testing", in *Proc. 1993 ACM Int. Symposium on Software Testing and Analysis (ISSTA)*, (Cambridge, USA), pp.99-109, 1993.

[201] P. Thévenod-Fosse, H. Waeselynck and Y. Crouzet, "An Experimental Study on Software Structural Testing: Deterministic versus random input generation", in *Proc. 21st IEEE Int. Symposium on Fault-Tolerant Computing (FTCS-21)*, (Montreal), pp.410-7, 1991.

[202] H. Waeselynck and P. Thévenod-Fosse, "An Experimentation with Statistical Testing", in *Proc. 2nd European Int. Conference on Software Testing, Analysis & Review (EuroSTAR'94)*, (Bruxelles, Belgium), 1994.

[203] J. Xu, "The t/(n-1)-Diagnosability and its Applications to Fault Tolerance", in *Proc. 21st Int. Symp. on Fault-Tolerant Computing (FTCS-21),* (Montreal), pp.496-503, IEEE Computer Society Press, 1991.

[204] J. Xu and S. Huang, "Sequentially t-Diagnosable Systems: A characterization and its applications", *IEEE Trans. Computers*, C-44 (2) 1995.

[205] J. Xu, B. Randell, A. Romanovsky, C. M. F. Rubira, R. J. Stroud and Z. Wu, "Fault Tolerance in Concurrent Object-Oriented Software through Coordinated Error Recovery", in *Proc. 25th Int. Symp. Fault-Tolerant Computing (FTCS-25),* (Los Angeles), IEEE Computer Society Press, 1995.

[206] J. Xu, B. Randell, C. M. F. Rubira and R. J. Stroud, "Toward an Object-Oriented Approach to Software Fault Tolerance", in *Fault-Tolerant Parallel and Distributed Systems* (D. R. Avresky, Ed.), IEEE Computer Society Press, 1994.

[207] R. Zainlinger, "Building Interfaces for CASE Environments: An object-oriented interaction model and its application", in *Proc. IFIP Int. Conf. on Human Factors in Information Systems Analysis and Design,* (Schärding, Austria), pp.65-80, 1990.

[208] R. Zainlinger and G. Pospischil, "DIAMOND: An object-oriented graphics library for software development environments", in *Proc. Autumn 1990 EUUG Conf.,* (Nice, France), pp.157-66, 1990.

# ESPRIT Basic Research Series

J. W. Lloyd (Ed.): **Computational Logic.** Symposium Proceedings, Brussels, November 1990. XI, 211 pages. 1990

E. Klein, F. Veltman (Eds.): **Natural Language and Speech.** Symposium Proceedings, Brussels, November 1991. VIII, 192 pages. 1991

G. Gambosi, M. Scholl, H.-W. Six (Eds.): **Geographic Database Management System.** Workshop Proceedings, Capri, May 1991. XII, 320 pages. 1992

R. Kassing (Ed.): **Scanning Microscopy.** Symposium Proceedings, Wetzlar, October 1990. X, 207 pages. 1992

G. A. Orban, H.-H. Nagel (Eds.): **Artificial and Biological Vision Systems.** XII, 389 pages. 1992

S. D. Smith, R. F. Neale (Eds.): **Optical Information Technology.** State-of-the-Art Report. XIV, 369 pages. 1993

Ph. Lalanne, P. Chavel (Eds.): **Perspectives for Parallel Optical Interconnects.** XIV, 417 pages. 1993

D. Vernon (Ed.): **Computer Vision: Craft, Engineering, and Science.** Workshop Proceedings, Killarney, September 1991. XIII, 96 pages. 1994

E. Montseny, J. Frau (Eds.): **Computer Vision: Specialized Processors for Real-Time Image Analysis.** Workshop Proceedings, Barcelona, September 1991. X, 216 pages. 1994

J. L. Crowley, H. I. Christensen (Eds.): **Vision as Process.** Basic Research on Computer Vision Systems. VIII, 432 pages. 1995

B. Randell, J.-C. Laprie, H. Kopetz, B. Littlewood (Eds.): **Predictably Dependable Computing Systems.** XIX, 588 pages. 1995

Printing: Mercedesdruck, Berlin
Binding: Buchbinderei Lüderitz & Bauer, Berlin